THE NEW ILLUSTRATED COMPANION TO THE BIBLE

THE NEW ILLUSTRATED COMPANION TO THE BIBLE

J. R. PORTER

DUNCAN BAIRD PUBLISHERS
LONDON

The New Illustrated Companion to the Bible
J.R. Porter

First published in the UK and Ireland by
Duncan Baird Publishers Ltd
6th Floor, Castle House
75–76 Wells Street
London W1T 3QH

Conceived, created and designed by Duncan Baird Publishers

Material from this book was first published in the United Kingdom
and Ireland by Duncan Baird Publishers in two separate volumes:
The Illustrated Guide to the Bible (1995) and *Jesus Christ* (1999).

Senior Editor: Peter Bently
Editor: Mike Darton
Consultant editor: Michael D. Coogan
Assistant editors: Lucy Rix, Daphne Bien Tebbe
Designer: Paul Reid
Assistant designer: Gail Jones
Picture research: Julia Brown, Jan Croot, Julia Ruxton
Commissioned artwork: Ron Hayward
Commissioned photography (see pp.431–2): Eitan Simanor
Map illustration: Lorraine Harrison and Neil Gower
Decorative borders: Lorraine Harrison and Iona McGlashan

Book-by-Book Summary compiled by Mike Darton

A CIP catalogue record for this book is available from the British Library.

ISBN: 1-904292-87-9

1 3 5 7 9 10 8 6 4 2

Typeset in Sabon
Colour reproduction by Scanhouse, Singapore
Manufactured in China by Imago Publishing Limited

The pictures on pp. 1–3 are credited on page 431.

ABBREVIATIONS

The following abbreviations are used in this book:

General abbreviations

CE	Common Era (the equivalent of AD)
BCE	Before the Common Era (the equivalent of BC)
ca.	*circa* (about)
ch./chs.	chapter/chapters
ff.	and following
fl.	*floruit* (flourished, active)
p./pp.	page/pages
v./vv.	verse/verses
NRSV	New Revised Standard Version (1989)
KJV	King James (Authorized) Version (1611)

Quotations from the Scripture and other Ancient Writings

The books of the Bible are referred to according to the list of short forms and abbreviations set out below; the abbreviations are used only in parentheses within the text. Chapter and verse are separated by a period (.), and a sequence is indicated by a dash (–). Thus, 1 Samuel 9.24 (or, in brackets, 1 Sam. 9.24) = chapter 9, verse 24 of the first book of Samuel; Acts 3.7–10 = chapter 3, verses 7 to 10 of the Acts of the Apostles; Matthew 5–10 (or Matt. 5–10) = chapters 5 to 10 of the gospel according to Matthew. Very occasionally, subdivisions of verses are indicated by letters. Thus, Genesis 2.4a = the first part of verse 4 of Genesis chapter 2.

Short form	Abbreviation
Acts of the Apostles	Acts
Additions to Esther	Add. Esth.
Amos	Amos
Baruch	Bar.
Bel and the Dragon	Bel
1 Chronicles	1 Chron.
2 Chronicles	2 Chron.
Colossians	Col.
1 Corinthians	1 Cor.
2 Corinthians	2 Cor.
Daniel	Dan.
Deuteronomy	Deut.
Ecclesiastes	Eccles.
Ephesians	Eph.
1 Esdras	1 Esd.
2 Esdras	2 Esd.
Esther	Esther
Exodus	Exod.
Ezekiel	Ezek.
Ezra	Ezra
Galatians	Gal.
Habakkuk	Hab.
Haggai	Hag.
Hebrews	Heb.
Hosea	Hos.
Isaiah	Isa.
James	James
Jeremiah	Jer.
Job	Job
Joel	Joel
John *or* Fourth Gospel	John
1 John	1 John
2 John	2 John
3 John	3 John
Jonah	Jon.
Joshua	Josh.
Jude	Jude
Judges	Judg.
Judith	Jth.
1 Kings	1 Kings
2 Kings	2 Kings
Lamentations	Lam.
Letter of Jeremiah	Let. Jer.
Leviticus	Lev.
Luke	Luke
1 Maccabees	1 Macc.
2 Maccabees	2 Macc.
3 Maccabees	3 Macc.
4 Maccabees	4 Macc.
Malachi	Mal.
Mark	Mark
Matthew	Matt.
Micah	Mic.
Nahum	Nah.
Nehemiah	Neh.
Numbers	Num.
Obadiah	Obad.
1 Peter	1 Pet.
2 Peter	2 Pet.
Philippians	Phil.
Philemon	Philem.
Prayer of Azariah and Song of the Three Young Men (Jews)	Song of Thr.
Prayer of Manasseh	Pr. of Man.
Proverbs	Prov.
Psalm(s)	Ps(s).
Revelation	Rev.
Romans	Rom.
Ruth	Ruth
1 Samuel	1 Sam.
2 Samuel	2 Sam.
Sirach (Ecclesiasticus)	Sir.
Song of Solomon	Song of Sol.
Susanna	Sus.
1 Thessalonians	1 Thess.
2 Thessalonians	2 Thess.
1 Timothy	1 Tim.
2 Timothy	2 Tim.
Titus	Titus
Tobit	Tob.
Wisdom of Solomon	Wisd. of Solomon
Zechariah	Zech.
Zephaniah	Zeph.

CONTENTS

Part of the scroll of the book of Isaiah found at Qumran and dated to ca. 100 BCE. It is the longest and oldest of the so-called "Dead Sea Scrolls."

THE MAKING OF THE BIBLE

Categories of Literature in the Hebrew Bible

The word "Bible" comes from the medieval Latin *Biblia,* originally a Greek plural, meaning "books." This is a good description of the character of what we know as the Bible, which consists of a number of different writings dating from approximately 1000 BCE to 100 CE or a little later. The books are very diverse in nature, and most of them have undergone a considerable amount of editing, reinterpretation, adaptation, and expansion in the course of their transmission. This process can be elucidated only by the techniques of biblical criticism developed since the nineteenth century. Such study is highly complicated, its results often remain hypothetical, and individual scholars differ in their assessments of the evidence.

Narrative

The books of the Hebrew Bible (also called the Hebrew Scriptures or Old Testament) can be classified into several broad categories, which do not necessarily correspond to those of earlier ages. The first seventeen books, from Genesis to Esther (in the order found in the Christian Bible), are typically viewed as narrative works. The first five, Genesis, Exodus, Leviticus, Numbers, and Deuteronomy, have always been recognized as a distinct section, the Torah or Pentateuch, forming a continuous narrative from the creation of the world (see pp.20–1) to Moses' death (see pp.60–1). The next seven books, Joshua through 2 Kings, recount the Israelite nation's development from the conquest of Canaan (see pp.62–5) through the Babylonian capture of Jerusalem (see pp.104–05), and are generally recognized as a coherent history, by one or more authors of the Deuteronomic school (see p.100). A similar work is 1 and 2 Chronicles, which appears to make use of the Deuteronomic history, while the books of Ezra and Nehemiah (see pp.110–11) continue Jewish history into the period after the return from the Exile. Esther, a kind of historical novel, tells the story of Jews being liberated from their oppressors in Persia (see pp.124–25).

Law

The Pentateuch also represents a second major category of works in the Hebrew Bible: Law. The Ten Commandments (Decalogue) and the Book of the Covenant, originally separate law codes, appear in Exodus (20.1–17 and 20.22–23.19). Deuteronomy contains the Decalogue (6.6–21), as well as another extensive law code (12–26). Priestly regulations, the Holiness Law, make up Leviticus 17–26, and similar material plays a large part in the later chapters of Exodus and Numbers.

Prophetical Books

Prophetical books form a third important category in the Hebrew Bible. Known as the "Latter Prophets" in Jewish tradition (the

"Former Prophets" being the books of Joshua, Judges, Samuel, and Kings), these are the books of Isaiah, Jeremiah, Ezekiel, plus the "Twelve Prophets" (Hosea through Malachi); the Christian tradition includes Daniel as well. They cover a period from the eighth century BCE to the early postexilic age, but other traditions attest to the deeds and words of earlier prophets. Because the dates and circumstances of individual prophets can usually be established with considerable certainty, the prophetic books provide valuable information about the political and social conditions of particular periods.

In most cases, the book bearing the name of a prophet purports to contain that prophet's own oracles. However, in the process of preserving and collecting the prophet's sayings, these original words were often combined with other material, such as biographical narrative. Also, in the course of literary transmission, the original oracles were often reinterpreted to adapt them to new circumstances. Other elements may also have been added, including later material from other prophets. This complex compositional process is especially apparent in the three major prophetic books, Isaiah, Jeremiah, and Ezekiel (see especially the discussion of Isaiah on p.99, p.106, and p.111).

Wisdom Literature

Proverbs, Job, and Ecclesiastes, together with the apocryphal works Sirach (Ecclesiasticus) and the Wisdom of Solomon, represent another category of the Hebrew Bible: Wisdom literature (see pp.120–21). The beginnings of this genre are seen in the bulk of the material making up the book of Proverbs: brief, pithy, proverbial sayings which enshrine popular understanding of life and society. But other sections of Proverbs show the development of Wisdom as a more profound theoretical concept. Later Wisdom works, such as Job (see pp.122–23), Ecclesiastes, Sirach (Ecclesiasticus), and the Wisdom of Solomon, wrestle with some of the fundamental problems of the human condition, particularly the existence of evil and suffering.

Other Categories

There are many other ways of categorizing the books of the Old Testament: Daniel, for example, is also an apocalypse, a type of literature that is related to classical prophecy but goes far beyond it in its cosmic and eschatological speculations (see pp.130–31). One of the most fruitful results of modern biblical study has been the identification of more of the wide range of linguistic and literary resources that biblical authors drew upon in composing their works. These include myths, sagas, legends, etiologies (origin stories), popular etymologies, and legal works. This study has greatly illuminated the character of the most important surviving collection of Hebrew poetry, the Psalms (see p.115), which can now be classified into a number of different types, according to the occasions for which they were produced.

CATEGORIES OF LITERATURE IN THE NEW TESTAMENT

While the composition and collection of the material in the Hebrew Bible spans a period of over a thousand years, the writings of the New Testament were probably produced in the space of less than a century. They can be classified into two main categories: historical narratives with strong biographical features, such as the gospels and Acts; and letters. Revelation (see pp.392–94) is certainly a Christian apocalypse, possessing many of the features that had become traditional in the Jewish genre of literature known as "apocalyptic" (see main text), but nevertheless it is in the form of a letter.

Many of the considerations that arise in the study of the Hebrew Scriptures are also applicable to the New Testament. Each of the gospels represents its author's own understanding and interpretation of the basic tradition about Jesus, and each has its own special material. The Synoptic Gospels (Matthew, Mark, and Luke; see pp.182–86), at least, are largely constructed from small units, such as healing stories, conflict stories, and parables. Many of the writings of the apostle Paul are genuine letters, but several of those which have been attributed to him and to other apostles are really different kinds of compositions. Often they reflect features of contemporary Hellenistic literature, such as the treatise, encyclical, diatribe, or what is known as *parenesis* (see pp.376–77).

Moses and Pharaoh's Daughter *(Exod. 2.10), from the* Golden Haggadah, *a Hebrew manuscript of 1320. The story of the Israelite Exodus from Egypt was central to the development of the Hebrew Bible.*

The Evolution of the Pentateuch

The first five books of the Hebrew Bible, the Torah or Pentateuch, were traditionally regarded as the product of a single author, Moses, who is the main human character in much of the story. Parts of the material may, indeed, have been contributed by Moses, but it is now generally accepted that the Pentateuch is a complex, anonymous work, developed from traditions dating from before and, especially, after the time of Moses himself.

Since the late nineteenth century, the dominant theory of the origins of the Pentateuch has been Julius Wellhausen's "Documentary Hypothesis," although this has been increasingly questioned by scholars. The Documentary Hypothesis proposes that the books of the Pentateuch are in the main a combination of four separate literary sources, which were written at different times. The first source, the Yahwist (or "J," from *Jahwe*, the German spelling of Yahweh), may have originated in Jerusalem and is generally dated to the tenth or ninth century BCE. The Yahweist is so-called because this author uses the word "Yahweh," the personal name of God. The "E" document, which uses the Hebrew word *elohim* for God in Genesis, appeared a little later, in the ninth or eighth century BCE, and reflects the traditions of the northern Israelite kingdom of Israel. The book of Deuteronomy, or "D," a separate work which gives a distinctive picture of the figure of Moses, was written in the southern kingdom of Judah in the seventh century BCE, although it too preserves northern traditions (see p.100). There may also have been a priestly source, "P," which was added after the Babylonian Exile, in the sixth or fifth century BCE (see pp.20–1). The final stage in the evolution of the Pentateuch was the combination of all these sources into the existing whole, a task probably carried out by a priestly editor who worked in Jerusalem in the period after the return from Exile.

FORM CRITICISM

Form criticism, a type of analysis that looks at individual units of the text, suggests that a long period of transmission may lie behind the existing written material. It is possible, for example, that the myths, sagas, etiological tales, and sanctuary legends of Genesis were orally composed and transmitted, though some of these may well have been written down at an early stage. Scholars came to recognize that what had been thought of as the nation of "Israel" was in fact a confederation of originally separate groups, and they were able to isolate within the Bible the distinct traditions of particular tribes or groups (see also sidebar, opposite).

The Canon of the Hebrew Bible and Old Testament

Not all the literature that was produced in Judaism or the early Church by the end of the first century CE is included in the Bible. Many other Jewish religious writings exist: the Hebrew Bible mentions books that are now lost, such as the book of Jashar (Josh. 10.13; 1 Sam.1.18), apparently a collection of ancient Hebrew poetry. The New Testament speaks of letters that are also no longer extant.

The list of biblical books is known as the "canon," a Greek word meaning "rule," but how and why the books in the Bible acquired this unique authority remains a subject of much scholarly speculation.

Three distinct sections comprise the canon of the Hebrew Bible: the Law, or Torah, consisting of the first five books, the Pentateuch; the Prophets, including the "Former Prophets" (Joshua through 2 Kings) and the "Latter Prophets" (Isaiah, Jeremiah, Ezekiel, and the twelve short prophetic books known as the Twelve or Minor Prophets); and the Writings, a collection of the rest of the works in the canon (Ruth, Chronicles, Ezra, Nehemiah, Esther, Job, Psalms, Proverbs, Ecclesiastes, Song of Solomon, Lamentations, and Daniel).

The Law has always been regarded as having special authority in Judaism: the other books repeat, amplify, and explain the Law. It seems likely, then, that this was the first section to be recognized as canonical. The prophetical books were probably collected together about the time of the return from the Exile (see pp.108–11), when the Deuteronomic history (Deuteronomy through 2 Kings) was also produced. When the two were combined, they formed the next portion of the canon. The third section, the Writings, seems to have taken longer to become fixed, with various books being added to it over a long period. The threefold division of the Hebrew Bible seems to have been settled by the second century BCE, when it is referred to in the prologue of Sirach (Ecclesiasticus), dating from about 130 BCE.

The Septuagint, the Greek translation of the Hebrew Bible, includes apocryphal writings (see sidebar, p.12) which are absent from the canon. This may mean that Hellenistic Jews recognized a wider canon than the Palestinian Jews. The Septuagint became the dominant Christian version of the Old Testament, and so these additional books were at first included in the Christian canon. The different order of books in the Septuagint, which has become standard in Christian Bibles, represents a specifically Christian theological arrangement: Israel's history is viewed as reaching its fulfillment in the coming of Christ. In the Christian arrangement, the Pentateuch is followed by most of the books in the third section of the Hebrew canon, and the Prophets bring the work to a close. With this arrangement, God's promise in Malachi 4.5–6 to send the prophet Elijah provides a transition to the New Testament, which begins with the appearance in the gospels of the second Elijah: John the Baptist (see pp.214–15).

The Canon of the New Testament

The first Christians inherited the Jewish canon and knew no other. Their own writings were intended to give pastoral guidance and instruction to emerging congregations and were not envisaged as sharing the canonical authority of the Jewish Scriptures.

The idea of a New Testament canon, parallel to that of the Hebrew Bible, began to emerge in the second century CE. By this time, the four gospels, with their basically similar pattern, were increasingly recognized as authoritative, and Paul's letters had been collected. The concept of a canon – a fixed body of authoritative works – was first applied to Christian writings by Marcion, who died around 160 CE.

Israel in Egypt *(Exod. 1.11), from the* Brother Haggadah, *Barcelona, ca. 1350.* Haggadahs *are collections of Bible stories telling the events of the Exodus from Egypt. Readings from them are traditionally made during the Jewish Passover supper.*

THE PENTATEUCH IN RECENT SCHOLARSHIP

In recent times, biblical scholars have tended to concentrate on the purpose and background of the Pentateuch in its final form. They generally agree with the claim of the Documentary Hypothesis (see main text, p.10) that the last stage in the development of the Pentateuch took place in the postexilic period. But they have emphasized that the final editors were attempting to convey a message tailored to the needs, hopes, and fears of people of their own time. The Pentateuch may be viewed as aiming to encourage and warn Jewish exiles faced with the challenge of returning to the Promised Land, and its themes can be seen as providing a program for the restoration of Israel. These themes are: the abiding covenant with God; the promise of the land in perpetuity to Israel; and the trials of the people in the wilderness before the settlement of the Promised Land.

This view has led some scholars to challenge the Documentary Hypothesis. Some have even argued that there is nothing to show that the Pentateuch uses any existing bodies of material, such as "J" and "P." This probably goes too far. The Pentateuch is a literary and theological product of the postexilic age, but it may well have drawn on earlier material, even if this cannot be identified with certainty.

He rejected the entire body of Jewish Scripture and accepted only Luke's gospel and an expurgated version of ten of Paul's letters. In reaction to Marcion, the mainstream Church emphasized the authoritative character of all four gospels and the thirteen letters attributed to Paul, thus implicitly excluding the many other Christian writings that had appeared by this time.

The main outlines of the New Testament canon were now fixed, but uncertainty remained about various other books, such as the letter to the Hebrews (see pp.388–89), Revelation (see pp.392–94), and some of the non-Pauline letters. A decisive stage was reached when Athanasius of Alexandria listed all twenty-seven books of the existing New Testament in a letter of 367 CE. Athanasius was the first person to use the word "canon" to refer to the Bible. His canon was widely accepted in the eastern Church, and in succeeding years it was also authorized by a number of synods in the West. Thereafter the New Testament was generally accepted as the second part of the Christian biblical canon.

THE APOCRYPHA

The Greek word *apocrypha* refers to some fourteen or fifteen writings whose canonical status has long been disputed. The term means "things hidden away," but, in fact, the books in question were never considered secret.

Some apocryphal books were originally in Hebrew, but they were excluded from the Hebrew canon and, until recent discoveries, survived only in Greek. Because they were included in the Septuagint, the Bible of the early Church, they were accepted without question by Greek-speaking Christians for most of the first four centuries CE. A great change occurred in 382 CE, when the Pope commissioned the scholar and churchman Jerome to make a new translation of the Bible into Latin. Jerome's translation is known as the Vulgate, from the Latin *vulgata editio*, roughly meaning "edition for common circulation." Jerome was convinced that only the Hebrew canon could be regarded as authentic, and hence he rejected the books found only in Greek, labeling them "apocryphal." But his views were not accepted, and the Vulgate retained the apocryphal books in the Old Testament.

In the sixteenth century, during the Reformation, Protestants universally agreed with Jerome. They either removed the apocryphal books from the Bible altogether, or placed them in a separate section between the Hebrew Scriptures and the New Testament. In recent years, a new appreciation of the apocryphal writings has developed, as scholars have increasingly realized their importance for both biblical interpretation and the understanding of the development of Judaism and early Christianity.

The Text of the Hebrew Bible and New Testament

Until the end of the first century CE, the main contents of the Hebrew Bible were transmitted in various forms or families: there was no single text. But after the fall of Jerusalem in 70 CE, as part of the restoration of Judaism under the Pharisees, one particular textual tradition emerged and became accepted as the official Hebrew Bible. As it now exists, it is known as the Masoretic text, from the learned scribes, the Masoretes, who compiled it from ca. 900 CE. They took their name from the Masorah, a body of notes that they appended to the text. They also added Hebrew vowel signs to a Hebrew text that had until then been written only with consonants. The work of the Masoretes gradually replaced other forms of the text, and so the earliest manuscripts of the complete Hebrew Bible date only from the tenth century CE. However, some of the biblical documents from Qumran, the so-called "Dead Sea Scrolls" (see p.139), some of which are basically the same as the Masoretic text, confirm its early antecedents.

Although the New Testament is a quarter of the length of the Hebrew Bible, its textual history is much more complicated, largely because there were so many more early witnesses to the text. About five and a half thousand manuscripts are known, ranging from the late second or early third century CE to the thirteenth century. Compared to the relatively small number of manuscripts of other writings from the ancient world, this number is remarkable. The oldest evidence is provided by a number of papyri from the second and third centuries CE, but many of them are fragmentary and contain only portions, sometimes quite brief, of the New Testament. The earliest manuscripts were in the form of a scroll, but around the beginning of the second century CE, the codex, or book form, began to be used in the Church, and parchment or vellum (calfskin) took the place of papyrus. This led to the production of a number of handsome Greek texts, containing the entire New Testament, and sometimes also the Septuagint. The most complete of these is the fourth-century CE Codex Sinaiticus, discovered in Saint Catherine's monastery in Sinai. Other important manuscripts of the same date or a little later include the Codex Alexandrinus, Codex Vaticanus, and Codex Bezae.

New Testament scholars are faced with a situation similar to the one that would have existed in the case of the Hebrew Bible before the production of the standard Masoretic text. Confronted with the large number of variations among the New Testament manuscripts, they have been led to distinguish three main textual families. One is associated with Alexandria in Egypt, a second is described as "Western," because the chief witnesses for it are Latin sources, and a third, later, form is known as the "Byzantine." The majority of manuscripts belong to this last tradition, and they became the basis for the most generally accepted *textus receptus* ("received text"), being reproduced in the first printed editions of the Greek New Testament, and in subsequent editions until the late nineteenth century.

Modern editions of the New Testament seek to reconstruct the original writer's words by comparing variant readings and attempting to decide which are the most authentic. However, the significance of the manuscript variants should not be exaggerated: all the manuscripts are witness to the same basic New Testament writings, most of which were probably written within a century of Jesus' death, by authors who belonged to the first generations of Christians. These writings are distinguished from the many apocryphal gospels (see p.190), acts of the Apostles, and letters, which were generally written much later than the New Testament canon and lack its authenticity.

THE BIBLE IN ENGLISH

The first complete English Bible was produced in 1382 from the Latin Vulgate by John Wycliffe, John Purvey, and Nicholas of Hereford. In 1526, William Tyndale produced the first English New Testament from Greek, and later translated Genesis–2 Chronicles from Hebrew.

Several complete English Bibles, all indebted to Tyndale, appeared in the reign of Henry VIII (1509–1547), notably the Great Bible, which was placed in all English churches by royal order. The Catholic Mary I (1553–1558) banned English Bibles, but one was produced by exiled Protestants in Geneva. The "Geneva Bible" (published 1560), the first English Bible with verse numbers, was very popular, but its extreme Protestant annotations offended the bishops of Elizabeth I (1558–1603). In 1568 they revised the Great Bible, and this "Bishop's Bible" was the basis of the "Authorized" or "King James Version" (KJV), commissioned by King James I and published in 1611. The KJV took four decades to replace the Geneva Bible in popularity, but thereafter its cultural influence was immense. By 1870 biblical scholarship had indicated many places where the translation could be improved, and the KJV was revised. But it remained the basis of the Revised Version and of the American Standard Version and its successor, the New Revised Standard Version. Many recent translations have aimed to be independent of the KJV, notably the New and Revised English Bible, the Good News Bible, and the New International Version.

Translations of the Bible

One of the most striking phenomena in connection with the Bible is the tremendous extent of its influence through translations into many different languages. The earliest of these was the translation of the Hebrew into Greek, the Septuagint, an undertaking unparalleled in the ancient world (see p.126). Each of the three great early translations, the Septuagint, the Latin Vulgate, and the Syriac Peshitta, became the standard Bible of one of the three main areas of medieval Christendom, respectively the Greek Orthodox, the Roman Catholic, and the Syrian.

In Western Europe, the Latin Vulgate remained the dominant version of the Bible throughout the Middle Ages. But, from an early period, there were numerous renderings of Scripture into vernacular

BIBLE TRANSLATION TODAY

In recent times Bible translation has been most vigorously pursued in Asia and Africa. In Asia, translators are often dealing with languages that already possess a considerable literature – for example, Japanese, Burmese, and the main Chinese and Indian languages. In Africa, on the other hand, they may face the task of creating a written language from a purely oral tradition. The same problem faces translations into the indigenous languages of South America. Translators also have to find terms to convey biblical concepts and images to peoples for whom they may be misleading, unfamiliar, or even unintelligible. The work of Bible translation continues to be a major task.

The title page of the 1534 edition of Luther's translation of the Bible. Martin Luther (1483–1546), was declared an outlaw in 1521 by the authorities of the Holy Roman Empire (a confederation of central European states) for his reformist religious views. Justifiably fearing for Luther's life, one of his aristocratic patrons organized his "kidnapping" and hid him for his own safety for several months at the Wartburg castle near Eisenach in Thuringia, Germany. It was there, in disguise and going by the name "Squire George," that Luther undertook his translation of the New Testament from the original Greek. The work was not Luther's alone; he succeeded in assembling a committee of advisers to check and, if necessary, improve his work. The Old Testament was completed after Luther left the castle.

languages. Sometimes these took the form of glosses on the Latin text, as with the famous gospels produced at the monastery of Lindisfarne off the coast of northeast England (ca. 950 CE). There were also many separate vernacular versions of the Bible in circulation. However, these renderings were generally somewhat free paraphrases, rather than strict translations, and they were only of certain biblical books.

In Eastern Europe, the first translations of the Bible into the Slavonic languages were made by the Greek missionaries Cyril and Methodius in the 860s. The language of their translations, known as Old Church Slavonic, became the liturgical language of the Orthodox Church in Slavonic-speaking lands. An edition of the Old Church Slavonic Bible published in St Petersburg, Russia, in 1751 (the Bible of Elizabeth) is the standard Bible of the Russian and other Slav Orthodox churches.

The sixteenth-century Reformation in Western Europe was a great motivating force behind many vernacular translations. The most important may well have been Martin Luther's translation of the Bible into German from the original Greek and Hebrew (from 1522). The influence of Luther's work was probably even more profound than that of the English Bible of 1611 (see sidebar, p.13), with which it has been compared. It was the first real literary work in modern German prose, and it created the vocabulary of literary German. It also served as the model for translations into other European languages, including English. None of these versions (in this context, "version" means "translation," as in "Authorized Version") achieved the same authority as the German and English standard Bibles. Nor did they have as great an influence on the cultures within which they appeared.

Protestant versions of the Scriptures led the way, but Catholics soon responded to a demand for Bibles in the vernacular. German Catholic Bibles appeared in Luther's own lifetime, and English Catholic exiles in Europe published an English New Testament in 1582 and an Old Testament in 1609–1610. French Catholic translations vied in popularity with Protestant ones: the seventeenth-century Catholic Bible of de Sacy was widely used by Protestants as well, and in some respects was the nearest French equivalent of the Luther or King James Bibles.

It has been estimated that the Bible has been published, either complete or in part, in more than two thousand languages, representing eighty percent of the world's population. Many translations have resulted from the Church's missionary work outside Europe, which, in modern times, began with Roman Catholic missions in the seventeenth century. Protestant missionaries were notably active in the era of European imperial expansion, and further work was undertaken by the Bible societies founded in the eighteenth and nineteenth centuries. The first translation of the Bible into an indigenous language of the New World was produced in 1663 by a Protestant missionary, John Eliot, in the now extinct Massachusetts Native American language.

History, Archaeology, and the Bible

Previous generations of scholars often linked archaeology very directly with the Bible: they spoke of "biblical archaeology" and saw it as a means of establishing the credibility of Scripture. It was felt that the archaeological evidence could demonstrate the historical veracity of, for example, the Ancestors, the Exodus, and the Israelite occupation of Canaan (see pp.62–5).

But these claims have not carried conviction. Scholars now recognize the complex relationship between archaeology and the biblical record, and there is no consensus about the course and historical setting of Israel's early existence. Archaeological evidence will rarely correlate neatly with the biblical record, but, with careful interpretation, it can often become a valuable supplement.

Archaeological investigation in Palestine, the primary setting of most of the biblical narratives, was ever more intensively pursued during the later twentieth century. The excavation of ancient towns there, and the discovery of both written and non-written remains, has revealed a great deal about the circumstances of Israelite daily life. Details of ordinary living and customs found in the Hebrew Bible have been invested with a new reality. The tenth-century "Gezer Calendar," discovered in 1908, has shown how Israelite farmers pursued their agricultural operations; and, at other sites, the layout of houses and streets, and the mass of domestic artifacts, have revealed a good deal about how the Israelites actually lived. Sometimes, findings will directly illuminate the biblical text. For example, the discovery of a weight labeled *pîm* has helped scholars understand 1 Samuel 13.21, the only verse in the Bible that includes the term; as the names of different weights were used to indicate value, it is clear that the verse is referring to a payment made to the Philistines. Other examples of such finds are the remarkable carved ivories of ca. 800 BCE found at the site of the royal palace of Samaria, capital of the northern kingdom of Israel (which existed 922–721 BCE). These illuminate such passages as 1 Kings 22.39, which refers to the "ivory house" of King Ahab.

Discoveries that show the nature of popular Israelite religion are of particular significance. At Arad, excavations have uncovered the only known Israelite temple and temple cult objects from the era of David and Solomon. Most remarkably, in the eighth-century site of Kuntillet Ajrud, archaeologists have found a painting of a half-nude female figure with an inscription mentioning "Yahweh of Samaria and his Asherah." Although the exact significance of this discovery is a matter of dispute, it may reflect the continuing veneration in Israel of Asherah, the great Canaanite mother goddess, in spite of the official state religion, which recognized Yahweh as the one and only God.

THE BIBLE AND HISTORY

The books of the Bible are all historical documents, produced by real people writing for their contemporaries against the background of their own times. One of the main aims of scholarship is to discover the historical setting of biblical texts and to show how the writers were responding to the circumstances of a given time and place. One aid in this task is the presence of references in the Bible to historical events, for example in the prophetical books. These references can often be corroborated by, and correlated with, evidence from extra-biblical sources.

Other approaches are concerned less with the historical truth behind the scriptural narratives than with the way in which the narrative framework determines the significance of the material as a whole. The chronological narrative in the Pentateuch and the historical books is the product of the collection and arrangement of a mass of traditions and documents into a single corpus, and the choice of events recorded may have been determined by the need to reflect and support the faith of the community. Many scholars today would consider that the Hebrew Bible's presentation of Israel's history is a reflection of a concern to understand the nation's destiny, and to preserve Israel's unity and identity in the light of the crisis brought about by the Exile.

HISTORY AND DIVINE REVELATION

The Bible has been seen as fostering the view that the way in which God has made himself known to humanity (divine revelation) has not been through ideas, concepts, or theological propositions, but rather through concrete acts, such as the deliverance of the Israelites from Egypt. This view of history as the medium for divine activity has often been claimed to be unique to the Bible. However, the idea of historical events as divine revelation was part of the common thinking of the ancient Near East and Hellenistic world. Much of the material in the Hebrew Bible seems to have little to do with revelation through history. It has to be asked whether an event was revelatory in itself or became so as a result of its interpretation. For example, what makes the Exodus so central to the Hebrew Bible is not the event itself but its significance as God's act. God himself communicates this to Moses before the crossing of the sea, and his explanation determines the meaning of the episode for the nation thereafter.

MYTHOLOGY AND SCRIPTURE

It is generally recognized today that myths and mythological concepts figure prominently in the Bible. The Hebrew Bible in particular can be set in the context of ancient Near Eastern religion, in which mythical thinking played an important part. The Bible contains myths in the strict sense: sacred stories set in an indeterminate "time of beginnings," in which the actors are divine or superhuman beings. These stories seek to account for the fundamental origins of the world, humanity, and social institutions. Such myths occupy a very small portion of the Bible – they are confined almost exclusively to the first eleven chapters of the book of Genesis – but they are significant because they express how the Israelites understood the universe.

The mythic character of Genesis 1–11 is confirmed by comparing the material in these chapters with the mythologies of some of the cultures surrounding Israel. There are parallels between Genesis 1 and the Babylonian creation epic (see p.21), and between Genesis and the theology of the ancient Egyptian cult center of Memphis. There are similarities between some themes in the narrative of the Garden of Eden, such as the molding of humans from soil (see p.21), the tree of life (see p.22), and the serpent (see p.23), and the Mesopotamian epics of Atrahasis and Gilgamesh. These epics furnish close parallels with the biblical story of Noah and the Flood (see pp.26–7), and the tale of the building of the Tower of Babel (see p.28) also has its roots in Mesopotamian sources. In Genesis, the ancient sacred myths have been revised in the light of Israel's own distinctive theology.

The language and structure of myths can be used to recount and interpret historical situations. Particularly significant in the Hebrew Bible is the widespread Near Eastern myth of a great conflict between a deity, and a water, or sea monster. For exaample, the Babylonian creation epic tells how Marduk, the supreme god of Babylon, killed a female dragon, Tiamat, the primal saltwater ocean. There is no conflict between God and an enemy in the first creation story in Genesis (see pp.22–3), but the idea of a watery chaos appears in Genesis 1.2: "darkness covered the face of the deep, while a wind from God swept over the face of the waters." Tehom, the Hebrew word for "the deep" in this passage, may be related to the name Tiamat. The deity's victory is often viewed as the prelude to his creation of the universe. There are numerous references to this myth in the Bible and it is found in the religion of the Canaanites, Israel's immediate neighbors, from whom it may well have been derived (see sidebar, left).

MYTHOLOGY AND THE NEW TESTAMENT

The extent to which the New Testament has a mythic character is much disputed. Revelation, as an apocalyptic work, certainly encompasses a wide range of mythical concepts, although it draws much of its inspiration from other apocalyptic books, especially Daniel and Ezekiel (see pp.392–94). The remainder of the New Testament also inherits many of the mythical themes and resonances of the religion of Israel. These were probably mediated through the apocalyptic writings, although in the main less obviously than in the case of Revelation. Attention has often been drawn to the New Testament's mythological conception of the universe, derived from the Hebrew Scriptures, and to the cosmic dimension to the presentation of Jesus, who is seen as a being outside time and space – creator, primordial man, and victorious king – which is so central to the thought of Paul and the Fourth Gospel.

CANAANITE MYTHOLOGY

The discovery in the twentieth century of a series of mythical poetic texts at the site of Ugarit (modern Ras Shamra), on the coast of Syria, provided first-hand evidence of the religion of the Canaanites. They gave details of the deities of the Canaanite pantheon, such as El, Baal, and Asherah – all names which occur in the Bible (see p.66). From the Ugaritic evidence, it appears that many of the characteristics of these deities were appropriated by the Israelite god Yahweh. The most important Canaanite myth deals with the fight for world kingship between Baal, the great storm god, and the chaos monster Yam, "the Sea," a being also called "River," "Dragon," "Serpent," and "Leviathan" in Ugaritic texts. Yam was the equivalent of the Mesopotamian chaos monster Tiamat. Baal was victorious, and his triumph guaranteed his control of the rains, the regular round of the seasons, and the world order. Much the same is said about God's defeat of the sea monster in Psalm 74.16–17.

After his triumph, Baal proclaimed himself king and was rewarded by the supreme god, El, with a palace: this was the great temple of Baal at Ugarit. The Baal epic was probably meant to be recited at a great autumn festival celebrating the end of the agricultural season and the coming of the new year. It is clear that the outlines of this myth were familiar to the Israelites. A number of the Psalms that speak of Yahweh's kingship and his victory over the waters of chaos may also be liturgical texts designed to accompany an annual celebration in the Temple of Jerusalem.

Noah releasing the animals from the ark after the Flood, a mosaic from St. Mark's Basilica in Venice, Italy (built 1071). The rainbow illustrates God's words to Noah: "I have set my bow in the clouds, and it shall be a sign of the covenant between me and the earth" (Gen. 9.13). This passage echoes the Babylonian creation myth, where the god Marduk hangs his bow in the sky after his defeat of Tiamat, a monster representing the waters of chaos (see also p.26).

A good example of mythologized history is the story of the Israelite Exodus from Egypt (Exod. 1–15). Whether the events narrated in these chapters have any basis in fact is virtually impossible to know. As it stands, the Bible interprets the episode in terms of the storm god's victory over the sea, especially in the culminating passage Exod. 15.1–18. This may originally have been a liturgy commemorating the Israelites' deliverance from Egypt. In many cultures, the mythical events of primordial time are often re-enacted through regular ritual celebrations. Some of Israel's festivals reflect this idea. For example, the feast of Tabernacles or Booths (see p.114) is considered by many scholars to contain elements representing the renewal of creation, Yahweh's victory over the forces of chaos, and his enthronement as king. This is the same pattern that is found in the case of Marduk in the Babylonian creation epic, or Baal in the Ugaritic texts. Myths are also a fruitful source for religious poetry, and for the inspired mystical utterances of prophecy (see p.88) and the genre known as "apocalyptic". There are numerous echoes of mythological themes in the Psalms, the prophetical books, and the apocalyptic writings.

וישא העם את בצקו טרם יחמץ משארותם צרורת בשמלותם על שכמם
וירדפו מצרים אחריהם וישיגו אותם חונים על הים כל סוס רכב פרעה

THE HEBREW SCRIPTURES AND APOCRYPHA

Left: Scenes from the Exodus, *from the* Brother Haggadah, *a Hebrew manuscript produced by the Jewish community in Barcelona, Spain, ca. 1350.* Top: *the Israelites leave Egypt (Exod. 12.50-51); the prominent bearded figures on the left are Moses and Aaron who are both holding onto a staff, one of the symbols of their office* *(see pp. 50-1)*. Bottom: *Pharaoh and his pursuing army (Exod. 14.8-9).*

ORIGINS

The first eleven chapters of the book of Genesis present a series of origin stories which prepare the ground for the appearance of the Israelites, the chosen people of God. Genesis is not concerned with the idea of creation out of nothing, but rather with how the world, as perceived by human beings, came into being. The concept of absolute beginning only occurs later in the Bible (for example in 2 Maccabees 7.28). The origin stories in Genesis describe the creation of the cosmos and the first people, the destruction of the world in a great flood, the re-emergence of humanity, and the origin of the different peoples and languages of the world.

THE CREATION

The opening chapters of the Bible describe God's creation of the ordered world and of humankind. It is widely agreed today that there are in fact two creation stories in Genesis. The first account, which runs from Genesis 1.1 to 2.4a, is usually said to be the work of an anonymous priestly writer ("P") of the sixth century BCE. This author's account draws on ancient mythological traditions and aims primarily to glorify the majesty and greatness of God rather than to give a scientific explanation of how the universe began. The creation story has a seven-day structure and ends with the institution of the Sabbath, the seventh day, when God rests to contemplate all that he has made. There are repeated refrains after each of the first six days ("And there was evening and there was morning, the first day," and so on), which suggest that the story was originally a hymn or poem. It may have formed part of the liturgy of a great annual festival in the Temple of Jerusalem before the time of the Exile in Babylon (see

God in the Act of Creation, *from the French* Bible Historiale *of 1411. Western European artists sometimes depicted God as a cosmic architect, measuring out the universe with a pair of compasses. The image is derived from passages such as Job 38.4–7. He is surrounded by flames, an image which evokes his manifestation in a pillar of flame, as in Exodus 13.21.*

pp.106–07). The festival probably celebrated God's victory over the primal chaos, a theme which was derived from older Near Eastern mythology (see p.16). The Bible retains some features of the ancient myth, such as the primeval waters, but the idea of a literal, physical, battle between the deity and chaos has disappeared. God overcomes chaos and establishes the ordered world simply through his free and unrestrained word or command, as expressed in the typical formula: "And God said, 'Let the earth bring forth living creatures.' " The belief that a deity's words possessed an almost magical power was widespread throughout the ancient Near East. The creative divine word is celebrated in Mesopotamian hymns and also in Egyptian myth, where the ordered universe is said to have come into existence through the word of the god Ptah.

This clay tablet of ca. 700 BCE is inscribed with part of the much older Babylonian creation myth, and relates the fight between Marduk, the great god of Babylon, and Tiamat, the dragon of chaos. It is written in Mesopotamian cuneiform ("wedge-shaped") script.

God separates the elements of the universe to produce an orderly, habitable cosmos in which plants, animals, and humans (see sidebar, right) can live. He divides the light from the darkness (Gen. 1.4); the waters below the dome of the sky from those above the dome of the sky (Gen. 1.6–8); the dry land from the seas (Gen. 1.9); and the day from the night (Gen. 1.14). Creation by separation occurs in early Sumerian texts and in the Babylonian creation epic, where the supreme god Marduk defeats Tiamat, the dragon of chaos, and cuts her in two, making one half of her corpse into the sky and the other half into the earth.

The second, and older, account of creation runs from Genesis 2.4b to 2.25 and is generally attributed to an author who is called the Yahwist or Jahvist ("J"), because this writer adds *Yahweh*, the personal name of God (see p.48), to the more abstract term *Elohim* ("God"). This creation story is basically similar in outlook to the first one, but its form is very different. It reflects the interests and concerns of a peasant society: before creation, the world is an arid desert without either rain or the farmer to make it suitable for life (Gen. 2.5). Genesis 2.6 describes how, before the existence of rain, "a stream would rise from the earth, and water the whole face of the ground." In the Hebrew original this "stream" is described by a word of Mesopotamian origin that denotes the underground waters that play a prominent part in Sumerian cosmology.

God molds the first man (*adam* in Hebrew) "from the dust of the ground" and breathes into him "the breath of life." This divine breath gives the man a unique closeness to the deity that corresponds to the idea in the first creation account that humans are "in the image of God." The concepts of the breath of life and of creation in the divine image are found together in a document written in the twenty-second century BCE for the Egyptian pharaoh Meri-ka-re. The formation of humans from soil or clay is common in the creation mythology of the peoples surrounding the Israelites. In Egyptian myth, for example, the god Khnum is said to have made gods, humans, and animals on a potter's wheel and then, like God in the Bible, breathed life into them. The first creation story in Genesis ended with the religious institution of the Sabbath; the second ends with the social institution of marriage: "Therefore a man leaves his father and his mother and clings to his wife, and they become one flesh" (Gen. 2.24).

In the garden of Eden (see p.22), God presents the animals to the man to be named (Gen. 2.19), an act which on one level serves as a simple explanation of how animals got their names, while also implying that the man controls them. It corresponds to the passage in Genesis 1 in which God grants humankind dominion over all creatures.

THE ORIGIN OF HUMANKIND

The first creation story relates how humans were created on the sixth day as the crown of creation. God does not create people through his simple command (there is no formula: "Let there be humans"), but he prefaces the creation of humanity with the words "Let us make humankind" (Gen. 1.26). The plural here probably indicates that God is taking counsel with the divine beings who, elsewhere in the Bible, form his heavenly court, for example in Nehemiah 9.6 and Job 1.6. Humanity is created "in the image of God." This probably means that, unlike other creatures, humans can communicate with God and respond to his word.

The creative act of separation (see main text) is present in God's creation of humankind as male and female. This establishes the essential complementary nature of the sexes: one cannot exist without the other, and both are equal in the eyes of God. God blesses humanity and grants it dominion over the future of the world and other creatures (Gen. 1.28).

The creation of humanity is central to the second creation story (see main text). In this older narrative the first woman is created after the first man (Adam), from his body (Gen. 2.21–22), a situation which no doubt reflects the dominant position of males in a patriarchal society. But the implied inferior status of women becomes explicit only after the fall from grace in Eden (see p.22), when God tells the woman: "your desire shall be for your husband, and he shall rule over you" (Gen. 3.16). Adam then gives his partner a name, Eve, an act that echoes his naming of the beasts, which expressed his dominion over animalkind. However, this account stresses, even more strongly than the first, the unity of the sexes and their mutual need. God says: "It is not good that man should be alone; I will make him a helper as his partner" (Gen. 2.18). Only woman proves suitable for this role.

THE GARDEN OF EDEN

According to the second chapter of Genesis, God planted a garden in a geographical region called "Eden" that is the source of a great river. The river flows into the garden and then divides into four branches, two of which, the Pishon and Gihon, are unidentified. The other two are the real rivers Tigris and Euphrates, which would therefore appear to locate Eden somewhere in the Mesopotamian region (the garden is described as "in the east," a phrase that is used to refer to Mesopotamia elsewhere in the Bible). However, although numerous more or less plausible suggestions have been put forward as to where the author intended Eden to be, the question is of secondary importance because the Bible's geography is essentially mythical and symbolic. The most significant point was that the fertility of the world known to the author depended on rivers flowing from the garden of God.

God created Eden as a habitat for newly created humanity (see p.21), but there are indications that the Israelites had a different, older, concept of Eden. In Ezekiel 28.13–19, it is referred to as the "garden of God" but also as a "holy mountain," full of precious stones. The description recalls the mountain between the source of two rivers that was said to be the abode of the god El, the head of the Canaanite pantheon (see p.66). This garden was the home of a supernatural being who was driven out for his presumption by a "guardian cherub." Such a myth probably lies behind the Genesis account, in which Adam and Eve are expelled from Eden and prevented from returning by cherubim (Gen. 3.24). Adam was probably in origin a supernatural or an angelic figure, as indeed he appears in some Jewish literature.

The garden of Eden occupied an important place in Jewish thought. For some of the prophets, it symbolized the renewal of Israel after the Babylonian Exile (see pp.106–09). The Greek translation of Genesis renders "Eden" as "paradise." Paradise, as the New Testament shows, came to be viewed as the final destiny of the righteous, who would return to the original state of perfection and harmony that was enjoyed by the first human pair in Eden.

THE FALL OF HUMANKIND: THE TWO TREES

The first man and woman live in a state of primeval leisure and innocence in the garden of Eden until, tempted by the serpent (see box on opposite page), they eat the fruit of the "tree of the knowledge of good and evil" in defiance of God's wishes. It was one of two trees in the garden, the other being the "tree of life," that is immortality (Gen. 2.9).

These trees are thought to represent two originally separate traditions which the biblical author has brought together to express his view of the origin of the human condition. The first tree belongs to a distinctly Israelite tradition. The "knowledge of good and evil" probably means the capacity for rational and ethical judgment. This attribute belongs supremely to God, who forbids humans to acquire it. After the first human pair has defied his command, God condemns them and their descendants to a life of toil and pain. He drives them from the garden in order to deny them the fruit of the tree of life, which would bestow the other divine attribute, eternal life (Gen. 3.22–24). Thus humans are like God in one respect but, unlike him, they die. In this distinction lies the vast potential but also the limitation of human existence. A sacred tree that confers eternal life occurs in many mythologies and is common in Near Eastern iconography. Numerous myths of the region explain that humanity is mortal because one person failed to eat a magical food that would have made them live forever (one example is found in the Mesopotamian epic of Gilgamesh). But the story in Genesis is alone in stressing that humans continue to suffer death as a direct consequence of their disobedience to God's command.

A reconstruction of a mural from the palace of Mari on the Euphrates River in Syria (ca. 1750 BCE). Some of its features strikingly recall details of the Genesis description of the garden of Eden. In particular, the mural depicts two types of tree (compare Gen. 2.9), guarded by mythical winged animals or cherubim (compare Gen. 3.24). The lower half of the central panel shows figures holding jars from which flow four streams (compare Gen. 2.10). The upper scene may depict a king being invested by the Mesopotamian fertility goddess Ishtar: Eve has been associated with such divine figures (see box on opposite page).

The serpent

Adam and Eve with the Serpent, *Spanish school, 12th century. Adam and Eve cover their nakedness after eating the fruit of the tree of knowledge (Gen. 3.7).*

The serpent in Genesis 3 is an ambiguous creature. In one respect, it is simply the snake, one of the animals made by God, and its physical characteristics and behavior are explained in Genesis 3.14–15. Here, in accordance with folktale, the serpent is represented as a cunning creature that causes trouble and is punished. It can also speak.

However, the serpent in Eden probably also represents a demythologized version of what was originally a much more significant being. Archaeologists have revealed that the serpent was widely venerated in Egypt and the Near East, not least in Canaan. There was also at one time a cult of the serpent in Israel, as demonstrated by the bronze serpent that is reported in the Bible to have once stood in the Temple at Jerusalem. (This serpent was destroyed by King Hezekiah: see 2 Kings 18.4.) The serpent was seen as the bringer of life, because it was able to shed and renew its skin annually: according to the Mesopotamian epic of Gilgamesh, it acquired this ability through eating the magical plant of immortality. The creature was particularly associated with fertility, and fertility goddesses are often shown accompanied by serpents. It has been suggested that "Eve," the name of the first woman in the biblical account, is related to a word for snake, and that she was originally a serpent goddess, the goddess of life and fertility.

In ancient tradition, the serpent is also a more sinister being that is associated with the underworld and its waters. In the Bible and elsewhere, the hostile monster that embodies primal chaos is frequently described as a serpent. When the author of Revelation identified "that ancient serpent" with the Devil or Satan (Rev. 12.9), he established this manifestation of the serpent as the enemy of God.

THE LAND OF DILMUN

It has been suggested that the biblical author meant to place Eden somewhere in the region of the northern end of the Persian Gulf. If so, it could be related to the land of Dilmun, which appears in the Sumerian myth of Enki and Ninhursag. In this myth, Dilmun, perhaps identifiable with present-day Bahrain, is a mythical place, a potential rather than a real world. Sickness and old age are unknown there, but it lacks the fresh water that is necessary to sustain plant and animal life. The god Enki therefore creates rivers with water from beneath the earth, and Dilmun becomes a rich and fruitful place. According to later Babylonian myth, a similar ideal land was the home of the few humans who became immortal.

CAIN AND ABEL

THE FAMILY OF ADAM AND EVE
The descendants of Adam and Eve, as presented in the two genealogies of Genesis chapters 4 and 5.

ADAM AND EVE

Cain	Seth
Enoch	Enosh
Irad	Kenan
Mehujael	Mahalalel
Methushael	Jared
Lamech	Enoch
	Methuselah
	Lamech
	Noah

A clay mask from the city of Ur depicting an ancient Mesopotamian demon. Before Abel's murder, God warns Cain that "sin is lurking at the door" (Gen. 4.7). This may refer to a well-known Babylonian demon, the rabisu *or "croucher."*

The story of Adam's and Eve's descendants down to the time of Noah is recounted in Genesis 4–5. The account represents one or more traditions that were originally separate from the preceding three chapters of Genesis, as is revealed by a number of logical discrepancies. For example, the farmer Cain murders the shepherd Abel out of jealousy (Gen. 4.8) and God condemns Cain to be "a fugitive and wanderer on the earth." But God puts a mark on him "so that no one who came upon him would kill him." However, there is no indication of how, if Cain is the only surviving child of the first man and woman, there can be anyone else who might kill him. Similarly, Genesis 4.17 states that "Cain knew his wife," but does not explain where she came from. More generally, the narrative presupposes the existence of an organized society, civilization, and culture. There is no solution to such inconsistencies, because the biblical writer did not consider them to be of primary importance.

The narrative is otherwise carefully integrated with what precedes and follows it. It marks the culmination of the Eden story (see pp.22–3) and presents Cain, the first murderer, as the representative of primeval humanity. As in the story of Adam and Eve, the tale of Cain and Abel follows the pattern of wrongdoing, penalty, banishment, and mitigation of God's punishment. It begins a series of narratives in the first eleven chapters of Genesis which chart the increasing violence and presumption of humankind after the Fall and expulsion from Eden. In each case, humanity incurs severe divine judgment, and its very existence is threatened. But God always shows mercy and takes steps to ensure that, in spite of everything, the world and the human race will continue. This pattern determines the general shape and meaning of the story of Cain.

The account is constructed from various motifs, many of which are rooted in myth and folktale. One is the motif of God favoring a younger son over his elder brother, a situation which often leads to jealousy and violence. Genesis 4.4–5 recounts how each brother presents an offering to God, who prefers Abel's gift of animal flesh to Cain's gift of crops. Cain is angry at the rebuff and murders his brother out of jealousy. No reason is given for God's choice, although later writers suggested that God knew of Cain's inherent wickedness. As in the case of Isaac and Ishmael, Jacob and Esau, and Joseph and his brothers, the biblical author sees no need to account for the divine selection. However, the passage may allude to the Hebrew sacrificial system, in which animal sacrifice was more prominent and more highly valued than cereal offerings (see pp.116–17).

Other ancient ideas are present in the narrative. After the murder, Cain is no longer able to cultivate the land because his victim's blood is said to have made it barren, a common concept in the Bible and other ancient traditions. Another theme is the age-old tension between the pastoral and the agricultural ways of life, which is also seen in the Sumerian tale of Dumuzi and Enkimdu. Dumuzi the shepherd and Enkimdu the farmer are rivals for the hand of the goddess Inanna. As in the story of Cain and Abel, the deity prefers the shepherd to the farmer, although in this case the two rivals are reconciled.

The story does not present Cain in a wholly negative light. God sets a mark on Cain to protect him, and he is banished to "the land of Nod," a word which simply means "wandering" and indicates the life of a nomad. This part of the story serves to explain the existence of the Kenites, a nomadic people traditionally said to be descended from Cain. The Kenites lived on the fringes of settled civilization, but had close connections with the Israelites.

After Eden: the decline of civilization

Between the stories of Cain and Noah there are two genealogies, one of Cain, and one of Adam. These are usually said to be by different authors, but the coincidence and similarity of some names (see sidebar on opposite page) suggest that both genealogies have a common source. The account of Cain and his descendants shows him as a founding father rather than the brooding murderer presented in the preceding narrative. He establishes the first city, called Enoch for his son, and his descendants are pictured as the originators of the human skills that characterize a settled existence: cattle-rearing, music, and metalworking (Gen. 4.17–22). The genealogy ends with the family of Lamech, a figure of violence who takes two wives and boastfully declares how he has killed a man (Gen. 4.23). He is probably meant to show how far humankind has degenerated morally from its primeval state, in spite of all the positive aspects of human development. A similar view of the development of humanity is found in the *Works and Days* by the Greek poet Hesiod, ca. 700 BCE.

Musicians playing horn and drum on a stone relief from Carchemish in northern Mesopotamia, ca. 800 BCE. According to the Bible, the first musician was Jubal, a son of Lamech and descendant of Cain.

Adam's genealogy (Gen. 5) through his third son Seth, serves a similar purpose to that of Cain, although nothing is said explicitly about the spread of evil among humankind. But the fact that the genealogy leads up to the picture of universal evil in the days of Noah suggests that it, too, intends to portray humanity's progressive moral degeneration. This genealogy has often been compared with the Sumerian "King List," a catalog of rulers before the great Flood. However, it is much closer to the work of Berossus, a Babylonian priest of the third century BCE, who lists ten rulers before the Flood and also gives an account of the deluge. Like Adam and his descendants, including Noah, each of these rulers has a fantastically long lifespan.

Tilling and sowing, a mural from Thebes, Egypt. Cain, "a tiller" (Gen. 4.2), was the ancestor of those who "have livestock" (Gen. 4.20).

THE FLOOD

The progressive corruption of the world after Eden culminates in God's decision to destroy "all flesh in which is the breath of life" by a great deluge, the story of which is told in Genesis 6–9. However, in accordance with the general pattern of divine judgment in Genesis, God mitigates his punishment. One man, Noah, "found favor in the sight of the Lord," because he "was a righteous man, blameless in his generation" (Gen. 6.8–9). God decides to spare Noah and his family to make a new start for the human race. He instructs Noah to build an ark (ship) to contain his family and at least one male and one female of every species of animal, so that the world can be repopulated after the Flood. Most authorities accept that the flood story as it stands is the work of two authors, "J" and "P" (see pp.20–1). This is revealed by some discrepancies in the story: for example, in Genesis 6.19 God tells Noah to take "two of every kind" of creature into the ark, but in 7.2 this becomes seven pairs of all clean animals, one pair of all unclean animals, and seven pairs of each species of birds. But both sources tell fundamentally the same tale, and they have been skillfully woven together to form a generally consistent whole.

The story functions as a kind of second creation, and the language it employs often recalls the original creation account. The flood waters come from both above the dome of the sky and below the earth, undoing the creative act of separation described in Genesis 1.6–7, and allowing the primitive state of chaos to return. When the deluge subsides, the appearance of the dry land is emphasized (Gen. 8.13–14), which recalls Genesis 1.9–10. The outcome of the narrative is the establishment of the world as we know it, when God promises that the earth will never again be destroyed. In one sense, the original creation is restored: the alternation of the seasons is assured (Gen. 8.22) and humanity will be fruitful and multiply (Gen. 9.1). But the post-Flood world does not mean a return to Eden. God now accepts that "the inclination of the human heart is evil from youth" (Gen. 8.21) and that the human behavior which caused the Flood can be controlled, but not abolished.

The dominion of humans over the beasts now means that animals will fear and dread humans, who can kill them for food (Gen. 9.2). However, humans may only eat meat from which the blood has been drained, and human life is stringently protected. These regulations form the core of what are called the Noachide ("of Noah") commands, which for the Jewish rabbis constituted a basic law for all humanity. The perpetuity of this new world order is guaranteed by a covenant, a unilateral promise by God that "never again shall all flesh be cut off by the waters of a flood, and never again shall there be a flood to destroy the earth" (Gen. 9.11). The term covenant, which makes its first appearance in Genesis 6.18, plays a central role in Israelite religion. Here, it brings humans and all other creatures into a direct relationship with God. The sign of the covenant is the "bow" which God sets in the clouds to remind him of his inviolable promise. This is usually taken to mean a rainbow, but it may also represent the weapon of a warrior god similar to Marduk in the Babylonian creation epic (see p.21). Marduk hangs his bow in the sky as a sign of his victory over Tiamat, the goddess of chaos. Perhaps at one time the end of the Flood was seen as the taming of the waters of chaos: Genesis 8.1 describes how a divine wind makes the floodwaters recede ("And God made a wind blow over the earth, and the waters subsided"), which recalls the Creation story (Gen. 1.2: "a wind from God swept over the waters"). In this case, the hanging up of the bow would signal the restoration of peace and harmony.

THE SONS OF GOD AND THE DAUGHTERS OF HUMANS

Genesis 6.1–8 forms the introduction to the story of the great Flood. It is in two sections, the first of which had no original connection with the Flood narrative. However, the author uses both sections to explain why God sent the deluge.

The first section (Gen. 6.1–4) gives a brief summary of an ancient myth that relates how divine beings mated with human women and produced offspring. In Hebrew thought, the human and the divine ought not to be confused, so these children violate the whole structure of the world. As punishment, God frustrates any attempt on humanity's part to attain divinity and immortality by declaring "my spirit shall not abide in mortals forever," and restricting their lifespan to one hundred twenty years. The children are described as "mighty men of old," who appear in a later chapter as the embodiment of absolute power in the ancient world. But they are also described as "Nephilim," which probably means "fallen ones." This is one source of the myth of the fallen angels that plays a prominent part in such books as Enoch and Jubilees, works that stand outside the Bible and Apocrypha. Jewish thought came to see these angels, rather than the sin of Adam, as the source of sin in the world.

The second section (Gen. 6.5–8) presents a picture of universal wickedness and evil that is the climax of humanity's increasing degeneracy (see main text).

Noah's Ark, *an illustration from the Nuremberg Bible of 1483. The shape of the ark has been the subject of much debate. In Genesis 6.15, God gives the dimensions of the ark as 300 by 50 by 30 cubits (one cubit is about 18 inches or 45 cm). This was often taken to mean that the vessel was rectangular, as here and on the coin below, rather than with a pointed prow and stern. The word for "ark" in Hebrew,* teba, *means "box" or "chest," and is otherwise used only of the basket in which the baby Moses was laid. In the epic of Gilgamesh (see box, below), Utnapishtim builds a box-like boat in the form of a perfect cube, although it differs from Noah's ark in other respects.*

Deluge myths of the ancient Near East

Stories of a great deluge occur widely in mythology throughout the world. The biblical story of Noah is a version of a flood myth that originated in Mesopotamia and was familiar throughout the ancient Near East from the time of the Sumerians (ca. 2500–2000 BCE). All the known versions of this myth have the same basic outline: a deity or deities send a deluge to destroy the world, but one righteous man is forewarned of the disaster and builds a ship in which he and his family survive the flood. After the flood has subsided, the world continues to exist and is repopulated.

Before God sends the Flood, the Bible tells us that human beings "began to multiply on the face of the ground" (Gen. 6.1). A similar expression occurs in the flood story in the Mesopotamian epic of Atrahasis, where the reason for the deluge is the gods' desire to curb human overpopulation. There are striking resemblances between the Genesis story and the account of a great flood related by Utnapishtim, who is the equivalent of Noah, in the Babylonian epic of Gilgamesh. For example, Utnapishtim survives the flood by building a ship. The vessel finally comes to rest on Mount Nisir, which is in the same region as "the mountains of Ararat," where Noah's ark comes to rest (Gen. 8.4). Utnaphishtim opens a window of his ship and sends out a dove, a swallow, and a raven to reconnoiter the ground, much as Noah opens the window of the ark and sends out a raven and a dove.

On emerging from the ship, Utnapishtim offers a sacrifice which propitiates the gods when they smell its sweet savor, and they agree that in future humanity should be punished if it behaves wickedly, but not destroyed. Noah likewise offers a sacrifice, and after smelling its "pleasing odor," Yahweh promises: "I will never again curse the ground because of humankind ... nor will I ever again destroy every living creature as I have done" (Gen. 8.21). Finally, both Utnapishtim and Noah are blessed and rewarded. Utnapishtim is granted immortality, while Noah lives for another three hundred fifty years and is granted a fecund progeny that will repopulate the whole world.

A Greek coin (artist's reconstruction below) of the 3rd century CE *showing Noah and his wife, both outside and inside the ark.*

THE TOWER OF BABEL

The story of the Tower of Babel (Gen. 11.1–9) begins with the ideal primeval situation in which everyone in the world speaks the same language. Humanity is presented as a small, homogenous group which travels from "the east" to the plain of Shinar, a region in what is now southern Iraq. There, people prepare to build a city and a tower "with its top in the heavens" (Gen. 11.4) to give them both identity and security. Yahweh, alarmed that "nothing that they propose to do will now be impossible for them" (Gen. 11.6), aborts the operation by causing the people to speak in different languages and scattering them over the earth. Genesis says that the city is named Babel from the Hebrew *balal* "to confuse," because Yahweh "confused the language of all the earth" (Gen. 11.9).

The narrative portrays the development of civilization, the change from nomadism to city life, and seeks to explain the existence of different languages and nations. It also attempts to account for the existence of a particular city, Babylon, and a particular tower: the description of the Tower of Babel in Genesis is probably based on the great ziggurat of Babylon (see opposite page and also p.31). The aim in building such a tower is to allow men to climb up to heaven and challenge the authority of the gods, an act of impiety and presumption that is frustrated by divine intervention.

The Building of the Tower of Babel, *by Abel Grimmer (1570–ca. 1619).*

Babylon

The materials used to build the Tower of Babel were the same as those employed for the construction of the great ziggurat of Babylon and similar ziggurats, according to ancient building inscriptions. The golden age of Babylon arrived when the Assyrian empire fell in 612 BCE. It became the dominant imperial power in the Near East, and the restoration of the city by Nebuchadrezzar II (605–562 BCE) transformed it into one of the seven wonders of the world in Greek eyes. Babylon fell to the Persian king Cyrus in 539 BCE and while it remained an important city under the later Achaemenid, Seleucid, and Parthian empires, it never again played an independent political role.

Babylon becomes in the Bible much more than a historical reality. After Nebuchadrezzar destroyed Jerusalem and exiled many of its inhabitants (see pp.104–07) it was viewed as the embodiment of all evil, a kingdom of wickedness set against God and his chosen people, a powerful and complex symbol of pride, oppression, wealth, luxury, sexual license, and idolatry. As such, Babylon is doomed to final destruction.

In Isaiah 14, the king of Babylon is described, in terms of an ancient myth, as Lucifer, the morning star, who aspired to scale heaven and challenge God himself. For his arrogance, Lucifer is cast into the underworld. The underlying theme of this story – the penalty paid for presumption – is similar to that of the Tower of Babel, as well as to that of the "fallen ones" (see p.26). The book of Isaiah mocks the idols which played so prominent a part in Babylonian religion and sees the city's chief deities, Marduk and Nebo, being carried away into captivity (Isaiah 46.1–2). The prophet depicts Babylon as a female prisoner of war, who was once a "lover of luxury" and a practitioner of sorceries and spells, but who is now stripped of all her splendor and forced to sit in the dust (Isaiah 47). For the prophet, the imminent capture of Babylon by Cyrus is evidence that the Persian king is the chosen agent of God's vengeance (Isaiah 45.1–7).

The name "Babylon" came to be applied to any empire that was seen as the enemy of God and the persecutor of his servants. The author of the book of Daniel tells stories of the humiliation of Nebuchadrezzar and the death of Babylon's last ruler, Belshazzar (see pp.128–29). Their fates serve as models for the destiny awaiting the Greek ruler Antiochus IV Epiphanes, the persecutor of the Jews in his own day (see pp.132–33). Subsequent Jewish writers identified Babylon primarily with the Roman empire. This identification is applied to the situation of the early Church in the book of Revelation, written in the shadow of the emperor Nero's persecution of Christians (see pp.392–94). There, Babylon is Rome, "the mother of whores and every obscenity" (Rev. 17.3–6), that will soon suffer complete and dramatic destruction (Rev. 18).

Ironically, the deportation to Babylon of the leading citizens of the kingdom of Judah in the reign of Nebuchadrezzar signaled a more positive evaluation of Babylon in Jewish life. The presence of the exiled Jews in Babylon made the city a great Jewish intellectual center. The massive Babylonian Talmud acts, even to this day, as an authoritative source for Jewish religion.

An inscribed basalt block describing the restoration of Babylon ca. 670 BCE by the Assyrian king Esarhaddon (681–669 BCE).

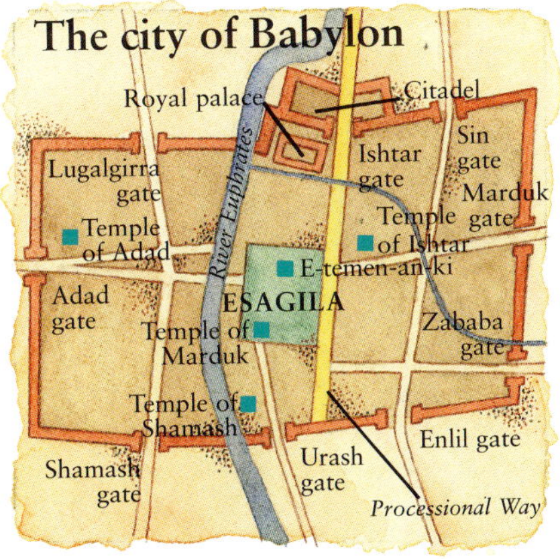

Babylon in the time of Nebuchadrezzar II. At its heart was Esagila, a huge sanctuary complex which contained the temple of Marduk, and E-temen-an-ki, the great ziggurat of Babylon, probably the prototype of the Tower of Babel.

THE ANCESTORS

The end of the first stage of the biblical story is marked by the episode of the Tower of Babel. The succeeding chapters of Genesis move from the universal perspective of cosmic origins to the origins of a single people, the Israelites. Israel's beginnings are recounted through the lives of the founding ancestors of the people. The patriarchs Abraham, Jacob, and Joseph are each the focus of a major story cycle, and there is also a considerably more concise account of Isaac. It seems likely that these four individuals originally represented different tribal groups, with their own specific traditions. But they have been united into a single family to present a family history traced through four successive generations.

THE CALL OF ABRAHAM

The episode of the Tower of Babel (see p.28) leaves humanity divided into competing nations, and God's choice now falls on one particular people. In Genesis 12.1–2 he speaks to Abraham, the son of Terah and a descendant of Noah's son Shem: "Go from your country and your kindred and your father's house to the land that I will show you. I will make of you a great nation." The subsequent obedience of Abraham (who is called Abram in the early part of the story) reverses humanity's previous disobedience and establishes him as the ancestor of Israel.

In the present century, many experts have become confident enough in their knowledge of the ancient Near East to place the ancestors of Israel in the second millennium BCE. Recently, however, this conclusion has been challenged. Some features of the biblical stories seem to indicate a period later than the second millennium. A number of alleged parallels between the archaeological evidence and the Bible narrative have turned out, on more careful examination, to be much less close than has often been claimed. Also, many customs and beliefs that supposedly characterized the second millennium BCE continued into later centuries. This reexamination has led some authorities to claim that the traditions of the ancestors were largely produced by the Israelite community of a much later date, perhaps even during the period of the Exile (587/6–539 BCE). But this does not mean that the ancestors never existed. Later generations may have retained authentic memories of these figures, who play a significant part in Israel's history and religious development.

The story of Abraham begins in the ancient Sumerian town of Ur in southern Mesopotamia, which was an important city until its destruction in 1740 BCE. The decision of Abraham's father Terah to leave Ur with his family (Gen. 11.31) has been linked with a supposed migration from the region of the nomadic Amorite people as a result of the upheavals of the time. But Ur revived under the Neo-Babylonian or Chaldean empire (ca. 625–539 BCE), and the Genesis description "Ur of the Chaldeans" would appear to indicate this later period. Terah set out for Canaan but settled

in the city of Haran, in northern Mesopotamia. Haran was linked with Ur by a long-established trade route, and both cities were important centers of the cult of the moon god Sin. Like Ur, it was prominent both in the second millennium BCE and under the Neo-Babylonians. In Haran, Abraham received God's call and apparently set out from there on his journey. In fact, the real home of Abraham's family seems not to have been Ur, but the region of Haran. His brother is called Haran, and he has relatives called Terah, Nahor, and Serug, which are also the names of towns near Haran. Later in the story, Abraham sends his servant to find a wife for his son Isaac, from among what Abraham calls "my kindred" who live in "my country." This turns out to be not southern Mesopotamia but Nahor, where the servant finds Rebekah, Abraham's great-niece (Gen. 24). Later still, Isaac's and Rebekah's son Jacob takes refuge in Haran with his uncle Laban (Gen. 28), and marries into his family.

Numerous features of the story of the ancestors (such as their wanderings with livestock and living in tents) hint at the life of pastoral nomads. It has been suggested that the biblical authors were city dwellers who regarded nomads with some disdain, and sought to stress that the founders of Israel originally came from areas of settled urban civilization.

The much-restored remains of the great ziggurat or sacred tower of ancient Ur, in southern Iraq. Such structures probably inspired the Tower of Babel (see pp.28–9).

God's promises to the ancestors

The main concern of the biblical writers who related the story of the ancestors was not historical accuracy but the theological significance of the founders of the nation. The most common motif running through the narrative of Genesis 12–50 is God's pledge for the future. He makes two promises to the ancestors: that they will possess the land of Canaan and that they will become a great nation. These are brought together in God's announcement to Abraham before he sets out on his journey from Haran. The promise of the land appears to be the more important: the entire narrative of the ancestors begins with the divine command to Abraham to go to the land of Canaan, and ends with the divine assurance that his descendants will return to the land "that he swore to Abraham, to Isaac, and to Jacob" (Gen. 50.24).

The ancestors, in fact, did not take possession of Canaan, which only happened later under Joshua (see pp.62–3). This delay in the fulfillment of the promise meant that the family line had to be continued, so that there would be someone to whom the Promised Land could be given in due course. A prominent theme in the whole saga of Abraham and his successors is the need to produce a direct heir (see p.36).

A caravan of migrating Asiatics, from an Egyptian wall painting of ca. 1890 BCE. The wanderings of Abraham have sometimes been linked to the migration of nomadic Near Eastern peoples.

ABRAHAM'S TRAVELS

THE JEOPARDY OF THE MATRIARCH
When Abraham and Sarah arrive in Egypt, an episode occurs that reflects a folktale motif described as "the jeopardy of the female ancestor" (Gen. 12.11–20). Abraham fears that Sarah's beauty will cause the Egyptians to kill him so that someone can take her as a wife. He asks her to say that she is his sister. Sarah does so and becomes Pharaoh's wife. Plagues afflict the royal house, as a result of which Pharaoh discovers the deception. He is angry that Abraham has caused him to marry another man's wife unwittingly, but shows clemency. He orders Abraham and Sarah to leave Egypt with their possessions. The plot of this episode is repeated twice, once again in connection with Sarah (Gen. 20), and then with Rebekah (Gen. 26). Both of these later incidents involve a certain King Abimelech, probably a different ruler in each case.

The biblical account of Abraham's career may appear to be made up of a string of disconnected episodes, but there are several distinct themes running through them. The patriarch's story in many ways encapsulates the subsequent history of Israel. After God's call to Abraham, he leaves Haran together with his wife Sarah (who is called Sarai at this stage of the story; see p.36) and their nephew Lot, and the group journeys into Canaan. Abraham erects altars and invokes Yahweh at Shechem and Bethel. Later, after leaving Egypt, he puts up another altar at Mamre near Hebron. These places were ancient Canaanite places of worship, and there are two references (Gen. 12.6 and 13.18) to oaks (or terebinths), the sacred trees often found at Canaanite shrines. At Shechem and Mamre, Abraham erects altars in response to a theophany (a manifestation of the deity), in which God promises the land in perpetuity to the patriarch and his offspring. Establishing a new cult is one method of laying claim to territory, so Abraham's altar-building paves the way for Israel's eventual occupation of Canaan. It also sanctions the newcomers to maintain the holy places of the former inhabitants for their own worship.

Abraham, Sarah, and Lot move on to Egypt as the result of a famine. Abraham becomes a wealthy merchant, mainly on account of Pharaoh's patronage after Sarah enters his household (see sidebar, left). However, Abraham, Sarah, and Lot are eventually compelled to leave Egypt and return to Canaan. These travels recall the tradition of the migration of the Israelite tribes into Egypt at the time of Joseph, and the subsequent Exodus under Moses.

Once back in Canaan, Abraham and Lot decide to go their separate

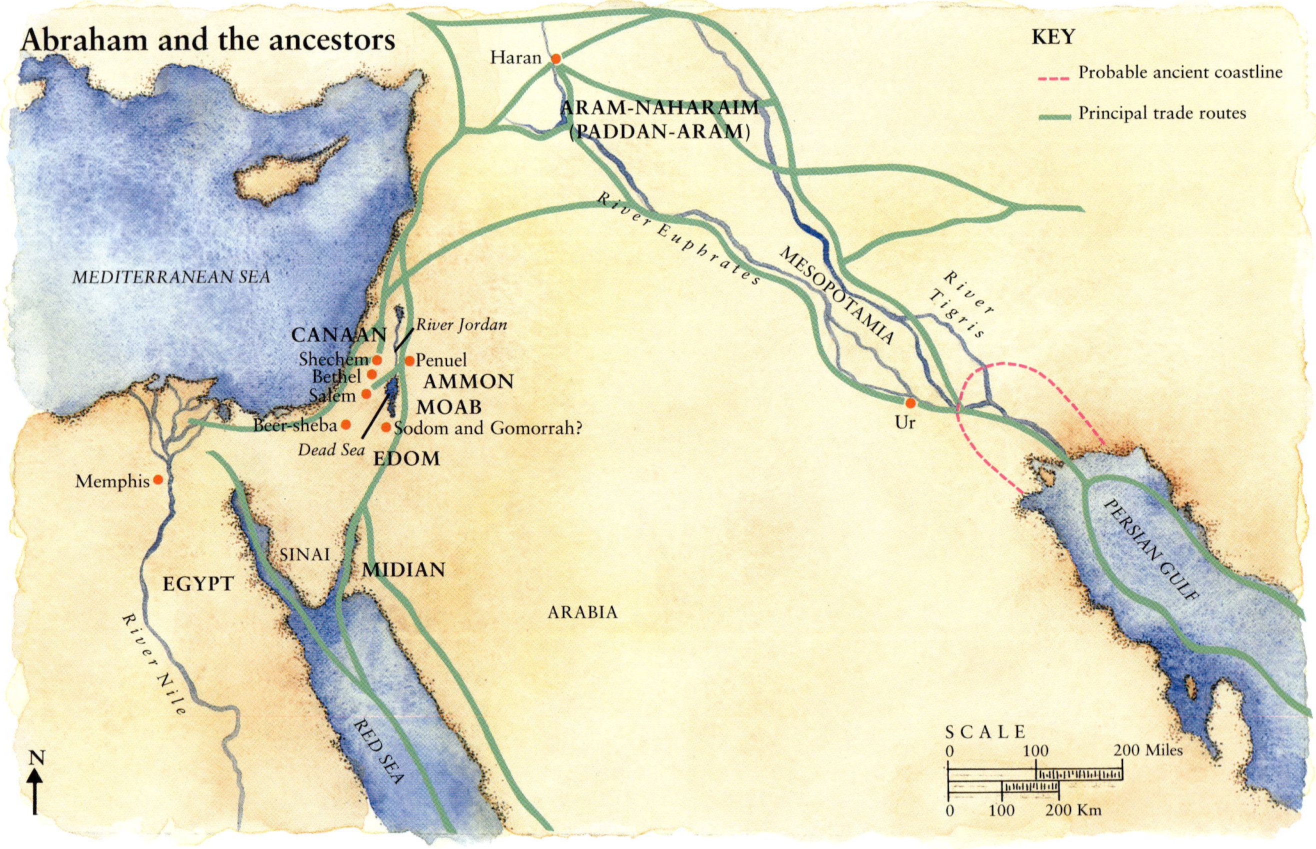

Abraham and Melchizedek

The narrative of Genesis 14 presents Abraham as a military commander, a picture that is very different from the other traditions about him. It tells of a coalition of four kings who campaign against five rulers of the area where Lot, Abraham's nephew, has settled. Two of the five rulers, the kings of Sodom and Gomorrah, are routed, and Lot is taken prisoner during the sack of Sodom, where he lives. Abraham collects three hundred eighteen retainers, defeats the four kings, and frees his nephew. Some of the names of the four kings are attested in non-biblical sources of the early second millennium BCE. But such a great military coalition is improbable, and the Bible account cannot be taken as historically reliable.

After his victory, Abraham is greeted and blessed by Melchizedek, the king of Salem (later Jerusalem) and priest of "God Most High," that is, El Elyon, the high god of pre-Israelite Jerusalem. Abraham identifies El Elyon with Yahweh and gives Melchizedek one-tenth of the booty he has won. The whole episode helps to explain the situation after the conquest of Jerusalem by David. El Elyon was assimilated to Yahweh, the Israelite monarch assumed the position of the former Canaanite priest-king, and the Israelites began to pay tithes for the upkeep of the ancient sanctuary. In the New Testament, the figure of Melchizedek is compared to Jesus in the letter to the Hebrews (see p.389).

The circumcision of two boys, from an ancient Egyptian relief of ca. 2200 BCE. The hieroglyphics above the man performing the operation on the left translate as: "Hold him, do not let him faint!"

ways, and Lot heads for the southern shores of the Dead Sea to settle in the plain of the Jordan River. It appears that Abraham originally intended to share Canaan with Lot, but Lot chooses part of the Jordan valley that lies outside the territory promised by God. Subsequently, in Genesis 19, Lot is said to be the ancestor of the Transjordanian Moabite and Ammonite peoples (although this Lot may originally have been unconnected with Abraham's nephew; see p.35). The parting of the patriarch and his nephew represents the separation of the direct descendants of Abraham from their ethnic relatives: Israel alone is the rightful heir of the divine pledge. God's promises to the ancestors (see p.31) are guaranteed by a covenant with Abraham, the first male ancestor. This covenant is found in two versions, one said to be by the biblical author "J," the other by the priestly author "P" (see p.20). The first, vividly described in Genesis 15, takes the form of God's unconditional commitment to give the patriarch all the land "from the river of Egypt to the great river, the river Euphrates," the ideal extent of Israelite rule. The covenant is effected in an ancient ritual in which an oath is confirmed by someone passing between the divided pieces of one or more sacrificial animals. In Genesis 15.17, Yahweh does this in the shape of a smoking brazier and a flaming torch. A similar rite is mentioned in a document of ca. 1775 BCE from the Mesopotamian city of Mari, which describes a treaty-making ceremony between two peoples.

"P"'s version of the covenant, in Genesis 17, involves an obligation not only on God's part but also on Abraham's. Abraham and his descendants are commanded to circumcise every male in the community, including slaves, on the eighth day after birth. Circumcision was an ancient custom practiced by many of Israel's neighbors. Originally, it was probably performed at the onset of puberty or before marriage, but the priestly writer reinterprets it as the mark of the covenant, the sign of belonging to God's chosen people. For this reason it should be performed at the earliest possible moment of a person's life (see also box on p.49).

A 19th-century photograph of the sacred oaks at Mamre, Hebron, reputed to be where Abraham erected an altar (Gen. 13.18) and where three divine beings appeared to him (Gen. 18.1; see also p.37).

SODOM AND GOMORRAH

One of the "pillars of salt," the craggy salt-rock formations that characterize the landscape around the Dead Sea. The sea is shown in the background.

God's destruction of "the cities of the Plain," which centers on the fate of Sodom and Gomorrah, is recounted in Genesis 18–19. The story was originally unconnected with the Abraham saga, and appears there because it is also concerned with Abraham's nephew, Lot. Its central theme recalls the story of the great Flood (see pp.26–7): the disaster is a divine punishment for the wickedness of the people, all of whom are destroyed except for one man. The downfall of Sodom and Gomorrah is mentioned more frequently in the Hebrew Scriptures and the New Testament than any other event in the book of Genesis. However, the language of the references suggests that they are not derived from the narrative in Genesis but reflect a popular tradition of a great calamity that occurred in primeval times. The story of what happened to Lot and his daughters, after the destruction of the cities (see sidebar on opposite page) also contains hints of a more cosmic myth, in particular the idea of the renewal of humanity following a universal disaster. This interpretation of the tale is found as early as the time of the Jewish commentators Philo (ca. 15 BCE–50 CE) and Josephus (37 CE–ca. 100 CE).

Just as the Flood story probably reflects the real inundations of the Tigris and Euphrates rivers, the story of Sodom and Gomorrah may have its source in some natural disaster in the region around the southern Dead Sea (see map on p.32). To some extent it serves to explain the bizarre appearance of the landscape in the area. The agents of destruction are described as "sulfur and fire" (Gen. 19.24), and there are large local deposits of sulfur and asphalt, which according to one theory might have been ignited, with great explosive effect, by an earthquake. However, there is nothing in the narrative to support another view, that the cities

Part of the southern shore of the Dead Sea. The sea is so salty in this region that white crusts of salt form on its surface, as can be seen on the right of this picture.

Abraham before the Lord

The discussion between God and Abraham about the fate of Sodom (Gen. 18.22–33) is a unique element in the book of Genesis. It reproduces the pattern of the various other dialogues between the patriarch and the deity, but it also represents an attempt at a theodicy – a vindication of God's goodness in a world where he permits evil to exist – by a theologian of the period after the Exile. In this era, God's justice was sometimes questioned, for example in the book of Job. Society was viewed in terms of the righteous and the wicked, as seen in Proverbs and the later Psalms, and there was an awareness of God's responsibility for the world outside Israel, as found in the book of Jonah.

The biblical author discusses these issues in the context of the destruction of Sodom, which indicates the deep impression that the event made on the Israelite consciousness. Abraham questions whether it is just that the fate that God plans for the city should also befall any righteous inhabitants. He addresses the problem in general terms and does not mention his relatives, Lot and his family, who live there. God says he will spare Sodom if there are "fifty righteous in the place." Abraham indulges in a piece of marketplace bargaining with the deity, who finally agrees that, if there are just ten righteous in the city, he will spare it. But the destruction of Sodom goes ahead, and so the reader is to assume that God could not find even this minimum number of righteous in the city (Lot and his family were warned by angels and escaped before the calamity, Gen. 19.15–16). Sodom is truly one mass of wickedness and fully merits its doom. The justice of the Lord is vindicated.

were overwhelmed by the waters of the Dead Sea. The fate of Lot's wife, who looks back at the destruction and is turned into a pillar of salt (Gen. 19.26), explains the origin of one of the natural pillars of salt that are on the top of Mount Sodom. It is also an instance of the widespread taboo, found in many cultures, on looking back. It occurs, for example, in the ancient Greek story of Orpheus and Eurydice.

The form of the narrative reproduces a widespread folktale of how a supernatural being goes incognito among mortals and receives hospitality from people who recognize a special quality in the stranger. There are two versions of the tale in Genesis. In one, the host is rewarded, often with the promise of a son and heir: this version underlies Abraham's reception of three divine beings immediately before the disaster (Gen. 18). In the other, attention is focused on the host's neighbors, who are severely punished for their lack of hospitality. This form is preserved in the story of Lot (Gen. 19), to which there is a close parallel in a narrative in the book of Judges (Judg. 19).

In the biblical tale, two of the three divine beings enter Sodom and are offered hospitality by Lot, who has settled in the city. But, while they are at his house, the men of Sodom – every male is implicated – gather in front of his house and demand that he hand over the strangers "so that we may know them" (Gen. 19.1–5). It is this threat of mass homosexual rape that triggers God's punishment. Elsewhere in the Bible, the "sin of Sodom" is pictured in more general terms as injustice, moral laxity, or disregard of the needy. Even the Genesis writer appears to be less concerned with the particular sexual proclivity of the men of Sodom than with the fact that it incites them to violate what is considered to be the sacred duty of hospitality.

The Angels Visiting Lot *(Gen. 19.1), from an illustrated Bible produced in 1279 for King Philip II of France.*

LOT AND HIS DAUGHTERS

After the destruction of Sodom and Gomorrah, Lot and his two daughters take refuge in a cave in the hills (Gen. 19.30). The daughters are concerned that they will not find husbands, so each in turn gets her father drunk and has intercourse with him. They both become pregnant and each bears a son.

Although the episode appears as a direct sequel to the destruction of the cities of the Plain, it is really an independent folktale, and the Lot here originally had no connection with Abraham's nephew. He may well have been identified with a local spirit of the cave where he was supposed to have taken refuge. The story is primarily an explanation of the origins of the peoples of Moab and Ammon, lands to the east of Israel. The elder daughter bears a son called Moab, who is the ancestor of the Moabites, and the younger has a son called Ben-ammi, the ancestor of the Ammonites. The sons' names are explained by popular etymology as meaning respectively "From father" and "Son of my kin."

The story may be an Israelite gibe at the supposed origin of two of their neighbors. But it seems more likely that the account is actually of Moabite and Ammonite origin, and that the action of Lot's daughters was originally seen as positive, a way to ensure that their descendants had no foreign blood. Whatever its source, it serves to demonstrate that these peoples were not direct descendants of Abraham, and had no claim to the land west of the Jordan (see p.33).

SARAH AND ISAAC

HAGAR AND ISHMAEL

As Abraham's firstborn child, Ishmael could claim to be his father's heir and thus frustrate God's purpose of continuing the line through Sarah. This danger appears to be averted when the pregnant Hagar is expelled from the household into the desert (Gen. 16). However, God commands Hagar to return. After the birth of Isaac, the threat that Ishmael may stake a claim to his father's inheritance recurs. Ishmael and his mother are finally driven out by divine permission. God allows this because he intends that a nation should spring from Ishmael, who now appears as a typical nomad, inhabiting the desert of Paran, on the border of Egypt. Hagar, herself an Egyptian, secures Ishmael a wife from Egypt. Hagar, in fact, is at the center of the story and is sympathetically depicted.

The divine promise to Ishmael is fulfilled when he becomes the ancestor of the twelve Arab tribes of the Syro-Arabian desert (Gen. 25.12–18), who are thus seen as having a close ethnic bond with the Israelites. Ishmael plays a significant part in Muslim tradition, not only as the ancestor of the North Arabian tribes, but also as a messenger and prophet. He and Abraham are said to have built the Holy House at Mecca. There are parallels between the stories of Ishmael and Esau (see pp.38–9).

The divine messengers who visited Abraham and Sarah (Gen. 18), part of a mosaic in the church of San Vitale, Ravenna, Italy (ca. 540 CE). Christians have found much symbolism in the episode; for example, in the Orthodox churches the messengers represent the Holy Trinity.

A central theme in the saga of Abraham is the repeated threat to God's promise to Abraham that he will be the founder of "a great nation" (see p.31). The Bible states frequently that his wife Sarah is infertile (for example, Gen. 11.30). Abraham decides to remain childless and make one of his household slaves his heir (Gen. 15.3), which may reflect an ancient Mesopotamian custom. Sarah, perhaps following another ancient custom, gives Abraham her Egyptian slave girl, Hagar, so that he may have an heir. In the early part of the story, the patriarch is called Abram (which may mean "exalted ancestor"), but at this in the narrative point God reassures him of the abundance of his future progeny and gives him a new name, Abraham, which Genesis interprets as "ancestor of a multitude" (Gen. 17.5). However, the precise meaning of Abraham and Abram is uncertain, and they are probably both variants of the same name.

However, it turns out that the chosen people are not to be descended from Ishmael, the son of Hagar (see sidebar, left). God promises a son to Sarah, although the matriarch is said to be ninety at this time and her husband ninety-nine. Until this point she has been called Sarai: now she receives the name Sarah as a token of God's renewal of his promise. Sarai and Sarah are variants of the same word, which is generally taken to mean "queen" or "princess."

The birth of Sarah's son is announced to Abraham in Genesis 17 by a divine oracle, which provides the model for several very similar birth oracles, in both the Hebrew Scriptures and in the New Testament, relating to barren women. God says that Sarah "shall give rise to nations; kings of peoples shall come from her" (Gen. 17.16). The literary form of the oracle is of Canaanite origin, and the account of Isaac's birth may have echoed the birth of a royal child, following well-attested "sacred marriage" rites of the ancient Near East. In these rites, a deity, who was represented by the king, had intercourse with a woman, generally the queen or a priestess. Love songs chanted on the occasion of the sacred marriage often praised the bride's beauty. Sarah's name has royal significance, and her great beauty is mentioned several times, for example in Genesis 12.11. It was for this reason that Pharaoh desired her, although she was about sixty-five at the time. Jewish tradition came to put great emphasis on Sarah's beauty, especially in a paraphrase of Genesis in Aramaic found among the Dead Sea Scrolls at Qumran (see p.169).

The idea of the sacred marriage has further echoes in Genesis 18. Three divine messengers or angels, who are identical with Yahweh himself, visit Abraham in human form (Gen. 18). One of them announces: "I shall return to you in due season and your wife shall have a son." Sarah overhears and laughs, but Genesis 21.1 relates that she indeed conceived after Yahweh "dealt with Sarah as he had said," a phrase that may have a sexual connotation. When the son is born, he is named Isaac, which means "he laughs." In Canaanite writings and elsewhere, laughter is said to accompany the birth of a child to a deity or royal figure.

The Sacrifice of Isaac

The threat to the continuation of Abraham's line did not disappear with the birth of Isaac. It surfaces again in the famous story in Genesis 22 usually called "the Sacrifice of Isaac," although in fact he is not sacrificed. The story, a masterpiece, tells how God asks Abraham to offer up his beloved son Isaac. The patriarch obeys, but at the last moment God halts the sacrifice and gives Abraham a ram to slaughter instead.

In rabbinic texts and in Jewish liturgy, the episode has the title *Aqedah*, "binding," and is interpreted as a perfect self-sacrifice by Isaac that atones for the sins of his descendants. In Genesis, however, no reason is given for God's demand that Abraham should sacrifice his son. The emphasis lies on the terrible challenge that the death of his son poses to the continuation of the line of Israel. It also presents Abraham as a paragon of righteous obedience, for which he is rewarded with a divine blessing.

In two respects the story serves as an explanatory myth. According to Hebrew law, the firstborn offspring of humans and animals had to be offered in sacrifice to God but, in the case of human beings, an animal victim could be substituted. The episode explains the origin of this practice and also the origin of the place-name Yahweh-yireh (traditionally rendered Jehovah Jireh). It is said to mean "Yahweh will provide," referring to the ram that is given by God. This follows a pattern that occurs frequently in the Bible, in which a particular place is authenticated as sacred through what is commonly referred to as a theophany, a manifestation of the deity.

The Sacrifice of Isaac, *a Turkish painting of 1583. An angel who is bearing a sacrificial ram calls out to Abraham at the precise moment at which he is preparing to murder his son (Gen. 22.10–13).*

Detail from a 6th-century Byzantine painting of Rebekah at the well. It is here that she encounters Abraham's servant on his way to find a bride for Isaac (Gen. 24.10–15).

ISAAC AND REBEKAH

Isaac appears regularly alongside his father Abraham and his son Jacob as one of the founding fathers of Israel. However, there is comparatively little about him in Genesis, and events involving Isaac mainly double episodes in the Abraham saga. For example, the theme of "jeopardy of the female ancestor" (see sidebar on p.32) recurs in the case of Isaac's wife Rebekah (Gen. 26.6–11). Like Abraham in Genesis 21, Isaac in Genesis 26 has a dispute over water rights with the Philistines, but subsequently makes a covenant with the Philistine king Abimelech. Each episode is said to account for the name of the city of Beer-sheba.

There is one unique narrative dealing with Isaac, although he plays only a small part in it: the tale, in Genesis 24, of how he obtains a wife, Rebekah. The story is the longest in Genesis, and its main features reappear in the accounts of how Jacob and Moses found brides. Its narrative structure, which parallels the Canaanite epic of King Keret, involves a journey to a distant land, marriage negotiations, departure for home, and finally a wedding. Abraham appears not as a simple nomad but as a wealthy ruler who possesses camels, flocks, herds, gold, and silver. He has a large household of servants, one of whom is sent, laden with rich gifts, to find Isaac a bride from among Abraham's relatives. They live in the area of Haran, the town from which the patriarch had originally set out. In this story, the region is called Aram-naharaim, which indicates a period after the expansion of the Arameans in the early first millennium BCE.

Under God's direction, the servant's mission is brought to a successful conclusion and Rebekah is betrothed to Isaac. There are reminiscences of royal wedding ceremonies. Rebekah is decked out in jewelry and rich clothes, and urged to leave her family for her new husband's land (Gen. 24.53–58). She receives a blessing (Gen. 24.60) and is led away to meet her husband, accompanied by her maids. These events resemble the royal marriage song in Psalm 45.10–17. There is a romantic glow throughout, not least in the final scene where the couple meet, with the concluding statement that Isaac loved Rebekah.

Masseboths, *sacred stone pillars, at the ancient Canaanite shrine of Gezer (see box on opposite page).*

Like Isaac's mother Sarah, Rebekah is said to be barren, but her infertility is cured after Isaac prays to God (Gen. 25.21), and she conceives twins. The story reflects the frequent motif in myth and folklore of the hostility between twins, even in the womb. The Genesis narrative is primarily concerned with accounting for two related peoples, the Edomites and Israelites. Rebekah's and Isaac's first child, Esau, emerges "red" and "hairy," the Hebrew words for which play respectively on the names Edom and Seir, another name for Edom. Esau's brother is born gripping Esau's heel and is called Jacob, which is said to mean "he takes by the heel." It can also mean "he supplants," which foreshadows the following episode, in which Esau sells Jacob his birthright for a stew (Gen. 27.27–34). The story contrasts the lifestyles of the nomadic hunter and the pastoral tent-dweller, and shows Esau's unworthiness to assume the legal status of the firstborn, which he dismisses with the words "of what use is a birthright to me?" The stew for which he sells his birthright is red, emphasizing again the origin of the name Edom.

Later, Jacob deceives Isaac, who is blind and near death, in order to receive his blessing in place of Esau (Gen. 27). The idea of Jacob as a trickster, and the rivalry between hunter and herder, color the narrative, but otherwise the story seems to represent a ritual ceremony of patriarchal blessing. There is a similar moment in Genesis 48, when Jacob blesses the sons of Joseph; on that occasion, too, the younger brother is preferred to the elder. Jacob brings Rebekah two goat kids for her to prepare for her husband. She tells Jacob to take the food to Isaac and receive his blessing (Gen. 27.9–10). Jacob tricks Isaac by wearing kidskins on his hands and neck to imitate Esau's hairiness: Isaac feels the skins and, convinced that Esau is before him, gives his blessing (Gen. 27.23). The kidskins are probably meant to be a slightly comic touch, but the episode may preserve memories of a sacrificial ceremony by which a younger son became the heir in place of his elder brother. The story also reveals the power of a verbal blessing for the ancient Israelites: even when Isaac knows that he has been deceived, he cannot cancel his blessing and can only compensate Esau with a rather second-rate promise of survival.

Esau plots to kill Jacob in revenge, but Rebekah learns of the threat and urges Jacob to leave home. Jacob flees and begins a perilous journey, a common feature in folktales of heroes. As the one designated to carry on the line of Israel. Jacob journeys to his distant kin to find a wife. Isaac tells him to wed one of the daughters of Laban, Rebekah's brother.

Jacob's dream

Jacob sets out from Beer-sheba on the heroic journey which forms the central structure of his story. The first episode on the journey takes place at an uninhabited spot where he stops to spend the night (the site is later said to be an existing Canaanite city, Luz). This is an instance of incubation, a practice that is found in the Hebrew Scriptures and in other religions, in which a person passes a night in a holy place in order to obtain a revelatory vision. In his dream, Jacob sees what is traditionally referred to as a "ladder" reaching to heaven with angels ascending and descending on it. The word for "ladder" can also be rendered "stairway" or "ramp." The description of it recalls the Tower of Babel and suggests a Mesopotamian ziggurat (see p.28 and p.31). In the Akkadian myth of Nergal and Ereshkigal, the gods are said to climb up "the long stairway of heaven," and the biblical account of "the gate of heaven" (Gen. 28.17) is paralleled in an Egyptian text that describes the ascent to heaven of a dead king by means of a ladder.

When Jacob wakes up, he erects a stone pillar and pours oil over it as an offering to the holy spirit of the place. Such sacred pillars, known as *masseboth*, were a regular feature of Canaanite shrines (see illustration on opposite page). Jacob names the place Bethel, which means "House of God" or "House of El." The Bible appears to be aware of the fact that the ancestors of Israel did not actually worship Yahweh. The story of Jacob's ladder, together with much other evidence, suggests that they venerated El, who was the head of the Canaanite pantheon, in his local manifestations at various Canaanite shrines. The episode is also one of several "sanctuary legends" in the Bible which justify the Israelite appropriation of Canaanite holy places in the Promised Land.

Jabob's Ladder, *by William Blake (1757–1828): "And he dreamed that there was a ladder set up on the earth, the top of it reaching to heaven; and the angels of God were ascending and descending on it" (Gen. 28.12).*

WRESTLING JACOB

On his return from Haran to Canaan, at the ford of the Jabbok River, Jacob encounters a man who "wrestled with him until daybreak" (Gen. 32.24). It is now generally accepted that this "man" was the guardian spirit of the ford. To move from one region to another is often regarded as a dangerous procedure, and crossing places are often said to be haunted by dangerous spirits or demons. The story was originally a local legend that may have became attached to Jacob because of the assonance between the names Jacob and Jabbok.

As day breaks the man makes to leave: the idea that a spirit loses power at daybreak and must then depart is very common in myth and folklore. Before Jacob lets him go, the man gives Jacob a new name, Israel, which is explained as meaning "The one who strives with God" or "God strives." To know someone's name is a step toward controlling them, so Jacob's assailant refuses to say who he is. Jacob calls the site of his encounter Peniel, "The face of God;" in other words, it was originally a Canaanite holy place where worshipers could come into direct contact with the local manifestation of El. The spirit dislocates Jacob's hip by hitting him on "the hip socket at the thigh muscle." This is said to be the reason why the Israelites do not eat the thigh muscle on the hip socket, a taboo not otherwise attested in the Hebrew Scriptures. The "thigh" may be a euphemism for the genital area, as in Genesis 24, when Abraham's servant took an oath by putting a hand "under the thigh of Abraham."

The so-called "Face of Baal," a terracotta cult mask of ca. 1300 BCE discovered at Hazor in northern Israel. It has been thought by some to represent the important Canaanite god Baal.

JACOB AND RACHEL

When Jacob reaches the land of his relatives (here called Paddan-aram), he finds himself in a situation similar to that of the servant who found a bride for Isaac in Genesis 24. Jacob's uncle Laban is still the head of the family in Haran, and Jacob meets his prospective wife, the beautiful Rachel, at a well. But from this point the course of the narrative is very different. Unlike Abraham's servant, Jacob has nothing to offer by way of a bride-price and, in order to win Rachel, he must work for Laban for seven years (Gen. 29.18). What follows is a lively folktale told with a degree of humor that would appeal to an audience. In the course of the story Laban cheats Jacob, Jacob cheats Laban, and Rachel cheats her father. Laban substitutes Leah for Rachel on the wedding night, justifying his action with the claim that custom forbade a younger daughter to be married before her elder sister. Such a custom is certainly widely attested, but the background may be a folklore motif known as the "false bride," in which another woman is substituted for the bride to foil the demons who were thought to threaten the marriage bed. A week after the wedding of Leah and Jacob, Laban permits Rachel and Jacob to marry, but in return Jacob has to work for Laban for another seven years.

Jacob increases his share of the family's flocks through quasi-scientific magic (Gen. 30.37–42), although the story attributes the outcome to God (Gen. 31.9). He becomes as rich as his grandfather Abraham. This arouses the jealousy of Laban's sons, and Jacob determines to return home secretly, with his family and possessions, to his father in Canaan. On this occasion, Rachel secretly steals her father's household gods or *teraphim* (Gen. 31.19), small idols similar to the *Lares* and *Penates* of the Romans. Her motive is unclear, but the theft has been related to a supposed custom of the people known as Hurrians, found in a legal document from the Mesopotamian city of Nuzi of ca. 1400 BCE. According to one interpretation of this document, the possession of the household gods conferred a right of inheritance. But the meaning of the Nuzi text is disputed, and the *teraphim* may simply have been thought to guarantee the safety, prosperity, and perhaps also the fertility, of their possessor.

Rachel's action leads to another example of the "jeopardy of the female ancestor" motif (see sidebar on p.32). When Laban catches up with Jacob and complains about the theft, Jacob, unaware that Rachel has taken the gods, pronounces the death penalty on the unknown thief (Gen. 31.32). Rachel averts the danger by another trick: she hides the idols in a camel bag and sits on it, pretending that she is menstruating and so cannot be approached: "Let not my lord be angry that I cannot rise before you, for the way of women is upon me" (Gen. 31.35). Laban's search proves fruitless and Jacob roundly rebukes him for what he sees as his false accusation (Gen. 31.36–42).

The sequel to the episode suggests what really lies behind this story of family hostility. Laban and Jacob make a treaty, which they ratify by erecting a pillar and a cairn of stones. These are given Aramaic and Hebrew names, meaning "cairn of witness." The deity enshrined in the stones, as at Bethel (see p.39), is the witness and guarantor of the pact. There is a parallel here to the well-known Mesopotamian *kudurrus* or boundary stones, which bore emblems of protecting deities. As the narrative brings out, the stones were to mark the frontier between Aramean and Israelite territory. The account reflects the politics of a much later period when, in spite of the old ethnic relationship between the two peoples, Aramean expansion posed a serious and long-lasting threat to the Israelite kingdoms.

The twelve tribes of Israel

The account of the birth of Jacob's twelve sons during his stay in Paddan-aram links together various originally separate groups, who federated together to make up the later nation of Israel. In the ancient Near East, the tie of blood was regarded as the closest bond of union, so the story gives the twelve tribes of Israel a common ancestor, Jacob. Benjamin, the twelfth son, is born after the family's return to the land of Canaan (Gen. 35.16–18), although his birth is probably anticipated in Rachel's prayer "may the Lord add to me another son" (Gen. 30.24).

The twelve-tribe system could not have originated in the age of the ancestors, whenever that may have been (the ancestors represent an individual family rather than groups of families or tribes), and probably not even in the early period of the Israelite settlement in Canaan. It is more likely to date from the time when Israel became an organized state. Even then, it always remained to a considerable extent a theoretical system. The tribal names were originally geographical names of parts of Palestine, but in Genesis they become the names of persons (similarly, the names of towns in northern Mesopotamia became those of members of Abraham's family; see p.31). The names of the tribal ancestors are all given popular etymologies, which in no way correspond to historical reality.

The sons are born to four different mothers, Leah, Rachel, and their respective maids, Zilpah and Bilhah (see family tree, below). Rachel is Jacob's first and greatest love, and Jacob shows most affection for her offspring, Joseph and Benjamin, who are his youngest sons. One of them, Joseph, subsequently achieves great fame (see pp.42–5). Jacob is recorded as having one daughter, Dinah, by Leah. The story of the rape of Dinah and her brothers' revenge is told in Genesis 34 (see sidebar on p.43).

The curious story of Reuben's mandrakes (Gen. 30.14–16) probably derives from a belief that mandrakes enabled Rachel to conceive her first child, Joseph, which happens shortly after the episode (Gen. 30.22). The mandrake root often resembles the human form, and it was once believed in many cultures to possess aphrodisiac powers and to be an aid to fertility. The Hebrew term for mandrake is connected with the verb "to love."

Jacob : Leah	Jacob : Bilhah	Jacob : Zilpah	Jacob : Rachel
Reuben	Dan	Gad	Joseph
Simeon	Naphtali	Asher	Benjamin
Levi			
Judah			
Issachar			
Zebulun			
Dinah			

This family tree shows the children of Jacob by his four partners Leah, Bilhah, Zilpah, and Rachel. According to the Bible, each son was the ancestor of one of the tribes of Israel.

A clay fertility figurine that may represent the Canaanite goddess Astarte (ca. 1300 BCE). The household deities or teraphim *that the still childless Rachel stole in Genesis 31 may have been similar figures, the possession of which was thought to confer fertility (see main text).*

JOSEPH

The sagas of Abraham and Jacob are constructed from a variety of traditions, explanatory myths, local and sanctuary legends, which may have passed through successive stages of composition. However, the history of Joseph, which occupies the last fourteen chapters of Genesis, is the product of a single author and is best described as a short story or historical novelette. It displays considerable literary skill.

There have been frequent attempts to discover a historical setting for the story by asking whether the Egyptian customs and practices it mentions are characteristic of a certain period of Egypt's history. In particular, the great position achieved by Joseph (see pp.44–5) has often been explained with reference to the time of the Hyksos (ca. 1670–1562 BCE), foreign rulers of Egypt under whom a non-Egyptian could have risen to prominence. But the story of Joseph does not give the name of any particular pharaoh, and the general conservatism of ancient Egyptian society meant that the same beliefs and customs remained virtually unchanged over many centuries. However, it has recently been argued that some of the cultural features present in the Genesis story can hardly have existed before the late first millennium BCE. Beyond this, it is difficult to establish any unquestionable connection between the Joseph narrative and a specific period of Egyptian history.

While it is obviously fascinating to try to relate Joseph's story to historical events, this is a diversion from the true nature and purpose of the biblical narrative. At the heart of the tale is the common folklore theme of the insignificant character, in this case one of Jacob's two youngest sons, who rises to greatness. The same theme occurs again in the story of the anointing of David as future king of the Israelites (1 Sam. 16.1–13; see pp.74–5). The story of Joseph can also be seen as part of the Israelite Wisdom tradition (see pp.120–21). It illustrates its teachings about divine providence and retribution, and Joseph can be compared with a figure such as Daniel, who is a wise man and an interpreter of dreams (see pp.128–31). The narrative employs several themes which characterize the saga of the ancestors as a whole: sibling rivalry which is finally reconciled; the birth of sons; the superseding of the firstborn; and the theme of exile and return. This last theme is particularly expressed in the dying words of Joseph (Gen. 50.24), which foreshadow the following phase of the history of the Israelites.

DIVINATION

Not all dreams have a self-evident meaning, as Joseph's seem to have had (see box on opposite page). Often they contain strange images and apparent portents which the dreamer cannot understand and which cause acute anxiety, as happens with Pharaoh's cupbearer and baker (Gen. 40), and with Pharaoh himself (Gen. 41). Dream diviners were well-known and widely employed throughout the ancient Near East to interpret the significance of dreams. The pharaohs had a body of what were called "dream interpreters," and a papyrus of the New Kingdom period (ca. 1540–1070 BCE) gives a detailed key to dream interpretation.

Joseph has a silver cup "for divination" (Gen. 44.5). This indicates that he is also a professional diviner, a practitioner of leconomancy, divination by means of liquid in a vessel.

Above and opposite: Scenes from the Life of Joseph, *by Giovanni di Bartolommeo (1483–1511).* Left to right: *Jacob sends Joseph to his brothers (Gen. 37.14); Joseph is sold to the Midianites (37.38); Joseph and Potiphar's wife (39.12); Joseph in prison (39.20–21).*

Joseph and his brothers

The story of Joseph and his brothers unfolds alongside that of Joseph's rise to power in Egypt. The opening of the story relates that the seventeen-year-old Joseph is the favorite of Jacob, who has "a long robe with sleeves" – not "a coat of many colors," as it is traditionally rendered – made for him (Gen. 37.3). In 2 Samuel 13.18 "a long robe with sleeves" is said to be the dress of a princess, so Jacob can be seen as conferring a quasi-royal status on Joseph that sets him above his brothers. The coat introduces the motif of Joseph's special dress as an indication of his position, which the author follows through in the rest of his narration. Jacob's favoritism causes his other sons to be jealous of Joseph: "they hated him, and could not speak peaceably to him."

The same picture is presented in the following episode, which relates Joseph's two dreams (Gen. 37.5–11). (Such pairs of events are characteristic of the narrative: the dreams are paralleled later by the two dreams of Pharaoh's servants and the two of Pharaoh himself.) Joseph dreams that the brothers are in the fields binding sheaves: his sheaf stands upright and the others bow down to it. In his second dream, the sun, the moon, and eleven stars bow down to him. Dreams in the Hebrew Scriptures are not fantasies or illusions but realities that point to the dreamer's innermost nature. Joseph has a king's dreams, something which can only happen to someone who is in fact a king. What happens later, therefore, when Joseph is the virtual ruler of Egypt and his brothers prostrate themselves before him, comes as no surprise.

The dreams reveal clearly to his brothers that Joseph aims to be king and they resolve to kill him so as to prevent him from becoming their ruler. However, Judah urges mercy, "for he is our brother, our own flesh." The others agree and instead they sell Joseph to some Midianite traders bound for Egypt (Gen. 37.28). They present Jacob with the long-sleeved robe as evidence of Joseph's death. In Egypt, the Midianites sell Joseph to Potiphar, the captain of the royal guard, and he ultimately rises to a position of great power, second only to Pharaoh himself (see pp.44–5). The brothers' initial humiliation of Joseph brings about his ultimate elevation.

THE END OF JACOB'S TRAVELS

Jacob's return to Canaan (Gen. 33–37) rounds off his career and that of his brother Esau. Like Ishmael (see p.36), Esau is not viewed wholly unfavorably in Genesis. When he and Jacob meet again, he treats his brother magnanimously and the final territorial separation between them is amicable. Esau's importance as the ancestor of the Edomites is shown by the list of his eighty descendants.

Of the patriarchs, Jacob was connected primarily with central Palestine and Transjordan, while Abraham and Isaac represented a more southerly group. From Genesis 33.18, Jacob is associated with two important northern sanctuaries, first Shechem and then Bethel. There is further patriarchal altar-building at these originally Canaanite holy places, as well as two interesting additional stories. One, told in Genesis 34, relates a savage attack on Shechem by two of Jacob's sons, following the rape of Dinah, the daughter of Jacob and Leah. This seems to be an episode of conflict with the native population at a time when groups forming the later "Israel" were occupying the land. The other episode, in Genesis 35, describes Jacob's journey from Shechem to Bethel. He prepares for this by burying the people's "foreign gods," such as Rachel's *teraphim* (see p.40) under the sacred tree at Shechem. The biblical author believed that the worship of Yahweh had to be purged of foreign elements. But some ancient cult ceremony also lies behind the story: at various sanctuary sites, archaeologists have found figurines of deities that were deliberately buried, although it is unclear why.

Finally, Jacob and his family are depicted moving peacefully throughout the country until they settle at Hebron, the home of Isaac. Isaac dies at the age of one hundred eighty, and the narrative moves on to the story of Jacob's sons.

(Continued from opposite page:) *The brothers before Joseph, the high official of Pharaoh (Gen. 15); the brothers' donkeys are loaded for the return journey (44.1); the discovery of Joseph's cup in Benjamin's sack (44.12).*

JOSEPH IN EGYPT

Just as Joseph's dreams led to his enslavement (see p.43), they were also a direct cause of his rise to a supreme position in Egypt. During his false imprisonment (see box, below), Joseph correctly explains the dreams of two of Pharaoh's servants (Gen. 40). His ability to interpret dreams comes to the attention of Pharaoh, who has had two vivid but puzzling dreams (Gen. 41). Joseph tells the monarch that his dreams presage seven years of plenty followed by seven of famine. He suggests measures to alleviate the effects of the famine and Pharaoh, impressed, puts him in charge of the relief effort. He grants him enormous powers "over all the land of Egypt" (Gen. 41.43). Although the annual flooding of the Nile usually guaranteed agricultural prosperity, famine was not unknown in Egyptian life. An inscription of ca. 100 BCE tells of a seven-year famine caused by the failure of the Nile floods in the reign of the pharaoh Djoser, who ruled some time around the twenty-eighth century BCE. The purpose of this inscription is to validate a claim by a group of priests for exemption from property tax. Similar priestly privilege is found in the Joseph story: when the Egyptians are compelled to surrender all their possessions to Pharaoh as a result of the famine, the priests are exempted (Gen. 47.22).

When the famine arrives, it is not confined to Egypt but is universal, and Jacob sends ten of his sons from Canaan to Egypt to get grain from the Egyptian storehouses. The narrative of Joseph's dealings with his brothers now becomes intertwined with the account of his rise to power. When they arrive in Egypt, the brothers do not realize that this great official is Joseph (he is at least twenty years older and speaks through an interpreter). But he recognizes them, and the intricate scenes by which the story is played out represent Joseph's plan to reunite his entire family, now much increased, in Egypt. He wants them to share in the good fortune that his wealth and position now make possible.

However, before this final reconciliation, Joseph plays a game with his

Judah and Tamar and Potiphar's wife

Two episodes in the story of Joseph stand apart from the main narrative of a hero's rise and his relations with his siblings. The first is the tale of Joseph's brother Judah and Judah's widowed daughter-in-law Tamar, which is related in Genesis 38, just after Joseph is taken to Egypt. The tale recounts how Judah mistakes Tamar, who is veiled, for a prostitute, and has intercourse with her. She becomes pregnant with twins and is denounced as a whore, until she reveals the identity of the father, who admits his fault. The story contains several of the recurring motifs in the history of the ancestors: the overcoming of childlessness, the birth of twins, the suppression of the firstborn, and problems with the local Canaanite population. The episode has often been seen as an insertion, misplaced from earlier in Genesis. However, just before the story Judah saves Joseph from death (Gen. 37.26–27), so perhaps the biblical author felt that it was appropriate to tell a story about Judah at this point.

The second episode is the attempted seduction of Joseph by the wife of Potiphar, the head of the royal guard and his first Egyptian employer (Gen. 39). The author may have used a well-known Egyptian story called "The Tale of the Two Brothers." In this tale, the elder brother is married and the younger works as his servant. One day, as the younger brother is going about his duties, his sister-in-law tries to seduce him. He rebuffs her, and when her husband returns she accuses his brother of rape. The biblical story has an almost identical plot, except that Joseph is falsely imprisoned until his sudden rise to power under Pharaoh. In the Egyptian tale, the accused man is able to convince the husband of his innocence and the two brothers are reconciled.

brothers that is a just retribution for their past behavior, and the narrator skillfully increases the suspense before the eventual happy ending. Finally Joseph reveals his identity to his brothers (Gen. 45.4) and, to allay their fears, he gives a theological explanation of their original misdeed. It was God who was responsible for his journey to Egypt, not Joseph's brothers. God sent Joseph ahead of his brothers "to preserve life," and "to keep alive for you many survivors." The area in Egypt where the Israelites are to settle, the land of Goshen, is allotted to them (Gen. 45.10). It remains their place of residence until the Exodus.

The last section of the story of Joseph (Gen. 48–50) centers on the deaths of Jacob (Israel) and of Joseph himself. On his deathbed, Jacob is once more shown as a great source of blessing. He blesses the two sons of Joseph, typically preferring the younger, Ephraim, over the elder, Manasseh. He is then credited with a lengthy poem in which he foretells the destiny, not invariably a happy one, of each of the twelve tribes in turn. When he dies, he is embalmed in the usual Egyptian manner and his corpse is taken by Joseph to Canaan to lie in the cave at Machpelah, which Abraham purchased as a family burial plot.

Joseph returns to Egypt and lives there for many years. The book of Genesis ends significantly with his last words, which look to the future of the Israelite nation: "Then Joseph said to his brothers: 'I am about to die; but God will surely come to you, and bring you up out of this land to the land that he swore to Abraham, to Isaac, and to Jacob.' "

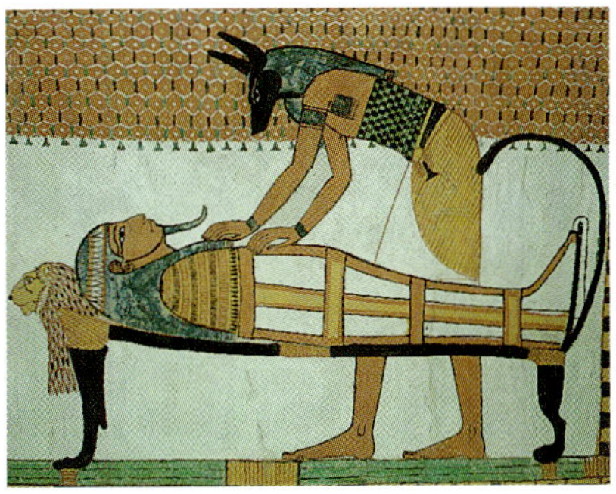

Anubis, the Egyptian god of embalming, prepares a body for burial, from a wall painting of ca. 1300 BCE. Embalming was usual Egyptian practice. The Bible says that after his death Joseph "was embalmed and placed in a coffin in Egypt" (Gen. 50.26).

Egyptian elements in the Joseph narrative

There are many apparently genuine Egyptian details in the narrative of Joseph's rise to power. Several Egyptian words are used, for example the shout "*Abrek!*" uttered before Joseph's chariot (Gen. 41.43). This is usually translated as something like "Bow the knee," although the exact meaning is uncertain. The new name given to Joseph, Zaphenath-paneah (Gen. 41.45), is genuinely Egyptian, as are the names of his bride, Asenath, her father Potiphera, and Potiphera's city of On, "City of the Pillar." On, better known by its later Greek name of Heliopolis, was a center of sun worship that was famous for its obelisks.

Pharaoh confers on Joseph authority "over my house." This phrase seems to be a direct translation of the title of the highest post in the Egyptian administration, which is accurately described in the biblical account as a position second only to that of Pharaoh himself. Pharaoh says to Joseph: "Without your consent no one shall lift up hand or foot in all the land of Egypt" (Gen. 41.44). Joseph is invested with Pharaoh's ring and a golden chain (Gen. 41.42): this was the regular practice for high Egyptian officials and is attested in a text from the reign of Ramesses II (ca. 1279–1212 BCE). Joseph later acquires all the land in Egypt for Pharaoh (Gen. 47.20). This seems to reflect the situation under the New Kingdom (ca. 1540–1070 BCE), when Egypt became a despotic state and everything was held to belong to the pharaoh.

These details, however, do not point unambiguously to any particular period of Egyptian history (see p.42). Not everything related about Egyptian customs in the Joseph story is accurate. For example, it is said that "the Egyptians could not eat with the Hebrews, for that is an abomination to the Egyptians" (Gen. 42.43) and that "all shepherds are abhorrent to the Egyptians" (Gen. 46.34). But there is no support for these statements in Egyptian sources.

MOSES

The books of Exodus, Leviticus, Numbers, and Deuteronomy are dominated by the figure of one man, Moses. There is little doubt that Moses was a real person, though of limited status. He may originally have been a significant local figure, perhaps a member of the tribe of Levi operating especially in the region of Kadesh-barnea in the extreme south of Canaan. In the Bible he is transformed into the idealized leader of Israel and given an overriding theological significance. He is the agent of God, and through him God acts to determine for all time the fundamental character and structure of the nation of Israel. His story transcends any particular historical epoch, and Moses appears as the human source of the fundamental features and institutions in the life of Israel: the worship of the one God, Yahweh; the Covenant; the Law; prophecy; kingship; and priesthood.

THE FIGURE OF MOSES

Moses first rises to prominence during the oppression of the Israelites in Egypt, described at the beginning of the book of Exodus. This oppression is often said to have taken place under the pharaoh Ramesses II (ca. 1279–1212 BCE), with the Exodus itself occurring under his son and successor Merneptah (ca. 1212–1204 BCE; see table on p.52). Ramesses was a great builder, who founded the city of Rameses in the eastern Nile delta. According to Exodus 1.11, Rameses was constructed by Israelite forced labor. However, Moses' historical background is not the Bible's main concern. The unnamed pharaoh of the narrative is presented as a stereotypical oppressive ruler. His actions seem improbable, especially his desire to wipe out his large Hebrew slave workforce, as related in Exodus 1.15–22.

The account of the Egyptian oppression is a carefully constructed narrative in three stages of increasing severity. Its purpose is to pave the way for the emergence of the heroic figure of Moses. After the death of Joseph and his brothers (see pp.44–5), their descendants flourished in Egypt (Exod. 1.7). A new pharaoh succeeds who is alarmed at their size and power and enslaves them. But their numbers increase at an even greater rate, so Pharaoh instructs the Hebrew midwives, Shiphrah and Puah, to kill all newborn Israelite males (the narrative may be using the number two as a storytelling device rather than seriously implying that the entire Hebrew population had only two midwives). The midwives cleverly succeed in disobeying this command, but Pharaoh simply orders all Hebrew males to be thrown into the Nile at birth (Exod. 1.22).

At this point Moses is born to parents of the house of Levi, who are later named as Jochebed and Amram. His mother keeps his birth secret until she can no longer hide the baby, then lays him in a waterproof basket and places him among the papyrus reeds on the banks of the Nile. Moses' sister Miriam (not named until Exod. 15) watches as Pharaoh's daughter finds the child and sees that it is a Hebrew baby. Miriam goes to the princess and offers to find a Hebrew nurse for the child. This nurse is Moses' own mother, who brings the child up. He is then adopted by the princess, who names him Moses (Exod. 2.10). The name Moses is really Egyptian, meaning "son," a shortened form of names such as Thutmose. But the narrator did not know the true origin of the name and shaped the story so that it backed up his own explanation, as frequently occurs in the Bible. The writer derives the name (*Mosheh* in Hebrew) from the Hebrew *mashah*, "to draw out," referring to Moses being lifted out of the Nile.

Parallels to this story occur in many cultures. The closest is the legend of King Sargon of Assyria (ca. 2334–2279 BCE), whose mother, it was said, bore him secretly, placed him in a basket of rushes sealed with bitumen, and threw him into the river. He was rescued by a certain Akki, "the drawer of water," who adopted him as his son. In due course Sargon won divine favor and became a great ruler. The Moses story concentrates on legendary themes and does not address puzzling questions such as how Moses has an elder sister when he is apparently his parents' first child.

The pharaoh Ramesses II (reigned 1279–1212 BCE) dressed for war. He has been proposed as the despotic ruler who initiated the oppression of the Israelites, as related in Exodus.

Papyrus flags depicted on a piece of Egyptian faience of ca. 1350 BCE. Many European artists assumed that the "reeds" in which Moses was laid (Exod. 2.3) were bulrushes, but they would almost certainly have been papyrus reeds.

Moses in Midian

Moses is raised in the Egyptian royal household, but as a young adult he becomes aware of the plight of his own people. He kills an Egyptian for beating a Hebrew (Exod. 2.12), and then flees for his own safety to Midian, on the eastern side of the Gulf of Aqaba. Moses' stay in Midian illustrates the common folktale idea of the hero's withdrawal into the wilderness before his return to the land where his destiny lies. Moses' encounter at a well with the daughters of the Midianite priest (Exod. 2.15–17) is a scene found also in the stories of Isaac and Jacob (Gen. 24 and 29). As on those occasions, the encounter leads to the hero's marriage, and the birth and naming of a son.

The tradition of Moses' marriage into the family of the Midianite priest shows that the biblical author was aware of close ethnic ties between Midian and Israel. Moses' father-in-law (variously called Jethro, Reuel, and Hobab), is described in Judges 1.16 and 4.11 as a Kenite, a descendant of Cain (see pp.24–5). The "mark" that God put on Cain (Gen. 4.15) may have meant that the Kenites stood out from their neighbors as Yahweh worshipers. Jethro may be a type of high priest of Yahweh: in Exodus 18 he presides at a sacrificial feast attended by the Israelites, and then instructs Moses in the administration of justice. The mountain where the name of Yahweh is revealed to Moses (see p.48), appears to be in the Midianite or Kenite area.

Some have concluded that the Midianites or Kenites were the original devotees of Yahweh and that the Israelites took over the worship of Yahweh from them after they had left Egypt. But the theory creates many problems, because Yahweh is intimately involved in events before and during the Exodus. Perhaps the most that can be said is that the Midianites or Kenites had a tradition, reflected in the Bible, that they shared a common cult with the Hebrews.

THE BURNING BUSH

During his stay in Midian (see p.47), Moses goes up to Mount Horeb (Exod. 3), where he encounters God in the form of a burning bush. God reveals his divine name, Yahweh, which is usually rendered "the LORD" in English Bibles. He calls on Moses to return to Egypt and lead his people from servitude to the Promised Land of Canaan.

The revelation of the name of Yahweh probably refers to the adoption of a new deity, but the Bible emphasizes that the being who speaks to Moses is "the God of Abraham, the God of Isaac, the God of Jacob." When Moses asks God to give his name, he answers "I am who I am," apparently an explanation of the divine name (Exod. 3.14). There has been much debate about the real meaning of this enigmatic phrase, which can also be translated "I am what I am" or "I will be what I will be." Much of this discussion may be beside the point, as God, like many divine beings, is reluctant to say his true name (compare Jacob's encounter at the ford in Gen. 32), and "I am who I am" is simply a negative answer to Moses' question. The Hebrew verb "to be," *hayah*, has a similar sound to the word "Yahweh," and the narrative skillfully makes the connection (Exod. 3.14–15): God says "I am who I am," then "I am" (a single word in Hebrew), and finally reveals the name Yahweh itself. This passage may represent part of the liturgy of an ancient cult initiation ritual.

God assures Moses that he will remain with him and, using a well-known Near Eastern formula for the appointing of a messenger, commissions him as an envoy to Pharaoh (Exod. 3.18). This formula was also used when a person was called as a prophet (compare 1 Kings 18.1), and the Jewish prophetic tradition has probably influenced the tradition of Moses' call. God empowers Moses, as he did the later prophets, to demonstrate the divine origin of the mission by various miraculous signs. The objections that Moses raises to his mission in Exodus 4 parallel those often uttered by prophets when faced with the divine summons.

The episode on Mount Horeb is partly a sanctuary legend. It follows a common pattern in which a holy place is legitimized by a manifestation of the deity. "The angel of the Lord" that appears in the flaming bush means the visible presence of God himself, who was believed in Israel to manifest himself in a fiery flame (see picture on p.20).

Aaron

At the burning bush, Aaron appears for the first time as Moses' brother and his spokesman. In the earliest parts of the Pentateuch (the first five books of the Bible), he is depicted as Moses' helper and joint leader of the Exodus and the desert wanderings, and there is little sign that he has specific priestly functions. Aaron may once have played a distinct or even an independent role in these events, perhaps indicated by traditions which show him in an unfavorable light because of his opposition to Moses. But he is clearly subordinate to Moses as his agent and displays many features that double those of the greater leader: he too has a miraculous rod, with which he causes the Egyptian plagues; both he and Moses face hostility from the Israelites; both are denied entry to the Promised Land; and both die on a mountain outside it.

The later parts of the Pentateuch give Aaron much greater prominence as the founder of the Israelite priesthood and guarantor of the only true priestly line. In particular, Aaron represents the high priest and his position as the head of the Temple of Jerusalem after the Exile. In Exodus 28, the installation of Aaron with the vestments and regalia of a high priest is described in detail.

Moses and the Burning Bush, *from a French illuminated manuscript of ca. 1210. It illustrates Exodus 3.5: "Then he said, 'Come no closer, remove the sandals from your feet, for the place on which you are standing is holy ground.' "*

The bridegroom of blood

After Moses and his family set out to return to Egypt (Exod. 4.20), they camp for the night at a place where Yahweh, apparently, seeks to kill Moses. This episode (Exod. 4.24–26) is highly mysterious and difficult to interpret, no doubt because the biblical narrator no longer knew its real meaning. It seems to be a fragment of a once independent tradition and betrays archaic features, such as the representation of Yahweh as a kind of hostile night demon, and the use of a flint knife for circumcision. Although Moses is alluded to through the context, his name does not appear in the Hebrew text of this episode. Originally the threat was probably to his firstborn son, who escaped death by being circumcised. God's threat to kill Pharaoh's firstborn precedes the story, and in Israelite thought the life of the firstborn male belonged to God.

The narrative reveals the original significance of circumcision as a rite of puberty and preparation for marriage. Moses' wife Zipporah touches the feet (possibly a euphemism for the genitals) either of Moses or her son – it is not clear which – with the foreskin, saying "Truly you are a bridegroom of blood to me." The story explains the origin of the rite known as "bridegroom of blood by circumcision."

MOSES AND AARON AND THE TEN PLAGUES

On Mount Horeb (see p.48), God commissioned Moses to bring the Israelites out of Egypt into Canaan, the Promised Land. Acting in obedience to this commission, Moses and his brother Aaron confront Pharaoh in Exodus 5. However, at this stage they request only that the Israelites be allowed to make a three-day journey into the desert in order to celebrate a sacrificial feast to their god. This again suggests that there may have been a connection between the Israelites in Egypt and ethnically related groups, such as the Kenites or Midianites, who lived in the desert regions of the far south of Palestine (see p.47). It may be significant that the Bible calls the deity "the God of the Hebrews" (Exod. 5.3), a term with a wider sense than "Israelites."

The first meeting with Pharaoh is unsuccessful and only brings greater hardships to the Israelites (Exod. 5.4–21). Moses complains to God, who once again reveals his name Yahweh (Exod. 6.3). In this passage, which is usually ascribed to the priestly biblical author "P" (see p.20), God reassures Moses and Aaron that his promise of deliverance will prevail. He says that he did not appear to Abraham, Isaac, and Jacob as Yahweh, but as "God Almighty," in Hebrew *El Shaddai*. This title probably means "El of the mountains," which would confirm the view that the ancestors worshiped the supreme Canaanite deity, El (see p.66). The epithet *Shaddai* is attested in Aramaic inscriptions of the ninth or eighth century BCE from Deir Alla in Transjordan.

Moses and Aaron go back to Pharaoh and once more ask him to let the Israelites go. God commands Aaron to give a sign or portent to convince the monarch that their request comes from God. Aaron enters into a kind of magical competition with Pharaoh's own magicians. He turns his staff into a snake, a feat which is immediately duplicated by the Egyptians, but Aaron's staff swallows up those of his adversaries (Exod. 7.8–12; see also sidebar on opposite page). Aaron's feat does not move Pharaoh, so God commands Moses to turn the waters of Egypt into blood. Aaron does so by wielding his staff, but the Egyptian magicians repeat the miracle and Pharaoh is unimpressed. Through Moses and Aaron, God sends more plagues: frogs, gnats (or mosquitoes), flies, livestock pestilence, boils, hail, and locusts. In each case, Pharaoh either remains unmoved by the plague, or relents and promises to release the Israelites, but then goes back on his word. It is only after the tenth and most drastic plague, the death of all the firstborn of the Egyptians, that Pharaoh needs no further convincing of God's power. He summons Moses and Aaron and does not simply promise to free the Israelites but actually commands the brothers to conduct their people out of Egypt (Exod. 12.31).

The narrative of the plagues is thought to represent a conflation of the work of the two biblical authors who are referred to as "J" and "P" (see pp.20–1), each of whom originally told of seven plagues, the number given in Psalm 105. According to one of the writers, it is Moses who wields his staff to bring about the plagues. The other writer gives much greater prominence to Aaron, who uses his own staff in the course of a contest with the Egyptian sorcerers. During the plague of boils (which was originally the fourth and central plague), the Egyptian magicians are afflicted with boils and therefore become ritually unclean, so they must withdraw. The two traditions could be successfully woven together because they both served to demonstrate the irresistible power of the god of the Israelites, Yahweh.

This drawing from an ancient Egyptian relief depicts a figure called "Seth of Ramesses-Beloved-Of-Amon." Some scholars have suggested that it represents a magician turning his staff into a serpent, which appears behind him.

Serpents featured in all areas of Egyptian culture. This alabaster and jasper gaming board of ca. 250 BCE *is for a game called* Mehen.

AARON'S STAFF

In Israelite tradition, Aaron's staff (see main text on opposite page) was venerated as the sign of his superiority and symbolized the exclusive claim of Aaron and his descendants to the priesthood (see p.48). The book of Numbers (Num. 17–18) relates how God sought to end wrangling among the Israelites and asked Moses to obtain twelve staffs, one from each of the leaders of the tribes of Israel. The one bearing Aaron's name, for the tribe of Levi, produced buds, blossoms, and "ripe almonds." (Such miraculous sproutings are common in folktales.) As a result, God granted Aaron and his sons sole control of the priesthood. The staff was laid up in a holy place.

It is significant that God should first try to impress Pharaoh by turning Aaron's staff into a snake. Snakes were potent symbols in the ancient Near East (see also p.23). In Egypt, they were regarded as the embodiment of chaotic forces, and the magic which could control and harness them was greatly valued.

Natural phenomena

The plagues that God imposes on the Egyptians (see main text on opposite page) are often explained as natural phenomena that occur from time to time in Egypt. The first plague, in which the Nile turns to stinking blood, may refer to the occasional reddening of the river owing to volcanic deposits and algae from the White Nile and Blue Nile. In his account of the seventh plague, hail, the biblical author notes that the wheat and the spelt were not destroyed because they had not yet ripened (Exod. 9.31–32). This is probably an accurate reflection of the Egyptian annual planting schedule. The ninth plague, "darkness over the land," could refer to the thick dust clouds caused in March by the hot winds from the Sahara known as the *Khamsin*. Exceptionally severe infestations of frogs, gnats, flies, and locusts are characteristic of North Africa, and no doubt afflicted Egypt with some regularity.

Moses Conjures Up the Plague of Locusts *(Exod. 10.12–13), from the Nuremberg Bible of 1483.*

The biblical plagues may reflect ancient memories of real occurrences, but they are also of theological significance. The Nile waters do not simply become red but actually turn into blood, which possesses profound symbolism in the Bible. Goshen, where the Israelites lived, is spared from the plagues of hail and darkness: this seems more an instance of God's care for his people than something that really happened. The unique severity of the plagues is frequently stressed.

The plagues appear to represent a tradition of God's judgment taking the form of natural calamities. There are other examples in oracles that prophesy divine judgment, such as chapter 4 of the book of Amos.

CROSSING THE SEA

PASSOVER AND UNLEAVENED BREAD
Exodus 12 and 13 explains the origin of the ancient spring festival of Passover and Unleavened Bread. There were originally two separate celebrations. Passover was the ritual sacrifice of an animal in order to ward off evil from the home, and may have been connected with the migration of pastoral nomads to summer pastures. Unleavened Bread was more characteristic of a settled population. It was a communal festival at the start of the harvest of barley, the first crop to be gathered.

The Bible brings the festivals together as commemorations of the events of the Exodus. Passover (*Pesah* in Hebrew, whence the word "paschal;") is so called because Yahweh "passed over" the Israelite dwellings (Exod. 12.27), which were protected from the last of the ten plagues, the death of the firstborn (see p.50). The festival once began with the sacrifice at dusk of a kid or lamb, a practice still observed by the Samaritans (see p.119). Exodus explains that the blood of the sacrifice protected the Israelite firstborn from God's plague (Exod. 12.21–23). The Passover is a night of vigil, because God kept vigil to bring the people out of Egypt (Exod. 12.42). It is followed by a week in which no leavened bread is eaten; the lack of leavened bread is attributed to the Israelites' hasty departure (Exod. 12.39).

After their release from captivity (see pp.50–1), Moses and the Israelites head southwest from the city of Rameses (see map on opposite page), taking the bones of Joseph with them. God goes before them in the form of a pillar of cloud by day and a pillar of fire by night, which are symbols of the divine presence elsewhere in the Bible. The quickest route to Canaan is "by way of the land of the Philistines," but God chooses to lead the people "by the roundabout way of the wilderness towards the Red Sea." This will discourage the Israelites from turning back if they face war (Exod. 13.17), and will make Pharaoh believe that the former captives are "wandering aimlessly" in the wilderness (Exod. 14.3). God encourages the Egyptians to pursue the Israelites because, as he tells Moses, he plans to "gain glory for myself over Pharaoh and all his army." In doing so, God will show the Egyptians that he is "the Lord."

The Egyptian army catches up with the Israelites at the Red Sea. There is understandable fear among the fugitives, but Moses reassures them: "The Lord will fight for you" (Exod. 14.14). During the night, the two pillars move between the Israelites and the Egyptians. On God's instruction, Moses raises his staff and God sends a strong east wind which drives back the sea and lays bare the seabed. The Israelites cross the sea "on dry ground." The Egyptian army follows, but in the morning God throws the pursuers into a panic and clogs the wheels of their chariots. Moses raises his staff again and the sea flows back, drowning Pharaoh's army.

The events of the crossing of the sea are pictured in terms of the ancient creation myth (see p.16 and pp.20–1), with the dividing of the waters and the defeat of the hostile forces of chaos, represented by the pursuing Egyptian army. Like many other narratives in the Bible, the story derives from two different traditions, represented by the authors "J" and "P" (see pp.20–1). In the "J" tradition, Yahweh acts alone, while "P" gives Moses much greater prominence. The two traditions have been skillfully woven together to produce a coherent narrative, the purpose of which is to awaken Israel's faith in the divine warrior who fights for his people. After

KINGS OF THE NINETEENTH DYNASTY
The Exodus is often dated to the time of the Nineteenth Dynasty of Egyptian pharaohs (below), in particular the reigns of Ramesses II, who built the city of Rameses (see map), and Merneptah. All dates are approximate.

Ramesses I	1292–1290 BCE
Sethos I	1290–1279 BCE
Ramesses II	1279–1212 BCE
Merneptah	1212–1204 BCE
Sethos II	1204–1198 BCE
Siptah	1198–1193 BCE
Tewosret	1193–1190 BCE

Egyptian troops on the march, a sculpture of the period 1990–1786 BCE from a tomb at Assyut, Egypt.

The route of the Exodus

The Israelites are said to have escaped across the "Sea of Reeds," in Hebrew *Yam Suf*. There is no agreement on exactly where this is, although elsewhere in the Hebrew Scriptures *Yam Suf* refers to the Red Sea. But few scholars believe that it means Red Sea in the Exodus story, and alternative routes have been proposed (see map). For example: a northern route across Lake Sirbonis; two central routes across either the marshes of Lake Timsah or the Little Bitter Lake; and a southern route near the Gulf of Suez. The itinerary of the Israelites after the crossing is also much disputed. It is impossible to identify with certainty many of the place-names in the narrative and the Bible itself does not seem to be consistent about the route of the Exodus. Different biblical authors were probably influenced by different ancient trails across Sinai.

It appears likely that the book of Exodus includes elements of various different nomadic traditions in a story that originally related the movements of just one of the groups that made up the later nation of Israel: the Bible hints that other, related, groups also moved from Egypt and wandered around the Sinai peninsula. The wandering people of the Exodus story are thus made the representatives of the entire Israelite nation.

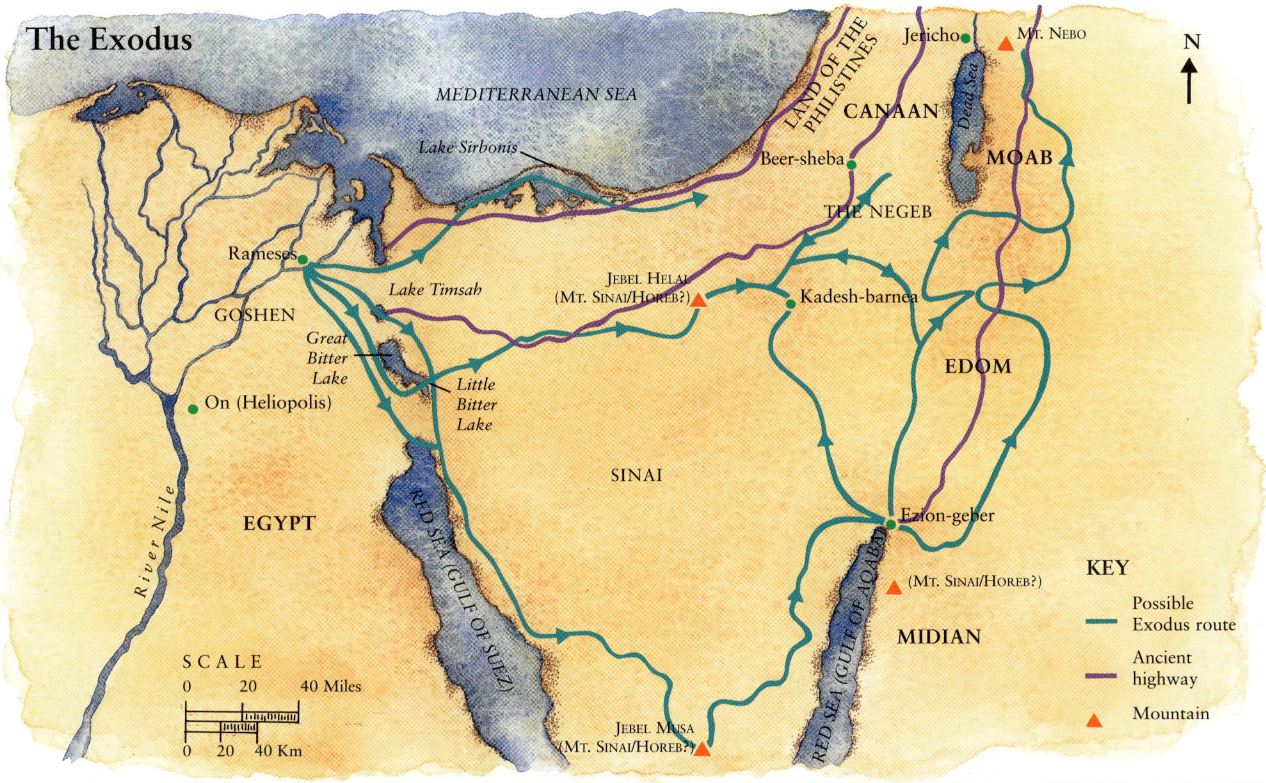

their deliverance from Pharaoh, the Israelites put their faith in Yahweh and his servant, Moses.

Both accounts agree on one essential point: something miraculous happened at the sea through divine agency, and that this was of fundamental importance for the nation of Israel. The episode is followed by a poem known as "The Song of the Sea" (Exod. 15.1–18). It is said to have been uttered by Moses, but in fact it is a later composition, possibly a liturgical hymn commemorating the Exodus. The first part of the text (verses 1–12) recounts the crossing of the sea and praises Yahweh's supremacy over all other deities. The second part (verses 13–18) shows how this event delivered Israel to become God's people, conquer the Canaanites, and establish the divine sanctuary on Mount Zion, Jerusalem.

MOSES ON MOUNT SINAI

After the crossing of the Red Sea (see pp.52–3), the Israelites journey into the wilderness until they come to Mount Sinai, where God transmits to Moses the divine laws by which the people of Israel will be governed. The giving of the law is the central element in the whole of the Pentateuch, as is implied by the amount of space devoted to it: twenty-one chapters of Exodus, the whole of Leviticus, and a considerable part of Numbers. The most important section, which determines all that follows, is the account beginning in Exodus 19 of the great theophany (manifestation of God) after the people arrive at the holy mountain (Exod. 19.2). This lengthy and complicated section is made up of a variety of components of different dates and backgrounds, but its significant themes are clear.

The narrative stresses the unique role of Moses as the mediator of the divine word. He alone is able to speak directly to God and to receive the divine instructions for transmission to the people. This is expressed by the repeated visits of Moses to the mountaintop to meet with the deity. The biblical picture of Moses includes features reminiscent of later kings, priests, and prophets who also appear as mediators. He sets a pattern for an important aspect of the future life of the Israelite nation. At Sinai,

Moses with the Tablets of the Law, *by Rembrandt (1659).*

THE TEN COMMANDMENTS

The basis of the covenant between God and Israel are the Ten Commandments, also called the Decalogue. They represent a type of law in the Hebrew Scriptures that consists of absolute ethical imperatives ("apodictic" law). There are two full versions of the commandments, in Exodus 20 and Deuteronomy 5, and they are summarized or quoted elsewhere in the Bible, especially in the prophets. They are also found in a papyrus of ca. 100 BCE and in fragments from the Dead Sea Scrolls (see p.139). The variations in these versions suggest that they all derive from an original catechism of ten brief sayings, or "Words," as the Hebrew describes them, which in some cases have been expanded. The basic commandments may go back to Moses, but their final form could have been influenced by Near Eastern treaties in which terms were imposed on a vassal by a sovereign. Alternatively, they may have originated as a cult liturgy of the sort also found in Psalms 15 and 24, setting out ethical conditions for participation in worship. Religious groups differ in their numbering of the commandments (see below).

THE COMMANDMENTS (EXOD. 20.1–17)

"I am the Lord your God who brought you out of the land of Egypt, out of the house of slavery." *[Prologue: the first commandment in Judaism.]*

"You shall have no other gods before me. You shall not make for yourself an idol." *[The second commandment in Judaism; the first commandment in the Roman Catholic and Lutheran churches; the first commandment – with the prologue – and second commandment in the Orthodox and Protestant Reformed churches.]*

"You shall not make wrongful use of the name of the LORD your God."
"Remember the sabbath day, and keep it holy."
"Honor your father and your mother."
"You shall not murder."
"You shall not commit adultery."
"You shall not steal."
"You shall not bear false witness against your neighbor."
"You shall not covet your neighbor's house; you shall not covet your neighbor's wife ... or anything that belongs to your neighbor." *[The tenth commandment in Judaism and in the Orthodox and Protestant Reformed churches; the ninth and tenth commandments in the Roman Catholic and Lutheran churches.]*

Moses is specifically the mediator of the Covenant, the formal agreement between God and the people that defines Israel as a nation. The terms of the Covenant are expressed as laws given by God that the Israelites must obey, and may well follow the general model of Near Eastern treaties between an overlord and his vassal. God promises that if the people abide by the terms of the Covenant, they will become "a priestly kingdom and a holy nation" (Exod. 19.6). Moses reports the divine promise and the people assent to it (Exod. 24.7). The narrative includes the giving of the Ten Commandments (see sidebar on opposite page) and other legal provisions. In fact, the Bible takes the view that all basic Israelite law was handed down by God to Moses on Mount Sinai (see also pp.112–13).

The Sinai episode appears to have been shaped by Israelite cult traditions, perhaps by a recurring festival of Covenant renewal. For example, the detailed purification rites before the theophany (Exod. 19.10–15) are a preparation for participation in worship. The theophany itself is accompanied by storm, fire, and earthquake (Exod. 19.16–18). These phenomena have sometimes prompted the view that Mount Sinai was a volcano, but they are in fact stereotypical features of a divine manifestation. The sounding of a trumpet, which is mentioned several times, represents the summons to a religious ceremony, and the cloud of smoke that hides Yahweh from the people (Exod. 19.18) may be based on an incense rite. Finally, the sacred meal and the sprinkling of sacrificial blood to seal the Covenant (Exod. 24.5–8) suggest a cult ritual.

The holy mountain

As far as the Bible is concerned, all that can be said for certain is that God's abode, the mountain where Moses received the Law, was outside the Promised Land, somewhere to the south of Canaan. Mount Sinai is traditionally identified with the mountain called, in Arabic, Jebel Musa ("Mount of Moses") in the south of the Sinai peninsula (see right and also map on p.53). But this identification seems originally to have been made by Christians and to go back hardly beyond the fourth century. It has been suggested more recently that the mountain was somewhere in northwestern Arabia, in what may have been a Midianite area, while some passages in the Bible locate Yahweh's dwelling in Edom (Seir), to the south of Palestine. There are various other terms for the holy mountain, notably Mount Horeb, but also "Mountain of God" or simply "the mountain." The concept of the holy mountain may have been applied to different sites in the interest of pilgrims after its exact location was forgotten.

Jebel Musa in southern Sinai, identified as Mount Sinai by Greek Christian monks in the 4th century CE.

In the Bible, there are several descriptions of Israel's history from the Exodus to the occupation of Canaan that make no mention of Mount Sinai. This is remarkable, given the focal role of Sinai in the Exodus narrative. In particular, there are strong indications of a tradition that Kadesh-barnea, an oasis in the desert region south of Beer-sheba, occupied the central place in the movement to Canaan and was the site of the giving of the Law. This tradition would have represented the experiences of one of the groups that made up the later nation of Israel. According to this theory, it was displaced by the tradition of another group, which located the lawgiving and Covenant-making on Mount Sinai.

THE BOOK OF THE COVENANT

Immediately after the giving of the Ten Commandments (see p.54), God instructs Moses to set a further, and much longer, series of laws before the Israelites (Exod. 20.22–23.33). When Moses reads them out, they are referred to as the "book of the Covenant" (Exod. 24.7), a term by which the collection of laws is usually known. The episode illustrates how all Israelite law came to be attributed to the work of Moses. It seems to be an insertion into the Sinai narrative, because it evidently refers to a time when Israel is a settled community, that is, after it has already moved into the land of Canaan: the ordinances refer to houses, cattle, fields and vineyards, slaves, silver, chattels, and the use of money. The book of the Covenant is thought to be the oldest of the biblical law codes and to reflect conditions soon after the occupation of Canaan, or perhaps even in the early days of the monarchy. Among the sacrificial laws is a prohibition on boiling a kid in its mother's milk (Exod. 23.19). There may be a parallel to this curious rule in a Canaanite text, so it is possible that the regulation is directed against a Canaanite rite. In fact, the book of the

Early Israelite religion

One section of the book of the Covenant (Exod. 20.22–26) provides some important insights into aspects of Israel's early religious practices. God states that he will come to bless the people "in every place where I cause my name to be remembered." This condones the existence of many sanctuaries, in contrast to the situation in the later Israel. It also appears to sanction the Israelite adoption of ancient Canaanite shrines, as seen in the ancestral legends of Genesis and elsewhere (see, for example, p.32 and p.39).

There are three divine regulations concerning the construction of an altar. The first is very ancient and states that altars must be made simply of earth (Exod. 20.24). This may reflect a preference for materials that were in their wholly natural state as they were created. A similar idea may underlie the second regulation, which allows altars of stone as long as hewn stones are not used, because a chisel would profane them (Exod. 20.25). This is probably directed against Canaanite altars, which were made of dressed stone. When Joshua builds the first Israelite altar in accordance with these prescriptions, the Bible states specifically that "no iron tool" was used on its stones (Josh. 8.31). There is no mention of iron in the book of the Covenant, so the law may go back to a time when ironworking was not yet known to the Israelites.

The third regulation prohibits the making of steps up to the altar (Exod. 20.26). It is likely that this law was originally aimed at the widespread ancient Near Eastern cult of the "high god," which involved the construction of altar steps. In the Bible, the reason for the prohibition is "so that your nakedness may not be exposed" on the altar, that is, so that the genitals will not be directly over any part of the altar. This reflects the Israelite abhorrence of any association between the sexual and the holy. A later regulation insisted that priests had to wear linen shorts beneath their robes to cover their genitalia.

Exodus 20 says "You shall not go up by steps to my altar," an ordinance probably designed to counter altars similar to this one at Petra, the center of the ancient Nabatean kingdom. Stepped altars were a characteristic of pagan worship.

Covenant as a whole may have been composed mainly to combat the religious and cultural influence of the indigenous Canaanites during the early period of Israelite settlement in Canaan (see p.66).

The book of the Covenant falls into two main sections that are distinguished by their literary style. The first section consists mostly of ordinances or case law, *mishpatim*, beginning with "if" or "when." For example: "When a slaveowner strikes the eye of a male or female slave, destroying it, the owner shall let the slave go, a free person, to compensate for the eye" (Exod. 21.26); and "If a thief is found breaking in, and is beaten to death, no bloodguilt is incurred; but if it happens after sunrise, bloodguilt is incurred" (Exod. 22.2–3). This is the most common form of ordinance found in other ancient Near Eastern law codes (see box, below). The second section is largely religious in content and combines humanitarian injunctions, standards for the administration of justice, directions for three great annual pilgrimage festivals, and sacrificial regulations. Like the Ten Commandments, this section is apodictic (imperative) in form, for example: "You shall not spread a false report. You shall not join hands with the wicked to act as a malicious witness ... when you bear witness in a lawsuit, you shall not side with the majority so as to pervert justice" (Exod. 23.1–2); and "Six days you shall do your work, but on the seventh day you shall rest, so that your ox and your donkey may have relief, and the homeborn slave and the resident alien be refreshed" (Exod. 23.12).

A Byzantine wall painting depicting Moses, from St Catherine's monastery on Jebel Musa, the traditional Mount Sinai (6th century CE*). From the Middle Ages onward, artists portrayed Moses as an older, bearded figure (see picture on p.54).*

Near Eastern law codes

The practice of codifying laws was common in the civilizations of the ancient Near East. In the last century, a number of law codes were discovered that display numerous points of contact with the legal texts of the Hebrew Scriptures, suggesting that they provided inspiration for the biblical codifications.

Seven ancient Near Eastern law codes are of particular importance. Four are royal codes, three of which date from the Sumerian period: the code of Ur-Nammu, the founder of the third dynasty of Ur (ca. 2100 BCE); the code of Lipit-Ishtar of Isin from the early nineteenth century BCE; and the code from the kingdom of Eshnunna of about the same period. The fourth is the famous law code of King Hammurapi of Babylon (ca. 1728–1686 BCE; see right). All except for the Eshnunna code have poetic prologues and epilogues praising the king and threatening divine retribution for anyone who seeks to alter his law. Three later codes, also containing parallels to biblical material, are not directly ascribed to monarchs. They are the Middle Assyrian Laws (twelfth century BCE or earlier), the Hittite laws from Asia Minor (fourteenth century BCE), and the laws of the Neo-Babylonian empire (ca. 625–539 BCE). The book of the Covenant resembles these codes in its largely secular subject-matter and in its businesslike tone, and there are many parallels. For example, the law that describes what happens when an ox is killed by another owner's animal (Exod. 21.35) is almost identical to one in the laws of Eshnunna.

These numerous parallels do not mean that the book of the Covenant depends directly on any particular Mesopotamian texts. It is more likely that the Israelites came to know the common Near Eastern pattern of setting out the law through their contact with the Canaanites, although no Canaanite law code has yet been discovered.

A Babylonian stela of ca. 1700 BCE *inscribed with the law code of King Hammurapi.*

THE TABERNACLE

A statue of king Gudea of Lagash. He was said to have had a dream in which the god Ningursu gave him details of a temple he had to build, together with a sketch of the structure.

Following the account of the giving of the Ten Commandments and the book of the Covenant (see pp.54–7), the remainder of the book of Exodus is devoted mainly to the building of a sacred dwelling place for God among the Israelites. This sanctuary takes the form of a tent or tabernacle that will also house the tablets of divine law handed down to Moses on Sinai. The concept of the tent-shrine was not unique in the ancient Near East. The Canaanites designated the abode of El, their supreme god (see p.32 and p.39), and other deities as a tabernacle or tent, the same terms used in the Bible for the sanctuary of Yahweh. God showed Moses on Mount Sinai "the pattern of the tabernacle and of all its furniture" (Exod. 25.9). In the Near East, it was commonly thought that the design and dimensions of the earthly temple of a deity were divinely ordained, and corresponded to those of the deity's sanctuary in heaven. Gudea, the ruler of the Sumerian city of Lagash (ca. 2060 BCE), was said to have received divine instructions for the building of a temple.

Chapters 25–40 fall into two broad sections: God's detailed directions to Moses on the building of the tabernacle, followed by an account of how these instructions were carried out. The tabernacle consisted of a rectangular court around a central sanctuary structure. The court was enclosed by curtains supported on poles, and its dimensions have been estimated as one hundred forty-five feet long, seventy feet wide and seven feet high (44 x 21 x 2.1m). The exact length of a cubit, the biblical unit of measurement is uncertain, but it has sometimes been put at eighteen inches (45 cm). The furnishings were made from the finest and costliest materials by two expert craftsmen, who are named in Exodus 31 as Bezalel and Oholiab. The structure of the tabernacle is the focus of the narrative, but there are also details of its contents, such as the altars and, above all, the ark of the Covenant, the sacred chest in which the tablets of the Law will be laid up (see p.70). Instructions are also given for the consecration of Aaron and his sons to the priesthood (see p.48).

The tabernacle was designed to be portable, and when the Israelites moved about during their wanderings in the wilderness, the whole structure was dismantled by the Levites, who re-erected it wherever the tribes pitched camp. The constant movement of so large a structure is hard

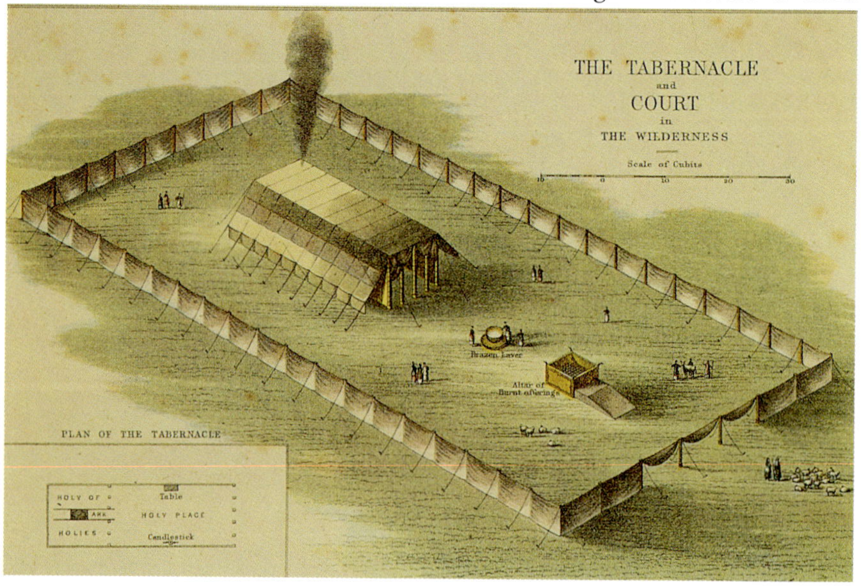

A 19th-century reconstruction of the Israelite tabernacle and court.

The Golden Calf

In between the two halves of the Tabernacle narrative is the episode of the Golden Calf (Exod. 32–33). Moses comes down from the mountain to discover that in his absence the people, led by his brother Aaron, have made an image of a calf in gold and erected an altar before it. When he sees them worshiping the idol, he smashes the tablets of the Law and destroys the calf.

The Tabernacle can only be built when the Israelites have been purged from this sin and the commandments have been reiterated. The text is essentially a mocking polemic against idolatry, the making of gods of silver or gold, which the book of the Covenant condemns as characteristic of Canaanite religion. The Israelites put their trust in a mere calf, and we are surely meant to laugh at Aaron's lame excuse that he only threw the gold into the fire and a calf emerged.

A bronze cult bull of the 12th century BCE *from Samaria in northern Palestine.*

However, the episode may represent what was originally a more favorable tradition of the fashioning of the calf. The story appears to be related to the account in chapter twelve of the first book of Kings of the setting up of two golden calves, at Bethel and Dan, by King Jeroboam I of Israel (see p.87). In Exodus the Israelites utter a ritual cry: "These are your gods, O Israel, who brought you up out of the land of Egypt" (Exod. 32.4). This cry is almost identical to Jeroboam's statement in the account in 1 Kings 12.28. The "calf" would have been a bull, a symbol of power that was commonly used to represent deities in the ancient Near East. Although Jeroboam's actions are condemned as sinful, his bulls would not have represented a foreign deity, but Yahweh. He may have been reviving a long-established cult which legend ascribed to Aaron.

to imagine in desert conditions, and it is unlikely that the Israelites, who were probably a relatively small group, then had the craftsmen, materials, or wealth to erect it. One explanation is that the account of the tabernacle stems from much later priestly sources, probably in the time of the Israelite monarchy, and in fact presents a description of Solomon's Temple at Jerusalem (see pp. 84–5) in the guise of a portable shrine. This is in accordance with the view that all Israel's religious institutions originated at the time of the Exodus.

The priestly writers were aware that no permanent sanctuary building existed before the occupation of Canaan, but this does not mean that the wilderness tabernacle was merely a fiction of the biblical narrators. As well as using the word "tabernacle," *mishkan*, the account also employs – some one hundred thirty times – the expression "tent of meeting," *ohel mo'ed*. This refers to a much simpler type of shrine (Exod. 33.7–11 and elsewhere) that was more likely to have existed in the wilderness. It was a real tent that one person could pitch, outside the camp, and functioned for the receiving of oracles. On these occasions, when Moses entered the tent to meet with God, the divine presence would descend in the form of a pillar of cloud. The priestly authors transferred the most significant features of the tent of meeting to their representation of the tabernacle, so the divine cloud descends on the tabernacle, and the meeting with God takes place over the ark within it.

The two traditions of desert tent and urban temple are brought together in the curious depiction of the "tent over the tabernacle" in Exodus 36.14. The materials from which it was made, tanned rams' skins and goats' hair, are in marked contrast to the rich fabric drapes of the rest of the tabernacle, and reflect a genuine desert tradition. The same materials are found in a Bedouin tent and, especially, in the Bedouin portable shrines or *qubba*s.

Il Nebi Musa, a Muslim shrine marking the spot on Mount Nebo where Moses is thought to have died (see box, below).

THE WILDERNESS YEARS

The account of the Israelites' wanderings in the wilderness, both before and after the stay at Mount Sinai, is made up of a number of separate episodes from different backgrounds and dates, some of which are repeated more than once. Their framework seems to have been the itinerary preserved in Numbers 33, which may well be an old pilgrimage route to and from Mount Sinai. Unfortunately, it is hard to identify with any certainty many of the names in the itinerary.

Certain themes characterize the narrative as a whole. The most prominent is what has been described as the "murmuring" motif, the repeated complaints of the Israelites against Moses, Aaron, and Yahweh himself (such as Num. 14.1–10). The complaints reflect internal dissent among the people as well as the hardships of desert life, such as the lack of food and water and the danger of attack from snakes and human enemies. The lack of trust which the murmurings betray often provoke Yahweh's anger and, in these stories, Moses appears as the supreme intercessor. For example, in the episode of the Golden Calf (see p.59), he averts God's wrath and persuades the deity to alleviate the condition of the people.

In some of the wilderness stories, Moses is also seen as a worker of divine wonders linked with particular localities or natural phenomena. He purifies the waters of Marah by casting a piece of wood into them (Exod. 15.23–25), and produces water from a rock at a place called Massah and Meribah (Exod. 17.6–7; Num. 20.11). Through Moses, God sends an abundance of quails and manna, which are phenomena characteristic of the Sinai peninsula (Exod. 16). In a battle with the Amalekites, victory is achieved through the power of Moses' uplifted hands (Exod. 17.8–13). When God sends a plague of snakes to punish the Israelites, Moses ends it by setting up a bronze serpent on a pole: anyone bitten by a snake could

The deaths of Moses and Aaron

Moses and Aaron both died outside the Promised Land of Canaan. This was an undeniable fact of Israelite tradition, but it was felt that some explanation was needed as to why these two great figures had not shared in the fulfillment of God's promise to the people. In the book of Deuteronomy, the explanation is that Moses was punished for the repeated sins of the people in the wilderness. In Numbers 20, Moses and Aaron repeat the miraculous provision of water from the rock at Meribah (Kadesh), after which God tells them: "Because you did not trust in me, to show my holiness before the eyes of the Israelites, therefore you shall not bring this assembly into the land that I have given them" (Num. 20.12). The reason for this is unclear. Perhaps Moses and Aaron were guilty of presumption by not giving God credit for the miracle (Num. 20.10). It may be that the story is deliberately vague about the offense so that Moses and Aaron are not incriminated too greatly. In any case, much care is taken to preserve the brothers' reputation. They install successors to carry on their work: Aaron's son Eleazar as the chief priest (Num. 20.28) and Joshua, son of Nun, as the national leader (Deut. 31.7). Both brothers die on mountains, Aaron on Mount Hor near Kadesh (Num. 20.28) and Moses on Mount Nebo in Moab (Deut. 34.5). When Moses ascends Mount Nebo (see picture, above left), God shows him the whole of the Promised Land (Deut. 34). It is now known that such a survey was a way of establishing a right of territorial possession, so that, in a sense, Moses does achieve his final goal.

At the end, Moses is presented like one of the ancient patriarchs. He dies, full of vigor, at a great age, and before his death he blesses all the Israelite tribes, as Jacob had done. Yet his stature is unique, as the final words of the Pentateuch make clear: "Never since has there arisen a prophet in Israel like Moses, whom the Lord knew face to face."

The Israelites gathering manna in the wilderness (Exod. 16.16–17), by the Master of the Manna, ca. 1470. The Bible derives the word manna from the question "Man hu?" *(Hebrew for "What is it?"), which the Israelites are said to have asked when they first saw the "fine flaky substance, as fine as frost" (Exod. 16.14). The true origin of the word, like the identity of the substance itself, is not known for certain.*

look at the serpent and be cured (Num. 21.6–9). This is the origin of the bronze serpent that stood in the Temple of Jerusalem (see pp.84–5). It was originally a symbol of Canaanite religion, but is here attributed to Moses, although its original significance as part of a cult involving serpent worship has been neutralized.

Moses' leadership does not go unchallenged, even by his sister Miriam and brother Aaron. They question Moses' unique role of mediator, but God reaffirms his position (Num. 12). Similarly, the stories of the rebellion and deaths of Korah, Dathon, and Abiram (Num. 16), and of Aaron's staff (Num. 17; see also p.51), reflect challenges by groups within the priesthood to the exclusive authority of the line of Aaron.

On their way to Canaan, the Israelites enter Moabite territory east of the Jordan River (Num. 22.1). Balak, the king of Moab, realizes the threat they pose and summons the seer Balaam to lay a curse on them. The account of Balaam's failure (Num. 22–24) is marked by folklore motifs and much ironic humor, as in the episode of the angel and the talking donkey (Num. 22.22–35), and in the way that Balak's schemes fail. Every time he asks Balaam to curse Israel, the seer obeys God's instruction and utters a blessing (see also sidebar, right).

BALAAM

Balaam is described as coming from Pethor on the Euphrates River, and his divinatory activities (see main text) show him as a typical Mesopotamian seer-priest, the kind known as *baru*. In the Bible he acts under the direct inspiration of Yahweh, and what is recounted of him represents various conventions of Israelite prophetic legend.

Recent discoveries suggest that Balaam may have been a real person of the Transjordan region. Fragmentary Aramaic texts of the ninth century BCE from Deir Alla refer to a Balaam who, as in the Hebrew Scriptures, was the son of Beor. He is said to have a vision of a disaster that befalls his city, at which he weeps. This revelation is received from an assembly of divine beings described as *Shaddin*, which recalls the title *Shaddai*, "Almighty," an archaic name for God in the Hebrew Scriptures (see p.50). The name *Shaddai* occurs more than once in the biblical story of Balaam, for example in Numbers 24.4.

THE PROMISED LAND

The Bible relates that, following the death of Moses (see p.60), the Israelites crossed the Jordan into Canaan. The book of Joshua gives an account of their first conquests and ends with a reaffirmation of the supremacy of Yahweh. But, according to the book of Judges, Israel repeatedly broke faith with God, for which it faced divine anger. Each time the people repented, God appointed a leader or "judge" to vanquish the nation's enemies. The greatest of them, Samuel, paved the way for a new institution: the monarchy.

The valley of the River Jordan.

THE INVASION OF CANAAN

According to the book of Joshua, after the death of Moses the Israelites conquered the Promised Land under his successor, Joshua, in three rapid campaigns: in the center, then in the south, and finally in the north. Archaeology has frequently been used to support and approximately date the biblical picture of a speedy and violent conquest. It has been claimed, for example, that four of the towns taken by Israel (Lachish, Debir, Bethel, and Hazor) suffered great destruction between ca. 1300 BCE and ca. 1200 BCE. This may be so, but there is no direct proof that the Israelites destroyed these particular towns or any others, because most cities in Palestine were devastated many times between 2000 BCE and 1000 BCE. Also, other cities said to have fallen to Israel could not, on the evidence, have been destroyed in the century 1300–1200 BCE. According to the Bible, Joshua and the Israelites captured and burned Jericho and Ai, but recent discoveries show that Jericho, while not uninhabited, was barely occupied during that century and certainly did not possess a city wall, while Ai had been abandoned hundreds of years before. Most of the territory conquered according to the book of Joshua is in the area later allotted to the tribe of Benjamin. The core of the book may represent how just one tribe came to possess its own particular territory.

Before the Israelites reach the land of Canaan, the book of Numbers gives an account of their conquest of Transjordan, the territory east of the Jordan. The narrative is confusing, because it is constructed from a variety of traditional elements and motifs. Transjordan is shown as a region contested by a number of peoples – the Edomites, Amorites, Moabites, and Midianites – who had settled in the area before the arrival of the Israelites. (It remained a much disputed area throughout the later history of the region.) The region is depicted as being somewhat strange and sinister. God's anger is provoked when some of the Israelites have relations with Moabite women and start to worship the local god, Baal of Peor (Num. 25). This apostasy is blamed in Numbers 31.16 on the seer-priest Balaam (see p.61), who is killed for it (Num. 31.8). In the book of Joshua, the Transjordanian Israelite groups build an altar, which the other tribes view as a departure from the true worship of Yahweh. According to Hebrew tradition, Transjordan had once been populated by Rephaim, a race of giants. The word is also found in Canaanite texts, where it refers to divine beings. King Og of Bashon, who was defeated and killed by the Israelites (Num. 21.33–35), was remembered as one of the Rephaim and his iron bedstead, nearly fourteen feet long and six feet wide (4.5m x 2m), was said to exist in the Ammonite city of Rabbah. It may have been a sarcophagus, or perhaps a basalt dolmen in the vicinity of Rabbah.

According to the Bible, Moses allotted the Transjordanian region to the tribes of Reuben and Gad, and to the half-tribe of Manasseh (Josh. 1.12–15). This probably points to what was in fact an independent movement of Israelite groups across the Jordan, perhaps originally from the west of the river.

The crossing of the Jordan

The crossing of the Jordan River into the Promised Land, recounted in Joshua 3, is of great symbolic and spiritual importance for the Israelites. In preparation for it, the people are told to undergo the regular ritual purification before a religious ceremony, and the passage over the river is led by the priests and the sacred ark. The story draws an explicit parallel between the crossing of the Jordan and the crossing of the sea during the Exodus (Josh. 3.15–17 and 4.23). Both events hark back to the language of the creation, when the waters of chaos were divided and the dry land emerged. The story is followed by an account of the origin of the sanctuary of Gilgal, which concludes with a circumcision rite at a spot called "the Hill of the Foreskins," and a celebration at Gilgal of the spring festival of Passover–Unleavened Bread (Josh. 5).

The character of the Gilgal legend indicates that it was a pre-Israelite holy place, probably the site of a Canaanite festival, which reenacted the victory of a deity over the forces of chaos, as in the stories of the gods Baal and Marduk (see p.21). The events at the Jordan and at Gilgal may well be the real source of the tradition of Israel's crossing of the sea.

THE FALL OF JERICHO

The Fall of Jericho, *an illustration by Jean Fouquet (ca. 1425–1480) from* Antiques Judaïques, *a French translation of the work of the 1st-century Jewish historian Flavius Josephus.*

A stone tower of the Neolithic period (ca. 7000 BCE*), discovered during excavations on the site of ancient Jericho, close to the modern town. Jericho is the oldest continuously inhabited city in the world; it was first settled ca. 8000* BCE*.*

The book of Joshua records the capture of a chain of cities in the central plateau of Palestine. Jericho, situated by an important ford over the Jordan, is the first and most influential of these cities and becomes a symbol of the conquest. The Bible combines two stories of the city's fall. The first is told in chapter 2. Joshua sends two men on a spying mission to Jericho. They are hidden from the king of Jericho's men by a prostitute, Rahab. In gratitude, the spies promise her that if she ties a crimson cord in the window of her house, she and her family will be spared by the Israelites. The sending of spies is a common feature of military planning and implies that Jericho was captured by military attack. Rahab's house is said to be in the city wall, and it has been plausibly suggested that the crimson cord in fact indicated the point at which an army could breach the wall. The crimson cord is also reminiscent of the blood applied to the doors and windows of Israelite houses to protect them from God's plague during the first Passover (see p.51).

The walls of Jericho did not fall to a military onslaught but as the result of a great seven-day ritual, which is recounted mainly in Joshua 6. The second story of the capture of Jericho begins with a meeting between Joshua and the commander of the heavenly army, who promises to lead the attack (Josh. 5.14). On God's orders, a procession of priests and soldiers walk around Jericho for six days accompanying the ark of the Covenant. On the seventh day, the Israelites utter a great shout and the walls of Jericho collapse. The Israelite force charges into the city and the inhabitants are slaughtered. All the booty goes into Yahweh's treasury, a regular feature of "the wars of Yahweh," known as the *herem* or "ban."

The fall and capture of the city is represented as a liturgical act, a processional encirclement of Jericho of the ark and its attendants, accompanied by ritual blowing of trumpets, in a seven-day festival. The story may have its origins in a rite celebrated at the sanctuary of Gilgal, which means "circle of stones" (see p.63). The rite may have reenacted a legend that the Benjaminites captured Jericho, a city whose broken down walls were still to be seen nearby.

After Jericho, the narrative of the occupation largely consists of a chain of local traditions from the area later assigned to the tribe of Benjamin. Following the story of the crime of Achan (Josh. 7), which explains the existence of a cairn of stones in the valley of Achor and the valley's name, there is an account of the capture of Ai (Josh. 8.1–29). This city was destroyed ca. 2400 BCE and remained a ruin until ca. 1200 BCE, so it was at most a small unwalled settlement during the likely period of the Israelite occupation of Canaan. In Hebrew, *ai* means "ruin" and the narrative may have served to explain that a prominent heap of ruins at Ai was the result of a destruction by Joshua.

The story of the Gibeonites accounts for the treaty relationship between Israel and four Canaanite cities, in the same way that the story of Rahab accounts for the friendly relations with a Canaanite group considered to be her descendants. A later tradition describes the Gibeonites as a group of temple servants, who were assigned to this position by Joshua. This, together with other indications of amicable relations between the newcomers and some of the indigenous inhabitants, suggests that the Israelite occupation of Canaan was not always accompanied by the wholesale conquest, destruction, and slaughter, which characterize the Bible narrative.

In fact, contrary to the biblical tradition, the "conquest" was probably a slow, gradual process, achieved by separate but ethnically related groups

Northern and southern campaigns

Compared with the detailed episodes relating to the central region, only highlights are given of the conquest of the rest of Palestine. These are the battle at Gibeon in the south and the destruction of Hazor in the north (see map on p.63).

One passage in the story of Gibeon refers to a series of unusual natural phenomena (Josh. 10.12–13). Part of this passage is a fragment of an old poem imploring the sun and moon to stand still. Gibeon was an ancient sanctuary, important in later Israelite history, and there is evidence that Shamash, the sun god, was worshiped there. The poem was originally addressed to Canaanite astral deities but was transferred to Yahweh by the Israelites.

Hazor was the leading city-state in Galilee, as the book of Joshua indicates (Josh. 11.10). Recent excavations have revealed the city's great size and strength. There seems to have been a partial destruction of Hazor by fire in the late thirteenth century BCE, but it is unlikely that the Israelite tribes would have had the military capacity to take such a well-fortified city. Also, the defeat of Jabin, king of Hazor, is ascribed in the book of Judges to a coalition of tribes, after Joshua's death. The story in Joshua probably represents a local tradition of the tribes that settled in Galilee, originally independently of the process of settlement in the rest of the country.

The site of ancient Hazor in northern Israel. According to the Bible, it was taken by Joshua (Josh. 11.10) and later by Deborah and Barak (Judg. 4.2 and 4.24). The city was rebuilt and fortified by Solomon (1 Kings 9.15) and Ahab.

After the conquest of the whole of Canaan, much of the remainder of the book of Joshua is taken up by a lengthy account of the division of the land among the twelve tribes. Many of the details of this account may derive from old materials, but it is generally agreed that the precise demarcation and assignment of Israelite territory would hardly have been of interest before the period of the unified kingdom of David and his successors.

over some hundreds of years (see p.68). At the time of the Israelite occupation of Palestine, the country was divided into a number of small city-kingdoms, inhabited by peoples known as the Canaanites and Amorites. This situation is reflected in letters written between ca. 1450 and 1350 BCE from the rulers of various Canaanite cities to the Egyptian pharaoh, their nominal overlord. Some of the letters, which were discovered at Amarna in Egypt, mention attacks by a people called *Hapiru*, a word that is probably closely connected with the name "Hebrew." The disturbances were obviously on a limited scale and it is too simplistic to equate the *Hapiru* attacks with the biblical record of the Israelite conquest. It seems likely that the movement of the *Hapiru* formed just one part of the long and piecemeal process which saw the settlement of various Israelite groups in Canaan.

The Bible unifies the traditions of a number of these groups, under the influence of the group that came out of Egypt. In Joshua 24, there may be a clue as to how this one tradition became dominant. Joshua gathers a great assembly of the Israelite tribes at the sanctuary of Shechem. Addressing them, he states clearly that their ancestors "served other gods." The aim of Joshua's speech is to win over the whole body of the Israelites, many of whom also worship other deities, to Yahweh, the one true God of Israel. The climax of the assembly is reached when all the people recognize Yahweh as the god who guided Abraham, Jacob, and Moses, and led the people into the Promised Land: "The Lord [Yahweh] our God we will serve, and him we will obey" (Josh. 24.24).

THE JUDGES

The book of Judges deals with the fortunes of the Israelite tribes in Palestine before the establishment of a unified state and kingdom. At Shechem, the tribes had pledged themselves to the worship only of Yahweh, but after Joshua's death the nation began to worship the Canaanite deities (see box, below). As a result, the Israelites incurred divine judgment and fell under the power of foreign enemies. When this occurred, the nation repented and turned back to Yahweh, in consequence of which Yahweh chose a "judge," who first led the people to victory over their oppressors and then governed Israel during his or her lifetime. But after each judge's death, Israel again turned from God and the same sequence of events recurred. This pattern was repeated many

The religion of the Canaanites

A basalt relief depicting Baal, the Canaanite god of storms. Baal was the guardian of the rains and therefore ensured the fertility of the soil. He is the central figure in an important cycle of myths that are probably intended to mark the end of the agricultural year and the coming of the autumn rains.

Before the twentieth century, what was known of Canaanite religion depended on the Hebrew Scriptures, some Phoenician inscriptions, and ancient Greek authors. This situation changed with the discovery, from 1929 onward, of a great number of written texts at Ras Shamra in northwest Syria, the site of the Canaanite city of Ugarit. These texts (often called "Ugaritic"), written in the cuneiform script widely used in the ancient Near East, give a first-hand picture of the Canaanite pantheon, mythology, and cult.

The Canaanites worshipped a group of deities, the most important of which were El (the creator god and head of the pantheon; see p.33 and p.39), Baal (the young god of storms and the most active deity), and Baal's consorts, the goddesses, Anath, Ashtaroth, and Asherah (see pp.16). There are references to all these gods and goddesses in the Bible, for example, in Judges 2.13 and 3.7. Canaanite religion was centered on fertility, on how to ensure an abundance of crops, animals, and children. Fertility is the underlying theme of most Ugaritic myths, which were probably recounted or reenacted in ritual form each year in order to guarantee the continued fruitfulness and prosperity of the land and its people.

It is not difficult to see why a religion of this kind appealed so powerfully to the Israelites, who had to survive in a strange environment and adapt to a new agricultural way of life. Agriculture was the central concern of the local Canaanite gods, so it was perhaps only natural for the Israelite farmer to turn to them or to transfer their functions to Yahweh.

The ruins of Ras Shamra, the ancient city of Ugarit. It was at its most prosperous in the 15th–13th centuries BCE, *the period to which the most significant discoveries of Ugaritic mythological texts belong.*

The walls of ancient Shechem, which features prominently in the Bible. The city occupied a strategic position in the pass between Mount Gerizim and Mount Ebal. It was destroyed by the Hasmonean ruler John Hyrcanus in 107 BCE *(see p.136). The Roman town of Neapolis (modern Nablus) was later built nearby.*

times until the appearance of the last judge, Samuel. Through him, a new system of government, the monarchy, came into being.

As its title suggests, the book centers on the figure of the "judge," who was not primarily a judge in the modern legal sense. The word "leader" gives a more accurate impression of the role, and the Bible sometimes describes the judge as a "deliverer" or "savior." The regular and permanent leadership of the tribes was in the hands of "elders," senior men entrusted with the conduct of affairs on account of their wisdom and experience. The judges, however, emerged in response to a severe crisis that almost always took the form of a dangerous attack from outside. They were marked out for their mission when they became possessed by the "spirit of Yahweh," a violent seizure that enabled them to perform superhuman feats of strength and military prowess. The judge represents a form of leadership that characterizes tribal societies and is often described as "charismatic." The judges disappeared with the formation of the unified state, when overriding authority was transferred to the king.

The book of Judges portrays the judge as the ruler of the entire Israelite people, but this picture represents the outlook of a later editor, who almost certainly belonged to the school of writers who produced the book of Deuteronomy (see p.100). These writers always view Israel as a single entity, and constantly emphasize the point that disobedience to Yahweh automatically courted national disaster. On closer examination, the stories of the judges that the editor used in fact deal only with the popular heroes and heroines of individual tribes and particular localities. These heroic figures emerged to save their own group when it was threatened with attack (probably on a relatively small scale) by neighboring groups.

An alternative view of the Israelite occupation

The opening chapter of the book of Judges presents a markedly different account of the Israelite occupation of Palestine from that found in the book of Joshua. In Judges, individual tribes, or even smaller groups, act independently of one another, each moving separately into a particular area on its own initiative. For example, the towns of Hebron and Debir are said in Joshua to have been captured by a united nation under the leadership of Joshua. But, according to Judges, Hebron fell to the tribe of Judah and Debir to the small clan of Othniel, and there is no mention of Joshua at all (Judg. 1.9–13).

The account in Judges also reveals that in a number of places the Israelites settled alongside the indigenous inhabitants. The newcomers did not attempt to expel or exterminate the natives, and the Bible suggests that they were regularly used as a source of forced labor (Judg. 1.27–35). As this passage indicates, the region of Israelite occupation was restricted to the hilly districts and did not extend to the Canaanite city-states of the plains, which long retained their independence (see also Judg. 1.19). Relations between these cities and the incoming Israelites no doubt varied from place to place. Often there would be mutual hostility, but Judges indicates that the two groups frequently lived in a state of relatively peaceful cohabitation. There are even instances of actual confederations between them, recalling the alliance between Joshua and the Gibeonites in Joshua 9 and 10 (see p.64). The alliance between Gideon and Abimelech and the Canaanite city of Shechem, which is recounted in Judges 8 and 9, is one example. The story of the dealings between the tribe of Benjamin and the Canaanite city of Shiloh (Judg. 21) probably has the same explanation.

HEROES AND HEROINES

A Syrian-Hittite stela of ca. 850 BCE, thought to depict Gilgamesh (center), the greatest hero of ancient Mesopotamian literature. Tales of his exploits were popular throughout the Near East and may have influenced the story of Samson.

Mount Tabor, where Barak is said to have defeated Sisera (Judg. 4.14–15).

When the Israelites looked back on the time of the judges from the more settled days of the monarchy, they recognized a distant past very different from later times. It was an epoch marked by heroic individuals who took the initiative in great deeds of arms, a situation that is well summarized in the statement: "In those days there was no king in Israel; all the people did what was right in their own eyes" (Judg. 21.25). In terms of outlook and literary character, the closest parallel to the book of Judges is the *Ayyam al 'Arab*, "The Day of the Arabs," the collection of Arab tribal traditions of the pre-Islamic heroic age. Like Judges, the *Ayyam* is almost entirely concerned with warfare.

At the heart of Judges are five originally separate story cycles about individual heroes and heroines, once local figures who came to be looked on as national symbols. In most of these, three basic details are given: the person of the heroic figure; his or her tribe, which remembered the hero or heroine in its traditions; and a sanctuary with which the figure is linked, where those traditions would have been preserved and recounted. In each case, this bare outline has been filled out with local legends, folklore, and cultic features, to produce the existing biblical form of the story.

The first cycle concerns Ehud (Judg. 3.15–30), who assassinates King Eglon of Moab, the oppressor of the Israelites. This story began as a typical folktale of a tribal hero, told with some broad black humor (such as the gruesome details of the killing of the "very fat" king in 3.22). But, in its final form, Ehud has become a national symbol, a "deliverer" of the Israelites who ends the divine punishment of foreign oppression.

The next narrative deals with the military campaign of the prophetess Deborah, the only woman judge, and Barak (Judg. 4–5). Mount Tabor, the border sanctuary of the two tribes primarily involved in the battle, features prominently, and the great poem sung by Deborah (Judg. 5) is probably a psalm of thanksgiving for victory that was sung at a solemn festival there. The poem begins with a vivid description of a manifestation of God, and victory is gained when even the stars and the torrential waters of the Kishon join the fight against Israel's foes (Judg. 5.20–21).

The third narrative tells the story of Gideon (see box, below). It is

Gideon

The third great story cycle in Judges is long and elaborate and centers on Gideon (Judg. 6.11–8.32). He seems to have been originally a simple folk-hero of a small clan group, who was remembered as one who upheld the fundamental social institution of the blood-feud by slaughtering the two kings of Midian who had killed his brothers (Judg. 8.18–21).

However, in the bulk of the scriptural traditions about him, Gideon is a national hero who rises from obscurity to greatness as the result of divine choice and inspiration. He leads his tribe in battle and, as often happens in such legends, he earns a new name, Jerubbaal (Judg. 6.32). As a reward for his exploits, the Israelites ask Gideon to be king (Judg. 8.22), an offer that he rejects, according to the narrative. But the rivalry for the throne between two of his sons following his death implies that he did in fact accept the kingship and rule Israel.

Interwoven with the account of Gideon's call by Yahweh is a legend about Gideon's foundation of the Manassehite sanctuary at Ophrah (Judg. 6.24), which plays a significant role in this saga. He is also said to have erected a golden ephod (in this case the word means a cult image rather than a priestly garment) at Ophrah, and his story ends with the mention of his tomb there. It seems fairly clear that the story of Gideon's life originated at the sanctuary, where it was probably recited on ritual occasions.

Samson

The fifth extended saga in Judges is the famous story of Samson (Judg. 13–16). He is a remarkable and complex figure. At one level, he is a simple clan folk hero, the son of Manoah of the tribe of Dan. But Samson's birth recalls that of several of the great ancestors (see pp.30–45): his barren mother is given a divine promise that she will conceive (Judg. 13.3). The announcement of the conception takes place at Zorah and is interwoven with the legend of the foundation of the sanctuary there (Judg. 13.15–24).

Unlike the other judges, he is not elected at a moment of crisis to lead the Israelite armies to victory over their oppressors. Instead, Samson's greatness is divinely ordained and foretold (Judg. 13.5), and he inflicts defeat on the Philistines (see p.71) through extraordinary feats of strength, such as the killing of a thousand men with the jawbone of a donkey (Judg. 15.15). Like the "labors" of the Greek hero Herakles (who has been compared to Samson since at least the fourth century CE), these feats are derived from a variety of sources. Some are local legends, while others derive from religious rituals and common mythological themes of the ancient Near East, such as the killing of a lion (Judg. 14.6). The source of Samson's amazing strength is his long hair, in accordance with a widespread popular belief, particularly among Semitic peoples. He is a trickster, as is seen in his riddle (Judg. 14.14), and in his repeated deception of his treacherous wife Delilah when she pesters him to reveal the secret of his strength (Judg. 16.6–14). Samson also embodies another well-known character of folklore, the man who constantly gets involved with women and is regularly deceived by them.

Samson carrying off the gates of Gaza (Judg. 16.2–3), from an early 15th-century Biblia pauperum *("Paupers' Bible"). Such Bibles were largely pictorial and aimed at the illiterate poor.*

God temporarily abandons the hero to his fate after he finally tells Delilah his secret: Samson's hair is cut off as he sleeps and he is captured and blinded by the Philistines. When they parade their prize during a great festival at the Philistine temple, Samson makes an appeal to God (Judg. 16.28) to grant him a final victory. He recovers his strength and pulls down the two pillars of the Philistine temple, killing everyone inside, including himself. This heroic act of suicide is a sign that Samson is received back by God. It resembles the apotheosis of Hercules (the Roman name for Herakles) in the work of the same name by the Roman writer Seneca: Hercules mounts his own funeral pyre, speaks to his father in heaven, and hears his reply. Samson's story comes to an end with his burial in the family grave at Zorah.

followed by an account of Jephthah (Judg. 11.1–12.7), which appears to represent a collection of tales from the sanctuary of Mizpah. It contains several common mythological and folklore themes, such as the hero's lowly birth (Jephthah's mother was a prostitute) and the vow with tragic consequences (Judg. 11.30–31). This vow results in Jephthah's sacrifice of his virgin daughter, which is said to have initiated an annual women's festival of lament for Jephthah's daughter. In fact, the festival marked the death of the spirit of fertility during the dry season.

The fifth, and probably most famous, of the heroic narratives is the story of Samson (see box, above).

SAMUEL

The focal point of the pre-Israelite shrine at Shiloh may have been similar to this round altar in the Canaanite temple at Megiddo in northern Palestine, dating from ca. 2000 BCE.

The last and greatest of the line of judges was the prophet Samuel. The announcement of his birth (1 Sam. 1) follows the common biblical pattern of the promise of a son to a barren woman, but there are indications that this story originally referred to the future King Saul (see pp.72–5). Hannah, Samuel's mother, names her child because she "asked" the Lord for him (1 Sam. 1.20), and says that the boy is "lent" to the deity (1 Sam. 1.28): both verbs play on the name Saul. Hannah's thanksgiving prayer (1 Sam. 2.1–10) has nothing to do with the birth of a child but is in fact a royal psalm. A biblical editor of a later period may have sought to exalt the office of prophet, which Samuel represented, above that of king. This may be why Samuel is credited with the subjugation of the Philistines, which is unlikely to be historical. Like his predecessors, Samuel is linked with a particular sanctuary, in this case Shiloh, a former Canaanite holy place. Its chief celebration was a great autumnal pilgrimage feast, during which women performed a ritual dance to enhance the fertility of the vineyards (Judg. 21.21). It is on this occasion that Hannah is granted her prayer for a child. Shiloh had a temple to Yahweh (1 Sam. 1.9), the Bible's first mention of such a permanent structure.

The temple housed the ark of the Covenant (see also p.58), from which oracles could be obtained. The Hebrew word usually translated as "ark" properly means "box" or "chest," and it is likely that various sanctuaries possessed such an object. Its most essential feature was that it could be carried about from place to place: portable shrines are known from ancient Egypt, Mesopotamia, and Canaan, and a portable tent-shrine, the *qabba*, is a feature of Bedouin and pre-Islamic Arab culture. In particular, the Shiloh ark was a sort of protective war standard, leading the Israelite army into battle, as in 1 Samuel 4. It was a manifestation of Yahweh's presence and was virtually identified with him: when the ark is brought to the Israelite army, the Philistines cry: "Gods have come into the camp" (1 Sam. 4.7). All these elements occur in a section of 1 Samuel known as the "history of the ark," that tells how the Philistines captured the ark and laid it up in the temple of their god Dagon at Ashdod. But Yahweh, in the shape of the ark, destroyed Dagon's image (1 Sam. 5.4), and the Philistines sent the ark away (1 Sam. 6.11–12). It halted at two Israelite shrines, Beth-shemesh and Kiriath-jearim, at the second of which it remained under a custodian, Eleazar. This episode may reflect memories of a time when the ark went on circuit to neighboring sanctuaries.

There was a hereditary priesthood at Shiloh, which probably came to an end through the Philistine destruction of the city, although the Bible attributes it to God's displeasure at certain ritual practices, such as cultic prostitution (1 Sam. 2.22). God was known at Shiloh by a title, "Lord of hosts" (as at 1 Sam. 1.3), that was possibly also Canaanite in origin. "Hosts" refers primarily to the heavenly powers that came to Israel's aid in its battles, although it may include the earthly Israelite forces as well.

The figure of Samuel has been much inflated in the biblical tradition. The most authentic information about him indicates that he was a local seer-prophet at the shrine of Ramah, where he is said to have built the altar and presided at sacrificial feasts, and where he was buried. From there he went on an annual circuit, dispensing justice at three sanctuaries (Bethel, Gilgal, and Mizpah) within a comparatively small area of central Palestine (1 Sam. 7.16–17). In the Bible, Samuel is transformed into a judge over the whole nation, a great military leader, and a prophet, as that office was understood in later Israelite tradition (see p.88). As the Bible sees it, it fell to Samuel to inaugurate the next stage in Israel's history, the monarchy.

The Philistines

The Philistines, who gave their name to the land of Palestine, formed part of a great ethnic upheaval that took place in the Aegean area in the last decades of the thirteenth century BCE. This upheaval is known as the movement of the "Sea Peoples," groups (probably Indo-European) that descended on the eastern Mediterranean coasts and destroyed the Hittite empire and the Canaanite city of Ugarit (see p.66), and menaced Egypt itself. They were finally checked, ca. 1190 BCE, by the pharaoh Rameses III, who settled the Philistines along the southern coast of Canaan.

In Canaan, they organized themselves into a league of city-states, made up of Ashdod, Ashkelon, Ekron, Gath, and Gaza, where a rich and complex culture developed. They rapidly sought to penetrate into the hinterland, where they encountered the Israelites. They were a grave threat to Israel because they presented a unified military force against the less well-organized individual Israelite tribes. As a result, the Israelites fell under Philistine domination for a long period, and it was only when Israel became a unified state under King David that the Philistines were defeated and confined within their own territory. After this, the Philistines no longer posed a serious threat, but intermittent warfare continued for many years between them and the Israelite kingdoms, until the Philistine rulers and people were deported by King Nebuchadrezzar II of Babylon at the same time as the exile of the Israelites in the early sixth century BCE.

The Israelites were aware of the Aegean origin of the Philistines (Amos 9.7 says they came from "Caphtor," that is, Crete) and that they were a non-Semitic people: in contrast to the Israelites, the Philistines are regularly described as "uncircumcised." But the Philistines assimilated the divinities of local Canaanite religion: of the three Philistine deities that are referred to in the Hebrew Scriptures, Dagon and Ashtaroth are found in Ugaritic texts, and Baalzebub, a name whose meaning is disputed, is clearly an epithet of the great Canaanite god Baal (see p.16 and p.66).

A decorated Philistine beer jug of the 12th century BCE. Philistine ceramics show Mycenaean influences.

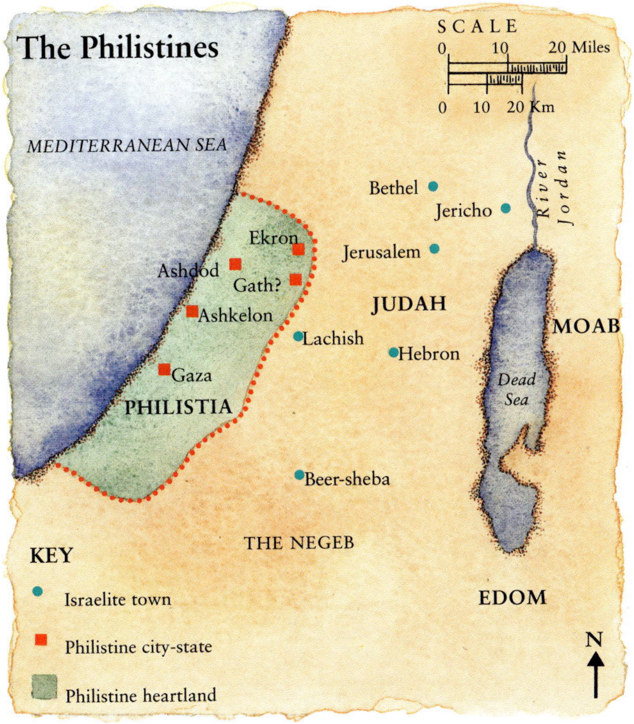

Philistine prisoners being led into captivity, from the temple of the pharaoh Ramesses III at Madinet Habu, Egypt.

THE FIRST KINGS

It is widely believed that the monarchy was established in Israel as a response to Philistine pressure, and certainly Samuel was promised that Saul's calling would deliver God's people from the Philistines. But it seems more likely that the Philistine threat only brought to fruition an internal development that was already under way. Israel was undergoing the same evolution from a tribal society to a unified state that was occurring among neighboring peoples. The rule of Saul was the prelude to the reigns of David and Solomon, under whom the united kingdom of the Israelites reached the zenith of its power and prestige. During this period, Jerusalem and its Temple became the focal point of Israelite civilization and belief.

SAUL

The rise of the first king of the Israelites, Saul, is told at considerable length (1 Sam. 8–11). It is generally agreed that the narrative combines three different versions of how events unfolded. One account views kingship in a positive light, seeing it as an institution introduced to Israel on the initiative of God. It is essentially a folktale, in which the young Saul is described in idealized terms (1 Sam. 9.2). He is guided by divine providence to the home of the prophet Samuel at Ramah and, when he appears, Yahweh instructs Samuel to anoint him as king. The seer obeys (1 Sam. 10.1) and promises Saul three signs to authenticate his unexpected election, including possession by the divine spirit. All of these signs duly occur, but at this point Saul keeps secret what has happened.

Saul's reign

The reign of Saul has generally been considered to be of minor importance in Israel's history. Although the Bible stresses the novel character of monarchy (see box on opposite page), in some ways Saul's rule only continued the old system of charismatic leaders or judges (see pp.66–7), confined to only a small group of tribes and lacking any concept of territorial expansion. Unlike other ancient Near Eastern monarchies, including the later Israelite kingdoms, Saul had neither a great royal city nor a civil service. He failed to defeat the Philistines or to establish a dynasty.

Nevertheless, it can be argued that Saul established the main features of future monarchical rule. The Bible sees him as inaugurating the idea of the "kingdom" as a distinct entity that thereafter passed from one successor to another. The "ways of the king," which Samuel explains to the people in 1 Samuel 8, correspond to the legal rights of Canaanite monarchs, and Saul was indeed responsible for most of the things listed by Samuel. He drafted young Israelites into a standing army; he appropriated and redistributed his subjects' property; he imposed taxes; and, like other kings of his time, he had a harem. His residence was "Gibeah of Saul" (1 Sam. 11.4), not exactly a royal capital like David's Jerusalem (see box on p.76), but Saul did build a large fortress there. Saul attacked four Gibeonite cities, traditional allies of Israel, because he aimed to create a consolidated state: the cities formed a block separating the tribes of Ephraim and Benjamin from Judah. He wore a diadem and bracelet, the characteristic insignia of Near Eastern kings.

It was Saul's sacred character that most distinguished him from the judges. The ritual of anointing endowed him with God's spirit, and rendered his person inviolable and holy: he became "the Lord's anointed."

The second account views kingship negatively. The Israelite elders go to Samuel and request a king (1 Sam. 8.5), but God tells Samuel that in doing so the elders have in effect "rejected me from being king over them." He instructs Samuel to warn the people of the oppressive nature of monarchical rule, which he does in some detail (1 Sam. 8.11–18). But the Israelites persist, and Yahweh agrees reluctantly to their request. Some time later (the episode of Saul's anointing comes in between), the Israelite tribes assemble at the sanctuary of Mizpah. Saul, who has hidden himself among the baggage, is picked out by sacred lot and made king by a ritual acclamation. In this account, no mention is made of anointing (1 Sam. 10.17–24).

An Ammonite attack on the town of Jabesh-gilead is the starting point of the third account of Saul's accession. The news is conveyed to Saul, who is apparently living as a simple farmer at his home in Gibeah (1 Sam. 11.5). Like one of the judges of Israel (see p.66), he is at once seized by "the spirit of God," as a result of which "his anger was greatly kindled." Saul musters the Israelite militia and breaks the siege. In gratitude, the people go to the sanctuary of Gilgal and invest him as king. Samuel's call to the people to "go to Gilgal and there renew the kingship" (1 Sam. 12.14) was probably inserted by the biblical editor to harmonize the three accounts of the rise of Saul.

The negative view of kingship in 1 Samuel 8 has often been attributed to a later Israelite school that blamed the monarchy for the disasters which befell Israel after the reign of Solomon. But it may well reflect contemporary debate at the time of the introduction of kingship, together with different traditions from the sanctuaries of Ramah, Mizpah, and Gilgal, all of which could lay claim to Saul. These and other elements have been woven together to present the formal process of accession which characterized Israel's developed monarchy. The accession took place in three stages: God's designation of the king through anointing, accompanied by a divine oracle assuring the king of divine favor and setting out his rights and duties; a victory over the king's enemies, whether actual or staged as part of a ritual; and, finally, public recognition and acceptance of him as Yahweh's chosen ruler.

The significance of the monarchy

Before the accession of Saul, the Bible provides evidence that the old system of judges was breaking down and proving unsatisfactory. Samuel appointed his sons to succeed him as "judges over Israel," but they "turned aside after gain; they took bribes and perverted justice" (1 Sam. 8.1–3). The Bible recounts that the Israelite elders confronted the elderly Samuel and asked him to appoint a new type of ruler, in imitation of foreign practice: a king (1 Sam. 8.5). The institution of monarchy had already existed for many centuries in the Near East and, although kingship differed significantly in character from nation to nation, many features were common to all the monarchies of the region. Above all, monarchy was a sacred institution, everywhere closely linked with a nation's deities. The king, it was believed, was chosen by the gods and goddesses, and represented his people before them. The deities, in turn, regulated all national affairs through the sovereign. It was this fundamental characteristic that made the establishment of monarchy such a new and revolutionary step for the Israelites to take.

Samuel anoints Saul, king of the Israelites (1 Sam. 10.1), from the Nuremberg Bible of 1483.

THE FATE OF SAUL

The story of Saul's life is very like that of a hero in an ancient Greek tragedy. In the course of the drama, there is often a crucial moment when the hero's previous good fortune is reversed. In the case of Saul, this occurs when God, through Samuel, abruptly rejects him as king after he fails to carry out a divine command (1 Sam. 15.26). Yahweh withdraws his benevolent spirit from Saul, and instead sends an "evil spirit" to torment him (1 Sam. 16.14). Mental and physical illnesses are often attributed to evil spirits, so the Bible is probably referring to a state of paranoia or depression. Saul is driven to a succession of violent actions, such as the wholesale massacre of the priesthood at Nob (1 Sam. 22.18), and ultimately to his doom. The narrator tells Saul's tale with a degree of sympathy for his plight and depicts him as a heroic figure, albeit a tragic one.

Saul is enmeshed in three conflicts. The first is the break with Samuel, the event which determines Saul's fate. The rupture occurs in two incidents which center on the authority claimed by the new institution of monarchy. In the first incident, Saul displeases Samuel when he offers a public sacrifice (1 Sam. 12.9). His fault is not that he, a layman, has usurped a priestly function, but that the king has taken control of the national religion from the figure of the judge, represented by Samuel. In the second incident, Saul does not complete the destruction of the Amalekites, as God has demanded (1 Sam. 15.3). In sparing the Amalekite king and all the valuable booty, Saul in effect claims the right to change an absolute religious decree, and for this he is condemned. His actions also display political expediency, something which would be less shocking to us than perhaps it would have been to Saul's contemporaries.

Saul's second conflict is with David (see sidebar, left). This is caused by Saul's obsessive jealousy of the younger man, which is provoked by the victory song of the Israelite women after the slaying of the Philistine giant Goliath: "Saul has killed his thousands, and David his tens of thousands" (1 Sam. 18.7). Saul interprets the song as a wish for David to replace him as king, and from this point onward Saul's dealings with David take the form of a succession of desperate attempts to kill him.

Lastly, there is conflict within Saul's own family. His daughter Michal falls in love with David and marries him. When Saul makes an attempt on

THE RISE OF DAVID
David's early career and character are depicted in various ways. The account of his secret anointing (1 Sam. 16.13) reflects a common folklore theme, in which the youngest and apparently least worthy family member is unexpectedly preferred over his or her siblings. The folktale quality pervades the whole story of David's rise to a high position at Saul's court.

The young David's most famous exploit is his killing of the Philistine giant Goliath (1 Sam. 17.48–51). Elsewhere (2 Sam. 21.19), Goliath is said to have been killed by Elhanan, another Bethlehemite, suggesting that the feat was only later attributed to David. David is portrayed as the ideal of chivalry, magnanimous toward Saul and twice sparing his life, at En-gedi (1 Sam. 24.7) and at Hachilah (1 Sam. 26.9). He arouses universal adulation and is capable of deep affection, especially in his feelings for Saul's son Jonathan (1 Sam. 20 and elsewhere). David is a skilled musician and composer of songs, whose lyre playing has an almost magical power (1 Sam. 16.23).

There is another, probably more historical, aspect of David. He appears as the leader of a band of outlaws in the Judean desert, astutely planning for his future by presenting gifts to the leading families of the region and making marriage alliances with them (1 Sam. 25.39–43). In pursuit of his aims David is even prepared to become a vassal of the Philistine king of Gath. However, in the story as it stands, he avoids actually giving help to the Philistines against the Israelites (1 Sam. 27.8–12).

Below, right: *The heights of En-gedi, where Saul hid from David (1 Sam. 24).*

Below: David and Goliath, *from an English manuscript of ca. 1020.*

The Death of Saul (1562), *by Pieter Bruegel the Elder (ca. 1515–1569). Saul (left), already badly wounded and facing defeat, falls on his sword (1 Sam. 31.4).*

David's life Michal foils it by means of a trick (1 Sam. 19.13). More poignantly, Saul's son and heir, Jonathan, develops an intimate friendship with David and protects him from his father's plots (1 Sam. 19.1–7 and elsewhere). Jonathan recognizes that it is David, rather than himself, who will succeed his father as king.

Before his final battle with the Philistines, Saul follows the regular custom of ancient warfare and seeks divine guidance on its outcome. During his reign he has carried out a religious reformation, as later Israelite monarchs were to do, by eradicating "mediums and wizards" who claimed that they could call up ghosts and spirits, a practice always opposed by the cult of Yahweh (1 Sam. 28.3; compare Lev. 20.6 and 20.27). But after Saul's rejection, Yahweh refuses to speak to him through the normal legitimate means of divination: dreams, the Urim and Thummim (sacred lots), and prophetic oracles. Saul is forced to resort to a practitioner at Endor, who has apparently escaped his ban (1 Sam. 28.7). She has an *'ob*, a word usually translated as "familiar spirit," that is, she is a medium. The appearance of Samuel's shade (1 Sam. 28.14) reveals how the ancient Israelites saw the fate of the dead: they retained the physical state, and even the clothes, in which they had died, and led a shadowy existence under the earth, cut off from real life. Living in this mysterious realm, they were considered to have a supernatural power to foretell the future.

Saul is overcome with terror at Samuel's dreadful prediction of his defeat and death (1 Sam. 28.19). But the narrative tells how he recovers himself, and the reader is left to assume that he accepts his fate and faces it bravely. When three of his sons, including Jonathan, have died fighting against the Philistines, and all is finally lost, Saul meets death in a typically heroic act of suicide on Mount Gilboa (1 Sam. 31.4), although it is later said that he enlisted a foreigner to end his agony as he lay dying (2 Sam. 1.9). David's great lament (2 Sam. 1.17–27) is in praise of two men he saw as heroes: "Saul and Jonathan, beloved and lovely! In life and in death they were not divided; they were swifter than eagles, they were stronger than lions."

DAVID

The pool of Gibeon (modern El Jib), where the armies of Ishbaal and David confronted one another (2. Sam. 2).

After Saul's death (see p.75), his kingdom continued under one of his sons, Ishbaal or Ish-bosheth, in the northern part of the country, while the royal seat was removed to Mahanaim, east of the Jordan, outside the area of Philistine occupation. Meanwhile, in the south, the clans whose support David had secured (see sidebar on p.74) anointed him as king over the house of Judah (2 Sam. 2.4). War broke out between Ishbaal and David, and at this time the really powerful figures were the formidable commanders-in-chief, Abner for Ishbaal and Joab for David. A vivid story tells how their two armies met at the pool of Gibeon (see picture, left), where, following a common custom of ancient warfare, each side produced twelve champions to engage in single combat to the death. The outcome was inconclusive (2 Sam. 2.16), and a full-scale battle ensued, in which Abner killed Asahel, one of Joab's brothers, and thereby incurred a blood feud.

Later, Ishbaal rebuked Abner for allegedly having intercourse with Rizpah, one of Saul's concubines. (According to a Canaanite text from Ugarit, the taking of a dead king's wife represented a claim to the throne; compare 1 Kings 2.22.) Abner was angry at the rebuke and negotiated with David to bring the northern confederation onto his side (2 Sam. 3.12). Abner visited David to finalize the compact, but he was killed by

Jerusalem

David's acquisition of Jerusalem (see main text, opposite) had far-reaching implications for the nation. It became a royal capital city, an essential feature of any Near Eastern monarchy, and something which Saul had lacked (see box on p.72). It was a strategic bridge between the northern and southern Israelite tribes, but was not attached to any of them.

Samuel anoints David, a wall painting from the synagogue of Dura Europos, Syria, ca. 245 CE. The Roman dress reflects the cosmopolitan character of this Greco-Roman frontier town on the Euphrates.

Until its capture, Jerusalem was a Canaanite enclave, inhabited by a people known as the Jebusites. David brought the city within the Israelite religious tradition by making it the permanent home of the ark of Shiloh (see p.70). Behind the detailed account of the transfer of the ark and the accompanying celebrations (2 Sam. 6–19), there probably lies a coronation rite. Through this rite, David assumed the role of the former Jebusite ruler, the heir of the priest-king Melchizedek who blessed Abraham in Genesis 18 (see p.33). A procession led by the ark was probably the climax of a great annual festival which celebrated God's choice of Jerusalem as his abode and of David's dynasty.

David did not exterminate the Jebusite population, and many of their religious traditions directly influenced Israel's faith. Yahweh was assimilated with the local deity of Jerusalem, El-elyon, and, significantly, the Israelite god was considered to have made a special covenant with the king that paralleled his covenant with the nation. The reign of David therefore marked a profound change in the whole nature and understanding of monarchy in Israel, which assumed the general character of Near Eastern kingship. In particular, this meant that each succeeding monarch was regarded as the adopted son of the deity, who guaranteed the continuation of the dynasty (see, for example, 2 Sam. 7; Pss. 2 and 89).

David's empire

Every ancient ruler was expected to be a war leader who sought to expand the territory of his state, and David was no exception. During his reign (ca. 1000–961 BCE), it was feasible for him to adopt an expansionist program, because there was something of a political vacuum in the Near East. The empire of the Hittites had disappeared ca. 1200 BCE, and, following the death of the great emperor Tiglath-pileser I in ca. 1078 BCE, the Assyrian state entered a period of weakness that lasted for some two centuries. Since ca. 1065 BCE, Egypt, too, had been impotent under the twenty-first dynasty. The field was free for the Israelites and other peoples to establish themselves as powerful states.

Following the final removal of the Philistine menace (2 Sam. 8.1), the Bible tells of a series of conquests by David of important neighboring states. He defeated the Ammonites and became their king (2 Sam. 12.30). Moab was made a client state (2 Sam. 8.2), and Edom was garrisoned as a province under direct Israelite rule (2 Sam. 8.14). David is said to have stationed garrisons in two of the rising Aramean kingdoms, although they were to remain a thorn in Israel's side for many years.

David also forged important diplomatic ties. He made an alliance with Hiram, the king of Tyre, one of the important group of Phoenician trading cities that had recently gained independence from Egypt and were entering on a golden age. The Phoenician alliance became a cornerstone of subsequent Israelite foreign policy (see p.83).

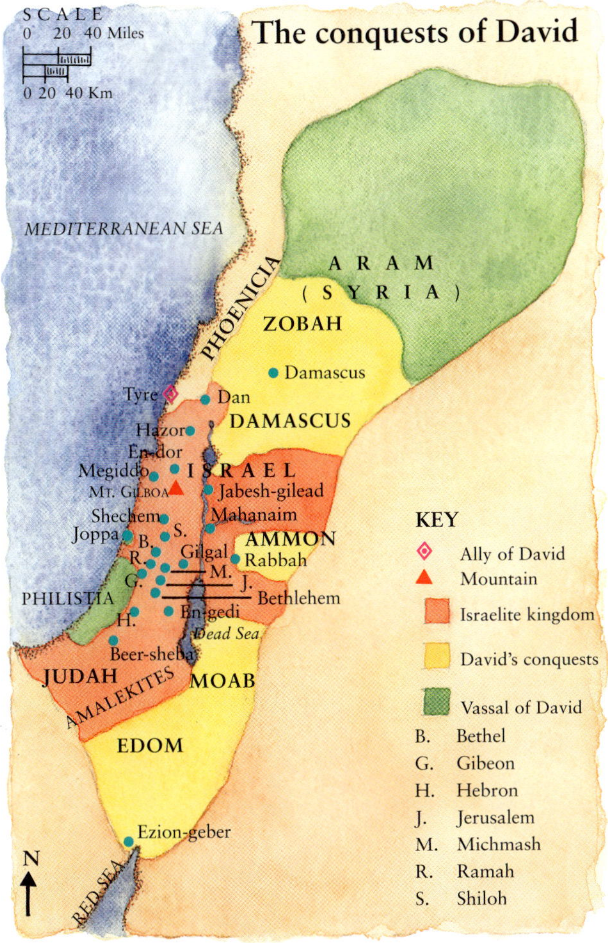

Joab in revenge for Asahel's death and the plan collapsed. With Abner gone, Ishbaal's entourage realized that his breakaway kingdom was no longer viable, and two of his officers assassinated him (2 Sam. 4.6–7).

Ishbaal's death opened the way for the second step in David's rise. David had always been careful to show respect and honor to Saul and his supporters. He sent a message of thanks to the inhabitants of Jabesh-gilead for giving Saul's corpse an honorable burial, laid a solemn curse on Joab for Abner's death, and executed Ishbaal's murderers. It was perhaps no surprise that the northern tribes now made an alliance with David and anointed him as their king (2 Sam. 5.3).

As the leader of a united kingdom, David was able, in two campaigns, to expel the Philistines from the central hill country and open the way for the third step in his rise to power, the taking of Jerusalem. Its capture is only briefly recorded, but the Bible indicates that it was taken by a stratagem, presumably because the Israelites had neither the experience nor the means for siege operations (2 Sam. 5.6–8). What is important is that Jerusalem was captured by David's personal troops and therefore became a private royal possession, held by David and his descendants by right of conquest. As if to emphasize this point, he renamed it the "City of David" and built a fortress there for himself (see also box on opposite page).

A clay figurine of a woman bathing, found at Achzib in Palestine and dating from ca. 1300–900 BCE. Bathsheba was bathing when David first saw her (2 Sam. 11.2).

DAVID'S REIGN

After David had established himself in Jerusalem (see p.77), he proceeded to organize his state. It was modeled on that of neighboring countries, particularly Egypt, and administered by a bureaucracy of court officials known as "servants of the king" after a Canaanite term. Its chief members were Joab, the commander of the native Israelite troops; Benaiah, the commander of the foreign mercenary forces (mainly Cretans and Philistines); two chief priests, Zadok and Abiathar; a royal herald, who announced the king's commands; and a secretary of state, who recorded the commands and other matters.

The internal history of David's kingdom is recorded in a number of chapters in 2 Samuel and the opening chapters of 1 Kings. These form a distinct section that may have been written by someone who was alive during David's reign. Its tone is markedly secular: God does not intervene directly in events and is not often mentioned, and the divine purpose is seen to operate through the interplay of human ambitions and motives. This section has been called "the court history of David" and "a narrative of the succession to the throne," and although it is unlikely that the narrative is as coherent and unified as is often supposed, both titles can claim some justification. It consists of tales of rivalry at court within the royal family, which is exacerbated by that invariable feature of ancient Near Eastern monarchy, the harem. A king and his several wives produced a large crop of ambitious siblings and half-siblings, all juggling for power

Opposition to David's rule

Later ages idealized the reign of King David, but the Bible shows that in fact it was subject to severe problems and tensions. David never succeeded in reconciling the supporters of Saul to his rule. One very serious rebellion was instigated by Sheba, from Saul's tribe of Benjamin, who roused the northern tribes with a war cry: "We have no portion in David!" (2 Sam. 20.1). Sheba was eventually betrayed by the citizens of Abel (2 Sam. 20.22).

Sheba's revolt followed the gravest crisis of the reign, the rebellion of Absalom, David's own son, and, after the death of Amnon (see main text, opposite), his expected heir. Absalom is a typical folk hero, renowned for his beauty and fabulously long hair (2 Sam. 25–26). By this time, David was growing old and losing his tight grip on affairs, and Absalom won the people's affection by promising redress of their grievances (2 Sam. 15.2–6). He proclaimed himself king at Hebron, cutting off David from his heartland. His uprising was serious, because he was followed not only by the southern Israelite tribes but also by the adherents of Saul's dynasty. The revolt drove David from his capital for a time, and he prevailed only with the support of mercenaries and other foreigners.

The Death of Absalom, *a 19th-century drawing of part of the floor of the 13th-century cathedral of Siena, Italy.*

Before the final battle, David ordered his generals to "deal gently" with his son. But the commander-in-chief, Joab, felt no such fatherly indulgence, and killed Absalom when he was caught by his hair in a tree (2 Sam. 18.9–15). The old king was grief-stricken and uttered a hauntingly brief, poetic lament: "O my son Absalom, my son, my son Absalom! Would I had died instead of you, O Absalom, my son, my son!" (2 Sam. 18.33).

David with the prophet Nathan (left) and kneeling in repentance (right), from a Byzantine Psalter of ca. 950 CE.

among themselves. As an account of the succession, the narrative shows how those of David's sons who might have succeeded to the throne are gradually eliminated, until only Solomon remains.

The first story in this section tells of David's adultery with Bathsheba, the wife of Uriah, a Hittite officer in the royal army (2 Sam. 11.2–12.25). To get Uriah out of the way, David orders Joab to place him "in the forefront of the hardest fighting" during a siege. Uriah is killed and David marries Bathsheba, who bears a son. But the king's actions anger God, and the prophet Nathan succeeds, by means of a parable, in getting David to condemn himself (2 Sam. 12.1–6). David acknowledges his sin, but Nathan says that although God will not strike David down, his house will be troubled and he will lose the child born to Bathsheba. The child dies, and the story ends with the birth of a second child, Solomon, who is assured of Yahweh's love. David's despotic behavior in taking Bathsheba for himself and arranging her husband's death would not have been unusual for a Near Eastern monarch. But it is sharply contrasted with the condemnation of his actions by Nathan, who speaks for older and simpler Israelite values.

The story that follows, told in 2 Samuel 13, centers on Amnon, David's eldest son. Abetted in a typical harem intrigue by his "very crafty" cousin Jonadab, Amnon lured his half-sister Tamar to his bedside and raped her. In revenge, Tamar's brother, Absalom, killed Amnon, thereby removing the man who would normally be expected to succeed to the throne. Absalom's banishment for his deed provoked a resentment in him which threatened David's throne but ultimately brought about his own downfall (see box on opposite page).

THE ACCESSION OF SOLOMON

When it became clear that David's powers were waning, a struggle to succeed him broke out between two parties, each with clearly defined interests and backing one of David's sons (1 Kings 1–2). The two factions embodied the tension that existed between the population of Judah and the royal city-state of Jerusalem, and which persisted until the fall of the kingdom.

On one side was a group with a background in Judah. Its candidate was Adonijah, the king's eldest surviving son, who was born during David's time in Hebron (2 Sam. 3.4). Behind him stood Joab, David's military commander, and the priest Abiathar, the sole survivor of Saul's massacre of the priesthood at Nob (see p.74), who took refuge with David during his years in the wilderness. The opposing faction was based in Jerusalem and backed Solomon, the son of David and the Jerusalemite Bathsheba (see main text). Behind Solomon were figures who had become prominent only after David established himself in Jerusalem: the priest Zadok, the prophet Nathan, and Benaiah, the captain of the foreign palace guard.

After the death of David (1 Kings 2.10) Solomon prevailed, and he took rapid and ruthless steps to dispose of the opposition. Adonijah was executed on a trivial pretext. (1 Kings 2.13–25). It would have been politically dangerous to kill a priest, so Abiathar was simply deposed and banished (1 Kings 2.27). Joab sought sanctuary by seizing the horns of the altar (see below) in "the tent of the Lord" but was slain by Benaiah (1 Kings 2.34), who also killed Shimei, a leading figure from Saul's tribe of Benjamin (1 Kings 2.46).

A horned altar of ca. 900 BCE from Megiddo (compare 1 Kings 1.50; 2.28).

SOLOMON

After succeeding to the throne (see p.79), Solomon did not embark on any expansionist campaigns, and his reign (ca. 961–922 BCE) was recalled as a time of peace and prosperity, when "Judah and Israel lived in safety, from Dan to Beer-sheba" (1 Kings 4.25). This description was used in later prophetic books to describe the perfection of the future Messianic age. Above all, Solomon was remembered as the embodiment of wisdom. In Israelite thought, wisdom was a practical quality, something that all people needed in order to evaluate the circumstances of their existence and to make a success of life (see pp.120–21). As the person responsible for the welfare of the nation, the king required wisdom more that anyone else. In this respect, Solomon was the ideal ruler (see box, below).

At the beginning of his reign, Solomon visited Gibeon, described as "the principal high place" (1 Kings 3.4): it had not yet been replaced by Jerusalem as the chief shrine. At Gibeon the king had a dream in which God appeared to him. Solomon's dream closely parallels the experience of the pharaoh Thutmose IV, to whom the Sphinx of Giza appeared in a dream. The Sphinx told Thutmose of his divine election in childhood and of the legitimacy of his succession to the throne, and on waking, the

Solomon's writings

Solomon Dictating the Proverbs, *from the French* Bible Historiale *of 1357.*

King Solomon's reputation for wisdom was so great that several later writings of a type known as "Wisdom" (see pp.120–21) came to be ascribed to him. The Wisdom of Solomon, one of the apocryphal books of the Bible, claims to be by him, and several sections of the book of Proverbs (see p.120). Solomon is said to have propounded some three thousand proverbs dealing with trees and animals (1 Kings 2.32). The Hebrew for "proverb" is *mashal*, from a verb which means "to be like" or "to compare." Solomon's "proverbs" were therefore similes and metaphors, pithy sayings (as seen in many examples in the book of Proverbs) in which an observation taken from the natural or animal world served to illuminate human behavior. To see the connection was evidence of a person's wisdom, and the ability to compose such proverbs was important for a monarch, because they were regularly used in diplomatic exchanges. The common stock of ancient Near Eastern wisdom consisted of such maxims. Since this wisdom was largely secular in character, it could be appropriated and adapted by different nations. This process was facilitated by the wide international contacts that were initiated by Solomon.

The traditions of Solomon's wealth and his love of women no doubt explain why the author of Ecclesiastes (see p.120–1) assumed his persona, and why Solomon was credited with the highly erotic Song of Songs (see p.125). The Bible claims that "his songs numbered a thousand and five" (1 Kings 4.33). Similarly, because of the tradition that Solomon wrote poetry, two of the Psalms (see p.115) were attributed to him.

The Queen of Sheba

The Queen of Sheba Arriving at the Court of King Solomon *by the Master of the Cassoni. Italian, late 15th century.*

Another story praising Solomon's wisdom is the famous episode of the visit of the Queen of Sheba (1 Kings 10.1–13). Ceremonial visits between royal houses, accompanied by the exchange of rich presents, were a regular feature of the ancient Near Eastern political scene. According to the Bible, the Queen had heard of Solomon's renowned wisdom and comes "to test him with hard questions"(1 Kings 10.1). The ability of one sovereign to demonstrate his or her wisdom and knowledge to another in a riddle contest was a valuable diplomatic tool. A similar example occurs in the story of Samson (Judges 14).

The stone head of a woman from Saba (Sheba), 1st millennium BCE.

Many fantastic and erotic features came to be attached to the story of the meeting of the two rulers in the Jewish, Islamic, and Ethiopic traditions, but the biblical account probably reflects sober political realities. The Queen's state was in southern Arabia, in the area of present-day Yemen. The countries in this region had a virtual monopoly of the immensely valuable spice trade in myrrh and frankincense, a vast quantity of which the Queen of Sheba presented to Solomon. Solomon had begun to break into the trade there by sending a fleet to the Red Sea, and an agreement to regulate relations would have been to the benefit of both parties. Solomon's empire embraced the north-south "King's Highway" in Transjordan and the east-west route across southern Palestine to Gaza, two arteries by which Arabian luxury goods were exported to consumer nations. The encounter between the monarchs may well have led to an agreement under which the Queen gave Solomon's fleet access to the ports she controlled, while Solomon guaranteed the security of the trade routes through his territory (see also p.83).

pharaoh offered sacrifices. All these elements are present in the story of Solomon's dream (1 Kings 3.5–15). The Bible's account is distinguished by the king's request for wisdom and Yahweh's promise to give him "a wise and discerning mind," which will bring him greater "riches and honor" than any monarch of his day.

Immediately afterward there is a very different story, a folktale to illustrate how the king's wisdom operated in the administration of justice. Two prostitutes came before Solomon with a baby boy, each claiming to be the child's mother. Solomon was faced with the two conflicting claims and no hard evidence, so he asked for a sword and proposed simply to cut the baby in two and "give half to the one, and half to the other" (1 Kings 3.25). One of the women pleaded for the boy's life, begging Solomon to give him to her rival rather than to kill him. The other woman said spitefully that the child "shall be neither mine nor yours" and told the king to go ahead and cut it in half. Through his understanding of psychology, Solomon saw in the first woman the compassion of the real mother and gave her the child. When the Israelites learned of the decision, they recognized that their new king truly possessed "the wisdom of God."

SOLOMON'S REIGN

Phoenician warships depicted on an Assyrian relief of the 7th century BCE. *The alliance with the Phoenicians, the greatest maritime power of the region, was central to Solomon's foreign policy.*

The kingdom under Solomon increasingly assumed the form and manner of a despotic ancient Near Eastern state. Striking evidence for this is the institution of the levy or *corvée*, by which the population could be drafted to labor on public works, as the Israelites had been forced to do in Egypt. Ugaritic texts reveal that this was also a Canaanite practice. One passage seems to indicate that forced labor only applied to the peoples that had been incorporated into David's kingdom (1 Chron. 22–1), but it is clear that native Israelites were also involved (compare 1 Kings 12.4 and 12.18). The probable explanation is that non-Israelites had the status of permanent serfs of the state, while Israelites were only drafted for labor in exceptional circumstances, such as Solomon's extensive building program. David may perhaps have considered introducing the levy, but it was in his son's reign that it became central to the administration of the state.

Although he did not wage any aggressive wars, Solomon was concerned to protect his realm from attack. There is mention of several cities where he carried out construction work and stationed garrisons of chariots and cavalry (1 Kings 9.15–19). Their positions are significant: Hazor protected the extreme northern boundary and Megiddo controlled a strategic pass from the coast to the central highlands. Gezer, which had been destroyed by an Egyptian pharaoh and then given to his daughter as a dowry on her marriage to Solomon, was rebuilt as a base from which to dominate the area of Philistine occupation. Excavations at all these sites have revealed extensive building during the Solomonic period.

The ruins of the Phoenician city of Byblos (biblical Gebal, modern Jebail, northern Lebanon). Solomon's extensive diplomatic and commercial connections enabled him to receive assistance from the inhabitants of Byblos, the Giblites, with the building of the Temple in Jerusalem (see pp.84–5).

The king also built a number of store-cities in connection with a wholesale reorganization of the state recounted in 1 Kings 4. His territory was divided into twelve administrative districts, each with a regional governor at its head. The division was to some extent based on the old tribal areas, but was not rigidly bound by them. The object of the reorganization was that each district should supply food to the royal household for one month in turn, so the twelve divisions were more probably determined by the twelve months of the year. Old Canaanite cities were also incorporated into the new regional districts. The monthly provisions, which each governor was responsible for organizing, were collected in the store-cities before being sent on to the court at Jerusalem.

Under Solomon, the Israelite empire became an important power on the international scene. The king was able to use his new prestige to extend his influence with neighboring states by diplomatic means. Solomon concluded a treaty with King Hiram of Tyre, continuing the alliance begun by David (1 Kings 5.12). One benefit of this treaty was that Hiram provided Solomon with timber from the famous cedars of Lebanon for his building operations, together with skilled craftsmen to fell the trees and transport them by sea.

Solomon's large harem is condemned in the Bible, which claims that it led the king to accommodate the deities worshiped by his foreign wives (1 Kings 11.1–8). The size of the harem is probably exaggerated to present the monarch, in typical Near Eastern fashion, as a paragon of wealth and virility. But the royal harem was an important part of diplomacy, because treaties between states were cemented by intermarriage of the respective royal families. Solomon almost certainly followed this practice: the Biblical narrative gives especial emphasis to his marriage with a daughter of the king of Egypt, who had her own palace in Jerusalem (1 Kings 7.8 and 9.16). In Solomon's day Egypt was in decline, but it was still recognized as a famous country. The fact that Pharaoh himself thought it worthwhile to seek Israel's friendship shows the considerable international prestige that Solomon's kingdom had acquired.

Solomon's trading activities

Most of the biblical references to Solomon's immense wealth possess a legendary or folktale quality, but they doubtless also have some historical basis. Some of the king's wealth would have come from the regular tribute paid by foreign parts of his kingdom, but the main source of the finance which paid for Solomon's many building projects was trade. Several of the region's most important trade routes crossed Solomon's empire, and he was able to exploit his control of the caravans that used them. In particular, he tapped into the lucrative commerce in spices and precious metals between southern Arabia and the north (see box on p.81).

Solomon's alliance with the Phoenician king Hiram of Tyre (see main text, above) proved vital, because the Israelites had no maritime experience. Solomon built a fleet to operate in the Red Sea, and Hiram, the head of a great sea-going power, supplied the Israelites with skilled sailors and ships of their own. The royal fleet had its headquarters at the port of Ezion-geber near Eloth (Eilat) at the head of the Red Sea, although its exact site is uncertain.

Trading activities on this scale led to the emergence of a new phenomenon in Israel, a class of merchant traders. A note in the Bible records how these merchants imported horses from Egypt and Kue (in present-day Turkey) for Solomon's army and sold horses on to the rulers of states north of Israel (1 Kings 10.28–29).

A cult tablet from southern Arabia, with an inscription in ancient Sabean script (1st millennium BCE).

THE TEMPLE

The most important of Solomon's building projects was the Temple in Jerusalem, which was to play a central role in the life and worship of the nation. In constructing it he was fulfilling one of the recognized duties of the ancient Near Eastern king, who was expected to build as splendid an edifice as possible in his capital city as a dwelling place for the national deity. The Jerusalem Temple was an innovation: when King David had planned to build a home for Yahweh, the prophet Nathan had forbidden him on the grounds that until then God had lived only in a moveable tent or tabernacle (2 Sam. 7.6 and 1 Chron. 17.4).

Since the Israelites had no experience of temple building, Solomon turned to King Hiram of Tyre, who supplied him with materials and labor, and in particular to one craftsman, also called Hiram, who made the Temple's cult furnishings (see box, below). The Temple was thus essentially a Phoenician or Canaanite construction: its tripartite ground plan is similar to the shrine of Tell Tainat in Syria and a temple at Hazor. The Temple was built to the north of the original city of David (see map on p.152), on an ancient Jebusite holy place traditionally connected with a threshing floor where David had built an altar (2 Sam. 24.18). This became the place for the open-air altar of the Temple. The Temple's walls, lined with Lebanon cedar, were adorned with cherubim, palms, and open flowers (perhaps lotuses), common religious symbols in the ancient Near East. Outside the vestibule were two free-standing pillars, a feature of Phoenician temples. The significance of these pillars is disputed but their names, Jachin ("Yahweh establishes") and Boaz ("In him [it] is strength"), suggest that they symbolized God's presence. They may have corresponded to the guardian figures of deities that stood at the entrance to Mesopotamian sanctuaries and palaces.

The Temple furnishings

The furnishings of Solomon's Temple had a cosmic symbolism. There was a large metal basin, called the "sea" (1 Kings 7.44), supported by twelve bull statues. One biblical text states that the basin was used for the priests' ablutions, but since it was over seven feet (2.2m) high, this is unlikely. The name "sea" parallels the Mesopotamian *apsu,* the name both of the subterranean ocean and of a temple basin that symbolized it. Bulls were a frequent symbol of fertility, and were associated with the Canaanite storm god Baal (see p.66).

The ark of the Covenant and two angels, from a 13th-century Hebrew manuscript.

In the Temple there were also movable lavers (basins for ritual washing), decorated with wreaths, bulls, lions, and cherubim. The main sacrificial altar was described by a term indicating that it was considered to represent the mountain of the gods and the world center, with its base resting on "the bosom of the earth."

At the Temple dedication ceremony, the ark of the Covenant was placed in the central sanctuary, the Holy of Holies. It ceased to be a portable object and Yahweh, as the opening words of Solomon's dedicatory prayer express, was believed from this time to reside permanently in the most holy place: "The Lord has said that he would dwell in thick darkness. I have built you an exalted house, a place for you to dwell in forever." (1 Kings 8.12–13). This belief led to the doctrine that Jerusalem and its Temple were inviolable. The ark was viewed as a throne on which God sat as an invisible deity. It is flanked by two large figures of cherubim, recalling a similar feature on the thrones of Phoenician rulers.

The building of the Temple (see 1 Kings 6) was accompanied by the construction nearby of Solomon's own (considerably larger) palace. This symbolized the Temple's role as both a national shrine and a royal chapel. The king was the head of the cult of Yahweh and led all important acts of worship. Solomon himself officiated at the consecration of the Temple, offering sacrifices and the dedicatory prayer.

In Canaanite religion the home of the gods was a mountain. The psalms used in worship at the Temple show that much of the mythology and symbolism of the divine mountain was transferred to Mount Zion, the dwelling place of Yahweh (see, for example, p. 42).

Later Temples of Jerusalem

Solomon's Temple was destroyed in the Babylonian sack of Jerusalem (587/6 BCE; see pp.104–05), but it was eventually restored by the returning exiles just over half a century later. The Second Temple seems to have been a more modest affair than the first and its significance was somewhat different (see pp.114–15). It was desecrated and despoiled under the Seleucid Greek empire (see pp.132–33) and later by the Romans (see p.136), and ca. 20 BCE Herod the Great, the client-king of Roman Judea (see p.136), embarked on the construction of an entirely new building. Descriptions of Herod's Temple, the bulk of which was completed in ten years, show that it reproduced the dimensions of Solomon's building. It followed contemporary Greco-Roman architectural fashions and its splendor was intended as a visual statement of the importance of Herod's kingdom to his Roman overlords. Herod was seen by many of his subjects as a usurper, and his lavish new Temple was an attempt to win them over.

There is considerable evidence, however, that Herod's motives were distrusted by the more devout and traditional elements of the population and that the new Temple did not win their affection and devotion. In any case, this last and grandest of the Jerusalem Temples had a comparatively short life: finally completed only in 64 CE, it was burned when the Roman emperor Titus took Jerusalem during a Jewish revolt in 70 CE and never rebuilt. However, the Temple site remains a holy one. Part of the ruins of the Temple complex, the massive Western Wall (the so-called "Wailing Wall"), is an important place of worship for Jews. On the site of the Temple's central sanctuary stands the Dome of the Rock, one of the holiest sites in Islam. It was built 685–691 CE to mark the spot where Abraham was said to have prepared to sacrifice Isaac (see p.37), and from where the Prophet Muhammad ascended to heaven.

Jews praying at the Western Wall, part of the few surviving remains of the Temple of Herod. The massive masonry is typical of Herodian architecture.

An artist's reconstruction of the southern façade of Herod's Temple.

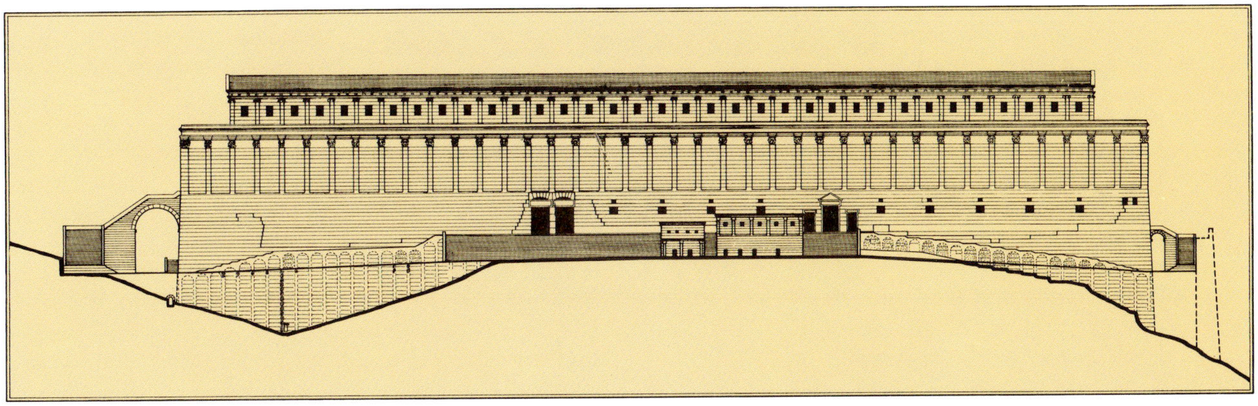

WEAKNESSES IN THE STATE

The Bible points to weaknesses and tensions in Solomon's kingdom which, while probably limited in their effects during his own lifetime, were to have serious consequences for the future. There was trouble in two dependent foreign territories, Edom and Aram (see map on p.77). The unrest there is represented as a divine punishment for Solomon's worship of foreign deities, as recounted in 1 Kings 11, and their significance may be exaggerated. One opponent, the Edomite prince Hadad, may have been no more than a minor irritant. Rezon, the Aramean rebel leader, certainly established an independent kingdom in Damascus, but this may have been in the period of Israelite weakness following Solomon's death. It has sometimes been claimed that Solomon faced financial difficulties, which is why he ceded twenty settlements in Galilee to his ally Hiram of Tyre for a large sum (1 Kings 9.11). But the story actually emphasizes Solomon's ability to bargain: Hiram is disappointed with his new property, and calls it "Cabul," which may mean "a land good for nothing."

More serious was the internal discontent, caused particularly by Solomon's institution of forced labor, the levy. Thirty thousand drafted male citizens worked abroad in shifts, spending one month in the Lebanon and two at home (1 Kings 5.14). The free Israelite farmers would have resented this state servitude, which must have brought serious disruption to farming. Thousands more were forced to work at quarrying and on Solomon's numerous building projects. Another source of internal pressure was the old tension between the north (Israel) and the south (Judah).

Egyptian influence on Israelite affairs

Egypt played an important role in the events of King Solomon's reign and immediately afterward. The country had long claimed hegemony over Palestine and, although an unnamed pharaoh of the weak twenty-first dynasty had thought it prudent to make an alliance with Solomon, the basic Egyptian policy did not change. The Egyptians were not averse to encouraging movements which might cripple Solomon's power. His opponents, Hadad and Jeroboam, received shelter and support from the pharaohs, and Hadad was even given the Egyptian king's sister-in-law in marriage.

Ruins of Megiddo, an important city under Solomon and his successors. It was captured by Sheshonk in the reign of Jeroboam I of Israel.

The Bible records that Jeroboam was welcomed by "King Shishak of Egypt" (1 Kings 11.40). This was the pharaoh Sheshonk I, who came to the throne ca. 945 BCE as the founder of a new Libyan dynasty. He was a strong ruler who revived his country's fortunes. In the reign of Rehoboam, Solomon's successor, Sheshonk sent an expedition into Palestine and reached Jerusalem. His campaign was on a considerable scale: a list of the cities he captured, carved on a wall of the temple of the god Amun-Re at Karnak, includes over one hundred fifty towns in Palestine. The list does not include Jerusalem, and the Bible's account, placed in the fifth year of Rehoboam's reign (see p.89), mentions only an attack on the city. Sheshonk was probably bought off by Rehoboam, who paid him tribute in the form of the treasures of the Temple and the royal palace. Further evidence of the extent of Sheshonk's raid are his victory column at Megiddo and a seated statue of the pharaoh found at Byblos in the Lebanon.

The two issues came together in the revolt of Jeroboam, a royal official from the northern tribe of Ephraim, who had first-hand experience of the effects of the levy: he was in charge of forced labor in his own tribal district. According to the Bible, Jeroboam received a divine promise from the prophet Ahijah that he would rule the ten northern tribes of Israel. The remaining two were the traditionally related tribes of Judah and Benjamin, which God reserved for David's dynasty (1 Kings 11.29–32). Ahijah's support for Jeroboam was significant, because Ahijah was associated with Shiloh, the original home of the national symbol, the ark (see p.70 and p.84): he represented the older Israelite religious tradition, which had been superseded by the new establishment centered on the Temple in Jerusalem.

Jeroboam's rebellion did not topple Solomon, because, as Ahijah said, God had promised that Solomon would be king "all the days of his life, for the sake of my servant David" (1 Kings 11.34). Jeroboam fled to Egypt to bide his time at the court of the pharaoh (see box, below).

The division of the kingdom

On the death of Solomon (1 Kings 11.43), his son Rehoboam succeeded automatically to two parts of the kingdom, Judah and Jerusalem. The dynasty's rule over Israel, in the north, rested on a treaty between King David and the tribes. Rehoboam had to renew this treaty and met with the northern tribal representatives at Shechem, traditionally the place where Joshua had allotted the Israelite tribes their territory. The result was a dramatic clash between the adherents of older and newer concepts of government, as recounted in 1 Kings 12. Rehoboam's older counselors approved of the assembly's demand for a relaxation of the harsh burdens of forced labor (see main text). But the king's younger advisers, who had grown up under Solomon's despotic system, persuaded him to refuse. In consequence, the assembly broke off with the ancient tribal cry: "To your tents, O Israel!"

The rebel Jeroboam returned from Egypt (see main text) and was made king of Israel. Rehoboam attempted to bring the breakaway kingdom to heel by sending Adoram, the head of the hated forced labor organization, to Israel. This was an unwise, even foolish, move: Adoram was stoned to death and from this time the nation remained divided between the two monarchies of Israel and Judah (1 Kings 12.19).

Jeroboam attempted to consolidate his new kingdom by setting up an independent national religious organization, so that the people of Israel would not have to worship at the great Temple in Jerusalem. He erected golden bulls at the sanctuaries of Bethel and Dan (1 Kings 12 28–29). The biblical narrative is written from the standpoint of Jerusalem and presents this as a sinful act. But Jeroboam was probably only reviving a long-established cult which represented God as a bull (see p.59), or perhaps depicted him riding on a bull in the manner of other Near Eastern deities.

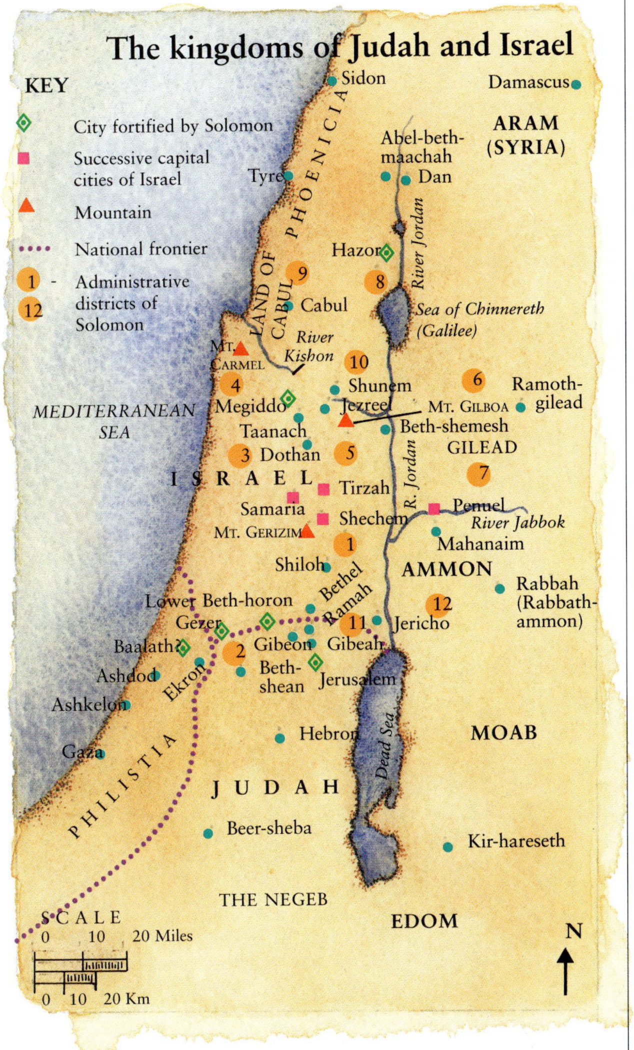

PROPHECY

Prophets and prophecy in the Israelite tradition emerged clearly on the biblical stage with Samuel's appointment of Saul as the first king of Israel (see p.72). Since prophets can arise in almost any society, they may well have been known to the Israelites before then. With the monarchy, Israelite society became more organized and prophets emerged as members of the recognized institutions, a process probably hastened by the existence of bands of prophets in Canaanite religion. It is not easy to define what makes a prophet or what distinguishes him or her clearly from other divinely-inspired figures, such as the judge or the priest. The prophets were individuals, not all of whom functioned in the same way, and the Bible provides considerable evidence of mutual hostility among different prophetic groups.

A Phoenician opal seal with symbols representing the name YZBL, "Jezebel," the 9th-century BCE *queen of Israel.*

THE PROPHET'S ROLE

The various terms used to describe prophets in the Bible indicate how they functioned to fulfill social needs, although they are to some degree stereotyped, to make it easier to recognize them. The general term "prophet" is a translation of the Hebrew word *nabi*, which probably means a speaker or spokesperson. Hence prophets were not primarily people who foretold the future, although they certainly had that power and exercised it, but proclaimers of the divine will, who spoke in God's name, with the regular introduction: "Thus Yahweh has said." Their essential function was to keep the nation in a correct relationship with God, and to streng-then that relationship by their words and actions. The verb derived from *nabi* means "to act as a prophet," and often denotes the uncontrolled behavior usually described as "ecstasy." Evidence of being possessed by the deity in some way, by Yahweh's "spirit" or "hand," was an essential characteristic of prophecy. It gave prophets an inner compulsion to deliver the divine message, even against their own will. Such behavior was not confined to the prophets of Yahweh: the eleventh-century BCE Egyptian story of Wen-Amon relates how a young man at the Phoenician city of Byblos was seized with prophetic frenzy during a sacrificial ceremony and delivered a message from the deity who had taken possession of him.

Prophetic figures were also called "seers," those who had the gift of second sight or who could discern omens from natural objects or phenomena. Another frequent appellation was "man of God," one who was in touch with the supernatural realm. Sometimes the prophet was said to have access to the court of heavenly counselors surrounding Yahweh. The prophet was thus a "messenger," and prophetic oracles often employed a formula by which an emissary spoke in the name of his or her superior.

Prophets functioned in a variety of social contexts. An individual prophet could serve the simple needs of a particular locality, usually centered on a shrine, as with Samuel at Ramah. But, particularly in the period of the early monarchy, there were also organized guilds of prophets, who moved about the country from sanctuary to sanctuary. Perhaps most significant were the court prophets, who were a common feature of ancient Near Eastern monarchies. They offered the king regular divine guidance in state affairs. Individual prophets are mentioned, such as Nathan and Gad at David's court, but the Israelite king maintained a large prophetic establishment, four hundred being mentioned in 1 Kings 22.6. This number closely parallels the four hundred fifty prophets of the Phoenician (Canaanite) god Baal in Jezebel's household (1 Kings 18.22), suggesting that the idea of the prophetic guild may have been borrowed by Israel from the practice of Canaanite monarchy. The Bible gives a vivid picture of the Baal prophets, on the occasion of their encounter with Elijah on Mount Carmel (1 Kings 18). In order to gain their god's attention, "they cried aloud and, as was their custom, they cut themselves with swords and lances until the blood gushed out of them. As midday passed, they raved on ... but there was no voice, no answer, no response." (1 Kings 18.28).

The divided kingdom after Solomon

After Solomon died, the Israelite monarchy was divided into the kingdoms of Israel, in the north, and Judah, in the south. There was more or less continual war between them, a situation that the new Aramean dynasty in Damascus was able to exploit under Ben-Hadad I (ca. 880–842 BCE). While Judah remained comparatively stable, continual disturbances wracked the north. Jeroboam I (922–901 BCE) was succeeded by his son, who was deposed by a military coup, three more of which followed. The Bible explains this instability as God's judgment for the sinfulness of Jeroboam (1 Kings 12.28–33 and 13.33–34), which his successors are seen as perpetuating. Two prophetic legends, full of vivid detail, recount how two prophets pronounced judgment on Jeroboam's house and ultimately on the northern kingdom itself (1 Kings 13).

The chaotic situation in the north was brought to an end with the accession of the final usurper, Omri (876–869 BCE), who was able to establish a powerful state and a stable dynasty centered on a new capital, Samaria. He checked the advance of Damascus and reconquered Moab, which had been lost during the years of Israel's weakness. Omri receives only a brief mention in the Bible, because the biblical editor regarded him as even more wicked than his predecessors. However, the great position he attained is indicated by the fact that Assyrian inscriptions refer to the kingdom of Israel as "the house of Omri," even long after Omri's dynasty had disappeared.

Rulers of Israel and Judah

Dates cannot be assigned to the reigns of the Israelite monarchs with absolute precision. This list follows the chronology of W. F. Albright, which is generally accepted as one of the most accurate. All dates are approximate and BCE.

THE UNITED KINGDOM		RULERS OF JUDAH		RULERS OF ISRAEL	
Saul	1020–1000	Rehoboam	922–915	Jeroboam	922–901
David	1000–961	Abijam	915–913	Nadab	901–900
Solomon	961–922	Asa	913–873	Baasha	900–877
		Jehoshaphat	873–849	Elah	877–876
		J(eh)oram	849–842	Zimri	876
		Ahaziah	842	Omri	876–869
		Athaliah	842–837	Ahab	869–850
		J(eh)oash	837–800	Ahaziah	850–849
		Amaziah	800–783	J(eh)oram	849–842
		Uzziah	783–742	Jehu	842–815
		Jotham	742–735	Jehoahaz	815–801
		Ahaz	735–715	J(eh)oash	801–786
		Hezekiah	715–687	Jeroboam II	786–746
		Manasseh	687–642	Zechariah	746–745
		Amon	642–640	Shallum	745
		Josiah	640–609	Menahem	745–738
		Jehoahaz	609	Pekahiah	738–737
		Jehoiakim	609–598	Pekah	737–732
		Jehoiachin	598–597	Hoshea	732–721
		Zedekiah	597–587/6		

PROPHECY IN THE NEAR EAST

Some of the most interesting information about prophecy in the period of the two Israelite kingdoms comes from the West Semitic and Mesopotamian areas. A stela of King Zakir (ca. 780 BCE) of the Aramean state of Hamath records how he received an oracle of victory from his god through prophets who are called "seers" and "messengers." Letters from the eighteenth-century BCE city of Mari on the Euphrates contain several examples of oracles given to King Zimrilim by diviners whose words and actions resemble those of biblical prophets. These oracles include revelations through dreams, visions, and trances, and the employment of the messenger formula. Parallels have also been discerned in a number of texts containing oracles to various kings, from the period of the Assyrian empire (ca. 680–627 BCE).

Elijah Visited by an Angel *(1 Kings 19.5), from an altarpiece in Louvain, Belgium, by Dirck Bouts (ca. 1420–75).*

ELIJAH

The prophet Elijah was prominent in the reign of King Ahab of the northern kingdom of Israel (869–850 BCE). The northern Kingdom was much more subject to Canaanite (Phoenician) influence than Judah, the southern Israelite kingdom. The prophets of Israel therefore shaped the story of Elijah's career so as to present him as the ideal champion of Yahweh against the worship of the Canaanite deity Baal. The Elijah tradition greatly exaggerated his historical role, such as his reputed massacre of the prophets of Baal at Mount Carmel (1 Kings 18.40), which is more likely to have occurred under King Jehu (842–815 BCE). Elijah was credited with miraculous powers: according to the Bible, when he was sheltered by a widow of Zarephath, he replenished her supply of meal and oil, and raised her son from the dead (1 Kings 17). This story was probably transferred from Elijah's successor, Elisha (see 2 Kings 4), who was much more firmly rooted in the events of his day (see pp.92–3).

Elijah is presented as a new Moses. His confrontation with the prophets of Baal on Mount Carmel, where he challenges their beliefs (1 Kings 18), recalls the incident in Exodus 32 where the Israelites construct and worship a golden calf, and are punished by plague for their idolatry. But the Moses tradition is most obvious in the account of Elijah at Mount Horeb, the site of Moses' revelation. There, Elijah heard the voice of God,

Ahab

The Bible presents King Ahab, the son and successor of Omri (see p.89), in a highly unfavorable light. In the biblical view, he was essentially a pawn of his wife Jezebel, serving and worshiping her god Baal, and doing "more to provoke the anger of the Lord, the God of Israel, than had all the kings of Israel before him" (1 Kings 16.33). The heated antagonism between him and the prophet Elijah is developed in 1 Kings 17–19. Several narratives which probably refer to later kings have been transferred to him to derogatory effect. For example, the story of the battle of Ramoth-gilead (1 Kings 22) tells of the death of a monarch referred to only as "the king of Israel." This may be an inserted episode that was not originally about Ahab at all, whose name is not mentioned in the chapter until verses 39–40. Ahab is then said to have "slept with his ancestors," which in the Bible usually means that he died peacefully.

A more objective view of Ahab would show that he maintained a strong and stable government. He built cities and secured his state by renewing the Israelite alliance with the Phoenicians of Tyre (see p.83). He dominated the southern kingdom of Judah through the marriage of his daughter, Athaliah, to Jehoram, the son of the Judean king Jehoshaphat (873–849 BCE). Ahab's importance is strikingly shown in an inscription of Shalmaneser III, king of Assyria (ca. 859–824 BCE), the first Assyrian monument to include an Israelite king's name. Ahab allied with Israel's old foe, Damascus, against Shalmaneser, and the allies met the Assyrians at Qarqar in the Orontes Valley in 853 BCE. Although Shalmaneser claimed victory, his advance was checked. His inscription records that Ahab had two thousand chariots and ten thousand infantry. Ahab's contingent of chariots was the largest among who told him to anoint Hazael and Jehu as new kings of Aram and Israel respectively, and a new prophet, Elisha, as his own successor (1 Kings 19).

Elijah seems to have spearheaded an attack on the worship of Baal, which was practiced by the Israelite king Ahab and his wife Jezebel, and to have initiated a new development in the worship of Yahweh. The ordeal on Mount Carmel shows that Baal is not just a usurper on Yahweh's territory, but that he is not a god at all: Yahweh alone is God. In Elijah's teaching, Yahweh acquires a universal aspect. He is the true lord of nature, a domain claimed by the Canaanite deities, and can control events in a foreign land. These insights are clearly expressed in the Mount Horeb episode, which also represents a genuine personal prophetic experience. At Horeb, Elijah had to recognize that his mission had failed and that Yahweh had decided to pass on his task to another.

Elijah's nemesis is Jezebel, who is depicted as a woman of great ability and determination. She exploited to the full the authority which her position allowed her, as in the episode of Naboth's vineyard (1 Kings 21), for which Elijah cursed her (21.23). It was accepted that foreign consorts worshiped their own deities, but Jezebel overstepped the mark by seeking to supplant Yahweh entirely with Baal, the god of her native Tyre. (This policy was also pursued in Judah by her daughter, Athaliah.) Her father Ethbaal, the Phoenician king of Tyre, was a priest of Astarte, and Jezebel introduced the worship of the goddess Asherah (1 Kings 18.19). Jezebel was accused of sorcery, and died a brutal death, pushed from her window by her own attendants during Jehu's coup d'état (see box, below), and, in accordance with Elijah's curse, devoured by dogs (2 Kings 9.30–37).

The Bible relates that before her death, Jezebel painted her face and looked out of the window in anticipation of Jehu's approach (2 Kings 9.30). Defiant in her religious beliefs to the end, she may have assumed the role of a goddess: "the woman at the window," possibly the goddess Astarte, is a motif of Assyrian art, as in the above ivory of ca. 800 BCE.

Palestine after Ahab

Ahab was succeeded in turn by his sons Ahaziah (850–849 BCE) and Jehoram of Israel (849–842 BCE), though their mother Jezebel (see main text) remained the power behind the throne. The policy of imposing the worship of Baal continued. Although Jehoram removed Ahab's sacred pillar of Baal in Samaria, the fact that it was later destroyed in Jehu's reformation may mean that he removed it only to replace it.

Jehu prostrated before the Assyrian king Shalmaneser III, from a monument known as the "Black Obelisk of Shalmaneser." It is the only known contemporary depiction of an Israelite ruler.

Omri's dynasty was finally overthrown by Jehu (842–815 BCE), a commander of King Jehoram's army. His brutal revolt, described in 2 Kings 9 and 10, took place in the context of an apparently unsuccessful attack led jointly by the kings of Israel and Judah on the Aramean city of Ramoth-gilead. Jehu was backed by the prophetic office of Elisha (see pp.92–3) and by the Rechabites, an Israelite group that stood out against the settled life of Canaan, abstaining from wine and agriculture and living in tents. But Jehu's usurpation seriously undermined the kingdom. He brutally extirpated the cult of Baal and murdered Jehoram of Israel, Jezebel, and all the royal family (Jehu may also have instigated the massacre of Baal prophets attributed in the Bible to Elijah; see main text). In doing so he broke Israel's alliances with the Phoenicians and Judeans, whose families had intermarried with that of Ahab. After the death of Ahab's and Jezebel's grandson, King Ahaziah of Judah, Ahaziah's mother Athaliah seized power. Athaliah, the widow of King Jehoram of Judah (849–842 BCE), imposed the same religious policies on Judah that her mother, Jezebel, had instigated in Israel.

As a consequence of his state's weakness, Jehu could not withstand the ever-increasing pressure of Assyria. He was forced to become the vassal of the Assyrian ruler Shalmaneser III (ca. 859–824 BCE).

The Ascent of Elijah *(2 Kings 11.1), a Russian painting of the 16th century. The prophet hands his mantle to Elisha as an angel carries him aloft in a chariot of fire.*

ELISHA

The Bible's stories about Elisha, the disciple and then successor of Elijah (see pp.90–1), form a narrative that is characterized by folklore and legendary motifs. Unlike Elijah, who was unswerving in his hostility toward the kings of Israel, Elisha at times advised the powerful figures of his day, in addition to helping ordinary people in distress. Also unlike Elijah, a solitary figure, Elisha acted in the context of groups of prophets who were probably responsible for shaping and recording his saga.

He is first mentioned in 1 Kings 19, when Elijah is commanded by Yahweh at Mount Horeb to anoint Elisha as his successor. In fact, Elisha was not anointed, but was chosen as a prophet while he was plowing a field, when Elijah approached him and threw his mantle over him (1 Kings 19.19). Elisha officially succeeded Elijah after accompanying him from Gilgal to Bethel, Jericho, and the Jordan, where they were separated by "a chariot of fire and horses of fire" and Elijah then "ascended in a whirlwind into heaven" (2 Kings 2.11). Elisha inherited the mantle of Elijah, representing the prophetic office, together with a double portion of Elijah's "spirit," his mysterious quasi-physical power. Elisha divided the waters of the Jordan with the mantle (2 Kings 2.14), as Elijah had done before him (2 Kings 2.8), re-enacting the crossing of the Jordan by Joshua (see p.63). The "company of prophets" that had followed Elijah and Elisha from Jericho declared that "the spirit of Elijah rests on Elisha," and pledged themselves as his "servants" (2 Kings 2.15–16).

Many of the stories about Elisha in 2 Kings are essentially miracle tales, demonstrating the prophet's supernatural powers through magical acts. Thus, he purifies the spring at Jericho (2 Kings 2.19–22), brings a son to a Shunammite woman and resurrects him when he dies (2 Kings 4.8–37),

The Arameans

The Arameans were a people who, in the last quarter of the second millennium BCE, spread out from the desert over the Fertile Crescent. In the Bible, the Hebrew patriarchs and matriarchs (see pp.30–45) are closely linked with the Arameans, who established a cluster of independent states west and north of the Euphrates River. The most important of these came to be Damascus, where King Rezon founded a new dynasty in Solomon's time (1 Kings 11.23–25). This began a three-hundred-year relationship, generally hostile but sometimes friendly, between Israel and Damascus.

In the disturbed conditions of the early years of Israel, Damascus, under Ben-hadad I, was able to dominate the northern kingdom. Under King Ahab of Israel, however, the Assyrian menace brought the two states into an alliance, until Jehu's revolt reversed Israel's policy (see p.91). At about the same time, Hazael of Aram, motivated, according to the Bible, by Elisha, usurped the throne of Damascus and was able to conquer all Israel's territory east of the Jordan. The Bible records warfare with Hazael's successor, Ben-hadad III, involving attacks on Samaria, which according to one legend was saved by Elisha.

But from this period onward, Damascus was weakened by repeated Assyrian assaults. As a result, Israel, under kings Jehoahaz (815–801 BCE) and Jehoash (801–786 BCE), recovered the initiative. The last scene of Elisha's life has the dying prophet ensuring victory over Damascus to Jehoash, albeit on a limited scale, by a vivid act of prophetic symbolism: Elisha commands the Israelite king to shoot an arrow eastward, representing "the arrow of victory over Aram," and then to strike the ground with his remaining arrows. But Joash strikes the ground only three times, ensuring him only three victories over Aram; had he struck the ground five or six times, he would have definitively ruined his rival (2 Kings 14–19). Damascus was finally overcome by Jeroboam II (786–746 BCE) and thereafter declined in importance, until it was finally brought to an end by Assyria in 732 BCE.

and makes an iron ax-head float (2 Kings 6.1–7). The heavenly chariot and horses of fire which carried Elijah into heaven almost certainly originally referred to Elisha, who was also known by the title "the chariots of Israel and its horsemen" (2 Kings 13.14). Elisha was seen as having the power to summon God's heavenly host in support of the nation: on one occasion, when the king of Aram surrounded Elisha's camp, Elisha was ringed by horses and chariots of fire that far outnumbered the Aramean forces (2 Kings 6.15–17).

These acts all occur in connection with prophetic groups, and it was in these circles that the Elisha saga took shape, when his disciples collected together various local traditions associated with him. Fundamental to the picture of Elisha is his relationship with the prophetic group called "the company of prophets," literally "the sons of the prophets" (2 Kings 2.5; 4.1; 4.38; 5.22; 6.1; 9.1). "The company of prophets" appears to be a technical expression for the followers of Elisha, who are described as his "servants," with him as their "master." In the Bible, almost all instances of the term are confined to the period ca. 860–840 BCE and to a relatively compact geographical area that contained the old Israelite sanctuaries of Gilgal, Bethel, and Jericho, where these prophets lived and operated just inside the northern kingdom of Israel. It seems to have been a movement organized in response to a specific historical situation, namely the religious policy of the dynasty of Omri that ruled the northern kingdom, and of Queen Jezebel in particular (see pp.90–1). "The company of prophets" ceased to exist when, with the overthrow of the dynasty by Jehu (see p.91), its work was done.

An ivory carving of a god, from the state bed of Hazael, ruler of the Aramean kingdom of Damascus, ca. 840 BCE (see box on opposite page).

Moab

Elisha was also involved in events concerning the kingdom of Moab, which had been conquered by King David (see map on p.77) but had regained its independence some time later. A contemporary account of events from the Moabite standpoint exists on the "Moabite Stone," a three-foot (1m) high basalt pillar of ca. 830 BCE celebrating the exploits of Mesha, king of Moab. It records that Omri of Israel had regained Moab, but that, after Omri's death, Mesha had thrown off the Israelite yoke, taken the offensive, and captured various Israelite cities in Transjordan. In language closely resembling the way Israel ascribed its victories to Yahweh, Mesha attributes his triumph to Moab's national god, Chemosh.

The inscription on the Moabite Stone is unclear as to whether Mesha's revolt occurred during the reign of Ahab or after his death, but the very first verse of 2 Kings states: "After the death of Ahab, Moab rebelled against Israel." Mesha is described as a sheep-breeder, who had to pay a huge annual tribute of lambs and wool to the king of Israel, but withheld it after Ahab's death (2 Kings 3.4–5). As a result, Jehoram of Israel (849–842 BCE), Ahab's son and successor, launched a campaign against him, but the expedition soon ran out of water for its men and animals, and Elisha was summoned to help. A musician was also summoned and, as he played, Yahweh's "hand" came upon Elisha, and, in God's name, promised both water and the defeat of Moab. Water duly arrived and the Israelites advanced on their target, but their conquest was frustrated when Mesha, seeing no other recourse, offered his eldest son and successor as a burnt offering on the city wall. The sacrifice threw the Israelites into terror (2 Kings 3.27) and they were forced to retreat. It is striking that Israel here implicitly recognizes the power of a foreign god, Moab's Chemosh.

The Moabite Stone, which was discovered in Transjordan in 1868.

ASSYRIA

King Ashurbanipal riding his chariot into battle, on a relief from the Assyrian royal palace at Nineveh, ca. 650 BCE.

Attended by servants, Ashurbanipal reclines on a couch to dine with his queen, from a relief at Nineveh.

Assyria, the heartland of which was a rich agricultural area along the plains of the Tigris River, had a long history. But its greatest era, and the time when it came into direct contact with the two Israelite kingdoms, was the period of the Neo-Assyrian empire (ca. 911–609 BCE). Around the beginning of this era, at least one of the campaigns of Shalmaneser III (ca. 859–824 BCE) involved the northern kingdom, Israel (see box on p.90).

After Shalmaneser's death, Assyria entered a period of decline. The removal of the Assyrian threat, together with the weakness of Damascus, enabled Israel and Judah under, respectively, Jeroboam II (786–746 BCE) and Uzziah (783–742 BCE), to make significant territorial gains. However, the accession of Tiglath-pileser III (745–727 BCE) ushered in the Assyrian golden age and, under a succession of able rulers, Assyrian policy became one of permanent conquest, creating an empire of provinces and vassal states (see map on p.101), marked by an increasing use of deportation to control the conquered peoples. To administer the state, a highly efficient and responsible bureaucracy was created and the imperial cities were enlarged and embellished, especially Nineveh, which was made into a magnificent royal capital by Sennacherib (705–681 BCE). The northern Israelite kingdom of Israel was eventually incorporated into the empire (see box on opposite page) and its southern neighbor, Judah, was forced into vassalage. But Assyria's resources were overstretched, and its eventual disappearance was rapid and dramatic. Nineveh fell to the Medes and Chaldeans in 612 BCE, and the final outpost of Assyrian resistance, Haran, was wiped out in 609 BCE (see p.102).

Assyria had a more civilized side. Assyrian art, as seen in reliefs on the walls of temples and palaces, reached a very high standard, and the great library of King Ashurbanipal (669–627 BCE) at Nineveh preserved the religious and other writings of the Sumerians, the main cultural influence

The end of the kingdom of Israel

King Jehu (842–815 BCE) founded a dynasty that lasted for about a century, bringing a period of stability to Israel, the northern Israelite kingdom, despite some profound weaknesses in the state (see p.91). The absence of Assyria meant that neighboring states were free to advance their own ambitions and rivalries (see Amos 1–2). Israel was primarily involved with the Aramean state of Damascus. Under Jehoahaz (815–801 BCE), Hazael of Damascus (see p.92) reduced Israel's army to fifty horses, ten chariots, and ten thousand infantry. However, Jehoash (801–786 BCE), the son of Jehoahaz, recovered a number of towns that his father had lost.

The long reign of Jeroboam II (786–746 BCE) was a period of respite for Israel. Like Omri, he is only briefly mentioned in the Bible, but he restored his kingdom's frontiers to their full extent and Amos indicates considerable prosperity during his reign. After Jeroboam's death, various usurpers ascended the throne, causing internal instability. When a resurgent Assyria invaded under Tiglath-pileser III, one of these usurpers, Menahem (745–738 BCE), was forced to buy off the Assyrians with a huge tribute of silver and Israel became an Assyrian vassal. After Tiglath-pileser's death, Israel's last king, Hoshea (732–721 BCE), revolted and, with Egyptian support, denied tribute to the Assyrians. Disaster ensued: Tiglath-pileser's son, Shalmaneser V, invaded Israel and the capital, Samaria, fell after a three-year siege. Under his successor, Sargon II, the former northern kingdom became an Assyrian province, and, according to his annals, he deported nearly thirty thousand members of Israel's upper classes to the northern Euphrates region. The deportees, who never saw their homeland again, were replaced with foreigners from other parts of the Assyrian empire (2 Kings 17).

Naked prisoners taken captive by King Sargon II of Assyria (722–705 BCE).

on Assyrian civilization. Nineveh's splendor was renowned. It was surrounded by extensive fortifications sheltering palaces and temples, including the magnificent shrine of the goddess Ishtar, the city's patron.

The Bible sometimes views Assyria as an instrument of God's purposes (Isa. 10.5–11). Nevertheless, smaller states could only see the Assyrians as oppressors, with brutal methods of warfare and a policy that might nowadays be called "ethnic cleansing": controlling conquered peoples through mass deportations and population exchanges. In addition, the regular tribute they had to pay was burdensome. Above all, it was the heavy tribute imposed on vassals that led small states like Judah to rebel, in spite of the odds against them. Several passages in the Bible proclaim a divine judgment on Assyria and predict its imminent fall. A few verses in the prophecy of Zephaniah foretell the devastation of Nineveh (Zeph. 2.13–3.5), but its actual destruction in 612 BCE is celebrated in the book of Nahum, one of the finest products of Israelite literary genius. Nahum's brief work consists of two interlinked poetic compositions and has the character of a prophetic curse. Nahum was probably a prophet attached to the Temple of Jerusalem, and his writing may be described as a liturgy. The fall of Nineveh is pictured as a cosmic event, described in motifs drawn from the ancient Mesopotamian myth of the defeat of primeval chaos. The poem expresses Judah's rapture at its release from the Assyrian yoke, which leaves it free to celebrate its religious festivals, "for never again shall the wicked invade you" (Nahum 1.15). The final words of the book show what a great and welcome impression the fall of Nineveh made in the Near East: "All who hear the news about you clap their hands over you. For who has ever escaped your endless cruelty?"

RULERS OF ASSYRIA, 934–609
All dates are approximate and BCE.

Ashur-dan II	934–912
Adad-nirari II	912–891
Tukulti-Ninurta II	891–884
Ashurnasirpal II	884–859
Shalmaneser III	859–824
Shamshi-Adad V	824–811
Adad-nirari III	811–783
Shalmaneser IV	783–773
Ashur-dan III	773–755
Ashur-nirari V	755–745
Tiglath-pileser III	745–727
Shalmaneser V	727–722
Sargon II	722–705
Sennacherib	705–681
Esarhaddon	681–669
Ashurbanipal	669–627
Ashur-etel-ilani	627–624
Sin-shumu-lishir	624–623
Sin-shara-ishkun	623–612
Ashur-uballit II	612–609

THE CLASSICAL PROPHETS

The book of Amos (ca. 760 BCE; see sidebar, left) marks the advent of what may be called "classical" prophecy, which was to be of central and enduring significance for both Judaism and Christianity. Instead of collections of stories in which prophets (such as Elijah and Elisha; see pp.90–3) play a leading role, "classical" prophecy is represented in the Bible by fifteen books that consist largely of oracles attributed to a particular prophet. In most cases, only a few biographical details of the prophet are given. The three longest books are known as the "Major Prophets": Isaiah, Jeremiah, and Ezekiel. The other twelve are all much shorter and are hence known as the "Minor Prophets": Hosea, Joel, Amos, Obadiah, Jonah, Micah, Nahum, Habakkuk, Zephaniah, Haggai, Zechariah, and Malachi. It was once common to speak of the so-called "writing" prophets, but in fact the classical prophets did not write down their messages themselves. The books that go under their names represent the work of their followers, who collected and transmitted their sayings, and also adapted them to meet changing circumstances.

Behind the books, however, it is possible to glimpse individual figures and their particular teachings. The line between them and their prophetic predecessors and contemporaries is not clear-cut: the source of their inspiration and the way they operated were essentially the same. Nevertheless, the classical prophets were aware of a fundamental conflict between them and other prophets, whom they denounced as "false." The "false prophets," as successors of the earlier style of prophecy, saw their function as ensuring the welfare of the nation. In contrast, the great individual prophets, such as Isaiah and Jeremiah, proclaimed God's impending destruction of Israel, because of the people's failure to observe the terms of the Covenant (see pp.56–7). While announcing the nation's doom, though, they also promised that, through this destruction, God would bring his people to new life. (The term "Israel" is at times ambiguous in this period, because it may denote either the entire nation of Israel, covenanted with God, or the northern Israelite kingdom, to distinguish it from the southern kingdom of Judah.)

AMOS
All the features of "classical" prophecy (see main text) are present in the book of Amos. He was from Judah, but prophesied in the northern kingdom of Israel in its last great days under Jeroboam II (786–746 BCE; see box on p.95). He was probably a substantial landowner and his message reflects a wide acquaintance with Israel's religious and cult traditions. The book of Amos begins with a traditional feature, a series of oracles of judgment against foreign nations (Amos 1–2.3). But then Amos switches abruptly (2.4) to a proclamation of similar judgment against the Israelites. Israel has flouted the kind of divine laws found in the book of the Covenant (2.4), and is guilty of the oppression of the poor through corrupt commercial practices (2.6), the perversion of justice (6.14), and ostentatious luxury (6.4–7). The prophet also denounces worship at famous sanctuaries, such as Bethel and Gilgal (5.5), not on the grounds of idolatry, but because those who went there believed that zealous ritual observance absolved them from moral and ethical obligations (5.21–24).

Amos refers to the moment of his calling (7.14), an event that was an essential feature of the prophetic office, when God summoned him from his normal life to prophecy. However, he denies that he is a prophet in the sense of belonging to the regular prophetic guilds. In a string of dramatic visions, he foresees the end of Israel, yet the final words of the book, which may not be by Amos himself, are a promise of restoration. The Davidic empire will regain its full glory, and God assures his people that "they shall never again be plucked up out of the land I have given them" (Amos 9.15).

The Prophet Amos, *by Juan de Borgoña (ca. 1470–ca. 1535).*

Micah and Hosea

Micah was from Judah, but he prophesied against Samaria, the capital of the northern kingdom of Israel: this means that he must have been active before the fall of that city in 721 BCE. The original collection of his oracles has been much expanded with later material, in particular the work of another contemporary prophet from the north. There is no agreement as to the precise extent of the additional material.

Micah's own message consists of both optimism and doom, but all of it reflects the language and liturgy of the Jerusalem Temple. It begins with a traditional description of a manifestation of God, with Yahweh coming from his shrine (Mic. 1.3). But his judgment is directed not against the enemy, but against the Israelite kingdoms of Judah and Israel. Among those denounced are priests, official prophets, and traders, together with those who rely on military power, soothsayers, or idols. To do justice and walk humbly is worth more than innumerable sacrifices.

However, after Jerusalem has been destroyed on account of its sins, Micah claims that there will be a reversal of fortune. Micah takes up one of the themes of the Temple cult, the attack of the nations on Zion and their annihilation. He provides the first picture of a coming savior or Messiah, an idea which reflects royalist ideology: a future ruler will be a second King David. This ruler will be struck on the cheek, a rite that was part of the installation of the Israelite monarch, and he is described in terms of the first man, another motif of Israelite kingship (Mic. 5.1–5).

The prophet Hosea also prophesied in the northern kingdom, probably a little later than Amos (see sidebar on opposite page), during the confused period following the death of Jeroboam II in 746 BCE, which saw a rapid succession of six kings in fourteen years (see table on p.89). His primary concern was to combat the popular religion of Israel, in which Yahweh was associated with Baal and the sexual rites of Canaanite religion: recent archaeological discoveries have confirmed the truth of this situation. The rites of the Canaanite cult provide the prophet with the material for launching his attacks. In a biographical section at the beginning of the book, Hosea is commanded by God to "Go, take for yourself a wife of whoredom" (Hos. 1.2).

The prostitute becomes a symbol of Israel's unfaithfulness to Yahweh. Israel's adoption of Baal, who in Canaanite religion was seen as the husband of the land and the source of its fertility, represents Israel's desertion of its true husband, Yahweh. As a result, national life is poisoned, and most of the book of Hosea consists of a sweeping condemnation of all the institutions of the northern kingdom, which it sees as doomed to destruction.

However, there is another side to the idea of the ancient Covenant between God and Israel being seen as a marriage. Hosea is again told to love a woman, as "the Lord loves the people of Israel, though they turn to other gods" (Hos. 3.1). In this case, the woman is a sign of God's desire to bring the people that he has chosen above all others to repentance. The prophet's distinctive message is that Yahweh is a god of love: God has always loved his chosen people, Israel, and he will never desert the nation, however hard it is punished for its sins.

Far left: The Prophet Micah, *by André Beauneveu (ca. 1335–1410).*

Left: The Prophet Hosea, *from the Worms Bible (German, ca. 1148).*

THE END OF THE TWO KINGDOMS

After the fall of Israel, the remaining Israelite kingdom, Judah, had a checkered history. In spite of the efforts of Hezekiah, Manasseh, and Josiah, the kingdom was ultimately unable to withstand the pressure of its imperial neighbors. It fell to the Babylonian king Nebuchadrezzar II in 587 or 586 BCE, and much of its population was forced into exile.

HEZEKIAH

After a period of turbulence following the fall of the house of Omri (see p.93), Judah was able to reassert its independence from the northern kingdom of Israel and take advantage of the weakness of the Aramean kingdom of Damascus. Edom was recovered, and under the long reign of Uzziah (also called Azariah, 783–742 BCE), Judah enjoyed a similar period of stability and prosperity to Israel, which also revived under Uzziah's contemporary, Jeroboam II (786–746 BCE).

This era came to an end with the revived expansion of Assyria under Tiglath-pileser III. To meet the Assyrian threat, King Pekah of Israel (737–732 BCE) and King Rezin of Aram renewed the alliance of King Ahab's time and apparently tried to persuade King Ahaz (735–715 BCE), Uzziah's grandson, to join them. When Ahaz refused, they attacked him and, to counter this crisis, Ahaz became a vassal of Assyria, which removed the pressure on him by defeating the northern allies (2 Kings 16.9). Ahaz may not have been a wholly unwilling vassal because the Bible depicts him disapprovingly as a man who sought to assimilate the cult of Yahweh to the general Near Eastern religious pattern (2 Kings 17; 2 Chron. 18). In particular, when Ahaz met Tiglath-pileser at Damascus, Ahaz saw an altar, probably a Syrian one, which he ordered to be copied (2 Kings 16.10–11). He subsequently introduced it into the Temple at Jerusalem as his own cult object.

By contrast, Ahaz's son and successor, Hezekiah (715–687 BCE), is regarded very favorably in the Bible, which declares that "there was no one like him among all the kings of Judah after him, or among those who were before him" (2 Kings 18.5). He reversed the religious policy of Ahaz and instituted a reformation to remove Canaanite practices from the religion of Judah, notably the worship in the Temple of a bronze serpent that was traditionally said to have been erected by Moses (2 Kings 18.4; 2 Chron. 29). This reformation represented a reassertion of the national religion and identity. Through it Hezekiah attempted to win over the inhabitants of the former kingdom of Israel, which ceased to exist after its conquest by the Assyrians (2 Kings 18.9–10 and 2 Chron. 30; see p.95).

Hezekiah pursued a consistent anti-Assyrian policy throughout his reign. He is reported (2 Kings 20.12–19) to have received a delegation from the king of Babylon, Marduk-apal-iddina (Merodach-baladan in the

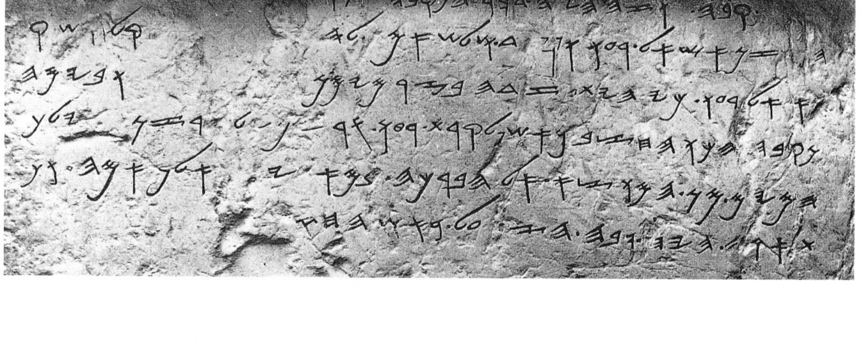

This Hebrew inscription of ca. 700 BCE commemorates the moment when two gangs of miners digging from either end of King Hezekiah's new water conduit broke through in the middle. The tunnel runs for 1750 feet (533m) from the Gihon Spring outside the city wall to the Pool of Siloam in the old City of David (see map on p.152). The inscription was installed at the point where the breach was made.

Bible), who had struggled, with some success, to free his own kingdom from Assyrian overlordship. The Judean king no doubt intended to coordinate a joint resistance against Assyria. To safeguard Jerusalem's water supply in the event of a siege, Hezekiah constructed a conduit that still exists (2 Kings 20.20; 2 Chron. 32.30). Eventually, soon after the accession of Sennacherib to the throne of Assyria in 705 BCE, Hezekiah joined an anti-Assyrian revolt by a broad coalition including Phoenicia, some Philistine cities, and probably also Moab, Edom, and Ammon. The revolt was supported by Egypt, where a new and vigorous Ethiopian dynasty had come to power ca. 715 BCE. The pharaohs saw that, if all Palestine fell, Egypt would be Assyria's next target. From this time onward, Egypt was regularly active against Assyrian expansionism in the region.

In response to Hezekiah's rebellion, King Sennacherib of Assyria invaded Judah in 702 BCE. He has left an account of the campaign in his annals, according to which he took forty-six Judean cities, including the strategic town of Lachish. The siege and capture of Lachish were depicted in reliefs at his palace in Nineveh. His annals relate that he then laid siege to Jerusalem, shutting up Hezekiah "like a bird in a cage." To prevent the sack of the city Hezekiah was forced to submit and pay a heavy tribute. The biblical narrative confirms the payment of tribute, but then says that the Assyrians demanded the handing over of Jerusalem (2 Kings 18–19; Isa. 36–38). Hezekiah conveyed the news to the prophet Isaiah (see sidebar, right), who delivered an oracle reassuring him that the city would not be attacked. According to the Bible, the enemy withdrew after the angel of God had struck down several thousand men in the Assyrian camp (2 Kings 18.35–36).

It is difficult to reconcile the account in the annals of Sennacherib with that in the Bible. The leading figure in the biblical account is Isaiah, and the text bears all the marks of a prophetic legend. The fact that Jerusalem was spared and Hezekiah remained on the throne may have seemed a miracle to the Jerusalemites. They may have interpreted events in the light of the official theology, which stated that God would protect his dwelling place (see Isa. 35, 37, and sidebar, right). However, the harsh reality seems to have been that Hezekiah became a vassal of the Assyrian king. Sennacherib distributed most of Judah's territory among those Philistine rulers who had remained loyal to him.

Israelite prisoners being led into captivity after the fall of Lachish to the Assyrians; from a relief in the palace of King Sennacherib of Assyria at Nineveh.

ISAIAH

The prophet Isaiah was an important figure in the reigns of Uzziah, Jotham (742–735 BCE), Ahaz, and Hezekiah of Judah. He was the confidant of kings, closely involved in the political movements of the day, and profoundly associated with the worship and theology of the Temple at Jerusalem. It was there that he received his prophetic call (Isa. 6). The book of Isaiah is a complex document containing material of widely different dates, but it is agreed that the voice of the prophet himself can be heard in the first thirty-nine chapters of the book. Even these chapters probably incorporate later material, although much less than has sometimes been supposed.

Like other prophets, Isaiah promises a mix of doom and prosperity. He strongly condemns the social abuses for which the nation's leaders are responsible, and announces a coming judgment. But, compared with earlier prophets, his note of reassurance is even stronger. He reasserts the doctrine that the home of the Lord is inviolable (Isa. 37, 35), as long as the nation repents of its offenses and puts faith in Yahweh's promises (Isa. 1–2). If the people place absolute trust in God, they will always be secure, so power-politics and the entanglements of foreign alliances are unnecessary. This message lies at the heart of his address to Ahaz when the king is faced with the coalition between Israel and Damascus (Isa. 7.3–15), and of his warnings against reliance on the new power of Egypt (Isa. 19–20, 31). His vision for the future is of a holy Jerusalem, where an ideal king of David's line will rule in peace and righteousness (Isa. 9, 11, 32).

Parts of the book of Isaiah are attributed to two different prophetic authors known as "Second Isaiah" or "Deutero-Isaiah" (see p.106) and "Third Isaiah"(see sidebar on p.111).

MANASSEH AND JOSIAH

Following Hezekiah (see pp.98–9), the Bible presents two sharply contrasted kings of Judah. Hezekiah's son and successor, Manasseh (687–642 BCE), is presented as the worst of all the Judean rulers, because of his wholesale reintroduction of pagan practices. The Bible sees this as the cause of the kingdom's fall (2 Kings 21.12–14; see p.104). However, Manasseh can be seen in a more favorable light as someone who sought to reverse his father's religious and political policies, which had led Judah to the brink of disaster (see p.99). He probably felt that the only hope of maintaining any kind of national existence lay in vassalage to the Assyrian empire (see pp.94–5). Assyria reached its height in the early part of Manasseh's reign with the overthrow in 671 BCE of the Egyptian pharaoh Tirhakah by King Esarhaddon (681–669 BCE). Assyrian texts show that Manasseh was in fact a loyal subject, at least for the majority of his long reign. As a result, he appears to have recovered territory lost by his father, because he was able to garrison "all the fortified cities in Judah" (2 Chron. 33.14). His religious policy aimed to restore the traditional situation that existed before Hezekiah's destruction of local shrines, which may have been unpopular and divisive.

According to 2 Chronicles, the Assyrians "took Manasseh captive in manacles, bound him in fetters, and brought him to Babylon" (2 Chron. 33.11). During his imprisonment, Manasseh apparently repented, and after his release he revoked his religious measures. Much of the biblical account is clearly legendary, but the episode of his capture and imprisonment suggests that he was not always a subservient vassal of Assyria. It may be that he rebelled when, in the later part of his reign, Assyria lost control of Egypt under Esarhaddon's successor, Ashurbanipal (669–627 BCE).

In contrast to Manasseh, his grandson and successor, Josiah (640–609 BCE), is portrayed as an ideal monarch, who reestablished the exclusive worship of Yahweh and restored the true kingdom of David. Josiah's father, Amon, "abandoned the Lord" and was assassinated in a palace conspiracy after ruling for only two years (640–642 BCE). But the conspirators were killed, and the eight-year-old Josiah was placed on the throne by "the people of the land," probably the free property-owning classes who were committed to Judean independence (2 Kings 21.23–24).

DEUTERONOMY

The "book of the law", found in the Temple in the reign of Josiah (see main text on opposite page), is an important landmark in the history both of the religion of Israel and of the Bible. Its appearance is the first mention of a written document containing essential regulations for life and worship. It represents the beginning of the development of the written religious Law (*Torah*), which became a fundamental feature of Judaism. The book also marks the first step in the compilation of a canon of Scripture.

The "book of the law" is generally thought to be related to the book of Deuteronomy in the Bible. Deuteronomy stresses the duty to eradicate all foreign elements in the worship of Yahweh (Yahwism), a message that may well have provided the impetus for Josiah's reform program. However, the biblical book as it now stands is the product of a complex process of composition that took place over many years. Whether Josiah's book really lay hidden in the Temple until it was "discovered" is questionable. Some features of Deuteronomy suggest that it originated among northern exiles who had fled to Jerusalem, the remaining center of Yahwism, after the fall of the northern kingdom of Israel in 721 BCE. Their work was a program for the nation's future faith and practice, and demanded a complete purification of Yahwism.

It is also possible that the work originated during the reign of Josiah's predecessor, Manasseh, as a response to his religious policies (see main text, right). It was with the accession of Josiah that the ideal political and religious climate arrived in which the book could be made public. The book "found" in the Temple probably consisted only of the "statutes and ordinances" that make up chapters 12–26. This may have largely been the work of prominent Judeans of Josiah's circle, such as Hilkiah, the chief priest, and the prophetess Huldah. They are closely connected with the book's appearance (see 2 Kings 22; 2 Chron. 34).

The angel of God striking down the Assyrians (2 Kings 19.35–37), from the Nuremberg Bible of 1483.

National independence seems to have been Josiah's consistent aim during his reign. He was able to pursue such a policy because in this period the Assyrian empire became too weak to intervene in the affairs of Palestine. The Bible concentrates on Josiah's religious reforms, which were part of this reassertion of national identity. According to 2 Kings, Josiah carried out an exhaustive purge of Judah's religion in response to the teaching of "the book of the law," which was found in the course of repair work on the Temple (2 Kings 22.8; see sidebar on opposite page). But 2 Chronicles states that the destruction of heathen cult objects and practices took place six years *before* the "discovery" of the lawbook (2 Chron. 34.14). This is probably closer to what actually happened. Once the nation's worship had been purified, the "finding" of the book was the occasion for the formal renewal of God's Covenant with his people. In particular, the Passover was properly celebrated for the first time since before the period of the monarchy (2 Chron. 35.18; 2 Kings 23.22; but see 2. Chron. 30).

Josiah's reformation has often been interpreted as the removal of the Assyrian deities and idols. The Bible does mention what are said to be typical Mesopotamian astral cult practices, such as the worship of heavenly bodies. However, there is no real evidence that Assyria imposed its own deities on vassal states. Besides, the divinities and cults that Josiah suppressed existed among neighboring peoples, such as the Canaanites, Sid-onians, Moabites, and Ammonites. Josiah's aim was to establish a cult of Yahweh, free from foreign taint. His reforms extended to the old northern kingdom of Israel. It was technically an Assyrian province, but the enfeebled Assyrian state was unable to resist Josiah's moves toward a restoration of the united kingdom of David and Solomon.

A letter of King Esarhaddon of Assyria about the Ethiopian dynasty of pharaohs. Esarhaddon ousted the dynasty in 671 BCE.

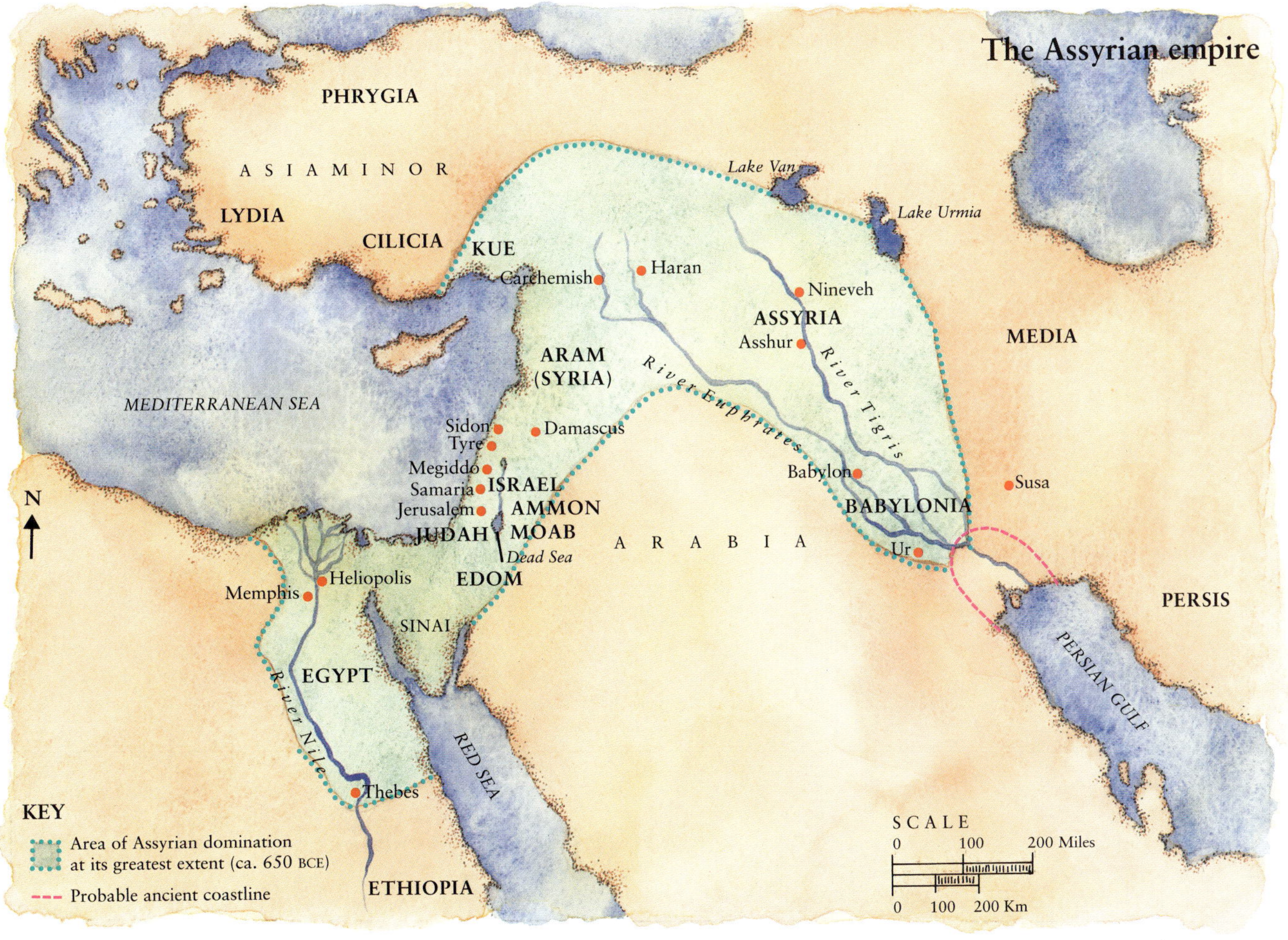

THE DECLINE OF JUDAH

RULERS OF THE CHALDEAN (NEO-BABYLONIAN) EMPIRE
Alternative spellings in round brackets; biblical spellings in square brackets. All dates are approximate and BCE.

Nabopolassar	625–605
Nabu-kudurri-usur II [Nebuchadrezzar, Nebuchadnezzar]	605–562
Amel-Marduk [Evil-merodach]	561–60
Nergal-shar-usur (Neriglissar)	559–56
Labashi-Marduk	556
Nabu-naid (Nabonidus)	555–39
Bel-sharra-usur [Belshazzar, Baltasar], regent	552–42

The achievements of King Josiah of Judah (see pp.100–01) did not last for long. He died in 609 BCE in battle against the pharaoh Necho II of Egypt, which had regained its independence from Assyria by 663 BCE under Necho's predecessor, Psammetichus I of the new twenty-sixth dynasty. In 612 BCE the Assyrian capital, Nineveh, fell to a coalition of the Neo-Babylonians and the Medes (see box, below), and Egypt changed its anti-Assyrian policy, realizing that a weak Assyria was less of a threat than the victorious Neo-Babylonian empire which had supplanted it. The Egyptians sought to bolster the Assyrian state of Asshur-uballit II (612–609 BCE), centered on Haran in northern Mesopotamia. To aid Haran, Egypt established a base at Carchemish on the Euphrates, and Necho was passing through Palestine with his army on his way there when Josiah confronted him. Josiah probably feared that, unless Necho was stopped, Assyrian domination of Judah would only give way to Egyptian rule. The Judean king attempted to check the pharaoh's advance at Megiddo, but fell in the subsequent battle (2 Kings 23.29; 2 Chron. 35.23–24).

Necho was unable to prevent the fall of Haran, but, for a time at least, he was free to assert control over Syria and Palestine. After Josiah's death, "the people of the land" anointed his younger son, Jehoahaz, as king in preference to his elder brother Eliakim, probably because they believed Jehoahaz would continue his father's policies in support of the national religion and political independence. Necho seems to have understood this,

The Neo-Babylonians and the Medes

The Ishtar Gate, one of the city gates built as part of the lavish redevelopment of Babylon by Nebuchadrezzar II. It is faced with glazed bricks including reliefs of guardian bulls and serpent-dragons.

During the first millennium BCE a number of tribal groups, known collectively as Chaldeans, infiltrated the extreme south of Mesopotamia and gradually gained control of the ancient towns of Babylonia. Here, Chaldean kings such as Merodach-baladan championed national independence from Assyria. In 2 Kings 20 and Isaiah 39, Merodach-baladan is reported to have sent a delegation to King Hezekiah of Judah (see pp.98–9). The Chaldean period of greatness began with Nabopolassar, who defeated Assyria, took over its empire, and founded a dynasty referred to as "Neo-Babylonian" to distinguish it from earlier Babylonian civilizations. Under his son, Nebuchadrezzar II (605–562 BCE), the state attained the height of its power and splendor, but Nebuchadrezzar's three successors had short and troubled reigns. The last Neo-Babylonian ruler, Nabonidus, was not a member of the royal family. In 539 BCE the Neo-Babylonian empire fell to the Persians. In the Bible, the Chaldeans also appear as magicians and soothsayers, professions for which they were renowned throughout the Near East.

Comparatively little is known about the Medes, an Indo-European people closely related to the Persians. Over several centuries, they occupied roughly what is now northwest Iran, the region known in ancient times as Media. Toward the end of the seventh century BCE, King Cyaxares established a strong Median empire, with its capital at Ecbatana (modern Hamadan, Iran), and joined Nabopolassar in his carve-up of Assyria. But Cyaxares' successor, Astyages, was defeated by the Persian king Cyrus in 550 BCE, and Media became a province of the Persian empire.

because after only three months, he deposed Jehoahaz and took him as a prisoner to Egypt, where he died (2 Kings 23.34). Necho replaced him with his brother, changing his name from Eliakim to Jehoiakim (609–598 BCE). On his accession, a king often received a new name from God; the fact that the name was conferred by the pharaoh emphasized Judah's vassal status, which was confirmed by the imposition of a heavy tribute.

Egyptian hegemony was shortlived, because in 605 BCE the Babylonian king Nebuchadrezzar II defeated Necho at Carchemish. Necho had to withdraw to Egypt and effectively surrender the whole Syria-Palestine region to the Babylonians. In the following year, Nebuchadrezzar sacked the Philistine city of Ashkelon and moved against Jerusalem, forcing the submission of Jehoiakim.

Jeremiah

Like other prophetic works in the Bible, the book of Jeremiah has been extensively edited, in this case notably by authors reflecting the outlook of Deuteronomy (see sidebar on p.100). Nevertheless, Jeremiah emerges as more of a distinct personality than any other of Israel's prophets. He was apparently the son of Hilkiah, the high priest in King Josiah's time, and his career spanned the time from Josiah until the fall of Jerusalem and the exile to Babylon (see pp.104–05). There are anguished passages where he gives vivid expression to his compulsion to prophesy, knowing that his message will be rejected. The book contains lengthy biographical passages (such as ch. 26), from which we can gain a reasonably authentic picture of the prophet's life, and information about the last days of Judah. Jeremiah used a scribe, Baruch, to write down his words, and much of the existing text may reflect Baruch's work.

The book of Jeremiah follows the common pattern of a prophesied divine judgment on Judah, and its eventual restoration. Jeremiah tells Judah that before its fortunes are restored, it must first accept the punishment of Babylonian domination (Jer. 27). This message brought him into conflict with the advocates of rebellion, not least with the anti-Babylonian King Jehoiakim. In one famous episode, Jehoiakim publicly cut up and burned the scroll on which Baruch had transcribed the prophet's oracles (Jer. 36.23). Jeremiah was imprisoned for his views, and even King Zedekiah, who greatly respected him, could only consult him in secret and finally felt unable to accept his advice.

If Judah submitted to its fate, this would not mean the end of all hope. For Jeremiah, the destiny of the nation lay in the hands of those exiled to Babylon. He has a vision of two baskets, one of good figs, representing the exiles, and one of rotten figs, representing those left behind (Jer. 24). In a letter to the exiles (Jer. 29), he exhorts them to seek Babylon's welfare and to make a new life for themselves there. If they do so, he says, God will hear them and bring them back home.

Jeremiah, portrayed as a scholarly medieval churchman by the Master of the Annunciation of Aix (ca. 1440).

THE FALL OF JERUSALEM

Nebuchadnezzar II and his Advisers, by Frans Francken the Younger (1581–1642).

The accession of King Jehoiakim (see p.103) ushered in the final act in the history of the kingdom of Judah. In 601 BCE, Nebuchadrezzar II of Babylon launched an expedition to conquer Egypt, but was defeated by an Egyptian army and forced to withdraw. His vassal Jehoiakim, who is depicted in the book of Jeremiah as a brutal and arrogant ruler, exploited this weakness to break away from Nebuchadrezzar, probably by withholding the payment of tribute. It took some time for Nebuchadrezzar to regroup his forces, but while this was underway he apparently took steps to weaken Judah. The Bible records that the country was devastated by guerrilla bands of desert tribes sent by God (2 Kings 24.2), but they probably acted on the instigation of the Babylonian king.

Jehoiakim died in 598 BCE and was succeeded by his son Jehoiachin (598–597 BCE). The transfer of leadership came at a bad time, because in the following spring Nebuchadrezzar invaded. Jehoiachin surrendered Jerusalem without any marked resistance and averted the destruction of the city by paying a heavy tribute (2 Kings 24.13). More importantly, Jehoiachin, his family, and his court, together with seven thousand of the leading classes in Jerusalem and a thousand skilled craftsmen, were deported to Babylon. Nebuchadrezzar replaced Jehoiachin with his uncle Mattaniah, a son of Josiah, and renamed him Zedekiah (2 Kings 24.17). Under this name he is known as the last king of Judah.

Zedekiah found himself in an impossible situation. Many Judeans continued to regard the captive Jehoiachin as their rightful king, and looked on Zedekiah as little better than a usurper. Some of those who remained in Judah probably felt this way, and it was certainly the view of the exiles in Babylon. Administrative tablets from the time of Nebuchadrezzar list the rations of oil given by the royal household to Jehoiachin and his sons. The documents call Jehoiachin "king of Judah," suggesting that even the Babylonians continued to regard him as the rightful Judean ruler.

The final verses of both 2 Kings and the book of Jeremiah record how Nebuchadrezzar's successor, Evil-merodach (Amel-Marduk: see table on p.102), released Jehoiachin from prison and gave him an honored position at the imperial court. In the Bible, this act of clemency serves as an assurance that God will not forever abandon the house of David.

In Judah, the deportation of the kingdom's most senior officials had gravely weakened the whole structure of the state. The book of Jeremiah presents a vivid picture of how Zedekiah was torn between different groups of advisers, some advising rebellion and others appeasement and submission to Babylon (Jer. 37–38). The rebel faction relied on the support of Egypt, which still harbored ambitions in Palestine. The prophet Jeremiah, who was among the appeasers, repeatedly warned against the folly of trusting the Egyptians and antagonizing Nebuchadrezzar. But the hawkish faction prevailed and led Zedekiah finally, and fatally, to rebel.

The fall of Judah is recounted in the last chapter of 2 Kings, 2 Chronicles, and Jeremiah. In response to Zedekiah's revolt, Nebuchadrezzar laid siege to Jerusalem. The strength of the city's defenses enabled it to hold out for eighteen months, and there was apparently a brief respite for the defenders when the appearance of an Egyptian army caused the Babylonians to break off the siege temporarily (Jer. 37.5). Like the Assyrian king Sennacherib (see p.99), Nebuchadrezzar preceded his attack on the capital by taking various strategic Judean towns. According to Jeremiah 34.7, eventually only Lachish and Azekah held out, apart from Jerusalem. A number of letters, written by Judean officers in surrounding outposts to the commander of the garrison at Lachish, report on

Judah after 586 BCE

The second book of Kings recounts the aftermath of the destruction of Jerusalem in 587/6 BCE much as it describes the misfortune which had befallen the city under King Jehoiachin a decade earlier (see main text). In both cases, the narrative claims, extravagantly, that most of the population was deported, leaving only "the poorest people of the land" (2 Kings 24.14 and 25.12). A more trustworthy source is preserved in the book of the prophet Jeremiah (see p.103), where it states (Jer. 52.28–30) that three thousand twenty-three Judeans were deported in 597 BCE, but only eight hundred thirty-two after Jerusalem's final fall and destruction. In fact, Babylon's policy toward its new province was relatively moderate, and life carried on in Judah.

The Babylonian king appointed a local man, Gedaliah, as governor: this name appears on a contemporary seal that identifies the owner as chief steward of the Judean royal palace. A number of prominent individuals and military commanders in the country rallied to Gedaliah at his headquarters at Mizpah. According to Jeremiah, Judean refugees returned home from the surrounding lands and were able to reap a good harvest (Jer. 40.12). The Bible also tells of a group of pilgrims from the north, who are murdered while taking sacrifices to "the temple of the Lord." This suggests that worship continued at the holy site of the ruined Temple in Jerusalem (Jer. 40.4–5).

Gedaliah was assassinated at Mizpah by Ishmael, a member of the deposed Judean royal family, who was also responsible for the slaughter of the pilgrims. Ishmael had returned from exile in Ammon, and probably intended to restore the deposed Davidic dynasty, with Ammonite support. Gedaliah's remaining followers were afraid of Babylonian reprisals in the wake of the murder and fled to Egypt, taking the prophet Jeremiah with them, against his will (a later legend claimed that the prophet had been stoned to death in Egypt).

The book of Jeremiah records that a second mass deportation to Babylon, involving over seven hundred Judeans, took place five years after the fall of Zedekiah, that is in 582/1 BCE (Jer. 52.30). This may represent the Babylonian response to the murder of Gedaliah. From this time, Judah was probably placed under the direct control of the Babylonian governor of Samaria, the province immediately to the north of Judah. But whatever happened, little further is known about conditions in the country for some forty years.

An Israelite seal inscribed "To Pedaiah son of the king." Pedaiah was a member of the Judean royal family in the last days of independent Judah (see 1 Chron. 3.16–17).

Babylonian troop movements. One letter indicates that the town of Azekah has fallen, while another complains of the activities of the antiwar party in Jerusalem. There is also mention of a senior army officer being dispatched to Egypt, presumably to seek assistance.

Jerusalem finally fell in 587 BCE or 586 BCE, and the punishment for its lengthy resistance was harsh. Zedekiah was taken to the Babylonian headquarters at Riblah in the Lebanon. There, the Bible relates, his sons were killed before his eyes, his officers were executed, and Zedekiah himself was blinded and taken in chains to Babylon (2 Kings 25.7; Jer. 52.10–11). In Jerusalem, Nebuchadrezzar's commander-in-chief, Nebuzaradan, supervised the destruction of the Temple, the royal palace, and the houses of prominent citizens. The Temple furnishings and remaining treasures were carried off as booty. It was the end of autonomy for Judah, the end of ancient Israel as an independent organized state.

EXILE IN BABYLON

The shock of the destruction of Jerusalem (see pp.104–05) is powerfully reflected in the dirges of the book of Lamentations, an anonymous work traditionally attributed to the prophet Jeremiah. The end of Judah's independence raised profound spiritual questions for Israel. The most important issue was whether the fate of Jerusalem meant that Yahweh had been defeated by more powerful deities, who now had to be worshiped in his place. The Bible implies that some Israelites accepted this opinion. In Egypt, Jeremiah and his fellow exiles argue vehemently over the cause of the national disaster. In a notable diatribe, the prophet blames it on the nation's worship of foreign gods, but his hearers attribute their lot to the fact that they had failed to worship the "queen of heaven," the great Near Eastern mother goddess, as their ancestors had done (Jer. 44). In the period after the first deportation of 597 BCE (see box, below), the prophet Ezekiel saw sun-worship and the rites of the Near Eastern vegetation deity Tammuz being carried out in the Temple (Ezek. 8.14).

Israel's faith and sense of nationhood seem to have been maintained

LAMENTS FOR JERUSALEM

The roads to Zion mourn,
for no one comes to the festivals;
all her gates are desolate,
her priests groan;
her young girls grieve,
and her lot is bitter.

Her foes have become the masters,
her enemies prosper,
because the LORD has made her suffer
for the multitude of her transgressions;
her children have gone away,
captives before the foe.

Lamentations 1.4–5

By the rivers of Babylon –
there we sat down and there we wept
when we remembered Zion.
On the willows there
we hung up our harps.
For there our captors
asked us for songs,
and our tormentors asked for mirth,
saying,
"Sing us one of the songs of Zion!"

How could we sing the Lord's song
in a foreign land?
If I forget you, O Jerusalem,
let my right hand wither!
Let my tongue cling to the roof of my mouth,
if I do not remember you,
if I do not set Jerusalem
above my highest joy.

Psalm 137.1–6

"Second Isaiah"

Chapters 40–55 of the book of Isaiah form a distinct section that contains the oracles of an anonymous prophet, commonly referred to as "Second Isaiah" or "Deutero-Isaiah." He preached in Babylon toward the end of the Exile and his message is one of joyful hope. Israel, he declares, has paid the penalty for its sins, and the era of divine mercy and restoration is about to dawn (Isa. 40.1–5). He pictures the return to the Promised Land as a second Exodus, even more wonderful than the first. In his teaching, monotheism is clearly expressed for the first time: God is not merely the greatest deity, but the only one (Isa. 44.6), and Second Isaiah mocks foreign gods and goddesses as lifeless idols with no real existence (Isa. 44.9–20). The one true God, Yahweh, alone controls the world and determines its history.

Second Isaiah was aware of the political situation of his time. Babylon was under threat from the Persian king Cyrus (see p.109), and the prophet looks forward to its imminent fall. He sees Cyrus as the Lord's anointed ruler (Isa. 45.1), who will return the Jewish exiles to their homeland after God has led him to victory (Isa. 45.13).

Second Isaiah's oracles speak of a figure called the "servant," whose identity has been much disputed. Early Christians saw him as the Messiah, and identified him with Jesus, notably in Isaiah 53 (see p.363). The picture of the servant appears to be made up of a number of traditional images. Certain aspects of him recall Moses, a typical Davidic king, and one of the prophets. But he stands primarily for Israel, with which he is explicitly identified in places, such as Isaiah 44.1. Israel is the nation that has been chosen by God, but endures contempt and suffering. This marks the emergence of a new and remarkable concept: Israel's vocation as a sacrificial victim for the whole world. The divine purpose for God's chosen people is that it should atone, by its sufferings, for the sins of all humanity. "The righteous one, my servant, shall make many righteous, and he shall bear their iniquities" (Isa. 53.11). (See also pp.99 and 111.)

and reinterpreted most effectively by the Judean exiles in Babylon. Conditions in Babylonia enabled them to preserve their identity. Governed by elders, the leading figures of the community, the exiles lived together in organized settlements, such as Tel-abib (Ezek. 3.15) and other places in the vicinity of the irrigation channel of Chebar, near the city of Nippur. One concern of the exiles was to preserve and record the traditions of Israel's past in writing, to create a body of Scripture upon which they could base their hopes for the future. It was during the exile that the Bible as we know it first began to take shape, in the form of the Pentateuch (the first five books); the history of Israel (Joshua to 2 Kings) by writers of the school that produced Deuteronomy (see p.100); and the prophetic writings. Living in a foreign environment, the exiles were anxious to stress the elements in Israel's religion which distinguished the Jews from other peoples. At this time, therefore, there was a new emphasis on such features as the Sabbath, circumcision, and the need for ritual purity.

The calamities which had befallen the Israelites came to be seen not as the result of Yahweh's powerlessness, but as his punishment for the people's repeated religious and social sins. This belief underlies the Deuteronomic school's interpretation of Israelite history. Similarly, the general message of the prophets, that a divine judgment would restore the nation by purging it, was presented as the norm. The Israelites began to see Yahweh as a truly universal deity, who controlled the destinies of all nations and remained with his people, even when they had been taken from his land. The exiles never abandoned the hope that God would eventually bring them back to their native country, and create Israel anew.

One of the most remarkable figures of the period of the Exile was the prophet Ezekiel. He was a priest who was taken to Babylon with King Jehoiachin in the first deportation of the Jews in 597 BCE (see p.104), and his whole message is couched in priestly terms and imagery. The book of Ezekiel paints a remarkable picture of the nature of prophetic inspiration, with visions, ecstatic experiences of levitation, and strange symbolic signs.

The book begins with Ezekiel's calling as a prophet, "among the exiles by the river Chebar" (generally identified with a canal that ran from the Euphrates near Babylon), in the fifth year since the first deportation (that is, ca. 592 BCE). It takes the form of a great vision of God, which became a central component of later Jewish mysticism. It has often been suggested that details of the vision, such as the winged cherubim (Ezek. 1.4–5), recall features of Mesopotamian religion. But they are perhaps more likely to reflect the cult of the Temple of Jerusalem, the main point being that Yahweh now manifests himself not only in Zion but also in a foreign land. Ezekiel's explanation of Jerusalem's destruction is that the actual presence of Yahweh, "the glory of the God of Israel," has left the polluted Temple, removing its divine protection (Ezek. 10.18–19). Restoration will only be achieved when the divine glory returns to the sanctuary.

Ezekiel's hope for the future is expressed in various ways. The people must accept responsibility for their own actions and no longer attempt to blame the disasters that have befallen them on the sins of their ancestors. He sees his defeated and exiled people as a heap of dry human bones, which is restored to life by the onrush of the divine breath or spirit. From this time the nation becomes a spirit-filled community (Ezek. 37.1–14). The book ends with a detailed description of a new and perfect Temple, the center and symbol of a newly revived Israel (Ezek. 40–48). The climax of the vision of the new Temple is the return of the divine presence (Ezek. 43.2–5), a sign of Israel's restoration. The divine voice tells the prophet that the Temple is the place "where I will reside among the people of Israel forever" (Ezek. 43.7).

Illustrations in the book of Ezekiel, from the Lambeth Bible, produced in England, ca. 1140–1150 (clockwise from top left): Ezekiel's calling (Ezek. 1.1–3); the vision of the scroll (2.9–3.3); six executioners, including "the man clothed in linen," receive God's instructions (9.1–5); the instructions are carried out (9.6–7).

A four-winged spirit from the palace of King Sargon II of Assyria (722–705 BCE) at Khorsabad. Such figures were common in Mesopotamian art and may have inspired the winged cherubim of Ezekiel's vision (compare Ezek. 1.5–6).

RETURN FROM EXILE

The book of Ezra (see p.110) opens with a decree of King Cyrus the Great of Persia, following his capture of Babylon in 539 BCE. He attributes all his victories to Yahweh, "the God of heaven," and states that Yahweh "has charged me to build him a house at Jerusalem." He goes on to authorize the return of Judean exiles to undertake the work (Ezra 1.2–4). The authenticity of this decree has often been doubted, largely because it has been thought unlikely that a Persian king would credit his successes to the god of a foreign subject people. However, in one genuine decree, Cyrus ascribes his victories to Marduk, the national god of Babylon. This document also parallels the Bible in stating that, in various areas, Cyrus has rebuilt temples and returned former populations. In Ezra 6 there is another version, often thought to be more reliable, of the decree concerning the Judeans. The decree was apparently found at Ecbatana in western Persia (Ezra 6.2). It is really a memorandum to the royal treasurer there, authorizing the expenses for the building of the Temple. It does not mention the return of exiles, but they would not have been the treasurer's responsibility.

According to the book of Ezra, following Cyrus's decree, a caravan of deportees returned to Judah. The number given is very large – about fifty thousand – and probably represents several groups that in fact returned at different times under different leaders. The new Temple is said to have been founded by Sheshbazzar, a Persian official who was apparently made governor of Judah (Ezra 5.16–18). Sheshbazzar was probably accompanied by a small group of Judeans, who were able to set up the open-air altar of burnt offerings on the Temple site, and to celebrate the autumn feast of Tabernacles or Booths (Ezra 3.3–4).

Construction was halted owing to opposition from those who had remained behind in Judah and from the ethnically mixed inhabitants of the former northern kingdom of Israel. The opponents of the Temple were supported by other Persian provincial officials. The result, although there is a good deal of confusion in the narrative, was that work on the Temple was stopped until 520 BCE, the second year of the later king, Darius. Then, at the instigation of the prophets Haggai and Zechariah (see below and sidebar, left), work resumed under two leading Judeans, Zerubbabel and Jeshua (Ezra 5.1–2). The royal governors consulted the king as to whether the Judeans had obtained proper authorization. Darius sent an affirmative answer, and the new Temple was completed in late March 516 BCE. The narrative of the book of Ezra is clearly designed to emphasize the favorable attitude of the Persian empire toward the Judeans, and to show that the rebuilding of the Temple had royal approval. In general, it presents a neat and unified picture of events, but it is likely that the reality was much more complicated.

Like Ezra, Haggai refers to a delay in rebuilding the Temple, but attributes it to a lack of enthusiasm among the inhabitants of Judah ("these people," Hag. 1.2), and does not mention returned exiles. In response to the prophet's message, the governor of Judah, Zerubbabel (a grandson of King Jehoiachin; see p.104), and the high priest, Joshua (Jeshua in Ezra), began work on the Temple in the second year of Darius's reign. Haggai addresses an oracle to Zerubbabel, in which God tells him "I have chosen you," and promises "to overthrow the throne of kingdoms." This corresponds well with the period of turmoil in the Persian empire at the beginning of Darius's reign. Haggai suggests that the oracle to Zerubbabel and the rebuilding of the Temple, far from having Persian approval, represented an attempt to restore the kingdom of Judah.

ZECHARIAH

Like Haggai (see main text), the prophet Zechariah was active during the reign of Darius I of Persia (522–486 BCE). The prophet also pins nationalistic hopes on Zerubbabel, who is promised royal dignity and lays the foundation of the new Temple (Zech. 2.6–10). He is crowned and given the royal title "Branch" (Zech. 6.12–13). In this passage, the name of the high priest, Joshua, has been substituted for that of Zerubbabel. Perhaps Darius, after securing his rule, deposed Zerubbabel, who disappears from history at this point. With the failure of this last attempt to reestablish the kingdom of Judah, much of the old royal ideology and ritual would have been adopted by the remaining senior figure of Judean society, the high priest. This would explain why the name Joshua has replaced Zerubbabel in Zechariah 6 and elsewhere.

The monumental tomb of King Cyrus II of Persia at Pasargadae, Iran.

Cyrus the Great and Darius I

The reign of King Cyrus II of Persia was a landmark in ancient Near Eastern history, and Cyrus probably deserves his epithet "the Great" more than many other rulers. He was the founder of an empire that was to last for over two centuries and bring the whole of the Near East, from India to the frontiers of Greece, under one ruler for the first time. Legends grew up around him, and ancient Greek writers, such as Herodotus and Xenophon, regarded him as a model ruler. This was largely because, unlike the Assyrians and Babylonians, he and his successors did not seek to eradicate long-established institutions, or to deport native populations. They preserved and restored the old legal and social systems of their subject territories, and paid particular attention to the upkeep of holy places. It is hardly surprising that Cyrus was welcomed as a deliverer, not only by the people of Judah, but also by the inhabitants of Babylon, who (according to his own annals) opened their gates to him without a struggle.

Cyrus's son, Cambyses, had a comparatively short reign, .but he succeeded in incorporating Egypt into the empire. The end of Cambyses' reign was marked by political unrest, and his successor Darius, whose origins are obscure, had a hard fight to secure his accession. Under Darius, the Persian empire reached its greatest extent, expanding as far as northern India, and the magnificent palace that he built at his capital, Persepolis, testifies to the wealth and splendor of his state. The only shadow on his reign was the failure of his expedition against the Greeks, who defeated the Persians at the battle of Marathon in 490 BCE. This abortive campaign was of profound significance for the future: the Persian empire eventually fell to the Greeks under Alexander the Great in 330 BCE.

RULERS OF THE PERSIAN EMPIRE
All dates are approximate and BCE.

Cyrus II ("the Great")	550–529
Cambyses II	529–522
Darius I	522–486
Xerxes I	486–465
Artaxerxes I	465–425
Xerxes II	425–424
Darius II	423–404
Artaxerxes II	404–359
Artaxerxes III	359–338
Arses	338–336
Darius III	336–330

A relief from the palace of Darius I of Persia at Persepolis, ca. 500 BCE, *which shows the enthroned Darius receiving a Median dignitary, behind whom stand two attendants.*

AFTER THE EXILE

The Exile in Babylon brought about a fundamental reappraisal of the spiritual life of Israel. This began among the exiles and was continued after their return to Judah, especially through the work of Ezra and Nehemiah. The life of the nation was now centered on the Temple, and Yahweh was increasingly seen not just as Israel's national god, but also as the one true and universal deity. In the postexilic period the biblical canon started to take shape. For most of this time, Palestine was dominated by the Persian empire and the Hellenistic empires which succeeded it. However, in the mid second century BCE*, more than four centuries after the fall of the last king of Judah, the Maccabees established an independent Jewish state.*

EZRA AND NEHEMIAH

According to the Bible, the leaders Ezra and Nehemiah brought about a fundamental reconstruction of the religion and society of postexilic Judah. Ezra's career is related in the last four chapters of the book which bears his name, together with two chapters now incorporated in the book of Nehemiah. The story of Nehemiah is told in the first person, but this does not mean it is an autobiography. The use of "I" throughout is a stylistic device modeled on Near Eastern royal inscriptions that were designed to glorify the national hero.

The traditions about the two men once existed separately, but they were brought together by the biblical author known as "the Chronicler" to form a sequel to the first and second book of Chronicles, the earlier retelling of Israel's history. It is not known for certain whether Ezra and Nehemiah were in fact contemporaries. In the Bible, both are dated to the time of a Persian king called Artaxerxes, who could be either the first or second ruler of that name (see table on p.109). It is generally agreed that Nehemiah was active under Artaxerxes I (465–425 BCE), but some have argued that Ezra came later, under Artaxerxes II (404–359) BCE. The current trend is to place both men in the time of Artaxerxes I and to see their careers as overlapping.

Ezra is described as a priest and as "the scribe of the law of the God of heaven" (Ezra 7.12), that is, he was the official in the Persian administration responsible for Israelite religious affairs. In accordance with the Persian imperial policy toward its subject peoples, Ezra was commissioned to investigate how Jewish law was being observed in Judah. On his arrival in Jerusalem, he at once put a stop to intermarriage between the returned exiles and foreigners. He saw this practice as polluting the land and "the holy seed" of Israel, and ordered that all foreign wives and their offspring be sent away in order to purify the nation and avert the wrath of God (Ezra 9–10). Later, as recounted in Nehemiah 8–10, he read out the law of Moses at a great ceremony that saw the revival of the feast of Tabernacles. This ceremony probably marked the first stage in the codification of the Pentateuch, the biblical books containing the divinely-given laws of Israel (see p.112). Ezra caused the leading inhabitants of Judah to bind themselves to the observation of the law by a solemn oath (Neh. 9.38–10.29).

Nehemiah's work was largely in the secular sphere. He was a cupbearer at the Persian royal court in Susa (modern Shush, Iran), when he received information that the fortifications of Jerusalem had been destroyed (Neh. 1.3). In 445 BCE, the twentieth year of Artaxerxes' reign, the king authorized Nehemiah to go to Judah (Neh. 2.6), apparently as imperial governor, a post he says he held for twelve years (Neh. 5.14). Behind this move may lie Persian concern to build a strong Judah in order to counter possible expansionist moves by the Egyptians.

Nehemiah's great achievement, recounted in a series of dramatic scenes (Neh. 3–6), was a rapid rebuilding of Jerusalem's walls, in the face of fierce opposition from neighboring leaders, led by Sanballat, the imperial governor of Samaria. There is an attempt to trick Nehemiah into seeking refuge from his enemies in the Temple (Neh. 6.10), but Nehemiah refuses, knowing that to do so would be sinful (Neh. 6.13). This episode has given rise to a theory that Nehemiah was a eunuch, and as such forbidden by the Jewish Law from entering the sanctuary (see Deut. 23.1).

Nehemiah also devised a new administrative structure for Judah and Jerusalem, tackled the issues of the proper observance of the Sabbath, and, like Ezra, sought to end mixed marriages (Ezra 10–13). Between them, Ezra and Nehemiah laid a firm religious and civil foundation for the future life of the Jewish community.

The Jews of Elephantine

Between 1906 and 1908, a number of papyri, written in Aramaic and dating from the Persian period, were discovered on the island of Elephantine or Yeb in the Nile in southern Egypt. The documents came from a colony of Jewish mercenaries in the Egyptian army, who, like the Judeans who fled to Egypt with Jeremiah (see p.103), had probably migrated as the result of the Assyrian and Babylonian invasions of Judah.

The documents show that they had a temple dedicated to Yahweh, but their cult also involved the worship of other deities, including the goddess Anath (see p.66). This probably reflects popular Judean religious practices in the time before the Exile. This temple was destroyed at the instigation of Egyptian priests ca. 410 BCE, and one of the texts is a letter to Bagoas, the Persian governor in Jerusalem, seeking support for its restoration. The authors of the letter say that they have also approached the sons of Sanballat, the governor of Samaria and the chief opponent of the prophet Nehemiah (see main text). Bagoas's reply, which is also preserved, sanctions the restoration of the Elephantine temple. The letter suggests that the postexilic religious authorities in Judah were beginning to claim Jerusalem as the sole legitimate sanctuary. The Elephantine sacrifices, Bagoas says, must only be offerings of food and incense. Animal sacrifice, a central element of the sacrificial cult because it involves the shedding of blood, is to be permitted only in Jerusalem.

The ruins of the temple on Elephantine dedicated to the deities Khnum and Anuket.

Ezra copying the Scriptures, from a 7th-century CE Italian illuminated manuscript.

MALACHI AND "THIRD ISAIAH"

Conditions in Judah after the return of the exiles, but before the arrival of Ezra and Nehemiah (see main text), can be reconstructed from two documents from this period, the book of Malachi and chapters 56–66 of the book of Isaiah (see p.99), whose author is often called "Third Isaiah." The prophet Malachi's main concern was the prevalence of intermarriage with women from neighboring nations, particularly among the upper classes and even the clergy. He believed such unions posed a threat both to Israel's national identity and to the uniqueness of its faith (Mal. 2.11–12). Malachi also attacked widespread abuses, such as the sacrifice of unclean animals and fraud in the payment of tithes.

Third Isaiah may have belonged to a faction that believed the destruction of the world was near, and was opposed to the established religion represented by the Temple and its clergy. He certainly paints a gloomy picture of the state of society. Its leaders are venal and drunken, there is social oppression, and the course of justice is perverted. In particular, he lists a whole catalog of religious abuses: neglect of fasting and the Sabbath; heathen religious practices; idolatry; child sacrifice; fertility cults; consulting the spirits of the dead; and eating the flesh of forbidden animals, such as the pig. Clearly, the expectations aroused by the ending of the Exile and the rebuilding of the Temple were not being realized.

THE LAW

The word "Law" is used to translate the Hebrew *Torah*, which means "instruction," "guidance," or "direction." It is used primarily to refer to the first five books of the Bible (Genesis through Deuteronomy), which are also called the Pentateuch, or "books of Moses." However, the Pentateuch contains much more than legal regulations. It includes the whole story of God's dealings with humanity from the Creation of the universe to the death of Moses (see pp.20–61).

The codification of the Pentateuch was central to how the Law of Israel came to be viewed in the postexilic period. The final version of the Pentateuch has generally been seen as a combination of three documents: a narrative from the period of the monarchy, the book of Deuteronomy (see p.100), and a work produced in priestly circles. Recently there has been a tendency to question whether any part of the Pentateuch as it stands dates from before the Exile, although the biblical authors certainly drew on many ancient traditions. In any case, the Pentateuch was written down in something approaching its present form during the period of Persian rule (539 BCE–330 BCE; see p.109).

The emergence of the written Pentateuch led to the codification of the other books of what Christians call the Old Testament. In this way there arose what is known as the "canon," a list of books which formed a body of authoritative Holy Scripture, in contrast to other religious writings. However, the Pentateuch was always regarded as supreme – the Samaritans, for example, have never recognized the other books in the Jewish canon (see p.119). The canon was built up in stages over several centuries and probably only reached its definitive shape toward the end of the first century CE.

The theory of an orally-transmitted Torah developed alongside the written Law. It was believed that God had given Moses not only a

Holiness and the Day of Atonement

One characteristic of the God of postexilic Judaism was his intrinsic holiness, a quality that his chosen people were to share. Those chapters in Leviticus that have been called "the Holiness Code" (Lev. 17–26) center on one key phrase: "You shall be holy, for I the Lord your God am holy" (Lev. 19.2). The nation's holiness was to be ensured by the faithful observance of the Law, and this brought about a new and far-reaching understanding of the purpose of worship. Sacrifice (see pp.116–17) came to be seen not so much as a rite that was effective in itself, but rather as a meritorious act of obedience that fulfilled the sacrificial regulations contained in the Law.

The whole system of sacrifice, and the one sanctuary where it was carried out (the Temple of Jerusalem), were seen as the means by which the nation could atone for its past failures to observe the Law. Sacrifice and the Temple were the focus of divine forgiveness. The Temple's center of holiness now became not the ark itself (see p.84), but its gold cover, the so-called "mercy seat." It was here that atonement was made, especially by the sprinkling of blood on the "Day of Atonement," Yom Kippur (Lev. 23.27–28; 25.9).

The Day of Atonement was probably an old observance, but it is only mentioned in writings from after the Exile, when it acquired the tremendous significance that it still possesses in Judaism. The rituals that marked this occasion had the effect of annulling all the sins committed by the nation during the previous year. As set out in Leviticus 16.6–22, the Temple and the priesthood were purified by the blood ritual. Afterward the high priest (see p.117) transferred the people's sins onto a goat (the scapegoat) in an ancient rite with many Near Eastern parallels. The animal was then released into the desert to carry its burden of sinfulness to a demonic spirit called Azazel.

written text but also a body of oral instructions that were handed down through a succession of teachers. In time, this body of teaching acquired almost the same status as the written Law. The oral Torah represented the work of the scribes, an important class of scholars that studied and interpreted the Law, and extended its scope to all areas of life.

The Pentateuch reflects the concerns of the Jewish community of the time. In the period after the Exile, Israel's Law came to be understood as an expression of God's will for the entire world, and obedience to the Law came to outweigh all other religious considerations and obligations. The Law tended to be viewed as something eternal, pre-existent, and independent, which had not come into being only when it was revealed to Moses on Mount Sinai (see pp.54–7). Some speak of the Law as an image of the cosmos, and the means through which the world was created.

After the Exile, the Jewish concept of God also became increasingly spiritual, transcendent, and universal. There was a growing tendency to avoid the use of God's personal name, Yahweh, which designated him specifically as the national deity of Israel, in favor of more abstract titles, such as "Lord" or "God of heaven." Alternatively, he might be referred to by circumlocutions such as "Name." The early Israelites pictured God essentially as a being that intervened directly in human affairs and spoke to men and women face to face. This picture became more and more unacceptable after the Exile, and the problem of how a transcendent being would communicate with his creation was resolved by assuming the existence of a number of intermediaries. For example, God's attributes, notably the divine Word, Wisdom, and Spirit, were personified as beings through whom he acted in the world (see also box, below).

Angels

Israel had always pictured Yahweh as surrounded by a court of heavenly spirits who acted as his agents and messengers. For example, when God says "Let *us* make humankind in *our* own image" in Genesis 1.26, he may be addressing these beings (see p.21; compare Pss. 29.1; 82.1). In postexilic Judaism there appeared a developed hierarchy of angels, with six or seven ranks. At the head of the angelic host were four senior angels (archangels) who had individual names containing the element *el*, meaning "god": Gabriel, Michael, Raphael, and Uriel. The functions of the angels were to praise God in heaven and to act as intermediaries between God and human beings (the word angel comes from the Greek *angelos*, "messenger"). They also protected Israel and other nations.

The influence of ancient Near Eastern religion can be seen in the way that angels are described. They are said to have wings, like the winged spirits that were a common feature of Mesopotamian belief. Their arrangement into six or seven groups recalls the seven Amesha Spentas, beings that personified aspects of the supreme Persian god Ahura Mazda. This is reminiscent of the seven heavenly bodies that were worshiped by the Babylonians.

A winged deity, armed with a sword and wielding lightning bolts, attacks a monster; a reconstruction of a relief from the Assyrian royal palace at Nimrud, ca. 870 BCE.

THE SECOND TEMPLE

King David playing the bells, from a 13th-century Psalter produced at Norwich, England.

When the exiles returned to Judah from captivity in Babylon (see pp.108–09) they found that their homeland had been devastated during the Babylonian occupation and reduced in size to a small region around the former royal capital, Jerusalem. However, this meant that King Josiah's policy of eliminating all foreign elements in the national religion (see pp.100–01) could now be implemented without great difficulty. The Temple of Jerusalem, rebuilt by the former exiles (see pp.108–09), was at the heart of this national religious revival and took on a new significance and character. The growing belief in one universal God (see box on p.106) found a parallel in the doctrine of one Temple. The single universal deity manifested himself nowhere else on earth except in the Temple of Jerusalem, and the Temple was the only place where worshipers could offer sacrifice to their God.

The Temple also took on a more practical role in the postexilic period. With the disappearance of the monarchy, responsibility for the country's internal affairs was transferred to the authorities of the Temple (see p.117), and Judah took on the form of a "Temple state" or theocracy. Civil and religious matters, in so far as the two can be distinguished, were administered by the Temple personnel, and the Temple also functioned as the national treasury. The central role of the Temple in national life was reinforced by the ancient obligation on every male to attend the sanctuary on the occasion of the three great annual festivals, Passover, Weeks, and Tabernacles (Deut. 16.16). At such times, Jerusalem was crowded with pilgrims, and later, during the period of Roman rule (from the late first century BCE), the religious celebrations often led to riots against the occupying power.

The feasts themselves were now integrated into the nation's history. Originally, Passover and Unleavened Bread had been a celebration in the home, but by this time the sacrificial Passover meal could only be eaten in Jerusalem, where the Passover lambs were slaughtered in the Temple (cf. Deut. 16.6). The ceremony had come to be seen as a commemoration of the Exodus from Egypt (see sidebar on p.52). The spring Israelite festival of Weeks (Deut. 16.9–12) marked the end of the wheat harvest, and although it always retained its agricultural character, it too came to be connected with events from Israel's past, such as the covenant with Noah after the great Flood (see p.27) or the giving of the Law to Moses at Sinai (see pp.54–5).

During the week of the great autumnal festival, the people were commanded to live in huts made out of branches, a custom which gave the celebration its name of Tabernacles or Booths. Agricultural laborers lived in

A PSALM OF DAVID
The Lord is my shepherd, I shall not want.
He maketh me to lie down in green pastures: he leadeth me beside the still waters.
He restoreth my soul: he leadeth me in the paths of righteousness for his name's sake.
Yea, though I walk through the valley of the shadow of death, I will fear no evil: for thou art with me; thy rod and thy staff they comfort me.
Thou preparest a table before me in the presence of mine enemies: thou anointest my head with oil; my cup runneth over.
Surely goodness and mercy shall follow me all the days of my life: and I will dwell in the house of the Lord for ever.

Psalm 23 (King James Version, 1611)

A view of present-day Jerusalem from the Mount of Olives to the Temple Mount. The golden-domed Mosque of Omar (the Dome of the Rock), Islam's third holiest shrine, was built in ca. 690 CE on the site of the Temple's central sanctuary.

The Psalms and music in the Temple

The Psalter or book of Psalms has been called the hymn book of the postexilic Temple. However, it includes material spanning several centuries, and many of the psalms date from before the Exile, at least in their original form. The book contains a number of collections distinguished by their titles, such as the seventy-three psalms – almost half the entire Psalter – attributed to King David, the Songs of Ascent (Pss. 120–134), pilgrimage songs, and psalms which represent texts used by two groups of Temple choirs, those of Asaph (Pss. 73–83) and the sons of Korah (the Korahites; for example, Pss. 44–49). It is possible to distinguish different types of psalms, as well as the occasions on which they were used. Many psalms are laments of an individual in distress (for example, Pss. 42–43), or laments uttered by the community in the face of a national catastrophe (Pss. 44 and (Pss. 116 and 118), and psalms celebrating God as sovereign (Pss. 96–99) and his choice of Zion, Jerusalem (Pss. 48, 87). Other psalms refer to the Davidic monarch himself.

Coins depicting instruments used in the Temple: trumpets (above) and a lyre (below). They were issued by the Jewish rebel leader Simon Bar Kochba during the anti-Roman revolt of 134–5 CE.

Most of the psalms are not the poems of particular individuals, but liturgical texts for use as part of the Temple cult. The Hebrew title of the Psalter is *Tehillim*, "Songs of Praise," which indicates the function of the Psalms in the Second Temple. During this period, the Psalms tended to be linked with the nation's past, and were given titles that related them to historical events, such as episodes in the life of King David (for example Pss. 51 and 63). The increasing predominance of the written Law (see pp.118–19) has also left its mark on the Psalter. The division of the Psalms into five books is probably a deliberate echo of the Pentateuch, the five books of Moses. Psalm 119, the Bible's longest chapter, is a glorification of the Law.

Music played a very important part in the worship of the Second Temple (the word psalm is from a Greek word meaning "song sung to the harp"). The rites of the Temple were not confined to the offering of sacrifice, but included prostrations, walking around the altar, processions in the sanctuary, and other rituals. These were generally accompanied by music. With the final destruction of the Temple in 70 CE, this liturgical music largely ceased, and we have very little idea of what it was actually like or how it sounded. The Bible provides a few clues, however. Psalm 68.24–27 speaks of a great ritual procession in the Temple, led by the ark, the dwelling place of Yahweh (alluded to in v. 24), and followed by singers, minstrels, and a group of girls beating tambourines. Other passages (such as Ps.150.3–5), refer to trumpets, stringed instruments, wind instruments, and percussion. Liturgical dancing was also a regular feature, and joyful cries and shouting (as in Ps.81.1), characterized most celebrations associated with the Temple.

Many Psalms apparently refer to the leader of a choir and to what are probably the names of tunes (Ps. 56), and suggest that the psalms were sung by guilds of professional singers. The author of 1 Chronicles 16 claims that King David organized these choirs under a director called Asaph, who led the singers in a hymn of praise (1 Chron. 16.36). The author is in fact referring to his own (postexilic) time. The membership of these choirs was hereditary and they were drawn from groups within the Temple's Levite personnel.

such temporary shelters while the fruit was being harvested. In the Bible, however, they are no longer a mere agricultural necessity, but are constructed as a reminder of how the Israelites had once lived in booths in the wilderness during the period in which God brought his people out of slavery in Egypt (Deut. 16.13–15).

The postexilic period saw the beginnings of the Diaspora ("dispersal"), the establishment of permanent Jewish settlements outside Palestine. The Jerusalem Temple became the central authority for the regulation of the religious life of the scattered Jewish communities abroad. A tax of half a shekel was levied annually on every adult Jew throughout the world for the upkeep of the Temple.

An ancient Babylonian plaque from Nippur depicting a priest offering a libation to a seated god (above); worshipers leading animals to sacrifice (below).

SACRIFICE

Sacrifice, the offering up to a deity of an animal or other object, was a universal feature of early religion, and it played a prominent role in the cult of the Israelites. Many attempts have been made to explain its meaning, but there is probably no single theory that can take into account every aspect of sacrificial ritual. The Bible takes sacrifice for granted as a practice and provides no clear rationale for it. However, each type of sacrifice and its accompanying ritual is described in great detail in Leviticus 1–7, and these descriptions may provide some insight into the original purpose of the sacrifice.

One theory of sacrifice is that it is a gift to the deity. Certainly, in the societies of the ancient Near East it would have been unthinkable for an individual to approach a superior, whether human or divine, without bearing some sort of gift. Most types of animal sacrifice were no doubt originally intended as offerings of actual food. This idea especially fits the type of sacrifice known as the holocaust (from Greek *holos*, "whole" and *kaustos*, "burnt"), so called because the sacrificial victim was burnt on the altar (it is also known as the "whole-offering" or "burnt-offering"). Leviticus describes it as "an offering by fire of soothing odor to the Lord" (Lev. 3.16). This is reference to an ancient concept whereby the deity literally smelled the fragrant smoke of the offering and therefore looked favorably on those providing it. It occurs in Genesis, which relates that Noah made a burnt-offering after the Flood (see pp.26–7), and "when the Lord smelled the pleasing odor, the Lord said in his heart, 'I will never again curse the ground because of humankind' " (Gen. 8.20–21). This in turn recalls the Babylonian flood myth recounted in the epic of Gilgamesh. After the deluge, Utnapishtim emerged from his boat to offer a sacrifice, and the gods gathered "to smell the sweet savor." After the Exile, the holocaust became the predominant type of sacrifice. Elaborate daily offerings were made in the Second Temple that were viewed as gifts presented in homage to Yahweh.

The idea that through sacrifice the worshiper communes with God underlies another type of sacrifice, the "shared-offering." It is called this because part of the offering was given up to the deity, the worshipers eating the remainder. It was the most common form of sacrifice in early times, when every animal slaughtered was intended for a meal, in which the deity had his share. This was believed to create a bond between God and the human participants in the offering. In Leviticus much of the old communal character of this type of sacrifice has been lost: most shared-offerings are shared only by the male priests (compare Lev. 6.29; 7.6).

In the postexilic period, it came to be understood that the main aim of all types of sacrifice was expiation and atonement. Sacrifice neutralized the consequences of sin and uncleanness, and restored the people's relationship with God. When an animal was sacrificed, expiation was achieved by applying the blood of the victim to the altar of the Temple. The blood was "life," and its shedding represented not only death, but also the release of a vital force. This idea was applied primarily to the "sin-offering" or "purification-offering," in which the blood ritual was particularly prominent (Lev. 4.5–7), and to the "guilt-offering" or "reparation-offering." The compilers of Leviticus saw these types of offering, which are described in chapters 4–7, as central to the entire sacrificial system. For them, the overriding purpose of sacrifice was to cleanse the nation of sin and its punishment. All sacrifices were seen as expiatory, even those that did not involve the shedding of blood, as in Leviticus 5.11–13 and elsewhere (see also p.37).

The priesthood of the Second Temple

The structure of the Temple administration following the Exile was completed after a long process of evolution. Membership of the Temple personnel was hereditary, and the entire company of officiants was traditionally descended from Levi, a son of Leah and Jacob (see p.41) and the legendary ancestor of the Levites, the Israelite tribe which provided all members of the priesthood.

One group of Levites, the Temple servants, were not priests. The prophet Ezekiel states that they had been demoted from their priestly status because of their idolatry (Ezek. 44.10–13). It seems likely that they were descended from priests who had officiated at regional shrines, where foreign elements may have crept into the cult of Yahweh. Such shrines were abolished by King Josiah of Judah (see pp.100–01), who probably brought their redundant ex-priests to Jerusalem. The Temple servants carried out the more menial duties in the Temple, acting as doorkeepers and slaying the sacrificial animals (Ezek. 44.11). Even so, these Levites had an honored position: they provided the Temple music (see p.115) and retained the ancient priestly function of teaching the Law to the people. Some of the speeches in 1 and 2 Chronicles may reflect Levitical sermons of this postexilic period.

The main sacrificial rituals of the Second Temple were carried out by the priestly Levites, who claimed descent respectively from Zadok and Abiathar, the two priests of King David (2 Sam. 20.25). In the Second Temple priesthood, Zadok and Abiathar were both credited with descent from Moses' brother Aaron (see p.48), the first high priest of the Israelites and a member of the tribe of Levi (Exod. 6.19–21). But the Zadokite line had the leading position, probably because of a postexilic agreement between the Zadokites, who had controlled the Temple priesthood before the Babylonian captivity, and the priesthood of the older Israelite shrines, such as Shiloh. During the Exile, the regional clergy had taken over the Jerusalem Temple priesthood from the Zadokites. When the Zadokites returned from Babylon, the two groups came to an arrangement that restored the leading role of the Zadokites, but also enabled the regional clergy to share in the running of the Temple.

Above: *Aaron turning the Nile into blood (Exod. 7.21), from a Hebrew manuscript produced at Barcelona, Spain, in 1320.*

Below: *Aaron portrayed as high priest of the Israelites; a stained-glass window in Chartres cathedral, France.*

Before the Exile, the Israelite cult was headed by the king, although there was also a leader of the Jerusalem clergy, who was usually called simply "the priest." With the disappearance of the monarchy, he came to be referred to by a new term, "high priest." The high priest took over from the king as the head of the nation and inherited much of the royal ideology. Originally, only the king was anointed: in the postexilic period the high priest was anointed at his installation. (Some passages in the Bible suggest that ordinary priests were also anointed, but this does not appear to have happened in practice.) The high priest dressed in splendid vestments like those once worn by the king (see, for example, Sir. 45.8–13). He wore a turban, a royal headdress, adorned with a gold medallion or "flower"; this seems to derive from the practice of the Egyptian pharaohs, where such an emblem symbolized the eternal life of the king. The high priest's breastplate, adorned with precious stones, recalls those worn by the pharaohs and the kings of Syria, alluded to in Ezekiel 28.13. According to the apocryphal Wisdom of Solomon, the whole world was represented on his mantle (Wisd. of Solomon 18.24). The impression made by these vestments is shown by the ecstatic description of the high priest Simon (Simeon II, who held office 219–196 BCE) in Sirach 50: "When he put on his glorious robe and clothed himself in perfect splendor ... he made the court of the sanctuary glorious" (Sir. 50.11).

THE GOD OF ALL NATIONS

The strict monotheism (see box on p.106) that became a distinctive feature of Judaism after the Exile involved a missionary task: to bring about the recognition of Yahweh by all peoples. In the Bible, this universalistic vision is expressed in some passages of the postexilic prophets. Zechariah (see p.108), for example, looked to a time when all nations would go on pilgrimage to Jerusalem to pay homage to Yahweh (Zech. 8.22), while Third Isaiah (see p.111) speaks of the Temple as "a house of prayer for all peoples" (Isa. 56.7). Malachi (see p.111) even claimed that Yahweh was actually worshiped by the gentile nations (Mal. 1.11).

It has sometimes been suggested that Ruth, the protagonist of the book of that name, is depicted as the ideal proselyte, a symbol of Israel's mission to convert the Gentiles. The charming story of Ruth is set "in the days when the judges ruled" (Ruth 1.1) and deals with the ancestors of King David. It is placed in the Christian Bible between the books of Judges and Samuel, although in the Jewish canon it comes between Song of Solomon and Lamentations in the books called the Writings (Psalms, Proverbs, Job, Song of Solomon, Ruth, Lamentations, Ecclesiastes, Esther, Daniel, Ezra-Nehemiah, and Chronicles).

At the beginning of the story, the Bethlehemite Naomi and her husband Elimelech leave Judah during a famine to go to the land of Moab. While they are there, their two sons marry local women, Orpah and Ruth. Elimelech and the two sons die, and when the famine in Judah is over, Naomi prepares to return to Bethlehem alone, instructing her Moabite daughters-in-law to return to their families (Ruth 1.8). But Ruth insists on accompanying Naomi, and when they arrive in Bethlehem the story of her devotion to her mother-in-law soon spreads. It is harvest time, and Ruth finds work gleaning in the fields of Boaz, a rich farmer and kinsman of Naomi's late husband. Boaz comes across Ruth and extols her virtues in caring for Naomi and seeking refuge under the wings of the God of Israel (Ruth 2.11–12). Ultimately they are married and, to Naomi's joy, Ruth

Jonah and the Great Fish *(top), an illustration from* The Fine Flower of Histories, *a Turkish manuscript of 1583.*

JONAH

The author of the book of Jonah presents a novel and remarkable picture of God: when sinful human beings show contrition, God himself can "repent," because his nature is always to be merciful to Jews and Gentiles alike.

The author weaves a tale around the prophet Jonah, who is mentioned in 2 Kings 14.25. God sends Jonah to the sinful city of Nineveh to announce its destruction. At first, the prophet tries to escape from this obligation by fleeing on a ship, but God sends a storm. Jonah admits that Yahweh is angry with him and asks to be thrown overboard. He is swallowed by a "great fish" (Jon. 1.17), but prays for deliverance (Jon. 2) and is released on dry land. He goes to Nineveh, but the inhabitants repent of their sins and God spares the city. By a sign, God shows Jonah that he cares for and pities even non-Israelites (Jon. 4.6–11).

Naomi Entreating Ruth and Orpah to Return to the Land of Moab, *a print (1795) by William Blake.*

The Samaritans

As God's unique gift to Israel, the Law set his people apart from all other nations, and defined what it meant to be a true Israelite, a question which was central to the spiritual life of the nation after the return from Babylon. But the Law required constant study and interpretation, and various groups within the community differed in their point of view. Postexilic Judaism was not a monolithic faith, but contained a number of sects and parties with different understandings of the Law. This gave rise to internal tensions that are perhaps most clearly illustrated in the case of the Samaritans.

The remains of the Samaritan temple on Mount Gerizim. The Samaritan community, which today numbers in the hundreds, still carries out its traditional Passover sacrifices on the mountain.

In the New Testament, the Samaritans appear as an ethno-religious community living in the area of the former northern kingdom of Israel (from the capital of which, Samaria, they took their name). They claimed to be the descendants of the northern Israelite tribes of Ephraim and Manasseh, but the Jews by this time had long regarded them as a foreign people (see, for example, Sirach 50.26). Nevertheless, there was an awareness of a shared heritage – the gospel story of Jesus and the woman of Samaria (see p.274) refers to their common ancestor, Jacob – and it is best to view the Samaritans as a sect that emerged from the religious situation after the Exile.

The written Pentateuch was the chief authority for both Samaritans (who regard nothing else as Scripture) and Jews, although the Samaritan Pentateuch differs in a few respects from the Jewish one. Both groups held that there was only one legitimate sanctuary where sacrifice could be offered: for the Samaritans this was not Jerusalem but Mount Gerizim, near the city of Shechem (modern Nablus).

When and how the final break between the two groups took place is difficult to determine. The Bible regards the Samaritans as an ethnically-mixed population originally introduced by the Assyrians after the fall of Israel in 721 BCE (see p.95). They were thus tainted by foreign religious influences. But Samaritan tradition dates the split to the much earlier time of the judges (see p.66), when the priest Eli, the predecessor of the prophet Samuel, established the sanctuary of Shiloh as a rival to Gerizim. Neither of these claims contains the whole truth, and two factors probably contributed to a separation which in fact occurred gradually over some centuries. Political considerations must have played a part. The opposition to the reconstruction of Jerusalem and its Temple was led by the authorities of the old northern kingdom (see p.108). They doubtless adhered to their ancient sanctuary of Shechem, which they claimed had been founded by Joshua. However, the first-century CE Jewish historian Josephus claimed that the split was begun by dissident priests from Jerusalem. This may explain how the Samaritans came to possess the Pentateuch, which had been codified in Jerusalem (see p.112). It may also account for the erection on Mount Gerizim of a Samaritan temple (destroyed by the Jewish ruler John Hyrcanus in 128 BCE).

The truth may involve a combination of both factors. Samaritanism possesses features of ancient Israelite tradition, such as the slaughter of Passover lambs (which occurs to this day on Mount Gerizim), alongside aspects of postexilic Temple-based Judaism, such as the Pentateuch.

bears a son to continue the line of Elimelech. That son is Obed, who was to become the father of Jesse and grandfather of King David.

The date of Ruth is not certain, but it seems likely to have been a postexilic work. It has often been claimed that the story is a conscious protest against the policies of Ezra, in particular his ban on marriages between Israelites and foreigners (see p.110), and is therefore to be dated around the period of his activity. The author's purpose was to present the Moabite heroine as one who is not only welcomed into the chosen people as a devout adherent of Yahweh, but who also becomes the ancestor of Israel's most famous king. However, there is no clear evidence of polemic in Ruth, which has a distinctly folktale flavor. The story is probably best seen as the product of a group of writers who took folktales as their models.

The Egyptian goddess Isis suckling the young god Horus, a bronze and gold statuette of the period 664–332 BCE.

A TIME FOR ALL THINGS

"For everything there is a season, and
a time for every matter under heaven:
 a time to be born, and a time to die;
 a time to plant, and a time to pluck up
  what is planted;
 a time to kill, and a time to heal;
 a time to break down, and a time to
  build up;
 a time to weep, and a time to laugh;
 a time to mourn, and a time to dance;
 a time to throw away stones, and a
  time to gather stones together;
 a time to embrace, and a time to refrain
  from embracing;
 a time to seek, and a time to lose;
 a time to keep, and a time to throw away;
 a time to tear, and a time to sew;
 a time to keep silence, and a time
  to speak;
 a time to love, and a time to hate;
 a time for war, and a time for peace.
What gain have the workers from their toil? I have seen the business that God has given to everyone to be busy with. He has made everything suitable for its time; moreover he has put a sense of past and future into their minds, yet they cannot find out what God has done from beginning to end."

Ecclesiastes 3.1–8

WISDOM

The book of Proverbs represents the Israelite fund of popular wisdom. As its title implies, most of the work consists of strings of proverbial sayings, such as "A soft answer turns away wrath, but a harsh word stirs up anger" (Prov. 15.1) and "Pride goes before destruction, and a haughty spirit before a fall" (Prov. 16.18). The Bible attributes the book to King Solomon, the archetypal wise man (see pp.80–1), but in fact it consists of several collections dating from different periods.

It has sometimes been claimed that the sayings in Proverbs originated among pre-exilic royal courtiers and reflect their concerns. This is unlikely, since the great majority of the proverbs deal with agricultural, family, and personal matters. Others have suggested that those referred to in the Bible as "the wise," as in Proverbs 1.5, were a professional group of scribes. According to this theory, the proverbs formed the teaching material of scribal schools, which were probably attached to the pre-exilic Judean court. There were such schools in ancient Egypt and Mesopotamia, but there is no evidence for their existence in Israel. The

Ecclesiastes

Israel's sages were optimistic: they perceived an order in the universe, which human beings could also discover. If people aligned themselves with it, they would find happiness and prosperity; if not, misery and disaster would be their lot. This teaching is challenged in the remarkable book of Ecclesiastes. The author is described by the Hebrew term *Koheleth*, which was translated into Greek as *Ekklesiastes* ("a person who addresses a gathering"), hence the title of the book. This is traditionally rendered as "Preacher," (NRSV: "Teacher"). *Koheleth* in fact probably means something like "Speaker," and the work perhaps represents notes made for public lectures, although the writer identifies himself as King Solomon, the ideal wise man. He presents a view of Solomon that is very different than the traditional image of the king. The book opens with a famous declaration: "Vanity of vanities! All is vanity" (Eccles. 1.2), a phrase which recurs near the end (Eccles. 12.8). Solomon's wealth and wisdom are said to be total futility, "vanity and a chasing after wind" (Eccles. 1.16 and elsewhere). A world order exists, but the human mind cannot discover it (see sidebar, left), and what happens in life is very much a matter of chance. Above all, every human achievement is frustrated by the inevitability of death, a theme which haunts the writer and finds expression in a moving poem on old age and death that rounds off the book (Eccles. 11.7–12.8).

There are parallels with Ecclesiastes in ancient Near Eastern culture. The inexorability of death is the central concern of the Mesopotamian epic of Gilgamesh, and several Egyptian and Mesopotamian writings express utter skepticism about the possibility of achieving the good life. But Ecclesiastes is not wholly pessimistic. Human beings are not able to discover the ultimate secret of existence, but because God sends both good and evil, they can still prepare themselves for whatever benefits he may grant. Israel's old body of practical proverbial wisdom (see main text) can help them to do this (Eccles. 12.9–14).

book of Proverbs itself makes clear (Prov. 4.3–4) that proverbial wisdom was learned in Israel in the context of the family. "The wise" should not, therefore, be seen as a distinct professional class.

Nevertheless, the sophisticated poetical form of the sayings in Proverbs suggests that they were transmitted among intellectuals, such as "the officials of King Hezekiah of Judah," to whom one of the collections in Proverbs is ascribed (Prov. 25.1). Such intellectuals would have been influenced by the broader Near Eastern wisdom tradition, and Proverbs contains two collections attributed to non-Israelite authors, who are possibly Edomite sages (Prov. 30 and 31). In addition, the thirty sayings in Proverbs 22.17–24.22 ("The words of the wise") are adapted from the thirty chapters of moral instruction by the Egyptian scribe Amenemope.

The influence of a wider wisdom tradition is apparent in Proverbs 1–9, which are very different in character from the rest of the book. They consist of extended discourses that are typical of the wisdom literature of the ancient Near East, and "wisdom" represents a concept of order that is to be found both in nature and human society. A prominent word in Egyptian wisdom texts is *maat*, "world order," which was also the name of a goddess embodying divine order, harmony, truth, and justice. There are some parallels between the goddess Maat and the female personification of Wisdom (the Hebrew word for "wisdom" is feminine) who appears in the first nine chapters of Proverbs (from Prov. 1.20). She has also been compared with the Canaanite goddess Asherah, whose symbol was the tree of life: in Proverbs 3.18 Wisdom is called "a tree of life to those who lay hold of her." Wisdom is contrasted with another female figure, the "foolish woman" (Prov. 9.13–18) or "loose woman" (Prov. 5.3 and elsewhere). She personifies stupidity and also has features that recall a type of Near Eastern goddess whose dangerous charms often lured young lovers.

The oldest wisdom tradition in Israel has often been described as human-centered rather than God-centered. But later texts developed the concept of wisdom as an inseparable attribute of Yahweh, functioning as God's agent in creation and in the government of the world. The personified figure of Wisdom is described in Proverbs 8.23 as existing before the universe was made (a concept commonly found in Egyptian and Mesopotamian texts), and in Proverbs 8.27 as being with Yahweh in his work of creation. In 8.30, according to one reading of the Hebrew text, Wisdom is also depicted as a "little child" playing in the divine presence, which recalls the goddess Maat's position as daughter of Ra, the great sun-god of ancient Egypt. Even more mythological elements surround another Wisdom figure, who appears in chapter 24 of the apocryphal book of Sirach (Ecclesiasticus). The chapter is headed "The praise of Wisdom." Like the great Egyptian mother goddess Isis, Wisdom praises herself in language which links her closely with nature and fertility. For example: "I will water my garden and drench my flower-beds" (Sir. 24.31). But in spite of these foreign mythological resonances, Wisdom is linked with the central elements in Israel's national life. Like Yahweh, her dwelling is in Israel (Sir. 24.8), and she is identified with the written Law (Sir. 24.23).

A distinctive picture of divine wisdom can be found in another apocryphal book, the Wisdom of Solomon, a product of the Greek-speaking Jewish community of Alexandria in Egypt (see sidebar on p.126). In this book, Wisdom is described in terms that are drawn from Greek science and philosophy. She is the creative agent, the expression of the divine presence in everything (Wisd. of Sol. 7.22–24), and the director of Israel's history, especially at the Exodus (Wisd. of Sol. 10). At the same time she is an emanation of God, the outpouring of the divine glory, the radiance of eternal light, the mirror, and the image of God himself (Wisd. of Sol. 7.25–26).

A pharaoh making an offering before the goddess Maat, a silver gilt statuette of the period 1303–1224 BCE. The large feather in the goddess's hair represents justice and truth. In Egyptian belief, the heart of every dead person was weighed against this feather on scales in the underworld. If the heart was heavier, it was burdened by sin, and the soul of the deceased was handed over to a monster to be devoured.

THE SUFFERINGS OF JOB

The book of Job tells the story of a righteous and wealthy man, Job, who never relinquishes his faith in God, in spite of suffering a series of terrible personal misfortunes. The work can be seen as a theodicy, a vindication of the goodness of God in a world where he allows the existence of evil (see also p.34). Its date of composition is uncertain, but it was probably inspired by the postexilic doctrines of a transcendent, wholly righteous deity and of the central role of the Law. At this time, society came to be seen as fundamentally divided between the pious, who were the faithful observers of the Law, and the wicked, who were not. Divine justice demanded that the pious should be rewarded with God's favor, but clearly this did not always happen. The question arose as to how the sufferings of the righteous could be squared with the justice that was to be expected from God. It is this particular issue that the book of Job addresses. The book is not concerned with the problem of suffering in general (in other words, why there is pain, disease and death in the world): the whole work takes for granted that Job's suffering is the result of divine action. The figure of Job himself appears in the book of Ezekiel (Ezek. 14.14, 20), together with Noah and Daniel, as the epitome of a righteous man. He is the symbol of those who suffer, wherever and whenever they live.

Most of the work is poetry, but the verse narrative is contained within a prose prologue and epilogue which, taken together, have often been seen as constituting an ancient folktale. Following a common strand of Israelite

Satan

In the central part of the book of Job it is taken for granted that the source of Job's afflictions is God himself. This is in keeping with the Israelite belief that everything, both good and evil, comes directly from Yahweh. However, according to the opening narrative, it is Satan who causes the disasters that befall Job (Job 1.12; 2.6). He is not a figure of evil, but one of the heavenly court (Job 1.6), who acts only with God's permission. "Satan" is in fact a title, meaning the "Adversary" or "Accuser" (Hebrew ha-satan), a legal term roughly equivalent to "prosecuting attorney."

The development of Satan into a negative character can be seen in the Bible itself. In 2 Samuel, God incites David to take a census (2. Sam. 24.1), a sin which results in a devastating plague on Israel. But in the parallel passage of 1 Chronicles, it is Satan – here the term has become a proper name – who prompts the census and the plague (1 Chron. 21.1). This reflects the view of postexilic Judaism that God is the only source of goodness, and that the source of evil must therefore be sought elsewhere. As the being who tempted humanity to act against the divine will, Satan became God's enemy. He subsequently appeared in Jewish writings as the chief of the fallen angels (see sidebar on p.26), who were expelled from heaven for rebellion against God, and are the cause of evil in the world.

In the New Testament, Satan is the head of a realm of evil that stands in opposition to the kingdom of God. The satanic kingdom is manifested in the activity of the demons who afflict humankind.

Satan and the Rebel Angels *(1808), by William Blake (1757–1827).*

Left: Job on the Dungheap, *from the* Heures d'Etienne Chevalier, *ca. 1445, by Jean Fouquet (ca. 1420–ca. 1480). Job sitting on his dungheap (a reference to Job 2.8) in the company of his friends was very commonly depicted in this period.*

NEAR EASTERN TRADITION AND THE BOOK OF JOB

The kind of problem which concerns Job was also present to the minds of thinkers elsewhere in the ancient Near East, and a series of writings from Egypt and Mesopotamia suggests that the book of Job was partly influenced by this wider tradition. The texts in question differ considerably among themselves, both in form and content, but they contain elements which resemble features in the biblical work. The dialogue form occurs frequently to present a debate or dispute between a sufferer and another participant. The Babylonian poem *A Dialogue about Human Misery* recalls the pattern of dialogue between Job and his three friends: the sufferer and his friend speak in alternate stanzas, the sufferer uttering bitter complaints against apparent divine injustice and the friend responding with moralistic admonitions and general observations. Like Job, the sufferer often protests his innocence.

Both in Egypt and Mesopotamia, such dialogues are sometimes framed by a narrative describing the nature of the sufferer's distress. This is not to say that the book of Job depends directly on all or any of these texts. Its extraordinary poetical power and beauty set it apart from any other composition, either in the culture of the ancient Near East or in the rest of the Bible.

Wisdom teaching (see pp.120–21), this folktale is said to present an individual who patiently accepts his sufferings and, as a result, is finally rewarded by God. According to this theory, the author of Job replaced the central part of the old tale with a long poetic dialogue (Job 38.1–42.6). However, it is probably better to consider the book as a whole. It has often been asked what solution it offers to the problem of suffering, but it should perhaps rather be seen as a work of poetical imagination that offers a variety of insights, all of which illuminate the problem. When Job is overwhelmed by a manifestation of God (Job 38.1–42.6), the author points to the ultimate mystery and freedom of God's actions, but also stresses the validity of the human quest to grasp that mystery.

Job's friends, Eliphaz, Bildad, and Zophar, go to "console and comfort" him (Job 2.11) but are so shocked by his state that at first they cannot speak to him. When they do, they try, unsuccessfully, to persuade Job that he must be in a state of sinfulness to have suffered so much. The friends are often viewed as straw men, who reproduce stock arguments for Job (and the author) to refute. But what they say, although certainly not the last word, has its own worth. They stress the positive value of acceptance and of trust in the ultimate divine benevolence. As Eliphaz says to Job: "Agree with God, and be at peace; in this way good will come to you" (Job 22.21).

Portrait of Queen Esther, *by Andrea del Castagno (ca. 1421–1457).*

POPULAR STORIES AND LOVE SONGS

The Diaspora – the dispersal of many Jews from Palestine to various areas of the Near East (see glossary) – brought the Jews into contact with a wider world. One result of this was the production of a number of short stories, intended as popular entertainment, based on supposedly historical events involving the Jews and other nations. Such stories recount, with humor and irony, dramatic and bloodthirsty episodes, court intrigues, and the perils undergone by beautiful and virtuous heroines. They showed the (Jewish) underdog getting the better of mighty oppressors, a common folklore theme. As well as providing entertainment, therefore, the stories served as encouragement to Jewish communities living abroad in a sometimes hostile environment.

The tale of Esther, told in the book of that name, is set at the splendid court of Ahasuerus, the historical King Xerxes of Persia (486–465 BCE). It probably originates from Jews living in Persia, and it may well be a Jewish adaptation of a Persian composition: the names of the Jewish heroine, Esther, and her foster-father, Mordecai, seem to be derived from the Babylonian deities Ishtar and Marduk. Also, the book never mentions God, a lack that was filled by additions to the Greek translation of the work, which are now found in the Apocrypha. Esther lives with her adoptive father in the Persian capital, Susa. Following the disgrace of the Persian queen, Vashti (Esther 1.19), Esther's beauty and charm captivate the king and he makes her his new queen (Esther 2.17). Esther is pictured as a national savior, who successfully defends Mordecai and her fellow

Tobit and Tobias

The apocryphal book of Tobit consists of two interwoven narratives about the elderly Tobit and his son Tobias. It combines two common folklore motives, that of "the grateful dead" and "the unfortunate bride," and it also draws on the non-biblical story of Ahiqar, a wise man at the court of the Assyrian kings Sennacherib and Esarhaddon (see pp.94–5). It is a product of the Jews of the Diaspora, and a version of the story was found among the documents of the Jewish colony at Elephantine in Egypt (see p.111).

The tale is set in Nineveh and Mesopotamia. Tobit, a righteous man, goes blind (Tob. 2.10) and is reduced to poverty as a consequence of fulfilling the pious duty of burying the dead. But in spite of everything, he preserves his integrity and his piety is rewarded. His sight and prosperity are finally restored and he meets with a happy and peaceful end.

A limestone amulet, dating from ca. 650 BCE, which depicts the Mesopotamian demon Pazuzu.

The story of the young Tobias is a typical folktale. It takes the form of the hero's quest for a bride, Sarah, whose seven husbands have been killed by a demon, Asmodeus, on their wedding night (Tob. 3.8). (The idea that the wedding night is a dangerous time, when evil forces may attack the partners, is common in folklore.) Tobias's quest involves a long journey and he encounters various dangers. He is accompanied and aided on his mission to exorcise the demon (and also to restore his father's sight) by a young man called Azariah, who is Raphael, one of the archangels (see p.113), in disguise. The figure of Asmodeus is typical of a postexilic Jewish concern with demons, and reflects a belief that a realm of evil powers exists which acts against the agents of the true God.

Jews against the plots of the anti-Semitic royal counselor, Haman. She displays both skill and courage in carrying out the advice of Mordecai and in confronting Xerxes when her people are threatened. Haman is a stock villain, vain and scheming, who in the end is hanged on the gallows he had originally erected for Mordecai (Esther 6.10). The author displays a sound knowledge of Persian customs, but is not recording actual history. Rather, the narrative explains the origin of the Jewish festival of Purim ("Lots"; see Esther 9.24–28), a popular celebration with the character of a lively carnival. Purim is not mentioned in the Law (see pp.112–13), and probably represents the Jewish version of a festival that occurs in many cultures at around the time of the spring equinox.

The apocryphal book of Judith has much in common with Esther, but its heroine is a considerably more vigorous character, who recalls such figures as Deborah and Jael in Judges 4–5. The book is set against the background of a massive invasion of Judah under the tyrant Holofernes, the commander-in-chief of "King Nebuchadnezzar of Assyria," presumably a reference to King Nebuchadrezzar II of Babylon (605–562 BCE), the ruler who exiled the Jews (see pp.104–05). However, the author probably has in mind the events of the time of Antiochus IV Epiphanes (175–164 BCE), the ruler of the Hellenistic Seleucid empire, who prompted the revolt of the Maccabees (see pp.132–35).

Judith, a wealthy widow, singlehandedly averted the threat to her people by offering herself to Holofernes. When he fell asleep, dead drunk, she beheaded him with a sword (Jth. 13.8), and returned with his head in a bag to her home town of Bethulia. The assassination put the Assyrians into disarray and they were routed by the Israelites, who celebrated with a great song in praise of God and his agent, Judith (Jth. 16.1–17). The story portrays her as a model of Jewish womanhood, beautiful, incorruptible, strict in all religious observance, and ready to "put away her widow's clothing" (Jth. 16.7) and risk danger for the sake of her people and religion.

FROM THE SONG OF SOLOMON

"My beloved speaks and says to me:
'Arise, my love, my fair one,
and come away;
for now the winter is past,
the rain is over and gone.
The flowers appear on the earth;
the time of singing has come,
and the voice of the turtledove
is heard in our land.
The fig tree puts forth its figs,
and the vines are in blossom;
they give forth fragrance.
Arise, my love, my fair one,
and come away.
O my dove, in the clefts of the rock,
in the covert of the cliff,
let me see your face,
let me hear your voice;
for your voice is sweet,
and your face is lovely.' "

Song of Solomon 2.10–14

The Song of Solomon

The Song of Solomon (or Song of Songs) is unique in the Bible. It is a series of poems celebrating, in remarkably exotic and erotic language, the physical love between a man and a woman. Not surprisingly, it was long debated whether or not it should form part of Holy Scripture, and it probably owed its place in the canon to its attribution to Solomon, who is mentioned several times in the text. The traditional interpretation, both in Judaism and Christianity, is that it is an allegory of Yahweh's love for Israel. As far as Christians are concerned, it also expresses the love of Christ for his Church.

The work resembles some Egyptian love poems and Arabic wedding songs praising the physical charms of the bride. There are also parallels with sacred marriage texts concerning the union of the Near Eastern goddess Ishtar and her consort Tammuz, a shepherd (or the union of a king and queen as their representatives). Some have seen the book as an actual liturgy for such a divine marriage, but this is unlikely. It is more widely accepted that the work simply celebrates human love.

A relief of ca. 1750 BCE from Ashur depicting a god, possibly Tammuz (who is also known as Dumuzi).

Nevertheless, if the Song of Solomon is not a royal marriage liturgy, it may well be derived from one. The poems form a kind of antiphonal exchange between the man, the woman, and a chorus of her companions, the daughters of Jerusalem. The man is sometimes identified as King Solomon and appears as a shepherd, a regular royal title that recalls Tammuz. The poems themselves may go back to the period of the monarchy, while their final version probably belong to the postexilic age.

HELLENISM

THE JEWS OF ALEXANDRIA

Jewish communities grew up in many Hellenistic cities (see right), but the most important of them, in terms of both its size and influence, was Alexandria in Egypt. The Jews there did not abandon their ancestral faith and distinctive ways, but at the same time they sought to learn and interpret them through the medium of Greek learning. One significant product of this process was the translation of the Scriptures into Greek. This translation, the Septuagint, was so called because it was said to have been carried out by seventy (Latin *septuaginta*) scholars at the request of King Ptolemy II of Egypt. It aimed primarily to serve the needs of the Greek-speaking Jewish community, and it reveals how they understood their ancient Scriptures. But it also served an apologetic purpose, demonstrating that Jewish monotheism was not inconsistent with Greek philosophy.

The Alexandrian Jews also produced new religious writings in Greek, including the apocryphal Wisdom of Solomon (see p.121). The work is steeped in biblical history and Jewish tradition, but it also draws upon Hellenistic universalist ideas and philosophical forms. Notably, it treats the concept of Wisdom in terms of the doctrine of the *Logos*, the controlling rational principle of the universe, propounded by the Stoic philosophers.

Alexander the Great (see box on opposite page) was more than simply a remarkable military conqueror. He wished to unite the East and West on the basis of the Greek civilization of which he was the champion. The result was that a new culture, broadly called "Hellenism," arose. It combined Greek and Oriental elements and was dominant in the Near East from ca. 330 BCE until the final establishment of Roman supremacy in 30 BCE. Greek language and culture remained significant factors in the civilization of the Near East for many centuries thereafter.

Hellenism created an intellectual climate dominated by Greek literature, science, and, especially, philosophy, through which the idea grew up of one world that was the common possession of "civilized" human beings. The leading Greek philosophical schools of the time, the Cynics, Stoics, and Epicureans, emphasized cosmopolitanism and individualism. Barriers between peoples were breaking down, not least through the widespread adoption of *koine*, the everyday Greek language, which became the lingua franca of the civilized world.

The main impetus for the spread of Hellenism was the building or rebuilding of Near Eastern cities on the model of the cities of Greece. Alexander established several new cities (see map) where he settled his mercenary soldiers, and this policy was continued by his successors. Hellenistic towns sprang up throughout the region; they were attractive, open places, typically with a marketplace (*agora*) surrounded by law courts, temples, a theater, and a gymnasium. They provided a humane and elegant environment, in contrast to the cramped squalor typical of earlier New Eastern towns. Chief among the new cities was Alexandria in Egypt, founded by Alexander in 331 BCE. Alexandria, with its famous Library and Academy built by the Greek king of Egypt, Ptolemy II, came to epitomize the best of Hellenistic culture. However, Hellenistic civilization was neither universally welcomed nor open to everyone. Its economy rested on slavery, which in turn disenfranchised many. Administrative power was confined to Greeks and to those who adopted Greek ways. This factor played a central part in the reaction to Hellenism among the Jews of Palestine.

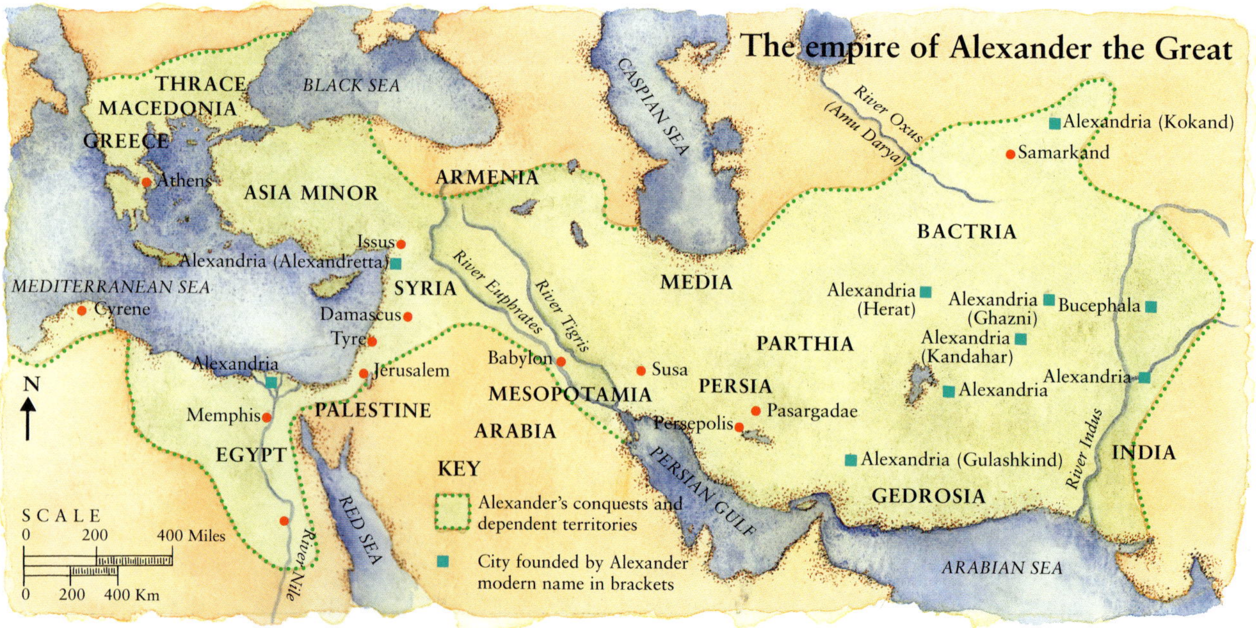

Alexander the Great and his successors

In 333 BCE, King Alexander III of Macedonia (Alexander the Great), defeated the Persian king Darius III at Issus in Syria (see map). In 331 BCE the whole Persian empire was in Alexander's hands, and, with visions of a world empire before him, he campaigned as far as India. Alexander's empire was shortlived: in 323 BCE he died in Babylon aged just thirty-three. His conquests were divided up among five of his generals, who embarked on several years of struggle. But by 312 BCE two of them, had emerged as the leading powers in the Near East. Ptolemy was established in Egypt, while Seleucus controlled roughly the territory of the old Babylonian empire (see p.102). Thus the old political pattern of the Near East was restored, with its two great imperial centers of Egypt and Mesopotamia. As in the past, Palestine lay between the two powers, and changed hands several times before the Seleucid ruler Antiochus III Megas ("the Great") won control of the area by his victory in 199 BCE at Paneas (later Caesarea Philippi; see map on p.145).

THE SELEUCID DYNASTY
All dates are approximate and BCE.

Seleucus I Nicator	312–281	Demetrius II Nicator (again)	129–125
Antiochus I Soter	281–261	Cleopatra Thea	125–123
Antiochus II Theos	261–246	Antiochus VIII Grypus	125–96
Seleucus II Callinicus	246–225	Seleucus V	125
Seleucus III Soter	225–223	Antiochus IX Philopator	114–95
Antiochus III the Great	223–187	Seleucus VI	
Seleucus IV Philopator	187–175	Antiochus X Eusebes	95
Antiochus IV Epiphanes	175–164	Antiochus XI Epiphanes	
Antiochus V Eupator	164–162	Philadelphus	
Demetrius I Soter	162–150	Demetrius III Philopator	
Alexander Balas (Epiphanes)	150–145	Soter	95–88
Demetrius II Nicator	145–139	Philip I	95–84
Antiochus VI Epiphanes	139–138	Antiochus XII Dionysios	87
Antiochus VII Sidetes	138–129	Philip II	84

Ruins of the Hellenistic city of Gerasa (modern Jerash, Jordan), one of a league of cities east of the Jordan known as the Decapolis (see map on p.137).

A mosaic from the Roman city of Pompeii depicting Alexander the Great at the battle of Issus. Alexander is on the left, his adversary, King Darius, in the center.

DANIEL

Daniel, the hero of the book of that name, begins as a legendary figure from the remote past. In the book of Ezekiel, he appears as a national hero, the embodiment of wisdom, perhaps from the city of Tyre. He is therefore of Canaanite origin: a figure called Daniel is the subject of one of the Canaanite texts from Ugarit (see p.66). In the Bible, he becomes one of the Jewish exiles in Babylon and the tales about him are of the same general type that became popular in the postexilic period (see, for example, pp.124–25). They illustrate how Jews ought to behave in a foreign and idolatrous environment, and how their trust in their faith and Law will be vindicated. In spite of severe crises from time to time, the Jews live mainly in peace, and some even attain high positions at the court of the Babylonians or their successors, the Medes and Persians.

The friendship and respect between Daniel and these foreign kings contrasts with the hostility between the Jews and the second-century BCE Hellenistic king Antiochus IV Epiphanes (see pp.132–33). Probably between 150 BCE and 100 BCE, an editor combined the popular cycle of Daniel tales with the remaining chapters of the present book, so that the stories became relevant to the persecutions of Antiochus IV. Nebuchadnezzar's golden image, which everyone was ordered to worship (Dan. 3.5), recalls Antiochus's decree that the Jews must "build altars and sacred precincts and shrines for idols" (1 Macc. 1.46), in particular his erection of "a desolating sacrilege" upon the sacrificial altar in the Temple of Jerusalem (1 Macc. 1.54). Similarly, Darius's claim of worship for himself (Dan. 6.7) may refer to Antiochus's assumption of divinity.

The stories reflect above all Daniel's traditional character as the supremely wise man. It is by his wisdom that he is able to interpret dreams, show his superiority to Babylon's magicians and soothsayers, and win the royal confidence, all of which is probably a conscious echo of the biblical story of Joseph (see pp.42–5). There is a powerful theological purpose underlying all the episodes: no adversary, however powerful, can successfully withstand the one true God, and even the greatest of kings are

BEL, SUSANNA, AND THE SONG OF THE THREE JEWS

As well as the work bearing his name, other stories about Daniel have survived. The apocryphal tales of Bel and the Dragon and of Susanna and the Elders, which are attached to the book of Daniel in the Septuagint, the Greek translation of the Hebrew Scriptures (see sidebar on p.126), display Daniel's wisdom not as the ability to interpret dreams, but rather as the practical astuteness reminiscent of King Solomon (see p.80). They have been described as the world's earliest detective stories.

The story of Bel and the Dragon is an example of Jewish propaganda against idolatry, which it mocks with a broad humor that would have delighted a popular audience. Similarly, the story of Susanna has elements that would appeal to popular taste: the attempted seduction of a beautiful young woman by two elders supposedly responsible for maintaining high standards in the community, and their clever unmasking by Daniel. The story ends with the comforting assurance that God will always protect and preserve virtue.

In order to lend the story of the three Jews in the fiery furnace a more overtly religious tone, the Septuagint inserts a prayer and a hymn (*The Prayer of Azariah* and *The Song of the Three Jews*) between Daniel 3.23 and 3.24. The inserted text, which is generally placed in the Apocrypha, is put into the mouths of Daniel's three Jewish companions (Azariah is the Hebrew name of Abednego) when they are thrown into the fiery furnace by Nebuchadnezzar. The three are made into models of Jewish piety, and their escape from the furnace is explained by the intervention of an angel who dampens the flames. *The Song of the Three Jews* (also translated as *The Song of the Three Children* and *The Song of the Three Young Men)* was adopted into the liturgy of the western Christian Church as two hymns known from their opening words in Latin as the *Benedictus es* (verses 29–34) and *Benedicite* (verses 35–68).

Susanna and the Elders *(ca. 1560), by* Iacopo Tintoretto *(1518–1594). Before the Renaissance, artists treated the scene of Susanna bathing with great modesty. However, from ca. 1500 the erotic aspect of the story tended to be emphasized.*

Belshazzar's Feast (1820), by John Martin (1789–1854).

compelled to recognize that their authority derives from God alone.

A recent discovery has thrown light on two of the most striking narratives in the book of Daniel. The first narrative relates how King Nebuchadnezzar of Babylon was afflicted with madness and banished from human society for seven years, until he turned to the God of Israel and was restored (Dan. 5.31–37). Nothing corresponding to this episode is known of the historical King Nebuchadrezzar II (605–562 BCE; see p.102). But something similar may have happened to Nabunaid or Nabonidus, the last Neo-Babylonian king (555–539 BCE), who left Babylon for ten years to live in the remote desert town of Teman in Arabia. Among the Dead Sea Scrolls (see p.139) there is a prayer attributed to Nabonidus, in which he relates that in Teman he suffered from an ulcer for seven years. After praying in vain to gods of gold, silver, bronze, iron, wood, and stone, he was cured by a Jewish exorcist, who ordered him to write his prayer to the glory of the true God.

There is another link with Nabonidus in the story of Belshazzar's Feast (Dan. 5). Nabonidus, not Nebuchadnezzar as in Daniel, was the father of Belshazzar (Bel-sharra-usur), who ruled as regent 552–542 BCE during his father's absence. In Daniel, Belshazzar holds a great feast at which the guests drink from sacred vessels looted from the Temple of Jerusalem and praise "the gods of gold and silver, bronze, iron, wood, and stone" (Dan. 5.3–4). Daniel condemns Belshazzar for exalting himself "over the Lord of heaven" (Dan. 5.23) and foretells the fall of Babylon. Belshazzar is killed "that very night" (Dan. 5.30). The gods praised at the feast are the same as those in Nabonidus' prayer, and the story of Belshazzar's idolatry and downfall may be adapted from a piece of propaganda by the Babylonian clergy originally aimed at the religious policies of Nabonidus' regime. The priesthood of Babylon objected to Nabonidus' preference for the moon god Sin over Marduk, Babylon's national god.

The Four Beasts and God Enthroned, *an illustration to Daniel's vision from the Beatus Apocalypse, produced at Santo Domingo de Silos, Spain, ca. 1100.*

APOCALYPTIC

In the later chapters of the book of Daniel, the figure of Daniel changes from an interpreter of other people's dreams to someone who himself has dreams and visions. The four visions which he sees represent a distinct literary genre known as "Apocalyptic." Daniel is probably the first fully apocalyptic work, although elements and anticipations of the genre are found in some of the prophets. The Greek term *apokalypsis* means the "revelation" or "unveiling" of some secret message at the point where it is about to be fulfilled. So Daniel is commanded to write down his words and keep them "secret and sealed until the time of the end" (Dan. 12.9). Daniel is associated with the Jewish Exile in Babylon in the sixth century BCE (see pp.106–07), but the apocalyptic message relates to the time of the persecution of the Jews by the Seleucid king Antiochus IV Epiphanes in the mid-second century BCE (see pp.132–33), when the book of Daniel was actually produced in its present form. Apocalyptic works often contain surveys of past world history in the form of predictions. Since these past events are known to have come true, they guarantee the seer's trustworthiness when he foretells what is yet to happen. All four of Daniel's visions are concerned with the empires of the ancient Near East, culminating in Daniel 11 with a detailed history of Palestine under the Ptolemies and the Seleucids and an even more detailed account of the career of King Antiochus IV Epiphanes.

It is widely accepted that Daniel represents the outlook of the Hasidean

The second book of Esdras

Daniel is the only apocalyptic writing in the canon of the Hebrew Bible, but the apocryphal second book of Esdras is a work with many resemblances and, indeed, references to it. Originally composed in Hebrew, it has extensive later Christian additions. It is attributed to the prophet Ezra (see pp.110–11), who is called Esdras in Greek. It is set in the time of the Babylonian Exile, but it was probably written ca. 100 CE and is actually concerned with the persecutions of the Roman empire and the fall of Jerusalem in 70 CE.

As with Daniel, the book mainly consists of the seer's visions. The most remarkable are the first four, in which Ezra engages in a dialogue with an angel, not simply about the sufferings of the Jews, but also about the general problem of the existence of evil in the world. The conclusion is pessimistic: the wrongs of the present can only be rectified in a new age still to come, which only a few will enjoy (2 Esd. 8.1). In other visions, there is animal symbolism. Rome is represented as an eagle, which is confronted by a lion, a nationalistic Messiah of the house of King David (2 Esd. 11.37–12.3), while the author takes up the human-like figure from Daniel and makes him into a pre-existent Messiah (2 Esd. 12.31–34).

Ezra becomes a second Moses, set to rewrite the Scriptures, which have been destroyed (2 Esd. 14.21). Five helpers produce ninety-four books in forty days. Twenty-four of these, representing the present Hebrew canon, are to be available for everyone, but the remaining seventy, representing apocalyptic and apocryphal writings, are only to be given to the "wise," for in them is "the spring of understanding, the fountain of wisdom, and the river of knowledge" (2 Esd. 14.47).

party, represented by the "wise" who alone will understand the significance of his message (Dan. 12.10). They expect deliverance through divine intervention rather than through the military prowess of the Maccabees (see pp.134–35), which the book dismisses as affording only "a little help." The work is written to encourage the faithful followers of the Law, by promising them that Antiochus's persecution will be short-lived and that the true religion will soon triumph.

Apocalyptic is the heir to the prophetic assurances that God will overthrow Israel's enemies and restore the nation, but its message of hope goes much further. It envisages a renewal of the whole cosmos, when the world will be restored to the ideal state in which it left the divine hand, and God's intervention will signal the final end of history. The powers of evil will be eradicated forever and the righteous dead will rise to enjoy eternal bliss. A belief in bodily resurrection appears for the first time in Daniel (Dan. 12.2), and the increasing acceptance of the doctrine probably owed much to the feeling that a just God would reward those, such as the Maccabee martyrs, who had died for their faith (see pp.134–35).

One immediately striking feature of Apocalyptic is its use of symbolic language and bizarre imagery. In part, this indicates the esoteric character of the Apocalyptic genre: its language is a code which only those who understand its secrets can unravel. However, the sources of this imagery lie in the myths and rituals of the ancient Near East. One example is the prevalence of animal symbolism, as in Daniel's opening vision, where the world empires are depicted as four terrible beasts: a winged lion; a tusked bear; a four-headed, four-winged leopard; and a "terrifying and dreadful" creature with iron teeth and horns (Dan. 7.3–7). They recall the fantastic monsters that appear frequently in Mesopotamian art, representing evil and demonic powers. In Daniel's vision they emerge from "the great sea," an image related to "the deep" of Genesis 1.2 and corresponding to the hostile watery chaos that appears in both the Babylonian Creation Epic and the Canaanite myth of Baal (see also p.16 and pp.20–1).

In such texts, the deity defeats the monster of chaos, and this motif is also found in Daniel. The last beast is destroyed, and then "one like a human being" is presented to the high god, "the Ancient One" (or "Ancient of Days") and given a universal kingship (Dan. 7.13–14). One epithet of the Canaanite supreme god El is "Father of Years," and the fact that the "one like a human being" comes with the clouds of heaven shows that he, too, is a divine being. The scene is based on El's grant of kingship to the young storm god Baal after Baal has defeated Yam, the Sea in a battle for sovereignty. An angel explains the vision to Daniel and identifies the "one like a human being" with "the holy ones of the Most High" – the pious of Israel – who "shall receive the kingdom and possess the kingdom forever – forever and ever" (Dan. 7.18).

The monstrous lion-headed bird Imdugud, whose beating wings were said to cause storms; a relief from the temple of the goddess Ninhursag at Tell-al-Ubaid (ca. 3000 BCE). Such fabulous beasts were common in Mesopotamian art and inspired the fantastic creatures in Daniel and other apocalyptic writings.

A Greek youth riding bareback and wearing a cloak, short skirt, and a wide-brimmed "cap of Hermes." This style of dress was widely adopted by young Jewish men in the hellenized cities of Palestine.

ANTIOCHUS IV EPIPHANES

Little is known of conditions in Judah after Ezra and Nehemiah (see pp.110–11), for the remainder of the Persian age, and the period of Ptolemaic Egyptian rule. It was probably a time of some stability for the Jewish population. Internally, the country was governed by a group of Jewish aristocratic and priestly families who formed the Sanhedrin or senate (Greek *synhedrion*, "council") under the high priest of the Temple.

With the coming of Seleucid rule (see p.127), dissension broke out among these families, some supporting the Ptolemies in Egypt and others the Seleucids in Syria. Rivalry was particularly intense between the Tobiads and the Oniads. The Ptolemies had appointed the Tobiads tax collectors for the whole of Palestine, while the Oniads held the high-priesthood and were usually pro-Syrian. However, both families switched allegiances whenever it seemed to their advantage. Their rivalry for the high-priesthood came to be a regular source of trouble, and was one cause of the repressive religious measures imposed on the Jews by Antiochus IV Epiphanes (175–164 BCE).

One dispute between the Tobiads and Oniads prompted a raid on the Temple treasures by Heliodorus, the minister of the Seleucid king Seleucus IV Philopator (187–175 BCE). The high priest Onias III objected to the raid on the Temple and was replaced by Jason, his brother. Jason paid higher tribute to Seleucus IV's successor, Antiochus IV, and promoted a policy of hellenization. He built a Greek-style gymnasium in Jerusalem, where even young priests took part in sports, running naked and sporting the Greek cap of Hermes. The Jewish enthusiasts for Hellenism (see pp.126–27), who were mainly among the Jerusalem upper classes, exchanged Hebrew names for Greek ones, abandoned circumcision, and regarded themselves in every respect as residents of a Greek city.

In 171 BCE, Jason was deposed in favor of Menelaus, who promised Antiochus even more tribute, which was paid for with some of the Temple treasures. When Jason attempted a return to power, Antiochus responded in

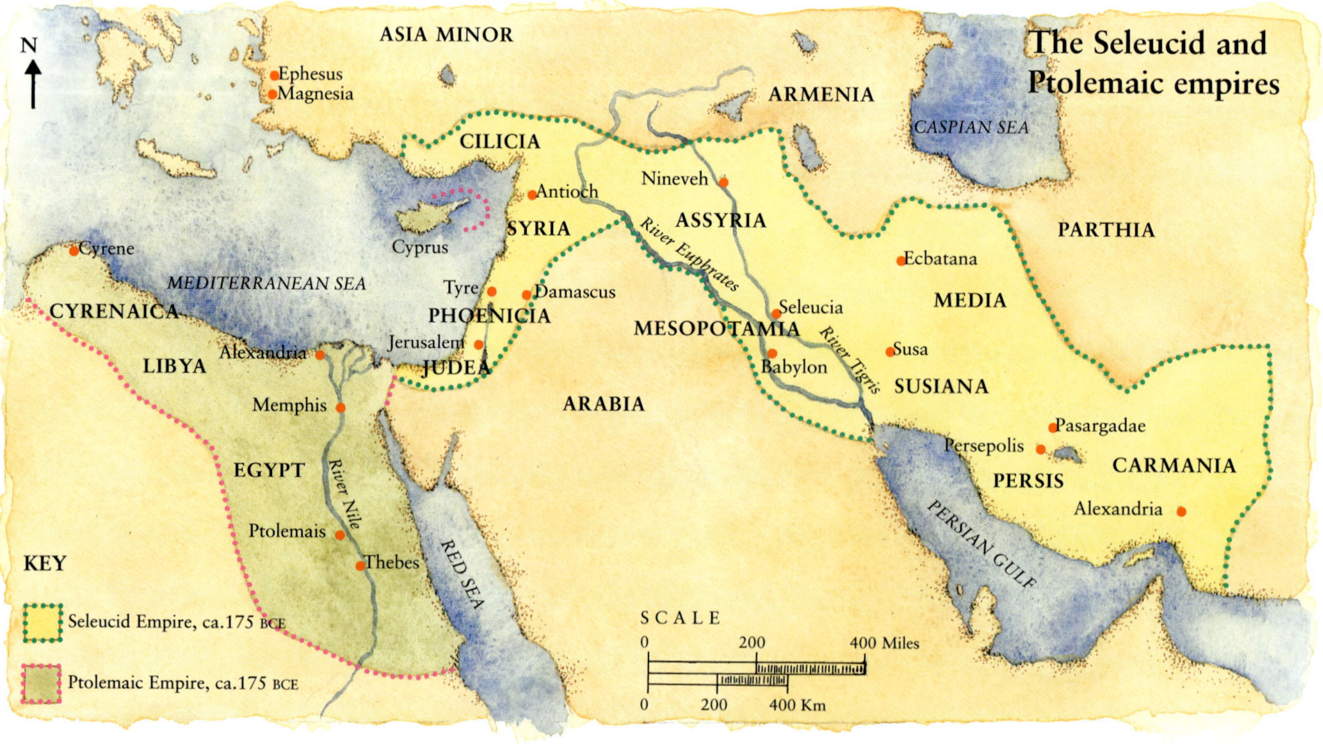

169 or 168 BCE by sacking the Temple. Then, in 167 BCE, he followed up this attack with a series of sweeping decrees that aimed to assimilate the Jews into his empire. Antiochus banned all the distinctive features of Judaism: circumcision, Sabbath observance, the keeping of feasts, and the purity laws. At the same time, sacred places were defiled, books of the Law were burned, and Jews were forced to attend sacrificial meals of pork (which was unclean to Jews) and ceremonies honoring pagan deities. In imposing these drastic measures, Antiochus would only have been in contact with the pro-hellenizing party in Jerusalem, who shared his objectives, and would not have anticipated any serious resistance. But in this he proved to be very much mistaken (see pp.134–35).

Unsurprisingly, Antiochus appears in the blackest light in Jewish tradition, but he was in fact an able and far-sighted ruler, who endeavored to counter the threat to his empire posed by the growing power of Rome. His father, Antiochus III, had been defeated by the Roman army at Magnesia in 190 BCE. Under the terms of the peace treaty, he had lost Asia Minor, been forced to pay a crippling indemnity, and had to send the young Antiochus as a hostage to Rome, where he remained for twelve years. The lesson was driven home for Antiochus himself when a Roman general ignominiously thwarted his hopes of conquering Egypt in 168 BCE.

To meet the Roman menace, Antiochus pursued a vigorous policy of hellenization in order to unite the various peoples of his heterogeneous kingdom. His aim was not to suppress the worship of local deities, although this was how it appeared to many Jews, but to assimilate them all to "Zeus," a name which had come to mean little more than "God." Antiochus himself took the title *Epiphanes* ("[God] Manifest"): he was the manifestation of God, by whatever name God might be worshiped.

The altar erected by Antiochus in the Temple of Jerusalem was called by the Jews "a desolating sacrilege" (1 Macc. 1.54). This is in fact a malformation of the name Baalshamaim, the Lord of heaven, a widely venerated Semitic god. Under Antiochus, the Temple was dedicated to Olympian Zeus, Zeus Olympios. Hence Antiochus sought to claim that Yahweh, Baal, and Zeus were the same deity under different names, depending on whether the worshiper was Semitic or Greek.

A silver four-drachma coin of Antiochus IV Epiphanes. The portrait of the king on the obverse (left) depicts him as the god Zeus; the reverse shows Zeus enthroned carrying the goddess Nike (Victory). The legend reads: "King Antiochus, God Manifest, Bearing Victory."

The Sack of Jerusalem *by Antiochus IV Epiphanes, a 15th-century French manuscript illumination.*

The Triumph of Judas Maccabeus *(1635), by Peter Paul Rubens (1577–1640).*

THE MACCABEES

Seleucid rule in Palestine came to an end as a result of the Maccabees, so-called from the rebel leader Judas Maccabeus. The Maccabee (or Maccabean) movement restored Jewish religious freedom after the repression of Antiochus IV (see pp.132–33), achieved political independence, and re-established a Jewish monarchy, albeit of a typically Hellenistic kind.

In one respect, the Maccabee rebellion was an expression of the long-standing tension between the more conservative Jews of the countryside and the cosmopolitan, hellenized capital. It was sparked off by a country priest, Mattathias, of a family called the Hasmoneans after his great-grandfather Hasmoneus. Initially, the struggle took the form of a guerrilla war to rescue the Law "out of the hands of the Gentiles and kings" (1 Macc. 2.48). The group around Mattathias and his family were joined by the Hasideans, the "pious" or "faithful," a group mentioned for the first time in 1 Maccabees 2.42. The Hasideans were specially devoted to the Law, and were prepared to die for it. They seem to have been the ancestors of similar groups within Judaism in the Roman period, such as the Pharisees and Essenes, and they always retained a separate identity from the Maccabees, from whom they eventually withdrew. The Maccabees were more concerned with the survival of the national religion than with the strict observance of the Law. When they heard of the massacre of a thousand people who had refused to take up arms on the sabbath, they resolved to retaliate if they were attacked on the day of rest (1 Macc. 2.41).

After the death of Mattathias, leadership passed to his third son Judas, nicknamed *Maccabeus*, "The Hammer," because under him the rebellion moved to full-scale war with the government forces, which Judas defeated in a series of battles. He eventually occupied Mount Zion (1 Macc. 4.37) and purified the Temple, which was re-dedicated, with great and joyful ceremony, on the twenty-fifth of Kislev (November–December) 164 BCE, the year Antiochus IV died. The day was ordered to be observed annually (1 Macc. 4.59), and remains as the Jewish feast of Hanukkah, "Dedication."

Recognizing Judas's success, Lysias, the regent of the boy king Antiochus V, rescinded Antiochus IV's religious decrees and deposed and executed the pro-hellenistic high priest Menelaus. Jewish religious liberty was at last restored, but it did not mean political freedom. The Jews were still subject to the Seleucid empire and obliged to pay taxes to it, and the Akra, the Greek garrison that Antiochus IV had established in Jerusalem, remained. The office of high priest continued to be in the Seleucid king's hands. On the appointment of the high priest Alcimus, who was of correct priestly lineage (unlike earlier royal choices), the Hasideans broke with Judas and backed the royal appointee. However, when they discovered that Alcimus was an ardent hellenizer, they soon returned to the Maccabee cause.

Independence now became the Maccabees' goal. The Seleucids still had enough force to defeat Judas, who fell in battle in 160 BCE (1 Macc. 9.18), but the kingdom then became increasingly weakened by dynastic rivalries. Jonathan, Judas's brother and successor, played one claimant to the throne off against another and, in return for his support, gained the office of high priest for himself and won more privileges for what was rapidly becoming a Jewish state. Full independence was achieved under the last Maccabee brother, Simon Hasmoneus. The Seleucid king Demetrius II (145–139 BCE) recognized Simon as high priest and granted him exemption from tax, effectively acknowledging the sovereignty of Judah. Simon secured his rule by taking the Akra, the last stronghold of foreign domination. The Jews began to date contracts and agreements from 142 BCE, "the first year of Simon the great high priest and commander and leader of the Jews" (1 Macc. 13.42).

A tomb built in Jewish-Hellenistic style in the Kidron valley, Jerusalem (see map on p.152). It is traditionally known as the "Tomb of Absalom," the son of King Saul, but it was probably built in the 1st century BCE.

The first two books of Maccabees

The apocryphal first book of Maccabees begins with the career of Alexander the Great and ends with the death of the Hasmonean leader Simon, under whom the Jews obtained effective independence (see main text), and whose reign is depicted in idealistic language. The book exists only in Greek, but it was almost certainly written in Hebrew by a supporter of the Hasmonean dynasty founded by the Maccabees (see main text). It is recognized as a basically reliable and sober narrative, but it has its own bias. Its aim is to present the Hasmoneans as the divinely chosen saviors of the nation, and the author models himself on earlier Hebrew historical writings, such as the books of Samuel and Kings. Not surprisingly, he tends to exaggerate the successes of his heroes and to play down their defeats.

The second book of Maccabees is a Greek writing, both in language and style, an abridgement of a five-volume work by Jason of Cyrene in North Africa. This kind of Hellenistic historiography, as the author himself tells us in a preface, aimed to give pleasure to readers and to incite their emotions by concentrating on incidents of drama and pathos (2 Macc. 2.29–32). The book is marked by a number of highly rhetorical set pieces, such as Heliodorus's attempt to despoil the Temple and, especially, the account of the martyrdom of a mother and her seven sons.

The author sees the Maccabean revolt as a religious conflict between Hellenism and Judaism, and he is the first writer to use these terms in contrast. He carries the story no further than what he presents as the final decisive victory of Judas Maccabeus.

THE COMING OF ROME

There is no biblical record for the period between the accession of the Hasmonean ruler John, son of Simon, in 134 BCE (1 Macc. 16) and the reign of Herod the Great. Like the Seleucids, whose rule they had thrown off, the Hasmoneans ultimately fell victim to dynastic rivalry and infighting that was exploited by the growing imperial power of the Mediterranean region, Rome. By the period of the New Testament, Judea had become part of the Roman empire, governed by a new dynasty of client kings: the Herods.

HYRCANUS TO HEROD

In the final years of Hasmonean rule, those who had begun as the opponents of Hellenism ended as typical Hellenistic princes, although always with a clear Jewish identity. John, the son of Simon (see p.134), succeeded in 134 BCE, took the Greek name of Hyrcanus, and embarked on a policy of aggression. He extended his borders and destroyed the Samaritan temple on Mount Gerizim (see p.119). Like other Hellenistic rulers, he minted coins bearing his name and Greek fertility symbols. He was opposed by the Pharisees, the spiritual descendants of the Hasideans (see pp.134–35), who plagued the dynasty from now until its fall. The Pharisees accused the Hasmoneans, who were not of priestly lineage, of profaning the office of high priest out of a desire for military and secular power.

John died in 104 BCE, but his son, Alexander Jannaeus (103–76 BCE), continued his militaristic tendencies. He acquired a reputation for his brutal suppression of internal opposition. By conquest and forced proselytization, he restored the Jewish state to its extent under David and Sol-omon. As well as being high priest, he assumed the title of king, which appeared in Greek (*basileos*) on his coins. But after Jannaeus died the Hasmonean state lapsed into prolonged dynastic rivalry. Increasing popular unrest was spearheaded

Herod the Great

Whatever his personal faults, and they were many, Herod was an outstanding figure among Rome's client kings and not undeserving of his epithet "the Great." He strengthened his realm economically and extended its borders (see map). He understood that his authority rested on Rome's favor and preserved his position by skillful diplomacy in the face of the power struggles that took place in Rome during his reign.

The remains of the fortress and palace of Herodium, built on an artificial hill by Herod the Great who was also buried here.

Herod's state had a very mixed population, which he sought to unify by a thoroughgoing and largely successful policy of hellenization. He founded a number of splendid cities as standard bearers of Hellenistic culture, with theaters, baths, marketplaces, gymnasia, and temples. However, unlike the Seleucids (see pp.132–33), he respected Jewish religious sensitivities: he rebuilt the Temple on a magnificent scale (see p.85 and map on p.152), and recognized the respect in which the Pharisees were held by the people. He tried to win the Pharisees' favor by observing their ritual laws, and exempted them from taking an oath of allegiance to him.

In spite of all his efforts, Herod never really won the hearts of the Jews, who regarded him as a foreigner (he was half-Idumean), and resented his dictatorial rule, control of the high-priesthood, and hellenizing ways. His ruthless suppression of potential opposition within his own family meant that he was unable to organize an orderly succession. In the following century, this failure ultimately spelled disaster for the nation.

by the Pharisees, who campaigned for the abolition of the kingdom and the establishment of a theocracy under a high priest of the legitimate line. The collapsing Seleucid state was powerless to intervene in Judah, so the Hasmoneans survived for a time. In 64 BCE, a brilliant young Roman consul, Pompey, captured Antioch in Syria and finished off the Seleucid empire. The arrival of the expanding Roman empire sealed the fate of the Hasmoneans. Pompey turned to Judah, where Jannaeus's sons, Hyrcanus II and Aristobulus, sought to outbid each other to win Roman support. Pompey sent the legate of Syria, Scaurus, who supported Aristobulus, but then Pompey himself took Jerusalem after a siege. He entered the Holy of Holies in the Temple – a sacrilege which pious Jews never forgot – but also restored the regular sacrifices and confirmed Hyrcanus II as high priest, exercising authority under the Syrian legate.

The real power behind Hyrcanus II emerged as Antipater from Idumea, whose people, the descendants of the Edomites, had been forcibly converted to Judaism by John Hyrcanus I. When Julius Caesar supplanted Pompey as Roman leader, Antipater was appointed Roman procurator of Judea (the Roman name for Judah) and his son, Herod, became military governor of Galilee. Herod's success in this post led the Roman Senate to appoint him king of Judea in 40 BCE. Although a client of Rome, Judea was once again a kingdom (see box on opposite page).

THE SYNAGOGUE

One of the most significant developments in Judaism by the beginning of the Roman period was the rise of the synagogue. Its origins are obscure: it is first mentioned in texts from the first century CE, and the earliest remains of synagogues in Palestine date from this time. But by then it was clearly a well-established institution, and had probably come into being during the two preceding centuries. In any case, synagogues were widespread both in Palestine and in the Diaspora.

The synagogue reflected the central place held by the Law in Judaism of the period, for its focal point was the reading of Scripture and the exposition of the Law. It was thus essentially a place of instruction, not of worship. Synagogue worship developed fully only after the destruction of the Temple in 70 CE, when aspects of the Temple cult, such as psalmody and prayer, were transferred to it. Synagogue and Temple should not be seen as in opposition to one another, but rather as complementary, not least because the Law taught in the synagogue authorized the sacrifices and priesthood of the Temple. The synagogue was one sphere of activity of the Pharisees (see p.164), who employed it to teach the Law, and their interpretation of it, to the mass of the people. After the fall of the Temple, Pharisaic doctrine and the synagogue were key elements in the development of Judaism.

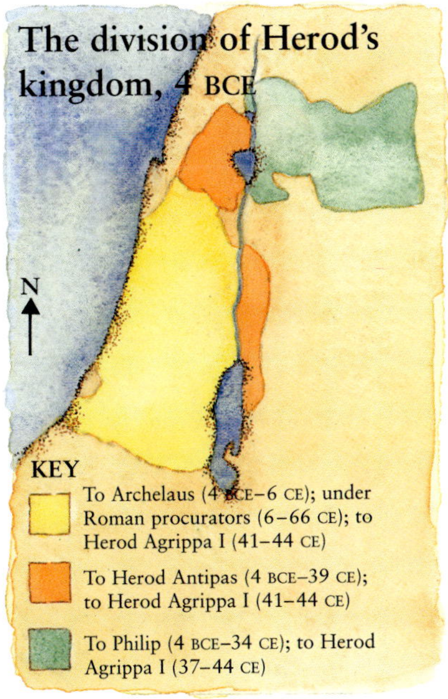

THE HERODIAN DYNASTY
(See also maps on p.137.) All dates are approximate and CE *unless stated.*

Herod the Great, *king of the Jews*	37–4BCE
Archelaus, *ruler of Judea*	4BCE–6
Herod Antipas, *ruler of Galilee, Perea*	4BCE–39
Herod Philip (Philip), *ruler of lands east of Galilee*	4BCE–34
Herod Agrippa I, *king of lands east of Galilee*	37–44
king of Judea, Galilee, Perea	41–44
Herod Agrippa II, *king of lands east of Galilee*	53–100
king of part of Galilee, Perea	56/61–100

Herod the Great
- Aristobulus (died 7 BCE)
  - Herod Agrippa I
    - Herod Agrippa II
- Archelaus
- Herod Antipas
  - Philip

Two "suicide lots" (above) found at Masada (right), the last outpost of Jewish resistance to the Romans during the war of 66–73 CE*. When faced with defeat, the Zealots defending Masada wrote their names on shards of pottery and drew lots to determine the order in which they would commit suicide. On the top right of the aerial view can be seen the ramp built by the Romans to break the siege.*

JUDEA UNDER THE ROMANS

In his will, Herod the Great specified that his kingdom was to be divided among his three surviving sons (see map on p.137). This arrangement was ratified by the Roman emperor Augustus, but he withheld the title of king from Herod's successors: there was to be no danger of their claiming independence from Rome. Archelaus was given Judea, Samaria, and Idumea; Antipas received Galilee and Perea; and Philip gained the mainly non-Jewish region to the north and east of Lake Galilee.

All three behaved as typical Hellenistic rulers, and while this worked well for areas with mixed populations, Archelaus was no more acceptable to the strongly Jewish populace of Judea than his father had been. After a troubled reign, complaints from his subjects led to his deposition by Augustus in 6 CE, and Judea became an imperial province under a Roman procurator, who resided in Caesarea. It remained a procuratorial province until 66 CE, apart from the period 37–44 BCE, when the emperor Caligula made Herod's grandson, Herod Agrippa I, king of the region.

Procuratorial rule proved a disastrous failure. Most of the procurators proved deeply insensitive to Jewish religious feelings, and their actions were often tactless or even deliberately provocative. The most famous procurator, Pontius Pilate (in office 26–36 CE), took Roman military standards bearing pagan images into Jerusalem, and plundered the Temple treasury to build an aqueduct. Such acts inevitably provoked riots, and the procurators tended to overreact and put them down with great brutality. There was often disorder during the great festivals, when Jerusalem was crowded with pilgrims. Things might have gone better if the Romans had

been able to govern, as they did elsewhere, through a ruling class that was acceptable to the people. But the Judean aristocracy enjoyed little popular support, and the high priests and the Sanhedrin (see p.132) were regarded as Roman puppets. Economic troubles added to the general misery, and Roman taxation was a heavy burden on small farmers and merchants.

As a consequence, there were constant attempts at rebellion, led by individuals with messianic claims, who gathered large followings by promising that God was about to overthrow the hated Romans. Law and order became precarious: sources speak of outright banditry and of the *Sicarii*, "Dagger Men," who assassinated those associated with the Romans, including, on one occasion, the high priest. The procurators countered the unrest with harsh measures that only fueled Jewish resentment, setting the scene for the final catastrophe. The great Jewish War (66–73 CE) broke out when the last procurator, Gessius Florus, requisitioned a heavy payment of gold from the Temple treasury and provoked a riot which proved uncontrollable. Florus was forced to abandon the city to the rebel. The revolt was in part a civil war, a popular uprising against the Jewish upper classes, whose authority in Jerusalem was destroyed.

Rebellion spread to the whole country and at first the Jews were successful, defeating an army sent by Cestius Gallus, the military governor of Syria. In Rome, the seriousness of the situation was quickly realized, and the emperor Nero (54–68 CE) dispatched a general, Vespasian, to quell the revolt. He first subdued Galilee, and by 68 CE prepared to advance on Jerusalem. There was a respite for the rebels when, after Nero's death, Vespasian left for Rome to assume the throne, leaving his son Titus (later emperor) to continue operations. In 70 CE, after a long siege, Titus captured Jerusalem, destroyed the Temple, and took its treasures as booty. Resistance to Rome was now led by the Zealots, a fanatical nationalist party. They held out until 73 CE, when their last stronghold, Masada, the former mountain fortress of King Herod, finally fell. Almost the whole garrison – a thousand men, women, and children – committed suicide rather than surrender. Jewish hopes for an independent state in Palestine were to remain unfulfilled for another nineteen hundred years.

Part of the arch erected in Rome in honor of the emperor Titus (79–81 CE). It shows Temple treasures paraded through Rome after Titus's sack of Jerusalem in 70 CE.

ROMAN PROCURATORS OF JUDEA
All dates are approximate and CE.

Coponius	6–8
Marcus Ambivius	9–12
Annius Rufus	12–15
Valerius Gratus	15–26
Pontius Pilatus (Pilate)	26–36
Marullus	37
Herennius Capito	37–41
[King Herod Agrippa I ruled]	37–44
Cuspius Fadus	44–46
Tiberius Alexander	46–48
Ventidius Cumanus	48–52
Marcus Antonius Felix	52–60
Porcius Festus	60–62
Clodius Albinus	62–64
Gessius Florus	64–66

Qumran and the Dead Sea Scrolls

Not everyone in Judea responded to Roman rule with violence, and one group in particular simply withdrew into its own idealistic community. They were the Essenes, whose writings – the so-called "Dead Sea Scrolls" – and ruined buildings have been recovered since 1947 at the remote desert site of Qumran by the Dead Sea.

The Essenes probably began as a protest movement by priests of true, that is Zadokite, priestly descent (see p.117), against the non-Zadokite priesthood of the Hasmoneans (see p.134). They were a strongly ascetic group, with strict disciplinary rules, holding possessions in common and with their own distinctive worship, in which communal meals figured prominently. Their scrolls show that their main occupation was the study of the Scriptures, which in their own writings they interpreted according to the teachings of their founder, who was called the Teacher of Righteousness. They regarded themselves alone as the true Israel, and their separation from the rest of Jew-ish society was absolute. Essentially, they were a quiet-ist apocalyptic sect, preparing themselves for the coming judgment, when they would inherit God's promises for Israel. A new Temple, they believed, would then take the place of the unclean Temple of Jerusalem.

Not all Essenes lived at Qumran and there were many Essene communities all over the country. It has been suggested that both John the Baptist and Jesus may have been linked with the Essenes, at least for part of their careers. There are a number of similarities between the outlook of the Essenes and the teachings of John (see p.214), Jesus, and the early Church. However, there are also many profound differences, and any close connection is unlikely.

THE NEW TESTAMENT

Left: The Tree of Jesse, *from the Ingeborg Psalter (French, ca. 1210). The descent of Jesus from Jesse, the father of King David (Matt. 1.6–16; compare Luke 3.23–38) was commonly represented in European illuminated manuscripts of the 12th–14th centuries. The genealogy was shown as a tree with Jesse sleeping at its roots and Jesus at the top. Between them are (from below) David, Solomon, and Mary.*

JESUS CHRIST: THE SETTING

Above: The Holy City of Jerusalem, *part of a famous 6th-century Byzantine mosaic depicting the Christian sacred sites of Palestine.*

Opposite: *The Sea of Galilee near Tiberias. Galilee, especially its lake margins, provided the setting for much of Jesus' ministry.*

THE LAND OF PALESTINE

The main events of Jesus' life took place in Palestine, a region that may conveniently be understood as the land west of the river Jordan, from Dan in the north to Beersheba in the south—the traditional "land of Israel" as defined in the Hebrew Scriptures (for example, Judg. 20.1)—and the territory immediately to the east of the Jordan. Ironically, perhaps, the name "Palestine" comes from the Philistines, Israel's great enemies, who in fact occupied only the southwestern coastal area. The term was first used of the wider region by the Greek historian Herodotus (fifth century BCE). In spite of its small size, Palestine's strategic position as a bridge between two continents gave it a pivotal role in the international politics, commerce and culture of the ancient Near East. However, there is little awareness of this wider context in the gospels as compared with the Hebrew Scriptures.

The region is delimited by the natural boundaries of the Mediterranean to the west, Mount Hermon to the north, and the Syrian and Negeb deserts to the east and south. Within these bounds, Palestine falls into four natural regions, each running roughly from north to south. First, the coastal plain stretches from the Phoenician city of Sidon (just north of Palestine as defined here) down to Gaza, interrupted only by the highlands of Mount Carmel and the Ladder of Tyre. There are brief mentions of a visit by Jesus to the region of Sidon and its southerly neighbour, Tyre (Mark 3.8 and parallels), but generally speaking the Mediterranean seaboard lay outside the sphere of his activities.

To the east of the coastal plain, the central mountain range runs from

The Jordan river in the north of Israel. It forms part of Palestine's natural eastern frontier and features prominently in Israelite history. It was the setting for the ministry of John the Baptist and for the baptism of Jesus.

Galilee to Judea. In ancient times this was the heart of the country. It was the center of its trade and agriculture—although some parts were more fertile than others—and the setting for almost the whole of Jesus' ministry. At the southern end of the range lie the hill country and wilderness of Judea. The hill country encompasses Jerusalem, Bethlehem, and other sites associated with Jesus. The wilderness, to the east of the city, is where John the Baptist began his ministry (see pp.214–15) and Jesus was tempted by Satan (pp.218–19). Adjoining the lower Jordan and Dead Sea region, it is not true desert, but rather uncultivated pastureland, which could provide the Baptist with a sparse diet of locusts and wild honey (Matt. 3.4 and parallels).

An ornate column capital from Beth-Shean (Scythopolis), the only Decapolis city west of the Jordan. In the 1st century CE these Greco-Roman cities were places of great wealth and splendor.

It was well enough watered to allow some basic agriculture.

The third region is the Palestinian section of the Afro-Asiatic great Rift Valley, through which the Jordan pursues a meandering course from north of Lake Huleh via the sea of Galilee down to the Dead Sea. The Jordan valley—which is below sea level for most of its length—is arid terrain except for the verdant margins of the river and freshwater lakes. The Baptist's main activity took place on one or both banks of the lower Jordan, in an area that includes the unlocated sites of "Aenon and Salim" (John 3.23), "Bethany cross the Jordan" (John 1.28), and of Jesus' own baptism (see pp.216–17).

Transjordan is the name given to the fourth broad region of Palestine, the hilly terrain lying east of the Jordan and the Dead Sea. In the north of this region, which is physically quite similar to the central mountain range, the snow-capped heights of Mount Hermon may have been the scene of the Transfiguration (see p.236). It was in Transjordan that Jesus drove an army of demons into a herd of swine, in the region of the Decapolis (Matt. 8.28–33; Mark 5.1–13; Luke 8.26–33; see sidebar, left). The gospel accounts suggest that on his final journey to Jerusalem, Jesus went over the Jordan (Matt. 19.1; Mark 10.1) into the area called Perea ("Land Beyond [the Jordan]"), where he attracted large crowds and performed healings, before crossing the river once more to enter Judea at Jericho (Mark 10.46).

There were two main types of settlement in first-century Palestine: the "town" or "city" (Greek *polis*) and the "village" (*kome*). They were not sharply distinguished in terms of size. A *kome* could have a larger population than a *polis* and perhaps the only real distinction was that "villages" were usually unwalled while "towns" were walled, such as Nain in Galilee, at the gate of which Jesus restored a young man to life (Luke 7.11–17). Archaeological evidence suggests that most settlements were quite small and inhabited mainly by Jews, while the bigger cities were more cosmopolitan, with large non-Jewish populations.

Towns and villages had a simple ground plan. Narrow streets and alleyways lined with modest houses converged on a large open marketplace, the hub of social and commercial life, which lay just inside the town gate if the place was walled. Mark 6.56 records that the sick were regularly brought into the marketplaces for Jesus to heal. The gospels frequently mention the presence of a synagogue in the towns Jesus visited, but otherwise there seem to have been few, if any, public buildings.

Apart from Jerusalem and its environs (see pp.150–53), Jesus is associated with several other towns in Palestine that were very different from those he frequented in Galilee (see pp.148–49). All the gospels relate an important episode that Matthew and Mark locate in the vicinity of Caesarea Philippi (Matt. 16.13; Mark 8.27), in which Jesus is acknowledged as Messiah (see pp.236–37). It was a major city at the foot of Mount Hermon in the far north of Palestine, in the tetrarchy of Philip (4BCE–34CE; see pp.156–57). A typical Greco-Roman settlement, Caesarea Philippi was the

THE DECAPOLIS

Jesus is recorded as crossing the Sea of Galilee to a region known as the Decapolis. This comprised a league of ten Hellenistic cities, originally independent but assigned by the Romans to the province of Syria. The Decapolis is the setting of the famous episode in which Jesus sent a band of demons into a herd of pigs (see pp.226–27). Early texts of the gospels variously locate this story in the land of "the Gerasenes," "the Gadarenes," and "the Gergesenes." The Decapolis city of Gerasa (Jerash, Jordan) in fact lay a considerable distance from the Sea of Galilee; Gadara, on the other hand, was just six miles (10km) from the lake. Gergesa was also near the lake, but was not in the Decapolis. The confusion suggests that, despite the numerous followers he is said to have had from the region, Jesus' connection with the Decapolis was essentially peripheral.

site of a sanctuary to the god Pan (hence the city's older name of Paneas, modern Banias) and most of its inhabitants would have been pagans. Jesus may have felt able to move freely in this environment, away from his Jewish detractors. But there is no evidence that he visited the town itself.

The gospels attest to a strong tradition that Jesus went to the non-Jewish region of Tyre and Sidon in Syria-Phoenicia, and even visited the latter city. But he is only said to have gone "by way of Sidon" (Mark 7.31) on his way back to Galilee and it would appear that he made a comparatively brief stay in the region, perhaps in an attempt to extend his influence there—the gospels relate that some of the inhabitants had been attracted to his teaching in Galilee (Matt. 4.24; compare Mark 7.26).

On his final journey from Galilee to Jerusalem (see pp.238–39), Jesus is said to have passed through Jericho, from where a direct road led through the Judean hill country to the capital. New Testament Jericho—situated in a fertile oasis just south of the site of the city of the Hebrew Scriptures—was granted ca. 30 BCE by the Roman emperor Augustus to Herod the Great, who adorned it with splendid palaces. Luke records that Jesus spent the night there at the house of Zacchaeus, "a chief tax collector" (Luke 19.2)—a title indicating that Jericho was a regional administrative center.

Orchards in winter in the north of Palestine. In the distance are the heights of Mount Hermon, which may have been the setting for the Transfiguration of Jesus (see p.236).

GALILEE

JESUS' GALILEAN ITINERARY
The gospels record that Jesus taught in the open and mention no visits to the larger Galilean towns, such as Sepphoris, the former capital of Galilee, just four miles from Nazareth, and Tiberias, the new capital founded ca. 18 CE. Jesus had good reason to avoid both cities: they were the power centers of Galilee's ruler, Herod Antipas (see p.157), who executed John the Baptist and was reportedly keen to question Jesus (Luke 9.7–9).

However, the evangelists do speak of Jesus regularly visiting other villages and towns, teaching in their synagogues and healing. The mission of his disciples was also directed toward population centers (Matt. 10.23; Luke 9.5–6). As well as Capernaum (see box, opposite) and Bethsaida (see main text), Jesus visited smaller Galilean towns such as Chorazin (Matt. 11.21; Luke 10.13), Gennesaret (Matt. 14.34; Mark 6.53), and Cana (John 2.1–11). Cana, near Nazareth, was also the hometown of the disciple Nathanael.

Galilee, a region in the north of Palestine, was the principal setting for the ministry of Jesus, especially the area around its lake, commonly known as the Sea of Galilee or Lake Galilee. In Jesus' lifetime Galilee was governed by King Herod the Great (37–4 BCE) and then his son, the tetrarch Herod Antipas (4 BCE–39 CE), both clients of Rome (see pp.156–57). It had long had a mixed population of Jews and Gentiles and was described in the Hebrew Bible as "Galilee of the Nations" (Isa. 9.1). According to one theory, this may have been the original name of the region—Galilee simply means "district" (Hebrew *galil*). The non-Jewish population increased around the beginning of the Common Era as Galilee's rulers founded new Hellenistic cities. Galileans were distinguished by their accent (Matt. 26.73), and the Pharisees (see pp.166–69) apparently looked down on them as lax in their observance of the Jewish law and incapable of producing the Messiah (John 7.52). The area was also known as a source of political unrest (see p.233).

Galilee includes the most northerly section of the central Palestinian mountain range (see pp.144–45) and is divided into Lower Galilee, the principal area of settlement and main focus of Jesus' ministry, and the largely mountainous Upper Galilee. In the gospels the most important feature of Galilee is the lake and its environs. The Hebrew Scriptures suggest that its earliest name was Lake Chinnereth ("lyre") which derived either from its shape or the name of a town at its northwest corner. In New Testament times, it was sometimes called Lake Tiberias or Lake Gennesaret

The Sea of Galilee near Capernaum, focus of Jesus' Galilean ministry. The Church of the Twelve Apostles (Greek Orthodox) commemorates the calling of the disciples.

Nazareth and Capernaum

The Galilean towns most closely associated with Jesus are Capernaum and Nazareth. Jesus' hometown of Nazareth was a small and insignificant village, and virtually nothing of Jesus' time has been preserved. It was a satellite of Herod Antipas's splendid city of Sepphoris, the largest city in Galilee and just an hour's walk away. It has been suggested that the young Jesus and his family may have had contacts with Sepphoris and been influenced by its Hellenistic civilization. As carpenter-builders, Jesus and Joseph may conceivably have worked on the reconstruction of the city following its destruction in a rebellion in 4 BCE. One early Christian tradition claimed that Mary came from there.

Jesus chose Capernaum (Hebrew, Kefar Nahum, "Village of Nahum") as the headquarters for his ministry in Galilee. He frequently resided there, probably in the house of his disciple Peter. At this time Capernaum was a modest but thriving commercial center, with a toll office and probably a small Roman garrison under a centurion. The town was close to the border of Philip's tetrarchy and on the Via Maris ("Sea Road"), an important highway linking Damascus in Syria with the coast.

When the site of Capernaum was excavated in the early twentieth century, the ruins were discovered of a fourth-century CE synagogue that had replaced one of the first century, in which Jesus may have preached.

Ruins of 1st-century Capernaum. In spite of the miracles he performed there, Jesus eventually felt rejected by its inhabitants.

Close by, under the ruins of an octagonal fifth-century CE church, lay the remains of a first-century CE house owned, according to objects discovered there, by fisherfolk. The early Christians revered this house as that of Peter—hence the church built on the site—and many modern scholars support this identification. It is certainly the kind of dwelling in which Peter and Jesus would have lived.

after two other towns. It is below sea level and surrounded by high hills, a combination that could produce the sudden squalls mentioned several times in the gospels. The lake was rich in fish and its shores formed a fertile agricultural area that attracted a large population.

Apart from Capernaum (see box, above), the place most frequently mentioned as the scene of Jesus' activity in the region bordering Lake Galilee is Bethsaida, just over the political frontier in the tetrarchy of Philip (ruled 4 BCE–34 CE), another son of Herod the Great. In Jesus' time Bethsaida would have been only a small place, and Mark calls it a "village." But the later gospels call it a *polis* ("town" or "city"), which may reflect its elevation by Philip in 30 CE, when it was renamed Julias in honor of Livia Julia, the mother of the Roman emperor Tiberius. The name Bethsaida means "House of fishing" and archaeologists have confirmed that it was a fishing settlement. According to John's gospel, three of Jesus' original disciples—at least two of whom, Peter and Andrew, were fishermen—came from there. Jesus ultimately curses Bethsaida (Matt. 11.21; Luke 10.13) for failing to respond to the miracles he had performed there (for example, Mark 8.22–26).

JERUSALEM

The most important city in Palestine, then as now, was Jerusalem. Well away from the main regional trade routes and areas of population, it was not a great economic center but primarily a religious and political capital. The New Testament provides comparatively little information about the city in Jesus' day, and the identification of most of the places traditionally associated with him, such as the sites of the Last Supper and the Crucifixion, derives from later Christian sources. But some of these writings may rely on good tradition, while archaeological discoveries and sources such as the historian Josephus (first century CE) and the Mishnah (second century CE) sometimes shed light on the gospel record of Jesus' activities in the city.

Jesus and the Temple Mount

At least two episodes that took place in Jerusalem are illuminated by what is known of the topography of the Temple Mount in the first century CE. According to the gospels, Jesus sat down opposite the Temple "treasury," where he observed people making monetary offerings (Mark 12.41; Luke 21.1) and where, according to John, he taught (John 8.20). As a great economic institution (see pp.162–63), the Temple had a treasury chamber, where the bulk of its wealth was stored, but when the gospels speak of the worshipers "putting money into the treasury" they probably mean the thirteen collection chests which, according to the Mishnah, were placed round the walls of the Court of the Women. Each was inscribed with the purpose to which the offerings inside were to be devoted. The specific mention in the gospels of people selling doves or pigeons for sacrifice (as at Matt. 21.12) may imply that these were the main offerings at this time for individual worshipers.

The famous episode of the Cleansing of the Temple (see pp.240–41) probably took place in or near the Royal Portico, or Stoa, a magnificent basilica-like covered colonnade which stood at the southern end of the Court of the Gentiles and towered high above the city and the Kidron valley. It was copied by Herod from similar structures that stood adjacent to temples in the Greco-Roman world and served as meeting places for merchants, worshipers, and pilgrims (see pp.84–5). On the occasion of the cleansing, Mark makes a reference (Mark 11.16) to Jesus forbidding the carrying of objects through the Temple precincts—in other words, using it as a short cut. But Jesus' action is supported by Josephus, who says that the practice was officially prohibited.

Jesus is recorded in John as walking in another vast colonnade, known as Solomon's Portico, on the east side of the Temple Mount (John 10.23). The portico, also mentioned in Acts (3.11 and 5.12) and by Josephus (although not by name), was a place where speakers would address the crowds that gathered there. It was therefore a very likely location for Jesus' teaching activities in the Temple.

A reconstruction of the Royal Portico at the southern end of the Temple Mount. The steps (foreground) led down to the Triple Hulda Gate, the Temple's main southern entrance.

A view westward across Jerusalem. The golden Dome of the Rock marks the site of the Temple sanctuary. The nearest walls follow the eastern and southern sides of the ancient Temple Mount.

The city that Jesus knew was above all the creation of King Herod the Great (see p.156), who constructed a wall around the quarter known as the New City, and built a theater, an amphitheater, a hippodrome, and also a fine palace for himself in the Upper City, the aristocratic quarter. The most impressive of all Herod's achievements was the rebuilding of the Second Temple to create one of the largest and most magnificent religious buildings in the Roman world. The central sanctuary was constructed from massive blocks of masonry and many parts of it were overlaid with gold and silver—the gospels record the wonder of onlookers who beheld its fine large stones and rich ornaments (Mark 13.1; Luke 21.5).

Relating the episode of the Cleansing of the Temple (see pp.240–41), John's gospel says that the building had been under construction for forty-six years (John 2.20). Josephus states that it was begun in 20–19 BCE, which would date the cleansing incident to the late 20s CE, a very feasible date for the ministry of Jesus. The sanctuary itself was completed in only eighteen months but work continued on other parts of the Temple Mount, the great platform on which the Temple stood (see box, opposite), almost up to the outbreak of the First Jewish War (66–70 CE)—during which the entire Temple complex was destroyed by the Romans.

Situated high in the Judean mountains, Jerusalem is surrounded by hills, of which the Mount of Olives is the most significant for the gospel story. On his final visit to Jerusalem, and perhaps before, Jesus is recorded as spending the night either in Bethany, a village two miles (3.2 km) from the

THE *PRAETORIUM*

In Jesus' day, the Roman prefect (governor) of Judea was based at Caesarea on the coast, but came to Jerusalem on the occasion of the major Jewish festivals. While in the city he resided at the *praetorium*, mentioned in the gospels (Matt. 27.27; Mark 15.16; John 19.9) as the place where Jesus was tried by Pilate. It is generally accepted that the *praetorium* was either the former palace of Herod the Great or the Antonia, a fortress built by Herod on the site of an earlier citadel at the northwest corner of the Temple Mount and named after his early Roman patron, Mark Antony (died 31 BCE). According to Josephus, Pilate stayed at Herod's palace, but it is possible that he moved to the Antonia, the city's main Roman garrison, for at least some of this time, since it was closer to the Temple, where any civil unrest was most likely to erupt.

Jerusalem in the time of Jesus

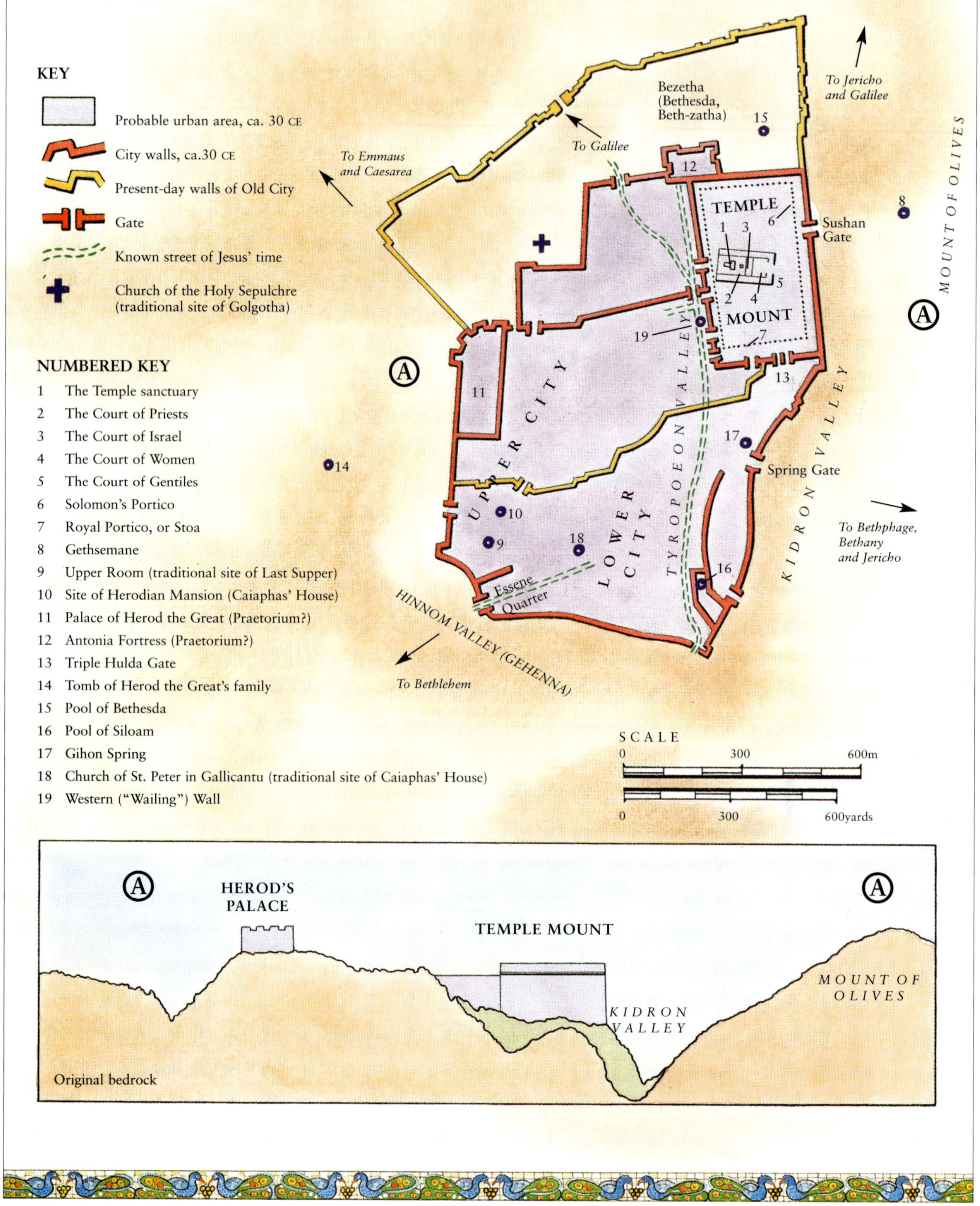

city on the eastern slopes of the Mount of Olives, where apparently he had a group of friends (Mary, Martha, and their brother Lazarus); or on the mount itself, probably in the estate of Gethsemane (Hebrew *gath sehnamim*, "Olive Presses") on its lower slopes, where he was arrested. As the name implies, the Mount of Olives was covered by extensive olive groves. On the occasion of his triumphal entry into the city (see sidebar, p.240), Jesus appears to have journeyed from Bethany over the mount, via the village of Bethphage, where he acquired the donkey on which he rode.

Whatever the date and authorship of the gospel of John (see pp.182–83), it is now widely accepted that it contains good historical and topographical information about first-century Jerusalem, which is supported by archaeological and other evidence. The evangelist appears to have known the city well, and he refers to a number of features not mentioned in the other gospels, such as the Sheep Gate and the adjoining pool of Bethzatha (or Bethesda), where Jesus cured the paralytic (John 5.2–9). There is archaeological and other evidence that the water in the pool—which was located in 1866 and discovered to have five porticoes, as John describes—was believed to possess healing properties. Similarly, only John mentions the pool of Siloam, where Jesus sent the blind man to be cured (John 9.7).

The evangelist also knew that the route from the city to the Mount of Olives crossed the valley of the Kidron brook, which he accurately describes by a word denoting a seasonal river, or wadi (John 18.1). This valley was much deeper in Jesus' day than now (see opposite).

John alone refers to the stone pavement (paved area) outside the *praetorium*, the Roman military headquarters (see sidebar, p.151). It was on this paved area that Pilate sat in judgment over Jesus, and John gives its Aramaic name, Gabbatha ("Raised Place") (John 19.13).

THE POPULATION OF JERUSALEM

It is difficult to assess how many people lived in Jerusalem at the time of Jesus. One estimate has put the number of permanent residents at no more than thirty thousand. But some four times this figure may have flocked to Jerusalem on the occasion of the major Jewish festivals, accounting for the crowds of which the gospels speak (for example, John 12.12) and for the regular presence of the Roman prefect in the city at Passover and possibly other times.

This view across Jerusalem, taken ca. 1950, captures much of the atmosphere of the Old City in the premodern era. In the distance, left, is the tower of the Lutheran Church of the Redeemer; the tower in the foreground is that of a mosque of the Turkish period.

HELLENISM

Hellenism may be defined as the essentially Greek pattern of civilization that came to dominate the Near East in the wake of the conquests of Alexander the Great (ruled 332–323 BCE). It embraced language, lifestyle, education, economy, philosophy, and religion. Its general effect was to bring diverse existing societies within a common culture. It encouraged "syncretism"—the equation of one god with another as forms of the same deity.

Hellenism in Palestine was largely confined to the urban upper classes, while the Maccabean revolt (see p.134) ensured that Jewish religious culture always remained fiercely independent. Under Hasmonean rule, the propagators of Hellenism were regularly forced to reiterate their loyalty to their ancestral Judaism. The later Hasmonean rulers acted as typical Hellenistic monarchs but remained strong Jewish nationalists. Herod the Great, who succeeded them, was a client of Rome and an ardent hellenizer, who built Greek-style cities that even incorporated pagan temples. Herod

Jesus and the Cynics

Jesus would have had few, if any, links with the sophisticated Hellenism of the Palestinian upper classes. But it has recently been argued that he may have been directly influenced by the Cynics, who followed the principles of the Greek thinker Diogenes (ca. 410–320 BCE). The Cynics—their name is the origin of the term "cynical" and literally means "canine" (Greek *kunikos*) because of their snappish attacks on conventional society—were itinerant preachers who, in the late first century CE, were found all over the Roman empire. In vivid and challenging language they proclaimed a lifestyle of austerity and radical self-sufficiency, calling on men and women to renounce all claims of the state, the social order, the family, and the accepted practices of religion in favor of a simple, free life in accordance with nature. The Cynics were often seen as a threat to order and morality, and were frequently expelled from Rome. Like them, Jesus and his disciples were itinerant preachers to ordinary folk, and asked their followers to renounce family ties and material possessions; and Jesus was often at odds with the authorities.

A bust of the ancient Greek philosopher Diogenes of Sinope, founder of the Cynic movement in the 4th century BCE.

However, the Cynic movement largely died out between ca. 100 BCE and the mid-first century CE. It then underwent a great revival, but it is uncertain how far this had begun in Jesus' lifetime. Apparent Cynic resonances in the New Testament (notably Matt. 6.25–29ff., Luke 12.22–27ff.) are more likely to derive from Cynic influence on the early Church. Unlike Jesus, the Cynics were not exorcists or healers, and nothing in their teaching corresponds to his central message of God's kingdom (see pp.280–83). Jesus remained an observant Jew and an heir of Israel's ancestral faith. The world-renunciation of the Cynics also characterized first-century CE Jewish ascetics, such as the Essenes and John the Baptist (see pp.169, 214–15) and it is with these that Jesus can more fruitfully be compared.

A Greco-Roman mosaic from the Hellenistic city of Sepphoris (Hebrew Zippori), 4 miles from Nazareth. Destroyed in a revolt that followed the death of Herod the Great in 4BCE, Sepphoris was magnificently rebuilt in the early years of the 1st century.

built an amphitheater and a hippodrome in Jerusalem and fostered Greek intellectual culture at his court. However, he also rebuilt the Temple of Jerusalem, the center of Jewish religious life, and maintained its distinctive religious practices. He was careful, too, to observe the Jewish law and to conciliate the most powerful religious faction, the Pharisees (see pp.166–67). The Roman prefects who ruled Judea in the first century CE likewise avoided offending Jewish religious sensibilities, with occasional exceptions—notably under Pontius Pilate (see p.158).

Many Jews were never reconciled to Hasmonean, Herodian, or Roman rule and repeatedly caused trouble for the authorities. They continued to view Hellenism as an alien culture and resented the wealth of its supporters. Such opposition encompassed various groups that responded to Hellenism in diverse ways. Jesus' own outlook is to be placed within this general climate. It has recently been suggested that he may have been affected by the Greco-Roman culture of the city of Sepphoris, which was close to Nazareth. While there is no solid evidence for this, Jesus did regularly criticize the rich and powerful, as in the famous story of the rich man and the poor man (Luke 16.19–31). His opinion of the typical Hellenistic lifestyle of a Herodian ruler is shown in his contrast between John the Baptist and those in royal palaces who "put on fine clothing and live in luxury" (Luke 7.25; compare Matt. 11.8).

THE HERODIAN DYNASTY

Palestine came under Roman control in 63 BCE, when the general Pompey captured Jerusalem and ended Hasmonean rule (see p.154). During Jesus' lifetime, imperial authority was exercised either directly, through Roman prefects, or indirectly, through client rulers of the dynasty founded by King Herod the Great (ruled 37–4 BCE). According to Matthew and Luke, Jesus was born in Herod's reign—at least four years before the traditional start of the Christian era. Whether historical or not, Matthew's dramatic story of Herod's massacre of the infants of Bethlehem (Matt. 2.16; see pp.204–05) faithfully reflects the king's notorious ruthlessness in preserving his throne. Toward the end of his life—when the massacre story is set—Herod's paranoia led him to execute several members of his own family.

After Herod's death, his territory was divided among three of his surviving sons, Archelaus, Herod Philip, and, most significantly for the story of Jesus, Herod Antipas (see sidebar, left). The Roman emperor, Augustus, granted them not the coveted title of "king" but the lesser status of "ethnarch" ("ruler of the people") or "tetrarch" ("ruler of one-fourth")—although the fact that Matthew and Mark call Antipas "king" (Matt. 14.9; Mark 6.14) suggests that the Roman titles were popularly ignored.

Judea fell to Archelaus (ruled 4 BCE–6 CE), who shared most of his father's vices but few of his talents. When King Herod died, Archelaus went to Rome to claim his inheritance and encountered a delegation of Jews opposed to his appointment; on his return to Judea as ethnarch he had many of these opponents executed. These events appear to be reflected in

HEROD ANTIPAS

The most prominent Herodian ruler in the gospels is Herod Antipas (ruled 4 BCE–39 CE), tetrarch of Galilee and Perea and commonly called simply Antipas to avoid confusion with his father. He was a typical Hellenistic princeling, building the splendid Galilean cities of Sepphoris, four miles from Nazareth, and Tiberias, his capital.

Antipas first appears in the gospels in connection with his execution of John the Baptist (see pp.234–35). According to Luke, some Pharisees warned Jesus that Antipas would kill him, too, if he remained in Galilee (Luke 13.31). In response to the warning, Jesus called Antipas "that fox," a term which in Jewish rabbinic writings denotes a fool—that is, one who cannot prevent Jesus from completing his mission.

Some passages in the gospels are not wholly unfavorable to Antipas. Prime responsibility for the Baptist's death is attributed to Antipas' wife, Herodias. The tetrarch is said to have recognized John as a holy man and to have imprisoned him only for his own safety (Mark 6.17–20 and parallels). Similarly, Antipas regards Jesus, with a kind of superstitious awe, as a reincarnation of John (Mark 6.14); and wants to meet and hear him (Luke 9.9).

Luke alone records that Pilate sent Jesus to Antipas (Luke 23.7) and that Antipas was involved in Jesus' condemnation (Acts 4.27). Luke notes that, as a result of their dealings over Jesus, the prefect and tetrarch became friends, having previously been enemies (Luke 23.12). This enmity probably dates from the occasion when Antipas joined in a complaint to the emperor Tiberius over Pilate's disregard for Jewish religious sensibilities (see p.158).

Some of Antipas' courtiers were among Jesus' followers (Luke 8.3, Acts 13.1).

In 39 CE, Antipas was deposed by the emperor Caligula on what were probably trumped-up charges and exiled to Gaul.

This monumental aqueduct was built by King Herod the Great to supply the coastal city of Caesarea with water. It was one of many remarkable large-scale building projects undertaken during his reign.

Luke 19.14 and 19.27. Archelaus was hated for his despotic rule and his unsavory reputation probably explains why Matthew says that Joseph was afraid to settle in Judea after his sojourn in Egypt (Matt. 2.22). In the end, Augustus deposed Archelaus and exiled him to Gaul.

By contrast, Herod Philip, or Philip (ruled 4 BCE–34 CE), was renowned for his justice and benevolence. His tetrarchy bordered the eastern shore of the Sea of Galilee and he built the cities of Bethsaida-Julias and Caesarea Philippi, which are associated with Jesus. Philip was a Jew, but his subjects were mainly Gentiles, and it was probably because of Philip's tolerance that Jesus felt able to move and preach freely in his territory.

THE "HERODIANS"
The gospels provide the only known reference to a group called the Herodians (Matt. 22.16; Mark 3.6, 12.13). They may have been supporters of the Herodian dynasty, perhaps specifically of Antipas (see opposite); they probably shared his view of Jesus as a danger to public order. The gospels associate the Herodians with the Pharisees, but perhaps only because both factions, for different reasons, were remembered as being hostile to Jesus.

Roman Palestine was linked to the rest of the empire by a network of fine roads. This Roman milestone still stands in the Ela valley, Israel.

A replica in situ *of the "Pilate Stone" discovered at Caesarea in 1963. It bears a dedicatory inscription in Latin from a "Tiberieum" (building in honor of the emperor Tiberius) that includes the words* [Pon]tius Pilatus ... [Praef]ectus Iudaeae *("Pontius Pilate, Prefect of Judea"). The original stone is in a museum.*

PALESTINE UNDER THE ROMANS

In Jesus' day the whole of Palestine was under direct or indirect Roman control. Following the deposition of Archelaus (see p.156), Judea became a subprovince of the Roman province of Syria, under an official called a prefect (*praefectus*). The prefect was in command of auxiliary military units, had full powers of criminal and civil jurisdiction, and was responsible for the collection of imperial taxes. He resided at Caesarea on the coast, but came to Jerusalem on the occasion of the major Jewish festivals.

Little is known of the first four prefects but there is considerable information about the fifth, Pontius Pilate (in office 26–36 CE), and not only from the gospels. Pilate's rule was marked by repeated confrontations with his Jewish subjects and this troubled situation forms an important part of the background of the career of Jesus, and especially his trial (see pp.250–51). Pilate showed contempt for Jewish religious feelings by bringing into the holy city of Jerusalem military insignia bearing the emperor's portrait and golden shields bearing his name. Because the Romans revered the emperor as a god, such images were idolatrous to Jews. He also attempted to use the Temple's funds to build an aqueduct. Each of these actions provoked serious riots in Jerusalem. Around the time of Jesus' condemnation, Pilate evidently faced a bloody disturbance in Jerusalem (Mark 15.7), for which Barabbas and other rebels were imprisoned. Jesus was crucified alongside two "bandits," the term that John's gospel uses of Barabbas, and this suggests that they were probably revolutionaries. Pilate's ruthlessness is shown by the reference in Luke to a bloody incident involving Galileans (Luke 13.1). Nothing is known of this event from other sources, but the involvement of the notoriously restive Galileans is probably significant (see p.233).

As Jesus himself pointed out, conquerors inevitably imposed taxes on their subjects. When Judea came under direct Roman rule, the imperial tax system was introduced (see box, opposite), and it appears that the client rulers Antipas and Philip (see pp.156–57) also adopted the Roman system.

Understandably, Roman military might made a great impression on the Jewish world and this is reflected in the New Testament. Matthew 8 and Luke 7 record how Jesus healed the slave of a centurion at Capernaum in Galilee. Such an officer, in command of a comparatively small detachment of troops, would be stationed in an important center to keep order. Centurions were well paid and however much Luke's account may be colored, as is generally thought, by a desire to present Roman authority in a favorable light, there is nothing improbable in his picture of the centurion at Capernaum as a notable citizen of the town and a generous benefactor.

The military was able to requisition individuals for public duty, as when the gospels relate how Simon of Cyrene was ordered to carry Jesus' cross (Matt. 27.32 and parallels; see p.253).

Mark alone uses the proper word "centurion" for the officer who supervises the Crucifixion. The demons who possess a man and are exorcised by Jesus (Mark 5; Luke 8) call themselves "Legion" (Latin *legio*, a large military unit) owing to their great number. According to Matthew, Jesus in Gethsemane declared that he could, if he chose, call on the assistance of "more than twelve legions of angels" (Matt. 26.53). John uses the technical term "cohort" (Latin *cohors*, "tenth of a legion") for the troops who arrest Jesus, although the author may be using the word loosely (NRSV: "detachment").

Roman taxation

The Roman tax system was quite extensive, involving taxes on crops, a poll tax, and a levy on the transportation of goods. However, during the lifetime of Jesus these taxes do not seem to have constituted an unduly heavy burden.

The job of collecting the taxes was farmed out to tax gatherers (publicans), who were organized under a head official stationed in a commercial center, such as Zacchaeus in Jericho (Luke 19.2). Tax collectors were highly unpopular, not least because they were suspected of exacting more than the tax actually due. The gospels and the Mishnah (see glossary) lump tax collectors with robbers, sinners, and pagans. A Jew who engaged in this occupation was regarded as a traitor, so many tax collectors would probably have been Gentiles. Nevertheless, the gospels speak of Jesus' regular association with tax collectors and one of them, Matthew or Levi, was a disciple. Such links caused offense to pious groups such as the Pharisees.

When Jesus was interrogated about the legitimacy of paying taxes to Rome, his response—"Give to the emperor the things that are the emperor's, to God the things that are God's" (Mark 12.17 and parallels)—is perhaps best understood in the light of a similar episode when he was asked about the payment of the Jewish Temple tax (Matt. 17.24–5). Here, Jesus teaches that his followers, who belong to the spiritual kingdom of God, are free from the obligation but should meet it to avoid giving unnecessary offense.

Zacchaeus the tax collector climbs a tree to catch a glimpse of Jesus in this Russian painting of Jesus' entry into Jerusalem. As was common in the Middle Ages, the artist has conflated this scene with that of Jesus' arrival at Jericho.

THE SANHEDRIN
Central Jewish judicial authority was exercized in Jesus' day by the Sanhedrin, from the Greek *synhedrionis* ("council"). There has been much discussion about the nature of this body and its powers, but its basic function was to administer Jewish law for those subject to it.

According to the gospels, the Jerusalem Sanhedrin tried and condemned Jesus, and the evangelists detail its composition. With the high priest (see main text) as president, it comprised three groups: members of the high-priestly family; lay elders, who were the city's other leading Jewish citizens; and "scribes," legal and religious experts (see p.162). It appears that by the time of Jesus many of the scribes would have been Pharisees (see pp.166–67).

The gospels also indicate that there were local Sanhedrins in different parts of the country, made up of elders and presided over by a judge. Jesus predicts several times that his disciples will be hauled before such bodies (for example, Mark 13.9).

JEWISH INTERNAL GOVERNMENT

Under the Hasmoneans (142–63 BCE), the last independent Jewish heads of state in Palestine before modern times, the ruler was the supreme civil and religious authority in the land. He could describe himself as "king" to the outside world, which viewed him as a typical Hellenistic monarch (see pp.154–55), but for his Jewish subjects he was also the high priest.

This arrangement came to an end with the Roman occupation and the accession of Herod the Great (see pp.155–56), who appointed high priests from different families and deprived them of many of their political powers. This practice continued under the Roman prefects (see box, below). There was only one high priest at any one time, so when the gospels speak of "high priests" or "chief priests"—the Greek term is the same—they are referring collectively to the members of such notable families, including those who had held the office of high priest.

The high priests, who presided over the Jerusalem Sanhedrin (see sidebar, left), derived much of their wealth and influence from their control of the Temple treasury. The Temple accumulated enormous wealth that made it the most significant single element in the economic life of Palestine. Alongside the Roman revenue system there were specifically Jewish taxes levied by the Temple, in particular a tithe on agricultural produce and a half-shekel tax collected annually from every male Jew in Palestine and the

The high priests and Roman rule

The Romans chose high priests from a small number of wealthy aristocratic families, apparently five in all. Acts 4.6 lists several members of the family of Annas (or Ananos as the historian Josephus calls him), the high-priestly family of the period. Just how influential this dynasty was is shown by the fact that Annas, five of his sons, and his son-in-law Caiaphas all held the high priesthood.

Rome looked to the high-priestly group to keep the populace quiet under their authority, especially in Jerusalem. Thus the prefect Florus (governed 64–66 CE) demanded that the high priest and the leading citizens should arrest eighteen agitators and hand them over to him—this probably explains the procedure for the arrest of Jesus.

The high-priestly families are generally considered to have been members of the Sadducean party (see p.167), whose policy was essentially one of collaboration with Rome for the sake of preserving Jewish religious institutions and as much autonomy as possible. The attitude of these priestly groups is well expressed by the statement attributed to them in the Fourth Gospel: if they did not take steps to restrain Jesus, the Romans would sweep away both the Temple and the nation (John 11.48)—this is precisely what happened as a consequence of the Jewish revolt of 66–73 CE.

The collaborationist position of the high priests and their supporters made them unpopular with many Jews, especially those who advocated resistance to the Romans. They were also accused of corruption, in that they were known to offer large bribes to the prefects to secure their appointment.

The Tribute Money, by Masaccio (1401–28), a fresco in the Brancacci Chapel in the church of Santa Maria del Carmine, Florence. Jesus (center) instructs Peter to catch a fish (left) containing a coin to pay (right) the Temple tax (Matt. 17.24–27).

Diaspora (see sidebar, right). In addition, many people made voluntary offerings, as seen in the gospel accounts of the widow and the rich man (Mark 12.41–44; Luke 21.1–4). The Treasury also acted as a kind of bank, where the wealthy deposited valuables for safekeeping.

The high priest's power rested on his position as head of the Temple, its personnel, and religious functioning. He performed a number of religious rituals that were believed to ensure the welfare and prosperity of his people, especially through his unique role in the ceremonies of the great Day of Atonement. The gospels say virtually nothing of these specifically religious functions. Perhaps the only hint is provided by the statement in the Fourth Gospel that Caiaphas was able to prophesy the death of Jesus (John 11.51)—the writings of Philo and Josephus suggest that the high priest was believed to possess prophetic abilities.

Unlike much of the Temple priesthood, the high priest did not live in the Temple precincts but had his own residence, which figures prominently in the accounts of Jesus' final ordeal. According to Josephus, the high priests lived in the Upper City, a wealthy quarter inhabited by the ruling class of Jerusalem (see plan, p.152). Excavations in this area have revealed the remains of a number of grand houses of the Herodian period, the architecture of which corresponds to what the gospels record about the house of the high priest Caiaphas. In particular, they were constructed around a large courtyard, such as Peter would have entered and where Jesus was apparently kept during the night of his arrest.

The houses of the Upper City had space for a considerable number of domestics, both male and female, and boasted one particularly large chamber, sometimes elaborately decorated. Such a room could have accommodated a meeting of the Sanhedrin to interrogate Jesus.

THE TEMPLE TAX

In Jesus' day, every male Jew aged twenty and above had to pay half a shekel annually to the Temple. This payment had to be made with the Tyrian *didrachma*, the finely minted silver two-drachma piece from the Phoenician city of Tyre. Like other Tyrian coins, it bore the head of the city's patron god, Melgart (see illustration, p.170), and the presence of this pagan image in the Temple clearly infringed the Jewish law against other gods and idols (Exod. 20.3–4, Deut. 5.7–8). That the Temple authorities evidently turned a blind eye to this fact illustrates how highly the Tyrian *didrachma* was valued.

Matthew uses the precise term for this coin (Matt. 17.24; NRSV: "Temple tax"). Later in the same passage, when Peter catches a fish with a single coin in it to pay the Temple tax for both Jesus and himself, Matthew again uses the correct term, *stater* (Matt. 17.27; NRSV "a coin"). A stater—also called a *tetradrachma*—was another Tyrian coin, worth two *didrachmas*.

THE LAW AND THE TEMPLE

The two fundamental institutions of first-century CE Judaism were the law and the Jerusalem Temple (see box, opposite). In the gospels, the word "law" refers to the written text of the first five books of the Hebrew Scriptures, variously known as the Torah, the Pentateuch, "the law of Moses," and "the Mosaic law." The strict rabbinic teaching on the law is well expressed by Jesus' statement that "until heaven and earth pass away, not one letter, not one stroke of a letter, will pass from the law" (Matt. 5.18; compare Luke 16.17): its words are unalterable and it has perpetual validity.

By the time of Jesus, other writings had also achieved canonical status in mainstream Judaism. The gospels (for example, Matt. 7.12) regularly link the law with "the Prophets," what are now usually called the historical and prophetic books of the Hebrew Bible, such as 1 and 2 Kings and Isaiah. Other works that later came to be included in the Jewish canon of scripture also seem to have been gaining recognition in Jesus' day. When Luke speaks of "the law of Moses, the prophets, and the psalms" (Luke 24.44), the word "psalms" may refer not just to the Book of Psalms but to the other works that make up the "Writings," the third subdivision of the Hebrew canon as we know it. This comprises the following books, given here in the order in which they appear in the Jewish Bible: Psalms, Proverbs, Job, Song of Solomon, Ruth, Lamentations, Ecclesiastes, Esther, Daniel, Ezra-Nehemiah, and Chronicles. Jesus himself is represented several times as quoting from the Psalms.

Thus there was in Jesus' time a large body of sacred scripture, which teachers read and expounded in the synagogues, as Jesus is said to have done at Nazareth (Luke 4.16ff.) By this period the law and the rest of the scriptures were already ancient and needed to be taught and explained in a contemporary context. The Pharisees (see pp.166–69) emerged as the most important interpreters and teachers of the law, and their work—later enshrined in the collections called the Mishnah and the Talmud—was predominant in forming the character of later rabbinic Judaism.

This scholarly activity aimed to clarify, safeguard, and protect the written law, and could be seen as part of the law itself in the literal sense of Torah ("instruction" or "direction"). Jesus is represented as dealing with both the written scripture and its interpretation, and also with the "oral Torah"—customs not found in the law but considered important by teachers. He was recognized as a teacher (see pp.292–93) and there is nothing unlikely in his being challenged by other teaching groups, even if the gospel accounts are colored by later relations between the Church and Judaism. The question of Jesus' attitude to the law is crucial for assessing the nature of his teaching and his place in the Judaism of his day (see pp.272–73).

THE SCRIBES

Each of the various parties or sects in first-century Judaism (see pp.166–69) had its own approach to interpreting the law. Those who undertook such interpretation were the "scribes," who appear frequently in the New Testament. They are often linked with the Pharisees (see pp.166–69), but not all scribes were Pharisees and the gospels present a somewhat complicated picture of the relationship between them. Scribes were essentially scholars and teachers of the Jewish law, and as such they might belong to one or other of the various religious parties. The gospels and Acts mention specifically Pharisaic scribes (Luke 5.30; Acts 23.9), and it was natural that groups such as the Pharisees should have their own legal experts to expound and defend their special doctrines.

Mark mentions scribes who apparently belonged to the Sanhedrin in Jerusalem (Mark 14.53; see p.28), and he twice speaks of scribes coming from the city to Galilee (Mark 3.22, 7.1). This probably refers to a body that interpreted and applied the law as it was understood by the Temple authorities. But there were scribes in the villages, too, as indicated at Luke 5.17, where the evangelist uses the synonym "teachers of the law." Luke also uses the term "lawyer" (as at Luke 10.25) for "scribe," possibly because it conveyed the sense better to his Gentile readers.

Like the Pharisees, the scribes are generally depicted as opponents of Jesus, but Matthew 8.19 records a scribe's wish to follow Jesus, and Mark 12.28 tells of one impressed by his teaching.

The Temple

Jesus was accused at his trial of predicting the destruction of the Temple and, as with the Jewish law, his attitude toward it as a central institution of contemporary Judaism is of great importance for an understanding of his teaching.

The gospels frequently refer to the Temple and its precincts, which were rebuilt by Herod the Great and must have been a magnificent sight. The evangelists also show knowledge of the Temple's rituals and organization. Its primary significance was its claim to be the only place where Jews could offer sacrifices to God. Luke depicts Jesus' parents, as observant Jews, going to Jerusalem to sacrifice on the occasion of Mary's purification (Luke 2.22), and the gospels refer to an individual bringing his sacrificial offering to the altar in the Temple.

Worship in the Temple was carried out by a large body of priests, organized into twenty-four divisions, each of which served for a week in rotation. The father of John the Baptist, Zechariah, belonged to one such division, the order of Abijah, and Luke 1.9 records that he had been chosen by lot from the members of his group to officiate, in accordance with regular Temple practice. Zechariah's particular task was to burn incense on the golden altar in the central sanctuary, just outside the Holy of Holies, a ritual carried out every morning and evening. Luke notes how ordinary worshipers, who were not allowed to enter the shrine proper, had to wait outside (Luke 1.10).

Most priests lived outside Jerusalem and only came to the Temple when they were required for duty. Thus Zechariah returned home to his house in the Judean hills after his tour of duty (Luke 1.23). When Jesus ordered a leper to show himself to the priest in confirmation of his cleansing (Matt. 8.4; Mark 1.44), he was not instructing him to go to Jerusalem but referring to a priest who lived locally.

The central sanctuary of the Temple, from the scale model of the city in Jesus' day at the Holyland Hotel, Jerusalem. The reconstruction is based partly on written descriptions and depictions of the Temple on, for example, coins and mosaics.

The Levites constituted the other main element in the Temple personnel. They served as singers, doorkeepers, and also as a kind of police force that kept order in the Temple precincts and could also operate in the city at large. It was this force that the Sanhedrin (see p.160) despatched to arrest Jesus in Gethsemane (see pp.244–45) and which, according to John 7.32, had also sought to apprehend him before.

The Temple was not only a place of sacrifice. Jesus quotes Isaiah in calling it "a house of prayer": there were three daily set times for prayer in the Temple, one of which probably provided the occasion for Jesus' parable of the Pharisee and the tax collector (Luke 18.9–14).

Teachers also went to the Temple, where they would find a large audience for their messages, in and around the great colonnades and porticos that surrounded the Temple Mount (see p.150). Jesus is reported to have taught regularly in the Temple during his time in Jerusalem.

The Pharisee and the Tax Collector Praying in the Temple, *a mosaic in the church of Sant' Apollinare Nuovo in Ravenna, Italy (ca. 520 CE), illustrating Jesus' parable about righteousness and humility (Luke 18.9–14).*

The synagogue at Bar'am in Galilee is later than Jesus' time, but may have replaced one that stood in his day (see Matt. 4.23).

THE SYNAGOGUE AND SOCIETY
The synagogue fulfilled an important social function. Josephus speaks of communal meals there and an inscription of the second or third century CE records a donor building an inn, guest rooms, and ritual baths for a synagogue in Jerusalem. It also functioned as the seat of the local law court—Jesus warned his followers that they would be handed over to local Sanhedrins, or councils (see p.160), which met in the synagogues, and condemned to be flogged. According to the Mishnah, this penalty was administered by a synagogue official, the *hazan*.

THE SYNAGOGUE AND JEWISH FESTIVALS

Jesus' main contact with his ancestral religion was through the institution of the synagogue (Greek *sunagogos*, "place of meeting"). Its origins are extremely obscure, but by the time of Jesus there were synagogues in Jewish communities throughout the Roman empire. The remains of over a hundred ancient synagogues have been discovered in Palestine, especially in and around Galilee. It has been suggested that the synagogue was the main means through which Judaism was revived in Galilee, which had been largely heathen at the time of the early Maccabean rulers in the late second century BCE (see p.154).

The great majority of the excavated synagogues of Palestine date from much later than the time of Jesus but many of them will have replaced earlier buildings on the same site, as was certainly the case at Capernaum. However, at least three synagogues can confidently be dated to the first century CE: one at Gamala in Galilee and two within Herod the Great's fortresses of Masada and Herodium. All these buildings have much the same plan and so indicate the kind of synagogue that Jesus would have known. They are rectangular, with stepped stone benches around the walls, facing into a central space where the scriptures would have been read and expounded. It was most likely in this area, too, that Jesus sometimes performed healings and exorcisms. In the gospels, the scribes and Pharisees are condemned for monopolizing the best seats in the synagogues (Matt. 23.6; Mark 12.39; Luke 11.43), perhaps those of the uppermost tier. Matthew 23.2 speaks of the scribes and the Pharisees sitting on "Moses' seat," probably a place of honor occupied by experts while expounding the Mosaic law; a basalt chair found in the synagogue of the third or fourth century CE at Chorazin may represent such a seat.

Unlike the Temple, the synagogue was primarily a place of instruction in the Jewish law. The main activity was a weekly assembly on the Sabbath for readings of the Torah and homilies based upon it, although other scriptures were also read. Jesus is recorded as attending the synagogue on the Sabbath and being involved in controversy about the observance of the day of rest. The gospels associate the synagogue with the Pharisees in particular, and this, along with other evidence, indicates that the institution had become very much a Pharisaic preserve—the chief means for propagating and popularizing the Pharisees' distinctive doctrines (see pp.166–67).

A synagogue was headed by an official called "the leader of the synagogue," a prominent citizen like Jairus in the gospels (Mark 5.22; Luke 8.41). He was responsible for the upkeep of the building and the regulation of its meetings. Luke tells of a synagogue leader who angrily rebuked Jesus for healing on the Sabbath (Luke 13.14). There was also an assistant, the *hazan*, who, as seen in the synagogue at Nazareth, had charge of the scrolls of the sacred scriptures and delivered them to the chosen reader for the day.

The reading of scripture always remained the principal purpose of the synagogue. Later Judaism developed annual or triennial reading cycles, whereby certain passages of scripture were assigned to a particular Sabbath or festival day. Some scholars have claimed that such a system was in operation in the first century CE and have even proposed that the structure of one or more gospels follows the pattern of the cycle of synagogue readings. But these suggestions have not gained wide acceptance.

The Jewish festivals in the gospels

If Sabbath worship was mainly centered on the synagogue, this was not the case for the major festivals. These were all occasions of pilgrimage, when the law required all male Jews to visit Jerusalem for the ceremonies in the Temple. The most popular festival was Passover, or Pesah, when huge crowds converged on the holy city. Its observance had two parts: the ritual slaughter of paschal (Passover) lambs in the Temple; and their consumption in a domestic meal that had to be held in Jerusalem. The gospels are only concerned with the second part (the meal) and their accounts generally correspond to what is known of the custom at the time. For example, those at the Passover meal lay on cushions to eat, and in their description of the Last Supper, Matthew and Mark use a verb meaning "to recline."

As well as Passover, the Fourth Gospel lists three other festivals for which Jesus is said to have visited Jerusalem. One, simply described as "a festival of the Jews," may have been Pentecost or possibly the Jewish New Year. The second is Tabernacles or Booths, which was marked by the ritual drawing of water and the illumination of one of the Temple courts. On this occasion, according to John, Jesus appropriately speaks of himself as the water of life and the light of the world. The third is the feast of the Dedication or Hanukkah, held in December to commemorate the rededication of the Temple in 164 BCE after its profanation by Antiochus (see p.154). Here, Jesus describes himself as the one whom God had sanctified, which may be intended to indicate that he, as the Messiah, replaces the Temple that is soon to be destroyed.

The Last Supper, *by the Master of Perea (15th century). The paschal (Passover) lamb is on the table in front of Jesus.*

SECTS AND PARTIES

Judaism in the first century CE was by no means homogenous. It was made up of various groupings with their own views and outlooks, and they were often very hostile to each other. The gospels mention a number of such sects, most notably the Pharisees, but also the Sadducees (see box, opposite), the Samaritans (see box, p.168), scribes (see sidebar, p.162), Herodians (see sidebar, p.157), and Essenes (see sidebar, p.169).

The attitude of the gospels toward the Pharisees (Greek *pharisaioi*, from Hebrew *perushim*, "separated ones") is mainly hostile and polemical, most notably in the blistering attack in Matthew 23 that includes the catalogue of seven "woes" against them. But allowing for this hostility—which scholars have often regarded as biased and unfair—the New Testament's characterization of Pharisaism broadly corresponds with that found in Josephus and other sources. According to Josephus, the Pharisees were the dominant religious group within Judaism, and this is how

Jesus in the House of Simon the Pharisee, *a fresco of 1072 in the basilica of Sant' Angelo in Formis, Capua, Italy, depicting the episode of Jesus and the woman who had sinned (Luke 7.36–50). Although the gospels project a generally critical view of the Pharisees, Jesus is depicted on amicable terms with some of them and he was invited to dine by Pharisees on more than one occasion (see also Luke 11.37).*

The Sadducees

One group with whom Jesus came into contact, the Sadducees, are known only from Pharisaic texts, Josephus, and the New Testament—all of which display a somewhat negative attitude toward them. It is generally considered that they were members of the priestly aristocracy, with the Temple as their base, and perhaps the likeliest derivation of their name is that it comes from Zadok, whom Solomon installed as chief priest (1 Kings 2.35). Zadok's successors, the Zadokites, controlled the priesthood until the second century BCE.

However, it would be wrong to overemphasize the specifically priestly aspects of the Sadducees. Not all priests, and certainly not all members of the Jerusalem Sanhedrin (see p.160), were Sadducees. In the New Testament, as in Josephus, they appear alongside Pharisees as a clearly religious party with its own particular interpretation of the Mosaic law, on which they challenge the teaching of Jesus. They were conservatives, who accepted only the written Pentateuch as scripture (as did the Samaritans), and hence opposed those novel Pharisaic doctrines which they did not find there, in particular belief in the resurrection of the dead or an elaborate hierarchy of angels and spirits. Although they rejected the oral law, they were, like the Pharisees, a learned group with their own interpretative tradition. The Mishnah and later writings record disputes between them and the Pharisees over such issues as the religious calendar and sacrificial regulations.

With the destruction of the Temple in 70 CE, the Sadducees largely vanish from history. This is consistent with Josephus' description of them as those who held the highest offices but had little following among the general population.

This superbly crafted column capital from Herod's Temple testifies to the wealth of the Temple and the priestly hierarchy that ran it.

JESUS AND THE PHARISEES

Although many things tended to divide Jesus and the Pharisees, they shared a number of important views, especially in contrast to those of the Sadducees (see box, left). The Pharisees actively propagated developments that had arisen in Judaism in the last centuries BCE. They accepted as scripture the Prophets and the Writings (see p.162) as well as the Pentateuch; they had expectations about the end of the present world age (including belief in a future Messiah, who would be preceded by the coming of the prophet Elijah and the general resurrection of the dead); and they possessed a highly developed belief in angels and demons.

The Sadducees rejected all these doctrines, but Jesus shared them, although he might differ in his interpretation of specific issues, such as whether the Messiah had to be descended from King David, and the significance of John the Baptist.

The gospels provide evidence of friendly relations between Jesus and at least some Pharisees (see illustration, opposite). Matthew's statement about the Pharisees sitting on "Moses' seat" (Matt.23.2; see p.164) recognizes them as the authoritative spokesmen for the law, and they are represented as recognizing Jesus as a true teacher of the way of God (John 3.2). It is Pharisees who warn Jesus about Herod Antipas (Luke 13.31).

they appear in their contacts with Jesus. Again, Josephus states that the Pharisees were distinguished on the one hand by their accurate exposition of the written Mosaic law, and on the other by their teaching of the "oral Torah," certain regulations handed down from earlier generations but not in the law as recorded in the Pentateuch. The gospels illustrate the observance of both types of law (see p.162).

Some of the confrontations between Jesus and the Pharisees turn on the correct understanding of the Mosaic law, such as what was meant by the prohibition of work on the Sabbath and the legality of divorce. The Pharisaic position on these and other issues was determined by the unwritten law, "the tradition of the elders" as the gospels call it (Matt. 15.2). According to the Mishnah, a compilation of these oral regulations made ca. 200 CE, Moses received the written commandments at Sinai, but also the oral law, which he committed to his successor Joshua, who in turn passed it on to a body of elders, from whom it was handed down by a succession of teachers. The Mishnah sums up the basic message of the unwritten law in three obligations that are a good description of how the Pharisees envisaged their task: "Be deliberate in judgment" (carry out the law's provisions faithfully and accurately); "Raise up many disciples" (bring as many people as possible to the proper observance of the law); and "Make a fence around the law" (employ the oral regulations to preserve and safeguard the written law).

The Pharisees sought to ensure the proper keeping of the law by clarifying various aspects of it. The gospels mention some of the issues that the Pharisees dealt with, for example the degree of cleansing required to avoid ritual impurity; precisely which products of the soil were liable to tithing; and what exactly was involved in vowing property to the Temple.

Josephus states that the Pharisees had the support of the masses and

The Samaritans

The Samaritans, who feature in several important episodes in the gospels, had much in common with other groups. They accepted only the Mosaic law (the Pentateuch) as scripture, like the Sadducees (see p.167), and rejected the Temple, as the Qumran community may also have done.

The Samaritans were marked by three features in particular, all of which are attested in the gospels. As their name indicates, they lived in villages in Samaria, a region that Jesus, like other devout Jews, apparently avoided on his last journey to Jerusalem. They were a distinct ethnic group, all descendants of old northern Israelite tribes, and thus Luke can describe a Samaritan as a "foreigner" (Luke 17.18). Thirdly, they recognized Mount Gerizim, not the Jerusalem Temple, as the sole legitimate place for sacrificial worship, as the Samaritan woman says in the Fourth Gospel (John 4.20).

The Good Samaritan *by the Spanish artist Rafael Tejeo (1798–1856). Jesus' famous parable of the Samaritan who, alone of three passers-by, goes to the aid of a man who has been robbed and beaten, is recounted in Luke 10.30–35.*

The gospels' attitude toward the Samaritans varies. For example, in Matthew 10.5, Jesus forbids his disciples to evangelize among them, but elsewhere—especially in Luke—he is more welcoming. In Luke 17.18–19, Jesus commends a Samaritan leper for his piety and likewise praises the Good Samaritan of the famous parable (Luke 10.30–37) for his charity.

This ambivalence was probably reflected more widely in contemporary Judaism. In the Mishnah lawcode, Samaritans are classed among the Jews and are able to enjoy table-fellowship with them. However, Pharisaic Judaism came to harden its attitude towards the Samaritans. John's gospel appears to echo this later situation in its statement that Jews do not share things with Samaritans (John 4.9), and the denunciation of Jesus as a Samaritan possessed by a demon (John 8.48).

The caves at Qumran, 9 miles (14km) south of Jericho, where the Dead Sea Scrolls were discovered by local Arab shepherds in 1947.

that, unlike the Qumran community (see sidebar, right), they were not an exclusive sect but engaged with the population at large. In contrast to the scribes, the Pharisees in general were concerned to move from the passive study of the law toward greater activity in bringing people to its proper observance, as they saw it. Their missionary zeal is highlighted by Matthew's statement that they "cross sea and land to make a single convert" (Matt. 23.15).

The devout Pharisee contrasted himself with "the people of the land," (*'am ha'aretz*), described by the Pharisees in the Fourth Gospel as those who did not know the law (John 7.49). This expression was particularly applied to the Galileans (see p.233) and so would have characterized Jesus and his disciples, who did not follow the prescriptions of the oral law in such respects as fasting (as at Luke 5.33) and washing (as at Matt. 15.2). In any event, it would often have been difficult for the ordinary peasant or artisan to fulfill all the detailed Pharisaic regulations. Hence, the gospels accuse the Pharisees and lawyers of loading people with burdens hard to bear and of being "hypocrites," who "do not practice what they teach" (Matt. 23.3) —an accusation also found in some Jewish sources. Paul, originally a Pharisee himself, calls them "the strictest sect of our religion" (Acts 26.5).

In sum, the Pharisees might be described as a bourgeois group, on a social level between the Temple aristocracy and the mass of the populace. They had the support of many ordinary people, and with the synagogues as their base, they were crucial to the survival of Judaism following the loss of the Temple as the center of Jewish worship in 70 CE. It is generally agreed that the activities of the Pharisees laid solid foundations for the development of rabbinic Judaism in the early centuries CE.

JESUS AND THE ESSENES

The Essenes existed throughout Palestine and it is likely that Jesus and his followers would have come into contact with them, although there is no unambiguous reference to Essenes in the New Testament. Their own writings were thought lost until the dramatic discovery in 1947 of the remains of a community and its literature—the Dead Sea Scrolls—at Qumran on the shores of the Dead Sea. Most scholars believe that the people of Qumran were Essenes.

According to the scrolls, Qumran was founded by a "Teacher of Righteousness," who revealed the true interpretation of scripture and ushered in the final age of history. It has been asserted not only that the Dead Sea Scrolls represent the Teacher as a slain and resurrected Messiah, but even that he and Jesus were the same person. However, the great majority of the scrolls predate the first century CE and so cannot refer to Jesus and his followers.

A more plausible theory is that Jesus (and John the Baptist) started out as Qumranites before leaving to embark on their own distinctive missions. Qumran was a closed body of initiates, similar to a monastery, whereas Jesus and John preached to the whole population and did not exhort their hearers to withdraw from society. Again, central to Qumran was an exact observance of Mosaic law—in contrast to Jesus' more relaxed attitude.

Nevertheless, many ideas and expressions in the gospels have parallels in the Dead Sea Scrolls that illuminate the teaching of Jesus and highlight more clearly the Jewish roots of his teaching (see pp.343, 346–49). In short, Qumran and Jesus represent two independent and distinctive developments within Judaism that draw on a common intellectual and theological background.

TRADE AND COMMERCE

Palestine's geographical position gave it an important role as an intermediary between the Mediterranean and the Middle East, and several major roads used by traders and merchants traversed Palestine and Transjordan (see map, opposite). There is hardly any reference to this international commerce in the gospels, although Matthew's image of a merchant in search of fine pearls (Matt. 13.45) no doubt indicates someone engaged in the importation of precious minerals and gems from a region such as southern Arabia. The gifts brought by the wise men to the infant Jesus (see p.202) also indicate the sort of exotic luxury goods that international traders brought to Palestine.

Jesus appears to have avoided the main highways—paved Roman roads such as that linking Galilee with Jerusalem. Along the minor routes, Jesus and his disciples traveled on foot, as was usual for the poorer classes. Most riding was done on the back of the humble donkey—horses are not mentioned once in the gospels, although Jesus does refer to the camel (Matt. 19.24, 23.24; compare Mark 10.25; Luke 18.25). Along the way, there were inns, as in Luke's accounts of the Nativity (Luke 2.7) and the Good Samaritan (Luke 10.34). These would have been typical Eastern caravanserais, providing accommodation for both travelers and their animals. The parable of the Good Samaritan also shows that crossing sparsely populated areas could often be dangerous for lone travelers.

The gospels make frequent, and knowledgable, reference to the wide variety of gold, silver, and bronze coins in circulation. In addition to the Roman imperial currency used throughout the empire, there were coins minted for local use by the client rulers Antipas (see p.235) and Philip, and by the Roman prefects of Judea, such as Pilate (see p.250). Some important commercial cities, such as Tyre, also minted their own coins.

The small imperial silver *denarius* was apparently the most widely circulated coin, probably because this was the standard day's pay for an agricultural laborer (Matt. 20.2; NRSV: "the usual daily wage"). The Good Samaritan generously gave two *denarii* for the care of the man he had rescued (Luke 10.35). The *denarius* was also the main denomination used to pay Roman taxes. It bore the name and portrait of the emperor (see illustration, p.188), as Jesus noted when challenged about the payment of tax to Caesar (Matt. 22.20; Mark 12.16; Luke 20.24).

Also in circulation were small bronze or copper coins of little value. In Mark, the two coins given by the poor widow to the Temple treasury are said to make up one *denarius* (Mark 12.42; NRSV:

MONEYCHANGERS AND BANKERS
The great range of coins and other monetary units in use in Palestine required the services of moneychangers. They were to be found throughout Palestine, but the gospels mention only those who sat at tables in the Temple precincts in order to convert worshipers' money into the Tyrian silver coins that alone were acceptable as Temple donations (see p.240).

The evangelists also mention bankers, but they were probably little different from the moneychangers: the Greek term used of them, *trapezitai*, derives from *trapeza*, "table." The parable of the Talents or Pounds (Matt. 25.14–30; Luke 19.11–27) indicates that the primary function of bankers was lending money at interest, the profits being partly passed on to the bank's investors (Matt. 25.27; Luke 19.23). Jewish law supposedly forbids usury between Jews (Exod. 22.25; Deut. 23.19), and it was considered an act of charity to make a loan to someone in need expecting no return, as Luke says (Luke 6.35). But, as the gospels also show, the acquisition of debt—both financial and in kind—was a common problem, especially for farmers who required help in planting their crops. This situation seems to provide the background to the parable of the Dishonest Manager (Luke 16.1–8).

Silver tetradrachmas *(4-drachma pieces) from the Phoenician city of Tyre. Tyrian coins were renowned for the purity of their silver content and were preferred for many payments and transactions.*

"a penny"). The Temple was the wealthiest institution in Palestine and the focus of a specifically Jewish monetary and taxation system (see pp.160–61).

Coins were a comparatively recent medium of exchange and the gospels show that the older system of using precious metals measured by weight still survived. One such measure was the talent, the equivalent of some seventy-five pounds (thirty-four kilograms) of silver. In Matthew's version of the parable of the Talents (Matt. 25.14–30), the man gives his slaves the extraordinary sum of eight talents. This is probably an exaggeration for dramatic effect: Luke's version of the parable is more realistic in its substitution of the talent with the *mina* (NRSV: "pound"), equal to one pound of silver (Luke 19.12–28).

TRADERS AND ARTISANS

The gospels presuppose a mainly agricultural society (see pp.173–74). Otherwise, the Palestinian economy was one of small-scale craftworkers and traders, often operating from the home, who would sell their wares in little shops surrounding the marketplaces of villages and small towns. It was to such people, who tended to be looked down on by the upper classes, that Jesus addressed his preaching and with whom he was chiefly associated.

Tanners produced leather objects such as the sandals, pouches, and wineskins which figure in the gospels, and potters made common objects for domestic use—bowls, cups, dishes, plates, jars, and ovens —as well as more expensive objects, such as the alabaster vase from which oil was poured over Jesus at Bethany (Matt. 26.7; Mark 14.3).

Stonemasons were no doubt engaged in the Greco-Roman cities and on great public works, such as the Temple, which were under construction during Jesus' lifetime. However, many builders worked with mudbrick, which meant that houses were liable to be washed away by a sudden rainstorm, as one of Jesus' parables depicts (Matt. 7.24–27; Luke 6.47–49).

Jesus and Joseph were apparently carpenters, although they may have engaged in more general building work in both wood and stone (see pp.212–13).

FARMERS AND FISHERS

Palestine was a primarily agricultural land and this is reflected in the many New Testament metaphors and images drawn from the practices of farming. To quote just two examples, divine judgment is symbolized by the cutting down of unfruitful trees (Matt. 3.10; Luke 3.9), and the growth of a mustard seed parallels the spread of the divine kingdom (Mark 4.30–32 and parallels).

At the time of Jesus, political conditions in Palestine were reasonably stable, allowing agriculture to be a potentially prosperous occupation. In Luke, Jesus depicts a farmer so successful that he has to demolish his barns and build new ones to accommodate all his crops (Luke 12.18). However, the repeated division of landholdings among a family's sons—Luke also

Wine production

The cultivation of vineyards for wine was the third great staple of Palestinian agriculture, and figures prominently in the gospels. Jesus' description of a vineyard in the parable of the Evil Tenants (Matt. 21.33–46; Mark 12.1–12; Luke 20.9–18)—however much it may owe to the "Song of the Vineyard" in the book of Isaiah (Isa. 5.1–2)—accurately reflects contemporary practice. There would be a hedge and watchtower for protection and a pit would be dug as a winepress for treading the grapes. The term used for the tenants to whom it was rented probably means "vinedressers." These were skilled agriculturalists, like the gardener in Luke 13.6–9 who knew how to preserve a barren fig tree by digging round it and manuring it. Wine was a common drink—Jesus drank it and was even denounced as a drunkard (Matt. 11.19; Luke 7.34). He quotes what is perhaps a popular saying about the superiority of a mature vintage (John 2.10) and was aware that a worn-out wineskin would burst if filled with newly fermenting wine (as at Matt. 9.17; Mark 2.22; Luke 5.37).

In Judaism, the vine had long been a symbol for the nation of Israel and Jesus continued this idea for the new community of his followers. The kingdom he preaches is a vineyard in which his disciples are laborers. The image is particularly developed in John's gospel: Jesus is "the true vine," his father is the vinegrower, and his disciples are the branches, who, if they prove unworthy, will be pruned and burned (John 15.1–8).

Harvesting the vine and treading grapes. A mosaic from a 5th-century Byzantine church on Mount Nebo in Perea (Transjordan).

The rich agricultural landscape of the shores of Lake Galilee near Bethsaida.

tells of Jesus being asked to decide an inheritance dispute between brothers (Luke 12.13)—coupled with the burdens of taxation and bad harvests, meant that many individuals lost possession of their own farms. Sometimes they were forced to sell out to wealthy aristocrats and become tenants, paying rent in kind, often to absentee landlords—a situation presupposed by the parable of the Unjust Steward in Luke 16. Or they were compelled to eke out a precarious existence as day laborers, forced to wait about in the marketplace of a local town each morning for someone to hire them, as in the parable of the Generous Employer (Matt. 20.1–16). Again, many people had to commit themselves to serve as slaves—the Greek term in the gospels usually translated as "servant" often really denotes such an indentured slave.

Farmers in Palestine cultivated three main types of crop: grain, olives, and vines (see box, opposite). Wheat was the staple diet and the principal crop. Barley was also grown, although it was of less importance and in the gospels it is specifically mentioned only once, in John's narrative of the Feeding of the Five Thousand (John 6.9–13).

Plowing and sowing took place in late October or the beginning of November, when the early rains (see sidebar, right) had softened the ground after the hot summer. Lack of water was a major problem, so the farmer would habitually scan the sky carefully to see whether it promised rain or drought, as Jesus said (Matt. 16.2–3). Seed was broadcast by hand, as the parable of the Sower indicates (Mark 4.3–9, 13–20 and parallels), either preceded or followed by plowing. Harvest time was May or June, when sickles were used to reap the crop. After threshing to remove the stalks, the ears of wheat were tossed into the air with a winnowing fork. The wind

THE CLIMATE OF PALESTINE

Palestine is broadly subtropical, with very hot dry summers and mild damp winters. There are two main rainy seasons, "the early rain and the later rain" (Deut. 11.14). The "early rain," which begins in October and can occur until March, may produce heavy downpours. In this period the ground is plowed and sown. The "later rain," in April, consists of lighter showers, sufficient to ripen late crops. Rain comes on western winds from the Mediterranean, as Jesus remarks (Luke 12.54). The rains were not always dependable and water was often scarce. In Jesus' day it was courteous to offer a guest or stranger a drink or a basin of water to wash dusty feet.

In contrast, hot, dry air is blown in from the desert south of Palestine (Luke 12.55). Palestinian summers are very hot (Matt. 20.12), but at other times the climate can turn chilly, especially at night in hilly areas, where it may even snow. The night of Jesus' arrest, around Passover in the Jewish month of Nisan (March/April), was cold enough to warrant a fire being lit in the high priest's courtyard.

Above: *An ancient olive oil press at Tabgha (ancient Heptapegon) near Capernaum.*

Right: *An olive grove in northern Israel near Mount Hermon.*

blew away the chaff, leaving the heavier grain, which was then cleared from the threshing floor and stored in a granary. The chaff was then burned, as John the Baptist carefully describes (Matt. 3.12; Luke 3.17). Before being stored, the wheat was sieved to remove any remaining impurities, such as small stones—a scene evoked by Jesus when he warns Simon Peter that Satan will sift the disciples "like wheat" (Luke 22.31). Finally, the grain was ground into flour using a large millstone, a process often carried out by women, as the gospels indicate (Matt. 24.41).

After wheat, the most significant staple crop was the olive. Palestinian olive oil, mentioned several times in the gospels, was of renowned quality and one of the region's major exports. It was used for a variety of domestic purposes, including as fuel for lamps, as in the parable of the Ten Bridesmaids (Matt. 25.1–13), and for healing (Mark 6.13; Luke 10.34). The Mount of Olives was, as its name implies, an area of olive groves that included Gethsemane ("[Place of] Oil Presses").

Fishing

Jesus was well acquainted with the fishing trade that was central to the Galilean economy. It was a prosperous activity and those of Jesus' disciples who were engaged in it were men of substance who worked in family partnerships, owning several vessels and employing hired hands. The remains of a first-century CE Galilean fishing boat have been recovered. It has a rounded stern, such as Jesus would have rested on during one of his voyages across the lake (Mark 4.38).

The gospels mention three types of fishing. One method involved throwing a small net from the shore into the water—this was what the brothers Simon and Andrew were doing when they were first recruited by Jesus. A fish could also be taken by angling with hook and line, as in the story of Peter catching a fish containing a coin to pay the Temple tax. Larger nets could be dropped from boats in deeper water and either hauled on board or pulled toward the shore if the catch was too heavy to lift.

Jesus' first disciples were fishermen and the gospels draw vividly upon the symbolism of their profession. In Matthew's gospel (Matt. 13.47–50), the dragnet is the heavenly kingdom that sweeps up all sorts of human beings. The catch is sorted and the "good" fish are kept while "bad" fish are thrown away, prefiguring the last judgment. John 21.11 records a great catch of one hundred fifty-three fish. Ancient Greek zoologists held that there were precisely this number of species of fish in existence, so the catch can be seen as representing the entirety of humankind and the universality of the gospel.

John places the story of the great haul of fish after the Resurrection, but in Luke it occurs at the beginning of Jesus' ministry and prompts Jesus to promise his fishermen disciples that henceforward they will be catching people (Luke 5.10–11). Luke says that the net was so full it began to break, a realistic detail—the gospels describe James and John carrying out the chore of repairing their nets (Matt. 4.21; Mark 1.19). John's account pointedly remarks that the net remained intact, emphasizing the miraculous nature of the catch (John 21.11).

As Christianity developed, fish acquired eucharistic symbolism. This may derive from the gospel accounts of the feedings of the four or five thousand, in which fish feature prominently (see pp.228–29).

The Miraculous Draft of Fishes *by Konrad Witz (1400–1447). It illustrates the episode in John 21 when Jesus, to the disciples' astonishment, tells them to cast their net on the right of the ship and it at once fills with fish. Peter is shown both trying to haul up the net and then jumping into the water to swim toward Jesus on the shore.*

MARRIAGE AND THE FAMILY

Among the Jews of Jesus' day marriage was regarded as virtually an obligation. The Bible records that some of Israel's patriarchs were polygamous, but by the time of Jesus the monogamous family was the social norm. Marriage was essentially a legal contract between two individuals, initiated by their parents. The key stage was the betrothal, when the bridegroom executed a written document, the Ketubbah, in which he undertook to assign his bride a sum of money in the event of his death or if he should divorce her. Betrothal made the woman legally the man's wife, but the marriage could not be consummated until she moved into her husband's house. Unfaithfulness on the part of the woman during the betrothal period was regarded as adultery and grounds for voiding the Ketubbah—this is the situation apparently faced by Joseph when Mary became pregnant while the couple were still betrothed (Matt. 1.18).

After some time, the bride was taken to her husband's house, just as Joseph took Mary as his wife after the angel had allayed his fears. The occasion was marked by a lavish wedding feast, such as the one Jesus

The Wedding Feast at Cana, *by Paolo Veronese (ca. 1528–88). Jesus and his mother are seated at the center among disciples; the chief steward (in white, right foreground) tastes the water that Jesus has miraculously turned into wine (John 2.9).*

The position of women

Women in Jewish society were largely confined to the home, but within the household they had a vital and central place, since they were mainly responsible for the whole domestic economy. Jesus sometimes alludes to the activities of women in the family, for example baking (Matt. 13.33; Luke 13.21) and grinding meal (Matt. 24.41; Luke 17.35). Martha, "distracted by her many tasks," represents the typical busy housewife (Luke 10.40).

A wife possessed legal rights that her husband had to respect, including the right to own and control her own property. But it was above all as mothers that women were honored. Normally, the childless woman was an object of scorn and pity, and it is a sign of particular divine favor that the barren Elizabeth becomes pregnant when past the normal age of childbearing (Luke 1).

*A coin issued to mark Rome's defeat of the Jewish revolt (70 CE). "Captive Judea" (*Iudaea Capta*) is depicted as a Jewish widow in mourning.*

The situation of a widow was an unhappy one but her condition was alleviated by a law, mentioned in the gospels, whereby if a man died without issue his brother had to marry the widow and provide for her (Mark 12.19 and parallels). If a man married his brother's divorced wife during the brother's lifetime it was viewed as incest, hence John the Baptist's opposition to the marriage of Antipas and Herodias, his brother's ex-wife (Mark 6.17–18 and parallels).

Women were exempt from many religious obligations, but they worshiped at the Temple, where they had their own court (see plan, p.152). They were often prominent in the synagogues, at least in the Diaspora, as Acts and Paul's letters indicate.

attended at Cana (John 2). The gospels do not mention whether Jesus himself was married. It has been suggested that the Cana celebration was his own wedding, but there is no evidence for this. The bridegroom was escorted to the feast at night in a torchlit procession of young women, as described in the parable of the Wise and Foolish Bridesmaids (Matt 25.1–13). Once in their marital home, it was usual for the couple to consummate their union, but Matthew is careful to note that Joseph and Mary had no sexual relations until after the birth of Jesus (Matt. 1.24–25).

Divorce was theoretically easy (see sidebar, right) but it was probably relatively infrequent. The rabbis discouraged it and stressed the blessings of the married state, chief among which were children. Boys and girls were expected to submit to parental authority—Luke mentions that Jesus was obedient to his parents (Luke 2.51) and Jesus reiterates the biblical commandment to honor father and mother (Mark 7.10 and parallels).

The father was definitely the head of the household, but he was bound by the Ketubbah to provide for his family. This obligation underlies Jesus' point when he says how incredible it would be for a father to give a hungry child a stone, a snake, or a scorpion instead of food (Matt. 7.9–10; Luke 11.11). The eldest son had a special status that gave him a double share of the inheritance, and he became head of the family on his father's death. If it is in this capacity that Jesus, on the cross, provided for the welfare of his mother (John 19.26–27), she must have already been a widow.

DIVORCE

Strictly speaking, in Jewish law the initiative for divorce rested with the husband, as suggested by a question that some Pharisees put to Jesus: "Is it lawful for a man to divorce his wife?" (Mark 10.2; Matt. 19.3). A man could give his wife a document stating that he had no further rights over her and that she was free to remarry. He could do this if she had ceased to please him for any reason, as Moses commanded (Deut. 24.1–4).

However, it was also possible for a wife to end her marriage, as Jesus implies (Mark 10.12), by a kind of legal fiction. She could petition the courts to compel her husband to give her a divorce, thus preserving the letter of the biblical law.

The differences between the Pharisees and Jesus on divorce appear to reflect a genuine debate on the issue in first-century Pharisaic circles. The school of the teacher Hillel adhered to Deuteronomy, but the followers of Shammai, another renowned teacher, taught that a wife could be divorced only for unchastity—precisely Jesus' position in Matthew (Matt. 19.9).

LANGUAGES OF PALESTINE

First-century Palestine was a markedly multilingual society. At all social levels, the most common language was Aramaic, a Semitic tongue closely related to Hebrew. It was originally spoken by Aramean tribes of northern "Aram," a term variously used to denote parts of ancient Syria and northern Mesopotamia. These tribes were conquered by the Assyrians, who took Aramean scribes into the imperial bureaucracy. Aramaic subsequently became an official—and the most widely used—language of the Assyrian state and of the Persian empire that supplanted it.

As a consequence, Aramaic was adopted by various peoples at the expense of their native tongues, and it rapidly became an everyday language throughout Syria and in Palestine. Judean exiles returning from Babylon in the sixth century BCE adopted Aramaic in place of Hebrew (see sidebar, left) as the most widely understood tongue in their homeland.

This situation prevailed in the period of the New Testament and it is therefore very likely that Jesus' native tongue was Aramaic. The gospels attribute a number of authentic Aramaic words and phrases to him, such as "*Talitha cum*" ("Little girl, get up!") (Mark 5.41) and probably also "*Ephphatha*" ("Be opened") (Mark 7.34). Both expressions may have been preserved as healing formulae by Jesus' disciples. Mark's version of Jesus' saying from the cross, "*Eloi, eloi, lema sabachthani*" ("My God, my God, why have you forsaken me?") (Mark 15.34), represents the opening of Psalm 22 in Aramaic and not the biblical Hebrew. This may indicate that Jesus acquired his scriptural knowledge from hearing sacred texts read out in the synagogues in Aramaic paraphrases (Targums), which were being made at this time for congregations that no longer understood Hebrew.

The gospels include Aramaic place names, such as Golgotha ("[Place of a] Skull") and Gethsemane ("Oil Presses"), and the Aramaic element *bar* ("son of") rather than the Hebrew *ben* occurs in personal names such as

THE SURVIVAL OF HEBREW

While Aramaic was current throughout Palestine and was certainly predominant in Galilee, it would be wrong to think that Hebrew had disappeared as a vernacular language. There are references in rabbinic sources to the use of Hebrew among ordinary people, and it is now known that the Hebrew of the Mishnah, the body of oral Jewish law and tradition that was first written down ca. 200 CE, was not devised by scholars as once believed but represents a living form of the language that developed in the last centuries BCE. This variety of spoken Hebrew is also found in some of the Qumran scrolls and in letters and other documents from the time of the Second Jewish War of 132–5 CE.

The evidence suggests, therefore, that in Jesus' day Hebrew continued to be spoken in the more southerly areas of Palestine, and it is likely that Jesus would have known some Hebrew, at least, and perhaps spoke it particularly on his visits to Judea. When Jesus addresses God as "Father," "*Abba*"—a word that subsequently passed over into the early Christian communities (Rom. 8.15; Gal. 4.6)—and employs the phrase "*Ephphatha*" (see main text), he could be speaking either Hebrew or Aramaic, because the two were very closely related. Matthew's version of Jesus' utterance from the cross, "*Eli, eli, lema sabachthani*" (Matt. 27.46), is partly in Hebrew and partly in Aramaic (see p.256).

The name "Jesus" is the Latin form of the Greek Iesous. *This in turn represents the common Jewish name Yeshu or Yeshua, which is inscribed in Hebrew letters on this ossuary of the late 1st century* CE *("YSHWA," reading from right to left).*

Greek

As a result of the conquests of Alexander the Great in the fourth century BCE, Greek came to be widely spoken in the ancient Near East (see p.154). Herod the Great and his successors fostered the use of the language in Palestine, especially in Jerusalem. The city had a synagogue for Greek-speaking Jews and numerous inscriptions reveal how common the use of Greek was there.

The Greek spoken in this period was not Classical Greek, but a simpler and more colloquial form known as the *koine* ("common [dialect]"). The language of the New Testament is basically *koine*, and it seems probable—if the gospels are to be trusted—that Jesus could speak it. He conversed with foreign officials who would almost certainly have spoken Greek, such as Pilate and the Capernaum centurion, and with a Syro-Phoenician woman whom Mark describes as "Greek" (Mark 7.26; NRSV: "Gentile"). As a craftsman, Jesus would also have found Greek useful in his trade among Galilee's mixed population. The names of the disciples Andrew and Philip are Greek, and those of Thaddeus and Bartholomew are Aramaized Greek.

Many Greek words passed into Aramaic and many people would happily have conversed in a *patois* of these two languages. But given the much stronger evidence that Jesus' main language was Aramaic (see main text), it is doubtful whether he was either fully bilingual or —as some scholars have proposed—sometimes even taught in Greek.

The Crucifixion, *French school, ca. 1452. The inscription on the cross (see p.337) is in Greek, Latin, and what the gospels term "Hebrew"—although this probably means Aramaic.*

Bartholomew, Bartimaeus, Barabbas, and Bar-Jonah (Matt. 16.17; NRSV: "son of Jonah"). Jesus would probably have been known in his own tongue as Yeshua bar Y(eh)oseph ("Jesus son of Joseph"). He and his disciples would have spoken the Aramaic dialect of Galilee, which differed from that of Jerusalem, as Matthew's gospel indicates (Matt. 26.73). According to rabbinic texts, Galileans were unable to pronounce guttural consonants properly.

Some scholars have attempted to go behind the Greek of the gospels (see box, above) to recover the original Aramaic words of Jesus. It has even been suggested that there once existed an Aramaic collection of his sayings, which may have been the earliest form of the hypothetical document known as "Q" (see p.189). While such attempts must always be tentative, some passages in the gospels can plausibly be illuminated by reconstructing an Aramaic substratum. It is notable that such instances occur most frequently in the words of Jesus himself. When many of his sayings are turned "back" into Aramaic from Greek, they assume the typical forms of Semitic poetry, with such features as wordplay, parallelism, alliteration, and assonance.

IC
XC

JESUS CHRIST: THE LIFE

Christ Pantocrator ("All-Ruling"), *one of a series of 14th-century mosaics in the Byzantine church of St. Savior in Chora (now Kariye Camii mosque), Istanbul, depicting the life of Christ. Surrounded by Israelite patriarchs, prophets, and kings, Jesus is presented as the bringer of the new law, which he holds in his left hand. His right hand is raised in a gesture of blessing.*

WHAT IS A "GOSPEL"?

"REDACTION CRITICISM"
In recent years, "redaction criticism" has countered the view of the form critics (see main text) that the gospels are basically collections of pre-existing fragments of material. Redaction critics, in contrast, see them as unified works by individual authors, each with its own plan and underlying assumptions. According to redaction critics, the gospels can be viewed in the light of an ancient biographical tradition. There are "biographies" in the Hebrew Scriptures (for example, the life of Moses) and such Jewish literature inspired other biographies of prophets and righteous individuals. The rabbinical writings (ca. first–seventh centuries CE) contain nothing corresponding directly to the works of the evangelists, but stories about individual teachers in these texts are often similar in form and content to stories in the gospels.

The term "gospel" literally means "good news" and translates the Greek *euangelion*. In this straightforward sense, *euangelion* was in regular secular usage in the Greco-Roman world, but in the New Testament the word takes on a specifically Christian meaning to designate the story of Jesus and his teaching. For Paul, this "good news" is primarily the salvation brought by Jesus' death and resurrection. In the four books known as gospels, it represents the message that the kingdom of God is coming, brought by Jesus.

Until the early twentieth century the four gospels of the Christian canon (see box, opposite) were mainly interpreted as biographies, a view introduced by the writer Justin Martyr (ca. 155 CE). It was often thought possible to construct a "life" of Jesus from the gospel evidence, although the pictures produced by different scholars often varied dramatically.

From the 1920s, a school of thought called "form criticism" powerfully challenged the concept of the gospels as biography, portraying them instead as a literary genre with no real parallel. Form critics emphasized that before the appearance of the first written gospels, traditions about Jesus' life and teaching would have circulated orally in small anecdotal units that would have been adapted to meet the needs of individual congregations. Each evangelist assembled these fragments to reflect his own theological interpretation of Jesus' message, and so the gospels cannot be relied on to create a factual, chronologically accurate biography of the historical Jesus.

Much of the work of the form critics remains of permanent value, especially their elucidation of individual episodes and teachings. However,

St. Paul Preaching, *from a Bible produced in France 843–51 CE. Before the gospels were written down, the traditions and teachings of Jesus were transmitted orally by the apostles and other early preachers.*

Gospels in the canon of Scripture

The Greek term "canon," meaning a "rule" or "standard," is used to denote the collection of writings that the Church accepts as possessing a unique and special status. The first canon that corresponds exactly to the New Testament as we know it was drawn up in 367 CE, after three centuries in which various writings gradually acquired authority.

The four gospels began to be perceived as a distinct group in the late second century CE. At this time, there were numerous other gospels in circulation, including the Gospel of Thomas (see box, p.191) and three Jewish-Christian works (see box, p.327). It is not easy to determine exactly why only Matthew, Mark, Luke, and John achieved canonical status, but the Muratorian Fragment (late second century CE), the earliest "draft canon" of the New Testament, indicates two key reasons. Firstly, in spite of their differences, these four gospels present the same basic account of the life of Jesus. Second, they were the earliest gospels written and their authors would have been in contact with Jesus' first followers. There was a sense, too, that these four texts alone were in accord with the emerging consensus about the true nature of the faith.

It has also been suggested that the Christians' remarkably rapid adoption of the newly-invented codex (bound book) played a part in the four gospels being fixed as a group. Unlike a scroll, a codex could contain all of them in a single volume.

Christ in Majesty, *in a church in Capua, Italy. The winged beasts around Jesus derive from Revelation 4.7–8 and Ezekiel 1.5–14 and symbolize the evangelists: man or angel (Matthew); lion (Mark); calf or ox (Luke); and eagle (John).*

most scholars today would agree that form critics tend to overstress the propensity of early Christian communities to modify a tradition to suit their particular needs. Nor does their skepticism about recovering an authentic picture of the historical Jesus really appear justified.

The gospels can certainly be compared with Jewish writings (see sidebar, opposite), but the most illuminating comparison is with the Greco-Roman genre of popular biography, where the authors related the careers of contemporaries or near-contemporaries with—like the evangelists—a polemical or apologetic purpose. The gospels resemble this type of writing closely enough to be considered a subgenre of it.

Regardless of how they resemble, or differ from, other forms of literature, the works attributed to Matthew, Mark, Luke, and John continue to be identified by the peculiarly Christian word "gospel," instead of the terms "life" and "memoir," which are used of contemporary works. In the end, it is their particular aim—to proclaim the "good news" of Jesus and the salvation he brings—that gives them their unique character.

THE FOUR EVANGELISTS

THE ORIGINS OF MARK'S GOSPEL
There was an early Christian tradition that Mark was written in Rome, a view based on the assumption that the author was connected with Simon Peter (see main text). This claim has been supported by the presence of some Latin terms in the gospel, but these words (such as *quadrans*, the name of a coin) would have been known throughout the Roman empire.

The commonly accepted earliest date for Mark, ca. 65 CE, depends on a statement by the late second-century churchman Irenaeus that Mark wrote after the death of Peter, which was assumed to have occurred during the persecution under the emperor Nero in the mid-60s CE. There are somewhat stronger grounds for fixing the latest possible date for Mark. The evangelist's apocalyptic chapter (Mark 13) contains a deliberately mysterious statement (13.14) that is generally taken to be a near-contemporaneous reference to the Roman capture and destruction of Jerusalem in 70 CE during the First Jewish War (66–70 CE). If so, the gospel would have been written either while the city was already under siege or shortly after its fall.

The gospel of Mark is widely—though not universally—believed to be the earliest of the four (see sidebar, left). Like all the gospels, except perhaps John, the work itself offers no clues as to the identity of its author. The first person to attribute it to someone called "Mark" was the churchman Papias (ca. 130 CE), who claimed to have received this information from a figure called "the Elder." The name Mark (Latin Marcus, Greek Markos) was very common in the ancient world, but most scholars believe that Papias means John Mark, who is mentioned several times in the New Testament (as at Acts 12.12, 12.25). John Mark was a minor figure—Papias notes that the evangelist did not know Jesus directly—and this itself argues for the likelihood that he was the author of the gospel. Obscure persons were rarely credited with famous writings unless a very strong tradition demanded it.

For most of Christian history, Mark was seen as basically an abridged version of the gospel of Matthew (see box, opposite). Mark's work came to be assessed as a comparatively simple and reliable account of the life and work of the Jesus of history, based on the reminiscences of the apostle Peter. Papias states that Mark was the interpreter of Peter, but this connection with the chief apostle is now rejected by many critics. It has been pointed out, for example, that John Mark was associated mostly with Paul, not Peter. On the other hand, the first letter of Peter refers to "my son Mark" (1 Pet. 5.13) and in Acts, when Peter is freed from prison, he is said to have gone to the house of John Mark's mother (Acts 12.12).

It was only in the nineteenth century that Mark came to the forefront of New Testament study, with the widespread recognition that it was in fact the first gospel, and that both Matthew and Luke depended on it. "Form

The ruins of the ancient Forum of Rome. According to a very early Christian tradition, the evangelist Mark accompanied the apostle Peter to the imperial capital and composed his gospel in the city.

Matthew: the "Jewish Gospel"

Long considered the earliest of the four gospels, Matthew represents the outlook of Jewish Christianity (see pp.326–27) and is largely concerned with the relationship of Jesus to Judaism. It is written in Greek, but may have drawn on Hebrew and Aramaic sources. If the reference to a burned city in Matt. 22.7 alludes to the Roman sack of Jerusalem, the final form of the gospel must be later than 70 CE.

There seems little basis for the traditional attribution of the gospel to the apostle Matthew, although the work does indicate a special interest in him—it alone narrates his calling and records that he was a tax collector. It is also the only gospel to mention how the fame of Jesus spread to Syria (Matt. 4.24): according to another theory the evangelist may have belonged to a Jewish Christian church founded by the apostle at Antioch in Syria (modern Antakya, Turkey).

Although it is basically a story, tracing the career of Jesus from his conception to the Resurrection, teaching is prominent in Matthew, notably in five great discourses of Jesus. Much in the gospel suggests that the author may have trained as a scribe (see p.162). For example, the way he often quotes the Hebrew Bible resembles the Qumran texts, while the Sermon on the Mount (Matt. 5–7) perhaps parallels the rabbinic procedure of modifying a biblical commandment to apply it to fresh circumstances. Matthew's polemic against the scribes and Pharisees is much stronger than in the other gospels, and this should probably be seen as an attack on rival Jewish teachers who did not accept the authority of Jesus.

The evangelist Matthew, from an illuminated gospel book produced ca. 1020 in England. His traditional symbol, the figure of a man or an angel, appears at top right.

criticism" (see pp.182–83) demonstrated that Mark was largely composed of small narrative units handed down in the early Church and not of material derived from a single eyewitness. At the same time, other scholars emphasized that, viewed as a whole, the gospel is clearly the work of a conscientious and sophisticated author with a deliberate theological purpose.

In spite of the undeniable validity of these and other assessments, scholars continue to differ widely in their judgments of Mark's aims and the extent to which he provides authentic historical information about Jesus.

Luke's gospel stands out in many ways, not least because it is the first part of a two-volume work, the second being the Acts of the Apostles. The opening words of the gospel are intended as a preface to both books, in which Luke presents the story of Jesus as part of a broader view of all human history, in successive phases: the epoch of Israel; the epoch of Jesus (from the Baptism to the Ascension); and the epoch of the Church as it

St. Luke, *from the 9th-century MacDurnan Gospels produced at Armagh, Ireland. The evangelist holds a book (his gospel) in one hand and a bishop's crozier in the other. He has cloven hooves instead of feet, an allusion to his symbolic creature, the calf or ox (see illustration, p.183).*

awaits the return of its Lord. The gospel is less a biography than a work belonging to the Hellenistic genre of general history. Luke avoids the term "gospel" (*euangelion*) and prefers to describe his work as a narrative in chronological order. His preface, in elegant Classical Greek idiom—he writes the most polished Greek of all the evangelists—conforms to a common type of introduction found in Hellenistic histories, where the author claims to have studied his predecessors in order to produce his own definitive account of events.

For Luke, Jesus' career and its sequel in the growth of the Church were not things that happened in obscurity, or "done in a corner" to use Paul's words in Acts 26.26. To emphasize this, at key points Luke synchronizes the life of Jesus with events in a wider historical perspective. In contrast to Mark and Matthew, he seeks to fix the period of Jesus' Galilean ministry to a definite time by introducing four references to the tetrarch Herod Antipas (see p.156).

The early Church identified the educated and polished historian who wrote the gospel with the Luke who appears in Acts as Paul's traveling companion, and claimed that his work embodied Paul's teaching, just as Mark reflected that of Peter.

Paul's mission was primarily to Gentiles (non-Jews) and the whole tenor of Luke's gospel suggests that it, too, is aimed at Greek-speaking Gentiles. The work was certainly so understood by the anti-Jewish writer Marcion (ca.140 CE), who excluded all the gospels except Luke from his canon. But even Marcion only accepted Luke in an expurgated form, since there is a pervasive influence of the Hebrew Bible in many parts of Luke's work. It has also been objected that Luke's portrait of Paul in Acts is very different from that which emerges from Paul's own letters. But biography and autobiography can often differ in the light they cast on the same subject, so this does not necessarily preclude a close link between Luke and Paul.

Luke clearly wrote at a time when the eyewitnesses he mentions had died, and a need had arisen for a reliable account of Jesus. His "predictions" of the destruction of Jerusalem, as in Luke 21, may be after the fact and thus imply a date post-70 CE. However, the statement that the city's inhabitants "will be taken away as captives" (Luke 21.24) may be a genuine prophecy, constructed along the lines of the account of the city's destruction in the book of Jeremiah.

Jesus is always the central figure in Luke. Unlike Mark or Matthew, Luke calls him "savior" and pictures him distinctively as a prophet, guided by the Spirit. Above all, Jesus is a being of gracious tenderness and compassion, not least in those parables peculiar to Luke. He shows a forgiving love toward outcasts, sinners, and Samaritans, poignantly expressed in the words from the cross at Luke 23.34 and 23.43. Luke's account possesses a universalism summarized by Jesus' final promise that "repentance and forgiveness of sins is to be proclaimed in his name to all nations."

John's gospel, also referred to as the Fourth Gospel, is an enigmatic work that is in some ways very dissimilar to the other gospels. It received a mixed reception in the early Church, and experts continue to give very different assessments of its theology, composition, and background. There has been much discussion as to whether the author of John (see sidebar, right) used one or more of the other gospels, but it is perhaps more likely that he drew upon similar traditions and developed them in his own way.

Scholars have often attempted to uncover other possible sources for John, such as a "book of signs" or an independent Passion narrative. These remain highly speculative, but if John does largely depend on sources distinct from those used by the other evangelists, much of it could predate the late first century CE, the period usually proposed for its composition.

The content of John may differ, but its differences in form should not be exaggerated. For example, the long discourses of Jesus in John have often been said to constitute the principal feature distinguishing this gospel from Matthew, Mark, and Luke. But—as the five discourses in Matthew demonstrate—lengthy speeches are also ascribed to Jesus in the other gospels.

THE AUTHORSHIP OF JOHN

The issues of the authorship and date of the final form of the Fourth Gospel are highly complex. The gospel itself claims to rest on the testimony of an eyewitness, referred to as the "beloved disciple," and it is not impossible that the first stage of writing did indeed consist of an oral transmission of Jesus' sayings, deeds, death, and resurrection by John, the apostle to whom it is attributed. The gospel has often been seen as a product of the Greco-Roman world, and the traditional place for its composition is Ephesus in Asia Minor. However, it is now generally agreed that the background of the gospel, or at least of many of the traditions it uses, is Palestine. Archaeology has confirmed that the author gives accurate information about sites and customs of the region. The Qumran texts (see p.169) contain many striking parallels with the language and ideas of John's gospel, and there are other similarities. In fact, the whole book, like Matthew (see p.185), can be seen as rooted in Judaism. Although John refers to "the Jews" as those who should have acknowledged Jesus but rejected him, he also states that "salvation is from the Jews." Jesus is regularly compared with the great figures of Jewish history, such as Abraham and particularly Moses. There are links with Jewish Wisdom theology and considerable concern with the Mosaic law, the Temple, and the Messiah.

However, none of this precludes Hellenistic influence, since it is now known that Palestinian Judaism was deeply affected by Hellenism in the centuries around the birth of Christ (see p.154).

The ruins of the Greco-Roman city of Ephesus in Asia Minor (Efes, Turkey), where the gospel of John is traditionally said to have been written. Paul founded an important Christian community here, and it is to this church that the letter to the Ephesians is addressed.

THE GOSPEL EVIDENCE

A silver denarius *of Tiberius (ruled 14–37 CE), Roman emperor when Jesus was active (Luke 3.1). As with Jesus, what we know of his life is based on four accounts, each with its own distinct outlook, most notably those of Tacitus (ca. 55–ca. 120 CE) and Suetonius (ca. 69–ca. 140 CE).*

One of the most assured results of modern New Testament scholarship is that the evangelists provide virtually all that we know about Jesus, and that therefore we can approach him in no other way than through the gospels. Many scholars would assert that these reveal more about the early Church than they do about Jesus himself, since they present Jesus as the object of early Christian belief and preaching—the "Christ of faith" rather than the "Jesus of history."

While few scholars would deny that Jesus ever existed—although this view is still occasionally advanced (see p.347)—the more skeptical would claim that little, if anything, can be known of the man Jesus beyond that he lived, taught, and died in Palestine. However, in assessing the value of the gospels as historical evidence various other factors need to be considered. For example, our knowledge of first-century Palestine has greatly increased in recent years and it can now be seen that much of the gospel picture of Jesus reflects an authentic historical background.

Also, it may be argued that the apparent dichotomy between the Christ of faith and the historical Jesus can be pressed too far, and that what the early Church believed must surely have borne some relation to the actual work and sayings of Jesus. Disciples of a Jewish *rabbi* were expected to memorize their teacher's sayings and transmit them faithfully to future generations. Jesus' followers may have done the same, perhaps even making written notes of his words and deeds in the period before the evangelists composed their accounts.

Much is often made of the discrepancies between the gospels—such as their different versions of the same sayings—and the possibility that much attributed to Jesus may be a creation of the early Church and the gospel writers. While there are obvious legendary elements in the gospels, and no doubt words are attributed to Jesus that he is unlikely to have uttered (see sidebar, left), the same may be said of other biographies of antiquity (not to mention more recent times). It has been pointed out, for instance, that there are also four surviving ancient biographies of Jesus' contemporary, the emperor Tiberius. These disagree very considerably among themselves—two are even biased against him—but scholars find it perfectly possible to produce a generally acceptable historical account of his life.

The extent of the divergences among the gospels can be exaggerated. For example, the wording of the Lord's Prayer varies in Matthew 6.9–13 and Luke 11.2–4, but the prayer is recognizably the same. Similarly, while the present forms of Matthew's Sermon on the Mount and Luke's Sermon on the Plain are no doubt creations of the evangelists, many of the individual sayings of which they are made up could well go back to Jesus himself.

THE JESUS SEMINAR

All the gospels are certainly written "that you may come to believe that Jesus is the Messiah, the Son of God" (John 20.31). But John also claims to be telling the "truth" (21.24)—describing what Jesus really did. This claim must be judged by testing the gospels according to the same criteria applied to similar ancient texts. Notable recent endeavors in this respect include the work of the "Jesus Seminar" of the Westar Institute in the United States, a group of scholars who subjected the words ascribed to Jesus in the four gospels and the Gnostic gospel of Thomas (see p.190) to systematic examination.

Their conclusions (published 1990–93) judged only two percent of the sayings attributed to Jesus to be "most probably genuine" and fourteen percent to be "probably genuine." The Seminar's work is not free of controversy (see Introduction), but on the other hand it is unlikely that any attempt to discover "genuine" evidence about Jesus will ever be the subject of scholarly unanimity.

The "synoptic problem"

The question of how each evangelist sourced and shaped his material arises particularly with the gospels of Matthew, Mark, and Luke. These texts have many resemblances that permit them to be set out in parallel and closely compared, and hence they are often referred to as the "synoptic" gospels (Greek *sunoptikos*, "seen together") and their authors as the "synoptists." New Testament scholarship seeks to describe how and why they are so similar.

At present, the most widely accepted explanation of their similarity is the so-called "Two-Document" hypothesis, although this is not an entirely adequate description. According to this theory, Mark was written first and established the distinctive genre of "gospel." Mark was used by the other two synoptists, but some resemblances between Matthew and Luke cannot be explained by their common use of Mark. Scholars have therefore postulated that they employed another source, known as "Q" from the German *Quelle* ("source"). The hypothetical "Q" was not a gospel in the usual sense, but a collection of sayings of Jesus, with some narrative, and could have reached the gospel writers in either written or oral form. It has been compared with the Gospel of Thomas, which also consists of sayings (see box, p.191).

Finally, as well as Mark and "Q," Matthew and Luke also use matter that is peculiar to each of them, referred to as "M" and "L" respectively.

The "Two-Document" theory has attained a wide degree of acceptance but is not without powerful challengers. For most of Christian history, Matthew was considered the earliest and basic gospel, an opinion that still has strong advocates. If this view is adopted, the most plausible account of the relationship between the synoptic gospels is perhaps what is known as the "Two-Gospel" hypothesis. According to this, the three synoptic gospels were written in the order Matthew-Luke-Mark, with Luke dependent on Matthew, and Mark using both Matthew and Luke. Among the evidence used to support this theory is the fact that Mark sometimes seems to abbreviate passages that appear in full in Matthew.

It must be emphasized that there is no surviving independent text of "Q" and many scholars would deny that there ever was such a document. Even if its existence is accepted, there are widely different assessments of its character and purpose. For example, was its original language Aramaic or Greek? Can successive strata, with different characteristics, be discovered within it? Most significantly, does it represent the preaching of a community outside what came to be

St. Mark, *from the early 9th-century gospel of St. Médard of Soissons, France. Above the figure of the evangelist is his traditional attribute, the winged lion.*

mainstream Christianity, which had its own particular approach to Jesus? To judge by the sayings that "Q" supposedly included, this group would appear, for example, to have had no interest in Christ's death and resurrection.

Such questions mean that the "synoptic problem" remains an issue. It must always be recognized how much is uncertain about the development of early Christianity, such as the fact that there is no hard evidence for the chronological order of the gospels.

Perhaps it is best to conclude that the evangelists employed a wide variety of documents and oral traditions, and were selective in what they used. The author of John acknowledges that he knew of many other acts of Jesus than he records (John 20.30, 21.25). Similarly, Luke's preamble to his "orderly account of the events that have been fulfilled among us" (Luke 1.1) shows that he was aware of many writings already in existence on the life and works of Jesus.

JESUS IN OTHER WRITINGS

EARLY PAGAN AND JEWISH SOURCES
There are a number of early references to Jesus in non-Christian writings. For example, the Roman historian Tacitus (ca. 55–ca. 120 CE) relates that the emperor Nero blamed the great fire of Rome in 64 CE on the "Christians," who took their name from "Christus." He had been executed by "one of our procurators," Pilate, but his "pernicious superstition" had survived and spread to Rome. Suetonius (ca. 69–ca. 140 CE) refers to Jews causing trouble at the prompting of "Chrestus" under Claudius (41–54 CE). Jesus is also described in a famous passage in the *Antiquities* of the Jewish historian Josephus (ca. 90 CE). Statements such as "He was the Messiah" have led to the dismissal of the entire passage as a Christian interpolation. But stripping out the more obviously Christian words produces a plausible original: Jesus was "a wise man" who "did surprising things"; "a teacher" who "won over" many Jews and Greeks. He was crucified by Pilate at the instigation "of men of the highest standing among us."

Apart from the four canonical gospels, there are numerous references to Jesus and his teaching in other very early sources, the great majority of them Christian, although some are non-Christian (see sidebar, left). The Christian sources include several "apocryphal gospels" of the second to fifth centuries CE, which contain legendary episodes from Jesus' infancy (for example, the second-century Protevangelium of James); narratives of the Passion; or accounts of Jesus' descent into Hell between his death and resurrection. Others reflect the outlook of Jewish Christianity, but survive only as brief extracts in later Christian authors (see p.327).

Among other notable but fragmentary apocryphal gospels are the Gospel of Peter and the Egerton Gospel, which date from the mid-second century. Especially significant in terms of recent discussion are the *agrapha* (literally "things not written"), sayings of Jesus not found in the canonical gospels but occurring elsewhere in the New Testament, in the works of the Church Fathers (see pp.328–29) or in other sources, above all the Gospel of Thomas (see box, opposite).

It would be widely agreed that there is little of historical value in the apocryphal gospels of Christ's infancy and Passion. They are obviously imaginative products, composed in order to supply perceived deficiencies in the information in the New Testament, and to stimulate popular devotion. A number of them were written to present the specific theological viewpoint of Gnosticism (see pp.330–31).

It has been claimed that the Gospel of Peter and the Egerton Gospel predate Matthew, Mark, Luke, and John. But a closer examination reveals that both writings consist of material that represents either a development, or a reproduction from memory, of material in the canonical gospels.

Anna and Joachim at the Golden Gate, *by Fra Filippo Lippi (1406–69). It illustrates a scene in the life of the legendary parents of the Virgin, St. Anna (Anne) and St. Joachim, whose story derives almost entirely from the apocryphal Protevangelium of James.*

A stronger case can be mounted for some, at least, of the *agrapha*. Even after the four gospels were written down, traditions about Jesus continued to be transmitted orally and remained highly valued. It is certainly possible that some *agrapha* depend on this oral tradition and preserve Jesus' authentic words. Examples include the saying attributed to Jesus by Paul in Acts 20.35 ("It is more blessed to give than receive") or Paul's poetic quotation of Jesus' words at the Last Supper (1 Cor. 11.24–25).

There is an increasing tendency among New Testament scholars to whittle down to quite a small number any extracanonical sayings that might claim to be genuine words of Jesus, and it is rarely easy to decide in any particular case. In the final analysis, the important conclusion must be that—whatever their interest—the noncanonical sources for Jesus add virtually nothing to the New Testament view of him, and still less require any fundamental revision of it.

The Gnostic gospel of Thomas

Among the cache of ancient Gnostic documents discovered in 1945 at Nag Hammadi in Upper Egypt (see pp.330–31) was the "Gospel of Thomas." The manuscript dates from the fourth century CE and is written in Coptic, the Egyptian language of the time, but there is evidence to show that it is actually a translation of a Greek original dating perhaps to the second century CE.

The gospel is unlike the canonical gospels: it contains no narrative but consists of one hundred and fourteen sayings, or "secret words," that Jesus is supposed to have passed on to the disciple Thomas, the purported author. In this respect it could be compared to the hypothetical "Q" document (see p.189).

As it stands, Thomas is clearly a Gnostic text and many of the sayings express Gnostic theology, even when they appear to be drawn from the canonical gospels (seventy of them have New Testament parallels, for example "Let him who seeks not cease seeking until he finds"; compare Matt. 7.7; Luke 11.9). But not all the sayings exhibit this tendency and it has been claimed that the Gnostic coloring was added to the Greek original. Thus the possibility exists that some sayings with no parallels in the canonical gospels may go back to Jesus. But even scholars who would wish to press this claim believe that the number of plausible cases is very small—perhaps no more than five in all.

The Apostle Thomas, *whom the Gospel of Thomas claims as its author, by Nicolas Frances (ca. 1424–68).*

Some of the parables in Thomas lack the allegorical interpretations appended to them in the New Testament gospels (see pp.267–68) and so, in the opinion of some, are likely to represent Jesus' own words. Yet even here caution is necessary. For example, the parable of the Great Net (Matt. 13.47–50) occurs in Thomas shorn of Matthew's eschatological interpretation: "And he said, 'The man is like a wise fisherman who cast his net into the sea; he pulled it up from the sea full of small fish; among them he found a large good fish. That wise fisherman threw all the small fish back into the sea, he chose the large fish without regret. Who has ears let him hear'" (Gospel of Thomas 8).

Matthew's parable about the end of the world has become one about human nature, in accordance with Gnostic concerns. It is thus doubtful whether Thomas's version, an apparent example of Gnostic editing, is either original to Jesus or independent of the canonical text.

JESUS' LIFE AND TIMES

The evangelists, with the possible exception of Luke, were not greatly concerned with chronology. Nevertheless, they provide a number of clues that make it possible to place the life of Jesus somewhere within a reasonably certain timespan, from sometime before 4 BCE to ca. 30 CE or a little later.

Jesus' birth is placed—by Matthew explicitly and Luke implicitly—in the time of King Herod the Great (ruled 37–4 BCE). Matthew gives no indication of how long after Jesus' birth Herod died (see pp.204–07), so all that can be said is that Jesus was probably born shortly before 4 BCE.

Luke dates Jesus' birth to the time of a census of the Roman empire under the emperor Augustus (ruled 27 BCE–14 CE) (Luke 2.1). There was never a single, simultaneous census of the whole empire: Augustus intended to carry out a census of all his domains, but on a province-by-province basis. Thus when Luke refers to "the first registration" (Luke 2.2), he means

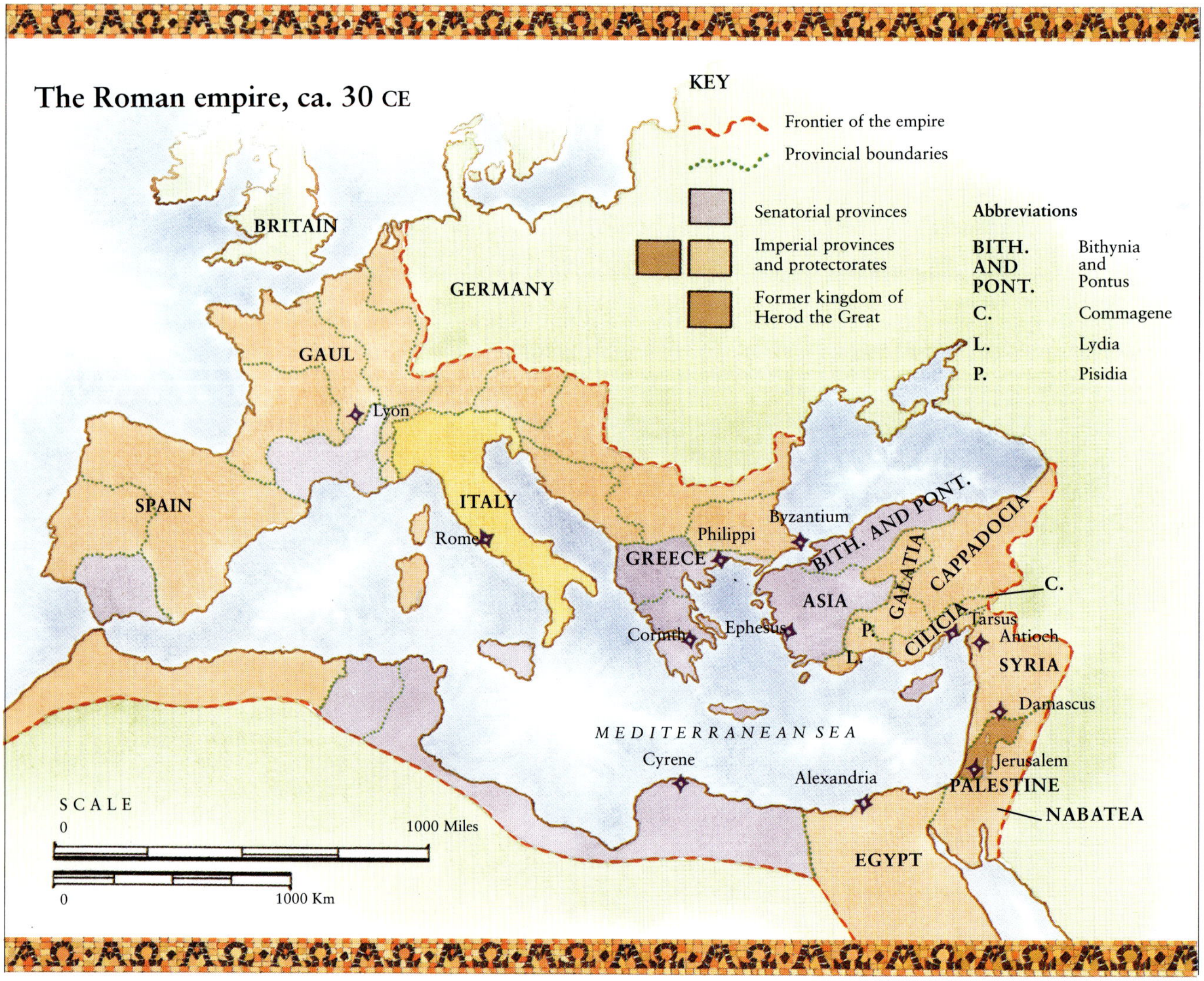

the first census of Judea, for which Quirinius, the legate (governor) of Syria (Luke 2.2), was administratively responsible.

Quirinius was legate of Syria in 6–7 CE, but Luke 2.1 says that the census took place "in those days," which in context means around the time of the birth of John the Baptist, which Luke places in the reign of Herod (Luke 1.5). Perhaps Luke believed that Jesus was born ten years after Herod's death, at the time of the census, but also wanted to put the Messiah's birth into the same general time frame as that of his herald, John, who was known to have been born under Herod. At first sight it seems unlikely that Luke, as a careful historian, really believed that the Judean census had taken place under Herod, because it sparked an anti-Roman revolt that was well remembered in Luke's day: he himself mentions it again in Acts 5.37 (see p.336). His contemporary, the historian Josephus, gives the date of the census as 6 CE, and there is no evidence that Quirinius held the same post a decade earlier—which in any case would have been highly unusual.

On the other hand, there were also riots after Herod's death, and it has been suggested that Luke erroneously conflated the unrest following the census with these earlier disturbances.

Luke 3.1–2 states that John's ministry began in the fifteenth year of the reign of Tiberius (ruled 14–37 CE), probably 28–29 CE. This gives an approximate date for the baptism of Jesus and the beginning of his own ministry. Luke 3.23 says that Jesus was "about thirty" when his ministry commenced, which seems very unlikely if Luke is seriously suggesting that Jesus was born in 6 CE and began his work ca. 29 CE. The age fits better with a birth in ca. 4 BCE. But Luke may use the figure of thirty only to indicate that Jesus had arrived at years of maturity (compare Gen. 41.46; Num. 4.47).

All the gospels agree that Jesus was crucified on a Friday, which was either Passover proper (the day that the Passover lambs were sacrificed in the Temple) (John), or the day after Passover (Matthew, Mark, Luke). The sacrifices took place on the fourteenth of the Jewish month of Nisan, and the Passover meal—the synoptists' Last Supper—was eaten at the start of Nisan 15 (in Judaism, days begin and end at sunset). It has been calculated—and the uncertainties of any such calculation must be stressed—that Nisan 14 ended on a Friday evening (April 3) in 33 CE, and that Nisan 15 ended on a Friday (April 7) in 30 CE. Either year fits Luke's assertion that Jesus died during the prefecture of Pilate (26–36 CE), the high-priesthood of Caiaphas (ca. 18–36/37 CE), and the reign of Antipas (4 BCE–39 CE). John's claim that Jesus died on Passover itself, Nisan 14, probably has a theological motive (see p.242–43). So, assuming the synoptists are correct, it may well be that the Crucifixion took place on Friday, April 7, 30 CE.

THE LENGTH OF JESUS' MINISTRY
It is often supposed that Matthew, Mark, and Luke assume a one-year ministry, while John presents a ministry covering two or even three years. But the evidence is inconclusive. The three synoptists provide no chronological scheme for the episodes that they select from Jesus' career and these may have occurred over more than a single year. The theory of a longer ministry in John rests on his reference to various Jewish feasts, but the order in which he presents them may be based on theological reasons rather than a concern for strict chronology.

The Baptism of Christ, *by Fra Angelico (ca. 1400–55). This event, which heralded the start of Jesus' ministry (see pp.216–17), is dated by Luke to sometime around the year 29 CE.*

THE GENEALOGY OF CHRIST

There are two genealogies of Jesus in the gospels (Matt. 1.1–17; Luke 3.23–38), and there are precedents for both in the Hebrew Scriptures. Recent studies of ancient Near Eastern genealogies show that they were compiled for political or religious reasons rather than as straightforward historical records. Genealogies of, for example, a ruler could be adapted to meet changing concerns and different versions might exist side by side without any sense of incompatibility. In postexilic Judaism, such genealogies became important as part of the picture of the expected Messiah.

Similarly, the genealogies in Matthew and Luke are not intended to present a factual family tree and so one should not attempt to harmonize them. Rather, they are artificial constructions with a theological aim, and may have been adapted from earlier Jewish messianic genealogies.

That they are literary creations can be seen most clearly in the case of Matthew. His list is based on a structure of three epochs: from Abraham to David, from David to the Jewish exile in Babylon, and from the exile to Jesus (1.17). Each epoch is of fourteen generations, although the last apparently comprises only thirteen. The evangelist may be reckoning "Jesus ... who is called the Messiah" (Matt. 1.16) as two names.

The Tree of Jesse, *an 18th-century icon from the Ionian Isles, Greece. It shows the descent of Jesus from Jesse, the father of King David.*

The numerical structure stresses God's careful providential plan. Hebrew letters are also used as numbers, and it may be no coincidence that the three letters that spell the name of David add up to fourteen, because David and Abraham are the two most important figures in the genealogy. Abraham is the father of the nation, and thus Jesus is seen as the true Israel, while his descent from King David shows that the divine promise to the Jews of a Messiah from the royal line of Judah has been fulfilled.

A remarkable feature of Matthew's genealogy is his introduction of four women (Tamar, Rahab, Ruth, and Mary). The purpose of this is to demonstrate the precedent in God's plan for the role of Mary, who appears as Jesus' mother at the end of the genealogy. It has often been noted that the first three of these women were morally ambiguous, even scandalous characters. But perhaps too much can be made of this, because by the first century CE Judaism had come to view them in a more positive light. For example, one rabbinic text speaks of Rahab as the ancestor of prophets and righteous men and of Ruth as the ancestor of kings.

The "priestly lineage" in Luke

In Luke's genealogy, several of the names that appear for the period after the Babylonian exile, such as Levi and Mattathias, imply descent from the Israelite priestly house of Levi (the Levites) rather than the royal house of David. According to Julius Africanus (ca. 220 CE), some people saw this feature as highly significant and held that while Matthew's genealogy asserted Jesus' royal descent, Luke emphasized his levitical, priestly, lineage.

It is unlikely, on closer analysis, that the genealogies can really be distinguished in this way. Interestingly, however, Luke presents Elizabeth, the mother of John the Baptist, as a woman of priestly stock, descended from Aaron (Luke 1.5). Mary is Elizabeth's kinswoman, so this could perhaps be taken as indicating that Jesus was of levitical descent on his mother's side. Curiously, in Luke, Jesus is said to be descended from King David not through the famous King Solomon but through another son, Nathan. Luke may have confused this Nathan with Solomon's contemporary, Nathan the prophet, because the evangelist intended to introduce a prophetic element into Jesus' background. Or Luke may have wanted to avoid referring to Jehoiakim and Jehoiachin, the last two legitimate kings of Judah, because of a prophecy in the book of Jeremiah that they would have no descendants.

The shrine under the altar in the 6th-century Church of the Nativity, Bethlehem. Beneath the silver "Star of Bethlehem" is a grotto in which, according to one Christian tradition, Jesus was born.

Luke's genealogy is less schematic than Matthew's and has more of the character of historical writing. Between David and Jesus he lists forty-two generations, which better suits the time span involved (about one thousand years) than the twenty-eight generations of Matthew. The Lukan genealogy is in the reverse order to that of Matthew, beginning with Jesus. Unlike Matthew, Luke places the genealogy not before Jesus' birth in Bethlehem but at the beginning of his ministry. Here Luke may be following the pattern in Exodus, where the list of Moses' ancestors follows the narrative of his birth and his summoning to God's mission (Exod. 6.16–25).

The other great difference between the two genealogies is that Luke traces Jesus' descent back beyond Abraham to the first man, Adam. This may reflect the universalistic orientation of Luke's gospel (see pp.186–87): Jesus is to be seen as the savior not just of the Jews—unlike Matthew, Luke does not use the term "Messiah" in his genealogy—but of all humanity. Adam is described as "son of God," an expression that may reflect speculation within Judaism about Adam as a heavenly figure. For Luke, though, this description explains why Adam's descendant, Jesus, has been declared the Son of God at his baptism, an event that immediately precedes the presentation of his genealogy (Luke 3.22).

THE NATIVITY

Both Luke and Matthew present the events surrounding Jesus' birth from their own standpoints, but the basic matters on which they agree (see sidebar, opposite) may well point to a reliable early tradition that predates them both. Matthew's version of the birth of Jesus is comparatively brief and colorless: it merely states that Jesus was born, without any accompanying details. Nevertheless, it is not just a factual account but a theological interpretation of events, reflecting ideas present in the Hebrew Scriptures. For example, the heavenly messenger appears in a dream, a regular medium for divine revelations in the Bible.

Also, Matthew draws out the meaning of the name Jesus, in much the same way that the Hebrew Scriptures frequently attach a special significance to personal names. Jesus (Hebrew Yeshu or Yeshua) is a form of "Joshua," which means "Yahweh Saves," and Mary's child is therefore

The figure of Joseph

In both Matthew and Luke, Jesus' descent from King David is traced through Joseph, which raises the question of whether Joseph was originally regarded as Jesus' actual physical father. In the gospels, Mary and Joseph are referred to as his parents, while Matthew calls Jesus the "son of the carpenter" and Luke refers to him as the "son of Joseph."

However, in their present form, the genealogies of Jesus (see pp.194–95) seem to refute this view. Matthew emphasizes only that Jesus was born of Mary (Matt. 1.16); in one Syrian manuscript this verse makes Joseph the father, but it is very unlikely that this reflects Matthew's original text. Again, when Luke calls Jesus the son of Joseph, he adds "as was thought," and there is no evidence to support the opinion that these words are a later insertion in the gospel.

The early Christians, such as Paul, wished to affirm that Jesus was a descendant of King David and thus the awaited Messiah. Joseph was known to be of Davidic lineage and it is probably reasonable to suppose that Matthew and Luke present Joseph as Jesus' legal father—as he would have been in Jewish law—in order to give Jesus a claim to Davidic descent.

Bethlehem, the home of Joseph according to the gospels. One theory proposes that Joseph moved to Nazareth to work on the rebuilding of nearby Sepphoris (see p.155).

Joseph's family connections were evidently with Bethlehem, the traditional home of David. Matthew describes Joseph as a "righteous" man and a devout observer of the Jewish law. He was therefore particularly favored to receive angelic messages through the medium of dreams, as Matthew relates (Matt. 1.20–23; 2.13; 2.19). It is possible that the evangelist may be consciously influenced here by the story of the Israelite patriarch Joseph, the great dreamer in the book of Genesis (see pp.42-5).

Joseph is only mentioned in the birth narratives. His absence from the rest of the New Testament may indicate that he died before Jesus began his ministry.

The Annunciation, *by Fra Angelico (ca. 1400–55). This illustrates Luke 1.26–38, where the archangel Gabriel announces to Mary that she will conceive by the Holy Spirit (represented here by the white dove).*

named because "he will save his people from their sins" (Matt. 1.21).

One characteristic of Matthew's gospel is the evangelist's frequent quotations of biblical prophecies that he sees as being fulfilled in Jesus and his work. These are especially prominent in the opening chapters, where there are no less than five. The purpose of the quotation from Isaiah in the birth story (Matt. 1.23) is not only to confirm Mary's virginal conception but also to attest another significant name for Jesus, "Emmanuel." The author goes on to translate this for his Greek-speaking readers as "God is with us," probably to be understood as indicating a special relationship with God, and Jesus as God's representative.

For Matthew, the main protagonist in the Nativity story, and in the events immediately following Jesus' birth, is Joseph (see box, opposite). He names the child, a very significant event in the Hebrew Bible and Judaism generally, while in Luke it is Mary who does so. The narrative is almost entirely devoted to Joseph's doubts about the proposed marriage and how they are allayed. Perhaps Matthew is developing a tradition of Jewish Christian origin, and is thus concerned to present Joseph as a typically devout Jew, careful to observe the law and customs of his faith. In Matthew he is clearly presented as the patriarchal Jewish head of the family, who could therefore be considered as Jesus' father, whatever his actual physical relationship to his son may have been.

Luke's Nativity account is a moving text of considerable beauty that has always appealed to later writers and artists. Combining poetic imagination and theological interpretation, it is carefully composed with the author's characteristic narrative skill from a series of idyllic scenes pervaded by the ambience of the Hebrew Scriptures. The introduction to the

THE NATIVITY STORIES IN MATTHEW AND LUKE

The accounts in Matthew and Luke of the birth of Jesus have significant divergences, but nonetheless reveal a number of shared features. These suggest that both evangelists drew upon and adapted much the same basic tradition, which—since each author was writing within a different Christian community—must have been well-established for some time. The most notable parallels are as follows:

- The names of Jesus' parents, Mary and Joseph
- The designation of Mary and Joseph as a betrothed couple
- The claim that Joseph is descended from King David
- The annunciation by an angel of the birth of a son (in Matthew to Joseph, in Luke to Mary)
- The angel's message that Mary's conception is by the Holy Spirit, and a command to call the child Jesus
- The representation of Mary as a virgin at the time of conception
- The location of the birth at Bethlehem.

To this list should probably be added the assertion that Jesus was born in the reign of Herod the Great, explicit in Matthew and apparently presupposed in Luke, who synchronizes the births of Jesus and John the Baptist (see pp.192–93).

The town of Ein Karem near Jerusalem, traditionally identified as the "Judean town in the hill country" (Luke 1.39), where Mary went to visit Elizabeth, the mother of John the Baptist.

THE BIRTHS OF JESUS AND JOHN THE BAPTIST

Luke's accounts of the events preceding the births of the Baptist and Jesus are carefully composed and display marked parallels:

- The angel Gabriel appears to Zechariah (Luke 1.11)
  The angel Gabriel appears to Mary (1.26–28)
- Zechariah is troubled at the sight of Gabriel (1.12)
  Mary is troubled by Gabriel's greeting (1.29)
- The angel reassures Zechariah, tells him that God has accepted his prayer, promises him a son, and tells him his name (1.13)
  The angel reassures Mary, tells her that she has found favor with God, promises her a son, and tells her his name (1.30–31)
- The angel foretells John's future in exalted poetic language (1.14–17)
  The angel foretells Jesus' future in a passage of similar quality (1.32–33)
- Zechariah queries the angel: "How will I know that this is so? For I am an old man, and my wife is getting on in years" (1.18)
  Mary queries the angel: "How can this be, since I am a virgin?" (1.34)
- Gabriel gives Zechariah a confirming sign: he is struck dumb (1.20)
  Gabriel gives Mary a confirming sign: her relative Elizabeth is pregnant (1.36).

Further parallels may be discerned in the events that follow the two births:

- John is circumcized and named (1.59–6)
  Jesus is circumcized and named (2.21)
- Events surrounding John's birth cause wonder (1.63, 65–66)
  When the shepherds recount the message of Jesus' birth, "all who heard it were amazed" (2.17–18)
- Zechariah blesses God for John in the form of a prophetic poem (1.67–79)
  Simeon and Anna bless God for Jesus, Simeon with a prophetic poem (2.28–32).

whole gospel is written in good Classical Greek (see p.186), but the author's style then changes dramatically, becoming full of Semitisms and biblical allusions, although Luke does not quote Scripture directly in the way that Matthew does. It has sometimes been supposed that this first section of Luke's gospel has an original Hebrew or Aramaic source, but its linguistic parallels and resonances are with the Septuagint, the Greek version of the Hebrew Bible, rather than the original, and the narrative is best viewed as a literary creation of the evangelist himself.

A distinctive feature of Luke's Nativity story is its close proximity to the story of the birth of John the Baptist. The two accounts come together directly in the meeting of Mary and Elizabeth, who is described as her relative. But the two accounts also have a common form (see sidebar, left), based essentially on various biblical legends in which an angel promises a child to a barren woman (as before the birth of Samson in Judges 13).

That Jesus was in some way closely connected with John, and that Jesus' baptism was of great significance in his own life (see pp.214–17), is one of the most soundly based facts about Jesus. Luke's purpose, perhaps drawing on a tradition current among the Baptist's disciples, seems to be to show that the two men were linked from the very moment of their conceptions, and that they were brought together as part of a great divine plan. However, like all the other evangelists, Luke is also at pains to make clear the superiority of Jesus, which is acknowledged both by Elizabeth and by the child in her womb (Luke 1.41–42). Luke's special contribution is to claim that this was known from the very beginning.

Mary is central to Luke's narrative and his opening chapters have appropriately been described as "the gospel of Mary." It is she to whom Gabriel comes and she who goes to Elizabeth as a kind of messenger of salvation. Her purification after childbirth is mentioned (see p.208), and the righteous Simeon addresses a special prophecy to her (Luke 2.34–35).

Later, Mary takes the lead in speaking to her son when he goes missing and is finally found among the teachers in the Temple (Luke 2.48; see p.208). She is depicted as the perfectly obedient servant of the Lord, suggesting that she is the ideal model of Christian discipleship. Twice the evangelist notes that Mary treasured what she had heard and seen and kept them in her heart (Luke 2.19, 51)—probably an implicit claim that his knowledge of what he records had come from her. It is not impossible that Luke is indeed giving his own version of traditions that go back to Mary herself.

Luke's presentation includes two famous poetic canticles known as the *Magnificat* (Luke 1.46–55) and the *Benedictus* (Luke 1.68–79) from their opening words in Latin translation. They are very probably the evangelist's own composition, based on a string of verses from the Septuagint (the Greek version of the Hebrew Bible). They celebrate the redemption of God's ancient people, Israel, which has now been realized. The *Benedictus* speaks of John as a prophet preparing the way of the Lord. In the *Magnificat* —the position of which is probably suggested by that of the song of Hannah, the mother of the prophet Samuel (1 Sam. 2.1–10)—Mary is the agent whom all future generations will call blessed.

The Adoration of the Magi, *by Jan Gossaert (Mabuse), ca. 1508. The artist depicts the wise men (Matt. 2.11; see pp.202–03) paying homage to Jesus in a picturesque ruin serving as the stable of the inn (Luke 2.7)—note the traditional detail of the ox and ass behind the figure of Mary.*

BETHLEHEM AND NAZARETH

The general evidence of the gospels is that Jesus' hometown was Nazareth in Galilee, but both Luke and Matthew record that he was born in the town of Bethlehem, south of Jerusalem. Matthew implies that Bethlehem was also the actual residence of Mary and Joseph (Matt. 2.11)—the couple only move to Nazareth later (Matt. 2.23). In Luke, the couple live in Nazareth (Luke 1.26–27) but go to Bethlehem for a census (Luke 2.4–5). Jesus is born there and the family returns to Nazareth (Luke 2.39).

It is difficult to reconcile these two accounts, and scholars have questioned whether Jesus can really have been born in Bethlehem or whether this assertion rests on theological considerations rather than historical truth. Bethlehem was the birthplace of King David, from whom the Messiah would be descended. Matthew 2.6 quotes a passage of scripture stating that the Messiah would come from Bethlehem.

Luke's account of the census as the reason for the move to Bethlehem also poses problems (see pp.192–93). However, Luke seems to have no ulterior theological motives for the details he gives of Jesus' birth in Bethlehem: the overcrowded inn, the bands of cloth, the manger (Luke 2.7). This may imply—assuming they are not products of Luke's imagination—that they represent an authentic tradition.

Indeed, perhaps the strongest argument in support of Matthew and Luke is the weight of the consistent, and very early, tradition that Jesus was born at Bethlehem. Luke's claim that Joseph's family was from there (Luke 2.4) is hardly implausible, and as a master craftsman he may well have traveled to find employment (see box, p.196). Mary's relative, Elizabeth, also apparently lived not far away (Luke 1.39).

THE VIRGIN BIRTH

"JESUS, SON OF PANTERA"
It has been argued that the early Christians may have invented Matthew's portrait of a pregnant, unmarried Mary, in order to counter scandalous rumors about Jesus' origins that circulated in non-Christian circles. For example, the early Christian writer Origen (ca. 185–254 CE), together with the Talmud and other Jewish sources, record an allegation that Jesus was the offspring of an adulterous liaison between Mary and a Roman soldier, variously called Pantera, Panthera, or Pandera.

Intriguingly, the tombstone of a Roman bowman called Pantera, who served in Tiberius' reign, was found in Germany in 1859. He is described as coming from Sidon, close to Galilee, demonstrating—if nothing else—that the name given to Jesus' alleged "real" father was neither anachronistic nor invented.

Alone in the New Testament, Matthew and Luke relate that Mary was a virgin when she bore Jesus (Matt. 1.18–25; Luke 1.26–35). The historical and literary evidence both for and against the virgin birth—or, more precisely, the virgin conception—is evenly balanced and there are arguments on both sides. Any judgment about the "truth" or otherwise of this event probably has to rest on such considerations as the possibility of the miraculous; the assessment of the gospel texts and what they really mean; and, not least, the religious viewpoint of the individual commentator.

Matthew says that Mary will conceive "from the Holy Spirit" (Matt. 1.18, 20) and Luke that "the power of the Most High will overshadow" her (Luke 1.35). It has sometimes been claimed that neither of these statements necessarily precludes ordinary sexual intercourse, because the evangelists may simply be indicating that God would be present at the moment of conception. Support for this opinion can perhaps be seen in the book of Genesis where Eve, after intercourse with her husband, cries: "I have produced a man with the help of the Lord" (Gen. 4.1).

But the evidence that the evangelists do indeed intend to assert that Mary conceived without human intervention is very strong. Much has been made of the fact that *parthenos*, the Greek word in the gospels usually translated as "virgin," primarily means only a girl who has reached sex-

Virgin birth: a pagan concept?

The notion of virgin conception is unknown in Judaism. The possibility of such a phenomenon is in no way implied in the numerous biblical legends of miraculous births to barren mothers—although these accounts certainly influenced the gospel stories of Jesus' birth. Nor can the prophecy of Isaiah (Isa. 7.14) quoted by Matthew (see caption, opposite) be taken as firm evidence of a Jewish belief in the possibility of conception without a human father.

However, the idea of virgin conception was widely current in the Greco-Roman world. Famous royal figures such as Alexander the Great and the emperor Augustus were commonly said to have been born from the union of their mother with a deity, and similar claims were made on behalf of charismatic religious figures. According to later writings, Simon the magician, a figure who appears in Acts 8, claimed that his mother was a virgin when she conceived him.

The idea of Jesus' virginal conception has therefore often been attributed to the influence of paganism. But it is uncertain how far such ideas would have been acceptable to first-century Christians with a Jewish monotheistic heritage. Also, the pagan parallels with the New Testament stories are not as close as they may seem. Pagan legends tell of intercourse in the usual human manner, between a woman and a god who takes human form.

But the gospels exclude any suggestion of divine anthropomorphism, speaking of the "descent of the Holy Spirit" and the power of God "overshadowing" Mary in language reminiscent of the Hebrew Scriptures. Such terms reflect the Jewish idea of the Shekinah, the divine presence on earth, a concept deliberately designed to exclude anthropomorphism.

The Virgin Annunciate (Our Lady of Expectation), *by Naddo Ceccarellli (died ca. 1347). The pregnant Mary reads the verse of Matthew that cites a prophecy in Isaiah 7.14: "Look, the virgin shall conceive and bear a son"(Matt. 1.23). Matthew is quoting from the Greek Septuagint, which translates as "virgin" (Greek* parthenos*) an original Hebrew word that means "young woman." At least as early as the 2nd century, it was claimed that Mary had remained a virgin even after Jesus' birth—an idea that led to the medieval doctrine of her perpetual virginity.*

ual maturity and not necessarily one who has never had intercourse. But it is clear from the context that the evangelists understand the term to mean "virgin" in the usual sense. For example, when the angel Gabriel announces Mary's pregnancy she expresses surprise: "How can this be, since I am a virgin?" (Luke 1.34.)

Luke describes Mary as a "virgin" betrothed to Joseph (Luke 1.26). In Judaism, an engagement could be swiftly broken if a bride was found not to be a virgin, just as Joseph plans to dismiss Mary when he discovers her pregnancy. But the angel reassures Joseph that his bride has not slept with any man (Matt. 1.18–20).

THE VIRGIN BIRTH IN THE NEW TESTAMENT AND EARLY CHURCH

One of the strongest arguments against the authenticity of the virgin birth is that apart from Matthew and Luke the New Testament never refers to it—in contrast to the central position of the Resurrection. Of course, this is an argument from silence and it may be that the virgin birth began as a private tradition within Jesus' own family, and only became more widely known with the increasing desire to learn more of Jesus' early life (see pp.190–91).

The two evangelists who do not mention the virgin birth may have had very strong reasons for beginning their gospels as they did. Mark opens with the ministry of the Baptist, the new Elijah, perhaps to parallel the way that the prophet Elijah appears suddenly and unannounced in the Hebrew Scriptures. John's prologue could be viewed as an exploration of the implications of Jesus as Emmanuel, "God is with us" (Isa. 7.14; Matt. 1.23).

The absence of the virgin birth in Paul's letters has to be seen in the broader context of his almost complete lack of reference to any part of Jesus' earthly career.

Some Jewish Christian groups, such as the Ebionites (see p.327), rejected the virgin birth, as did the Christian writers Cerinthus (ca. 100 CE) and Marcion (ca. 160 CE). But Ignatius, bishop of Antioch ca. 112 CE, unquestioningly accepted it, suggesting that the belief was early and strongly held. In the succeeding century it became virtually universal among Christians.

THE PRECIOUS GIFTS
Christians came to interpret the three gifts brought by the wise men (Matt. 2.11) as each symbolizing an aspect of Jesus' character: gold denoted his royal nature as Son of David and Messiah; frankincense (used in sacred rituals) represented his priesthood (compare Heb. 9.11); and myrrh (used in the anointing of corpses) pointed to his saving death.

However, nothing in the gospel itself justifies this understanding. Matthew is probably reflecting an awareness that such luxury goods were staples of the extensive import trade from southern Arabia.

THE FIRST WITNESSES

The second chapter of Matthew recounts the famous story of the "wise men from the East" (Matt. 2.1) who, following a star, come to pay homage to the infant Jesus. This episode underwent considerable development in Christian thought. For example, the evangelist does not say how many wise men there were, and the tradition that there were three of them was deduced from the fact that they brought three types of gift (see sidebar, left).

The visitors are often thought of as kings, an idea that only developed when the Church applied verses in the Hebrew Bible to this episode. For example, there are references in Psalms (as Ps. 72.10–11) to kings bringing tribute to an Israelite ruler interpreted as the Messiah, while Isaiah speaks of kings coming to the brightness of the Messiah and of camels bearing gold and frankincense (Isa. 60.6). It is intriguing that Matthew himself does not cite such passages, in spite of his marked habit of quoting biblical predictions that he sees as referring to Jesus.

The shepherds

Luke's story of the shepherds who visit the infant Jesus parallels in some ways Matthew's story of the wise men. Both follow immediately the account of Jesus' birth, and both record a supernatural revelation to a group of people of the true character of the newborn child. In Luke 2, the revelation is to shepherds, the sort of simple folk for whom his gospel generally shows special concern.

The Annunciation to the Shepherds, *a stained glass panel of ca. 1300.*

The angel tells the shepherds of universal rejoicing at Jesus' birth (Luke 2.10–11) and of the divine gift of peace on earth to those whom God favors—probably meaning the future followers of Jesus (Luke 2.14). Jesus is the Messiah, born in David's city (Luke 2.11). Luke's terms "bringing good news" and "savior"—the sole occurrence of this word in the three synoptic gospels—echo some inscriptions in Asia Minor commemorating the birthday of the emperor Augustus.

The shepherds are described as living in the fields to guard their flocks at night (Luke 2.8). This was the usual practice in Palestine, where sheep were turned into the fields after the June wheat harvest to graze on the remains of the crops. If Luke's account has any historical basis, therefore, Jesus is likely to have born in the summer.

Luke's story is a beautiful idyllic tale, perhaps influenced by pagan legends that link shepherds with the birth of famous men such as Romulus and Remus. However, Bethlehem, the city of David, is prominent in the narrative. David began his career as a shepherd. Genesis mentions a place nearby called "tower of flocks," where, according to a Jewish tradition, the king-Messiah would one day be revealed.

The Magi, *a 6th-century mosaic in the church of Sant' Apollinare Nuovo, Ravenna. It gives the "wise men" their traditional names of Balthasar, Melchior, and Caspar (or Gaspar). Each wears a Phrygian cap, a felt hat originally from the land of Phrygia in Asia Minor but widely used in Greco-Roman art to denote a person from the Orient.*

The eastern strangers have sometimes been depicted in art visiting the newborn Jesus in the manger at the same time as the shepherds, whose visit is described in Luke (see box, opposite). But Matthew says that they found Jesus and Mary in a domestic setting (Matt. 2.11), and the fact that Herod felt it necessary to massacre all children under two (see pp.204–05) would suggest that Jesus had been born some considerable time previously.

There have often been attempts to connect the guiding star with astronomical phenomena around the time of Jesus' birth, in particular with the appearance of a comet ca. 5 BCE. But it seems more likely that Matthew has developed an imaginative scenario out of a prophecy in the book of Numbers that "a star shall come out of Jacob" (Num. 24.17). Matthew does not quote this passage, but it also occurs in a collection of messianic texts from Qumran (see p.169). Simon bar Kosiba, the leader of the Second Jewish revolt against Rome (132–5 CE) was called "bar Kokhba" ("son of a star") by his followers, many of whom proclaimed him as the Messiah.

It has been suggested that the whole episode in which foreign wise men acknowledge Jesus deliberately anticipates the universal Christian mission with which Matthew's gospel ends (Matt. 28.19). If so, the reference is oblique: the *magi* are not depicted as evangelical converts, but simply return to their own country (Matt. 4.12). More likely, the evangelist is expressing the common Jewish expectation that when the Messiah appeared, he and Israel would receive the homage of all nations. Genuine speculation in learned Jewish circles in Jerusalem about the arrival of the awaited Messiah may find echoes in Herod's decision to convene all the chief priests and scribes and seek their advice (Matt. 2.4).

THE MAGI

Matthew describes the foreign visitors by the Greek term *magi* (singular *magos*; Latin *magus*), which is probably best rendered as "magicians." Originally of Persian origin, by the first century CE the *magi* had become widespread in the ancient world as a highly influential group of skilled practitioners in esoteric arts, such as astrology and oneiromancy (divination from dreams), both of which figure in the gospel narrative. They possessed secret and arcane wisdom and so may justifiably be called "wise men," the traditional English translation of *magi*.

The Jewish writer Philo commends the *magi* as adepts of "true magic" but elsewhere denounces them as charlatans, concerned only with charms and incantations. The same negative verdict appears in the New Testament in the depiction of other *magi*, such as Simon (Acts 8) and Elymas (Acts 13).

Matthew certainly recognizes the special abilities of the *magi*. Owing to their supernatural wisdom they understand that the guiding star manifests the royal status of Jesus (Matt. 2.2). They also receive a divine message in a dream (Matt. 2.12).

On the other hand, there may be an implied contrast with Jesus. In the gospels Jesus is accused of being a magician and performing miracles in the name and power of Beelzebub, the prince of the demons (Matt. 12.24 and parallels). In introducing the *magi*, Matthew may wish to imply that all practitioners of magic must admit the superiority of Jesus—just as the demons do (as at Matt. 8.29–30; Luke 4.34)—and acknowledge that as the Holy One of God, his power and authority are utterly different in nature from their own.

THE WRATH OF HEROD

This 1st-century tomb in Jerusalem was long thought to be that of King Herod the Great, but more probably belonged to a member of his family. Note the stone rolled to seal the entrance.

The figure of Herod the Great (ruled 37–4 BCE) features prominently in Matthew's story of the wise men, or *magi* (see pp.202–03), and its sequel. This culminates in the flight of Jesus' family to Egypt (see pp.206–07) and the mass slaughter of the infants of Bethlehem (see box, opposite).

There has been much discussion of how far, if at all, what is recorded of King Herod in Matthew has any genuine historical basis. That the king should have taken such *magi* seriously is by no means improbable, since Jewish interest in astrology is well attested, for example in the so-called *Treatise of Shem* (first century BCE), while horoscopes have been found among the Qumran documents. It has perhaps been too readily assumed that the *magi* were pagans, since by this time there were well-established Jewish communities in the East, notably in Babylonia.

Matthew's general picture of Herod as brutal, hot-tempered, superstitious, and cunning, with a strong instinct for self-preservation, accords well with what is known of his genuine character (see pp.156–57). Herod's expressed wish to pay homage to the newborn king (Matt. 2.8) is, of course, on one level to be understood as a trick. But for Matthew what Herod says, albeit unwittingly, is true: when the king-Messiah comes, the secular ruler must indeed submit to him.

Whatever their historical basis, it can hardly be denied that Matthew's stories involving King Herod are woven from various biblical themes. One of the most important of these is the life of Moses. For example, the Massacre of the Innocents is very likely based on the story in Exodus 1 that Pharaoh ordered the slaughter of all Israelite male children. Thus Matthew is casting Herod in the role of the Egyptian king, the oppressor of Israel.

HEROD AND ABRAHAM

Jewish embellishments of the story of Abraham in the book of Genesis may have influenced Matthew's narrative centered on Herod the Great. In the Abraham legends, his birth is marked by the appearance over his birthplace of a huge star, which astrologers recognize as presaging the advent of a great future ruler. They relate their prediction to the king, Nimrod, who in consequence slaughters seventy thousand innocent children.

As with the Exodus story of male Israelite babies being slaughtered (see main text), the parallels are not exact, but they may provide some of the elements out of which Matthew constructed his own story.

The Massacre of the Innocents

Herod the Great's most notorious act in Matthew's gospel account is to order the massacre of all the children of Bethlehem aged two or under in an attempt to get rid of the infant born there whom the wise men have hailed as Messiah and king of the Jews (Matt. 2.16). Some would assert that this event—known as the Massacre of the Innocents—may be authentic, since the victims would not have been numerous. Bethlehem was a small place and the event could have passed largely unnoticed in the fevered, bloody atmosphere that marked the last years of Herod's reign.

Nor, it is argued, were such acts unheard of in the contemporary world. According to the first-century Roman historian Suetonius, shortly before the future emperor Augustus was born, an omen heralded the birth of a king of Rome, so the republican Senate decreed that all males born that year should die. But this story may be just as legendary as similar Jewish tales. No other source mentions Herod's massacre.

Other scholars hold the view that here, as in all his post-birth narratives, Matthew has manufactured an episode based on a biblical passage, in this case a verse of Jeremiah that refers to a place near Bethlehem (Jer. 31.15), which Matthew quotes (Matt. 2.18). But it is hard to see how he could have drawn what he writes from Jeremiah alone. It is more likely that he relies on a broad range of biblical and other Jewish themes (see sidebar, opposite), introducing particular scriptural passages in order to stress that the events he relates form part of a longstanding divine plan.

The Massacre of the Innocents, *by Fra Angelico (1387–1455). While Matthew's portrait of a ruthless, paranoid monarch accords well with what is known of Herod's last years, there are various improbabilities in the massacre story. For example, Herod could have found out who the newborn king-Messiah was simply by ordering spies to follow the magi to Bethlehem.*

Similarly, when an angel tells Joseph that Herod is dead and that he can therefore return home from Egypt (Matt. 2.20; see p.207), the angelic words allude directly to God's instruction to Moses to return from exile in Midian (Exod. 4.19).

Matthew may also echo Jewish legends about Moses that were current in the first century CE, although they only occur in later *haggadahs* (accounts of the Exodus read during the Passover meal). According to one of these legends, Pharaoh was warned that the infant Moses would usurp the crown unless he was killed, but Moses was saved by the angel Gabriel. In the gospel, Jesus is preserved from Herod's destruction through the intervention of an angel, who warns Joseph to flee with his family from Bethlehem. Other themes with parallels in Jewish legends of Moses include prophetic dreams and even Joseph's proposal to divorce his bride.

THE FLIGHT INTO EGYPT

After the wise men had paid their homage to the infant Jesus, Matthew relates that an angel warned Joseph in a dream of King Herod's murderous intentions toward the child (Matt. 2.13). At the angel's command, Joseph took his wife and the boy to Egypt, where they remained until after Herod's death. The evangelist gives no details either of the journey or of the family's life in Egypt, and most scholars doubt that the episode has any genuine historical basis. Matthew relates the Egyptian sojourn to biblical prophecy, and cites Hosea 11.1, translating directly from the Hebrew: "Out of Egypt I have called my son" (the Septuagint has "my children").

The "son" represents Moses and, by extension, the Israelite people, whom Moses led from slavery in Egypt. Matthew appears to be alone in taking Hosea's words to refer to the Messiah, but the evangelist may simply wish to stress that Jesus' life echoed and recapitulated key events in the

Jesus the "Nazorean"

Matthew implies that Bethlehem, where Jesus was born, was the original place of residence of Joseph and Mary (see p.199). But he also knew that Jesus was brought up in Nazareth in Galilee and claims that Joseph was directed to go there in fulfillment of a prophecy that "He [the Messiah] will be called a Nazorean" (Matt. 2.22–23). By "Nazorean" (Greek Nazoraios) the evangelist appears to mean an inhabitant of Nazareth, and the word has this sense elsewhere in the New Testament; in Acts it is a name for Christians in general.

Matthew's "prophecy" does not correspond closely to anything in the Bible and many scholars think that it is based on Isaiah 11.1, a well-known messianic passage, where the Messiah is described as a "branch" (Hebrew nezer) of the tree of Jesse (the father of King David). But Matthew normally cites the Septuagint, the Greek version of the Hebrew Bible, which has nothing like Nazoraios at this point. However, he may be translating directly from the original Hebrew, as with his earlier quotation from Hosea (see main text).

There is another explanation. Matthew here claims to cite "the prophets," the term used for one of the three parts of the Jewish Bible (see p.162). In this sense it includes the book of Judges, and in some versions of the Septuagint, Judges 13.7 describes Samson as naziraios, a "nazirite" (Hebrew nazir), a person dedicated to God by special vows. This seems the most probable source of Matthew's Nazoraios. Samson may seem an unlikely model for Jesus, but he is one of the great Israelite heroes and, like Jesus in the gospels, suffered betrayal and agony—only to triumph in death over Israel's enemies. Luke makes a comment on the upbringing of Jesus (Luke 2.40) that may also be influenced by the story of Samson (Judg. 13.24).

The modern town of Nazareth in Galilee. Not mentioned in the Hebrew Scriptures, it was little more than a village in Jesus' day.

The harsh desert terrain of the Negeb desert in southern Israel. If Matthew's account has a historical basis, this is the sort of landscape through which Mary, Joseph, and Jesus would have passed on their journey to Egypt.

story of Israel. The idea that Christ had been present throughout Israel's history was certainly current in early Christianity (for example, 1 Cor. 10.1–4).

Other biblical figures may also be in the background. Most notably, Matthew probably intends to link Joseph of Nazareth with his great namesake, the patriarch Joseph, who was saved from death by being taken into Egypt, enabling God's promise to Israel to be fulfilled. The patriarch Abraham and the prophet Jeremiah—whom Matthew quotes a few verses later—also migrated to Egypt in order to avoid various calamities.

As Christianity developed, a growing interest in the details of Jesus' early life led Christian writers to embellish Matthew's bald account of the Egyptian interlude. These legends are found in the so-called "infancy gospels" (see pp.190–91) and are notable for giving much greater prominence in the story to Mary and the infant Jesus.

The account of the family's return from Egypt (Matt. 2.19–21) is also brief. It, too, is set in motion by an angelic message conveyed in a dream, and once more Joseph is the chief protagonist. Again, the angel's words link Jesus with Moses (see p.205). Matthew says that Joseph feared a return to Bethlehem because "Archelaus was ruling over Judea" (Matt. 2.22). On Herod's death, his son Archelaus became "ethnarch" of Judea and ruled (4 BCE–6 CE) with such brutality that the Romans deposed him lest he provoke a revolt (see pp.156–57). So Joseph and his family headed not for Bethlehem but for Nazareth in Galilee, outside Archelaus' domains (see box, opposite).

RITES OF CHILDHOOD

Following the visit of the shepherds to the infant Jesus (see box, p.202), Luke presents two attractive and moving scenes that display his narrative power and skill. He depicts the parents of Jesus as devout Jews, meticulous in carrying out "everything required by the law of the Lord" (Luke 2.39) with regard to the birth of a male child. The main rituals concerned were those of circumcision, purification, and presentation in the Temple.

Jesus' circumcision took place eight days after the birth, as prescribed by Jewish law (Luke 2.21), and was accompanied by naming the infant in accordance with the angelic command in Luke 1.31.

Childbirth placed a mother in a state of ritual impurity, which lasted for forty days. Luke 2.22 writes of "their" purification, apparently meaning both Mary and Joseph, although Jewish law refers to the mother alone.

Jesus and the Temple teachers

The differences between the second chapters of Matthew and Luke suggest that a variety of traditions about Jesus' early years were circulating soon after his death. Luke has selected one episode—the only story about Jesus' boyhood in the canonical gospels—in which the twelve-year-old child goes missing on a visit to Jerusalem at Passover and is found by his parents debating with religious teachers in the Temple (Luke 2.41–49).

Christ among the Doctors [Teachers] in the Temple, *a fresco by Giotto (ca. 1266–1337) in the Scrovegni Chapel, Padua. According to Luke 2.47, "all who heard him were amazed at his understanding."*

This story brings together Jesus and the Temple, a theme in which Luke shows special interest. Other key themes from the Presentation recur (see main text): Jesus' family as devout Jews; the prominence of Mary; and the recognition of Jesus' exceptional nature by representative Jewish figures. The setting is to be understood as the precincts of the Temple, where rabbinical teachers gave instruction, as Jesus himself did later in his career and as Luke represents the apostles doing in Acts.

In Judaism, a boy attains the status of religious maturity, bar mitzvah ("son of the commandment"), at thirteen, when he takes on the full duties required of males under Jewish law. Luke may intend to present Jesus as possessing a precocious understanding of religious matters that amazed his elders (Luke 2.47).

The meaning of the story emerges in the dialogue between Jesus and Mary (Luke 2.48–49), when, for the first time in the gospels, Jesus calls God his Father. Jesus' awareness of a special relationship to God is central to his self-awareness (see pp.166–7). That Jesus' parents do not understand his words at this stage reflects another gospel theme—the incomprehension of his family during his ministry.

Jesus' parents suffer considerable anxiety as a result of his absence. Luke is careful to balance this behavior with the statement that he was otherwise a model child, whose prime duty was obedience (Luke 2.51).

The Presentation of Jesus in the Temple, *by Giovanni Bellini (ca. 1431–1516). Mary (left) passes the infant into the arms of Simeon (Luke 2.28) as Joseph (center) and others look on.*

The time of purification was completed by a visit to the Temple in Jerusalem for the "presentation" of an animal sacrifice as an act of thanksgiving, which Luke describes as the type permitted for the poorest worshipers (Luke 2.24). This reflects both the "lowliness" of Mary—under Jewish law, the sacrifice would have been offered by the mother—as expressed in the *Magnificat* (Luke 1.46–55; see p.199) and perhaps also Luke's general interest in the poor and the humble.

However, for Luke, the term "presentation" refers primarily to the dedication of Jesus for his future mission. The evangelist quotes the law by which a firstborn child was "designated as holy to the Lord" (Luke 2.23). This passage is probably influenced by the biblical story of the dedication of the infant Samuel at Shiloh (1 Sam. 1). The theme is continued by the prophetic figures of Simeon and Anna, who may have been well-known personalities. Simeon in particular is filled and guided by the Holy Spirit. In the song known (from its opening words in Latin) as the *Nunc Dimittis* (Luke 2.29–32), he foretells the universality of the gospel message—a note that echoes throughout all Luke's work.

Luke's birth narrative is centered very much on Mary and this emphasis continues in his story of the presentation. Simeon has a special message for her (Luke 2.34–35), which strikes a more moving and somber chord than the triumphant note of the *Nunc Dimittis*: the child Jesus is a prophetic sign, which "will be opposed," and his mission will also bring extreme suffering to his mother.

Luke's account concludes with the peaceful return of the family to Nazareth. Jesus grows up blessed by divine favor and "filled with wisdom" (Luke 2.40)—words that prepare the way for the next vivid episode of Luke's gospel (see box, opposite).

THE HOME LIFE OF JESUS

Apart from the Nativity and infancy stories in Matthew and Luke, the gospels provide only incidental information about the childhood and youth of Jesus or the circumstances of his home life up until his baptism by John the Baptist and the beginning of his ministry. A number of early texts and "infancy gospels" (see p.190) sought to supply the missing details of Jesus' family background and upbringing, and while their authenticity is at best dubious, they were an important source of several medieval traditions.

Whether or not Jesus was born in Bethlehem (see sidebar, p.199), early nonbiblical sources, such as the second-century Protevangelium of James, claimed that he had family ties with Judea. The Protevangelium says Mary was born in Jerusalem, the home of her legendary parents, Anna and Joachim (see illustration, p.190). In the gospels themselves, Luke calls Mary a relative of John the Baptist's parents, Elizabeth and Zechariah, who lived near Jerusalem in the hill country of Judea (Luke 1.36, 1.39).

The Protevangelium also says that the family of Anna held estates in the region of Mount Carmel, and other early Christian traditions outside the canonical gospels connect Jesus with Galilee and the north of Palestine.

A stone oven dominates the kitchen area of this two-story house in the partly reconstructed village of Qatzrin in the Lower Golan. Although the extant remains at Qatzrin date substantially to the 5th century CE*, scholars believe that the form of its domestic buildings and those excavated at other villages in Galilee and the surrounding area, would have changed little since Jesus' day.*

A view of present-day Nazareth. The hill in the background, known as the "Mount of the Precipitation" or "Mount of the Leap," is traditionally said to be the place from which the enraged inhabitants of the town tried to hurl Jesus following his preaching in the synagogue, as described in Luke 4.29–30.

According to one such source, Mary was born in Sepphoris, a city near Nazareth (see illustration, p.155). Some commentators have suggested that for both Jesus and his mother to be invited to a wedding at Cana (John 2.1–2) it must have been a family occasion.

Such legends and speculation aside, it is universally accepted that Jesus was raised at Nazareth in Galilee, and archaeological evidence of life in Palestine in the first century CE means that several aspects of Jesus' early years can now be gleaned with reasonable probability. Recent excavations at a number of nearby sites have given an idea of the sort of house in which he and his family would have lived (see illustration, opposite). Basically, it consisted of a courtyard, around which were a number of rooms of one or two floors, the upper floor resting on wooden beams and reached by an inside ladder or outside stairway. If Jesus' house had accommodated all nine or more members of his family—mother, father, five sons, and at least two daughters—it would probably have required a second story. The gospels indicate that common household items included an oven, a lampstand, a meal tub or basket, and mats or mattresses on which to sleep.

Nothing is known directly about any education or intellectual formation which the young Jesus may have received. The fact that his learning later drew comment, and that his followers could address him as *rabbi* ("Teacher"; see pp.292–93), suggests that he was well acquainted with the Hebrew Scriptures as they were taught in contemporary Judaism. By this period, the Pharisees in particular had established schools attached to local synagogues, where children learned to read and write and received instruction in the Jewish law. Jesus might well have attended such a school: he could certainly read and expound a biblical passage during a synagogue service (Mark 1.21, 6.2). The only recorded episode from Jesus' youth, his discussion with the teachers in the Temple (Luke 2.42–51), took place when he was twelve. In later Jewish practice, which may well have applied

James, the brother of Jesus

One of Jesus' brothers, James, attained a position of special importance in the early Church. This would appear to have been largely on account of his blood relationship with his elder brother, although Paul also records that James was marked out because he experienced a personal vision of the resurrected Christ. He appears very early as a prominent leader in the Jerusalem Church, perhaps even its chief spokesman, as Acts and Galatians indicate.

In the New Testament, James is portrayed as the representative of the Jewish Christianity that characterized the Jerusalem Church, in contrast to the Gentile Christianity whose chief missionary was Paul (see pp.326–27). Later writings, reflecting the outlook of Jewish Christianity, claim that James had even greater authority, and state that he was the most important apostle, responsible for commissioning all the others. He is traditionally said to be the author of the letter of James and, while this is now disputed, it may well reflect his teachings.

A reliable tradition recorded by the first-century Jewish writer Josephus indicates that James and others were stoned to death in 62 CE on the orders of the high priest Ananus, during a power vacuum between the death of one Roman prefect and the arrival of his successor. The second-century Christian historian Hegesippus also has an account of James's death, but its vivid details are seen as largely legendary.

Hegesippus relates that after James's death, another relative, Simeon, assumed a leading position at Jerusalem. This suggests that a dynastic pattern of leadership developed for a time among the followers of Jesus in the city.

This ancient Egyptian bow-drill almost certainly differs little from the sort of carpenter's tool that would have been familiar to Joseph and Jesus. The Greek word tekton, *which is used in the gospels, has a wider sense than "carpenter," by which it is traditionally translated. It can mean someone engaged in construction work in wood, stone, and brick. It is easy to exaggerate the supposed poverty of Jesus' background: a family of general builders could have been quite prosperous.*

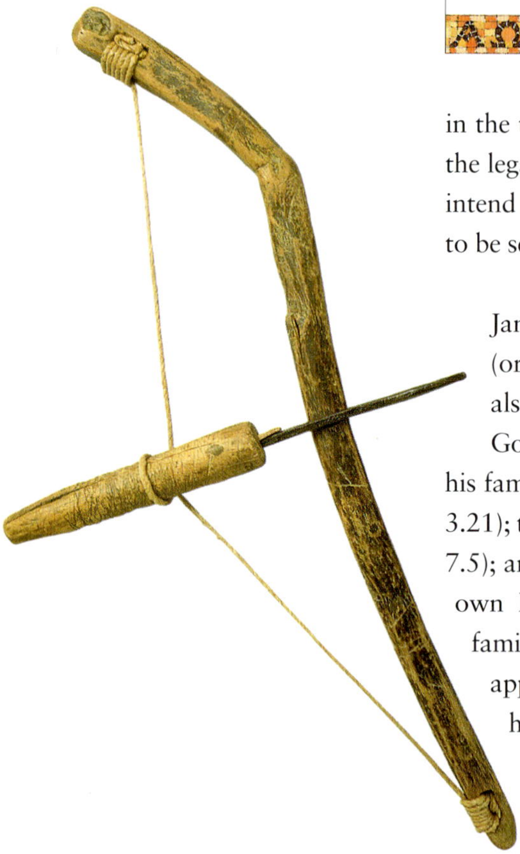

in the time of Jesus, a boy became a full adult at thirteen and assumed all the legal and religious responsibilities required of a Jewish male. Luke may intend the episode in the Temple either to demonstrate Jesus' precocity or to be seen as a preparation for his assumption of maturity (see box, p.208).

Mark 6.3 and Matthew 13.55 mention four brothers of Jesus: James (see box, above), Joseph (or Joses), Simon (or Simeon) and Judas (or Jude, possibly the author of the Letter of Jude). The two evangelists also refer to "his sisters," but provide no information about them. Gospel tradition is clear that during his lifetime Jesus was at odds with his family. They are said to have tried to apprehend him as a lunatic (Mark 3.21); the Fourth Gospel states that his brothers did not believe in him (John 7.5); and Jesus himself commented that a prophet had no honor among his own kin and his own house (Mark 6.4; Matt. 13.57). However, his family's attitude seems to have changed, especially after the risen Christ appeared to the eldest brother, James (1 Cor. 15.7). In Acts, Mary and her surviving sons emerge as a distinct unit in the Jerusalem Church (Acts 1.14), alongside the twelve apostles. The sons bear the honorific designation "brothers of the Lord."

From at least the mid-second century CE, the Church increasingly emphasized the concept of the perpetual virginity of Mary. This prompted considerable theological debate about the relationship of Jesus to his "brothers," which continues today. For example, it has been proposed that they were either stepbrothers (the children of a former marriage of Joseph), or else Jesus' cousins (the sons of a sister of Mary). The term "brother" in the Bible and elsewhere can signify no more than "kinsman," so neither of these two opinions can be judged wholly implausible.

In Mark 6.3, Jesus is described as "the carpenter" (Greek *tekton*), in Matthew as "the carpenter's son" (Matt. 13.55). It is possible that these descriptions amount to the same thing—in Jesus' time it was common for the eldest son to follow the profession of his father. However, it is clear from the gospels that in later life Jesus did not practice a trade, as Paul and Jewish teachers regularly did. It has also been suggested that the Greek word for "carpenter" in the gospels actually stands for an underlying Aramaic term that is used metaphorically in the Talmud (see glossary) to denote a scholar. But those who call Jesus a carpenter in Matthew and Mark evidently use the word literally, because they are questioning how a mere manual craftsman can display such learning.

The Holy Family with a Sparrow, *by Bartolomé Esteban Murillo (1618–82). The sparrow held by the infant Jesus refers to a popular legend from the apocryphal infancy gospels in which Jesus is said to have modeled sparrows in clay and made them come to life (see also p.309).*

JOHN THE BAPTIST

Wadi Ze'elim in the Judean desert. John the Baptist is said to have been raised in the desert; it has even been conjectured that the Essenes of Qumran (see main text) adopted him following the deaths of his elderly parents Elizabeth and Zechariah.

THE BAPTIST AND JOSEPHUS

Writing toward the end of the first century, the Jewish historian Josephus calls John by his main title, "the Baptizer" (compare Mark 1.4), and gives details about the form of baptism that was John's primary activity.

According to Josephus, John's baptism was not intended by itself to atone for sin, although it represented a physical purification of those genuinely resolved to change for the better. This parallels John's message in the gospels (see main text).

However, unlike the gospels, Josephus includes nothing of John's prophecy of the coming divine Judgment. This is because Josephus himself was distrustful of the fervent search by contemporary Jews for a Messiah, and desired to portray John as no more than a moral philosopher. Josephus nonetheless finally attests to John's great popularity, and records his execution by Herod Antipas.

One of the most solidly based facts in the New Testament is the close association of Jesus at the beginning of his ministry with John the Baptist (see box, opposite). The Baptist was certainly a historical figure. According to the gospels, John called upon his listeners to mend their sinful ways in advance of the coming Messiah and the advent of the kingdom of God. He performed an act of ritual cleansing called baptism (Greek *baptizein*, "to immerse"), which involved immersion in the waters of the Jordan river. This "baptism of repentance" (Mark 1.1–14 and parallels) was accompanied by the confession of sins. Much of this is confirmed by the description of the Baptist in the writings of the historian Josephus (see sidebar, left).

Most of John's audience were clearly expected simply to return to their ordinary lives and thereafter make a better contribution to society. But there were also those who committed themselves more deeply to the Baptist and became his disciples, thus inaugurating a movement which, according to Acts 19.1–4, spread as far as Asia Minor (and which apparently continued until some time after 200 CE). They adopted the ascetic lifestyle of their master, who came "eating no bread and drinking no wine" (Luke 7.33).

Since the discovery of the Dead Sea Scrolls, widely presumed to be the library of an Essene community based at Qumran in the Judean desert (see p.169), it has often been asked whether the Baptist may have been influenced by Essene doctrines, and even whether he and Jesus might have been members of the Qumran community. According to Luke 1.80, John passed his childhood in the desert, and Jesus spent time there (see pp.218-19). Like the Baptist, the Qumranites made much of Isaiah's words about the voice

Jesus and John

From the gospel evidence, it seems likely that Jesus began as a disciple of John the Baptist. John began his work east of the Jordan and Jesus was with him (John 1.28ff.). John 3.22 states that Jesus began his own work in Judea, baptizing at the same time as John. Following John's arrest, Jesus withdrew to Galilee (Mark 1.14, Luke 4.14) but he had apparently ceased baptizing in person (John 4.2), and the move may mark the point at which he began his distinct ministry as an exorcist and healer. Two of his followers are said to have begun as disciples of John (John 1.37).

In the gospels, Jesus credits the Baptist with a very special status. He is Elijah (Matt. 11.14), the herald of the Messiah foretold by Malachi 4.5, the "wilderness voice" of Isaiah 40.3 and more than a prophet (Luke 7.26). However, each of these utterances is carefully qualified. The Baptist is greater than any ordinary human "yet the least in the kingdom of heaven is greater than he" (Matt. 11.11 and parallels).

The early Christians recognized John's contribution and significance but sought to convince the Baptist movement (see main text) that John himself referred to Jesus as the Messiah in saying that he was not worthy to untie the sandals of the one for whom he prepared the way (Mark 1.7 and parallels). The gospels may increasingly downgrade John—by the Fourth Gospel he is only the wilderness voice and denies being the Messiah, Elijah, or any expected prophet (John 1.19–23)—but he remains a great witness to "the true light" (John 1.6–8). This policy seems to have been successful because the Church eventually absorbed most of the Baptist's followers.

Madonna and Child with John the Baptist, *by Sandro Botticelli (1445–1510). John, whom Luke presents as the relative of Jesus, wears his desert garb of camelskin (Mark 1.6).*

in the wilderness crying: "prepare the way of the Lord" (Isa. 40.3; Mark 1.2–3 and parallels). They too summoned Israel to repentance in the face of imminent divine judgment, and attached importance to ritual washings.

But there is no clear evidence of any direct connection. The Qumran community was only part of the much wider Essene movement, and other contemporary sects in Palestine specialized in baptism. Nor, as an ascetic teacher, was John unique. Moreover, while Isaiah 40.3 had a messianic significance when applied to John, at Qumran the "way of the Lord" meant the study of the Jewish law. The Baptist's ministry was to all the nation of Israel, but the Qumranites were conscious exiles from general society, concerned with their own salvation. At Qumran, washings were a daily ceremony to preserve religious purity, whereas John's baptism was a single, unrepeated rite to prepare for the coming Day of Judgment.

THE BAPTISM OF JESUS

The gospels make it clear that the baptism of Jesus was very different from other baptisms performed by John (see pp.214–15). On this occasion, the Spirit of God descended on Jesus "like a dove" when he emerged from the baptismal waters of the Jordan river. In Mark 1.10 and Matthew 3.16, the descent of the Spirit is a subjective vision, experienced by Jesus alone. For Luke, the dove appears "in bodily form" (Luke 3.22). In the Fourth Gospel (John 1.34), the Baptist himself witnesses the descent. The dove as a symbol of the Spirit would seem to be a distinctively Christian concept: there is nothing clearly comparable to it in the Hebrew Scriptures or other Jewish writings.

For the evangelists, Jesus' baptism marked his formal designation as the Messiah heralded by John, and it was the occasion on which Jesus himself realized the nature of his mission. Later in Luke, Jesus reads a passage from Isaiah that describes a figure anointed for the task of proclaiming God's good news (Luke 4.18). It was with this figure and his work that Jesus identified himself at his baptism, and this was affirmed by a voice from heaven.

In Mark 1.11 and Luke 3.22, the voice addresses Jesus himself, assuring him of his unique relationship with God, as his beloved son. Matthew 3.17 has a public proclamation, while in the Fourth Gospel (John 1.32) it is the Baptist who receives a divine oracle telling him the meaning of the descent of the Spirit on Jesus. The heavenly message combines part of Psalm 2.7 ("you are my Son") with one or more verses from Isaiah (Isa. 42.1, 44.2). Together they form a texture rich in messianic associations.

The Jordan river in evening light near the Dead Sea. The river was the focus of the baptizing ministry of John and was the scene of Jesus' own baptism.

John's role in Jesus' baptism

All the gospels record the baptism of Jesus and see it as an event of great significance, dedicating and empowering Jesus for his ministry. However, in some respects it was also a source of embarrassment for the early Christians. The disciples of John the Baptist (see p.214) could claim that Jesus' acceptance of baptism from John, by which he associated himself with John and technically became his follower, proved the superiority of their master.

Mark 1.9–10 gives a straightforward account of the baptism, but the other evangelists introduce elements which in various ways aim to play down John's importance in the event. Matthew 3.14–15, for example, creates a dialogue in which John asserts that it is he who should be baptized by Jesus, not the other way around. Jesus reassures him that their roles must be temporarily reversed, because the baptism is a joint act "to fulfill all righteousness." This seems to mean that it was part of the overall divine plan.

Luke does not explicitly state that it was John who baptized Jesus (Luke 3.21). He may even deliberately exclude the possibility, since he describes John's imprisonment before he mentions Jesus' baptism. However, the evangelist may not intend to provide a precise chronology.

The Fourth Gospel (John 1.32–33) says nothing about Jesus' baptism in the Jordan river but tells only of the descent of the Holy Spirit. The Baptist's declaration at this point that he came baptizing with water in order that the coming one "might be revealed to Israel" may contain the evangelist's own interpretation of Jesus' baptism: it was a revelatory act on the part of the Baptist, which, like the latter's whole ministry, pointed beyond him to his great successor.

The Baptism of Christ, *a mosaic (ca. 520 CE) in the baptistery of the Arians, Ravenna. As John baptizes Jesus, the Spirit hovers in the form of a dove. The Jordan is personified (left) as a pagan river god with water pouring from a jar.*

In some early manuscripts of Luke, the heavenly voice makes no reference to the text of Isaiah but instead quotes the sentence from Psalm 2.7 in full—"You are my son, today I have begotten you." Some groups in the early Church held that Jesus was the human son of Mary and Joseph and only became the Son of God at his baptism. This heretical view might account for text modifications to the Lukan variant, if that represents the evangelist's original words. Yet several early Christian writers knew this variant and saw nothing heretical in it. Moreover, the whole verse of Psalms is cited in Hebrews 1.5 in reference to the preexistent Christ and in Acts (13.33) in reference to the Resurrection. The New Testament evidently sees no contradiction between the supernatural birth of Jesus (as described in Matthew and Luke), his preexistence (as in the Fourth Gospel), and his designation as the divine Son at his baptism.

The Quarantal monastery (Greek Orthodox) is perched high on the sheer face of the peak near Jericho known as the Mount of the Temptation. It is the traditional site of Jesus' ordeal with Satan in the wilderness.

THE TEMPTATION

The three synoptic gospels all bear witness to the tradition that immediately following his baptism (see pp.216–17) Jesus withdrew into the desert, where he was tempted by the devil—that is, he was tested to see if he could be induced to misuse his powers (Mark 1.12–13, Matthew 4.1–11, and Luke 4.1–13). As often in the Bible, such a testing is viewed as part of the divine purpose: Jesus is led, or even driven, to his encounter with Satan by the Spirit that he received at his baptism. Many authorities have tried to suggest what this meant for Jesus, either as a personal experience or as a religious inspiration, but the New Testament provides no real information on the matter. The gospels contain two interpretations of the episode, on the one hand in Mark (see box, below), and on the other in Matthew and Luke.

Matthew and Luke present a dialogue between Jesus and his adversary in three scenes. In each scene Jesus spurns the devil's approach, quoting a verse of scripture in typical rabbinic fashion. Every temptation represents a theme of significance to Jesus' ministry. The first—that Jesus should turn stones into bread to eat—is rejected on the grounds that "one does not live by bread alone, but by every word that comes from the mouth of God" (Matt. 4.4). Later, Jesus was accused of being a magician in league with the ruler of the demons, but in the desert the Son of God demonstrates that he refuses to perform meaningless tricks at the prompting of Satan.

Next, the devil flies Jesus to the "pinnacle" (highest point) of the Tem-

The Temptation in Mark

Mark's account of the Temptation (1.12–13) is brief and enigmatic. The Spirit "drove" Jesus for forty days into the wilderness, where he was "tempted by Satan" and lived "with the wild beasts" while "the angels waited on him."

The two possible interpretations depend on the dual symbolism of the wilderness in the Bible. On the one hand, the desert is often a barren and hostile place, the haunt of demonic powers. Wild beasts frequently represent evil forces and the wicked people who assail the righteous. Thus Jesus' entry into the wilderness at once exposes him to the onslaught of satanic powers, and the angels may be understood as aiding him in this conflict (in Matthew 4.11 the angels seem to provide Jesus with sustenance only after his ordeal—perhaps an echo of the provision of food to Elijah in 1 Kings 19.4).

However, the wilderness may appear in a positive light. Israel's forty years of exile in the desert (see pp.60–1) can be seen as a time when the nation enjoyed an ideal relationship with God, which afterward decayed. It was in the desert that the relationship would one day be restored. Mark may intend to say that Jesus lived harmoniously with the wild animals, in allusion to Isaiah's beautiful depiction of the Messianic age (Isa. 11.6–9).

Or the gospel may be hinting at the restoration of Eden, where Adam lived in peaceful coexistence with the animals and where, according to some Jewish texts, he and Eve were waited on by angels. By Jesus' time the serpent of Genesis 3 was frequently identified with Satan. Mark may, therefore, view Jesus as the Second Adam, who reverses Adam's fall and regains paradise (see also pp.324–25).

ple and suggests that if Jesus jumps off, God will surely send angels to prevent him from plummeting to the ground. On his arrest in the garden of Gethsemane, Jesus will say that his heavenly Father, if asked, would at once send legions of angels to thwart his captors (Matt. 26.53). The point is that Jesus will not ask: God is not to be tested in this way (Matt. 4.7).

Finally, Satan offers Jesus dominion over "the kingdoms of the world," that is, secular overlordship like that of a Roman emperor. But in the gospels Jesus teaches that he is not to govern in the manner of Gentile rulers: "my kingdom is not from this world" (John 18.36). Jesus is in the world as the servant of God, and his followers must be the same (Matt. 4.10).

The order of temptations in Matthew is generally held to be the original, with the offer of world domination as an obvious climax. Luke's reversal of the last two temptations allows him to end with the hint at Jesus' passion and death, the climax of his earthly life. At the end, Satan departs "until an opportune time." He reappears again only when he enters into Judas Iscariot (Luke 22.3) and so prompts Jesus' arrest and crucifixion.

SATAN AND THE DEVIL

In the period following the Babylonian exile, Jewish religious thinkers became intensely preoccupied with the nature and origin of evil. The idea developed of a vast realm of evil ruled by a terrifying figure who was the arch-enemy of the good God and the source of all human woes. This evil principle was itself one of God's own creations. One widespread concept was that of the two ages: a present age controlled by the powers of evil, in which all the kingdoms of the world are given over to the devil (which is why he can offer them to Jesus; see main text); and a future age when evil will be banished forever.

The gospels give various names to the head of the evil forces, such as the devil, Satan, Beelzebul (KJV: "Beelzebub"), and tempter. His minions are the demons, such as those which Jesus exorcises on several occasions (see pp.226–27). Such exorcisms are not simply humanitarian cures, but also signs that a new age has arrived and the grip of evil on the world has been broken.

Satan Tempting Christ with the Kingdoms of the World, *by William Blake (1757–1827), an illustration to Book 3 of Milton's* Paradise Regained.

THE DISCIPLES

THE DUTIES OF DISCIPLESHIP
Jesus instilled in his disciples devotion to one task above all: to proclaim the coming kingdom of God. This was to supersede all human ties and concern for worldly possessions. The ideal disciple abandoned everything—home, wife, parents, children—for the sake of the kingdom, and no one who looked back wistfully to their old life was fit to enter the kingdom. Discipleship also involved sharing the nomadic way of life of Jesus and living in poverty, carrying no money and wearing a minimum of clothing. These restrictions were aimed more at aiding an unhindered dedication to the task than at imposing an ascetic lifestyle, because disciples might accept any hospitality offered, and eat and drink whatever their hosts provided.

The word "disciple" literally means a "pupil" and translates the Greek *mathetes*, a "pupil" or "learner" of the doctrine of a specific teacher or movement. Hence the Fourth Gospel describes the first five of Jesus' followers as committing themselves to the one they call *rabbi*, "teacher" (John 1.37–50). Many who were strongly influenced by Jesus' teaching might also be termed his "disciples," although they never joined him in his itinerant ministry. For example, Joseph of Arimathea is called a disciple (Matt. 27.57) and Nicodemus acknowledges Jesus as *rabbi* (John 3.2).

However, the primary meaning of "disciple" in the gospels is one who follows Jesus—literally accompanies him on his mission—and has made a radical break with a previous lifestyle in order to do so (see sidebar, left). In this sense Jesus appears not so much as a teacher as a charismatic prophet, who issues a direct summons to each disciple. A close parallel in the Hebrew Scriptures is the sudden call of Elisha by the prophet Elijah (1 Kings 19.19–21). Only when Elisha abandons his livelihood as a farmer does he become Elijah's disciple: this story is clearly the model for scenes in the gospels where Jesus rebukes individuals who ask for dispensation to meet

Jesus and the Apostles, *a Spanish painting of ca. 1250. The title "apostle" (Greek* apostolos, *"messenger," "ambassador") is given to the twelve leading disciples and Paul, who also appears in the picture.*

The names of the Twelve

Khirbet Qana in Galilee, now considered to be the probable site of Cana, where the disciples witnessed Jesus' first miracle (John 2.1–11). The disciple Nathanael came from here. (See p.223.)

Lists of the men who comprised the Twelve appear in all three synoptic gospels (Matt. 10.2–4; Mark 3.16–19; Luke 6.13–16). The lists are basically identical: Simon (called Peter, or Cephas) and his brother Andrew; James and John, the sons of Zebedee; Philip; Bartholomew; Matthew (or Levi) the tax collector; Thomas Didymus ("the Twin"); James, the son of Alphaeus; Simon the Zealot; and Judas Iscariot.

The twelfth disciple is variously called Thaddaeus, Lebbaeus, or Judas son of James (Matt. 10.3; Mark 3.18; Luke 6.16). These may be names for the same person, since some early Christians may have wished to distinguish him from Judas Iscariot. He is commonly referred to as Judas Thaddaeus, or Jude, and the letter of Jude has been ascribed to him, although modern scholars tend to ascribe it to Judas the brother of Jesus.

Peter is always listed first, corresponding to his central role in the whole synoptic tradition. His calling by Jesus is immediately followed by that of his brother Andrew and of his friends James and John, the "Sons of Thunder." Andrew plays little part in the synoptic gospels, but Peter, James, and John are a distinct trio, accompanying Jesus at particularly significant and intimate moments, notably at the Transfiguration (see p.236) and in Gethsemane (see pp.244–45).

John's gospel has its own traditions about the call of the disciples. Andrew is much more prominent: he brings Peter to Jesus and is named as one of two former disciples of the Baptist (the other is never named, but this may be another veiled reference to the "beloved disciple"—see sidebar, p.187). John also mentions the call of Philip, who in turn introduces a certain Nathanael to Jesus. Nathanael may be the same as the disciple Bartholomew of the synoptic gospels.

family obligations before joining him (Matt. 8.21–22, Luke 9.59–60).

The gospels state that Jesus had many disciples, from whom he chose a select group of a dozen men. To this body, referred to as "the Twelve," Jesus assigned the authority to exorcize, to perform cures, and to preach the kingdom of God (see pp.280–81). Their number corresponds to that of the tribes of ancient Israel. This is deliberate: Jesus promised the Twelve that their supreme reward, at the renewal of all things, would be to sit on twelve thrones and to judge the twelve tribes (Matt.19.28, Luke 22.30).

The Twelve were a fixed and unchanging body that was especially close to Jesus. After the death of Judas Iscariot the number had to be made up to twelve again by the appointment of someone who had accompanied Jesus throughout his ministry (Acts 1.16–26). The new Twelve continued the work of exorcizing, healing, and preaching.

JESUS' PUBLIC CAREER

According to the synoptic gospels, Jesus' public career fell into three distinct stages: the Galilean ministry; a journey to Jerusalem; and the final events of his life. During the ministry in Galilee, Jesus' activity was confined to a small area along the western shore of the lake and the surrounding hills; he also made occasional visits outside Galilee.

It is unlikely that the evangelists intended to present a precise chronological sequence in their accounts of the sayings and deeds of Jesus. The earliest witness to the gospel of Mark states that the evangelist did not set events out in order and, assuming that Matthew and Luke had Mark's work in front of them (see p.189), they evidently felt free to change the order and setting of the individual sections that make up Mark's narrative. However, all three synoptists agree that the Galilean ministry came to an end with Jesus' decision to go to Jerusalem, a journey that took him southward along the Jordan river (Mark 10.1; Matt. 19.1), probably in

The character of Jesus' ministry

The accounts of Jesus' ministry given in Matthew, Mark, and Luke on the one hand and in John on the other differ considerably. While the differences should not be overemphasized (see p.187), it is true that certain features found in the three synoptic gospels—parables, exorcisms, the Sermon on the Mount, the Lord's Prayer, and Jesus' words over the bread and cup at the Last Supper—are absent, or almost absent, from the Fourth Gospel.

Jesus' teaching in the synoptists is largely concerned with moral and religious guidance and is characterized by pithy sayings. In John, Jesus speaks in lengthy discourses and has extensive debates with opponents. These speeches aim to demonstrate the true nature of Jesus and to reinforce his claim to divine sonship.

Jesus does perform miracles in the Fourth Gospel, but mostly different ones from those that appear in the other three. They are "signs"—each with its own special message about the true nature of Jesus—rather than examples of his powers. Thus by giving sight to a blind man, Jesus is revealed as the light of the world (John 9.1–5).

In John, the opponents of Jesus are generally labeled simply "the Jews." He is presented as one who stands somewhat apart from Judaism, rather than as an essentially Jewish figure, as in the synoptists. This tends to suggest that the Fourth Gospel was written at a time when a clear split was starting to appear between Jewish Christianity (see pp.326–27) and the synagogue. However, like the other evangelists, John is unequivocal about Jesus' Jewish origins (John 1.45–46, 4.22).

The Light of the World, *by William Holman Hunt (1827–1910). It illustrates the words of Jesus in John 9.5.*

The Roman Catholic (left) and Greek Orthodox churches at Kfar Kanna, the traditional site of Cana in Galilee, both claim to mark the place where Jesus performed his first "sign" by turning water into wine at a wedding, according to John 2.1–11. John's gospel gives greater prominence to the south of Palestine, especially Jerusalem (see sidebar, below), but it is aware of Jesus' origins in Galilee and that he performed healings and other miracles there. Scholars now consider Khirbet Qana (see p.221) to be a more likely location for the Cana of the gospels.

order to avoid the direct route through hostile Samaria (Luke 9.51–56, 17.11). Luke develops this journey into an extended travel narrative (Luke 9.51–19.27; see p.239).

Taken as a whole, Matthew, Mark, and Luke present a markedly different picture of Jesus' ministry from that in John (see box, opposite). The Fourth Gospel implies a ministry of two years or longer (see sidebar, right), and this has often been contrasted with the synoptists, who mention only one visit to Jerusalem, at Passover, and seem to imply a ministry of a year or less. The differences may not be entirely irreconcilable, because each of the evangelists is more concerned with theology than precise chronology.

For John, each Jewish festival reveals something of the significance of Jesus. For example, Jesus represents the sacrificial Passover lamb (John 1.29, 36). In the synoptic gospels, Jesus' final journey to Jerusalem is significant not because he was keeping the Passover but because it was the occasion on which he was to meet his death (Mark 10.33 and parallels). The unique significance attached to this particular visit to Jerusalem does not necessarily exclude the possibility that Jesus, as a pious Jew, would have gone to the city on other occasions to observe certain Jewish feasts. The Jewish law (Deut. 16.16–17) called upon all males to visit the Temple at Passover, Pentecost, and Tabernacles, the so-called "pilgrimage festivals." While it seems unlikely, for practical reasons, that every single Jewish male really was obliged to leave home three times a year, it was doubtless considered an act of merit to fulfill the biblical commandment whenever circumstances permitted. This would have been easier for those, like Jesus and his disciples, who were not tied to home or workplace.

THE MINISTRY IN JOHN

In John, Jesus begins his ministry in Judea and the adjacent Transjordanian region of Perea (John 3.22, 26), and moves regularly between there and Galilee. But the greater part of Jesus' ministry, according to the Fourth Gospel, takes place in Jerusalem and its environs. Jesus visited the city on the occasion of Passover and other important Jewish festivals and on most of these occasions visited the Temple.

The evangelist mentions three Passovers and three other intervening festivals. If they are intended to be seen as occurring in strict succession, it is possible to reconstruct a fairly precise chronology of Jesus' life over two or more years.

The first year included a Passover visit to Jerusalem in the spring (John 2.13) and another visit on the occasion of an unspecified festival (John 5.1), either the feast of Weeks (or Pentecost, seven weeks after Passover) or, perhaps more likely, the New Year festival (early autumn).

In the following year, Jesus fed the crowd in Galilee near the time of Passover (John 6.4) and is said to have been in Jerusalem for the feast of the Dedication in December (John 10.22), perhaps having remained in the city since the autumn festival of Tabernacles.

In the third year, after visiting Perea (John 10.40), Bethany (John 11.1–43), and a town near the Judean desert (John 11.54), Jesus returned to Jerusalem for his final Passover (John 12.1, 13.1).

THE HEALINGS

PHYSICIANS AT THE TIME OF JESUS
The professional medical practitioners of Jesus' time are often given a bad name in both pagan and Jewish sources. The Mishnah lawcode quotes one rabbi: "the best among physicians is destined for Gehenna [hell]"; and Jesus cites an uncomplimentary proverb widely known in the ancient Mediterranean world: "Doctor, cure yourself!" (Luke 4.23.) The poor reputation of doctors is also reflected in the account of a woman cured by Jesus of chronic hemorrhaging (Mark 5.25–34 and parallels). For years she "had endured much under many physicians and had spent all that she had and was no better, but rather grew worse" (Mark 5.26).

In Jesus' day, illness and disease were regularly blamed on evil spirits or demons, and for this reason it is hard to distinguish absolutely in the gospels between healing and exorcism (the casting out of spirits that have possessed an individual; see pp.226–27). For example, Peter's mother-in-law suffers a fever that "left her" after Jesus "rebuked" it (Luke 4.39). However, several passages do seem to acknowledge a distinction between curings and exorcisms, especially in Matthew, who displays considerable diagnostic knowledge in his categorization of illness (Matt. 4.24, 10.8).

There were two main types of healer in the time of Jesus: professional physicians, who were held in low regard (see sidebar, left), and "wonder-workers," who enjoyed great popularity. The latter performed healings using age-old magical methods and media, such as spells, incantations, animal parts, potions, and blood. There is no indication that Jesus employed such practices, although on three occasions he is said to have healed a person by applying saliva (Mark 7.33, 8.23; John 9.6). No doubt this was a common folk remedy, but the essential point is that it created a physical bond between Jesus and the sufferer. Most accounts of Jesus' cures involve

The Blind of Jericho, *by Nicolas Poussin (1594–1665). According to Matthew 20.30–43, Jesus restored the sight of two blind men of Jericho by touching their eyes (compare Mark 10.46–52).*

Raising the dead

The gospels record three occasions on which Jesus brought a dead person back to life. In the New Testament, this miraculous ability is part of Jesus' role of prophet, linking him particularly with the biblical figures of Elijah and Elisha. Both of these great prophets restored to life the son of a widow (1 Kings 17.17–23; 2 Kings 4.18–36), and the accounts of these miracles parallel the gospel stories of the raising of the daughter of Jairus, a synagogue leader (Mark 5.22–24, 35–42 and parallels).

All three gospels quote Jesus as saying that Jairus' daughter "is not dead but sleeping." This could be understood literally, but each gospel is at pains to stress that the girl's death was real, as does John in his account of the raising of Lazarus, where Jesus utters similar words (John 11.11–14).

There may be an echo here of the book of Daniel, which says that "Many of those who sleep in the dust of the earth shall awake" (Dan. 12.2): the dead sleep peacefully, awaiting the general resurrection at the Day of Judgment. Paul's letter to the Ephesians has the summons: "Sleeper, awake! Rise from the dead" (Eph. 5.14).

The raising of Jairus' daughter, therefore, is a foretaste of the resurrection assured to all who believe in Jesus. This is also John's clear understanding of the revival of Lazarus, a story only found in this gospel (John 11.1–44): Jesus himself is "the resurrection and the life" (John 11.25).

The raising of the son of a widow at Nain, a miracle unique to Luke (7.11–15), is even more closely modeled on the Elijah and Elisha stories. The miracle prepares the way for Jesus' reply to John the Baptist's messengers (Luke 7.20–23) and marks out Jesus as a prophet as great as his two biblical predecessors. His presence brings God's favor on his people (Luke 7.16).

The village of Nain in Lower Galilee, the setting for Jesus' miraculous raising of a widow's son, recounted in Luke's gospel.

some sort of bodily contact, touching or laying on of hands. Similarly, the gospels record that people were cured by touching Jesus or even just his clothing, as with the woman with the hemorrhage (see sidebar, opposite). When Jesus healed, power came out from him (Luke 6.19); this is how he himself knew when someone in a large crowd had touched him (Luke 8.46). At such moments, Jesus appears as a holy man similar to several Israelite prophets, possessing a mysterious quasiphysical force that can be directed to the benefit of others.

For Jesus, an equally important means of healing is his authoritative word. Sometimes a simple utterance is enough: "Be made clean" (Mark 1.41 and parallels); "Stretch out your hand"(Mark 3.5 and parallels); "Stand up and take your mat and walk" (Mark 2.9, 11 and parallels). Jesus' word operates even at a distance (Matt. 8.5–13; Luke 7.2–10).

More usually, however, touching and utterance go together, which seems to correspond to the practice of popular healers. An example is the account of the healing of the blind man at Bethsaida, where Jesus both applies saliva to the man's eyes and lays hands on him (Mark 8.22–25).

The ruins of the splendid synagogue at Capernaum, constructed ca. 400 CE to replace the building where Jesus taught and cured a man possessed by an evil spirit (Mark 1.23–26).

THE EXORCISMS

A belief in the ubiquitous presence and malevolent activity of evil spirits—also called demons, devils, or unclean spirits—was virtually universal in the ancient world, and there are plentiful references to them in the gospels. Many natural and human calamities (including illness and injury) were attributed to demonic possession. In the synoptic gospels, evil spirits are associated primarily with a specific type of affliction that is accompanied by violent physical symptoms, described in three vivid narratives.

In the synagogue at Capernaum, an evil spirit throws a man into convulsions (Mark 1.26). On another occasion (Mark 9.17–27 and parallels) a boy is similarly hurled to the ground, where he foams, grinds his teeth, and becomes rigid—a combination of symptoms that is currently understood to describe an epileptic seizure. The boy is said to have been frequently impelled by the spirit to attempt suicide. Most dramatic of all are the accounts of the Gerasene, or Gadarene, demoniac, who lived naked in a graveyard and wandered the hills, howling and bruising himself. He possessed such supernatural strength that no chains or fetters could restrain him (Mark 5.1–13; Luke 8.27–33; compare Matt. 8.28–33).

Exorcists in Jesus' day

The limited medical knowledge that was current at the time of Jesus allowed little understanding of severe mental illness: "demonic possession" was the standard diagnosis. Over a long period there had developed a class of exorcists, to whom people turned in order to expel evil spirits and restore a sufferer's peace of mind. The techniques they used were essentially magical. Exorcists depended for their success (or at least their reputation) on the correct performance of elaborate rituals involving incantations and spells and the use of various substances believed to possess supernatural properties.

To people who did not know of him, Jesus may well have seemed like other Palestinian wonder-workers and exorcists. At one stage he was certainly accused by his opponents of being no more than a magician, and moreover one whose power derived from the prince of demons, Beelzebul (KJV: Beelzebub). But the purpose of such accusations was not to deny the success of his exorcisms but to attribute them to sorcery. Different as Jesus undoubtedly was, it is possible to discern parallels between his exorcisms and those of Jewish and pagan exorcists. Mark (9.38) and Luke (9.49) record that a man went around casting out demons in Jesus' name—that is, at least one exorcist had come to realize that Jesus' name could be used effectively in magical conjuration.

Jesus himself acknowledges the existence of other successful exorcists including, according to Matthew (12.27), some of the Pharisees, who, like many other Jewish religious teachers, may well have had a great interest in exorcism. The process of exorcism demanded that the exorcist wield self-evident authority over the evil spirits to be cast out, and a teacher might well be assumed to possess such authority.

For the synoptic gospels, Jesus' authority over demons is closely associated with his authority as a teacher, in that his healings and exorcisms confirmed the truth and power of his preaching. To the jealousy of his opponents, Jesus possessed authority over the demons because he was recognized by the people at large as a charismatic prophet who—like the prophets in the Hebrew Scriptures—was directly inspired by the spirit of God.

In contrast to other healers (see box, opposite), Jesus made no use of magical techniques, but cast out demons simply with words of power: "Come out!" There did not have to be physical contact with the demoniac—indeed, in the case of the daughter of the Syro-Phoenician woman (Mark 7.25–30), Jesus never even saw the sufferer. The reason that his methods were different, according to the gospels, was that Jesus had a special understanding of his activity as an exorcist: he saw the demons as not just random and individual spirits but as the agents of the mighty power of evil in the world. They worked under the direction of their leader, who is known by several names and titles, including the devil and Satan (see sidebar, p.219). Casting out the demons was in itself a prophetic sign, to those that could comprehend it, that the power of evil was losing its grip on the world—that the new kingdom of God was beginning, heralded and inaugurated by the mission of Jesus.

If most Jews, apart from Jesus' own followers, did not recognize this sign, some of the demons cast out by Jesus certainly did. They verbally acknowledged him as the Holy One or the Son of God, and were terrified at his power over them. In the case of the legion of spirits who possessed the Gerasene demoniac, they implored Jesus not to make them go back into the "abyss"—suggesting that the gospel writer equates the demons with the fallen angels who were placed in such a confinement. Jesus' response portrays the demons as in reality powerless and contemptible figures. He sends them not into the cosmic abyss but instead—and the narrative is not without a touch of humor—into a herd of pigs who, maddened by this invasion, rush headlong to destruction.

The Gadarene Swine, *depicted in the 6th-century mosaics of Sant' Apollinare Nuovo, Ravenna. Jesus (center) casts evil spirits out of a demoniac—ancient manuscripts of the gospels disagree on whether he was from the region of Gerasa or Gadara—into a herd of pigs (right), which hurtle down a bank into the Sea of Galilee.*

THE FEEDING MIRACLES

All four gospels relate how Jesus employed a tiny amount of food to feed a crowd of five thousand or more, and Matthew and Mark also describe a broadly similar feeding of four thousand people. If there is a relationship between the two episodes, as is commonly supposed, it is not easy to determine. The feeding of the five thousand seems to be aimed at a Jewish audience, especially in Mark's account (Mark 6.34–44). The setting is Galilee and the crowd is described as "like sheep without a shepherd"—an image for Israel in the Hebrew Scriptures. They are divided into groups of hundreds and fifties, which recalls the way Moses divided up the Israelites (Exod. 18.25), and the leftover food is collected in twelve baskets, recalling the twelve tribes of Israel.

Mark's account of the feeding of the four thousand (Mark 8.1–9) is preceded by a healing in the Decapolis (see p.154), a largely Gentile area. So it is possible that the two feedings originally symbolized the call, first to Jews and then to Gentiles, to share in the new life that Jesus bestowed.

The feeding narratives in the gospels are accompanied by passages that seek to bring out their deeper meaning. In Matthew and Mark, this takes the form of a discussion between Jesus and his disciples on the subject of food (Matt. 16.5–12; Mark 8.14–21). On a crossing of the Sea of Galilee, the disciples realize that they have brought no bread or, at most, a single loaf. Jesus warns them against "the yeast of the Pharisees," and the disciples take this as a reference to their forgetfulness. But Jesus upbraids them for their lack of perception and reminds them how, in each of the miraculous feedings, a small number of loaves had fed great multitudes and produced a vast quantity of leftover pieces.

In Mark, Jesus does not go on to explain what he actually means by "yeast"—the evangelist's primary concern is simply to show how the disciples repeatedly fail to understand their master's words and actions. In Jewish rabbinic writings, yeast is commonly used as a metaphor for human evil. One teacher of the third century CE concluded that what hindered people from doing God's will were oppressive pagan empires and "the yeast in the dough"—the evil impulse in all human beings. In the gospels, the term is broadly to be understood as the hostility of Jesus' opponents, of whom his followers are to beware. To the "yeast of the Pharisees" Mark adds "the yeast of Herod," while Matthew includes the Sadducees. In Matthew, "the yeast of the Pharisees and Sadducees" refers specifically to the teaching of these groups (Matt. 16.12). Luke, who has the "yeast" reference in a different context (Luke 12.1ff.), equates it with the Pharisees' hypocrisy.

Two other motifs emerge from the accounts of the feeding of the five thousand. Firstly, the setting is a desert place, and there is a clear analogy

DEEDS OF POWER

Scholars today distinguish between Jesus' miraculous cures, which may seem more credible to modern people, and the so-called "nature miracles" such as the feedings of great multitudes. It is doubtful whether Jesus' contemporaries would ever have made such a distinction. Charismatic Jewish teachers of the time were often thought able to control the forces of nature, and the same was true of biblical prophets such as Elijah, with whom Jesus was identified by some contemporaries. It is therefore quite understandable that Jesus should have been credited with various miraculous feats, even if some—such as the fish with a coin in its mouth (Matt. 17.27)—must be regarded as legendary.

How the gospels interpret the nature of miracles is significant. The accounts of Jesus stilling a great storm (Matt. 8.26 and parallels) and walking on water (Matt. 14.25 and parallels) recall God's power over the waters of the Red Sea (Exod. 14–23) and the crossing of the Jordan by the Israelites (Josh. 3.14–17) and the prophet Elisha (2 Kings 3.13–14). In Luke, the story of Peter and the miraculous draft of fishes (Luke 5.3–11) symbolizes both Jesus' divine authority and the mission of his followers to make converts.

Jesus sometimes warned against anyone being unduly preoccupied with his "deeds of power": his audience were to take note of his person and message rather than his miracles. Thus when the Pharisees asked Jesus for a miraculous prophetic sign, he simply refused (Mark 8.11–12). When he effected cures, he told those he had healed not to publicize what he had done.

The Sea of Galilee at Tabgha. The modern Church of the Multiplication of Loaves and Fishes (foreground) marks the spot where Jesus is said to have miraculously fed some 5,000 people with a mere 5 loaves and 2 fishes (Mark 6.38 and parallels). Dedicated in 1982, the church incorporates remains from a 3rd-century CE *Byzantine basilica that originally stood on the site.*

between Jesus' action and Moses' provision of food for the Israelites in the wilderness (Exod. 16). Second, Jesus' taking, blessing, breaking, and distribution of the bread and fishes foreshadow the events of the Last Supper (and probably the Christian Eucharist).

Both motifs are explicitly developed in the Fourth Gospel, especially in the accompanying discourse of Jesus (John 6.25–59). The miracle takes place at the time of Passover, when Jews eat a meal to commemorate the Israelite deliverance from Egypt. The food Jesus provides is contrasted with the manna of Moses: those who ate the manna eventually died, but Jesus himself represents the true bread from heaven, the gift of his Father who alone confers eternal life and the assurance of resurrection (John 6.48–50). The discourse moves on from the image of consuming bread to the eating of Jesus' flesh and drinking his blood (John 6.51–57), whereby a believer is united with him, the true source of life. The Fourth Gospel contains no account of the Last Supper, and John's narrative of the feeding is to be understood as its equivalent.

CONFLICTS AND CONFRONTATIONS

The gospels contain many accounts of opposition to Jesus and his teaching, and there is a distinct class of "conflict stories," such as the five grouped together at the beginning of Mark's gospel (Mark 2.1–3.6). These were preserved because they contained words of Jesus that were considered important to his message.

It has often been said that the stories of Jesus' confrontations with various Jewish groups, especially the Pharisees, really reflect later disputes between Christians and Jews that developed after Jesus' death. It is not impossible that the gospels may have been influenced by later circumstances, but many aspects of Jesus' message and actions would certainly have provoked hostile reactions during his lifetime.

To begin with, Jesus came into conflict with his own relatives, who even attempted to restrain him as a dangerous lunatic (Mark 3.21). This is something that the early Church would have been unlikely to invent, and that it caused embarrassment is shown by the fact that some New Testament manuscripts alter Mark's original to make the participants "the scribes and the others" rather than "his family." Jesus and his followers were dedicated to a peripatetic life of poverty, and he could be seen as challenging the ties of home and kinship, when he taught that his disciples were

Christ and the Woman Taken in Adultery, *by Lucas Cranach the Younger (1515–86). John 7.53–8.11 records that "the scribes and Pharisees" wanted Jesus to endorse the penalty—death by stoning—against a woman guilty of adultery. Jesus replied: "Let anyone among you who is without sin be the first to throw a stone." The crowd dispersed and Jesus dismissed the woman with a warning not to sin again.*

Ruins of the Roman-period synagogue at Chorazin in Galilee, one of the towns that Jesus cursed—together with Capernaum and Bethsaida—for rejecting the message of his "deeds of power."

his only true family (Matt. 12.49–50) and that discipleship meant the renunciation of family and possessions (Mark 10.28–30 and parallels; Matt. 10 37–39; Luke 14.26–27).

The gospels record the success of Jesus' Galilean ministry but they also show that this was by no means unmixed: Jesus was ejected from the synagogue at Nazareth, his own hometown (Luke 4.16–30), and could perform no miracles there because the inhabitants would not recognize his prophetic authority (Mark 6.1–6 and parallels). Jesus cursed several Galilean towns for their failure to respond to his message (Matt. 11.20–24; Luke 10.13–15).

The gospels record a number of confrontations on specific issues between Jesus and the Pharisees, the "scribes" (see p.162–63), and other experts in Jewish law closely associated with them. For example, they accused Jesus of being possessed by Beelzebul, the ruler of the demons, and performing exorcisms by his power (Mark 3.22 and parallels). This accusation—that Jesus was a false magician—was a way of isolating him as a threat to the established religious and social order.

However, the Pharisees represented a fairly wide range of religious opinion and the evangelists do show that they were not invariably hostile to Jesus. There was much in Jesus' teaching that corresponded with the Pharisaic outlook, such as his refutation of the arguments of the Sadducees (see p.167) against the resurrection of the dead (Luke 20.27–39). Jesus' words on this occasion gained scribal approval, and his definition of the supreme commandment of the Jewish law is also represented as being in harmony with that of the scribes (Mark 12.28–34; Luke 10.25–28).

The "woes" that Jesus pronounces against the Pharisees, especially in Matthew (Matt. 23.13–29), probably echo later tensions and largely represent the evangelist's version of similar lists of denunciations and prophesied woes in the Hebrew Bible (such as Isaiah 5.8–24 and Habakkuk

Jesus in the House of Simon the Pharisee, *by Jean Fouquet (ca. 1420–ca. 1481), from* The Hours of Etienne Chevalier. *According to Luke 7.36–50, Jesus was invited to dine by a Pharisee, but criticized his host for giving him a poor welcome compared with that of a woman—described as "a sinner"—who washed and anointed Jesus' feet and dried them with her hair. The woman is traditionally identified with Mary Magdalene, the first person to see the resurrected Christ, as depicted in the inset scenes below (see John 20.11–17).* *(See also pp.166 and 340–41.)*

2.6–19). Jesus, like very many Jews of his day, apparently recognized the Pharisees as authoritative teachers (Matt. 23.2–3), and he is recorded as enjoying the hospitality of individual Pharisees. It is worth noting that the three synoptists make no mention of Pharisaic involvement in the moves leading to Jesus' arrest and condemnation.

All the same, there remain important differences in outlook between Jesus and the Pharisees. The fundamental issue is summed up in Jesus' complaint that the Pharisees have neglected "the weightier matters of the law: justice and mercy and faith" (Matt. 23.23). According to Jesus, Pharisaic rules about such matters as tithing, fasting, and priestly purity, which were intended to protect and strengthen the Mosaic law, went so far beyond it that they were in danger of obscuring its real priorities. The observance of such meticulous rules could become a burden and lead to an attitude of contempt toward the social and religious outcasts with whom Jesus so closely identified, as seen in the parable of the Pharisee and the tax collector (Luke 18.9–14). It is Jesus' priority of humanitarian concern, as in the healing of disease or relief of hunger, that is at stake in the controversies about the proper observation of the Sabbath (Mark 2.23–28 and parallels).

The Pharisees no doubt saw Jesus as a threat to their religious authority and teaching. In their eyes, he was a provincial (see box, below) with no background of religious training, and they inevitably questioned whether his teaching, so different from scribal learning (Mark 1.22; Matt. 7.29), could possess the authority of their own (Mark 11.27–33 and parallels).

Galilee: a land of rebels

Jesus and his immediate followers were natives of Galilee, particularly of the Galilean countryside, and as such they were a ready object of suspicion to both the religious and civil authorities. In the gospels, the Pharisees and scribes appear to have a background in Jerusalem (Mark 3.22, 7.1), where Galileans seem to have been widely regarded as boorish provincials with a marked regional accent (Matt. 26.73), ill-educated in the Mosaic law and lax in its observance. This attitude is reflected in John, where some of the Jerusalem crowd question whether the Messiah could come from Galilee (John 7.41) and the Pharisees describe Jesus' followers as "this crowd, which does not know the law" (John 7.49).

When a sympathetic Pharisee, Nicodemus, intervenes with the "chief priests and Pharisees" in Jesus' support, he is taunted with being a Galilean (John 7.51–52). From the Pharisaic point of view, Jesus could appear to be guilty of the religious impropriety that was seen to characterize Galileans in general: he accepted hospitality from the hated tax collectors; consorted with "sinners" and prostitutes; and his disciples did not observe the strict Pharisaic rules (see main text).

Galilee had long been a center of resistance to the Roman power and its client Jewish rulers. For example, the New Testament mentions a revolt led by "Judas the Galilean" (Acts 5.36–37) in 4 BCE, following the death of King Herod the Great (see pp.156–57). During the uprising the capital of Galilee, Sepphoris (see p.155), was looted and destroyed.

According to the Jewish historian Josephus, John the Baptist was executed by Herod Antipas, the ruler of Galilee (see p.156), because he was afraid that the success of John's preaching would provoke another rebellion. The evangelists suggest that Antipas saw Jesus as a similar figure (Mark 6.14–16 and parallels) and likewise sought to remove him (Luke 13.31–33). The gospels describe a group called the "Herodians" conspiring to destroy Jesus (Mark 3.6) or trying to catch him out on the issue of Roman taxation (Mark 12.13–17). It is possible that the Herodians were the partisans of the Galilean ruler, although Mark associates them with the Pharisees, who were generally hostile to the Herodian dynasty.

In the Fourth Gospel, the Temple authorities in Jerusalem are also afraid that Jesus' activities will earn him a large following and provoke a drastic intervention from the Romans (John 11.47–50). All four gospels record the "Cleansing" incident, a disturbance caused by Jesus in the Temple (see pp.240–41) near Passover—a time when the Roman military was on special alert in case of trouble in the crowded city.

A blocked-up triple arch has been identified as the Triple Hulda gate, the main south entrance of the Temple Mount and used by worshipers coming from the southern end of the Mount of Olives, Bethany, or Jericho. It was probably where Jesus made his entry for the Cleansing of the Temple (see pp.240–41).

THE FATE OF THE BAPTIST

The Beheading of John the Baptist, *by Massimo Stanzione (1585–1656), as recorded in Matthew 14.10 and Mark 6.27. According to Josephus, Antipas imprisoned and executed John at the fortress of Machaerus in southern Perea, near the Dead Sea (see map on p.157).*

The arrest and execution of John the Baptist made a profound impression on the early Christian community. It is mentioned several times in the gospels, and the fact that the Jewish writer Josephus, writing in the last quarter of the first century CE, also records it shows that the events remained well known.

The three synoptists claim that Herod Antipas, the tetrarch (ruler) of Galilee and Perea, arrested John mainly because the Baptist had condemned his marriage to his former sister-in-law while her ex-husband was still alive—an act that Jewish law regarded as incest (see sidebar, p.177). However, according to Josephus, Antipas imprisoned and executed the Baptist because he feared that his popularity would provoke an insurrection. Both stories are plausible, because Josephus wrote in Rome for a Gentile audience that would not have been concerned with the niceties of Jewish marriage law. Matthew, though, implies that John's popularity was why Antipas did *not* want to execute him—he feared the reaction of "the crowd," who regarded the Baptist as a prophet (Matt. 14.5).

Mark presents a vivid narrative of the death of the Baptist (Mark 6.17–29) and there is a more summary account in Matthew (Matt. 14.3–12). Both evangelists probably rely on a common tradition, preserved among the Baptist's disciples and perhaps told to people visiting his tomb (Mark 6.29; Matt. 14.12).

Mark's version has the character of a Jewish folktale, with echoes of the Hebrew Bible. The daughter of Herodias, Salome—it is from Josephus that we have her name—dances for Antipas, who makes her a rash promise: "Whatever you ask me, I will give you, even half of my kingdom." This promise occurs twice, in almost identical form, in the book of Esther (Esth. 5.6, 7.2), where the setting is also a great royal banquet. Esther's response to the monarch's promise brings about the execution of her enemy, Haman. In Mark, Salome is prompted by her mother Herodias to ask for "the head of John the Baptizer."

Mark's story also reflects the resentment of ordinary people, such as the followers of the Baptist and Jesus, at the splendor and intrigue of the courts of the Herodian dynasty (see pp.156–57). Elsewhere, Jesus contrasts the Baptist with those who put on fine clothing and live in luxury in royal palaces (Luke 7.25; Matt. 11.8). The decadence of the Herodian royal family is emphasized by the performance of a dance (probably understood to be of a lascivious character), by a royal princess (Mark 6.22)—this sort of entertainment was usually provided by professional courtesans.

A coin issued by Herod Antipas (ruled 4 BCE–39 CE). The obverse (right) bears the Greek legend "Herod the Tetrarch" and the reverse has the name of his capital city, Tiberias in Galilee.

JOHN AND ELIJAH

Mark's account of the Baptist's death has significant echoes of the biblical story of the prophet Elijah. In each case the ruler's wife is the prophet's real and determined enemy, while her husband displays a more ambiguous attitude. Herodias, like Queen Jezebel in 1 Kings, appears as the dominant partner in the marriage, and it is at her instigation that John is jailed (Mark 6.17; Matt.14.3). Again like Jezebel, it is she who plots the prophet's death (Mark 6.19; 1 Kings 19.2).

Some people believed that Jesus was Elijah (Mark 6.15; Luke 9.8), but Jesus himself identified Elijah as the Baptist (Matt. 11.14). In one key passage (Mark 9.9–13; Matt. 17.9–13), the disciples asked Jesus whether Elijah would return to usher in the messianic age, in accordance with scripture (Mal. 4.5–6). Jesus replied that Elijah had already come, but "they did to him whatever they pleased" (Mark 9.13)—a reference to the Baptist's execution that is explicit in Matthew (Matt. 17.12–13).

Matthew states that the "Son of Man"—Jesus—will suffer in the same way (Matt. 17.12) and that his fate and that of the Baptist-Elijah are foretold in scripture (Mark 9.12–13). In this respect, the gospels see the death of John as foreshadowing the inevitable fate of Jesus himself.

Salome with the Head of John the Baptist, *by Andrea Solario (ca. 1470–1524), illustrating Matthew 14.11 and Mark 6.28.*

PETER'S CONFESSION AND THE TRANSFIGURATION

All four gospels record an episode in which the disciple Peter made a confession (avowal) of faith in the special character of Jesus (Matt. 16.13–23; Mark 8.27–33; Luke 9.18–22; John 6.67–69). Matthew and Mark locate this scene in the vicinity of Caesarea Philippi, in the far north of Palestine. At the heart of Peter's confession is his declaration of the disciples' belief that Jesus is the Messiah. In Matthew, Mark, and Luke, Jesus never uses the term "Messiah" of himself, and in their accounts of the Galilean ministry it occurs only once, in the mouth of the demons (Luke 4.41). It is only after Peter's avowal of faith that the issue assumes significance.

There was a wide variety of messianic concepts in contemporary

The Transfiguration

Peter's confession is followed by the episode known as the Transfiguration, when Jesus appears transfigured—illumined in glory—on a mountainside in the company of Moses and Elijah (Matt. 17.1–8; Mark 9.2–8; Luke 9.28–36). The experience provides divine confirmation of Jesus' vocation as Redeemer and of his words (Mark 8.34–9.1 and parallels) on suffering as a condition of discipleship.

A privileged trio of disciples, Peter, James, and John, witness the event and perceive the reality of the divine world to which Jesus belongs. They are overshadowed by a "bright cloud" (Matt. 17.5), a sign of the presence of God, from which a heavenly voice utters words recalling Jesus' baptism (Mark 9.7 and parallels). Just as the Baptism (see pp.216–17) empowered Jesus for his earthly ministry, so the Transfiguration is a foretaste of the glory of the resurrected Christ.

The Transfiguration episode contains a variety of biblical motifs. Moses is clearly in mind (Exod. 24.15–18; compare also Exod. 34.29 and Matt. 17.2). He and Elijah are usually understood to symbolize the law and the prophets respectively, two of the three subdivisions of the Hebrew Bible (see p.162). They thus represent the old covenant with Israel, which Jesus supersedes. In rabbinic traditions, Moses and Elijah were expected to appear at the end of the world, so their presence may be intended to indicate that a new age—inaugurated by Jesus' death and resurrection—was about to commence.

Nonbiblical Jewish writings tell of individuals who ascend to the divine presence, where they are transfigured into heavenly beings and learn divine secrets. They become clothed in shining white garments, the dress of angels. Such accounts seem to be derived from the personal visions of seers, and the Transfiguration may represent a similar mystical transformation experience on the part of Jesus, which was also shared by the three disciples.

Mount Tabor in Galilee is identified in Christian tradition as the "high mountain apart" (Mark 9.2) of the Transfiguration. Many modern scholars tend to favor Mount Hermon.

The springs of Banias, ancient Paneas, in the Golan. It was an important town in the territory of the tetrarch Philip (ruled 4 BCE–34 CE), a son of Herod the Great (see pp.156–57) and halfbrother of Antipas, the ruler of neighboring Galilee. Paneas was in a largely Gentile region and was named from its important shrine to the Greco-Roman god Pan, around which Philip constructed the city of Caesarea Philippi ("Caesarea of Philip"). Jesus may have crossed into Philip's lands to escape the attentions of Antipas following the execution of John the Baptist (see Matt. 14.1–2; Mark 6.14–16).

Judaism, but almost all involved a belief in God's intervention in history through an intermediary who would "redeem Israel" (Luke 24.21) from its oppressors. At Caesarea Philippi, the disciples recognized Jesus as this intermediary: he is more than the Redeemer's forerunner, more than a prophet, teacher, or wonder-worker: he is the Redeemer himself.

However, Jesus saw his redeeming work as different from what most Jews expected of the Messiah (see pp.294–95). It was to be accomplished through his death and resurrection, a truth that Jesus drives home in the three predictions of the Passion (see p.238). He told the disciples that the Jewish religious authorities would reject him and, far from overthrowing the heathen oppressors, he would be handed over to them. When Peter cannot accept this Jesus rebukes him (Mark 8.32–33; Matt. 16.22–23).

A crucified Messiah would have seemed a contradiction in terms to most Jews and to announce Jesus as Messiah would have aroused false expectations. So Jesus insisted that this truth must be kept secret among his disciples, to be revealed only when he had been vindicated by actually rising from the dead (Mark 9.9; Matt. 17.9). Until then, not even the disciples would be able to understand the true meaning of Jesus' mission.

The confession marks the virtual end of Jesus' ministry in Galilee—he returns there only briefly—and the beginning of his final journey to Jerusalem. In Matthew and Mark, the content of the narrative also changes strikingly: they recount just two healing miracles and emphasize Jesus' teaching, which is imparted chiefly to his closest disciples. Luke also gives much prominence to Jesus' teaching, but the shift is less marked and his account of the journey to Jerusalem includes a variety of themes (see p.239).

From Caesarea Philippi onward, the gospels strike an increasing note of tragedy. Jesus becomes increasingly isolated and the narratives reach a climax when all his disciples have abandoned him (Mark 14.50; Matt 26.56).

THE ROAD TO JERUSALEM

The Jericho-Jerusalem road passes through the rugged landscape of Wadi Qelt, 8km (5 miles) west of Jericho. High above the valley floor is the Greek Orthodox monastery of St. George, originally founded in the 5th century CE.

THE MEANING OF FAITH
Another prominent theme at this point in the gospels' story is how faith is to be understood. Following the Transfiguration (see p.236), there is an account of Jesus curing an epileptic boy (Mark 9.14–29 and parallels). On this occasion, the disciples had tried to effect a cure but failed, and their failure is a sign of a faithless generation. Mark emphasizes the faith of the boy's father, and in Matthew and Luke the disciples are instructed about the supreme power of such faith. In Mark, the disciples are taught that exorcism must rely on prayer, presumably following the example of the boy's father, who prays to Jesus (see also box, opposite).

The synoptic gospels present varied accounts of the period in which Jesus and his disciples journeyed from Caesarea Philippi to Jerusalem, via Galilee and Jericho (Matt. 17.9–21.11; Mark 9.9–11.10; Luke 9.51–19.28). The versions of Mark and Matthew are broadly similar, while that of Luke is quite distinctive and much longer (see box, opposite).

In all three gospels, a growing shadow is cast by Jesus' three predictions of the Passion, before and after the Transfiguration (Mark 8.31, 9.31, 10.33–34 and parallels). The first prediction is followed by a warning that Jesus' disciples must also be prepared for rejection and even death. But such suffering will guarantee them the ultimate reward for true discipleship (Mark 8.34–9.1 and parallels; see pp.220–21).

The gospels relate disputes about leadership of the community of Jesus' followers (Mark 9.33–37 and parallels; Mark 10.35–45; Matt. 20.20–28). These lead to Jesus' teaching that members of the Christian community are to follow their master and seek to serve rather than to rule. To belong to the kingdom of God they must have the unquestioning trust of a child. The child represents the ordinary believer, whose welfare must be paramount to the community (Mark 9.42–48 and parallels).

Concern for the future community of believers is most clearly seen in one of the several discourses that punctuate Matthew's gospel (Matt. 18.1–19.2). It has been described as "a manual of Church discipline" and some of it seems to envisage a situation that must have existed only later than Jesus' lifetime, such as regulations for resolving disputes in the congregation (Matt. 18.15–17). For Jesus, the society of the faithful is to be characterized by unlimited forgiveness (Matt. 18.21–22). The parable of the Unforgiving Servant drives home this great truth (Matt. 18.23–35).

The parable of the Rich Man (Mark 10.17–31 and parallels) again illustrates the absolute demands of God's kingdom and both the hardships and eternal rewards of discipleship. In Matthew, the parable of the Vineyard Laborers is intended to make the same point (Matt. 20.1–16; compare Matt. 19.30 and 20.16).

Just prior to Jesus' arrival at Jerusalem occurs the episode of the healing of one or two blind men at Jericho (Mark 10.46–52 and parallels; see illustration, p.224). Here Jesus is hailed as "Son of David," anticipating the cry that will greet his entry into the Holy City (see sidebar, p.240).

The journey in Luke

Luke's extensive account of Jesus' journey to Jerusalem (Luke 9.51–19.28) forms the core of his gospel and it has been claimed that it is crucial for understanding his distinctive message. The dominant purpose of Luke is to present Jesus' career as "the way of the Lord" (Luke 3.4). As a travel narrative, it has been linked with Acts, the evangelist's second volume, which records the spread of the faith.

However, Luke's actual references to traveling are brief and generalized, very different from the detailed movements recorded by the same author in Acts. They are no more prominent than those in the accounts of the journey in Matthew and Mark, and Luke seems to have no more precise knowledge of the course of events than they do.

As with the other gospels, Luke's presentation of this part of Jesus' ministry focuses far more on Jesus' teaching than on healing miracles. The evangelist has grouped traditions of Jesus' teaching on such important topics as prayer, wealth, and forgiveness. Many of these teachings occur in the other gospels, but here they are brought together to provide a corpus of teaching for the followers of Jesus on their mission. Like Mark and Matthew, Luke has in mind the situation of the Church after Jesus' death.

Luke has also introduced his own distinctive contribution to his account of this period of Jesus' life, notably several famous, and striking, parables that occur in his gospel alone: the Good Samaritan, the Prodigal Son, the Rich Man and Lazarus, the Pharisee and the Publican (Tax Collector), the Unexpected Guest and many others.

The Return of the Prodigal Son, *by Rembrandt (1606–69). The father's joyous welcome for his errant son is among the most frequently depicted scenes from this famous parable, which is recounted in Luke 15.11–32.*

THE CLEANSING OF THE TEMPLE

JESUS' ENTRY INTO JERUSALEM
Matthew, Mark, and Luke place the Cleansing incident immediately after Jesus' triumphal entry into Jerusalem on a donkey's colt, accompanied by nationalistic enthusiasm from the crowds (Matt. 21.1–11; Mark 11.1–11; Luke 19.29–40).

In Matthew, the crowds hail Jesus as a prophet (Matt. 21.11), and the Cleansing of the Temple is probably to be seen as the sort of dramatic symbolic act that was typical of the prophets in the Hebrew Bible. They often criticized the Temple and looked forward to a time when the institution would be purged of the corruptions that they believed had invaded it. Jesus' action may have been influenced by a prophecy that, in the coming new age, there would "no longer be traders in the house of the Lord" (Zech. 14.21).

Almost immediately after his final arrival in Jerusalem, at Passover time, the synoptic gospels record that Jesus caused a public disturbance in the precincts of the Temple. John also records the event, but places it at the beginning of Jesus' ministry (see box, opposite). The incident is usually called "the Cleansing" but what happened is not altogether easy to interpret. It appears that Jesus carried out an attack on traders on the Temple Mount who catered to worshipers by changing money for them, because the Roman coins in common circulation were not acceptable for Temple donations as they bore images of the emperor—a Roman god—and other idolatrous symbols. The traders also sold animals for sacrifice (Matt. 21.12; Mark 11.15; Luke 19.45; John 2.14–16).

At one level, Jesus was no doubt making a protest against the commercialism surrounding Temple worship. The Jewish historian Josephus and rabbinic texts attest to a degree of corruption and intrigue among Temple personnel that merited Jesus' denunciation: "My house shall be called a house of prayer, but you are making it a den of robbers" (Matt. 21.13 and parallels, citing Isa. 56.7).

It has been suggested that in calling the Temple "a house of prayer"

The Cleansing of the Temple, *a fresco in the Scrovegni Chapel, Padua, by Giotto (1266–1337). Whatever Jesus' precise motives, there was certainly much popular resentment against the wealth and splendor of the Temple, which was lavishly rebuilt by Herod the Great partly as a monument to his dynasty. The scale of the undertaking was such that it was finally completed only half a dozen years or so before its destruction in 70* CE.

John and the "New Temple"

In its distinctive presentation of the Cleansing of the Temple (John 2.13–22), the Fourth Gospel develops certain themes that are only hinted at in the accounts of Matthew, Mark, and Luke. John places the incident at the beginning of Jesus' ministry, although its position in the other gospels, shortly before Jesus' arrest, is more likely to be historically correct. But the Fourth Gospel is primarily concerned with the theological significance of the event as an example of God's judgment against the Judaism of his day—a judgment that the evangelist sees as present in Jesus' actions from the very beginning. In John, the Cleansing demonstrates that Israel's existing religious practice, centered on blood sacrifice, is to be abolished—a fact emphasized by Jesus' driving out of all the sacrificial animals (John 2.15).

Unlike the other evangelists, John does not deny that Jesus spoke of the destruction and rebuilding in three days of the Temple (see main text), but characteristically provides his own interpretation. Here, as repeatedly in his gospel, "the Jews" fail to understand the true importance of Jesus' words. They take them to refer literally to the Temple building, whereas Jesus actually means "the temple of his body," which will suffer death but then be resurrected (John 2.21–22). Through Jesus' death and resurrection a new Temple—the Church—will arise. Elsewhere in the New Testament (for example, 1 Cor. 12.27) the Church is referred to as "the body of Christ." It represents a wholly new type of worship, "in spirit and in truth"—which supersedes all previous forms (John 4.19–26).

The el-Aqsa mosque stands over the main southern exit of Herod's Temple Mount. Traces of the Herodian gate can be made out (right of center).

Jesus was advocating an end to the institution's sacrificial practices. However, the gospels do not suggest that Jesus was opposed to sacrifices. The Isaiah quotation points to a future age, when (as the Qumran sect and others believed) the Temple would be replaced by a new, purified institution. It may be that Jesus himself shared this outlook.

The gospels certainly suggest that Jesus' negative attitude toward the Temple was a central factor in his subsequent condemnation by the priestly authorities. He was accused before the Sanhedrin (see pp.248–49) of claiming that he, personally, would destroy the Temple and rebuild it in three days (Mark 14.58, 15.29; Matt. 26.61, 27.39; Acts 6.14). But the New Testament regards this accusation as false and it does seem unlikely that Jesus would actually have made such a claim. His earlier prediction of the destruction of the Temple (Mark 13.2 and parallels) mentions no involvement on his part and introduces the so-called "Synoptic Apocalypse" (Mark 13.5–37), foretelling a general catastrophe for Jerusalem.

The best conclusion may be that Jesus did speak against the existing Temple in some way, and that his violent behavior there was understood by the religious authorities as some kind of prediction of its destruction. Certainly, Jesus' actions implied much more than simply ridding the Temple of commercial practices.

A POLITICAL ACT?

Scholars who see Jesus as a political revolutionary (see pp.336–37) have proposed that he actually occupied the Temple at the head of a band of militant followers. However, anything on such a scale would have provoked an immediate intervention by the Temple's own police force or by the Roman troops stationed in the nearby Antonia fortress. The Roman garrison was reinforced at Passover precisely to deter any disturbances among the crowds attending the Temple. Moreover, such a demonstration would certainly have led to a round-up of all Jesus' followers—but the gospels speak only of a plot to arrest Jesus himself.

THE LAST SUPPER

The gospels recount that Jesus and his twelve closest disciples had one final meal together before his arrest. Matthew, Mark, and Luke make it clear that the Last Supper was the Seder, the special meal that is traditionally eaten by Jews in celebration of the feast of Passover, or Unleavened Bread. All three gospels record that the proper preparations were made for this festival supper, including the sacrifice in the Temple of the paschal (Passover) lambs that would form the main part of the meal (Mark 14. 12–16 and parallels).

However, according to the Fourth Gospel, the meal cannot have been the Passover supper because Jesus was crucified at about noon on the day of Passover preparation (John 19.14). There have been many attempts to reconcile the discrepancy between John and the synoptic gospels. One theory is that Jesus and his disciples were following the practice of the Qumran sect, which had its own ritual calendar and sometimes celebrated Passover earlier than other Jews. The Qumranites were very likely Essenes (see p.169), and the traditional site of the disciples' final meal with Jesus is in the ancient Essene Quarter of Jerusalem (see plan, p.152). But all the

The Last Supper and the Eucharist

There has been a great deal of discussion about the significance of Jesus' words at the Last Supper (Mark 14.22–25 and parallels). The event is clearly related to the Christian sacrament variously known as Eucharist (Greek *eucharistia*, "thanksgiving"), Holy Communion, and Lord's Supper, and the extent to which Jesus intended to inaugurate such a rite is also the subject of much debate.

Jesus offers the disciples bread to eat with the words: "this is my body" (Mark 14.22 and parallels). He then offers them wine to drink, saying: "this is my blood of the covenant, which is poured out for many" (Mark 14.24; Matt. 26.28). Just as the old Israel was established by the "blood of the covenant" (Exod. 24.8), Jesus establishes a new covenant with the "many"—all humankind—whose sins, as Matthew 26.28 makes explicit, are forgiven through the sacrifice of Jesus' body.

Jesus says that it is only in the coming kingdom of God that he will again eat the Passover meal or drink wine (Mark 14.25; Matthew 26.29; Luke 22.16, 18). This suggests that he saw the Last Supper as prefiguring the great banquet presided over by the Messiah, which it was widely believed would mark the advent of the final age. In Matthew and Mark, Jesus implies that the Last Supper will be repeated only in the messianic age, and hence he does not appear to envisage the meal being commemorated by his followers in a regular rite. But the first Christians may have believed that they had already entered the final age, and celebrated the Eucharist as a foretaste of the imminent messianic banquet.

It is only in Luke that Jesus explicitly founds a new rite: most manuscripts of the gospel record that Jesus broke the bread with the command "do this in remembrance of me" (Luke 22.19). Some early manuscripts of Luke omit these words and many scholars think that they were interpolated from Paul's first letter to the Corinthians (1 Cor. 11.23–25). This is not to say that they are necessarily inauthentic: Paul's letters are the earliest documents in the New Testament and in the passage quoted he claims to describe a rite "received from the Lord"—indicating a very early Christian tradition.

The Last Supper (1480), by Domenico Ghirlandaio (1449–94), a fresco in the refectory of the Ognissanti monastery, Florence. Peter, depicted as a man of mature years, is on Jesus' right; reclining on Jesus' left is the "disciple whom Jesus loved" (John 13.23). Judas Iscariot, who will betray Jesus, sits apart, without a halo. The Latin legend around the walls quotes words spoken by Jesus to the disciples during the meal: "I confer on you, just as my Father has conferred on me, a kingdom, so that you may eat and drink at my table in my kingdom" (Luke 22.29–30).

references in the gospels point to a Passover celebrated in accordance with the practices prevalent in Jerusalem.

Christian tradition certainly closely associated the final events of Jesus' life with the Passover, and the anomalous timing of the meal in the Fourth Gospel probably arises from John's interpretation of the symbolic significance of the festival. In the Fourth Gospel, Jesus is presented prominently as the true sacrificial Passover lamb, and as such his destiny is accomplished when he dies at the time of the slaughter of the lambs in the Temple (John 19.36). In John's interpretation of the feeding of the multitude (John 6.4ff)—which in many respects parallels the accounts of the Last Supper in the synoptics—the evangelist also appears to view Jesus as the paschal lamb. The feeding takes place near Passover time (John 6.4) and the discourse that follows centers on Jesus' gift of his body and blood to confer eternal life (John 6.48–58; see also p.229). The synoptists may also see Jesus as the paschal lamb in offering himself as food to his disciples within the context of the Passover meal (Mark 14.22, 24 and parallels).

None of the gospels explicitly mentions the consumption of the lamb at the Last Supper, but they do refer to other rites that were, and remain, a part of the Passover meal: the blessing and sharing of unleavened bread and wine (Mark 14.22–23 and parallels). The gospel writers mention only those elements of Passover ritual to which Jesus' words gave a new and distinctive interpretation (see box, opposite).

BETRAYAL AND ARREST

THE KISS
In the synoptic gospels, the arrest of Jesus begins with the dramatic and poignant moment when Judas Iscariot (see box, opposite) identifies his former master with a kiss or attempted kiss (Mark 14.44–5 and parallels). The kiss emphasizes that Jesus alone is to be the victim, while his followers escape (Mark 14.56 and parallels).

Judas addresses Jesus as "Rabbi" (see p.292), and a kiss was the regular salutation of a disciple to his rabbinical master. The gesture may also be inspired by biblical passages where an apparently friendly kiss conceals treachery, for example, 2 Samuel 20.9–10 and Proverbs 27.6. It also serves to highlight Judas' responsibility for Jesus' arrest, in which his real role was probably comparatively minor—if obviously momentous.

The four gospels broadly agree in their accounts of the arrest of Jesus. Following the Last Supper (see pp.242–43), Jesus and his disciples set out for the garden of Gethsemane, an olive grove on the Mount of Olives, after singing the final part of the Jewish hymn sung at the end of the Passover celebrations (Mark 14.26; Matt. 26.30). The depiction of the group in Gethsemane suggests that on this occasion they intended to withdraw for a special time of prayer and meditation. During his time in Jerusalem, Jesus apparently spent all his nights outside the city, either on the mount (Luke 21.37) or at nearby Bethany (Mark 11.11; Matt. 21.17).

On the way to Gethsemane, according to Matthew and Mark, Jesus

The Agony in the Garden, *by Corrado Giaquinto (1690–1765), depicts Jesus' solitary vigil and prayer in the Garden of Gethsemane. The angel (Luke 22.43) bears a eucharistic chalice, a literal interpretation of Jesus' words: "Father, for you all things are possible; remove this cup from me" (Mark 14.36 and parallels).*

Judas Iscariot

The gospels and Acts all record that the disciple Judas Iscariot was instrumental in the arrest of Jesus. According to John, Iscariot was a surname, borne also by Judas' father, Simon (John 6.71, 13.2). It is commonly understood to mean "man of Kerioth," a village in southern Judea, and some manuscripts actually say "Judas from Kerioth" at John 6.71. John is well informed about Judean matters and this appears to be the best explanation of the name. Thus Judas was alone among the disciples in not hailing from Galilee.

The Roman Catholic Church of All Nations, constructed in 1924, adjoins the site of the Garden of Gethsemane and commemorates the events leading to the arrest of Jesus.

As for his motives, the gospels explain only that Judas was possessed by Satan (Luke 22.3; John 6.70, 13.2, 27) and betrayed Jesus for money (Mark 4.10–11 and parallels). John emphasizes Judas' interest in money and his cupidity (John 12.5–6). Recently, however, some scholars have suggested that Judas could not accept Jesus' coming death and wished to force him to show his power as Messiah. Another "rehabilitating" theory is that Judas wished to help Jesus to achieve his purpose—in Matthew and Mark, the mention of Judas' treachery immediately follows the scene at Bethany where he predicts his death (Mark 14.3–9; Matt. 26.6–13). However, perhaps all that can be said with certainty is that Judas showed the Temple priests how Jesus could be arrested away from the public glare (Mark 14.1; Matt. 26.4; Acts 1.16).

Whatever the facts, the gospels tend to depict Judas in the light of the fulfillment of scripture. Thus in Matthew he is paid "thirty pieces of silver," a reference to an obscure biblical prophecy (Zech. 11.12). The details of Judas' repentance and death (Matt. 27.3–10; Acts 1.16–20) are similarly constructed from biblical passages.

solemnly predicted that his followers would desert him and that even Peter would deny him (Mark 14.27–31; Matt. 26.31–35; compare Luke 22.33–35, John 16.32, and John 13.36–38). Peter's subsequent denial of Jesus is probably authentic—the early Christians are unlikely to have invented such an unflattering story about one of the Church's leading figures.

On arrival at the garden, Jesus withdrew for a moving prayer in which he accepted the destiny decreed by his heavenly Father (Mark 14.32–42 and parallels). He counseled his disciples to pray that they might escape the coming time of trial. John's gospel has no account of this "agony in the garden"; its equivalent is Jesus' final prayer at the Last Supper (John 17).

At this point a party arrived to arrest Jesus, guided by Judas (see box, above), who knew where Jesus might be found (John 18.2). All the gospels describe some kind of brawl, during which a sword was drawn and the ear of the high priest's slave was cut off (Mark 14.47 and parallels). Mark records the episode simply but the other gospels make clear that Jesus himself repudiated the violence. A somewhat obscure passage in Luke probably means the same thing: when the disciples produce two swords, Jesus says curtly "It is enough" (Luke 22.35–38).

THE ARRESTING PARTY

According to the synoptists, the body that arrested Jesus was an armed troop sent by the Temple authorities. The Fourth Gospel identifies this troop as the regular police force of the Temple and claims that it was accompanied by a Roman cohort under its commanding officer (John 18.3, 12).

There is nothing improbable in such cooperation between the Roman and Temple authorities, because it was in the interest of both to avoid disturbances at Passover time, when Jerusalem was very crowded. But it seems unlikely that so many people—a cohort consisted of two hundred men or more—would have been needed to apprehend a single individual. However, what they had heard about the manner of Jesus' entry into Jerusalem (see p.240) may have led both authorities to overestimate the scale of his following.

THE TRIALS OF JESUS

Jesus Before Herod, *by Duccio di Buoninsegna (ca. 1260–1318). Luke alone records that Pilate sent Jesus for a hearing before Herod Antipas, the ruler of Galilee (Luke 23.6–12). The gospel describes the scene: "Herod with his soldiers treated him with contempt and mocked him; then he put an elegant robe on him, and sent him back to Pilate" (Luke 23.11).*

JESUS BEN ANANIAS

Josephus records an interesting parallel to the gospel account of the two trials of Jesus from the time of the Roman prefect Albinus (62–64 CE). It concerns one Jesus ben Ananias who, during the feast of Tabernacles, repeatedly prophesied the destruction of Jerusalem in the Temple. As a result, he was arrested by some of the leading citizens and soundly beaten, but he persisted in his prophesying and was brought before the prefect, presumably for execution. When Albinus asked the man who he was, where he came from, and why he acted as he did, Jesus ben Ananias made no reply but continued his ranting. Albinus concluded that he was insane and let him go after a flogging—rather as Pilate is said to have wished to do in the case of Jesus.

Around one-fifth of each gospel is devoted to the Passion (Latin *passio*, "suffering")—the final days of Jesus' earthly existence, from the Last Supper to his burial (Mark 14–15; Matt. 26–27; Luke 22–23; John 18–19). While it is virtually impossible to fix any clear chronology of Jesus' earlier ministry, the Passion narratives present a detailed and remarkably consistent sequence of events. This suggests that the evangelists all relied on a narrative tradition that was well formed by the time they wrote; Luke and John also appear to draw on other, distinct, traditions.

The synoptic gospels—John is less clear on this point—record two consecutive trials and condemnations of Jesus, one before the high priest and Sanhedrin, or council (see p.160), and one before Pontius Pilate, the Roman prefect of Judea. Scholars have examined the accounts of the trials of Jesus in the context of what is known about contemporary Jewish and Roman legal processes (see pp.249–51). But such material has to be assessed with caution: for example, most of the evidence for Jewish legal practice comes from the Mishnah lawcode, which was compiled ca. 200 CE. While the Mishnah undoubtedly records numerous longstanding practices, it is not certain how many of these were in force in Jesus' day. Also, the Mishnah represents the outlook of the Pharisees (see pp.166–67), and it cannot necessarily be assumed that the Sadducee-dominated Temple

The death penalty in Roman Palestine

This ossuary dating from the 1st century CE was discovered in 1990 in a family tomb, 2km (1.2 miles) from the Temple Mount. It bears the name Yehoseph bar Qypa—Joseph Caiaphas—the high priest who tried Jesus, according to the gospels.

The Fourth Gospel explains that the Temple authorities had to hand Jesus over to Pilate because the high priest and the Sanhedrin did not have the power to impose capital punishment (John 18.31–32). There has been much argument as to whether this statement is historically accurate or whether it is an invention of the evangelist to confirm Jesus' own predictions that he would meet his end by being "lifted up" on a Roman cross.

It does seem to have been regular policy throughout the provinces of the empire to restrict the ability to pass a death sentence to the Roman authorities. But there may have been exceptions. For example, a famous Greek inscription from the Temple threatens death to Gentiles who trespass in areas restricted to Jews. This has been taken as evidence that, even under Roman rule, the Sanhedrin retained the right to carry out executions—a right it could certainly claim under Jewish law. Further support for this theory has been seen in the stoning of the first Christian martyr, Stephen (Acts 6–7), and later, in 62 CE, of Jesus' brother James.

But both deaths—and possibly the right to execute trespassers in the Temple—are best explained as special cases. The death of James, recorded by Josephus, seems to have been unauthorized: it took place between the death of one prefect and the arrival from Rome of another. Once in Judea, the new prefect deposed the high priest responsible for the execution.

authorities, before whom Jesus is said to have been tried, would have accepted Pharisaic rules. Nor are the evangelists the equivalent of today's court reporters. Their primary concern is a theological presentation of the facts of Jesus' suffering and death. Moreover, as history often shows, in a situation of crisis precise legal niceties may not always be observed.

However, while there is no inherent improbability in Jesus being tried twice in fairly rapid succession (see sidebar, opposite), there is considerable uncertainty about the gospels' claim that the priestly hierarchy of Jerusalem was primarily responsible for arresting and trying Jesus and accusing him before the Roman governor. Some scholars have proposed that the religious authorities only acted at the instigation of, and in collusion with, the Romans, or, more radically, that the whole story of the trial by the Sanhedrin is a Christian fiction designed to slander the Jews. While it is lamentably true that anti-Judaism and anti-Semitism have often sought justification from these and other passages in the New Testament (see pp.342–43), it is very hard to reject the unanimous gospel view that the Jewish priestly authorities, headed by the high priest, were involved in the arrest of Jesus and subsequently handed him over to the Romans. That Jesus was arraigned before Pilate is generally accepted, because it is almost certain that he alone could impose the death penalty (see box, above).

BEFORE THE COUNCIL

THE GROUNDS FOR JESUS' ARREST

The gospels note several different reasons why the Temple authorities ordered Jesus' arrest. But these accounts are not necessarily contradictory and all the factors mentioned by the evangelists may have contributed to the final decision to apprehend him.

Mark states that the priestly authorities reacted to Jesus' dramatic expulsion of the traders from the Temple by actively seeking a way to get rid of him (Mark 11.18; see pp.240–41). They may also have been alarmed by the circumstances of his entry into Jerusalem (see p.240), which in Matthew and Luke culminated in his entry into the Temple.

Luke states that "the chief priests, the scribes, and the leaders of the people" sought to eliminate Jesus because of his teaching in the Temple (Luke 19.47–48), and all the synoptics say that an attempt was made to arrest him because of a particular example of his teaching there: the parable of the Wicked Tenants (Mark 12.1–12 and parallels; see p.297).

According to the Fourth Gospel, the Sanhedrin was alarmed by Jesus' popularity—boosted by his raising of Lazarus from the dead at Bethany, just outside the city (see pp.312-13)—which was liable to lead to large gatherings, unrest, and severe Roman intervention as a consequence (John 11.45–53).

The gospels record that Jesus was taken under arrest before the high priest and the Sanhedrin, the Jewish governing council (see p.160), which judged him to be deserving of death. Various grounds are given for Jesus' arrest (see sidebar, left), but taken as a whole they suggest that Jesus was viewed as one who stirred up discontent with the accepted religious and social order, and as such posed a threat to the stability of the whole region. Luke in particular shows that this was the accusation made against Jesus before Pilate (Luke 23.2, 5, 14; see pp.250–51).

To justify a capital charge, the Sanhedrin had to prove that Jesus was guilty of a serious offense against the Jewish law. The priestly authorities may have been provoked by Jesus' alleged prediction of the destruction of the Temple (see p.241). This accusation was made at his trial, although Matthew and Mark relate that Jesus made no answer to this charge and, for whatever reason, it apparently could not be substantiated.

Christ's Entry into Jerusalem, *a Russian icon of the Novgorod School (14th century). News of this dramatic episode, recounted in all the gospels (see p.240), may well have been a factor in the decision to have Jesus arrested.*

The Roman Catholic Church of St. Peter in Gallicantu (St. Peter at the Cockcrow) was built in 1931 on the traditional site of the high priest's house, the scene of Jesus' trial in the gospel accounts. The church commemorates Peter's sorrow in the courtyard of the house when he realized that he had denied his master three times, just as Jesus had predicted: "Before the cock crows twice, you will deny me three times" (Mark 14.30, 66–72 and parallels).

According to the gospels, the high priest and council finally condemned Jesus after the high priest asked him whether he claimed to be the Messiah. Jesus' reply is variously given by the synoptists: "I am" (Mark 14.62); "You have said so" (Matt. 26.64); "If I tell you, you will not believe" (Luke 22.67–8). Whatever his actual words, his answer was judged to be affirmative. In Matthew and Mark, the high priest describes Jesus' response as "blasphemy." According to the Mishnah, blasphemy applied only to speaking the sacred and unutterable name of God (YHWH), but there is no evidence that Jesus did so. However, elsewhere in the gospels "blasphemy" seems to mean anything causing serious theological offense (Mark 3.28–29 and parallels).

A claim to be the Messiah was not technically against the Jewish law. However, in Matthew and Mark, the high priest's question couples "Messiah" with "Son of God," and this might be the more crucial term: "Tell us if you are the Messiah, the Son of God" (Matthew 26.63); "Are you the Messiah, son of the Blessed One [God]?" (Mark 14.61). In Luke, the Sanhedrin puts two separate questions to Jesus (Luke 22.67, 70), and it is only following the second ("Are you, then, the Son of God?") and Jesus' reply ("You say that I am") that he is condemned. The Fourth Gospel reports only an allegation that Jesus called himself "Son of God" (John 19.7).

The term "Son of God" had a range of connotations in contemporary Judaism. It was used by some charismatic wonder-workers to describe themselves, and such individuals were at times accused—like Jesus (see pp.226–27)—of performing magic through the agency of demons. If the Sanhedrin considered that "Son of God" denoted Jesus as a magician, they could condemn him as a false prophet, tempting the people of Israel to trust in miracles performed by supernatural beings other than the true God. For this, in the Mosaic law, the penalty was death (Deut. 13.1, 5; 18.20). (See also pp.296–97.)

THE TRIAL AND JEWISH LAW

The accounts of Jesus' trial before the Sanhedrin have often been examined in the light of Jewish process of law and the known powers of the Sanhedrin, especially as set out in the Mishnah. It has been proposed that Jesus' appearance before the high priest was only a preliminary hearing before he was referred to the Roman jurisdiction. But Matthew, Mark, and Luke all speak of Jesus before "the council," indicating a formal assembly.

The Mishnah states that a capital trial could not be held on the eve of a festival or the Sabbath. This conflicts with the gospel accounts, but this provision may not have been in force as early as Jesus' time. Matthew and Mark appear to suggest—it is not entirely explicit—that Jesus was tried at night in the house of the high priest, which would infringe another Mishnaic ruling, that capital cases had to be tried in the daytime in the council chamber in the Temple. Luke indicates a trial by day, before the full council (Luke 22.66).

John has no details of a trial before Caiaphas, the incumbent high priest, and the council, although some charges made against Jesus in the synoptic accounts appear in John in a different context (John 10.24–25, 33–36). He does include an interrogation by the ex-high priest Annas, who handed him over to Caiaphas (John 18.13, 19 –24). Annas had been deposed from office, but remained influential (Caiaphas was his son-in-law).

JESUS AND PILATE

A bronze coin issued in Judea by Pontius Pilate. One side (left) gives the date, in Hebrew, as "Year 17"—that is, 30–31 CE, the 17th year of the reign of the emperor Tiberius. The Greek legend on the other side (right) reads "[Of] Tiberius Caesar." The coins issued by Pilate have no imperial portrait, to avoid giving offense to Jews.

Jesus' final condemnation followed his appearance before Pontius Pilate, the Roman prefect of Judea. Scholars agree that the principal reason for Pilate's decision to execute Jesus is reflected in the placard fixed to the cross upon which he was crucified: he had claimed to be "King of the Jews" (see p.338). The wording of the whole inscription differs among the four gospels, but they all agree on this key phrase, and the issue of Jesus' kingship is central to all their accounts of his trial before Pilate (Mark 15.2, 9, 12 and parallels). This would be compatible with a judgment by the Sanhedrin that Jesus had claimed to be the Messiah (see pp.248–49), because it was popularly expected that the Messiah would be of royal blood, a descendant of King David, and would free Israel from Gentile domination. In Matthew and Luke, Jesus' messiahship is an issue in both his Sanhedrin trial and that before Pilate (Matt. 27.17, 22; Luke 23.2).

When Pilate asks Jesus if he is "king of the Jews," Jesus gives an evasive answer (Mark 15.2 and parallels; John 18.37), similar to the response he gives to the high priest when asked if he is the Messiah (see p.249). The Romans would have been well aware of the threat to public peace which a claim to kingship could pose. As the Jewish historian Josephus records, following the death of Herod the Great in 4 BCE, Palestine lapsed into a state of anarchy in which several dangerous rebels proclaimed themselves king and enjoyed considerable, if temporary, success.

Each gospel presents the Roman trial in its own way, but together they indicate that it followed regular judicial procedure as followed in the provinces of the empire, with certain exceptions (see sidebar, left). According to the gospels, the court was held in public outside the *praetorium*, or military headquarters, on a paved space—the local name of which, Gabbatha, is preserved in John 19.13—where the final verdict was pronounced. The trial began with formal charges being laid by the prisoner's accusers, after which the defendant was questioned and given the opportunity to respond. In Roman practice, the accused had three opportunities to make a defense before the presiding official gave his verdict. When, after repeated questioning, Jesus remained silent, Pilate had no choice but to find him guilty.

The gospels record that Pilate was reluctant to impose the death penalty, and it may well be true that he thought Jesus should be let off, again in accordance with Roman custom, with a warning flogging, as Luke says (Luke 23.16, 22). (Luke employs the precise Greek term for such a comparatively mild whipping; Mark 15.15 and Matthew 27.26 use a word that means the very severe flogging inflicted before execution.) It is also

LEGENDARY EPISODES OF JESUS' ROMAN TRIAL

While the gospel accounts of Jesus' trial before Pilate generally reflect regular Roman judicial procedure, some episodes are of more dubious historical value.

For example, there is no evidence for a Passover amnesty under which the prefect freed a prisoner of the people's choice, in this case a rebel called Jesus Barabbas (Mark 15.6 and parallels). Luke makes no mention of an amnesty and records the release of Barabbas without giving a reason for this concession (Luke 23.18–19).

In Matthew, Pilate washes his hands of responsibility for Jesus' death (Matt. 27.24–25). Again, this was not a Roman custom, but echoes scripture (Deut. 21.6–9) and, like the dream of Pilate's wife (Matt. 27.19), the episode is probably best regarded as the invention of the evangelist.

John has two exchanges between Jesus and Pilate inside the *praetorium* (John 18.33–38, 19.8–11). It is not impossible that Pilate, like Herod Antipas (Luke 23.8), was interested to find out more about Jesus, but John could hardly have known anything that was said between the two men in private. The dialogues contain distinctive themes of this evangelist and must be judged to be his own creation.

Ecce Homo, *by Antonio Ciseri (1821–91). The Latin title of this scene is taken from the words of Pilate when he presented Jesus to the crowd, according to the Fourth Gospel: "Here is the man!" (John 19.5).*

reported that the prefect sought to avoid responsibility for Jesus, either by returning him to the Sanhedrin court (John 18.31, 19.6) or by sending him for trial by Herod Antipas, the ruler of Galilee, Jesus' place of origin (Luke 23.6–12), who happened to be in Jerusalem (see illustration, p.246). Whether or not these episodes are historical, they were certainly legitimate options for a Roman governor.

If Pilate was initially unwilling to execute Jesus, he evidently changed his mind. All the evangelists represent his final decision as a response to the demands of the crowd, led and incited by the Temple authorities, for Jesus' crucifixion (Mark 15.15 and parallels). The chief concern of a Roman governor was the maintenance of public order, and the gospels state that Pilate's initial resistance to the crowd's demands threatened to provoke a riot (Matt. 27.24). Pilate knew the sort of trouble a mob could cause (see p.158), and probably felt that it was not worth risking a serious disturbance for the life of an individual whom he considered to be unimportant. According to John, he finally gave in to the crowd when accused of disloyalty to the emperor (John 19.12). Such accusations were not infrequent in the politics of the Roman empire and often had the gravest consequences for the accused.

JESUS CONDEMNED

All the gospels record that Jesus was mocked by Roman soldiers prior to his execution (Mark 15.16–20 and parallels). They also claim that Jesus had already been treated roughly during his appearance before the high priest, apparently by the Temple police, who engaged in a brutal game of blind man's buff designed to show that Jesus was not a genuine prophet (Mark 14.65; Luke 22.64).

Jesus' abuse at the hands of the Roman soldiers centered on his alleged claim to kingship, the charge on which he was evidently finally condemned. Luke locates the mockery of Jesus not in the *praetorium* during the trial by Pilate but during Jesus' interview with the Galilean ruler Herod Antipas. The Fourth Gospel places it not at the end of the Roman trial but in the middle of it. With characteristic irony, John depicts Pilate presenting Jesus as a parody of monarchy and a mere ordinary human being (John 19.4–5); but the gospel wishes it to be understood that Jesus is indeed a king, and one far greater

The Daughters of Jerusalem

Luke alone mentions an encounter on the journey to Golgotha between Jesus and a group of women who bewail his fate (Luke 23.27–31). There is nothing inherently improbable in this: mourners accompanying a condemned person remain a common sight in the Middle East. Jesus addresses the women as "Daughters of Jerusalem," a term with scriptural precedent, and movingly foretells the tragic end of the city.

Although Jesus is likely to have prophesied the destruction of Jerusalem at some point in his ministry, his words here seem rather to be those of Luke. The lament weaves together biblical reminiscences, influenced perhaps by a strange passage in Zechariah that describes a great mourning ceremony among the inhabitants of Jerusalem for "the one whom they have pierced"—where the sorrow of the wives is specifically mentioned (Zech. 12.10–14). The episode is related to another prediction of Jerusalem's fall, also unique to Luke, when Jesus weeps over the city (Luke 19.41–44).

This sculpture in a chapel on the Via Dolorosa—the traditional route followed by Jesus to Golgotha—marks the spot where Jesus is said to have fallen for the first time under the weight of the cross, shortly before meeting the women of Jerusalem.

Jerusalem on the Day of Christ's Death, *by Olivier Pichat (died 1912). The artist has imagined the expectant crowds lining the route to Golgotha (foreground, right). The city is his own reconstruction, but the landscape is accurately depicted. The three large towers—still partly extant—belong to the former palace of Herod (see plan, p.152).*

than any earthly sovereign (John 18.36–37).

The spectacle in which the Roman soldiers dress Jesus up as a mock sovereign has been compared with similar practices that marked the Persian festival of the Sacaea at Babylon and the Roman Saturnalia. But a much closer parallel is found in the account by the Jewish writer Philo of the lampooning of King Herod Agrippa I at Alexandria in 38 CE. On that occasion, a wretched lunatic was crowned with a piece of bark, given a scrap of papyrus for a scepter, and dressed in a rug for a royal robe, while the spectators pretended to pay him homage and addressed him as king.

Perhaps this anecdote became widely known in Palestine and the evangelists used it to elaborate a simpler story that Jesus had been derided and spat upon by the soldiers. However, it is not improbable that the soldiers acted on their own initiative, mimicking the imperial insignia by what they had to hand—a soldier's cloak and plants from the *praetorium* gardens—and parodying the regular greeting to the emperor, "Hail Caesar" (Mark 15.18 and parallels).

Crucifixion was carried out by the military. When the soldiers had ended their sport, they dressed Jesus in his own clothes and marched him to the place of execution, Golgotha, which means "Place of a Skull" in Aramaic. The preservation of the name in the gospels suggests that the site was well known, but it can no longer be certainly identified. Its description as a skull points to a small rounded eminence, probably just outside Jerusalem: both Jewish and Roman executions were carried out beyond the city walls, and later Christian tradition (for example, Heb. 13.12–13) recalled that this had been the case with Jesus. The Fourth Gospel states that near the place of crucifixion there was a garden with a tomb (John 19.41), and archaeology has confirmed that burials also took place outside the urban area.

In his narrative of the road to Golgotha, Luke mentions that Jesus was accompanied by two other condemned criminals, which suggests that Jesus' trial was part of a wider process of rounding up troublemakers (Luke 23.32). It is likely that Jesus was accompanied by a crowd, since various texts show that the practice of parading a criminal through the streets served to provide a visual warning lesson to the population.

SIMON OF CYRENE

A condemned man had to carry his cross to the place of execution and it seems that Jesus began by doing so (John 19.17). But Matthew, Mark, and Luke relate that Jesus could not continue, perhaps owing to the flogging and other privations he had suffered. A bystander, Simon, was thus "pressed into public service" to assist him (Mark 15.21; Matt. 27.32). He is said to have come from Cyrene in North Africa, where there was a Jewish community. Cyrenian Jews had their own synagogue in Jerusalem (Acts 6.9). The mention of Simon's sons, Alexander and Rufus (Mark 15.21), is strong evidence for the historicity of the event, because the casual and unadorned way in which Mark refers to them suggests that they were known to the community for which he wrote.

Mark and Luke state that Simon came "in from the country," which some have taken to imply that he was breaking the prohibition against journeying on the Passover and so could not have been a Jew. But the words are too vague to warrant this conclusion. Nor do his sons' non-Hebrew names prove that the family was Gentile, since Greek names were common among contemporary Jews (see p.179).

THE CRUCIFIXION

The heelbone, pierced by a nail, of a 1st-century CE crucifixion victim called John (Yehohanan), whose remains were discovered near Jerusalem in 1968.

In the Roman empire, crucifixion was regarded as the most humiliating and painful of all penalties. It was confined to slaves and foreigners, Roman citizens being exempt. Not the least reason for believing that the crucifixion of Jesus was a historical event, therefore, is that the first Christians were unlikely to have invented so degrading a fate for their master. They well knew how unfavorably the world viewed it (1 Cor. 1.23).

In depicting the Crucifixion, the evangelists include legendary features (see sidebar, left) and present their own special interpretation of events at Golgotha. Above all, they are concerned to demonstrate that the manner of Jesus' death had been foretold in scripture and so fulfilled God's purposes. They—Luke especially—seek to present Jesus as the perfect example of how they themselves should respond to suffering and persecution.

Notwithstanding their theological concerns, the gospels can also be shown to contain good historical information. Before being affixed to the cross, Jesus is said to have been given a drink (Mark 15.23; Matt. 27.34). The Talmud indicates that it would have been a narcotic, intended to deaden the pain. This was a Jewish custom, and while the gospels seem to imply that the drink was offered by the Roman soldiers, they do not explicitly say so. Matthew apparently understands the gesture as a fulfillment of Psalm 69.21 ("for my thirst they gave me vinegar to drink") and thus makes it a hostile act rather than a humane one. The gospels say that Jesus refused the drink, perhaps to demonstrate his own power to conquer pain.

In another preliminary act, Jesus was stripped of his clothing, since criminals were hanged naked on the cross. In Roman custom, the clothes and other small possessions of a condemned man were a perquisite of his executioners. The soldiers are said to cast lots for them (Mark 15.24; Matt. 27.35), but this scene may be influenced by Psalm 22.18, which John actually quotes at this point (John 19.23–24). John's reference to a squad of four soldiers may be authentic, since this was a regular Roman unit for guard duty (Acts 12.4), and his mention of Jesus' seamless tunic accurately describes the kind of loose garment commonly worn next to the skin.

There were various ways of crucifying a person, but it seems certain that Jesus was nailed to the cross. In John, the risen Christ explicitly shows the nail marks on his hands (John 20.24–27) and Luke 24.39 implies the same. Luke 24.40 indicates that Jesus' feet were also nailed, like those of a crucified man discovered recently in a tomb near Jerusalem (see illustration, above left). Josephus twice mentions victims being nailed to a cross.

The crucified Jesus is mocked by the crowd, the Temple authorities or (in Luke) the soldiers, and the two criminals (Mark 15.29–32; Matt. 27.39–44; Luke 23.35–39). It is very likely that passers-by would indeed

LEGENDARY ELEMENTS OF THE CRUCIFIXION ACCOUNTS

In their narratives of the Crucifixion, Matthew, Mark, and Luke describe supernatural events that can hardly be accorded historical value. They are designed to demonstrate that, contrary to appearances, Jesus' death on the cross was a victorious occurrence that heralded the messianic age, the final period of history.

The three hours of darkness from noon (Mark 15.33 and parallels) cannot have been an eclipse of the sun, as perhaps suggested in Luke 23.45, since this is not astronomically possible at Passover time. Rather, it represents one of the phenomena marking the great "Day of the Lord," the onset of the final age (Amos 8.9; Joel 2.31).

The tearing of the Temple curtain, the veil that shrouded the Holy of Holies (Mark 15.38 and parallels), represented the supreme desecration of the Temple—in effect its destruction, as Jesus had prophesied. In Matthew, the tearing of the veil is followed by an earthquake and the bodily resurrection of the righteous (Matt. 27.51–53), both of which were regularly expected in Judaism to accompany the arrival of the last age of history. For the evangelists, this is when Jesus will arrive in glory as the Son of Man, as they have described earlier in apocalyptic passages with many echoes of the Hebrew Bible (Mark 13.24–27 and parallels).

The Crucifixion, *by Antonello da Messina (ca. 1430–79). At the foot of Jesus' cross are his mother and the "beloved disciple" (a reference to John 19.26–27). In contrast to his two fellow victims, Jesus betrays no sign of his torments. Above his head is the titulus (Mark 15.26 and parallels), the placard on which the reason for execution was written. It would have been carried in front of him or hung around his neck as he was led to the execution ground. The letters INRI stand for* Iesus Nazarenus Rex Iudaeorum *(Latin, "Jesus of Nazareth, the King of the Jews"), the version of the inscription given in John 19.20 (see also p.337).*

THE TWO CRIMINALS
All the gospels state that Jesus was crucified between two other victims (Mark 15.27 and parallels) and there seems to be no reason to suppose that this is not historically accurate. Mark 15.28 quotes a scriptural precedent: "And he was counted with the lawless" (Isa. 53.12: "and [he] was numbered among the transgressors"). But it is widely accepted that this verse was not part of Mark's original text. It was probably added under the influence of Luke, who quotes the verse in a different context (Luke 22.37).

have insulted a crucified man, and the crowds abused Jesus for his alleged threat to destroy the Temple. But the gospel accounts at this point also include biblical reminiscences (for example, a reference to Psalm 22.7–8), and generally display the careful artistry of the evangelists.

According to the timescale in Mark's gospel (Mark 15.25, 34), which is broadly supported by Matthew and Luke, Jesus was alive on the cross for some six hours, from nine in the morning until three in the afternoon. John suggests an even shorter period, since in his account Jesus is hanged at least three hours later (John 19.14). Crucifixion victims often survived for a considerable time—even days—so when Pilate was asked to release Jesus' body, he is reported as expressing some surprise (Mark 15.44).

The early Christians remembered that Jesus had spoken from the cross,

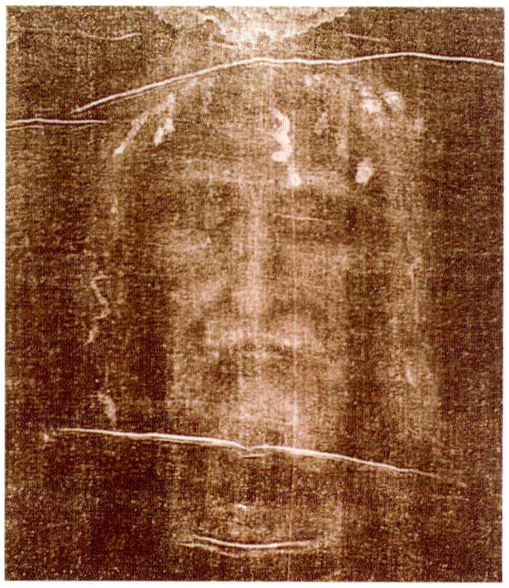

The image on the Turin Shroud is best viewed, as here, in negative. It accurately depicts the type of crucifixion wounds described in the gospels. Interestingly, the figure displays wounds to his wrists—this is widely accepted as a more likely method of crucifixion than nailing through the hands.

although it is unlikely that he spoke all seven of the utterances attributed to him in the gospels. The authenticity of one famous saying—"Father, forgive them; for they do not know what they are doing" (Luke 23.34)—is questionable, since it is absent from several early manuscripts. Also in Luke, Jesus' promise to one of the two criminals hanged alongside him ("Truly I tell you, today you will be with me in paradise"; Luke 23.43) may reflect the evangelist's own belief that the righteous enter a realm of bliss immediately upon death (Luke 16.22).

John 19.26–27 records a moving scene between Jesus and his mother and "the disciple whom he loved," who is referred to several times in the gospel (see p.187). Jesus says to Mary, "Woman, here is your son" and, to the disciple, "Here is your mother." The scene does not appear to be dictated by the theology of the Fourth Gospel and may reflect a tradition that, at some stage in his life, Jesus had made special provision for his mother.

The gospels include four utterances at the moment of death, all influenced by the Psalms. Mark and Matthew report only one of these, and it has perhaps the best claim to historicity: "My God, my God, why have you forsaken me?" (Mark 15.34; Matt. 27.46). The early Church may have come to understand this utterance—the opening line of Psalm 22—as God's rejection of Jesus, and hence the other gospels omitted or replaced it. But these words need not be taken as a cry of hopelessness: Psalm 22 goes on to reassure the sufferer of God's help. Mark gives the saying in Aramaic, Jesus' own tongue, which argues for its authenticity. Matthew replaces *eloi* ("my God") with the Hebrew *eli*, perhaps to make it clear why some bystanders thought Jesus was invoking the prophet Elijah (Matt. 15.35).

Mark and Matthew state that Jesus expired with an inarticulate shout, for which Luke substitutes the more edifying "Father, into your hands I commend my spirit" (Luke 23.46), which quotes Psalm 31.5.

The two last sayings of Jesus in John (19.28, 30) display the double meaning so frequent in that gospel. The first, "I am thirsty," is an apparently simple expression of human need but also echoes the spiritual thirst found in the Psalms (Pss. 42.2, 63.1). The second, "It is finished," is an acknowledgment both that Jesus' physical end has arrived and that the Savior has accomplished his mission.

All the gospels relate that Jesus received a drink of "sour wine," in Luke and John from the soldiers, in Mark and Matthew from an unspecified bystander (Mark 15.36 and parallels). This could be understood as a kindly act, since in Jewish sources "sour wine" is generally a refreshment (see, for example, Ruth 2.14). But Luke, at least, regards it as a mockery, and all the gospels probably have Psalm 69.21 in mind (see p.254). The reference to the sponge and reed with which the drink was proffered have no theological significance and may well be authentic. However, John says the branch was of hyssop, a herb used in the Passover ritual (Exod. 12.22), reflecting the evangelist's view of Jesus as the true paschal lamb (see p.243).

THE SHROUD OF TURIN

For centuries, a linen cloth preserved in the cathedral of Turin, Italy, has been venerated by many Christians as the very shroud in which Jesus was buried. The 4.5-meter (14-foot) length of cloth bears the faint but remarkably powerful image of a man who has apparently been crucified and laid out for burial.

In recent years, the cloth has attracted widespread world attention because of the possibility that modern scientific methods might determine its date and provenance. In 1988, a carbon-14 test dated the cloth to ca. 1260–ca. 1390 CE, with a margin of a century on either side, thus branding it a pious medieval forgery.

However, this verdict has not quite settled the issue. Other evidence suggests an earlier date, for example a number of early medieval images of Christ that closely resemble the facial features of the shroud image. It is not a painting and it has proved difficult to explain how it could have been created in late medieval times. Whether or not it dates back as far as the first century CE—let alone depicts the actual body of Jesus—the shroud retains, for many, its mysteries.

The Deposition and Entombment

Usually, a body was left hanging on the cross until it was devoured by vultures, but sometimes an influential person might secure the right to bury it. In Jewish law, a hanged man had to be buried before nightfall (Deut. 21.31), and John says that "the Jews"—probably meaning a delegation from the religious authorities—asked Pilate to have Jesus and his two companions removed from their crosses, so as not to desecrate the approaching Sabbath (John 19.31).

The delegation assumed that the victims would still be alive and requested that their legs be broken in accordance with the Roman custom (*crurifragium*). This caused the dying victim to collapse, putting unbearable weight on the chest and causing rapid suffocation and death. The soldiers broke the legs of the two criminals, but Jesus appeared to be already dead. Perhaps to make sure, one of them thrust a spear into his side, releasing a flow of blood and water. John claims that a reliable eyewitness vouched for this (John 19.35), and apparently the phenomenon is medically possible. But John invests this whole episode with a profound symbolism, and sees what happened to Jesus as the fulfillment of scripture (Exod. 12.46; Zech. 12.10). In the first letter of John, which was written in the evangelist's circle, water and blood reveal Jesus as the savior who has come (1 John 5.6).

A man executed as a criminal would hardly have received a decent burial, and Jesus' body and those of his companions would very likely have been thrown into a ditch. It was probably from there that Jesus' corpse was retrieved by Joseph of Arimathea who, notwithstanding Luke 23.53, would have found it very difficult to remove it from the cross on his own. This man was of sufficient standing to persuade Pilate to commit Jesus' body to him. Matthew and John make him an actual disciple of Jesus (Mark 15.42–45 and parallels).

John relates that Joseph and his companion Nicodemus embalmed the body in accordance with Jewish custom (John 19.39–40). But the synoptists say only that the corpse was wrapped in a shroud before immediate burial (Mark 15.46 and parallels). This seems more likely: the quantity of spices that John specifies is excessive, and there are hints that the looming Sabbath deadline imposed a degree of haste that precluded full burial rites (Luke 23.54; John 19.42; see also p.259).

All the gospels agree that Joseph interred the corpse in a hitherto empty rock tomb (Mark 15.46 and parallels), no doubt belonging to his own family (Matt. 27.60). The entrance was sealed by a large stone (Mark 15.46; Matt. 27.60; see illustration, p.258).

The Entombment, *Castile school, ca. 1475. Joseph of Arimathea and Nicodemus lay Jesus in the tomb; the other mourners are John (the "beloved disciple") and the "Four Marys," including the Virgin (center) and Mary Magdalene (right).*

THE RISEN LORD

The interior of a tomb in Jerusalem dating from around the time of Jesus. As in the gospel accounts of Jesus' burial place, the tomb was sealed by rolling a large stone in front of the entrance.

Each evangelist presents his own individual account of the events that followed the entombment of Jesus, and although scholars have often sought to reconcile the four narratives, this is not really possible. However, the four versions share underlying thematic and structural patterns, which indicates that they all rely on a common and well-established tradition.

Most significantly, the gospels all agree that, on the third day after his burial, Jesus' tomb was discovered to be empty. Matthew, Mark, and Luke are at pains to stress that those who made this discovery knew for certain that the tomb they went to was the one in which Jesus' body had been placed (Mark 15.47 and parallels). In Matthew, the Temple authorities bribe the tomb guards to say that the disciples have stolen the corpse (Matt. 28.15). This story is unlikely to be historical, but it strongly suggests that knowledge of the empty tomb was widespread and accepted.

A second shared element is that one or more women found that the heavy stone sealing the tomb had been rolled away, and that Jesus' body had gone (Mark 16.3–4 and parallels). They had visited the tomb because they were anxious that Jesus' body had not received a proper burial (see p.257). Such concern was consistent with the way female disciples had provided for Jesus during his ministry (Mark 15.40–41 and parallels). An element common to the synoptists is that the women were confronted by one or more supernatural beings, who assured them that Jesus had risen from the dead. In Mark and Matthew, the women were then commanded to tell the disciples that Jesus was going ahead of them to Galilee, where his followers would meet him (Mark 16.5–7 and parallels).

For women to be credited with the first testimony to the Resurrection is remarkable for the time, and this alone makes a strong case for accepting that the gospel accounts have some sort of historical basis. Under Jewish law, women were not permitted as witnesses in court, and the male disciples at first rejected what the women told them (Mark 16.11; Luke 24.10–11).

The gospels go on to record various appearances of the risen Jesus, and here they begin to diverge considerably. Very likely, each writer has chosen particular traditions of special theological interest to himself. Paul—whose

The ending of Mark's gospel

All the accounts of the appearances of the risen Jesus in Mark's gospel occur in its final verses (Mark 16.9–20). Scholars generally agree that these passages are a later addition and that the work originally concluded with Mark 16.7–8: an angelic being, having announced that Jesus "has been raised," commands the three women who have come to the tomb to tell the disciples that Jesus would be preceding them to Galilee. But the women fled "and said nothing to anyone, for they were afraid."

The Resurrection, *by Fra Angelico (1387–1455). "A young man, dressed in a white robe" (Mark 16.5) greets the women in the tomb. The risen Christ holds a banner symbolizing his resurrection.*

Did Mark never complete the gospel, perhaps because death intervened, or was the original ending lost? Both theories have been discussed, but many scholars now believe that Mark did indeed intend to conclude at 16.8. In doing so, he ends on a note that demonstrated simply the tremendous and awesome effect of the Resurrection on ordinary believers. It has been pointed out that Mark reports three times Jesus' prediction that he would rise on the third day (Mark 8.31, 9.31, 10.34). The angelic "young man" simply confirms the fulfillment of Jesus' promise and no further proof is needed. Moreover, accounts of Jesus' appearances would have been well known to his readers.

At an early stage, many readers evidently felt uncomfortable with Mark's apparently abrupt ending and lack of Resurrection stories. Verses were added that read like a digest of post-Resurrection appearances in the other gospels: the appearance to Mary Magdalene (compare Matt. 28.1–10); the meeting on the road to Emmaus (Luke 24.13–32); Jesus' appearance to the disciples and their commissioning (Matt. 28.16–20; Luke 24.36–53; John 20.26–29, 21.1–23). Its only distinctive feature—the promise that believers would possess special powers (16.17–20)—reflects the experience of the early Church (Luke 10.17, 10.19; Acts 2.1–4; 5.16, 28.1–6, 8; 1 Cor. 12.10).

The Miraculous Draft of Fishes, *by Antoniazzo Romano (fl. 1460–1506). The scene depicts the events surrounding the appearance of the resurrected Jesus recounted in John 21.1–8 (compare illustration, p.175).*

THE RESURRECTION IN JOHN

The Fourth Gospel describes appearances of the risen Christ that are not especially different in kind from those in the synoptics, but, as ever, John gives his own distinctive account of them. Only one woman, Mary Magdalene, discovers the empty tomb (John 20.1–2). She encounters the risen Jesus and attempts to touch him (John 20.11–17). Jesus later appears twice to the disciples, confirms that he is the crucified one, and commissions them for ministry, conferring on them authority to forgive sins by the gift of the Holy Spirit (John 20.19–29). The Fourth Gospel also records a meeting of the risen Jesus with seven disciples in Galilee, in a narrative that contains several reminiscences of episodes of the Galilean ministry (John 21.1–19).

Noteworthy throughout John's version is the prominence of Peter. He is the first to attest to the real emptiness of the tomb (John 20.6–7), a tradition also found in some texts of Luke (Luke 24.12), and he is the main protagonist in the events at the Sea of Tiberias. There, in a moving dialogue, Jesus grants Peter the supervision of the Christian flock (John 21.15–17). There was a well-attested tradition in the early Church that the first appearance of the risen Jesus had been to Peter (Luke 24.34; 1 Cor. 15.5).

letters probably provide the oldest evidence of the early Church's belief in the Resurrection—also lists a number of appearances of Jesus to various individuals and groups (1 Cor. 15.5–7).

Matthew provides a coherent account of the events that followed the discovery of the empty tomb, and displays a clear understanding of their significance. The women meet Jesus and take hold of his feet. This corresponds to the accounts in Luke and the Fourth Gospel of the physical reality of Jesus' resurrection (Matt. 28.9; Luke 24.36–42; John 20.20, 24–27).

For Matthew, and probably also Mark, the true setting for the revelation of the risen Lord is Galilee, where he commands his disciples to travel to meet him (Matt. 28.10; compare Mark 16.7). Jesus appears to them on a mountain, probably to be understood as the place where once he had enunciated the new Law in the Sermon on the Mount (Matt. 5–7; see pp.278–79). There, he delivers his final message: a program for the mission of the future universal Church (Matt. 28.16–20). For Matthew, the Resurrection establishes Jesus as the Lord of the Christian community, which is assured of its ultimate triumph by the power of his continuing presence.

In Luke, the appearances of the resurrected Jesus occur in Jerusalem, and he presents a string of episodes that all take place, somewhat improbably, on the first Easter day. But precise chronology is not Luke's primary concern at this point. His interest is the same as Matthew's: the needs and tasks of the Church, and he already has in mind his second volume, Acts, in which the mission of the Church begins in Jerusalem.

Luke emphasizes that the death and resurrection of Jesus have been foretold in scripture (Luke 24.25–27, 44–45), and this is the major theme of Peter's first sermon (Acts 2.14–36). The disciples are entrusted with preaching to all nations a gospel of repentance and forgiveness of sins (Luke 24.47; Acts 2.38, 5.31). They are to remain in Jerusalem until they receive the gift of the Spirit which will empower them for their task (Luke 24.49; Acts 1.4–5, 8; 2.1–4; see pp.262–63).

The risen Lord and the Church

From the very beginning, the Resurrection became the central article of Christian faith. The New Testament books are unanimous in describing it as a genuine historical event, but its significance cannot be fully expressed in merely historical terms. It is a mighty act of divine power, comparable to God's primal act of Creation (Rom. 4.16–24), and like the Creation it was not an observable phenomenon. No one saw Jesus leave his tomb and even the guards who, according to Matthew, were present at the time, only witnessed an angelic visitation (Matt. 28.2–4). There is no description of the actual moment of resurrection: the gospels infer that it took place from the evidence of the empty tomb and the appearances of Jesus afterward.

The Roman Catholic church at Emmaus commemorates the famous encounter between two disciples and the resurrected Jesus described in Luke 24.13–32.

Many authorities have suggested that the traditions of the empty tomb and of the appearances of the risen Christ originated separately. According to this theory, faith in Jesus' resurrection originally arose from his followers' belief that they had experienced Jesus' continuing presence after the Crucifixion; the story of the empty tomb was a later legend, designed to prove the reality of Jesus' physical resurrection.

It is true that only the evangelists refer to the empty tomb, and not Paul, whose letters predate the gospels. On the other hand, Paul may simply be taking the well-known story of the empty tomb for granted. Besides, his focal concerns were to validate his personal experience of the risen Jesus, and to emphasize the truth of the resurrection of all believers, which Jesus' own resurrection guaranteed.

Conversely, if the original version of Mark's gospel ends at 16.8, as many believe (see box, p.259), then this evangelist provided no record at all of the appearances of the risen Jesus and offered only the words of the angelic man at the empty tomb as evidence for the Resurrection. All in all, it is probably best to view the reported experiences of the risen Jesus and of the empty tomb as joint sources for the belief that Jesus rose from the dead.

Another suggestion is that the appearances of the risen Christ represent subjective mystical or visionary experiences of his followers, arising from their belief that he would rise from the dead.

However, the source of any such conviction is not clear. There is no firm evidence that contemporary Jews believed that the expected Messiah would die and rise again; and Jesus' own predictions of his death and resurrection, as recorded in the synoptic gospels, are regarded by most scholars as stemming from the evangelists and the early Church rather than from Jesus. In any case, the gospel accounts emphasize that the disciples were unable to understand or accept his words (Mark 8.32–33, 9.10, 9.32; Matt.16.22–23, 17.23; Luke 18.34).

THE ASCENSION

MYSTICAL ASCENT TO HEAVEN
According to the nonscriptural Jewish writings known as the Pseudepigrapha, a whole range of figures from Israel's past ascended to heaven, including Adam, Enoch, Abraham, Moses, and Isaiah. In heaven they were transformed into angelic beings, to whom divine cosmic secrets are revealed. Such accounts probably represent the actual subjective experience of Jewish mystics, as is suggested by some evidence from Qumran and by Paul's account of how he himself was mysteriously "caught up" to heaven and heard divine secrets (2 Cor. 12.1–7).

Some authorities claim that Jesus himself underwent the same kind of experience, and that this is seen notably in the description of his Transfiguration (see p.236). This has much in common with the New Testament references to his ascension, which have probably been shaped in part by mystical tradition.

Of all the writings of the New Testament, only Luke's second volume, Acts, describes Jesus' ascension to heaven as a genuine historical event and a visible phenomenon (Acts 1.2–11). Most often the New Testament speaks of the "exaltation" of Jesus, notably in an early hymn quoted in the letter to the Philippians (Phil. 2.6–11). The same image is dominant in the letter to the Hebrews (Heb. 1.3–4) and elsewhere: after his earthly sufferings, the Son is invested by God with supreme authority over the cosmos (Eph. 1.20–22). He inaugurates the new messianic age, and his followers share in his exalted status (Eph. 2.4–6). All this is achieved because Jesus has been carried into the heavenly realm and seated at God's right hand (Mark 16.19; Rom. 8.34)—that is, Jesus has returned to the divine state he enjoyed, as the agent of Creation, before his incarnation (Col. 1.15–17; Heb. 1.2).

As with Jesus' bodily resurrection (see p.261), the moment of Jesus' heavenly ascent remains largely undescribed. Luke's gospel states that Jesus "withdrew" from his disciples "and was carried up into Heaven" (Luke 24.51). According to Acts, as the disciples watched, Jesus was "lifted up, and a cloud took him out of their sight" (Acts 1.9). In the verses added to Mark (see box, p.259), Jesus is said to have been "taken up into Heaven," where he "sat down at the right hand of God" (Mark 16.19). However, Matthew speaks only of the supreme cosmic authority conferred on Jesus and of his continuing presence (Matt. 28.18–20). In John, Jesus announces to Mary Magdelene his imminent ascension, but its actual occurrence has to be inferred (John 20.17).

A view eastward across the Old City of Jerusalem toward the Mount of Olives, also known as Mount Olivet, the scene of Jesus' Ascension (Acts 1.12). Close to the traditional site stands the tall belfry of the 19th-century Russian Orthodox Church of the Ascension.

The gift of the Spirit

Only Luke (in Acts) and John record the gift of the Holy Spirit to the disciples (John 20.22; Acts 2.1–13, 33). It represents Jesus' final bequest: the Spirit is to take his place, as it were, after he withdraws to heaven. For Luke, the descent of the Spirit is a public, visible, and dramatic event. In John, the disciples receive the Spirit in secret (John 20.19–23) and it remains known only to them (John 14.17).

In five sayings, John sets out what Christians are to understand about the nature and operation of the Spirit, also termed "the Advocate" (John 14.15–17, 25–26, 15.26, 16.4–11, 12–15). The Advocate will focus on Jesus and his teaching (John 14.26, 15.26, 16.14), and will guide the disciples into "the truth," which is Jesus himself (John 16.13–15; see p.283). The promise of the Spirit in Acts and John corresponds to Jesus' promise in Matthew that he will always be with the disciples (Matt. 28.20).

According to the gospels, the Spirit was involved at key moments throughout Jesus' earthly existence, and indeed directed his entire life and teaching (John 3.34). It was the agent of his conception (Matt. 1.18; Luke 1.35) and descended on him at his baptism (Mark 1.10 and parallels; John 1.32–33); at the start of his ministry, Jesus claimed to be the Spirit-filled prophet foretold in Isaiah (Luke 4.16–21). Through the Spirit, Jesus performed deeds of power, such as casting out demons (Matt. 12.28). Similarly, the gift of the Spirit grants the disciples "power from on high" (Luke 24.49) to exorcise, heal, and perform other "signs" in Jesus' name (Mark 16.17–20).

The Ascension, *by Pietro Perugino (ca. 1448–1523). Jesus ascends amid angels and cherubs, as the apostles gaze up to heaven (Acts 1.9–10). Following an early tradition, the Virgin also appears (center), as does Paul (with sword).*

The special object of the Ascension narrative in Acts is to make clear that the post-Resurrection appearances have come to an end. Jesus leaves the earth, not to be seen again until his second coming at some unknown date. His presence will be replaced by that of the Holy Spirit which will empower and inspire the Church (Acts 1.8). Luke's account appears to be modeled on the ascension of Elijah as described in the Hebrew Scriptures (2 Kings 2.9–12). For example, the forty-day period between the Resurrection and the Ascension on the Mount of Olives recalls Elijah's forty days' journey to Mount Horeb (1 Kings 19.8); and the gift of the Holy Spirit is paralleled by the gift to Elisha of the spirit of Elijah.

The unique feature of Jesus' ascension is its eschatological significance. It symbolizes the end of the old world order and the inauguration of the last age; his final coming will bring into being a wholly new heaven and a wholly new earth (Rev. 21.1).

EGO VER
SUM TAS
VIA

JESUS CHRIST: THE TEACHINGS

Above: The Last Supper, *a mosaic in the church of Sant' Apollinare Nuovo, Ravenna, Italy. The gospel accounts of Jesus' final meal are central to Christian teachings on the Eucharist and the kingdom of God.*
Opposite: Christ the Redeemer *(detail), by Agnolo Gaddi (ca. 1350–96). Jesus holds open a passage (in Latin) from one of his discourses in John's gospel: "I am the way, the truth, and the life" (John 14.6).*

SAYINGS AND PARABLES

The gospels clearly present the "parables" of Jesus as central to his message and to the way in which he proclaimed it. What is less clear is how this word (Greek *parabole*) should be defined. Most often, it is used to refer to any of the numerous narratives with which Jesus illuminates his teaching (see sidebar, opposite). But *parabole* covers a variety of other meanings, for example it is used of a metaphorical saying in Mark 7.14–17 and is translated as "proverb" in Luke 4.23. Conversely, Luke records some of Jesus' most famous and characteristic parables—such as the Good Samaritan (Luke 10.30–37) and the Prodigal Son (Luke 15.11–32)—but does not call them parables.

In the Septuagint, the oldest Greek version of the Hebrew Scriptures, *parabole* translates the Hebrew *mashal*, a word that can indicate a proverb, an allusion, a gibe, a riddle, or a prophetic oracle. *Mashal* derives from a root meaning "to be like," and is often found in conjunction with a comparative phrase such as "It is like" and "It may be likened to" in the Hebrew Scriptures (for instance, Ezek. 16.44) and in rabbinical texts. Similar phrases occur in the gospels in association with *parabole* (as at Mark 4.30; Matt. 13.24, 25.1), and may also introduce what is clearly a parable even when the term itself is absent (Matt. 18.23, 20.1).

The Ten Bridesmaids, *by Frans Francken the Younger (1581–1642), illustrating Matthew's parable about the vigilance required of those seeking to enter God's kingdom (Matt. 25.1–13). The five wise bridesmaids (right) have filled their lamps in anticipation of the arrival of the bridegroom (the Messiah), unlike the five foolish bridesmaids (left). When the Messiah's arrival is announced, the foolish bridesmaids must go to buy oil and are shut out of the messianic banquet.*

A mosaic of a grapevine from the church of Santa Maria di Capua Vetere, Italy. The image alludes to Jesus' parable of the Vine and the Branches (John 15.1–10).

So a parable may be defined, in a wide sense, as any figure of speech containing an arresting and illuminating image, allegory, or analogy. In this light it is quite understandable for Mark to describe Jesus' popular preaching as consisting wholly of "parables" (Mark 4.34), which modern scholars would variously categorize as similes, proverbs, metaphors, aphorisms, fables, and so on.

In the Fourth Gospel, Jesus' teaching tends to be less figuratively expressed, but his style of instruction is not so radically different from that in the synoptists as is often supposed. Not only does John contain two passages that have the distinct character of parables as the term is ordinarily understood—the Good Shepherd (John 10.1–18) and the Vine and the Branches (John 15.1–10)—but the gospel also conveys Jesus' message by means of a whole range of metaphors and figurative expressions.

The question arises as to how far it is possible to recover Jesus' actual words and the meaning that he himself attached to his parables. The evangelists present the parables as they were preserved, used, and understood in different circles within the early Church. This is evident from the way in which the same basic parable may vary from one gospel to the next. An example is the parable of the Wedding Banquet, to which the guests choose not to come (Matt. 22.1–14; Luke 14.15–24). In Luke, the story provides a message for the present, a warning against a refusal to accept God's gracious summons. In Matthew, it refers to the future messianic wedding feast for God's own Son and forecasts the coming destruction of Jerusalem.

The gospels tend to group parables (for example, Matt. 13.1–50, 25.1–46; Mark 4.1–34; Luke 6.39–49, 12.35–59). This suggests that the evangelists considered such parables to share the same theme, whether or not this was originally the case. For example, some parables are carefully

NARRATIVE PARABLES OF JESUS

It is possible to list numerous examples of parables in which the element of narrative is characteristic—brief stories that illustrate one or more ideas. Most scholars would accept the following list:

PARABLES IN ALL THREE SYNOPTICS:
- A Divided House (Mark 3.23–26 and parallels)
- The Sower (Mark 4.2–9 and parallels)
- The Mustard Seed (Mark 4.30–32 and parallels)
- The Wicked Tenants (Mark 12.1–11 and parallels)
- The Fig Tree (Mark 13.28–29 and parallels)

PARABLES COMMON TO MATTHEW AND LUKE:
- The Two Builders (Matt. 7.24–27; Luke 6.47–49)
- The Yeast (Matt. 13.33; Luke 13.20–21)
- The Lost Sheep (Matt. 18.12–14; Luke 15.4–7)
- The Wedding Banquet (Matt. 22.1–14; Luke 14.15–24)
- Faithful and Unfaithful Slaves (Matt. 24.45–51; Luke 12.42–46)
- The Talents or Pounds (Matt. 25.14–30; Luke 19.11–27)

A PARABLE ONLY IN MARK:
- The Growing Seed (Mark 4.26–29)

PARABLES ONLY IN MATTHEW:
- The Sower of Weeds (Matt. 13.24–30)
- The Hidden Treasure (Matt. 13.44)
- The Pearl (Matt. 13.45–46)
- The Great Net (Matt. 13.47–48)
- The Unforgiving Servant (Matt. 18.23–35)
- The Vineyard Laborers (Matt. 20.1–16)
- The Two Sons (Matt. 21.28–31)
- The Ten Bridesmaids (Matt. 25.1–13)
- The Judgment of the Nations (Matt. 25.31–46)

PARABLES ONLY IN LUKE:
- The Creditor (Luke 7.41–43)
- The Good Samaritan (Luke 10.30–37)
- The Unexpected Guest (Luke 11.5–8)
- The Rich Fool (Luke 12.16–21)
- The Barren Fig Tree (Luke 13.6–9)
- Choosing a Seat (Luke 14.7–11)
- The Lost Coin (Luke 15.8–10)
- The Prodigal Son (Luke 15.11–32)
- The Dishonest Manager (Luke 16.1–8)
- The Rich Man and Lazarus (Luke 16.19–31)
- The Widow and the Unjust Judge (Luke 18.1–8)
- The Pharisee and the Tax Collector (Luke 18.9–14)

PARABLES IN JOHN:
- The Good Shepherd (John 10.1–18)
- The Vine and Branches (John 15.1–10)

Biblical and rabbinic parables

The parables in the Hebrew Scriptures were an important influence on the parables in the New Testament. The function of a parable is illustrated by the story told to King David by the prophet Nathan in order to open his eyes to the depths and consequences of his misdeeds (2 Sam. 12.1–15): to bring home to hearers the reality of their situation and to alert them to the response demanded from them (Luke 10.36–37). Much the same purpose inspired the parable told by King Jehoash in his confrontation with King Amaziah (2 Kings 14.8–10).

In these instances, the speaker adds an explanation of the story's thrust, so that it comes close to allegory, a feature that becomes increasingly prominent in the Hebrew Scriptures. For example, Ezekiel's parable of the Eagles and the Vine is described as a "riddle" and an "allegory" (Ezek. 17.1–21).

The way in which the rabbis used parables in their teaching also throws considerable light on the gospel parables. Most extant examples are later than the time of Jesus or the New Testament, but there are good grounds for believing that they reflect a well-established tradition. Like Jesus, the rabbis drew their examples from daily life, and many of their typical images correspond to those in the gospel parables.

The Prodigal Son *(detail), by the Master of the Female Half-Lengths (ca. 1490–1540). The parable of the son lost to his father but found again (Luke 15.11–32) draws upon themes in the story of Joseph.*

Rabbinic parables frequently illustrate passages of scripture. The only clear parallel to this method in the gospels is the parable of the Wicked Tenants (Mark 12.1–12 and parallels), which begins with a reference to Isaiah 5.2 and ends with the direct quotation of Psalm 118.22–23. But there are also indirect allusions to scriptural themes in Jesus' parables. For example, the story of the Good Samaritan interprets Leviticus 19.18, which is quoted (Luke 10.27), while the role of the Samaritan may recall 2 Chronicles 28.15. The parable of the Prodigal Son echoes the story of Joseph (Gen. 37–47), and the teaching about Choosing a Seat (Luke 14.7–11) is an interpretation of Proverbs 25.6–7.

explained in considerable detail as if they were allegories (Mark 4.13–20 and parallels; Matt. 13.36–43, 49–50). But it has been noted that in the parables unique to Luke, there is an absence of allegory, just a straightforward ethical message. The passages in the Gospel of Thomas (see box, p.191) that parallel the synoptic parables also lack allegorical features.

Consequently, some scholars have attempted to recover the "original" form and significance of Jesus' parables by stripping them of all elements of allegory and eschatology. However, if Jesus was influenced by the Hebrew Scriptures or by contemporary rabbinic practice (see box, above), he may well have used allegory on occasion. Indeed, it is hard to see how such parables as the Sower and the Wicked Tenants are intelligible except as allegories.

It has been suggested that Jesus' parables are primarily concerned with his central theme of the Kingdom (see pp.280–81), but he may have used them for a variety of purposes, sometimes perhaps simply to emphasize moral duties. The gospels imply that Jesus did not expect his parables to be widely understood, and revealed their real meaning only in private to the disciples (Mark 4.10–12 and parallels; Mark 4.33–34). But this may represent an attempt by the early Church to account for the fact that Jesus' public teaching had met with so little response in his lifetime. It seems clear that Jesus did indeed intend his parables as aids to getting his message across, not least because their imagery is overwhelmingly drawn from daily life.

Modern literary studies of the New Testament stress that the parables invite multiple interpretations and applications. The way in which they were transmitted in the early Church should perhaps be viewed, therefore, not as an obscuring or perversion of Jesus' teaching, but as a first witness to the continuing challenge to the Christian community to understand, and assimilate, his words.

The Sower of Weeds, *by Domenico Fetti (ca. 1589–1623). Like many of Jesus' parables, Matthew's story about God's kingdom (Matt. 13.24–30) draws upon everyday rural life: "The kingdom of heaven may be compared to someone who sowed good seed in his field; but while everyone was asleep, an enemy came and sowed weeds among the wheat." The weeds represent those who will be judged unworthy to enter the kingdom: "At harvest time I will tell the reapers, collect the weeds first and bind them in bundles to be burned, but gather the wheat into my barn."*

MIDRASH

Recent scholarship suggests that Jesus' use of scripture may be illuminated by comparison with the methods of biblical quotation and analysis current in the Palestine of his day. In mainstream Judaism, biblical interpretation and analysis were the prerogative of the rabbinical schools, whose wide variety of interpretative systems goes under the general description of *midrash* (from a Hebrew root meaning "to investigate").

Most of the extant rabbinic evidence is later than Jesus' time, but because the background of *midrash* has much to do with the scribes and the Pharisees, it could well have emerged by the first century CE.

The aim of *midrash* was to preserve the relevance and authority of the ancient scriptures in the life of every generation. To meet contemporary needs, additional legal regulations and moral teachings were drawn from the Hebrew Bible. This was done in various ways, for example by interpreting one scriptural passage in the light of another; by referring to oral tradition (see p.162); or by applying general theological or legal principles to extend the scope of a particular passage.

JESUS AND SCRIPTURE

Allusions to the Hebrew Scriptures abound in the gospels, and there are also many direct quotations. As these quotations illustrate, in the first century CE the scriptures existed in a multiplicity of textual forms. Most passages quoted by the evangelists are taken from one or other version of the Septuagint (the oldest Greek version of the Hebrew Scriptures), but some, especially in Matthew, seem to depend more on the original Hebrew, while others do not correspond precisely to any known Greek or Hebrew text. It is possible that the gospel writers may often have quoted inexactly from memory, or felt free to adapt a biblical passage in order to make a particular theological point. Another suggestion is that they may have been influenced by the Targums, the Aramaic paraphrases of scripture that were used in the synagogues at the time for the benefit of Jews who did not understand Hebrew (see p.178).

All the evangelists employ verses from the Hebrew Scriptures in the course of their narrative in order to bring out the significance of Jesus'

Christ Disputing with the Pharisees, *one of a series of 13th-century stained glass panels known as the "Poor Man's Bible" in Canterbury cathedral, England.*

words and deeds. They do this in ways that have parallels in the Judaism of their time (see sidebars), except, of course, when they interpret various biblical prophecies as being fulfilled by episodes in the life of Jesus. The question arises as to whether Jesus himself used scripture in similar fashion in his own teaching—which in turn involves the issue of the authenticity of the words attributed to him.

Jesus was clearly accepted as a teacher (see pp.292–93), and a recognized teacher would have been expected to be familiar with the scriptures and to turn to them in his instruction. The gospels certainly portray Jesus as a person who was generally well versed in the scriptures, and several of his sayings, parables, and prayers contain echoes of biblical phrases and themes. For example, Mark 13.24–26 and parallels allude to Isaiah 13.10 and 34.4 and Daniel 7–13; the conclusion of the parable of the Growing Seed (Mark 4.26–29) echoes Joel 3.13; and the prayer on the cross in Mark 15.34 and Matthew 27.46 quotes Psalm 22.1, while that in Luke 23.46 paraphrases Psalm 31.5.

However, Jesus was an itinerant preacher who did not belong to any of the more "official" Jewish teaching groups, and the chief priests, elders, and scribes (experts in Jewish law; see p.162) are represented as querying his qualifications (Mark 11.27–33 and parallels). The gospels specifically contrast him with the scribes—whose particular expertise was scriptural analysis and interpretation—as one who presents a new teaching that has "authority" (Mark 11.27–28 and parallels). This indicates that Jesus was regarded by his followers as a prophet who, like his biblical predecessors, was delivering a divine message direct from God. Such a message did not require biblical evidence to support it, so it is not surprising that the evangelists present Jesus as appealing to scripture comparatively infrequently.

Jesus had recourse to the Hebrew Scriptures to justify his teachings or actions primarily when he was challenged by various learned opponents. He then employed the kinds of argument that would have been familiar to his challengers and so might have been more likely to convince them (Luke 20.39). One technique was that of interpreting a biblical verse in the light of another, which was among the methods of *midrash* (see sidebar, left), as in his controversy with the Pharisees over divorce (Mark 10.2–9, Matt. 19.3–8) and his argument with the Sadducees over the doctrine of resurrection (Mark 12.26–27 and parallels).

Using the technique known as *pesher*, which was also employed by the Qumran sect (see sidebar, right), Jesus could point to events connected with his life as being the fulfillment of biblical prophecy—notably the role of John the Baptist as forerunner of the Messiah (Matt. 11.10; Luke 7.27) and the desertion of the disciples (Matt. 26.31; Mark 14.27). In particular, Jesus announced that he and his entire mission represented the realization of earlier prophetic writings (Matt. 12.39–40; Luke 4.16–21, 11.29–30, 22.37).

Part of the ruins of the settlement at Qumran in the Judean desert. These steps led to the pool used by Qumranites for ritual purification.

QUMRAN AND *PESHER*

Since the discovery of the Dead Sea Scrolls (see sidebar, p.169), scholars have devoted a great deal of attention to the analytical and interpretative techniques of the Qumran sect, particularly as they relate to Jesus' own methods of expounding the Jewish scriptures. The most characteristic method of biblical commentary at Qumran was *pesher* (Hebrew, "interpretation"), whereby a verse of scripture was quoted and then explained in a passage beginning with an introductory formula ("Interpreted, this concerns…").

Any verse thus cited was understood to be a prophecy and was usually taken from the prophetic books of the Hebrew Bible. The prophecies treated in this manner refer to events of the end time, which the Qumran sect believed had arrived. Through *pesher*, the Qumranites sought to identify contemporary persons and events in the life of the Qumran community to which the prophecies might be referring. The inner meaning of the prophecies, they believed, had been divinely revealed to the community's founder, the figure known as the Teacher of Righteousness.

THE LAW AND THE EVANGELISTS
The question must arise as to how far sayings about the law ascribed to Jesus represent his own teaching rather than the ideas of the evangelists and of various currents within the early Church. For example, Matthew's gospel contains Jesus' most positive statements about the law (Matt. 5.17–19) and even presents him as approving of the teaching—if not the actual practice—of the Pharisees (Matt. 23.2–3). Is Matthew here reproducing the attitude of contemporary Jewish Christians in Palestine?

By contrast, Mark's comment that Jesus' teaching "declared all food clean" (Mark 7.14–19) may reflect the particular outlook of Pauline Christianity, with its mission to win over the Gentiles (compare Rom. 14.14).

JESUS AND THE JEWISH LAW

It is possible to discern in the gospels a reasonably coherent and distinctive attitude on the part of Jesus toward the Torah, the Jewish law (see p.162). He is depicted as an observant Jew who regularly attended synagogue. He advocated obedience to the law's precepts, even in matters of ritual, such as sending gifts to the Temple (Matt. 5.23). But he warned against putting too much emphasis on the precise carrying out of such external regulations. Jesus perceived the deeper religious significance of the law as the means by which people can attain a good life in accordance with the will of God. While he was not alone in this among the Jewish teachers of his day, he laid special emphasis on it in his own teaching. Above all, Jesus emphasized that what was crucial was the correct intention on the part of the individual.

Much of Jesus' teaching on the Torah has parallels in Jewish thought of his time. The perpetuity of the law was a central dogma of Judaism, and the gospels may preserve the words that Jesus used to support that idea (Matt. 5.18; Luke 16.17), although they appear to modify its absolute character (Matt. 11.13; Luke 16.16). It may be that Jesus envisaged that the law would continue only for the comparatively brief period before the advent of the new age.

The law in contemporary Judaism

All Jews accepted the supreme authority of the Torah, but Judaism in the first century CE was not a monolithic system. By this time, the ancient law required interpretation and exposition to make it relevant to contemporary social conditions, and there were a number of different groups (see pp. 166–69) with their own expository methods. It is only to be expected that Jesus, as an independent teacher, would have had his own distinctive ways of interpreting the law.

A stone carving of ca. 400 CE from Capernaum of a wheeled Torah shrine, in which the scrolls of the law were kept in a synagogue.

At the same time, it has often been pointed out that there is something of a problem with the term "law" as translated in the New Testament. The Greek word *nomos*, used in the gospels, certainly means "law" but in no way conveys the full sense of the Hebrew word Torah, which means "instruction" or "direction." Torah comprises the whole of God's revelation to humanity—the entire corpus of scripture with associated religious tenets. For the Pharisees it included the oral law (the "tradition of the elders"; Mark 7.3, 5; Matt. 15.2), although this was rejected by other groups, notably the Sadducees (see p.167).

It sometimes appeared that Torah, in this wide sense, embraced inconsistent teachings, so that it was sometimes necessary to decide which should take precedence. Such a procedure is several times attributed to Jesus in the gospels (see main text and pp.162–63).

Christ and the Woman Taken in Adultery, *by Nicolas Colombel (1646–1717). In the gospel account (John 8.2–11), the Pharisees bring an adulterous woman before Jesus and challenge him to defy the biblical teaching that an unfaithful wife should be put to death (Deut. 22.22). Jesus' famous response—"Let anyone among you who is without sin be the first to throw a stone at her"—warns against paying too much attention to the external rituals of the law at the expense of monitoring one's own conscience. In the end, the crowd disperses, and Jesus forgives the woman with an injunction not to sin again.*

In the Sermon on the Mount there are six sections (Matt. 5.21–48) in which Jesus quotes from the law and apparently contrasts it with his own ruling, for example: "You have heard that it was said, 'An eye for an eye and a tooth for a tooth' [compare Exod. 21.24]. But I say to you, Do not resist an evildoer..."(Matt. 5.38–39). The formula "but I say to you" was also employed by the Pharisees (Matt. 15.4–6; Mark 7.9–13) and does not in itself imply that Jesus was attempting to contradict or supersede the law. Rather, Jesus often aimed to support and bolster the Torah by indicating the interior moral disposition that must be confronted in order to ensure the law's proper observance. Thus anger is the cause of murder (Matt. 5.22); lust is equivalent to adultery (Matt. 5.28); true love must embrace enemies (Matt. 5.43–48). A promise need not be reinforced by swearing to God (Matt. 5.34–35, 23.16–22; Jesus uses common rabbinic paraphrases for the divine name)—the simple word of an honest person is enough (Matt. 5.37). Philo and Josephus record that the Essenes held much the same view.

Elsewhere, Jesus interprets the law within the framework of regular rabbinic methods of interpretation and analysis. His teaching on marriage and divorce (Matt. 19.3–8; Mark 10.2–9) relies on an appreciation that one scriptural text (Gen. 2.24) is of greater weight than another (Deut. 24.1). Similarly, when Jesus is accused of breaking the Sabbath by healing on that day, he points to the generally accepted principle that the need to preserve life supersedes the Sabbath taboos (Mark 3.4 and parallels ; Mark 14.5 and parallels). The Pharisees' complaint against his disciples for plucking grain on the Sabbath (Mark 2.23–28 and parallels) seems to categorize the act as "harvesting," which was forbidden on that day. Jesus defends it by appealing, in typical rabbinic fashion, to scriptural precedent (1 Sam. 21.1–7; Matthew also mentions Num. 28.9–10)—which had greater authority than the rules of the Pharisees.

JESUS' SUMMARY OF THE LAW

On various occasions Jesus is represented as summarizing the whole of the law in brief, pithy statements. To this end he quotes the Ten Commandments (Mark 10.17–19 and parallels), pronounces the so-called Golden Rule (Matt. 7.12; Luke 6.31), and teaches that the whole of scripture can be summed up in just two commandments: to love God and one's neighbor (Mark 12.28–34 and parallels). The directness and clarity of Jesus' words, and the manner in which they embrace all the ethical and religious aspects of the Torah, strongly suggest that they embody his particular and authentic teaching.

Within Judaism there was a similar tendency to define the essence of the law in one or more simple statements, and parallels to all three of Jesus' summaries can be found in Jewish authors and early rabbinical sources. For example, Hillel, a great teacher of the first century BCE, is reported to have said: "What is hateful to you, do not to your neighbor. That is the whole Torah. The rest is commentary."

GENTILES AND SAMARITANS

Christ and the Woman of Samaria at the Well, *by Philippe de Champaigne (1602–74). When Jesus asked a Samaritan woman to give him a drink, she was initially wary (John 4.9), since the attitude of Jews and Samaritans was often one of mutual hostility. According to John 4.7–29, Jesus revealed himself to her as a prophet and as the Messiah, declaring that Samaritans would share in the "living water"—the gift of divine spirit that Jesus brought. Samaria was an early destination for the missionary apostles, and Philip is said to have had great success there (Acts 8.5–8). However, whether Jesus himself really sanctioned a mission to the Samaritans is debatable (see p.168).*

Within a few years of Jesus' death, the embryonic Church emerged as an active missionary body centered on Jerusalem. The traditional Christian view is that the Jerusalem leadership agreed to concern themselves with converting Jews, while the apostle Paul and his colleague Barnabas would embark on a mission to the Gentiles (Gal. 2.7–10).

There is considerable evidence to indicate that Jesus himself personally undertook no such mission to non-Jews. He said that he had been sent "only to the lost sheep of the house of Israel" (Matt. 15.24). On occasion he even displayed a distinct antipathy toward Gentiles, for example describing them as "dogs" (Mark 7.27 and parallels), an epithet also employed in rabbinic sources. When Jesus sends out the twelve apostles on their missionary journey, he orders them not to go either to Gentiles or to Samaritans (Matt. 10.5).

Such sayings seem to reflect the authentic attitude of Jesus himself, since they do not chime with the practice of either the Jewish or the Gentile wings of the early Church (see pp.326–27). It is worth noting that the first Christians, in their approach to the Gentiles and the question of circumcision, never appeal to any direct teaching of Jesus.

However, some words and actions of Jesus point in a different direction. He declared that the twelve disciples would sit on thrones at Judgment Day to judge only the tribes of Israel (Matt. 19.28; Luke 22.28–30), but both gospels also report his statement that those who will sit in the kingdom of God are in fact the Gentiles, who will supplant the Jews (Matt. 8.11–12; Luke 13.28–29). Jesus said that he found more faith in a Roman centurion than anywhere in Israel (Matt. 8.10; Luke 7.9) and recognized the truth of the Canaanite woman's claim that a Gentile might share in Jewish privileges (Matt. 15.27–28; Mark 7.28–29). Jesus is recorded as healing not only Jews but also crowds who flocked to him from non-Jewish areas (Mark 3.7–8).

These divergent attitudes toward Gentiles reflect Jewish thought of the time. Jesus may well have seen his min-

Jews and Gentiles in Jesus' time

Most Jews were keenly aware of their separateness from the Gentiles who surrounded them. Condemnations of the Gentiles for idolatry and immorality were frequent, and the regulations of the Torah—especially regarding clean and unclean food and circumcision—served, for Jews, to mark them off as the people chosen and set apart by God.

But there is also much evidence of a positive attitude toward Gentiles. Some were recognized as righteous, and were accordingly expected to observe the seven basic commandments that God is said to have given Noah after the Flood (Gen. 9). There were Jewish thinkers who believed that such righteous Gentiles would be rewarded with a place in the future messianic age. In the face of much Gentile hostility, some Jewish writers sought to defend and commend their faith to outsiders, to considerable effect. Judaism as a whole was not an active missionary movement, but converts and proselytes were often welcomed and apparently sometimes vigorously sought out (Matt. 23.15). A proselyte had to accept all the requirements of the Jewish law; many Gentiles felt unable to go so far, but remained attracted to Judaism on account of its strict monotheism, ethical concerns, and morality, which they learned about in the synagogues—places that were open to all. Many Gentiles, like the centurion at Capernaum (Luke 7.2–5), enjoyed friendly relations with Jews.

The attitudes toward Gentiles prevalent in Jesus' time find their roots in the Hebrew Bible. On the one hand, it betrays a strong exclusivist strain, especially in postexilic writings such as Ezra and Nehemiah, which forbid marriages with non-Jews.

A relief carving from the synagogue at Capernaum. According to Luke 7.5, the synagogue of Jesus' own day was built by a Gentile benefactor, a centurion in the occupying Roman army.

Elsewhere there is a note of universalism: Israel is a light to the nations (Isa. 49.6), with a mission to unite with the Gentiles (Isa. 55.5) so that they too become God's people (Zech. 2.11). This is symbolized by the image of peoples converging on Jerusalem (Isa. 60.3, 11; Zech. 8.20–21) to worship the one true God (Zech. 14.6). Thus, according to a verse quoted by Jesus, the Jewish Temple becomes "a house of prayer for all peoples" (Isa. 56.7; Mark 11.17).

istry as preparing Israel for the imminent advent of the perfect rule of God (Matt. 10.23), while conceding that this would also embrace all non-Jews.

So even if it is concluded that the idea of a mission to all the nations arose only after the Crucifixion (Matt. 28.18–20; Mark 16.15; Luke 24.47), such a mission can be understood as a legitimate development of Jesus' own words and deeds. There is a pronounced strain of universalism in his teaching, as in the idea that God cares for all men and women equally, and even embraces one's enemies (Matt. 5.43–48; Luke 6.27–28, 32–36). One of the most characteristic features of Jesus' ministry was his fellowship with, and concern for, those rejected by society: tax collectors, sinners who had put themselves outside the Jewish law, Samaritans, and the disabled. Here may be seen the root of the concept of a gospel for the whole of humanity, as expressed by Paul: "For there is no distinction between Jew and Greek; the same Lord is Lord of all and is generous to all who call upon him" (Rom. 10.12).

GOD THE FATHER

God the Father Enthroned, *from the Limoges Missal (late 15th century). The figure of God is depicted wearing the papal tiara; one hand is raised in blessing, while the other holds an orb with a cross, signifying the sovereignty of Christ over the world. He is surrounded by the evangelists and their symbols.*

The concept of God as father is central to the life and teaching of Jesus as presented in the gospels, and the concept was certainly known in the Judaism of his day. It derives from the Hebrew Scriptures, where God is described, for example, as the father of the Israelite nation (Deut. 32.6; Isa. 63.16; Jer 31.9) and of the Israelite king (2 Sam. 7.14).

However, "father" is much less common in the Hebrew Bible than other descriptions and titles of God, whereas Jesus employs "Father" almost without exception (although some examples of his use of the term may well have been shaped by the evangelists or the liturgy of the early Church). Conversely, although "king" is a frequent title for God in the Judaism of the time—and despite the fact that the kingdom of God is another constant theme of Jesus' teaching (see pp.280–81)—only once does Jesus refer to God as king (Matt. 5.35), and even this instance is questionable. There can be little doubt, then, that the notion of God as father is an authentic element in Jesus' thought.

For Jesus, the fatherhood of God means that he is a forgiving deity and forgiveness must be a special mark of true worshipers (Matt. 6.14; Mark 11.25). The description of the Father as "heavenly" or "who is in heaven"—especially frequent in Matthew—points to God's perfection, which again must be a mark of his true followers (Matt. 5.48), who will be aided by his spirit (Matt. 10.20; Luke 11.13).

Above all, Jesus teaches that the heavenly Father actively cares for his whole creation, for all human beings, good and sinful, and such compassion once more must be a pattern for every human life (Matt. 5.43–46; Luke 6.32–36). God's providence extends to the natural world (Matt. 6.25–34, 10.29; Luke 12.6, 12.22–30). He may be compared to a human father who will always seek to give the best to his children (Matt. 7.7–11; Luke 11.9–13) so that the children of the heavenly Father, unlike others, can be certain that he will always provide for their needs—if their priority is to seek to enter his kingdom (Matt. 6.31–34; Luke 12.29–31).

The "little ones"—probably not simply infants but all who believe with childlike openness, as an addition in some manuscripts suggests—are always in the Father's sight (Matt. 18.10, 14). The secrets of the human heart are known to God, with the result that it is not the outward actions involved in almsgiving, prayer, and fasting at which he looks but the inner intention of an individual that obtains his reward (Matt. 6.2–8, 16–18).

The gospels record five prayers of Jesus in which he addresses God as "Father," the best known of these being "The Lord's Prayer" (see sidebar, right). In his two prayers from the cross recorded in Luke (Luke 23.24, 46) Jesus also addresses his "Father": in the second case the word is added to a quotation from Psalm 31. Of special importance is Jesus' great thanksgiving prayer (Matt. 11.25–27; Luke 10.21–22), which certainly depicts a unique relationship between Jesus and his divine father. This passage characterizes Jesus very much as he is presented in John's gospel, and consequently it has been dismissed as a later addition, influenced by Hellenism (see pp.154–55) or even Gnosticism (see pp.330–31). But the idea expressed in this prayer that a special individual might be admitted to divine secrets and then in turn reveal them to others, is widely attested in Jewish writings such as the books of Enoch and some Qumran texts.

Jesus' fifth "father" prayer is spoken in Gethsemane (Mark 14.36 and parallels). Mark preserves the Aramaic term *Abba* (properly translated as "my father" or "our father"), and most scholars agree that this is the word Jesus would have used, both here and elsewhere. It also occurs twice outside the gospels (Rom. 8.15; Gal. 4.6), where it represents the practice of Greek-speaking churches—a fact that probably shows how deeply Jesus' own usage had embedded itself in Christian tradition.

A great deal has been read into the word *Abba*. Some have claimed that it represents a young child's way of speaking (the equivalent of "Daddy") and therefore indicates a special intimacy on the part of Jesus with his heavenly Father. But there is no real evidence that *Abba* means anything other than simply "father," and its precise significance must be determined by the context. For example, it was the regular title used when speaking to revered rabbinic teachers.

THE LORD'S PRAYER

Jesus' most famous prayer is The Lord's Prayer (Matt. 6.9–13; Luke 11.2–4). It might better be described as "The Disciples' Prayer," since it is intended as a brief and comparatively simple pattern for disciples to follow, in contrast to the "many words" apparently characteristic of Gentile prayers (Matt. 6.7). There is no fundamental difference in content between the versions in Matthew and Luke, and the petitions that come after the initial address reflect Jesus' general teaching about the nature of the heavenly Father (see main text).

The clause in Matthew "Your will be done" stresses the need for earthly life to correspond to the heavenly: in Jesus' teaching, those who desire to belong to the Father's family must seek first and foremost to carry out the divine purpose (Mark 3.35 and parallels; Matt. 7.21). The next petition, about "daily bread," probably refers to God's provision for ordinary human needs, of which Jesus speaks elsewhere. Commentators have proposed that the obscure Greek word translated as "daily" actually means "for tomorrow" and refers to the Day of Judgment expected shortly, but the likely Aramaic original suggests that Luke's "each day" gives the true sense—Jesus elsewhere discouraged any concern for "tomorrow" (Matt. 6.34).

Again, the prayer for the remission of debts or sins appeals both to the divine attribute of forgiveness and the requirement that human beings imitate it in their relationships with one another (see also Matt. 18.23–35; Luke 7.41–43, 47). The final petition, whatever its precise significance, reflects Jesus' assurance elsewhere (Matt. 18.14) that the Father will protect believers from harm.

The Lord's Prayer appears in 100 languages on the walls of the Pater Noster Church on the Mount of Olives. The church—the name of which is the Latin for "Our Father"—stands on the spot where Jesus is said to have spoken the prayer.

SERMONS AND DISCOURSES

THE SERMONS: A SUMMARY

MATTHEW'S SERMON ON THE MOUNT:
5.3–12 The Beatitudes
5.13–16 The new community
5.17–48 The fulfillment of the law
6.1–18 Duties toward God
6.19–7.12 How human life is to be lived
7.13–27 Challenges of choosing the right path

LUKE'S SERMON ON THE PLAIN:
6.20–23 The Beatitudes
6.24–26 The Woes
6.27–36 Love for enemies
6.37–45 Human life and relationships
6.46–49 Challenges of choosing the right path

According to the synoptic gospels, Jesus expressed most of his teaching in short, pithy sayings or in brief parables (see pp.266–69). This contrasts with the Fourth Gospel, in which Jesus' teaching is presented almost entirely in lengthy discourses (see pp.284–85). However, there are examples in the synoptic gospels of extended addresses attributed to Jesus, such as the so-called "Synoptic Apocalypse" (Mark 13.5–37 and parallels). In Matthew's gospel, in particular, there are at least five such discourses, which occupy a prominent place in the structure of the work (see box, below).

Nonetheless, although it is not impossible that Jesus occasionally made

Jesus' discourses in Matthew

New Testament scholars often claim that Matthew's gospel has a five-part structure based around five great discourses attributed to Jesus, each of which is rounded off with the phrase "when Jesus had finished" (Matt. chs. 5–7, 10, 13, 18, 23–25). It has been suggested that this pattern is intended to parallel the Pentateuch, the first five books of the Bible (Genesis–Deuteronomy, the books of the law) and that Matthew's gospel thus has the character of a code of religious instruction—the new law for the Christian community.

However, it is far from clear that there are only five important discourses in the gospel. For example, Matthew 11 is also an extended collection of Jesus' sayings. Also, if Matthew were understood as essentially a lawcode, the narratives of the Nativity, Passion, and Resurrection would fall outside its main structure, which seems very strange.

Other scholars propose that Matthew's framework echoes the Hexateuch, the first six books of the Bible. Thus the birth narratives parallel Genesis, the Passion parallels Deuteronomy (which ends with the death of Moses), and the Resurrection stories parallel Joshua (in which the Israelites enter the Promised Land and reaffirm their covenant with God).

But the evangelist himself provides no indication of any such conscious scheme. It seems better to conclude that Matthew intended to present his work as history: an account of the life and ministry of Jesus.

The Flight into Egypt, *by Gentile da Fabriano (ca. 1370–1427). Claims about the "Pentateuchal" structure of Matthew have been based on stories such as the Holy Family's journey to Egypt (see pp.206–07), which has echoes of the story of Joseph in Genesis.*

This hill near Capernaum, known as the Mount of the Beatitudes, is the traditional site of the Sermon on the Mount. On its crest stands the Roman Catholic Church of the Beatitudes, built in 1936.

orations in the manner of some of the prophets of ancient Israel, internal evidence suggests that, as they stand, all the discourses in Matthew, Mark, and Luke are actually compilations of individual sayings. For example, sayings that appear in a discourse in one gospel sometimes occur in another gospel in a quite different context.

The best known of such discourses appears in two related versions, traditionally called the "Sermon on the Mount" (Matt. 5–7) and the "Sermon on the Plain" (Luke 6.20–49), which deal with Jesus' challenging ethical demands. A comparison between Matthew's and Luke's versions suggests that they both derive from an earlier collection of sayings, either in oral or written form, which each evangelist has expanded and interpreted in his own way. In both gospels, the discourse is represented as being addressed to a general audience (Matt. 7.28; Luke 6.17, 7.1), but it seems likely that originally it was intended for the disciples alone (Matt. 5.1; Luke 6.20) and that it was preserved as a manual of instruction for the early Church.

In both Matthew and Luke, the discourse essentially represents the proclamation of the kingdom by the Messiah. This is clearer in Matthew, where the sermon opens the section of his gospel that sets out the message and teaching of Jesus (Matt. 4.17–16.20). To view it as primarily law—even as a new law for Israel—is to mistake its character. The moral and ethical teachings it contains represent the demands and obligations made on those who are prepared to accept the gift of the kingdom.

The position of the Beatitudes ("Blessings") at the beginning of the sermons is significant: they provide the keynote for all that follows. Luke has only four of the nine blessings cited by Matthew, and there are differences (probably unimportant) in the wording of those they have in common. The formal structure of the Beatitudes is modeled on similar sayings in the Hebrew Bible and other Jewish writings. (See also Sir. 25.7–10.)

BLESSINGS OF THE KINGDOM

The Beatitudes in Matthew's Sermon on the Mount and Luke's Sermon on the Plain seem deliberately to reflect the opening verses of Isaiah 61, and this provides the clue to their character. Isaiah 61 was the text upon which Jesus first preached in the synagogue at Nazareth (Luke 4.18–20), and the Beatitudes are prophetic and apocalyptic sayings that express the substance of Jesus' preaching in the synagogues of Galilee, where he proclaimed the gospel of the kingdom (Matt. 4.23). The millenarian connotations are more emphatic in Luke, who to the four Beatitudes adds four "Woes" that depict the fate of those who are deaf to the demands of the kingdom (Luke 6.24–26).

Matthew's first four blessings stress the reversals of fortune that the kingdom will bring to "the poor in spirit," "those who mourn," "the meek," and "those who hunger and thirst for righteousness." The remainder continue the theme of the rewards in a kingdom that is still to be consummated, although both gospels display the conviction that this consummation is close at hand. The discourses reach a climax with a call for people to act on Jesus' words in light of the coming Judgment. This is expressed in the parable of the houses built on rock and sand (Matt. 7.24–27; Luke 6.47–49), which is based on the Israelite idea of "the two ways" of righteousness and wickedness (Deut. 30.15; Ps. 1.6; Prov. 4.10–19).

THE CALL OF THE KINGDOM

Christ Pantocrator *("Ruler of All"), a mosaic in the dome of the Byzantine church at Daphni, Greece (ca. 1200). Jesus, as God the Son, is portrayed as king of kings, omnipotent sovereign of the universe, holding in his left hand the book of the new law that he brings.*

Jesus' preaching in Galilee centered on "the good news of the kingdom" (Matt. 4.23; Luke 8.1), and the synonymous expressions "the kingdom of God" and "the kingdom of heaven" occur around a hundred times in the synoptic gospels. Nowhere is the nature of this kingdom explicitly defined, which suggests that Jesus was talking about a concept familiar to his audience. At the same time, in spite of the many references to the kingdom, Jesus seems never to have spoken of God as "king," and there is a marked absence of royal imagery in his sayings about the kingdom.

Scholarly debate about the kingdom in the gospels has focused mainly on the issue of whether Jesus viewed it as a future phenomenon or as a reality already present. There are certainly passages which suggest that the kingdom has yet to appear, as in the petition "Your kingdom come" in the Lord's Prayer (see p.277), and in Jesus' promise to some of his disciples that they will live to witness the arrival of the kingdom (Mark 9.1 and parallels). At the Last Supper, Jesus says that he will not again drink wine until he drinks it anew in the kingdom of God (Matt. 26.29; Mark 14.25: see pp.242–43), referring to the great banquet that was expected to be held in celebration of the beginning of the messianic age. The banquet is also mentioned in a verse that tells of the future entry of all the nations into the kingdom (Matt. 8.11; Luke 13.29), which echoes ideas in the Hebrew Scriptures (Isa. 2.3; Mic. 4.3). The use of the future tense in Matthew's version of the Beatitudes (see pp.278–79) suggests that the disciples' enjoyment of the kingdom is yet to come.

On the other hand, numerous passages (such as Mark 1.15) speak of the kingdom as already present. Jesus' exorcisms are evidence that this is so (Matt. 12.28; Luke 11.20), and signs of the approach of the kingdom need not be sought, for it is here (Luke 17.21). The parables of the Growing Seed (Mark 4.26–29), the Mustard Seed (Mark 4.30–32 and parallels), the Yeast (Matt. 13.33; Luke 13.20), the Sower of Weeds (Matt. 13.24–30), and the Great Net (Matt. 13.47–50) all view the kingdom as a present reality.

In assessing whether the gospels view the kingdom as here or yet to come, commentators have often simply opted for one or other alternative. However, it is now increasingly recognized that the gospels are not necessarily self-contradictory, because the notion of God's kingdom as

The kingdom in Judaism

The nearest thing to the term "the kingdom of God" in the Hebrew Bible is "the kingdom of the Lord," which occurs once (1 Chron. 28.5) and refers to Israel. But the scriptures regularly refer to God as "king" and as "reigning," and speak of "his kingdom" (Ps. 145.12), "your kingdom" (Ps. 145.11, 13), and "my kingdom" (1 Chron. 17.14). Initially, the God of Israel was conceived, like other Near Eastern national deities, as the divine king of one people. However, as Israelite mono-theism developed, God's sovereignty came to be seen as both universal and eternal (Pss. 22.28, 103.19, 145.13; Wisd. of Solomon 10.10). But his rule was not universally recognized, so later Jewish writings developed the idea of God's kingdom as a hope for the future, to be realized either by his direct intervention or through his Messiah.

By the first century BCE, this hope had become particularly fervent, and was coupled with a belief in a present kingdom of evil at war with the kingdom of God. Contemporary disasters for the Jews, which appeared to be multiplying, were interpreted as signs that this conflict was close to its climax, when evil would be defeated and God's kingdom established. This was a central belief of, for example, the Qumran sect (see p.169).

The dual notions of a present and future kingdom also appear in rabbinic thought. The faithful Israelite can enter the kingdom here and now by taking on "the yoke of the kingdom of heaven": submitting to God and observing the law. On the other hand, in the Kaddish prayer, the worshiper asks for God's kingdom to be established "speedily and at a near time." The two concepts come together in a Targum (Aramaic paraphrase) of the Song of Moses in Exodus 15: "The Lord's is the kingdom in this world and his in the world to come."

The Mount of Olives from the walls of Jerusalem. According to Jewish tradition, the kingdom would be inaugurated by the arrival of God's Messiah on the Mount of Olives. It was here that the accompanying resurrection of the dead would begin—hence the thousands of Jewish graves that cover the hillside.

Christ and the Rich Youth, *by Bartolomeus Breenberg (ca. 1599–1657). A rich young man knelt before Jesus and asked how he could attain eternal life. Jesus replied that, as well as keeping the commandments, he must sell all he owned and give the money to the poor. Crestfallen, the youth departed, prompting Jesus' remark: "It is easier for a camel to go through the eye of a needle than for someone who is rich to enter the kingdom of God" (Mark 10.17–25 and parallels).*

JESUS' IMAGERY OF COMMITMENT
To drive home the necessity for absolute submission to the will of God, Jesus often employed vivid, even exaggerated images, as with his famous analogy of the camel and the needle's eye (see above). Just as a plowman should always look ahead, so no one entering the kingdom should look back to his or her old life (Luke 9.62). The kingdom even overrides the sacred duty of burying the dead, which must be left to the dead—Jesus' stark description of those who do not enjoy the new life of the kingdom (Matt. 8.22; Luke 9.60).

If a hand, a foot, or an eye "causes you to stumble" on the way to the kingdom, Jesus says, it is better they should be cut off or plucked out than be allowed to hinder one's entry (Matt. 18.8–9; Mark 9.43–48). Similarly, "there are eunuchs who have made themselves eunuchs for the sake of the kingdom of heaven" (Matt. 19.11–12).

both a present and future reality already existed in Judaism (see box, p.281). The thrust of Jesus' teaching is that the kingdom already exists but only becomes properly "activated" by his message and ministry, and this leads to its full and final consummation at some point in the near future. But the ultimate triumph of the kingdom depends upon men and women accepting its demands and devoting themselves wholly to its service (Matt. 6.33), not least as co-workers with Jesus in bringing others to repent and to acknowledge its claims (Matt. 10.7; Luke 9.2).

Most of Jesus' sayings about the kingdom address the religious and moral qualities that individuals require in order to enter it, and these form the core of his ethical teaching. As many people have observed, Jesus says nothing directly about social issues, nor is it possible to attribute any specific political doctrines to him. Rather than constituting a rounded, systematic, and universally applicable ethical system, Jesus' teaching as recorded in the gospels was prompted by *ad hoc* situations, often in response to particular questions put to him. This is not to say that many of his contemporaries did not regard his teachings as having significant social consequences. Jesus' radical demands were often an occasion of conflict in that they broke with convention and were seen to challenge accepted social priorities.

The first requirement that Jesus pressed on individuals was the need for repentance and belief in the good news that the kingdom had arrived. The gospels present this as the essential kernel of his preaching (Matt. 4.17; Mark 1.14–15). Repentance for past sins alone was not enough—and in this it is possible to detect a difference between Jesus and John the Baptist, for whom repentance was central (Matt. 3.6; Mark 1.4–5). Although the idea of turning from sin is certainly present in Jesus' teaching, his central concept is more positive: the turning around of a person's entire life toward the wholehearted service of God. This is the condition for entry into the kingdom, where the believer realizes and enjoys the divine forgiveness that is a leading theme of Jesus' message.

Entry into the kingdom must be complete and unconditional: its demands are overriding and nothing must stand in its way. It involves detachment from possessions and family ties, and a complete reversal of the usual social distinctions (Mark 10.29–31 and parallels). The striking language with which Jesus expressed how an individual should submit to God (see sidebar on opposite page) should not be understood as prescribing specific modes of external behavior. It points to the fact that Jesus' ethical teachings center primarily on one's interior disposition and commitment. Thus the Sermon on the Mount calls not just for the outward observance of the commandments of the law but for obedience to the spirit of those commandments (see pp.272–73).

Along with repentance goes utter trust in God, who, when people renounce everything except service to him, will supply all their needs, freeing them from all anxiety. The model for those hoping to enter the kingdom is the unquestioning trust of a little child (Mark 10.15 and parallels; Matt. 11.25; Luke 10.21). In their own personal behavior the kingdom's children are to exhibit the very nature of their heavenly Father, reflecting his perfection in themselves (Matt. 5.48, 19.21). Just as the Father is loving and merciful to all human beings, irrespective of their merits, so too all humans must practice universal benevolence, even toward enemies (Matt. 5.43–48; Luke 6.27–36), and show mercy toward all in need (Luke 10.29–37). The prime ethical principle of Jesus, therefore, is fundamentally one of love, crystallized in his summary of the law: "You shall love the Lord your God with all your heart, and with all your soul, and with all your mind, and with all your strength" and "you shall love your neighbor as yourself" (Mark 12.29–31 and parallels).

JESUS AND THE "END TIME"

Jesus' proclamation of the kingdom, according to the gospels, seems to have located that kingdom both in the present and in the future (see main text). Many scholars would say that it was the future kingdom that dominated Jesus' own convictions—that he believed that the present age would shortly come to an end, to be replaced by another inaugurated by God, and that this belief conditioned all his ethical teaching. Jesus very likely did expect an imminent time when the kingdom would be fully realized. Some of his ethical demands reflect this, for example, his teaching about the conduct needed to face the Last Judgment with confidence (Matt. 25.31–46)—although the attribution of this passage to Jesus is widely questioned.

But Jesus was not primarily a prophet of the end of the present world, nor did he teach that such an expectation should be a motive for right conduct. He discouraged speculation—widespread at the time—about "signs" that were thought to herald the advent of the kingdom (Mark 8.11–12; Luke 17.20). In fact, he declared that the hour of its appearance was unknowable, even to him (Matt. 24.36; Mark 13.32), so that people should be ready for it whenever it might occur (Luke 12.39–40).

Jesus' words reveal his belief that he and his followers were already living in the "end time," an epoch quite different from all that had gone before. His demands on men and women are determined not so much by the expectation of the imminent end of the world but by faith in the God who has brought salvation in Jesus and in the divine will that Jesus proclaims. The kingdom is already present, waiting only for individuals to discover it and respond to it (Matt. 13.44–46).

THE TEACHINGS IN JOHN

Jesus' teaching in the Fourth Gospel is conveyed largely through six extended speeches (John 3, 4.7–26, 5.19–46, 6.25–65, 8.12–59, 10), in addition to his farewell addresses to the disciples (John 14–17). Not only is the form of the teaching in John very different from that which characterizes Matthew, Mark, and Luke, but its content is also distinctive. However, such divergences must not be exaggerated, as there are also passages in John in which the evangelist seems to develop themes and concepts that are present in the synoptic gospels. Either the author knew one or more of the other gospels directly or he relied on a shared corpus of traditions.

In the synoptics, Jesus' preaching centers on the kingdom of God and the moral demands that it makes on those who seek to enter it (see pp.280–83). However, in the discourses of the Fourth Gospel, Jesus primarily expounds the real significance of his own person and what is involved in recognizing his true nature. John uses the expression "the king-

Faith and belief in the Fourth Gospel

The whole of John's gospel is written with the purpose of awakening faith (John 20.31): the evangelist uses the verb "to believe" more often than all the other gospels put together. Belief consists not so much in accepting a body of teaching but in the conviction that Jesus himself is the uniquely authentic revelation of the Father, and the only way to him. Jesus' miracles are not only works of power but, above all, "signs" that indicate who Jesus really is (John 9.3).

This rock in the Franciscan church at Cana (Kafr Kanna) is said to mark the precise spot where Jesus performed his first miracle, according to John 2.1–11.

According to the evangelist's complex theology, the gift that believers receive from Jesus is eternal life (John 10.10). Believers are incorporated into the life and body of Christ, and this concept is expressed in various ways. For example, they are branches of the "true vine" (John 15.1ff.). Incorporation into the life of Jesus is attained by partaking of his flesh and blood (John 6.53–57).

After Jesus has left the earth, the "Spirit of truth" will enter his disciples (John 14.16–17). The truth is Jesus himself (John 14.6), and so the Spirit will lead the disciples to a complete knowledge of Jesus, and thus of God, and enable them to continue to glorify Jesus and to bear witness to him (John 14.26, 15.26–27, 16.13–15).

During Jesus' incarnate life the world is largely in the darkness of error (John 3.19). To believe in Jesus, the "light of the world" (John 8.12), is to turn from darkness. Believers are children of light (John 3.21, 12.35–36, 46).

Above all, believers in Christ form a community distinguished by mutual love. Jesus' only explicit commandment in the Fourth Gospel is that his followers are to love one another (John 13.34, 15.12). This love creates a perfect union (John 17.23), because it is a response both to Jesus' love for his disciples and the Father's love for the Son (John 17.26).

dom of God" only twice, and in the same context (John 3.3, 5), and even then he gives it his own particular interpretation. Elsewhere in the Fourth Gospel, Jesus speaks of "my kingdom" and accepts the title "king" (John 18.36–37). But there are indications in the synoptic gospels, too, that the kingdom is bound up with the person and work of Jesus (Luke 11.20), and he appears as its sovereign in some sayings that Matthew and Luke attribute to him (Matt. 16.19, 16.28, 25.31–46; Luke 22.29).

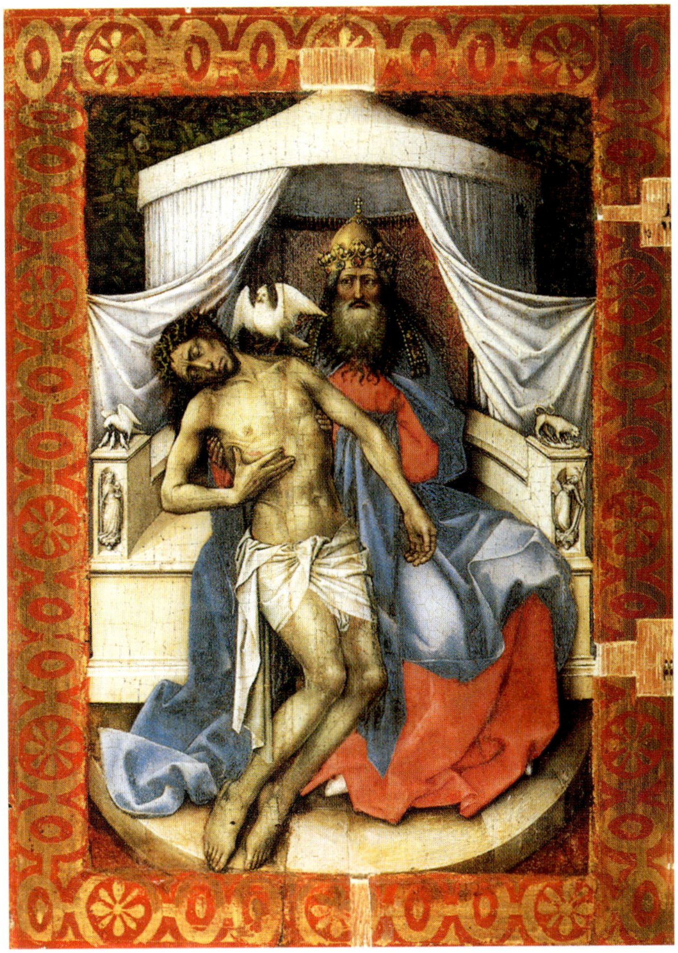

The Throne of God ("Mourning Trinity"), *by the Master of Flémalle (fl. 1410–1440). God the Father, enthroned in heaven, holds the body of the crucified Son; the Spirit hovers in the form of a dove. John's gospel contrasts the earthly world with the heavenly realm from which Jesus descended (John 3.13) to bring eternal life to believers (John 3.36, 6.47). His heavenly glory belonged to him before creation (John 17.5) and was visible throughout his earthly life (John 1.14). It was revealed in his miracles (John 2.11, 11.40) and was demonstrated supremely not so much in the Resurrection as in the Crucifixion (John 17.1).*

In the Fourth Gospel, Jesus predominantly refers to himself as the Son and to God as his Father. The synoptists also represent the Father-Son relationship as a central feature in their portrayal of Jesus (see pp.296–97), but the concept is carried much further in John. Here, Jesus is the Son of God in a unique sense: he is himself divine, and is described as such in the gospel's prologue (John 1.1–18), where the main themes of the work are outlined, and in the confession (avowal of faith) of the disciple Thomas (John 20.28), just before what was probably the original end of the gospel (John 20.31).

Jesus repeatedly says that God is unknown and unknowable to human beings (John 5.37, 6.46) but is revealed in his Son, and that this is the whole purpose of his ministry. For John, simply to see Jesus is to realize his identity as the Son of God and to receive his gift of eternal life (John 6.40) (see box, opposite), and the same reward is assured to those who attend to his words (John 5.24). Those who see the Son see also the Father (John 14.8–10); the Father can be approached only through the Son (John 14.6), because the two are in complete and perfect union (John 10.30, 14.11). The work of the Son is not his own and he does nothing of his own volition (John 5.19, 8.28–29), but he simply carries out the Father's will in utter filial obedience (John 5.30, 6.38). The Father entrusts the Son with total authority because he loves him (John 3.35). John's distinctive teaching about the Father and Son may represent the development of a tradition about Jesus that is traceable also in two of the synoptic gospels (Matt. 11.27; Luke 10.22).

It is hardly surprising that the title "Son of God" for Jesus is used more freely in John's gospel than in Matthew, Mark, and Luke. But John also brings out clearly the humanity of Jesus. Whatever is meant by the term "Son of Man" in the synoptic gospels (see pp.298–99), John gives this phrase a particular sense: it expresses the evangelist's distinctive doctrine about the person of Christ in which Jesus is perceived as the heavenly savior who descends from, and ascends to, the Father (John 3.13, 6.62).

ΘΕΟΡΡΥΤΩ ΑΙΜΑΤΙ ΚΕΝΩΘΕΝΤΙ ΔΕΣΠΟΤΑ ΧΡΙΣΤΕ

JESUS CHRIST: INTERPRETATIONS

Above: Christ Giving the Keys to St. Peter, *a mosaic (ca. 500 CE) in the Church of Santa Costanza, Rome. The scene is based on a disputed passage (Matt. 16.18–19), and the extent to which Jesus can be viewed as the founder of the Church remains the subject of debate (see pp.332–33).*
Opposite: *This chapel in the Church of the Holy Sepulchre, Jerusalem, is said to mark the site of the Crucifixion, an event that has been central to the interpretation of Jesus and his mission.*

Steps leading down to the ancient pool of Siloam in Jerusalem, where Jesus sent a blind man to be cured, according to the Fourth Gospel (John 9.7).

THE HEALER OF BODY AND SOUL

Jesus' acts of healing and exorcism (see pp.224–27) formed the major part of his activity and made the greatest impression upon those around him. In the first instance, Jesus' healings were a response to individual suffering—the gospels speak of him being moved with pity in the presence of afflicted persons. This reflects his particular concern for social outcasts, because those with physical disabilities, such as lepers, were often shunned by their fellow citizens.

The distinct structure of each healing story in the gospels (see p.224) represents the form in which such accounts were treasured and passed on in the early Church. To a certain extent they may be influenced by the standard ways in which the miracle cures of other contemporary healers, both Jewish and pagan, were described. Certainly, Jesus would have regarded himself in some respects as one among many charismatic healers and exorcists (see box, p.226) in Palestine, and the gospels indicate that some of his opponents viewed him in that light. He is recorded as recognizing the power of other miracle workers (Matt. 12.27; Mark 9.38–39; Luke 9.49–50, 11.19).

But Jesus was also significantly different from other wonder-working figures, because his healings had a great underlying purpose. When John the Baptist's disciples ask Jesus whether he is the "Coming One"—the Messiah—Jesus replies by referring to his healing miracles in words that are derived from messianic prophecies in the Hebrew Scriptures: "Go and tell John what you hear and see: the blind receive their sight, the lame walk, the lepers are cleansed, the deaf hear, the dead are raised, and the poor have good news brought to them" (Matt. 11.2–6 and Luke 7.18–23, citing Isa. 26.19, 35.5–6, 61.1). Much of what Jesus did, therefore, tended to prove that he was indeed the expected Messiah, and distinguished him from the Baptist, who performed no miracles (John 10.41).

Jesus saw his healings—especially the exorcisms—in an eschatological light. That is, they indicated that the present epoch was nearing its end and a new age was dawning as the kingdom of God was being realized (Matt. 10.7–8,12.28; Luke 10.9; 11.20). The healings and exorcisms were not simply remarkable cures of physical disorders but the means by which individual men and women received the kingdom, brought to them in the person of Jesus, with the consequence that their whole existence was transformed and the reign of God became a reality in their lives. For Jesus, faith in him as God's manifestation and the acceptance, through him, of divine forgiveness were the conditions required of a person who wished to be healed (see box, opposite).

HEALINGS
- Blindness (Mark 10.46–52 and parallels; Mark 8.22–26; Matt. 9.27–31)
- Leprosy (Mark 1.40–45 and parallels; Luke 17.11–19)
- Fever (Mark 1.29–31 and parallels)
- Hemorrhage (Mark 5.25–34 and parallels)
- Withered hand (Mark 3.1–6 and parallels)
- Deaf mute (Mark 7.31–37; Matt. 15.29–31)
- Paralysis (Matt. 8.5–13; Luke 7.1–10; Mark 2.1–12 and parallels)
- Crippled woman (Luke 13.10–17)
- Dropsy (Luke 14.1–6)
- Official's son (John 4.46–53)
- Crippled man (John 5.2–9)
- Blindness (John 9.1–12)

EXORCISMS
- Man at Capernaum (Mark 1.24–28; Luke 4.31–37)
- Gerasene/Gadarene/Gergesene demoniac (Mark 5.1–20 and parallels)
- Mute demoniac (Matt. 9.32–34)
- Blind mute demoniac (Matt. 12.22)
- Syro-Phoenician woman's daughter (Mark 7.24–30; Matt. 15.21–28)
- Boy with a spirit (Mark 9.14–29 and parallels)

It is remarkable that of all the numerous recorded wonder-workers of the time, none is credited with as many miracles as Jesus. Matthew, Mark, and Luke record a total of some thirteen incidents of healing and six cases of exorcism, covering a considerable range of physical and mental conditions that are summarized—with considerable medical awareness—by Matthew (Matt. 4.24). The narratives that describe the restoring to life of a dead person should perhaps be added to this list (Mark 5.35–43 and parallels; Luke 7.11–17; John 11.1–44; see box, p.225). There are also three accounts of healings in the Fourth Gospel, although John records no acts of exorcism.

Compared with the stories told of other healers, the gospel accounts of Jesus' cures are marked by sobriety and restraint. The evangelists report that Jesus appealed to those whom he healed to keep their cures secret (Matt. 9.30, 12.15–21; Mark 1.41, 5.43, 7.36; Luke 8.56), perhaps indicating that Jesus, unlike other wonder-workers, did not wish to claim personal credit for his miracles.

Healing, forgiveness, and faith

When Jesus says, in the account of the cure of the paralytic, "Your sins are forgiven" (Mark 2.5 and parallels), he simply means "You are healed." In the gospel accounts, this is regarded by the Jewish religious teachers as an extraordinary and blasphemous claim on his part, since only God could forgive sin. But Jesus would not necessarily have been presuming divine status. The idea that forgiveness of sin was a prerequisite of healing was familiar in Judaism. For example, a text from Qumran called *The Prayer of Nabonidus* relates how a Jewish exorcist cured a Babylonian monarch by forgiving his sins.

More notable is the fact that faith is several times said to be necessary for healing to take place. Either the actual sufferer must have faith, or those concerned for him or her, such as the centurion of Capernaum (Matt. 8.13; Luke 7.9–10) and the friends of the paralytic. At one level, "faith" means confidence in Jesus' ability to heal, but at another it probably means the recognition of Jesus' unique status and character. So the centurion has faith in Jesus' supreme authority, contrasted with the general lack of faith in Jesus among his fellow Jews. By the same token, lack of faith inhibits healing. Jesus is said to have been unable to perform more than a few cures in his own home town of Nazareth because of the unbelief of the inhabitants (Matt.13.58; Mark 6.5–6). This statement may well be reliable, since Christians are unlikely to have invented a tradition that showed Jesus as possessing limited powers.

Jesus Heals the Paralytic, *from the* Bible Moralisée *(French, ca. 1240). Jesus cured a paralyzed man with the words: "Stand up and take your mat [Matt. and Luke: 'bed'] and walk" (Mark 2.9, 2.11 and parallels; compare John 5.11–12).*

THE PROPHET

THE DISCIPLES AND JESUS THE PROPHET
Peter's confession at Caesarea Philippi (Mark 8.27–33 and parallels; see pp.236–37) sets Jesus on a higher plane than all other prophets. However, it seems that his disciples venerated him as a prophet for the most part because of his miracles and his teachings. Thus the two disciples on the road to Emmaus following the Crucifixion described Jesus as "a prophet mighty in deed and word before God and all the people" (Luke 24.19), and Peter in Acts speaks of him as one through whom God accomplished "deeds of power, wonders, and signs" (Acts 2.22).

The gospels attest that Jesus was widely regarded as a prophet. It was as a prophet that the crowds hailed him on his entry into Jerusalem (Matt. 21.11), and his miraculous healings led people to recognize his prophetic status (Luke 7.16; John 6.14, 9.17).

Such popular acceptance of Jesus as a prophet was something of which his opponents were very much aware (Matt. 21.46). They sought to disprove his entitlement to such a status by attempting to show that he lacked the superior knowledge or "second sight" that was believed to characterize a genuine prophet (Matt. 26.68; Luke 7.39, 22.64). Many biblical prophets had enjoyed this gift—for example, the blind Ahijah was able to penetrate the disguise of King Jeroboam's wife (1 Kings 14.1–18) when she asked him to foretell the future. In the gospels, Jesus demonstrates that he does indeed possess such abilities when he tells the Samaritan woman things about her past that he could not have known otherwise: she instantly acknowledges him as a prophet (John 4.16–19). Matthew, Mark, and Luke all record how, before he entered Jerusalem, Jesus told his disciples that there would be a donkey's colt for him to ride waiting on the Mount of Olives (Mark 11.2–4).

Although Jesus never explicitly called himself a prophet, the concept

The Transfiguration, *by Duccio di Buoninsegna (ca. 1260–1318). Jesus stands between the greatest prophets of Israel's past, Elijah and Moses, whom he both succeeds and transcends (see box, p.236). The disciples Peter, John, and James look on in awe. (Compare illustration on p.297)*

False prophets

There is evidence that the Jewish religious authorities regarded Jesus as a "false prophet" who was corrupting and disturbing the populace. He was accused before Pilate of "perverting" and "stirring up" the people (Luke 23.2, 5, 14), and of being an "impostor" and deceiver (Matt. 27.62–64). A similar charge of deception is leveled at him in the Fourth Gospel (John 7.12, 47). Such an allegation may well have constituted a formal indictment under the Jewish law, based on biblical descriptions of false prophets who entice the nation to apostasy or are otherwise unauthorized by God. Such individuals merit the death penalty (Deut. 13.1–5, 18.20).

Jesus himself is represented as denouncing false messiahs and prophets who would lead the people astray (Matt. 24.24; Mark 13.22). There was clearly widespread concern about such individuals at the time, and with good reason, because a whole string of them appeared in Palestine during the early years of the first century CE. They were a major contribution to the region's troubles: the Jewish historian Josephus mentions that a considerable number of self-styled "prophets" were in the service of those who led rebellions against the Romans. As well as insisting on the title "prophet," most of these figures foretold the deliverance of the Jewish nation by supernatural means, and claimed to perform prodigious miracles. Josephus labels them unequivocally as "impostors" and names two in particular, who are also referred to in the New Testament: Theudas, who was active sometime between 44 and 46 CE (Acts 5.36) and a man known as "the Egyptian," active between 51 and 60 CE, for whom Paul was mistaken (Acts 21.38).

These two men enjoyed mass support, and it is not surprising that Jesus' popularity among ordinary people should have led the educated classes to regard him as just one more prophetic troublemaker, who posed a threat to law and order and should therefore be suppressed. To a greater or lesser extent, the high priests, Sadducees, and Pharisees all stood for accommodation with the Roman authorities in the interests of avoiding the national catastrophe that rebellion would inevitably bring—and as indeed it finally did with the great Jewish revolt that began in 66 CE.

seems to have been an important element in his self-understanding. Twice, he is clearly referring to himself when he speaks of what a prophet may expect to experience and the ultimate fate awaiting him, (Mark 6.4 and parallels; Luke 13.33). When he rebukes Nazareth, he draws a parallel with the actions of the great prophets Elijah and Elisha (Luke 4.25–27), figures who had come to be revered in Judaism as the supreme wonder-workers (Sir. 48.1–14). Several of Jesus' miracles parallel those performed by these two figures, notably his revival of the widow's son at Nain (1 Kings 17.17–24; 2 Kings 4.18–38; see p.225) and the miraculous feedings of a great crowd with few provisions (2 Kings 4.42–44; see pp.228–29).

Jesus' awareness of himself as a prophet may well have been initiated and confirmed by his association with John the Baptist, another Elijah-like prophetic figure (Matt. 3.4; 2 Kings 1.8). John too had been acclaimed as a prophet (Matt. 11.7–9, 14.5, 21.26; Luke 7.25–26), but the gospels all emphasize that the Baptist's ministry was only preparing the way for the appearance of the even greater figure of Jesus, the final Judge and Savior. This idea probably derives from a passage of Deuteronomy in which God promises to raise up another prophet like Moses, through whom the deity will speak (Deut. 18.17–19). Peter cites these verses in reference to Jesus during his speech to the crowd on the Temple Mount (Acts 3.22–23).

MASTER, RABBI, LORD

On a number of occasions in the gospels Jesus is addressed by the Hebrew term *rabbi* or its Aramaic equivalent, *rabbouni* (Matt. 26.25, 26.49; Mark 9.5, 10.51, 11.21, 14.45; John 1.38, 1.49, 3.2, 4.31, 6.25, 9.2, 11.8, 20.16). The appearance of such non-Greek words in the gospels suggests that they represent a reliable tradition faithfully preserved by the evangelists. *Rabbi/rabbouni* literally means "my master," and in Jesus' time this was a reverential greeting to a person of authority—the term is also addressed to the Baptist (John 3.26). The Fourth Gospel explicitly translates *rabbi* and *rabbouni* as "teacher" (John 1.38, 20.16), and when Jesus is addressed as "teacher" (Greek *didaskale*, *epistata*) elsewhere in the gospels it probably represents one or other of these Semitic terms.

Like other teachers, Jesus taught in the synagogues, expounded on disputed points of the Jewish law, and gathered around him a body of students—this is the proper meaning of the word "disciple" (Latin *discipulus*, Greek *mathetes*, "pupil"). Commentators have often claimed that Jesus must therefore have been a "scribe," a highly trained and widely recognized interpreter of scripture (see p.162), and have seen evidence for this in the fact that his followers and others addressed him as *rabbi*. Similarly, occasional attempts by scholars to see Jesus as a dissident Pharisee have partly been based on the fact that he was called *rabbi*.

However, in Jesus' day, the term *rabbi* had not acquired the distinct sense it was later to possess of a religious teacher or scribe trained in the Pharisaic tradition (see sidebar, left). The great Pharisaic teachers who were Jesus' contemporaries or near-contemporaries—Hillel, Shammai, and others—were never called *rabbi*. There is also every reason to believe the

JUDAISM IN THE RABBINIC AGE

Soon after Jesus' time, the word *rabbi* was to become primarily a title, and one that genuinely and almost exclusively denoted a trained and officially authorized interpreter of the law. This was largely the consequence of the destruction of Jerusalem in 70 CE, when the Temple and its priesthood came to an end and most of the different sects and parties within the Jewish community (see pp.166–69) ceased to exist.

Only the Pharisees and their scribes (see p.162) survived, and it was they who subsequently were to determine the character of Judaism. They became the sole authoritative religious leaders and delivered binding judgments on a whole range of issues; their authority was accepted on account of their profound knowledge of scripture and their highly respected, and distinctive, tradition of interpretation.

The Pharisees established academies in which legal wisdom and expertise were passed on from one generation of scholars to the next. The interpretative work of successive scholars was eventually collected in the Mishnah (ca. 200 CE) and the Talmud (ca. 400–500 CE). In this period, commonly referred to as the rabbinic or Talmudic age, the word *rabbi* came to mean a person who had undergone extensive and exhaustive training in the Jewish law and emerged as a recognized teacher and spiritual guide. This status was acknowledged in a formal ordination rite that conferred on them the right and authority to teach.

Part of the North Palace at Masada, the stronghold of the Zealots during the 1st Jewish War (66–70 CE) and the last place to fall to the Romans (see p.337). The Zealots were one of several Jewish groups that disappeared after the war, leaving the Pharisees to lay the foundation of what is termed "rabbinic" Judaism, in which the word rabbi *came to refer to an authoritative teacher and interpreter of the Jewish law.*

Jesus the "lord"

According to the gospels, Jesus was regularly addressed as "lord" (Greek *kurios*, also transliterated *kyrios*). There is considerable debate over this word, particularly with regard to its use in Acts and the letters of Paul. Influenced by the fact that the title "lord" came to indicate Jesus' divinity, numerous authorities have concluded that the appearance of the term in the gospels must be attributable to the early Church. According to this theory, the title derives from after Jesus' lifetime: he never thought of himself as "lord" or was addressed as such either by his disciples or others.

However, in the time of Jesus, *kurios* and the corresponding Aramaic term *mar*—the phrase *maranatha* ("come, lord"; 1 Cor. 16.22) was probably an invocation current in the very early Church—both had a wide range of applications. Like *rabbi* and *rabbouni* (see main text), they basically designated a male figure of authority. *Kurios* was a common title for God, but it could also be used of the head of a family (Matt. 21.30), the owner of a large property (Matt. 13.27), or a ruler (Matt. 27.63). The vocative form *kurie*, used in direct address (as in another Christian invocation, *kyrie eleison*, "lord, have mercy"), could be little more than a polite way of addressing a man, and is often translated simply as "sir" (John 4.11, 5.7).

In the miracle stories, Jesus is addressed as "lord" by his disciples as an expression of awe at his supernatural power (Matt. 8.25, 14.28; Luke 5.8; John 21.7). *Mar* was similarly bestowed on other charismatic Jewish wonder-workers.

The Miraculous Draft of Fishes, *from the church of Sant' Angelo in Formis, Capua, Italy. In John 21.7, the disciples declare "It is the Lord!" in acknowledgment of Jesus' miraculous powers.*

In the gospels, Jesus only once describes himself as "lord" (John 13.13), but there is no evidence that he actively prevented others from doing so, and other passages suggest that the idea of his "lordship"—however defined—may well have formed part of his self-understanding. Like *rabbi* and *rabbouni*, both *kurios* and *mar* can have the sense of "authoritative teacher" (Luke 12.42, 18.6; John 6.68), and Jesus rebukes those who call him "lord" but are not prepared to obey his teachings (Matt. 7.21–23; Luke 6.46).

gospels' claim that Jesus' methods of teaching were in fact very different from those of the Pharisees. To begin with, there is no evidence that he ever received a scribal education, and contemporaries perceived his teaching to be different from that of the scribes (Matt. 7.29; Mark 1.22). The scribes themselves questioned Jesus' status as a recognized teacher (Mark 11.27–28 and parallels) and considered that his teaching betrayed a lack of formal training (John 7.15).

While *rabbi* eventually came to refer most often to religious scholars and teachers, in Jesus' day it had a wider application and could also be addressed to Jesus as, for example, a great miracle-worker (Mark 10.51; but note NRSV: "my teacher"). Jesus appears to have been happy to be called *rabbi*, and to have regarded the authority it denoted as applying to him in a unique sense. His followers are "not to be called *rabbi*," because there is only one teacher—the Messiah—and they are no more than his students (Matt. 23.8–10).

Ancient remains on the traditional site of Jesus' trial before the high priest, where he was accused of claiming to be the Messiah, according to the gospels.

Opposite: King David Enthroned, *a late 14th-century French tapestry. Over the centuries, a vast quantity of Christian art has been inspired by the dramatic story of David, the shepherd boy turned great king of Israel (ruled ca. 1000–ca. 965* BCE*) and traditional author of the Psalms. His revered status in Christianity derives above all from the belief that he was the ancestor, and prefigurement, of Christ (see sidebar, opposite). Thus David's defeat of the giant Goliath (1. Sam. 17.48–51) was held to prefigure Christ's triumph over Satan and his forces, and David's words about the shepherd who protects his flock (1 Sam 17.34–35) were seen as an annunciation of the coming of Jesus, the Good Shepherd.*

MESSIAH

It has been a central tenet of the Christian Church from its earliest beginnings that Jesus was the Messiah, or Christ. But nowhere in the gospels does Jesus state "I am the Messiah" or—publicly at least—accept the title. For this reason, commentators have often questioned whether the concept of messiahship formed part of his self-understanding at all, or whether it derives instead from the faith of the early Church.

According to Luke, Jesus perceived himself as one anointed by the Spirit, as set out in Isaiah 61.1–2, which Jesus reads out in the synagogue at Nazareth (Luke 4.16–21). Evidence from Qumran shows that in Jesus' day these verses were strongly associated with the coming Messiah; by using the passage at all, therefore, Jesus was effectively making a messianic claim. In Matthew, Jesus also alludes to Isaiah (Matt. 11.4–6), and the gospel explicitly refers to his deeds as those of the Messiah (Matt. 11.2).

However, Jesus spoke about only one aspect of popular messianic expectation, namely the reign of justice and renewal that the Messiah would bring (Matt. 19.28; Luke 22.30). The idea of the Messiah as a royal and military figure (see sidebar, opposite) are entirely absent from his words, but his followers do appear to have thought of him in such terms (Acts 1.6), and his opponents call him "Messiah" sarcastically, evidently believing that Jesus had falsely claimed that status (Matt. 26.68; Mark 15.32 and parallels).

Jesus seems never to have explicitly rejected the title Messiah, perhaps because people might have understood this as a denial that he was *any* sort of redeemer. But he did not promote its use and sought to discourage most of the expectations associated with it. Thus demons who recognize Jesus as the Messiah (Luke 4.41) are forbidden to speak, and a request for a place of honor in Jesus' "kingdom" (Matt. 20.20–23; Mark 10.35–40) elicits Jesus' refusal of the kingly role (Mark 10.41–45 and parallels). When some people ask him directly if he is the Messiah, Jesus does not give a direct affirmation but points to the testimony of his miracles (John 10.24–25). When Peter confesses his belief that Jesus is the Messiah (see pp.236–37), Jesus acquiesces, but forbids his followers to proclaim him as such. This is because—as Luke, at least, suggests (Luke 9.21–22)—Jesus' destiny as Messiah was not to lead Israel in kingly triumph, but to undergo suffering and death. Peter cannot accept this and receives a severe rebuke.

How Jesus perceived his messiahship perhaps emerges best from the accounts of his trials (see pp.248–51). In Matthew and Luke, Jesus gives an ambiguous answer to the question of whether he is the Messiah (Matt. 26.64; Luke 22.67–70). This is perhaps more likely to be authentic than Mark, who gives Jesus' reply as "I am" (Mark 14.62), because for Jesus either to admit or deny his messiahship outright would be to lay himself open to serious consequences—the wrath of the authorities or rejection by many followers. When Pilate asks if he is the "King of the Jews"—the messianic claim that was of most concern to a Gentile ruler—Jesus' response is again equivocal (Mark 15.2 and parallels).

The Fourth Gospel represents Jesus as explicitly claiming the messianic title on at least one occasion (John 4.25–26), albeit in a private conversation. In John's account of the trial, Jesus once more equivocates about accepting the designation "king." He acknowledges that he has a kingdom, but it is "not from this world"—it was not to be achieved by force, as most Jews would have expected of the Messiah, and as Pilate might have feared (John 18.33–37).

Perhaps the soundest conclusion is that Jesus regarded himself as the fulfillment of the general hope among Jews for a redeemer who would herald a new epoch (see sidebar, right). But he was aware that his own understanding of his person and mission did not truly correspond to any of the concepts of the Messiah then current, and he avoided the public use of the title "Messiah" because of its nationalistic and revolutionary implications. In the volatile political climate of Roman Palestine, anyone suspected of claiming to be the Messiah was unlikely to survive long, and so it proved with Jesus: the inscription affixed to his cross, which all four gospels record, makes it clear that he was crucified as a dangerous messianic revolutionary (see sidebar, p.337).

THE SON OF DAVID

In the first century CE there was a general expectation among Jews that God would shortly intervene to end the present age and usher in a new world of perfect righteousness. Some believed that God would act directly, others that he would send an intermediary: his "Anointed One," or Messiah (Hebrew *Mashiach*, Greek *Christos*). "Messiah" was a title given in the Hebrew Bible to Israelite rulers of King David's dynasty. The Savior was thus seen as a king, a "son" (descendant) of David, who would overcome Israel's oppressors.

The gospel genealogies of Jesus (see pp.194–95) presuppose an early belief that Joseph came from Bethlehem, David's city, and was of David's line. (Matt. 1.20; Luke 1.27, 2.4; Rom. 1.3). Jesus and his close disciples do not use the title Son of David, but others hail him as such (as at Mark 10.46–52 and parallels; Matt. 21.9).

At one point, Jesus apparently denies that the Messiah would be a Son of David (Mark 12.35–37 and parallels), perhaps to counter hopes that the Savior would be a military figure who would end Roman rule.

SON OF GOD

THE "SON" AS MIRACLE-WORKER
In the gospels, the phrase "Son of God" is also used to mark Jesus out as a worker of miracles, and there is evidence that the title was applied to other charismatic Galilean wonder-workers of the time. When Jesus exorcizes demons, they address him as Son of God in recognition of his miraculous healing power (Mark 3.11, 5.7 and parallels). Satan, too, expected the Son of God to be able to perform miracles, as the Temptation shows (see pp.218–19).

The one occasion on which Jesus' followers address him directly by the title is in the context of a miracle (Matt. 14.33), and the onlookers at Golgotha challenge him to prove his status as Son of God by freeing himself from the cross (Matt. 27.39–40, 42–43). The expression of awe uttered by the centurion at the Crucifixion ("Truly this man was God's Son!") is provoked by the marvels that accompanied Jesus' death (Matt. 27.51–54).

To profess that Jesus is the Son of God has been central to Christian faith from the earliest times, as the New Testament shows. Nowhere in the gospels is the title found on Jesus' own lips, but his habit of addressing God as his Father (see pp.276–77) implies not only that he saw himself as *a* son of God but that he perceived himself to be God's son in a special sense.

Twice in the gospels Jesus speaks of himself as "the Son" in reference to God as his Father, but scholars often debate whether these instances can be regarded as authentic sayings of Jesus. In the first passage, Jesus states that "neither the angels of heaven nor the Son" know when "the end" will come, but only the Father (Mark 13.32; Matt. 24.36). These may be genuine words of Jesus, since early Christians are unlikely to have created such an admission of ignorance on Jesus' part, placing himself on a lower footing than God. The phrase "nor the Son" is omitted in many early manuscripts of Matthew, which tends to support this idea.

In the second passage, Jesus says that the Son alone knows the Father and the Father alone knows the Son (Matt. 11.27; Luke 10.22). Although it is likely that the words as we have them are those of the early Church, they may well be based on an authentic expression by which Jesus affirmed his special intimacy with his heavenly Father.

The parable of the Wicked Tenants (Mark 12.1–11 and parallels) reaches its climax when the absentee landowner sends his son to collect his

The messianic son

The term "Son of God" is closely associated with the title "Messiah" (Matt.16.16, 26.63; Mark 14.61; Luke 22.67–70). In the Hebrew Scriptures the reigning monarch was called God's son (Ps. 2.7; 2 Sam. 7.14), but by the time of Jesus, such references were understood to refer to a future descendant of King David: the Messiah (see pp.294–95).

God's declaration in Psalm 2.7 ("You are my Son, today I have begotten you") was particularly significant for the first Christians (Acts 13.33), and Mark and Luke echo these words in their accounts of Jesus' baptism (Mark 1.11; Luke 3.22). It served as a formula whereby God adopted a person as his son and is also reflected in Luke's Nativity narrative, where the future child is to be a royal figure, who will be designated by God as "the Son of the Most High" and "Son of God," and will receive "the throne of his ancestor David" (Luke 1.32, 35).

The title "Son of God" is particularly characteristic of the Fourth Gospel, where it is also linked with the kingship of Israel and other messianic concepts (John 1.49, 11.27, 20.31). But the evangelist also carries the idea much further. Jesus' divine sonship is wholly unique (John 1.18). He is a preexistent entity who has always been with the Father (John 13.3), unknown to the world until revealed in his incarnation (John 6.42). This notion is comparable with some contemporary Jewish beliefs that the Messiah would remain hidden in heaven until he was revealed on earth.

For John, Jesus is literally God's son, "equal to God" (John 5.18), sharing his divinity and exercising full divine authority (John 3.35–36, 17.10). Jesus expresses it unequivocally: "The Father and I are one" (John 10.30).

The Transfiguration, *a 14th-century Russian icon (Novgorod School). Eastern depictions of this momentous event (compare the Western version on p.290) typically show Jesus within a* mandorla *(almond-shape) representing the "bright cloud" of heavenly radiance from which the divine voice declared "This is my Son, the Beloved!" The three disciples are shown physically hurled to the ground by the sight. The spearhead-shaped figure represents the mountain peak, but its three points tapering to one also symbolize the three-in-one Godhead of Father, Son, and Holy Spirit.*

dues from the tenants of his vineyard. All commentators agree that the parable is an allegory, and that the landowner represents God, the vineyard Israel, and the son Jesus. Jesus here speaks of himself as God's son in a unique sense. Jesus' followers are to become sons of God (Matt. 5.45; Luke 6.35), but they enjoy this status because they follow the teaching and example of Jesus: he is the first and true Son of God. The Hebrew Scriptures frequently describe the people of Israel as God's sons (Exod. 4.22; Jer. 31.20), and in later writings the righteous Israelite is specifically God's son (Sir. 4.10; Wisd. of Solomon 2.17–18).

Perhaps most significant for Jesus' self-understanding was the occasion of his baptism (see pp.216–17), when he was endowed with the Spirit, and the heavenly voice proclaimed him, for the first time, "My Son, the Beloved." This expression clearly implies uniqueness. In this way, according to the gospels, Jesus' real character and vocation were revealed to him—to be immediately tested and confirmed by his victorious encounter with the devil in the wilderness (see pp.218–19).

OFFSPRING OF THE DIVINE

It has been frequently observed that when people address Jesus as Son of God in the gospels, the title does not necessarily imply divinity in the sense that it was later understood in Christian theology, of a complete sharing in God's nature. In the Judaism of the first century CE, the concept of divinity was fairly broad and any heavenly supernatural being could be considered a "Son of God." For example, in the Hebrew Scriptures and other Jewish writings, "Son of God" can refer to angels and other celestial beings (Gen. 6.2, 4; Ps. 29.1; Job 1.6), and it is not impossible that Jesus was viewed in this light.

At his Transfiguration, when the voice of God proclaims Jesus "my son," he is transformed into a heavenly being, like Moses and Elijah (see pp.236–37, 340–41). It is notable that it was the exorcized demons, themselves supernatural entities, along with their leader Satan, who recognized the true nature of Jesus as Son of God (see sidebar on opposite page).

SON OF MAN

THE "SON OF MAN" BEFORE JESUS
It has been claimed that the concept of a messianic figure known as the "Son of Man" existed in Judaism before the time of Jesus. Daniel 7.13–14 speaks of "one like a son of man," who comes on clouds and receives universal dominion. Later rabbis certainly identified this figure with the Messiah, but there is no evidence that they did so as early as Jesus' day—nor did they use the term "Son of Man" as a distinct messianic designation.

Outside the Bible, the apocryphal book 2 Esdras has a passage obviously dependent on Daniel 7.13 that speaks of "something like the figure of a man" rising from the sea and flying on the clouds (2 Esd. 13.3). This being is subsequently identified with the Messiah, and no doubt this represents the beginning of rabbinic interpretation of the figure in Daniel—2 Esdras may date from as late as ca. 100 CE. But, again, "something like the figure of a man" does not in itself specifically denote the Messiah.

It is the writings known as the books of Enoch that have attracted most attention from New Testament scholars. Within 1 Enoch is a section called the "Similitudes of Enoch" that refers some sixteen times to a "Son of Man" figure as a divine messianic being. Again, however, this passage also derives from Daniel 7, using the same imagery, and cannot be taken to prove that "Son of Man" was a distinct concept or title. Recent evidence suggests that the Similitudes, too, may be very much later than Jesus' lifetime.

The expression "Son of Man" occurs more than sixty times in the gospels, yet it is found only three times elsewhere in the New Testament (Acts 7.56; Rev. 1.13, 14.14) and is used only in sayings attributed to Jesus. Debate over the significance of the phrase has been, and continues to be, very wide-ranging. The Greek term used by the evangelists does not sound idiomatic and almost all scholars now agree that it represents a literal translation of an original Aramaic phrase. The Semitic background leaves no doubt that "Son of Man" means primarily "the man" or "a man," and it can also be an indefinite pronoun, the equivalent of "one" as in "one does."

It has also been proposed that "the son of man" was employed simply as a circumlocution for "I." There are some complicated linguistic problems connected with this last proposal, but it appears to be gaining acceptance among New Testament scholarship. The Aramaic evidence suggests that a speaker might say "the son of man" instead of "I" out of modesty or

Banias, ancient Caesarea Philippi, where Peter acknowledged Jesus as Messiah (see pp.236–37). The gospel accounts of this episode provide strong evidence that Jesus used the Aramaic phrase "Son of Man" as a way of referring to himself. In Matthew, Jesus asks: "Who do people say that the Son of Man is?" but Mark and Luke give the question as: "Who do people say I am?" (Matt. 16.13; Mark 8.27; Luke 9.18).

Jesus and the apocalyptic "Son"

Even if the term "Son of Man" represents a colloquial idiom used instead of "I" (see main text), the question still arises as to whether, in using it, Jesus saw the phrase as holding a special significance. It was the description that he used most commonly of himself, which suggests that this was so.

It has often been asserted that the concept of the "Son of Man" as an apocalyptic figure already existed in some Jewish circles (see sidebar, opposite) and that Jesus employed the expression as a definite messianic title. Whether this is true or not, it is quite likely that Jesus did envisage both a present and a future role for himself, and that his view of his future role was influenced by the "Son of Man" figure in Daniel 7.13. The early Church may be responsible for the actual wording of Jesus' references to this passage—whether explicit (Mark 13.26, 14.62 and parallels) or implicit (Mark 8.38 and parallels)—but they may genuinely be founded on Jesus' own view of himself as the coming divine agent in the final Judgment. This is analogous to his teaching of the kingdom of God (see pp.280–81) as both a present and a future reality.

A fresco in the cathedral of Anagni, Italy. The central winged being derives principally from the vision of Ezekiel (Ezek. 1.1–14; compare Rev. 4.8), which may have influenced Jesus' understanding of himself as Son of Man.

It is also possible that Jesus was aware of God's repeated use of "son of man" (Hebrew *ben adam*; NRSV: "mortal") to address the prophet Ezekiel in the Hebrew Scriptures, and that the phrase therefore contributed to Jesus' awareness of his own role as a prophet. There is considerable evidence, particularly in John's gospel, that the book of Ezekiel influenced the New Testament.

reserve, and this could well be the case with Jesus, who often appears to have been cautious about making claims for himself, as he was with the title Messiah (see pp.294–95). "Son of man" could also be employed to soften an unacceptable or unpalatable statement. So when Jesus foretells his death to his disciples, he almost always refers to the fate of the "Son of Man" (Mark 8.31, 9.31, 10.33 and parallels; Luke 9.22).

According to one relatively recent hypothesis, "Son of Man" occurs in three distinct contexts: Jesus' activity and teaching during his ministry; statements concerning his death and resurrection; and passages dealing with his ascension and apocalyptic return. This categorization, however illuminating, has not convinced everyone. Some scholars continue to doubt whether Jesus himself ever employed the expression "Son of Man," while others view only the apocalyptic utterances as genuine: Jesus proclaimed the coming of the "Son of Man" (see box, above), but did not necessarily identify himself with this figure—this identification was only made later by his followers.

However, the fact that "Son of Man" is confined to the gospels and to the lips of Jesus, that it represents an original term in his own language, and that it rapidly fell out of use in Christian circles, tells against the view that it was a theological concept that developed in the early Church.

Opposite and below: The Good Shepherd, *an early 3rd-century fresco from the crypt of Lucina in the cemetery of Callixtus, Rome; and an ivory statuette, also from Rome, of ca. 300* CE. *One of the most popular early Christian motifs was that of Jesus as a shepherd tending his flock, a frequent image in the New Testament (for example, John 10.14–17; Heb. 13.20). The iconography of the Good Shepherd was adopted virtually unaltered from the common Classical images of the god Hermes (the Roman Mercury) carrying a ram in his role as the protector of flocks, and of the mythical figure of Orpheus charming the animals.*

EARLY CHRISTIAN ART

The earliest period of Christian art is commonly defined as the time from the mid-first century until the emperor Constantine's Edict of Toleration of 313 CE, which ended the persecution of Christians in the Roman empire. The most significant surviving examples of this period date mainly from the third century and come from the catacombs (underground cemeteries) of Rome and the remains of a Christian "house church" (a private house used for Christian worship) at the Greco-Roman city of Dura-Europos on the Euphrates in present-day Syria. Strikingly similar themes and images are found in both these places, suggesting that by this time there was already a common Christian artistic tradition throughout the empire.

Before Constantine's edict, Christianity's nascent artistic expression was largely an adaptation of existing models. It drew in large measure on the motifs and conventions of Greco-Roman art, which furnished Christians with numerous templates—many of them clearly pagan in origin—for the representation of Jesus. Third-century mosaics in a small mausoleum under St. Peter's basilica in Rome include, as well as a depiction of Jonah and the Whale—interpreted at one level as a metaphor of the resurrected Christ—the unmistakable figure of the Classical sun god Helios (or Apollo) riding in his chariot in the sky. This can perhaps be understood as representing Jesus in the terms of the biblical prophecy of the coming Messiah: "For you who revere my name, the sun of righteousness shall rise, with healing in its wings" (Mal. 4.2).

The other main influence on Christian artistic expression at this time was probably Jewish synagogue art. Early Christian decoration is dominated by motifs from the Hebrew Bible, some of which, such as Jonah and the Whale, were considered to prefigure aspects of Jesus.

Christian artists went on to develop representations of incidents from Jesus' life, of which some half-dozen occur frequently in the oldest catacombs: the visit of the Magi; the Baptism; the healings of the paralytic and the woman with a hemorrhage; the Samaritan woman at the well; and the raising of Lazarus. In addition, the Dura-Europos church has scenes of Christ walking on water and the visit of the three women to the tomb.

The earliest representations of Jesus himself are in the catacomb of Priscilla, dating from the mid-second century, and at Dura-Europos, from the first part of the third century. In these and other early depictions, Jesus appears as an ordinary human being, without any distinguishing marks, young, beardless, and shorthaired, wearing the regular dress of the time. Perhaps most striking in what has been preserved of early Christian art is the absence of any depiction of the Nativity or the Crucifixion, so central to the Christian art of all later centuries (see pp.302–03, 314–19).

THE NATIVITY

The elements of the Nativity scene came together gradually in the centuries following Constantine's Edict of Toleration. An early image of the swaddled baby lying in the manger between Mary and Joseph appears on a gospel-book cover (402 CE) in Milan cathedral. The ox and ass were also shown from the start, in fulfillment of Isaiah's words: "The ox knows its owner, and the donkey its master's crib" (Isa. 1.3). They bear witness that the child is no ordinary baby but the divine manifested in human form.

Apart from the ox and ass, the main features that appear in depictions of the Nativity in both the Eastern and Western Churches derive from the gospels of Matthew and Luke (see pp.196–207). The Magi (Matt. 2.1–12) were a separate motif in early Christian art, but by ca. 600 CE they appear

All the elements of the classic Orthodox depiction of the Nativity are present in this 16th-century Russian icon, for example the setting of a cave rather than a stable. The three kings are shown traveling and arriving at the scene. The foreground is dominated by two apocryphal motifs that are not derived from the canonical gospels: the Devil prompting Joseph (left) to disbelieve in the Virgin Birth; and midwives preparing a bath for the Child.

with the angels and shepherds (Luke 2.8–20) on *ampullae*, small flasks for holy oil, made in the Holy Land as souvenirs for Christian pilgrims. Magi, angels, and shepherds all became regular elements in Nativity scenes.

The Eastern Church took other Nativity motifs not only from the canonical gospels but also from apocryphal gospels and other writings. For example, following the Protevangelium of James (see p.190), Orthodox icons set the Nativity in a cave. The black cave symbolizes the darkness of the material world that the Godhead has entered; it also foreshadows Christ's tomb, while the swaddling clothes prefigure his shroud.

In the medieval West, texts focusing on the mystery of the God taking human form encouraged the naturalistic depiction of the baby. The Revelations of a fourteenth-century visionary, St. Bridget of Sweden, greatly influenced the depiction of the Christ Child in late medieval and Renaissance art. Among her visions was one of the painless birth of Jesus, in a sudden blaze of light, to Mary as she prayed.

The Adoration of the Shepherds, *by Georges de la Tour (1593–1652). A sturdy ordinariness characterizes Mary, Joseph, and their rustic visitors, who are dramatically lit, apparently by Joseph's candle. But the scene recalls the words of St. Bridget of Sweden, who saw a vision of the Christ Child "surrounded by a light so brilliant that it completely eclipsed Joseph's candle." The shepherds have brought the gift of a lamb, which prefigures Jesus' sacrificial role as the paschal lamb (see pp.242–43).*

MADONNA AND CHILD

The composite image of the infant Jesus with his mother, the Virgin Mary, forms a particularly rich vein in Christian iconography. The Virgin's central significance in Christian theology was defined at the ecclesiastical council of Ephesus in 431 CE, which formally bestowed on her the title *Theotokos* (Greek, "God-Bearing"), an epithet still employed in the Greek Orthodox Church. Artistic conventions then had to be devised for depicting Jesus' mother in a manner befitting her awesome role in mediating the incarnation of God on earth.

To begin with, the imperial imagery of the Byzantine court at Constantinople inspired images of Mary seated on a jeweled throne in the manner of an empress, with Jesus posed formally on her lap. Although Jesus is represented as the size of a baby in relation to his mother, his features are those of an older child, and his future role as lawgiver is symbolized by the scroll that he holds in his left hand. This tradition persisted into the

The date of this Russian icon of the Virgin and Child is uncertain, but the upright, full-face pose of the Child and the inclined head of the Virgin are hallmarks of the widespread Russian icon type known as "The Mother of God of Kazan" *(see p.306).*

Opposite: Madonna and Child, *by William Dyce (1806–64), a Scottish artist whose profound reverence for 14th- and 15th-century Italian sacred art anticipated that of the English Pre-Raphaelites. In this simple but refined portrait, the Virgin's book—a traditional symbol of wisdom—and the infant Jesus' extraordinarily intent concentration upon it, are the only hints that the subjects are more than just a young woman and her child.*

Opposite: Madonna of the Rose Bower, *by Martin Schongauer (1440–91). The predominance of red in this richly symbolic work refers to Christ's sacrifice and, as a royal color, to Mary's role as Queen of Heaven. The roses denote her as the sinless "rose without thorns."*

Below: Virgin and Child, *a 12th-century French silver-gilt statuette. Jesus raises his right hand to command attention and in his left holds the new law, inscribed with the Greek contraction of his name (IHS XRS, more correctly IHC XPC).*

Romanesque art of the early medieval West. The Eastern Church went on to develop a range of conventions for depicting the Virgin and Child. Some icons show Mary standing full-length, but the majority show her half-length, or just head and shoulders, with the Child in various hieratic (priestly) poses. Usually, Jesus has the domed head of an infant, but his face and posture are those of an adult.

Some individual icon paintings gave their names to whole classes of image. Of these, the most famous was the Virgin Hodegetria, named for the Hodegetrion church at Constantinople (Istanbul) where it was kept, and also known as "The Virgin who shows the way." In this painting and those based upon it, the Virgin holds the Child on her left arm and gestures towards him with her right hand; Jesus sits upright holding a scroll in his left hand and blessing with his right. Another widespread image is "The Mother of God of Kazan" (see illustration, p.304), which is based on a 16th-century Russian original at Kazan on the Volga River that was believed to possess miraculous properties.

In the West, the depiction of Jesus and Mary is commonly known as the Madonna (Italian, "My Lady") and Child. The holy mother and her baby are shown either by themselves or with saints, a type known by the Italian term *sacra conversazione* ("holy gathering"). Early medieval Madonnas retain much of the formality of their Byzantine counterparts, but from the fourteenth century onward the natural human bond was increasingly emphasized; Jesus and his mother became engrossed in each other, the child no longer engaging with the world through his priestly gesture of blessing.

Another ancient image is of Jesus being breastfed by Mary, a type known as the Virgo Lactans (Latin, "Suckling Virgin"). This is believed to derive ultimately from ancient Egyptian depictions of the goddess Isis—whose cult was widespread in the ancient Greco-Roman world—suckling her son, the god Horus. The Virgo Lactans won a new lease of life in the later medieval period, partly as a result of the many places of Christian pilgrimage that claimed to possess a phial of the Virgin's milk, among them Eton and Walsingham in England. The Virgo Lactans is sometimes combined with the image known as "The Virgin of Humility": the Virgin seated on the ground with the infant Jesus on her lap.

Artists established the sacred character of the Virgin and Child through their portrayal of the objects associated with them, such as the scroll or book held by Jesus, which represents the new law that he brings. The surroundings may also be of significance. A favorite late medieval type was the Virgin of the Rose Garden, in which the *hortus conclusus* (Latin, "enclosed garden": see Song of Solomon 4.12) symbolizes Mary's virginity.

SCENES FROM CHILDHOOD

"And the child grew, and became strong, filled with wisdom" (Luke 2.40). Beyond this simple statement the gospels have virtually nothing to say of Jesus' childhood and youth at Nazareth. The only incident narrated is the visit to the Temple at Jerusalem when he was twelve (Luke 2.42–50: see box, p.208). Thus, artists seeking to depict Jesus' early years have eagerly seized upon the smallest details, such as the reference to the adult Jesus as a carpenter (Mark 6.3) and the son of a carpenter (Matt. 13.55), which inspired them to portray Jesus as an apprentice in Joseph's workshop.

Apocryphal texts attempted to make good the silence of the canonical gospels, and the infancy gospels recount a sequence of wonders performed by the boy Jesus. Artists depicted many of these apocryphal acts, although

Our Savior Subject to his Parents at Nazareth, *by John Rogers Herbert (1810–90). Luke records that Jesus went missing on a visit to Jerusalem, but after he had been found, in the Temple, he returned home with Mary and Joseph and thereafter "was subject [obedient] unto them" (Luke 2.51, KJV). He goes quietly about his work, but Mary's intent gaze recalls the rest of Luke's verse: "His mother kept all these sayings [Jesus' momentous words in the Temple] in her heart" (KJV). The heap of wood on the ground prefigures the shape of the Cross.*

The illuminator of this late 15th-century Spanish manuscript presents the Holy Family as a model of domestic industry, paying detailed attention to Joseph's tools in his carpentry workshop and Mary's needlework. The bird may allude to an apocryphal story, recounted in the Infancy Gospel of Thomas, in which the 5-year-old Jesus modeled sparrows from clay and brought them to life.

some of them are hardly attractive, such as legends that he caused children to drop dead because they had angered him. Renaissance painters developed a type of group portrait known as the Holy Kinship, comprising the Holy Family (Mary, Joseph, and Jesus) with all or some of their close relatives, such as Elizabeth and the infant John the Baptist, as well as Anne (Anna) and Joachim, the—entirely legendary—parents of Mary.

The early nineteenth-century Nazarenes, a group of mainly German painters based in Rome, treated the Holy Family and other sacred themes in a naturalistic way that influenced the English Pre-Raphaelites. The portrayal of Jesus and his parents as, for example, a simple working family outraged those who expected an exalted academic style for religious subjects.

THE MINISTRY

Scenes from the ministry of Jesus were part of Christian art from its beginnings. Healing miracles were among the earliest subjects of catacomb art, and appeared with episodes such as the wedding at Cana and the multiplication of the loaves and fishes on fourth-century sarcophagi.

In the later Roman period, the decoration of churches assumed a more or less standard pattern, with certain images appearing at particular places within the building. Sequences of scenes from Jesus' ministry are found in mosaic or fresco on the walls of the nave or narthex (porch), such as the thirteen small mosaics above the windows on the north wall of the church of Sant' Apollinare Nuovo, Ravenna, Italy, which date from 500–520 CE. In these, Jesus has a halo inscribed with a cross, which was first depicted about a century earlier; it persisted in Byzantine, Romanesque, and Gothic art as the form of halo particularly associated with Christ. Also in the fifth

The Healing of the Man Born Blind *(John 9.1–7), part of the 11th-century Romanesque fresco cycle in the Basilica of Sant' Angelo in Formis at Capua, southern Italy. Jesus smears clay mixed with spittle on the blind beggar's eyes. Jesus' instruction, "Go, wash in the pool of Siloam," led to this miracle being interpreted as an allegory of baptism.*

century, Jesus was portrayed for the first time with shoulder-length hair and beard, an image that eventually superseded the Roman-style, clean shaven Jesus of late antiquity.

The Calling of Peter and Andrew, *an early 6th-century mosaic in the church of Sant' Apollinare Nuovo, Ravenna. Jesus summons the brothers from their task of fishing to be his disciples and "fish for people" (Matt. 4.18–20). At this period Jesus was still often represented beardless, and his formal stance and gesture recall the traditional pose of teachers or orators in Greco-Roman art.*

The healing miracles retained perennial appeal, but other events from the ministry that were charged with symbolic significance were also frequently depicted. The turning of water into wine at Cana and the miraculous feedings could, for instance, be seen as foreshadowing the Christian Eucharist. The two scenes are sometimes juxtaposed in such a way as to make the connection plain, as in the fourteenth-century mosaics in the church of St. Savior in Chora (Kariye Camii mosque) in Istanbul, where they face each other across the entrance to the church.

In his *Painter's Manual*, which codified earlier iconographical traditions and is still relevant to Orthodox iconographers today, the early eighteenth-century Greek monk Dionysius of Fourna gave minute instructions on how to paint several dozen episodes from Jesus' ministry. In practice, in both the

The Raising of Lazarus, *a northern Greek icon of 1611. Jesus, striding forward to perform the miracle, dominates the crowded scene. Lazarus' vertical rock tomb is a convention of Orthodox icons, as are the suppliant figures of his sisters Martha and Mary. Behind Jesus, the disciples, led by the white-bearded Peter, gesture their amazement, as does the crowd in the background, one of whom covers his face against the expected stench from the tomb.*

Eastern and Western Churches, only a few of these scenes appear regularly. Along with the miracles, the most favored episodes have a strong narrative and symbolic content, such as the summoning of the apostles; the Samaritan woman at the well; Jesus walking on the water and stilling the storm; and Jesus with the woman taken in adultery. These also appear in other media and as individual panel paintings.

The raising of Lazarus (John 11.1–44), Jesus' final miracle before the Passion, combines strong narrative with potent symbolism. It is a drama of suspense and emotional power, which foreshadows Jesus' own resurrection. Its frequency in Orthodox iconography is due to the commemoration of the miracle as one of the twelve great feasts of the Orthodox Church (Lazarus Saturday, the eve of Palm Sunday). The icon depicting the scene is displayed on the iconostasis, the "icon screen" that divides the nave from the sanctuary in an Orthodox church. It appears in the upper level of the screen, which is devoted to festival icons.

Opposite: The Raising of Lazarus, *by Juan de Flandes (ca. 1465–1519), part of an altarpiece for the church of San Lazaro in Palencia, Spain. The disciples, crowd, and Lazarus' sister Mary all feature in this intensely emotional composition. But the astonished gaze of Lazarus directs the viewer's attention to the true focal point of the picture: the calm, undramatic figure of Jesus.*

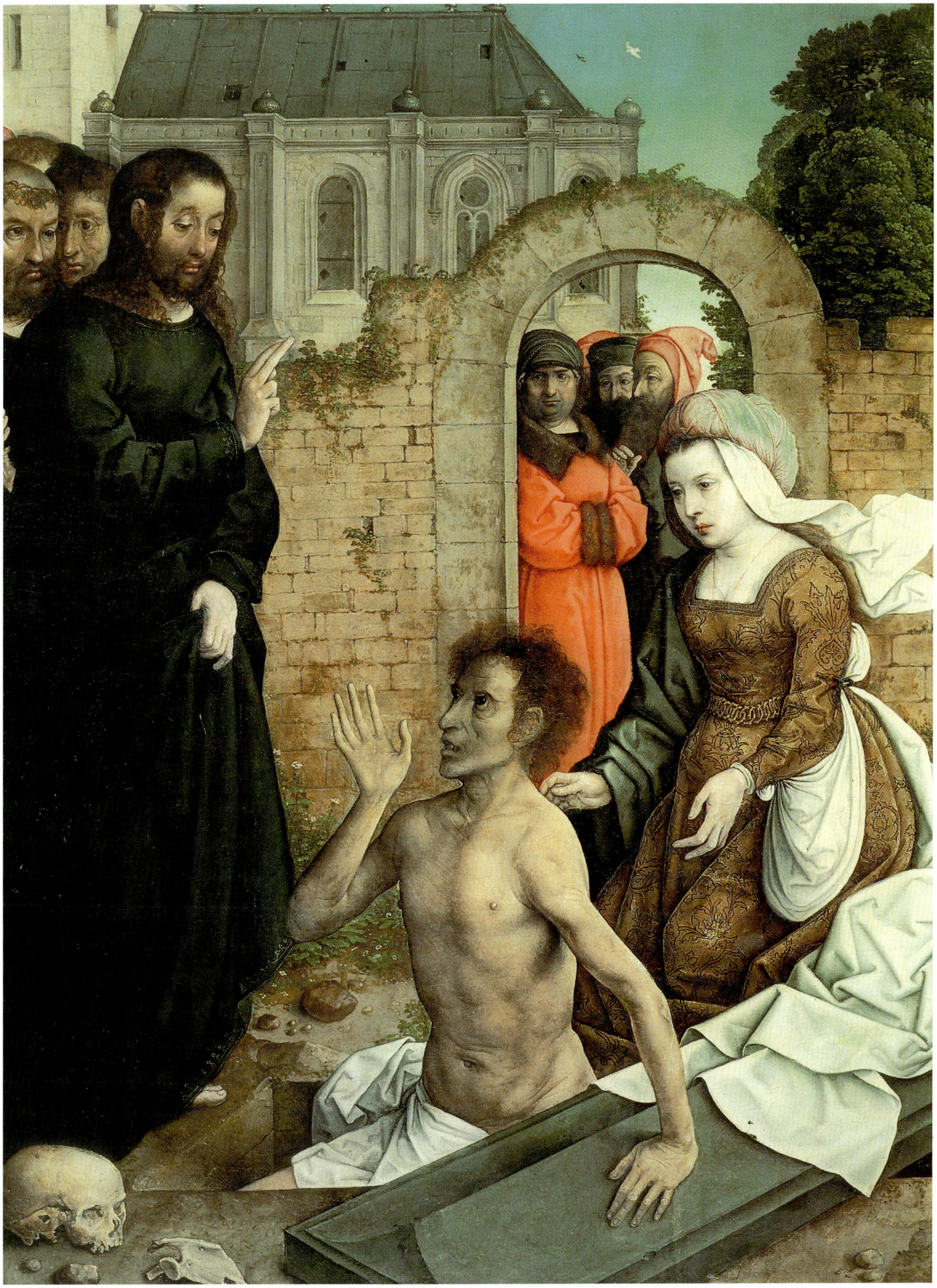

THE PASSION

The Betrayal of Christ, *a fresco in the Scrovegni Chapel, Padua, Italy, by Giotto (1366–1337). The dignified profiled head of Jesus expresses stillness and serenity amid a frenzied tumult of activity, during which Peter (left) cuts off the ear of one of the arresting party.*

The travails that marked the end of Jesus' earthly life are collectively known as the Passion (Latin *passio*, "suffering"). The importance of the Passion to Christian teaching is reflected in the vast range of artistic representations, in almost every medium, of the events following the Last Supper, from Jesus' arrest to his entombment. The climactic event of the Passion is the Crucifixion, but this scene, so common in later centuries, is absent from very early Christian art. The reasons are complex, but one factor was the pref-

The Mocking and Crowning with Thorns, *by Hans Holbein the Elder (ca. 1460–1534), from the Passion altarpiece painted in 1500–1 for the Dominican church of Frankfurt-am-Main, Germany. The soldiers are caricatures of brutish cruelty, while Jesus' face looks directly out at the onlooker, invoking pity at his suffering.*

Below: The Road to Calvary, *by Simone Martini (ca. 1284–1344). Outside the gates of Jerusalem, Jesus looks back sorrowfully at his mother, who is threatened by a guard. Following behind, Mary Magdalene (identifiable by her long red hair) makes a gesture of grief.*

erence for themes relating to the paradisial afterlife (which often found iconographical precedents in Greco-Roman art); the shameful nature of Jesus' execution was another. The earliest known attempts at the Crucifixion date from the fifth and sixth centuries and perhaps reflect doctrinal uncertainty about how this scene should be handled. Other early Passion scenes feature on an ivory casket at Brescia, Italy (ca. late fourth century), and in miniatures in sixth- and seventh-century gospel books. The Last Supper appears in early sixth-century manuscript miniatures and as part of a mosaic Passion cycle in Sant' Apollinare Nuovo, Ravenna.

The Passion story begins with Judas' betrayal of Jesus in Gethsemane. From the medieval period, this scene might form part of a virtuoso night-piece, complete with attendant crowd and Peter cutting off the ear of the high priest's servant; or it might consist simply of the two central figures embracing. The ensuing trial of Jesus could be handled similarly. Pilate's showing of Jesus to the crowd with the words "Here is the man!" (John 19.5)—usually known under its Latin title Ecce Homo—was commonly depicted by Renaissance artists with Pilate, the crowd, and others; otherwise the image might consist solely of the purple-robed Jesus wearing the crown of thorns (Mark 15.17 and parallels).

The gospels say little concerning the carrying of the cross to Calvary (Latin *Calvaria* = Golgotha) beyond recording that Simon of Cyrene was

A 19th-century Russian Crucifixion in brass and enamel is surmounted by the image known as the Mandylion. According to an ancient tradition, Jesus himself made the original Mandylion by miraculously imprinting his face on a cloth which he sent to King Abgar of Edessa (modern Urfa, Turkey).

Opposite: The Crucifixion, *attributed to Hubert van Eyck (died 1426). The* tau *(T-shaped) cross towers over a fantasy Jerusalem cityscape. Jesus is already exalted above the mortal emotions and concerns of the grieving Virgin and St. John, the anguished women, and the indifferent men chatting and riding back to the city.*

compelled to carry the cross for Jesus, and that Jesus spoke on the way to a group of lamenting women. These details were supplemented by, among other embellishments, the medieval tradition of a woman who wiped the sweat from Jesus' face with a cloth on which his likeness remained imprinted. The *vera icon* ("true image") of Jesus upon the fabric seems to have been the origin of this woman's traditional name, Veronica. Famous relics that claimed to bear the true imprint of Christ's features include the controversial Shroud of Turin (see p.256) and the Holy Mandylion of Edessa; the iconography of both of these promoted the now conventional image of Jesus as a bearded man.

The traditions surrounding Jesus' progress to Golgotha and the incidents that occurred on the way evolved in the late Middle Ages into the elaborate sequence known as the "Stations of the Cross," promoted especially by the Franciscans. Beginning with Jesus' condemnation and ending with his burial, the stations now usually number fourteen. They are represented in paintings, sculptures, or tableaux placed at intervals along the route to a church—most famously along the Via Dolorosa ("Way of Sorrows") in Jerusalem, the traditional route taken by Jesus to his place of execution—or inside, around the nave.

The treatment of the Crucifixion itself varies greatly, although certain elements nearly always occur. The way in which Jesus was to be depicted on the cross was a matter of debate throughout the early Byzantine centuries. At issue was how to convey the balance between the suffering humanity and impassive divinity that was believed to coexist in the person of Christ. One tradition, long maintained in the Romanesque art of the West, shows Jesus very much alive, open-eyed and with head erect, and clothed in a tunic (*colobium*). This was superseded around the ninth century in Constantinople by the convention of showing him naked except for a loincloth, with body bent and head slumped.

Around the eleventh century, the Crucifixion became the subject of the special festal icon for Good Friday in the Eastern Church. The icon usually depicts the Virgin and St. John the Apostle (traditionally identified as the "beloved disciple" of John 19.26 and as the evangelist himself), perhaps accompanied by another woman and the centurion (Matt. 27.54). As in Western treatments, a skull lies at the foot of the cross, a reference to the name of Golgotha ("Place of a Skull") as well as a symbol of Jesus' ultimate triumph over death.

In their portrayal of the crucified Jesus, Byzantine artists laid less emphasis on the extremes of physical suffering than was usual in the medieval West. Orthodox icons show Jesus' feet nailed to a slanting foot-

ihesus · nasarenus · rex · iudeorum

Pietà, *by Michelangelo (1485–1564). The naturalistic portrayal of the dead Christ and the poignant youthfulness of his mother are combined in a marble sculpture that the artist's biographer, Condivi (1553), described as "of so great and rare beauty that no one sees it without being moved to pity."*

board with two separate nails, rather than with a single nail to the upright of the cross, imparting a less contorted form to the body. The overall impression reflects the language of Orthodox liturgical texts that speak of Jesus as "falling asleep" rather than dying upon the cross.

In the post-Romanesque West, a concentration on the physical torments of the Passion aimed to elicit horror and sympathy in the onlooker. From the fifteenth century, a growing understanding of anatomy brought to the near-naked body of Jesus on the Cross a disturbing realism completely absent from the stylized torsos and musculature in Eastern icons.

A similar realism was displayed in Western depictions of the Deposition, or Descent from the Cross (the taking down of Jesus from the cross), and the Lamentation (the scene of mourning over the body). Although the Deposition is described by Dionysius of Fourna (see p.311), the fully elaborated form of the scene is a relative latecomer to Orthodox iconography, being based on Western prototypes of the sixteenth century. Earlier Eastern versions of the subject tend to limit the number of mourners to Joseph of Arimathea, Nicodemus, St. John the Apostle, and the Virgin, and to be more in the nature of a Lamentation. Since the fourteenth century these scenes, with the dead body of Jesus laid out on a cloth or slab, have been embroidered on the *epitaphios* (bier-cloth) used in the Holy Saturday ritual of the Orthodox Church.

The Lamentation and Entombment, the final stages of the Passion narrative, are often combined, and the mourners depicted are usually the same in both scenes. The Lamentation is related to one of the most powerful of all Christian devotional images, the Pietà (Italian, "Pity"), which developed in the thirteenth century. In it, the Virgin holds the dead body of her son in a tragic echo of the Madonna and Child. Associated with the Entombment is the scene referred to as the Man of Sorrows, known in Greek as the Akra Tapeinosis ("Peak of Humiliation"); both titles come from the description of the Suffering Servant in Isaiah 53.1–9. The dead Jesus, usually wearing the crown of thorns, stands in an open sarcophagus; only the naked upper part of his body is visible, often displaying the wounds in his hands and side.

The Avignon Pietà, *attributed to Enguerrand Quarton, or Charreton (fl. 1444–66). Absorbed in grief, the Virgin prays, while Mary Magdalene weeps, and John gently removes Jesus' crown of thorns. The stylized gold background and heavy draperies make a striking foil for the pallid, unnaturally curved body of Christ and the delicate, expressive faces of the mourners. The man who commissioned the work is depicted in the left foreground.*

THE RESURRECTION

The Supper at Emmaus, *by Caravaggio (1570–1610) captures the disciples' surprise at the instant when they recognized Jesus (Luke 24.31). The head of the standing man casts a shadowy halo on the wall behind the youthful Christ, whose dramatic gesture of blessing has the two disciples starting from their seats.*

Christ's resurrection is not described in the gospels, and the artistic traditions of East and West differ considerably in how they present this event. In early art it was alluded to symbolically, for example by a cross combined with the monogram of Christ to represent his triumph over death. The Western tradition of Jesus rising from his tomb, holding aloft the banner of the Resurrection (a red cross on a white background), did not appear until the eleventh century. The Eastern form of the Resurrection (Greek *Anastasis*) is the scene known in Western art as the "Harrowing of Hell," and depicts the resurrection of the righteous dead by the risen Jesus. The

The Resurrection (Anastasis). *The mosaics of the monastery church of Hosios Loukas in central Greece, include an early version of the classic* Anastasis *(ca. 1020). Christ, standing on the scattered doors, locks, and bolts of hell, plucks Adam from his sarcophagus. Awaiting their turn are Eve (whose hands are respectfully veiled according to Byzantine imperial protocol) and kings David and Solomon (who are crowned like Byzantine princes).*

scene is suggested by passages of the New Testament (Matt. 27.52–3; Eph. 4.9, 5.14; 1 Peter 3.18–19) and the Psalms (Pss. 24.7–9, 107.16), although its details derive from apocryphal texts. It first appeared in the eighth century, but it was only in the eleventh that it attained its classic form: the risen Christ, holding the Cross as the symbol of his triumph over death, tramples down the gates of hell and reaches out to the resurrected figures of "saints who had fallen asleep." Foremost among them are Adam and Eve, usually with David and Solomon. John the Baptist is also sometimes shown, and more elaborate compositions include biblical patriarchs and prophets.

The events of the forty days from the Resurrection to the Ascension provided artists with several subsidiary subjects, drawn from episodes related in the gospels. Two have in common the dramatic twist in which the disciples' initially fail to recognize their master, and these became popular in the Renaissance and later. The first is the meeting between Mary Magdalene and the risen Jesus in the garden near the empty tomb (John 20.11–18), known under the Latin title of Noli Me Tangere ("Touch me not"; NRSV: "Do not hold onto me") (John 20.17). The second is the journey to, and supper at, the village of Emmaus (Luke 24.13–35).

CHRIST TRIUMPHANT

The issues posed by the representation of Christ after the Ascension, when he takes his place in heaven in triumph as part of the glory of the Trinity, are bound up with the whole question of how, if at all, the Trinity should be represented. Standard Orthodox iconography portrays the three Persons of the Trinity only indirectly, under the guise of the three angels entertained by the patriarch Abraham at Mamre (Gen. 18.1–8).

The symbols associated with Christ triumphant appeared early: a relief carving (ca. 430 CE) on a door from Santa Sabina, Rome, shows him standing within a victory wreath, holding a scroll and with the Greek letters Alpha and Omega (ΑΩ; see Rev. 1.8) inscribed beside him. The scroll (or book) is a constant element, symbolizing Christ as the Logos, the eternal divine Word (John 1.1ff.), and bringer of the New Law. The Greek title Pantocrator ("All-Ruling") appeared from the twelfth century onward in

Christ Pantocrator, *a mosaic in the apse of the cathedral at Cefalù, Sicily (1148). Craftsmen working in the Byzantine tradition created this dominating apse mosaic of Christ as judge and ruler of all things. His countenance is stern, but he raises his right hand in blessing and proffers words of comfort and hope from John's gospel: "I am the light of the world. Whoever follows me will never walk in darkness but will have the light of life" (John 8.12).*

half-length representations of Christ as ruler and judge of the world. The Pantocrator embodies the attributes of both Father and Son—power, justice, mercy, and love. As a mosaic or fresco, it occupies a dominant position in a church, in the main dome or apse, or over the principal entrance.

The Western Church evolved different conventions for the depiction of the Trinity. Biblical hints were elaborated to produce the archetypes of God the Father as a robed, white-bearded old man ("the Ancient of Days," as Dan. 7.9), while the Holy Spirit takes the form of a dove (Matt. 3.16). Typically, the spatial arrangement of the three Persons is in descending order with the Father at the top, as in Raphael's *Disputà* (see above). A widespread form of northern European Gothic Trinity shows the Father crowned and enthroned, holding a figure of Christ on the Cross with the dove over Christ's head; less common is the Father and Son as crowned figures side by side, with the dove between them.

In the West, the book of Revelation (especially 4.2–10) inspired a subject popular in Romanesque sculpture: Christ crowned and enthroned between the four symbols of the evangelists and surrounded by the twenty-four elders (Rev. 4.4). An example is the tympanum at the abbey of Moissac in southern France, dating from before 1115.

Disputà, *by Raphael (1483–1520). This fresco for the Camera della Segnatura in the Vatican, Rome (1508–11) is a huge panorama representing the Church triumphant on earth and in heaven. God the Father (top) stands over the enthroned figure of Christ in glory showing his wounds, flanked by the Virgin and John the Baptist. Around his throne are seated Peter (far left), Paul (far right) and the other apostles. The Holy Spirit in the form of a white dove becomes present on earth in the Blessed Sacrament of the Eucharist, which stands on the central altar, surrounded by figures from the Church's history.*

Crosses placed by worshipers outside the Church of the Holy Sepulchre, Jerusalem, revered by Christians as the traditional site of the Crucifixion.

EARLY CHRISTIAN BELIEFS

Paul states that if Christ had not risen again, all Christian faith and teaching would be in vain (1 Cor. 15.12–19). Certainly, all the documents that make up the New Testament are written in the light of the firm conviction that Jesus rose from the dead, but it is the writings other than the gospels that most clearly express the early Church's belief in the resurrected Christ. The Acts of the Apostles and the Letters contain the first stages of what is known as "Christology": the continuing task of interpreting the significance of the person of Jesus Christ to the faith of the Church.

The New Testament authors use a wide range of titles and concepts to express this significance. One of the most basic themes is that the Resurrection was an act of divine exaltation, by which God had vindicated Jesus and conferred on him a position of supreme authority in the universe. Jesus had risen and been taken up to heaven, and would eventually return to restore all things (Acts 3.20–21; 1 Thess. 1.10). Jesus' Resurrection therefore both revealed and proclaimed him definitively as Messiah, Lord, and the Son of God (Acts 2.36; Rom. 1.4).

In interpreting the person of the risen Jesus, the early Christians naturally also turned to the Hebrew Scriptures. Paul compares Jesus with Adam:

"Wisdom Christology"

The New Testament writers identified Jesus with the biblical concept of Wisdom (1 Cor. 1.24, 30). In the Hebrew Scriptures and later Jewish texts, Wisdom is personified as the expression of the inner being of God and as his sole agent in the work of Creation. Wisdom is also the revelation of God and the means of salvation for human beings (Wisd. of Sol. 7.22–27). These characteristics are applied to Jesus Christ in several New Testament passages that are probably quotations from early Christian hymns. He is the visible image of the invisible God, the one through whom all things were created, who sustains all creation, and who, by his triumphal ascension to heaven, finally reconciles the world to the Father (1 Cor. 8.6; Col. 1.15–20; Heb. 1.2–4).

Wisdom Christology also inevitably meant that the early Church recognized its Lord as a preexistent divine being, who had been "with God" from before the Creation. This is most clearly expressed in the Fourth Gospel (John 1.1–18), but it is attested elsewhere in the New Testament, most notably in a hymn quoted by Paul, which describes Jesus as originally being "in the form of God" but then "taking the form of a slave, being born in human likeness" (Phil. 2.6–11). Similarly, Jesus—the exact imprint of God's being, superior to all angelic beings (Heb. 1.3–4)—was for a time "made lower than the angels" by sharing in ordinary human nature (Heb. 2.9, 14–17).

HEBREWS AND CHRIST CRUCIFIED

The letter to the Hebrews provides the fullest interpretation of Jesus' death, depicting it throughout in terms taken directly from the Hebrew Scriptures. It was an atoning sacrifice (Heb. 2.17) and the fulfillment of Jeremiah's prophecy of a new covenant (Heb. 8.6–13). Above all, it showed Jesus to be the true high priest according to the order of Melchizedek (Heb. 5.6–10).

Hebrews compares Christ's saving work with the great annual ritual of the Day of Atonement (Yom Kippur), the occasion when, in ancient times, the high priest entered the Holy of Holies of the Temple with the atoning blood of sacrificial victims (Lev. 16.11–17). The equivalent exaltation of Jesus occurs when he enters heaven to come before the presence of God with his own atoning blood (Heb. 9.12, 9.24, 10.12). Jesus' self-offering is the perfect, once for all, sacrifice for sin—an act that entirely supersedes the need for the sacrifices of the old Israel (Heb. 7.26–28).

but while the disobedience of Adam had brought death into the world, the perfect obedience of Christ brought eternal life for believers (Rom. 5.12–21). Again, Paul describes Jesus as "the last Adam": the first Adam was "a man of dust," a physical being made from the dust of the ground, but the resurrected Christ is a man "from heaven" and "a life-giving spirit"—a spiritual being who transmits this character to his followers. Just as every human bears "the image of the man of dust," he or she will be resurrected through Christ "to bear the image of the man of heaven" (1 Cor. 15.45–49).

If the early Church saw Jesus as an exalted heavenly figure, its members also knew that he had first suffered the shameful death of crucifixion. Despite the fact that such a death was seen as humiliating by both Jew and Gentile (1 Cor. 1.23), its significance was central to the thought of all the New Testament writers—especially Paul, who saw the crucified Christ as the essence of the whole gospel (1 Cor. 2.1–2). In what may be examples of the earliest Christian preaching, Jesus' execution is represented as Israel's rejection of its true Messiah, with the Resurrection as God's reversal of that judgment (Acts 2.23–24, 3.13–15, 10.39–40). But there are already suggestions of the developed Christian idea that the death of Jesus had a broader saving purpose for humans—it is said to be part of God's plan (Acts 2.23) and foretold in Scripture (Acts 3.18).

The Last Judgment: Christ Enthroned and the Resurrection of the Dead, *from the Ingeborg Psalter (French, ca. 1210).*

Most simply, it could be said that Christ died to atone for the sins of humanity (Rom. 3.25; 1 Cor. 15.3; 2 Cor. 5.14; Gal. 1.4; 1 Pet. 3.18). The faithful interpreted this basic conviction in various ways, mainly through the use of images and concepts from the Hebrew Bible. The blood that Christ shed is compared with the blood ritual of the annual Jewish sacrifice of atonement, through which God is able to wipe away sins (Rom. 3.24–25; 1 John 2.2). The New Testament letters present Jesus as the true Passover lamb (1 Cor. 5.7; 1 Pet. 1.19), and portray his suffering in the same language used in Isaiah 53 to describe the figure of the "Suffering Servant," a figure who, in his death, bore the sins of many (1 Pet. 2.21–25; Isa. 53.5–12).

The idea of Jesus' death as a sacrifice on behalf of others is especially developed by Paul. On the Cross, Jesus took upon himself the curse of the old law (Gal. 3.10–14). In a paradoxical statement, Paul says that the wholly sinless one was made sin (2 Cor. 5.21)—taking on the sins of others and making them "righteous" in God's sight. Not only did the Cross annul the divine penalty for human sin but it also marked a decisive victory over the cosmic powers of evil (Col. 2.13–15), a triumph to be finally realized at Christ's second coming (1 Cor. 15.23–25).

PAUL AND THE JESUS OF HISTORY

It has sometimes been asserted that Paul fundamentally transformed what had been the earliest Christian faith, substituting for the historical Jesus a heavenly redeemer on the model of similar figures in the religions of the Greco-Roman world. In support of this assertion, it has been pointed out that Paul's letters show little knowledge of Jesus' life and teachings. But this claim is exaggerated. Apart from the fact that he lays great emphasis on the Cross—acknowledging the climactic historical event of Jesus' career (see main text)—Paul knows of Jesus' human birth (Gal. 4.4), his betrayal, and the Last Supper (1 Cor. 11.23–26), and also refers to examples of his teaching (1 Cor. 7.10, 9.14).

OPPOSITION TO PAUL
In his letters to the churches of Corinth, Philippi, and especially Galatia, Paul writes about various groups who oppose his mission. A number of commentators have suggested that this opposition represented a united Jewish Christian assault on Paul's teaching, but the situation was in fact more complex and it is far from clear in every instance that his adversaries were Jewish Christians. This does seem to have been the case in Galatia—although again Paul's opponents there probably represented only one particular Jewish Christian group.

JEWISH AND GENTILE CHRISTIANS

Christianity began as one movement among the numerous currents within first-century Judaism (see pp.166–69). The first Christians regularly attended Temple worship (Acts 2.45) and some Pharisees who joined the Church continued to observe the Jewish law (Acts 15.5). Peter's first sermons were addressed to Jews (Acts 2.14, 3.12). What distinguished the Christians from other Jews was their conviction that Jesus was the expected Messiah (Acts 2.36, 3.20) and that he had fulfilled the messianic prophecies addressed to Israel in the Hebrew Scriptures (Acts 3.22–26).

Within the Christian community, the Church in Jerusalem—headed by James, the brother of Jesus (see p.212)—was accorded special preeminence and authority. But tensions arose early on, and there emerged a distinct group of "Hellenists" (Acts 6.1), Greek-speaking Christians who probably began as members of a synagogue for Diaspora Jews (Acts 6.9). One member of this group, Stephen, was executed by stoning for speaking against the Temple and the Jewish law (Acts 6.14, 7.44–50), and his views provoked a wave of persecution by the Temple authorities. This seems to have affected only the Hellenists, who were expelled from Jerusalem. The apostles and other Aramaic-speaking Christians appear to have been left undisturbed (Acts 8.1), presumably because they were still considered to be within the fold of Judaism.

The dispersal of the Hellenists took the Christian mission beyond the boundaries of Israel, beginning with the preaching of Philip to the Samaritans (Acts 8.4). But the real crisis was brought about by the extensive and successful evangelization of Gentiles by Paul, who had begun as a Pharisee (Acts 23.6, 26.5) and a zealous persecutor of Christians (Acts 8.1–3). Paul held that his new converts were not required to observe the full Jewish law—especially with respect to circumcision—and his teaching of universal salvation through the death and resurrection of Jesus represented a markedly new development of the Christian gospel.

The New Testament indicates that the split between Jewish Christianity and Gentile Christianity, as advocated by Paul, was formalized by a pact whereby the Jerusalem Church took responsibility for evangelizing Jews, while Paul undertook to convert Gentiles (Gal. 2.9). Under this agreement, according to Acts 15, Gentile converts would have to obey only the "Noahide laws"—seven basic commands said to have been handed by God to Noah after the Flood. Jews had to obey the whole Torah, but any non-Jew who observed the Noahide laws (for example, the rules quoted in Acts 15.21, 25) was counted among "the righteous of the nations of the world."

This 12th-century French reliquary of wood, silver gilt, semiprecious stones, and glass, portrays Stephen, a prominent member of the Hellenist group in the early Church, who is revered as the first Christian martyr.

Jewish Christian sects

The destruction of Jerusalem by the Romans in 70 CE was the principal cause of the decline in Jewish Christianity, and determined that in future the Church would be a predominantly Gentile body. One source reports that the Christians of Jerusalem migrated to Pella in Transjordan, and from this time Jewish Christianity was increasingly marginalized and fragmented. Various sects survived until at least 300 CE in different parts of the Near East. What little is known about them comes from references in the works of the Church Fathers (see p.328). They sometimes quote from Jewish Christian gospels, many of which were based on Matthew, the most "Jewish" of the canonical gospels. The Fathers regarded most of these groups as heretics, so their reports cannot always be wholly relied upon. But they convey a reasonable picture of three groups.

Ruins of ancient Pella in present-day Jordan, where the Jewish Christians are said to have fled following the destruction of Jerusalem by the Romans in 70 CE.

The best-known Jewish Christian group, the Ebionites, lived in Transjordan, and their name probably means "the poor." Their Greek gospel was a reworking of Matthew, but omits the nativity and infancy narratives because Ebionites rejected the virgin birth. They were "adoptionists," believing that Jesus became Messiah and Son of God only when the Spirit entered him at his baptism. While Ebionites observed many Jewish rites, as vegetarians they rejected the sacrifices of the Temple.

The group that produced the gospel of the Hebrews appears to have originated in Egypt in the early second century. Their distinctive gospel echoes Gnostic ideas (see pp.330–31) and at its core is the Holy Spirit—a female figure like the Gnostic Sophia ("Wisdom"). Again, the Baptism is the key moment in Jesus' life, when the Spirit descends on the preexistent Son and finds ultimate rest and fulfillment in him.

The Nazarenes, based at Aleppo in Syria, were not considered heretics. Their gospel, written in Aramaic in the second century CE, was also based on Matthew, with picturesque elaborations and popular legends.

Scholars disagree on whether the Christian mission really was formally divided up in this way. In any event, it did not settle the issue of the relationship between Jewish and Gentile Christians. Even within the Church at Jerusalem, some members were apparently prepared to compromise, while others insisted that Gentiles "be circumcized and ordered to keep the law of Moses" (Acts 15.5). The eventual dominance of Gentile Christianity—and this should not be considered simply as a synonym for the teachings of Paul—was largely the result of external factors rather than internal strife (see box, above). The Christian movement as a whole preserved, in its scriptures, several texts of a clearly Jewish Christian character, such as the gospel of Matthew (see box, p.185), the letter of James, and Revelation.

THE PATRISTIC PERIOD

THE CHURCH FATHERS

The eminent theologians known as the "Church Fathers" include Clement of Rome, Ignatius of Antioch, and Polycarp of Smyrna in the first century CE; Justin Martyr and Athenagoras of Athens in the second century; Clement of Alexandria, Origen, and Cyprian of Carthage in the third century; and Ambrose, Athanasius, Augustine of Hippo, Basil, Gregory of Nyssa, Gregory Nazianzus, Jerome, John Chrysostom, and Cyril of Alexandria in the fourth and fifth centuries.

The Church Fathers determined Christian orthodoxy and rejected other ideas and doctrines as heretical. They also established the final form of the New Testament, the authoritative canon of Christian scripture (see p.183).

From the first century CE until around the middle of the fifth century, the Church was engaged in a constant debate on the nature, character, and significance of Jesus. The great (male) thinkers who contributed to this debate are known as the "Church Fathers" (Latin *Patres Ecclesiae*; see sidebar, left) and the era of their activity is known as the Patristic period.

The key issue in the early Patristic period was Jesus' relationship to God. How could New Testament statements implying the divinity of Christ be reconciled with the Judaic belief in one God accepted by most Christians? The Apologists, a group of influential second-century writers who defended Christianity against pagan and Jewish attacks, perceived Jesus as the Wisdom of God and the Son of God, but above all as the creative Word (Greek *Logos*) that "was with God" and "was God" (John 1.1) (see sidebar, opposite).

The achievement of the Apologists was to present Jesus as both identical with, yet distinct from, the one God, much like the figure of Wisdom in Proverbs 8 and Sirach (Ecclesiasticus) 24. But this view was open to challenge on two fronts. Some strict monotheists held that Jesus the Logos was simply a human being on whom the power of God rested, or that he was one of a succession of temporary (not eternal or preexistent) "modes of operation" on the part of the unique Godhead. Others, such as Arius of Alexandria (ca. 250–336 CE) claimed that Jesus could not properly be called God, because he was created by God like all other things in existence, although Jesus was the first and greatest of creatures and the agent

Remains of the 2nd-century walls of the city of Nicea in Asia Minor (present-day Iznik, Turkey). A Church council met at Nicea in 325 CE to counter the Arian heresy and formulate the Nicene Creed, the statement of belief that forms part of Christian liturgies to this day.

Jesus as God and man

Christ [*right*] with Abbot Mena, *Coptic (Egyptian Orthodox) icon ca. 600* CE. *The Coptic Church was one of several groups that rejected the two natures of Jesus. It adhered to Monophysitism, the belief that Christ had one divine nature.*

The second great debate in Christianity during the Patristic period was over the problems of the Incarnation. If God had assumed human nature in the man Jesus, how were divinity and humanity to be viewed together in the one person? Arius (see main text) had used the numerous references in the gospels to Jesus' human weaknesses to argue that he could not be truly divine. Some thinkers seemed content to affirm the doctrine known as Nestorianism—that there were two separate personalities in the incarnate Son, one divine, the other human. Thus, Jesus' miracles could be ascribed to the former, his human fallibilities to the latter.

Opponents countered with the claim that Christ had one personality, but that his human nature was confined to the "flesh" while the divine element, the Logos, replaced his human soul or mind. It was objected that, if this were true, Jesus would lack the most significant elements of human nature and therefore could not be fully human. This in turn effectively nullified the purpose of the Incarnation: to restore humanity's true nature, lost by the fall of Adam and Eve in Eden. To quote one key Patristic phrase, Christ "became what we are in order that we might become what he is."

The subtle, complicated, and sometimes confused debate achieved a resolution at the Council of Chalcedon in 451 CE. The Chalcedonian Definition, which was generally—but not universally—accepted, does not explain precisely how two natures operate in the one being of Jesus. Rather, it states that a Christian must believe in the reality of a Christ who is inseparably human and divine: "one and the same Christ…recognized in two natures, without confusion, without change, without division, without separation."

through whom everything else was made. Arius pointed to passages of scripture that seemed to uphold his view that the Logos was indeed a created being and thus subordinate to the Father (for example, Prov. 8.22; John 14.28; Sir. 24.8).

Arius' teaching—Arianism—caused a crisis in the Church, not least because Arius' opponents failed conclusively to make their point: that universal salvation was not the work of a supernatural being distinct from the Father, but the revelation of God himself in the life of Jesus (2 Cor. 5.19). Unfortunately for the supporters of traditional Logos Christology, passages of scripture used to support their doctrine could also all too easily be given an Arian interpretation.

Arianism was finally condemned as heretical at a great ecclesiastical council held at Nicea in Asia Minor (325 CE), at which the Church settled on the nonscriptural formula that Jesus was "of one substance with the Father"—that is, they shared the same essential being. This formula was incorporated into the Nicene Creed, the fundamental statement of Christian belief, and thereafter became the orthodox doctrine of the Church.

THE LOGOS

The concept of the divine Logos as a kind of "world soul," a universal creative force, was common to much Greek philosophy and was also influential among some speculative currents within first-century CE Judaism. By identifying Jesus with the Logos, the Apologists were able to represent him as an expression of the innermost being of God, the Deity's reason projected into speech, the agent of both creation and revelation. He was close to the Father's heart and God's Son in that he was the only being that the Father had "begotten." In this way, the Father was the sole source of Jesus the Logos, who existed before the Creation and was the directing reason of the whole universe.

JESUS AND GNOSTICISM

"Gnosticism" is the modern term for a major religious movement of the early centuries CE. It existed in a bewildering variety of forms that collectively provided the principal challenge to the development of mainstream Christianity in the era of the Church Fathers (see pp.328–29). From at least the second century CE, Gnosticism was regarded by leading Christian theologians as a highly dangerous heresy.

The word Gnosticism derives from the Greek *gnosis* ("knowledge"), and a Gnostic is thus one who is considered to have attained to true knowledge. This concept was a basic feature of all the different Gnostic systems: an initiate had first to understand the condition in which human beings find themselves, and this understanding became in turn the means of deliverance from the human predicament.

In Gnosticism, humanity is akin to the divine. Every person represents a "divine spark" imprisoned in a material body. Salvation is the freeing of that divine element so that the individual may realize his or her heavenly nature. The basis for this doctrine is a radical dualism between "spirit" and "matter," whereby the material world is a realm of evil from which the individual needs to escape. Because the world is evil, the being that created it cannot be the one true God. Above this creator-being, or "demiurge," and sharply distinguished from it, there must be an unknown transcendent Deity.

The "knowledge" to which the Gnostic attains takes the form of an elaborate creation myth. This is recounted differently in the various Gnostic systems, but they all speak of an ultimate divine figure, the Father, from whom

GNOSTICISM AND THE NEW TESTAMENT

Concepts resembling those of Gnosticism appear in the New Testament, especially in John's gospel and the letters of Paul. For example, John regularly uses the verb "to know" and Paul the noun "knowledge." The frequent contrasts that both writers make between light and dark, flesh and spirit (Rom. 8.1–13) can be interpreted with reference to Gnostic dualism.

In reality, it is very doubtful how far these and other ideas in the New Testament have the same meaning as in the Gnostic systems, because such concepts were common in the general religious and intellectual climate of Jesus' time, both Hellenistic and Jewish. Moreover, the New Testament shows evidence of deliberately setting out to combat Gnostic beliefs. For example, it strongly asserts the reality of Jesus' bodily humanity (1 John 1.1–4; 1 Tim. 3.16; 2 Tim. 3.8), against the Gnostic view that, because all matter and flesh were evil, Jesus was human only in appearance.

The later New Testament letters rebut Gnosticism most clearly and strongly, indicating how serious a threat it was perceived to be to the emergent Christian orthodoxy. They denounce false myths (1 Tim. 4.7; 2 Tim. 4.3–4; 2 Pet. 1.16); the practice of asceticism and celibacy to avoid contamination by the evil material world (1 Tim. 4.1–5); and the Gnostic genealogy of "eons" (1 Tim. 1.4; Tit. 3.9). Jesus is unique, superior to all other spiritual beings (Heb. 1.1–14) and justly called "God" (Tit. 2.13).

Christ Giving the Word of God to the Apostles Paul [*left*] and Peter, *a mosaic of ca. 500 CE in the Church of Santa Costanza, Rome. Paul's letters have been said to echo Gnostic dualism, for example the contrast he makes between flesh and spirit. But this is better compared with the rabbinic doctrine of the good and evil inclinations within a single person. In reality, the early Church strenuously opposed Gnostic speculation.*

The Nile at Nag Hammadi in Upper Egypt. A cache of documents discovered here in 1945 provides firsthand evidence for Gnosticism, and has clarified references in the New Testament letters to "cleverly devised myths" (2. Pet. 1.16) and other aspects of Gnostic thought.

emanates a genealogy of spiritual beings known as "eons," who together constitute the *pleroma*, the "fullness" of divinity. The eons progressively move away from the divine center until one or other of them "falls," carrying spirit into the lower realm of matter. When this happens, the visible world comes into being (sometimes through the work of a demiurge) at the same time as the evil powers ("archons") that govern it.

According to this understanding, human beings are so enmeshed in matter that they can realize their authentic spiritual nature only through a supernatural revelation. Where Jesus appears in Gnostic speculation, this is the role he fulfills. He is a heavenly figure who descends to reveal to humanity the true and redeeming *gnosis*. He is not incarnate as a real human being, as Christian orthodoxy insists (although Gnostic texts are not consistent on this point), because that would corrupt him with the material world. The "Gnostic gospels" relate nothing of the ministry, death, and resurrection of the human Jesus but instead are either meditations on his message or collections of his sayings. His teaching is sometimes described as "secret words," hidden knowledge not granted to ordinary believers.

Until the twentieth century, knowledge of Gnosticism was largely confined to the hostile accounts of Church Fathers and such extracts as they reproduced from Gnostic writings. This situation was transformed by the discovery in 1945 of a quantity of Gnostic texts at Nag Hammadi in Egypt. Gnosticism can now be viewed not simply as a distortion of the true faith, but as a belief system in its own right that was widely attractive because it appeared to offer the hope of deliverance from humanity's sad condition. The Nag Hammadi documents, which include the Gospel of Thomas (see box, p.191), seem to indicate the existence of a pre-Christian Gnosticism that became largely Christianized while retaining its original basic outlook.

CHRIST THE REDEEMER

A central issue between the Church and Gnosticism was the uniqueness of Christ and the understanding of his redemptive work. The Gnostic Jesus was only one in the evolving succession of divine emanations known as "eons," and, since he was not viewed as physically human, there was no place in Gnostic thought for the notion of salvation through Jesus' bodily death and resurrection. By contrast, for the Church, the whole divine *pleroma* (see main text) was contained in Jesus (Col. 1.19, 2.9): he is *the* one through whom the universe came into being (John 1.3), the sole mediator between God and humankind (1 Tim. 2.5), who "was handed over to death for our trespasses and was raised for our justification" (Rom. 4.25).

The Catholic Church of the Primacy of St. Peter was built in 1934 on the foundations of a Byzantine church near Tabgha. The rock, called "Christ's Table," is traditionally where the disciples shared a meal with the risen Jesus, who designated Peter as the head of the body of believers with the words: "Feed my lambs" and "Feed my flock" (John 21.9–17). Whatever the authenticity of this scene, the New Testament certainly shows that Peter enjoyed a special position of leadership in the early Church.

FOUNDER OF THE CHURCH?

It is often asserted that Jesus had no intention of founding a Church in the sense of an enduring body of followers. Jesus, it is claimed, expected the imminent end of the present age, but was mistaken in this expectation and the Church and its mission came into being to meet a situation for which he had provided no guidance. The creation of the Church may be explained by the sociological theory known as "cognitive dissonance," according to which a group faced with the failure of its accepted beliefs retains their form—in this case Jesus' predictions of a speedy end of the world—but reinterprets their substance. Thus Jesus' anticipation of the impending end was replaced by the future hope of his Second Coming, the *Parousia*.

However, many scholars would still wish to claim that the foundation of the Church was central to the purpose of Jesus. The Greek word translated as "church" is *ekklesia*, which originally meant just "gathering" or "assembly." But the usage of the term in the New Testament seems to be derived from the Septuagint, the Greek version of the Hebrew Scriptures, where *ekklesia* frequently denotes the Israelite nation. The first Christians, therefore, saw themselves as the continuation and true realization of Israel, God's chosen people (Rom. 9.6–8; Gal. 6.16; Phil. 3.3; 1 Pet. 2.9).

It would seem that in calling the twelve leading disciples, Jesus aimed to set up a group that, with him as its head, would constitute the new twelve tribes of Israel at the renewal of all things (Matt. 19.28; Luke 22.28–9). In Jesus' preaching, the kingdom of God is both present and to come; those who enter it now will constitute a "little flock" (Luke 12.32), a society of the redeemed, when the kingdom is fully and finally realized. If Jesus identified himself with the "Son of Man" in Daniel 7 (see box, p.299), he may also have envisaged the creation of a new community of "the people of the holy ones of the Most High" (Dan. 7.27). The foundation of a community may also be implied in Jesus' conception of himself as Messiah (see pp.294–95).

It is possible to draw too sharp a distinction between Jesus' views on the imminence of the end of the world and those of the early Church. If the "Synoptic Apocalypse" (see pp. 334–35) is to be trusted, Jesus said that he did not know the exact time of the end (Matt. 24.36; Mark 13.32). He envisaged a community in a state of constant watchfulness for the unexpected appearance of the Son of Man (Mark 13.33–37 and parallels), and warned this community to take steps to survive the catastrophes that will usher in the final end (Mark 13.14–20 and parallels).

The members of the very early Church had much the same outlook and expectation: they believed that Jesus would return to establish his kingdom soon (1 Thess. 4.15–18), but the precise time was hidden from them, so all they could do was watch and wait (Acts 1.7; 1 Thess. 5.1–6).

It seems likely that Jesus understood his followers to constitute a distinct group within Judaism, a new synagogue that alone embodied the true Israel. The early church can be viewed as an organic development of this idea. The Qumran community (see p.169) provides an interesting parallel. It considered itself the only authentic representative of Judaism and its members believed that they were living in the last days, awaiting God's imminent intervention at an unknown time. The Church of the New Testament probably understood itself in the same way, as a body awaiting—in accordance with the teachings of Jesus—the divine consummation of all things.

A foundational rite: the Lord's Supper

Jesus' institution of the Lord's Supper, or Eucharist, can be seen as the formal foundation of the Church. In their accounts of the Last Supper, Mark and Matthew make no mention of the continuation of the rite, and difficult textual problems in Luke's version make it uncertain as to whether or not Jesus envisaged it. But Paul, an earlier witness than the evangelists, certainly knows the Supper as the central sacramental act of worship in the Church: it is what unites believers into a single body (1 Cor. 10.16–17, 11.23–26).

In any event, the gospels agree that Jesus' actions at the Last Supper were a rite of covenant-making, referring back to the covenant with Israel in the Hebrew Scriptures. That covenant designated Israel as God's chosen people: the covenant in Jesus' blood designated his Church as the new Israel. The Lord's Supper prefigures a great messianic banquet in heaven to celebrate Jesus' return—but it is also a sacrament to be respected continually by his followers on earth in remembrance of him.

The words and actions of Jesus can also be seen to replace the sacrificial cult of the Jerusalem Temple, which was the very heart of the religious life of Judaism. A new community is given a new mode of worship: a simple meal replaces the sacrificial food of the Temple, perhaps specifically the Passover meal (1 Cor. 5.7–8). (See also box, p.242.)

The Last Supper, *by Andrea del Castagno (1421–57), a fresco in the refectory of Sant' Apollonia monastery, Florence, Italy. The scene has long been a popular subject for the dining halls of Christian religious communities (compare illustration, p.243).*

THE APOCALYPTIC JESUS

The apocalyptic character of Jesus' message is revealed most clearly in the passages known as the "Synoptic Apocalypse" (Matt. 24.4–25.46; Mark 13.5–37; Luke 21.8–36). All three versions of this discourse are founded on the same basic tradition: Jesus predicted the destruction of the Temple and, in response to his disciples' question as to when this momentous event would happen, revealed that it would herald his second coming and the end of the age (Matt. 24.3).

Speaking in private to his closest disciples (Mark 13.3), Jesus told of the universal catastrophes that would mark the onset of the end of time (Mark 13.7–8 and parallels); these tribulations are described in language that recalls apocalyptic predictions in the Hebrew Bible and the Apocrypha (Dan. 2.2.8; Isa. 19.2: 29.6; Ezek. 5.12; 2 Esd. 13.31–32, 16.18–19). The climax of these calamities would be a profanation of the Temple, a "desolating sacrilege" (Matt. 24.15; Mark 13.14)—this term refers to the pagan

The Revelation to John

Jesus as an apocalyptic figure features most prominently in the book of Revelation. Like many Jewish writings of the apocalyptic genre, it claims to be the vision of a seer who has been vouchsafed heavenly secrets. Its author, traditionally identified with the writer of the Fourth Gospel, draws on the Hebrew Scriptures, the gospels, and a wide range of other sources, such as the books of Enoch, astrology, and myths current in the Greco-Roman world. His primary thematic starting point is the Synoptic Apocalypse (see main text).

A Byzantine mosaic from Carthage, Tunisia. On either side of the cross, alpha *and* omega *(ΑΩ), the first and last letters of the Greek alphabet, denote Christ as the eternal God (see Rev. 1.8).*

Revelation is not just a vision of the future, a view that has often led to a misunderstanding of its character and purpose. Like the book of Daniel, it addresses a particular historical situation of persecution, which is viewed as a prelude to the end of the world and the vindication of the faithful. It opens with messages from the risen Christ to the churches of Asia Minor (Rev. 1.11, 2–3), exhorting them to endurance in the face of persecution (compare Mark 13.9–13 and parallels). Calls for watchfulness occur throughout the work (Rev. 13.9–10, 13.18, 14.12, 16.15).

According to Revelation, Jesus was exalted to heaven by his death in order to assume universal authority. He alone controls the course of history and can open the seals on the scroll of destiny (Rev. 5.1–10). The birthpangs of the messianic age will be marked by war, famine, and pestilence (Rev. 6–11) and the appearance of false Christs and prophets (Rev. 12.13). But the forces of evil will soon be overcome by the victory of angelic beings (Rev. 14–18), heralding the return of Christ, the Last Judgment, a new heaven and earth, and a new Jerusalem (Rev. 19–21).

The Adoration of the Lamb, *from an 8th-century Spanish manuscript of the* Commentary on the Apocalypse *by Beatus of Liébana. The image is drawn from the vision in Revelation 5.6–14 of elders, angels, and "four living creatures" worshiping the divine Lamb (Christ). The description of the four creatures (Rev. 4.7) derives from apocalyptic writings in the Hebrew Scriptures (compare Ezek. 1.10).*

altar of Zeus erected in the Temple by the Hellenistic king Antiochus Epiphanes in 164 BCE (Dan. 9.27, 12.11; 1 Macc. 1.54). In Jewish thought, the Temple represented the universe, and any interference with its rituals brought a cosmic catastrophe. Instead of the profanation of the sanctuary, Luke substitutes a siege of Jerusalem (Luke 21.20). This is generally taken to refer to the events of 70 CE, although Luke may have been inspired by similar biblical prophecies (Isa. 29.1–3; Ezek. 4.1–8).

These woes are the prelude to the final deliverance, the coming of the Son of Man (Mark 13.26 and parallels), as prophesied in the book of Daniel (Dan. 7.13–14). His appearance is marked by further cosmic upheavals (Mark 13.24 and parallels), which also echo a number of biblical passages (Ps. 65.7; Isa. 13.10, 24.23, 27.13, 34.4; Zech. 12.12–24). Those who carry out the Son of Man's redeeming mission are the angels (Matt. 24.31; Mark 13.27), who play a central role in Jewish apocalyptic speculation. Matthew concludes his version of Jesus' discourse with a vision of the Son of Man enthroned at the Last Judgment (Matt. 25.31–46).

THE SYNOPTIC APOCALYPSE AND THE TEACHINGS OF JESUS

The Synoptic Apocalypse is closely linked with the eschatology of other New Testament writings, especially Revelation (see box, opposite), and differs in many respects from what the gospels generally record of Jesus' teachings. As it stands, it no doubt reflects the concerns of the evangelists and the communities for which they wrote, but the key question is whether it wholly misrepresents the thought of the historical Jesus, as many scholars have asserted.

While the language of the Synoptic Apocalypse resembles that of other apocalyptic writings, its outlook and content differ considerably. In typical apocalyptic texts, the "signs" enable the reader to predict the time of the end, but in the Synoptic Apocalypse this time is said to be unknowable (Matt. 24.36, 25.13; Mark 13.32). Jesus will return when least expected (Matt. 24.44), and his followers must not be misled by those who claim that he has already reappeared (Matt. 24.23–25; Mark 13.21–23).

Similar teachings are found on the lips of Jesus elsewhere in the gospels (as at Luke 17.20–23). His message is as much for the present as the future, as is shown by the admonitions to be watchful (Mark 13.33–37; Luke 21.34–36), driven home in Matthew by a series of parables (Matt. 24.37–25.30), most of which are found (in different contexts) in Luke. The demand for faithful discipleship and a readiness to accept wholeheartedly the demands of the kingdom are at the core of Jesus' entire teachings (see pp.280–81).

THE REVOLUTIONARY

"LIBERATION THEOLOGY"
The idea of Jesus as an essentially revolutionary figure is important for the modern phenomenon known as "liberation theology," a movement which emerged in the 1960s in Latin America and has been especially influential there. In liberation theology, a fundamental characteristic of God is that he takes the side of those, in particular the poor, who are oppressed or marginalized by the dominant social structures. The whole Bible is viewed as the record of God's action on their behalf—seen for example in the deliverance of Israel from Egyptian bondage and in the protests of the prophets against social injustices.

The life and teaching of Jesus stand in the same line. Jesus, it is claimed, deliberately chose an "option for the poor" and his message was primarily directed to them. Liberation theologians see Jesus' central proclamation of the kingdom as a message of liberation for the oppressed and downtrodden, and the promise of a free and just society. The response to Jesus today must take the form of a continuation of his struggle to establish this kingdom, through actual social and political activity—from which violence is not always excluded.

Opponents of this kind of theology have objected that it is unduly preoccupied with political activism, often of an avowedly Marxist brand, to the detriment of wider spiritual concerns. Perhaps, above all, it can be criticized for neglecting the work of biblical scholarship and viewing the historical figure of Jesus too exclusively in the light of present-day needs and concerns.

Since the end of the eighteenth century, some scholars have claimed that Jesus advocated armed resistance to free the Jews from Roman rule, and that he was linked with one or more groups that were actively engaged in such a struggle. The New Testament sometimes appears to suggest that Jesus may have been connected, directly or indirectly, with contemporary revolutionary groups. For example, one explanation of the mysterious name "Iscariot" given to the disciple who betrayed Jesus (see p.245) links it with the Sicarii, or "Dagger Men," Jewish fanatics who assassinated those they suspected of being Roman sympathizers or collaborators.

One of the disciples is referred to as Simon the Zealot (Luke 6.15; Acts 1.13). The Zealot party was behind the great Jewish revolt of 66–70 CE, and may have existed earlier (Zealot leaders included sons of Judas the Galilean, who had led a rebellion in Galilee in 6 CE in protest at a Roman census; see p.193). It has been claimed that some sayings of Jesus reflect Zealot thought, such as his statement that he had not come to bring peace but division (Luke 12.51), and his instruction to his followers at the Last Supper to buy a sword (Luke 22.36). But the Zealots and others held that humans had to assist God in establishing the messianic kingdom, whereas the general tenor of Jesus' teaching was that the kingdom would be brought about by God alone. The term "zealot" applied to a disciple may imply no more than that he was a zealous adherent of the Jewish law.

Perhaps the strongest evidence for Jesus' alleged revolutionary tendencies

The Kiss of Judas, *a 6th-century* CE *mosaic in the church of Sant' Apollinare Nuovo, Ravenna. Judas identifies Jesus for the armed men (left) sent to arrest him. The disciple Peter (John 18.10) draws a sword with which he subsequently cuts off the ear of one of the arresting party. In Matthew, Jesus rebukes this act of violence with the words: "Put your sword back in its place; for all who take the sword will perish by the sword" (Matt. 26.52).*

The Zealots, with whom Jesus has been linked, held out for 3 years after the end of the 1st Jewish War (66–70 CE) in the fortress of Masada. The Romans broke the siege by building a huge ramp (bottom left); most of the defenders committed suicide.

is the fact that the Roman prefect sentenced him to death on a political charge, namely of claiming to be "King of the Jews," a messianic pretender. According to Luke, the Sanhedrin accused Jesus before Pilate of "perverting our nation, forbidding us to pay taxes to the emperor, and saying that he himself is the Messiah, a king" (Luke 23.2). The charge that Jesus had claimed to be a king is no doubt authentic, as the inscription on his cross indicates (see sidebar, right). But this does not mean that the accusation was justified, any more than the charge that Jesus had forbidden payment of Roman taxes, which was certainly false (Matt. 22.17–21). The inscription may indicate only that Pilate went along with the Sanhedrin's claim that Jesus was a royal pretender who might spark political unrest (see pp.250–51, 294–95). A Roman prefect had to remain on good terms with the Jewish establishment, which could easily cause trouble for him at Rome.

The gospels' picture may have been influenced by later disputes between Christians and Jews, but even allowing for this it seems clear that Jesus' attacks were not political but religious. He was not concerned with how and by whom the Jews were governed, but with those fellow Jews—especially in the Temple authorities—who accused him of laxity in religious observances, and finally took the lead in arresting him. The Cleansing of the Temple (see pp.240–41) was not a signal for a political uprising, as some have suggested, but a symbolic prophetic act of opposition to the Temple as an institution. It was an opposition that Jesus expressed elsewhere and which he shared with other Jewish groups of the time.

THE INSCRIPTION ON THE CROSS

According to the gospels, the inscription on Jesus' cross—the *titulus*—recorded that Jesus had been found guilty of a political offense: claiming to be "King of the Jews" (Mark 15.26 and parallels). It is generally accepted that Mark's simple wording of the inscription ("The King of the Jews") is probably authentic. However, Matthew's version, "This is Jesus the King of the Jews" (Matt. 27.37), parallels the wording of the placard of a Christian martyr at Lyons, France, in 177 CE: "This is Attalus the Christian." John's account (John 19.19) may also contain good historical information. He stresses the official nature of the inscription ("Jesus of Nazareth, King of the Jews") as being authorized by Pilate, with the words "of Nazareth" added to identify the victim more precisely.

THE MYSTIC

To describe someone as a "mystic" implies that he or she regularly enjoys an individual religious experience of peculiar intensity, an intimate communion with the divine. Jesus would certainly seem to have been conscious of an especially close relationship with God (see pp.276–77, 296–97), which the gospels suggest was expressed and confirmed through his own practice of prayer.

Jesus' customary mode of prayer was essentially private and personal: he may have joined in the regular prayer sessions at the Temple (as mentioned in Acts 3.1) from time to time, but the gospels do not explicitly state this. He tended to withdraw to pray alone in isolated places, especially mountains (Mark 1.35, 6.46; Luke 4.42, 5.16, 6.12, 9.18, 9.28, 11.1). The

Jesus and the Holy Spirit

The New Testament clearly portrays Jesus as one endowed with the Spirit of God. The synoptic gospels contain comparatively few references to the Spirit in the earthly life of Jesus, but these occur at significant moments in his career, while elsewhere in the New Testament he is the source of the gift of the Spirit to believers (Gal. 4.6).

In the Hebrew Scriptures, the Spirit is primarily a supernatural force that empowers individuals to perform heroic deeds or to voice prophetic utterances. Traces of this concept are evident in the gospels. Thus Jesus comes to Galilee filled with the power of the Spirit (Luke 4.14). After his baptism, he was driven out into the wilderness (Mark 1.12), recalling the way in which the Spirit physically transported prophets such as Elijah or Ezekiel (1 Kings 18.12; 2 Kings 2.16; Ezek. 3.14, 11.1, 37.1, 43.5). Such Spirit possession was usually only temporary and partial, but in later writings prophets increasingly came to be viewed as the permanent bearers of the Spirit (Isa. 11.2, 61.1). In much Jewish thought, the future Messiah was similarly pictured as the bearer of the Spirit.

Jesus is represented as claiming to fulfill those passages in the scriptures that depict the prophet as the bearer of the Spirit (Matt. 12.18–21; Luke 4.18–19). The descent of the Holy Spirit at Jesus' baptism constituted a permanent endowment (John 1.32–33). Jesus possessed the Spirit in a unique and complete manner, and did so as the result of his personal relationship with the Father, who gave him the Spirit "without measure" (John 3.34)—fully and not in part, as was the case with earlier prophetic figures. His possession of the Spirit is identical with his divine sonship (John 3.35).

Jesus' whole ministry and preaching were authenticated by the power of the Spirit (Matt. 12.28), and those who failed to recognize the Spirit at work in him and blasphemed against it risked eternal damnation (Mark 3.28–30 and parallels).

The Judean wilderness, where the Spirit drove Jesus (Mark 1.12). His 40-day sojourn in the desert recalls the duration of Elijah's journey to Mount Horeb (1 Kings 19.8).

The Agony in the Garden, *by Andrea Mantegna (ca. 1430–1506). The artist depicts Jesus' anguished solitary prayer in the Garden of Gethsemane shortly before his arrest (Mark 14.32–42 and parallels; see pp.244–45). According to Luke, "an angel from heaven appeared to him and gave him strength" (Luke 22.43). The disciples Peter, James, and John lie sleeping a little way away; in the background, Judas leads the arresting party from Jerusalem toward the garden.*

gospels' repeated references to such acts of private devotion show how significant they were felt to be for a proper understanding of Jesus. According to Christian tradition, intense and dramatic experiences such as Jesus' prayer in Gethsemane (most vividly portrayed in Luke 22.42) were a regular mark of his life on earth (Heb. 5.7).

One characteristic of mystical experience is the reception of visions of the supernatural world, the revelation of divine secrets. In the gospels, Jesus tells of such a vision, in which Satan falls from heaven like a flash of lightning (Luke 10.18), although this passage may have been influenced by Jewish myths that were in turn inspired by Isaiah 14.12–15).

At least one authority has recently claimed that Jesus' spiritual experience can be linked with a tradition of Jewish mysticism. Some Jewish teachers of his time entered a trance-like state in which they claimed to "ascend to heaven" into the very presence of God. It seems likely that Paul had such an experience (2 Cor. 12.2–4), although the clearest picture of the mystical ascent to heaven is found in the nonscriptural writings concerning the figure of Enoch (see sidebar, p.298). In these, Enoch ascends to the throne of God, where his whole being is transformed. He is clothed in shining garments of glory and then returns to earth as a heavenly messenger.

Such a tradition may well underlie the description of the person and mission of Jesus at the beginning of Revelation (Rev. 1.1–16), and there are striking parallels with the Transfiguration (see box, p.236). A passage in the Fourth Gospel (John 3.31–33) can be interpreted as a declaration that Jesus' gospel was true because it contained what he had seen and heard in heaven. Other sayings of Jesus in John have been interpreted as providing a glimpse of his own awareness of a mystical ascent to heaven (John 3.13, 6.42, 8.23).

JESUS AT PRAYER IN LUKE

Luke's gospel especially emphasizes the role of prayer in the life of Jesus. Two references are particularly significant. After Jesus' baptism and the opening of heaven, Luke adds that Jesus was praying (Luke 3.21); and at the Transfiguration the appearance of Jesus is transformed as he prays (Luke 9.29). In both instances, the evangelist may be suggesting that the heavenly voice which proclaimed Jesus as God's Son at the Baptism and the Transfiguration was a mystical confirmation of his true nature, revealed to Jesus following his communion and union with the Father through the intimacy of prayer.

A chapel on the shore of Lake Galilee at Migdal, ancient Magdala, the hometown of Mary Magdalene, who always appears first in the list of female followers.

JESUS AND FEMINISM

Feminist theory shares with liberation theology (see sidebar, p.336) a concern for a marginalized group, namely women, whom it sees as continually ignored and oppressed throughout history by a male-dominated society. Although all feminist writers would share this outlook, there are considerable differences in their approach to the New Testament and to the ideas and intentions of Jesus in particular.

The gospels make clear the important place of women in Jesus' life and ministry. The names of some of those who accompanied him and provided for him on his Galilean mission (Matt. 27.55–56; Mark 15.40–41; Luke 8.1–3) are preserved, and it was also remembered that women had been the first witnesses of the Resurrection (Mark 16.1–8 and parallels; see pp.258–59). There is a marked emphasis on Jesus' healing of women, for whom he shows a special compassion: he healed a "daughter of Abraham" who had been crippled for eighteen years (Luke 13.10–17); a Syro-Phoenician Gentile (Matt. 15.21–28; Mark 7.24–30); and a woman whose condition made her unclean and a social outcast (Mark 5.25–34 and parallels). Strikingly, Jesus was accepting even of prostitutes, opening the kingdom of God to them (Matt. 21.31–32) and receiving their homage (Luke 7.36–50). Again, images drawn from the world of women and their occupations

The "androgynous Jesus"

To quote one feminist writer, "where God is male, the male is God." For some radical feminists, Jesus' manhood and the masculine language he employed in speaking of God mean that he cannot be seen as a savior for women. His message, they claim, excludes women, as the mainstream Judeo-Christian tradition has always done. Hence women must reject Christianity in favor of a religion that directly expresses female religious experience.

Other feminist scholars have sought to address this claim by arguing that the New Testament figure of Jesus is to be understood as both male and female. Their view is influenced by the revived interest in Gnosticism (see pp.330–31), which they would see as an authentic Christian movement, the significance of which was obscured as Christian theology became increasingly patriarchal in outlook. Many Gnostics, following ideas current in some Jewish circles, held that the first human being was androgynous. Christ, the second Adam, restores in his own person the primitive sexual unity of all humanity. This teaching is attributed to Jesus in some of the apocryphal gospels with a Gnostic background, such as the Gospel of Thomas and the Gospel of Philip.

Central also to many Gnostic systems is the figure of Sophia, or Wisdom, the female aspect of deity (see pp.330–31). In the Hebrew Bible, the personified figure of Wisdom is also described in female terms. Sophia is a mother and identified with the Holy Spirit; the Gospel of Thomas calls her the true Mother of Jesus, and Luke's account of Jesus' conception by the Holy Spirit can be understood in this light (Luke 1.35).

In the New Testament, Jesus is sometimes described as the Wisdom of God, and can thus be viewed as the incarnation of Sophia—in whom the fundamental feminine and masculine natures are united—and as her prophet to all human beings, both women and men.

Noli Me Tangere, *by Martin Schongauer (1440–91). It illustrates the account in John's gospel of the appearance of the risen Christ to Mary Magdalene (John 20.11–18). The Latin title given to this scene translates Jesus' words to Mary: "Touch me not" (NRSV: "Do not hold on to me"). Mary's prominence among Jesus' female disciples is probably based on the tradition that she was the first to see the risen Lord (compare Mark 16.9).*

occur in Jesus' parables and teaching (Matt. 13.33, 24.41; Luke 13.20, 15.8–10, 17.35). He also shows concern for widows, whose position in society was often an unfortunate one (Mark 12.42–44; Luke 18.2–8, 21.2–4).

Such facts would be recognized by all New Testament scholars, whether feminist or not, but caution is needed in assessing their significance. It is often suggested that Jesus' attitude marked a radical break from the subordinate position of women in contemporary Judaism. However, comparatively little is known of the place of women in first-century Judaism and they may have enjoyed a higher status than is often supposed. On the other hand, feminists would point out that all the gospels were written by male authors and that their outlook as a whole remains firmly patriarchal. They are therefore unlikely to have portrayed women playing such a special part in Jesus' career unless their role was indeed exceptional for the time.

JESUS AND FEMALE DISCIPLESHIP

Feminist scholars seek to read the gospels from the distinctive standpoint of women, and this approach has often produced novel and illuminating results, uncovering aspects hitherto unappreciated in the texts. For example, Jesus' honoring of the woman who anoints him—in the face of his disciples' disapproval—can be seen as affirming a central place for women in the life of the future Church (Matt. 26.6–13; Mark 14.3–9).

In the story of Martha and Mary (Luke 10.38–42), Mary listens to Jesus while her sister Martha busies herself with household tasks. When Martha complains of this to Jesus, he says that Mary "has chosen the better part." This episode may reflect a dispute about the proper role of women in the Christian community, with the favoring of Mary confirming the right of women to full discipleship.

Women in the gospels can be seen as those who humbly and faithfully accept the teaching of Jesus—in contrast to the frequent doubts and questionings of the male disciples. Much interest has focused on the figure of Jesus' mother, and feminist theologians have shown that she is not to be understood just as a passive recipient of the divine purpose but as an active proclaimer of liberation and a model of discipleship for all humanity.

JUDAISM AND THE CHURCH

The early Church in Jerusalem saw its mission as directed towards Israel, but all the evidence suggests that it gained only limited penetration among Jews, especially in Palestine. Jewish Christians—those who continued to observe the Torah while believing in Jesus and his mission—occupied a precarious position between Judaism and mainstream Christianity and were acceptable to neither. They fragmented following the dispersion of the Jerusalem Church in 70 CE and ultimately disappeared (see pp.326–27).

One issue dividing Christians and Jews was the Jewish rejection of Jesus as the Messiah. The Judaism of Jesus' day had no concept of a suffering, dying, and resurrected Savior. For Christians, Jesus was the prophet foretold in the Hebrew Scriptures, and those who did not heed his message would be held accountable by God (Deut. 18.18–19). In Acts, this warning is intensified: "everyone who does not listen to that prophet will be utterly rooted out by the people" (Acts 3.23). Thus the refusal by Jews (or anyone else) to accept Jesus and his teaching inevitably incurred divine judgment against them. However, in Judaism, it is not in itself unacceptable to claim to be the Messiah, and Jewish history has produced many messianic claimants (such as Simon bar Kokhba in the second century CE and Shabbetai Zvi in the seventeenth). What most offended mainstream rabbinic Judaism was the Christian belief that Jesus was God made flesh. In Judaism, it has been said, the human cannot be divine and hence the divine cannot be human.

As a result of Paul's teaching that Christ had superseded the Jewish law (Rom. 10.4), Christians no longer felt bound by the full requirements of the Torah. This was a decisive and fundamental break with Judaism, and it meant that the new faith could be preached to Gentiles. The Church soon became, and remained, an overwhelmingly Gentile body.

The break was further widened during the reorganization of national life after the catastrophe of 70 CE, when Jewish religious leaders—essentially the Pharisees, since the Temple and its priesthood had ceased to exist—demanded strict observance of the law, under rabbinic authority and teaching. The pluralism that had existed hitherto within Judaism (see pp.166–9)

"JESUS THE JEW"
Recent appreciations of the person of the historical Jesus on the part of both Jewish and Christian writers (see pp.332–33) have opened the way for a new climate of understanding between Christianity and Judaism. Since at least the eighteenth century, New Testament scholarship has increasingly recognized the essential Jewishness of Jesus, and that his life and teaching must be interpreted from within the context of the Judaism of his day.

Similarly, some strands of Jewish scholarly opinion, while obviously continuing to reject belief in Jesus' divinity, and resurrection, have come to view him in a more positive light. Some Jewish scholars—a very small minority, it must be stressed—would say that Jesus revealed what lies at the heart of the Law, the existential relationship between human beings and God, and that his identification with the outcast and oppressed constituted a universal challenge to all humanity.

The Synagogue, *an allegorical figure of ca. 1230 from Strasbourg Cathedral, France. Her eyes are bound, to indicate the "blindness" of the Jews to the gospel, and she carries a broken lance (one of the instruments of the Crucifixion, for which Jews were blamed), and a closed book (representing the Jewish law, which Jesus was considered to have superseded).*

was greatly reduced. Increasingly, Christians were arraigned before local Jewish tribunals and expelled from synagogues, as the gospels indicate (Matt. 10.17; Mark 13.9; Luke 12.11, 21.12). Paul believed that the Jewish rejection of Jesus would only be temporary (Rom. 11.26), but his hopes were not realized. The breach became ever wider, and the early Church understood the success of its mission to the Gentiles as a sign that Judaism had indeed been superseded (Acts 13.46–47, 18.6).

The further mainstream Christianity became distanced from its roots in Judaism, the less Christians understood the Jewish context in which Jesus had operated, and the more they came to see him and his disciples in contradistinction to "the Jews." In particular, Christians increasingly came to put responsibility for Jesus' death not on Pilate, nor on the Temple authorities and other Jewish groups that had opposed Jesus' teachings, but simply on "the Jews"—the entire Jewish people.

The Virgin and Child, *a panel from an Ethiopian Coptic icon diptych of the early 18th century. The infant Jesus holds the book of the new law, which renders obsolete the old law of Judaism.*

Early on, Peter could say that "the Jews" and their rulers had acted only through ignorance (Acts 3.17), but what Christians saw as the Jews' continued obduracy and refusal to acknowledge the truth about Jesus soon led to a hardening of attitudes. This is to be seen most starkly in the Fourth Gospel, where "the Jews"—here clearly meaning the whole nation—are pictured as seeking to destroy Jesus from the outset. The Jews' rejection of Jesus showed that they were not God's elect, not the children of Abraham, but the offspring of the devil (John 8.31–44).

Over the succeeding centuries, whatever sociological or economic factors may also have been involved, there can be little doubt that the widespread Christian belief that the Jewish people as a whole bore the guilt for Jesus' death lay at the root of Christian anti-Judaism, and of its baleful nineteenth-century racialist offspring, anti-Semitism. As a consequence, Judaism tended to see Jesus as the cause of its persecution and to depict him in the most unfavorable light (see sidebar, right).

Opposition between the two groups varied in its bitterness at different periods, but there was always a link between them in that the Church appealed to the authority of the Hebrew Scriptures, the Christian Old Testament. In medieval Europe there were frequent formal public disputations between learned rabbis and Christian teachers. These were staged by the Church in order to "prove" the superiority of its message, and centered on the Church's belief that various passages in the Hebrew Scriptures referred to Jesus, and on Christian claims that statements in the Talmud expressed a belief in Jesus' messiahship.

JESUS IN THE TALMUD

The Talmud contains brief references that may demonstrate Jewish attitudes toward Jesus in the early centuries CE. A prayer that probably dates from the first century CE petitions for the destruction of heretics, which may be a veiled reference to Christians. It is also alleged that Jesus had been hanged as a criminal for practicing sorcery, and that he had enticed Israel to apostasy. Both charges are reflected in the gospels, notably the sorcery accusation (Mark 3.22–27 and parallels). But the notion that Jesus had attempted to lead Israel astray was undoubtedly strengthened by the Church's abandonment of the full requirements of the Torah.

Another passage in the Talmud speaks of one who, though born of a woman, sought to make himself God—a fairly clear attack on the belief in Christ's divinity.

JESUS AND ISLAM

In the Qur'an, Jesus (Arabic, Isa) is one of a succession of individuals to whom God revealed his Word, beginning with Adam, Noah, and Abraham. The last and greatest of these figures was the Prophet Muhammad, who has no successor and is thus "the Seal of the Prophets." Between Abraham and Muhammad there were many other prophets (*nabi*s), of whom twenty-eight were selected to bear and propagate the divine Word. These special prophets are known as *rasul*s and include Moses and Jesus, who brought the Word to two specific communities, the Jews and the Christians respectively. As "Peoples of the Book"—those to whom God (Allah) has vouchsafed scripture—Jews and Christians thus possess a special status in Islam.

Jesus' distinguished position in the line of prophecy is reflected in the considerable range of titles and descriptions applied to him in the Qur'an, such as "Messiah" and "God's Word and Spirit." He is described most frequently as "Son of Mary," and the virgin birth is strongly emphasized. The Qur'an also has the story of the birth of John the Baptist, whose mission is to confirm Jesus as God's Word.

The Birth of Jesus, *a Persian miniature of ca. 1700. According to the Qur'an (*Sura *19, "Mary"), the pregnant Mary withdrew to a "distant place," where she gave birth to Jesus next to a palm tree. At the behest of the newborn child (right), Mary shook dates from the tree to eat, while a refreshing stream flowed from its roots.*

On his mission (see box), Jesus was strengthened by the Holy Spirit and raised to the highest rank among the prophets. He performed miracles by the power of Allah, healing the blind and the leprous and raising the dead, with the apostles as his helpers. Jesus was given the Gospel by God, and set about teaching its truths. All the "People of the Book" will come to believe in the truth of Jesus, and he will witness against their errors at the Last Judgment.

On the other hand, the Qur'an firmly rejects any notion of Jesus' divinity. Jesus is not God's son, only his servant and prophet—a "Messenger of God," a creature of dust, like Adam. Only those who lack true belief would say that the Messiah, the Son of Mary, is God. The Qur'an particularly condemns the doctrine of the Trinity, although mainstream Christianity would probably argue with the way in which the Qur'an represents Trinitarian doctrine: "They are unbelievers who say, 'God is the Third of Three.' No god is there but One God" (*Sura* 5, "The Table").

The Qur'an also denies the Crucifixion. It says that although "the Jews" claim to have executed Jesus, they did not actually slay or crucify him but only his double, who was put to death in his place, while Jesus was "raised up" by God to be with him. Later Muslim traditions speak of Jesus' future return to earth, when he will kill the Antichrist and inaugurate an age of harmony and prosperity under the true religion.

The components of this picture of Jesus reflect the canonical gospels, some of the apocryphal gospels, and debates in which Muhammad engaged with Christians. Christian scholars generally agree that Muhammad probably had no firsthand acquaintance with the four New Testament gospels. His own personal contact with Christians was probably restricted to wandering monks and ascetics, who had penetrated into southern Arabia largely from the adjacent region of Syria, and for whom the Qur'an shows considerable regard. Such people propagated what was essentially a popular form of Christianity, which over the course of time had acquired many legendary and folkloric features and was sometimes at variance with strict Church orthodoxy.

The life of Jesus and the Qur'an

The passages about Jesus in the Qur'an echo the New Testament and often also traditions found in some apocryphal gospels, which were evidently well known in southern Arabia, since they exist in numerous early Arabic translations.

In the Qur'an, the Annunciation to Mary is made by an angelic being in human form, to whom Mary responds as in Luke. Jesus' birth takes place under a palm tree (see illustration, opposite): a virtually identical account occurs in the apocryphal "Gospel of Pseudo-Matthew."

The Qur'an mentions Jesus' miracles of healing. He is also described as making birds of clay and bringing them to life, an episode found in many apocryphal sources (see illustration, p.309). In another miracle, Jesus, at the request of the apostles, causes a table laid with a festival banquet to be sent down from heaven for them. This may contain a reference to the Christian Eucharist or perhaps to the miraculous feedings recorded in the gospels.

There are also many allusions to Jesus' teachings. Jesus is said to confirm the Torah, but relaxes some of its prohibitions—this is reminiscent of Jesus' attitude to the law as portrayed in the New Testament (see pp.272–73). Parables of Jesus are also alluded to, such as those of the Sower and of the Ten Bridesmaids, and many Qur'anic phrases recall the language of the canonical gospels.

Several sayings and miracles of Muhammad recorded in the Hadith (Muslim traditions about the life of Prophet) are very similar to words and deeds that the New Testament ascribes to Jesus. Later Muslim historians and theologians often show a good knowledge of the gospels, not least in their debates with Christian opponents, and there are many sayings attributed to Jesus in the writings of Muslim mystics (*sufis*).

THE GOSPELS IN THE QUR'AN
In the Qur'an, the Gospel is a book given by God to Jesus, in the same way that the Torah was given to Moses. Muslim scholars who knew the four canonical gospels frequently claimed that they represented a corruption of this original Gospel. Part of the corruption, it was claimed, was the removal of Jesus' prophecy of the coming of Muhammad, which appears in the Qur'an:

> **"And when Jesus son of**
> **Mary said, 'Children of**
> **Israel, I am indeed the**
> **Messenger of God to you,**
> **confirming the Torah**
> **that is before me, and**
> **giving good tidings of**
> **a Messenger who shall**
> **come after me, whose**
> **name shall be Ahmad [Muhammad].'"**

(From *Sura* 61, "The Ranks," translated by Arthur J. Arberry, first published by Allen and Unwin Ltd, 1955; © HarperCollins Publishers; quoted with permission).

IN SEARCH OF THE JESUS OF HISTORY

The Church's doctrine, as formalized in the Patristic age (see pp.328–29), recognized the true humanity of Jesus and viewed him as a real historical person. His deeds and teachings, as recorded in the gospels, were accepted as authentic and authoritative for theology, and were taught to the people at large through preaching, art, and popular drama. In the Churches of East and West, the gospels were believed to be divinely inspired and thus of unquestioned accuracy: their apparent contradictions and variations were harmonized or virtually ignored. Belief that Jesus embodied the perfect union of divinity and humanity meant that there was no difficulty in accepting all the miracles attributed to him in the New Testament. He was seen very much as unique, set apart from Judaism and the world of his time, about which relatively little was known.

A substantial change in this situation began only with the rise of rational ideas and the beginnings of modern science in the seventeenth century. Science revealed a world that seemed to operate through autonomous laws. Assuming that God had ordained these laws at the Creation, questions arose as to the need for further divine interventions, such as miracles, which could appear to violate the laws of nature. Since the gospels record miracles, this inevitably led thinkers such as the English Deists (who sought a faith founded only on rational thinking), to raise fundamental questions as to the nature and origin of the gospels.

The entrance of an ancient tomb at Bethany near Jerusalem, traditionally said to be that of Lazarus, whom Jesus raised from the dead, according to John 11. The Fourth Gospel was formerly considered to provide little reliable historical information relating to Jesus. But this view is now seriously questioned, partly owing to the identification by archaeologists of hitherto undiscovered sites mentioned in John.

It is usually agreed that the modern search for the historical Jesus began with the work of the German scholar Reimarus (1694–1768). Although he was much indebted to his predecessors, such as the Deists, his work was marked by two original, and influential, contentions. First, in sharp contrast to orthodox Christianity, he differentiated between what Jesus really said and taught and what his later followers believed about him—that is, he distinguished between the "Jesus of history" and the "Christ of faith." Secondly, he held that Jesus could only be understood within the context of the Judaism of his day. Jesus, he proposed, was a typical Israelite prophet who had proclaimed the imminence of the messianic and political kingdom for which the Jews had long hoped.

Another important scholar, D. F. Strauss (1808–1874), made the same distinction between the real Jesus and the Church's Redeemer, but perceived this in the gospel texts themselves. Many of the individual stories

The Transfiguration, *from the Ingeborg Psalter (French, ca. 1210). While the dramatic accounts of Jesus' Transfiguration (Mark 9.2–8 and parallels) can be viewed in their present form as largely constructs on the part of the evangelists, it has recently been argued that this event may be rooted in a genuine mystical experience of Jesus (see p.339).*

about Jesus, he suggested, are mythical interpretations that reveal the significance that Jesus possessed for his followers. Here, to some extent, Strauss anticipated the views of later "form criticism."

At the same period, a further impetus was provided by the rise of historical criticism of the gospel texts, with particular reference to their dating and chronological order. The result included a general acceptance that Mark, not Matthew, was the earliest gospel and that John was comparatively late and of thus little historical value (see p.189). In consequence, Mark came to be regarded as providing the most authentic account of Jesus' life and ministry, one that presented him very much as a human figure, with a basically simple ethical message, in contrast to the dogmatic faith of the Church. Taking this view as a starting point, the later nineteenth century saw the appearance of numerous "lives" of Jesus, which sought to reconstruct his real personality and essentially reflected the dominant liberal Protestant theology of the time.

However, by the early twentieth century, fresh developments in New Testament scholarship appeared to signal the collapse of the whole search for the Jesus of history. The very influential work of Albert Schweitzer (1875–1965), author of *The Quest of the Historical Jesus* (1906), showed that the various liberal lives of Jesus were largely projections of their authors' own ethical ideals. The real Jesus, he claimed, was an apocalyptic prophet whose own ethical teaching was only intended for the brief period before the imminent advent of God's kingdom. It also became clear that Mark's gospel was not just a straightforward objective account of Jesus' life and ministry, but a highly theological work reflecting the beliefs of the early Church.

Above all, the methods of form criticism (see pp.182–83) led many to conclude that the gospel writers had no intention of producing a life of Jesus and that their work provides no material for any such undertaking. Rudolf Bultmann (1884–1976), the dominant form critic, dismissed works attempting to reconstruct Jesus' life, personality, and spiritual development as "fantastic and romantic."

However, interest in the Jesus of history was not seriously weakened by the findings of form criticism. Indeed, some of Bultmann's own followers embarked on what has come to be called the "New Quest" of the historical Jesus. The New Quest sought evidence of continuity between the real Jesus and the Christ of the Church's faith, pointing out that all the New Testament writers had assumed without question the identity of the earthly Jesus with their glorified Christ. The proclamation of Christ by

Recovering the "real" Jesus

Three criteria have assumed considerable importance in modern New Testament scholarship. The first criterion is known as "ecclesiastical embarrassment": sayings attributed to Jesus that could have caused embarrassment to early Christians—such as his confession of ignorance of the date of the End Time (Matt 24.36; Mark 13.32)—are highly unlikely to have been made up and the fact that the young Church felt obliged to preserve them is a strong argument for their authenticity.

The second criterion is that of "multiple attestation": sayings that are attributed to Jesus in several strands of the traditions represented by the gospels should be given considerable weight. Behind the different gospels and the material peculiar to each of them lie what was remembered of Jesus and his ministry in several different Christian communities. It is hard to imagine that each of them would have independently invented the same traditions about him.

The Sower, *a window in Canterbury cathedral, England. Jesus' parable of the Sower is likely to be authentic according to the criterion of multiple attestation: it is is found in all three synoptic gospels.*

The third criterion, that of dissimilarity, has proved the most contentious. According to this, if a saying or practice attributed to Jesus appears to be very dissimilar to anything in the teachings and customs of the Judaism of his day, or diverges significantly from the beliefs of the early Church, it may be accepted as good historical evidence for his distinctive outlook.

This procedure may well demonstrate the genuineness of certain sayings of Jesus, but it carries the danger of isolating Jesus from his Jewish background, so that anything in his teaching that conforms to Judaism tends to be regarded as inauthentic. Also, our knowledge both of first-century Judaism and of the primitive Church is still very limited and debatable. Without a fuller picture, it is hard to be sure how far some of the sayings of Jesus identified as "genuine" by the dissimilarity criterion really did or did not conform to the beliefs of his fellow Jews or of the first Christians.

the early Church was based, it was claimed, on the ministry and teaching of the historical Jesus, as presented in the gospels.

The problem remained of how far it was possible to discover a body of teaching that could confidently be accepted as representing Jesus' authentic outlook. Various criteria have been suggested for establishing authenticity (see box, above), but more recent scholarship prefers instead to rely on the general yardstick of "historical plausibility" that historians adopt toward all ancient texts. This places Jesus firmly within his Jewish context: traditions about him are likely to be historical if they fit into the known Jewish background of his ministry (see pp.298–99). Here, modern sociological studies have shown that much of what the gospels record of Jesus' activity mirrors conflicts and tensions in first-century Judaism. The approach of historical plausibility also involves a greater appreciation of the direct links between Jesus and the Christ of the early "Jesus movement." The group that Jesus formed around him during his lifetime preserved traditions of what its original members had actually learned from Jesus, and these formed the basis of the Church's mission and its preaching.

Historical plausibility on its own can never become historical fact, and even if an outline of the historical Jesus could be produced that was acceptable to most scholars, the real significance of the details would continue to be debated. Some writers would even question the whole attempt at a search for the "authentic" Jesus in favor of a concentration on the abiding religious value of the gospel stories, whatever their historical origin.

Yet Christianity has always claimed to rest on the life and teaching of a real figure in a particular time and place and it is unavoidable that every age should seek to discover more about Jesus with the investigative tools at its disposal. The great expansion of so many areas of knowledge and the appearance of new scholarly disciplines during the last two hundred years no doubt make the search for the historical Jesus ever more complicated and diverse. But accepted positively, and rigorously tested, this quest can only add to our understanding of Jesus of Nazareth, a figure whose fascination, for so many men and women, continues undiminished.

The Presentation in the Temple, *by the Master of St. Severin (French, fl. ca. 1485–1515). Luke 2.22–24 records that Jesus' parents observed the Jewish rite of Presentation, although the evangelist endows the event with a Christian significance (see p.209). Modern scholars of the historical Jesus must look behind such theological layers in order to set him more firmly in his Jewish context.*

THE "MYTHICAL" JESUS

Since at least the nineteenth century, there have been claims that Jesus never really existed and that the picture of him in the gospels is wholly fictional and mythical. The supporters of this view generally hold that the Jesus venerated by the early Church was essentially the creation of Paul: a heavenly figure who appeared in ecstatic visions to Paul and his fellow apostles.

To account for the wide acceptance of Paul's preaching, it has been suggested that his congregations were Essenes (see sidebar, p.169) who already revered a "Teacher of Righteousness," the founder of the Qumran community. Paul, it is claimed, identified the Jesus of his visions with this Teacher.

Such claims have failed to find favor with the consensus of New Testament scholarship. They depend heavily on speculative and hypothetical arguments and often seem to ignore evidence which tells against them. For example, while Paul did not know Jesus personally, he clearly had knowledge of Jesus' life and teaching (see sidebar, p.325). His letters offer no hint that his congregations were predominantly Essenes, and nor do the Qumran texts ever suggest that the Teacher of Righteousness was an object of worship.

Above all, if Jesus was really just a supernatural figure, it is difficult to understand how the gospels ever came to be written or why early Christians should have wished to produce such an elaborate fiction of a human being active in a very particular time, place, and society.

PETER, PAUL, AND THE EARLY CHURCH

Above: The Savior, *a 14th-century Russian icon. The austere majesty of the face of Christ epitomizes the Orthodox Church's vision of Jesus as Pantocrator, ruler and redeemer of the universe.*

Opposite: Pietà: Angels Support the Wounded Body of Christ, *by Antonello da Messina (ca. 1430–79). Associated with the theme of the "Man of Sorrows," such images were revered in the late Middle Ages as focusing on Christ's great suffering to redeem fallen humanity.*

THE EARLY CHURCH

The story of the growth of the early Church after the death of Jesus is related in the Acts of the Apostles. However, it cannot be said to give a complete picture of the early expansion of Christianity. It focuses on the career and work of the leader of the apostles, Peter, whom Jesus appointed to lead the Church, and Paul, who began his career as a fervent persecutor of Christians but became perhaps its greatest missionary after his dramatic experience on the road to Damascus (see pp.364–65).

THE ACTS OF THE APOSTLES

Above: *An early 13th-century Syriac manuscript of the Acts of the Apostles. Syriac is a dialect of Aramaic, which was probably the first language of Jesus and the twelve apostles. It became the standard language of many churches of the Near East. Although now largely supplanted by Arabic (to which, like Hebrew, it is related), it still survives in some rural areas of Syria.*

Acts is the second volume by Luke and is written as a sequel to his gospel. It begins with an account of the Ascension of Jesus (Acts 1.9; see pp.262–63). It then takes up the story of how, after the death of Judas Iscariot, the body of apostles was made up to the proper number of twelve by the choice of Matthias through sacred lot, in accordance with biblical precedent. For Luke, the title of "apostle" is reserved for the twelve, in contrast to Paul, who uses the term more widely. In Acts 1.22 Luke states that the replacement for Judas must have been a witness to Jesus' entire public ministry. The new twelve constitute the governing body of the first organized church at Jerusalem.

A more accurate translation of the title of Acts is "Acts of Apostles," because it does not describe the careers of all the twelve. Later Christian writers produced a considerable number of "Acts" of other apostles to redress this lack. Also, a significant role is played in Acts by figures who did not belong to the twelve, such as Stephen (Acts 6–7) and Philip (Acts 8). But the two leading characters in Acts are Peter, who is the hero of its first dozen chapters, and Paul, whose missionary work is recounted in the remainder of the work.

Just before the Ascension, Jesus commands his disciples to bear witness to him in Jerusalem, Judea, Samaria, and "the ends of the earth" (Acts 1.8), and this program is carried out in successive stages until the book's climax in Rome, the center of the empire of which Judea was then part. Acts is in many respects an apologia for the Christian movement, addressed to the Roman governing classes. This is seen especially in its account of the career of Paul (see pp.368–75).

Luke's two-volume writing, comprising his gospel and Acts of the Apostles, is the New Testament work that approaches most closely the standards and style of Classical (Greek and Roman) historians, although it has its own theological outlook (see sidebar, right). Luke follows common Classical convention in dedicating his books to a distinguished person, in this case a certain Theophilus, who may actually have been the author's patron. In the introduction to the gospel, which serves as an introduction to both volumes, Luke contrasts his work with that of his predecessors and hints that it is an improvement on them (Luke 1.1–4). In saying this he is writing in much the same vein as the great Greek historian Thucydides (lived ca. 475 BCE) at the beginning of his *History of the Peloponnesian War*.

ACTS AND HISTORY

In the past, the author of Acts has generally been seen as a careful and accurate recorder of events. But in more recent years his reliability has been questioned, and attention has focused on the extent to which Acts reflects Luke's own theological outlook. It is widely accepted that the author had a good knowledge of the contemporary geographical, social, and political setting of his narrative. He is strikingly accurate with respect to the names and titles of the imperial officials who appear in the course of his account, and he displays a sound knowledge of Roman legal procedure.

However, correct background information does not guarantee the reliability of all episodes and stories. It is perhaps the picture of Paul in Acts that has raised the most doubts. The author seeks to draw parallels between Peter and Paul and to show that they had a common theological outlook. But passages in Paul's letters show that their relationship was not always harmonious (see p.367). In the early Church, there were those who denigrated Paul in favor of Peter, and it may well be that Luke is consciously concerned to correct this attitude.

Christ and the Apostles; *Spanish (Catalonian), 13th century. The enthroned figure of Jesus is surrounded by the symbols of the four evangelists.*

The literary background to Acts

Acts cannot be seen simply as a work of Classical history writing, since the early Christian community, of which it is a product, had its own distinctive outlook. Nevertheless, it does employ several of the conventions of Classical historians, most notably the use of speeches, which occupy about a third of Acts.

As a famous passage from Thucydides states, Greek and Roman historians did not seek to reproduce verbatim what had been said on a particular occasion, but to give in their own words what they imagined the speaker would have said, had he been able to fully express himself. Although Thucydides claims to follow, as closely as possible, what had actually been uttered, later historians tended to treat such speeches as rhetorical exercises, paying less attention to historical probability. As they stand, the speeches in Acts are no doubt Luke's compositions, but they seem to be constructed for the particular audience to which they were addressed. Those which are written for Jewish ears are couched in the language of the Septuagint, the Greek translation of the Hebrew Scriptures, while Paul's speech to the pagan philosophers at Athens (Acts 17.22–31) is essentially a Hellenistic discourse about the knowledge of God.

The dramatic character of many episodes in Acts, especially Paul's journeys and their accompanying adventures, invites comparison with Hellenistic romances. The accounts of healing miracles, of escapes from prison, and of Paul's sea voyage to Rome are similar in form and vocabulary to many contemporary Greek writings. The voyage belongs to a great literary tradition going back to Homer's *Odyssey*.

THE DESCENT OF THE SPIRIT

The Descent of the Spirit at Pentecost, *a fresco by Giotto (ca. 1266–1337) in the Scrovegni chapel at Padua, Italy, ca. 1305.*

The gift of the Holy Spirit is of central importance to the author of Acts, because the Spirit is the motivating force of the whole story that he tells. The Spirit wins new converts, empowers the working of miracles, and gives wisdom and courage to the leaders of the young Church. It guides them to undertake significant initiatives, such as Peter's visit to the Gentile Cornelius (Acts 10; see pp.366–67), and missionary journeys.

The fact that the gift of the Spirit occurred on the feast of Pentecost, the Jewish festival of Weeks (see Exod. 34.22; Deut. 16.10), may be of particular importance. Weeks was originally an agricultural celebration, marking the end of the wheat harvest and the offering of its first fruits. However, it became a commemoration of the giving of the Law on Sinai (see pp.54–5), and the depiction of the day of Pentecost in Acts has sometimes been interpreted as the moment when the old Jewish Law was replaced by a new spiritual revelation for all humanity. This theory is complicated by the fact that the association of Pentecost and the Law does not seem to be older than the third century CE, although the book of Jubilees, a text of the second century BCE, makes the Pentecost a commemoration of the "Noachide commandments," which were held to bind all humankind, Gentiles as well as Jews (see p.26).

The actual account of the descent of the Spirit is couched in biblical imagery typically associated with a divine manifestation. The "sound like a rush of violent wind" (Acts 2.2) and the "divided tongues, as of fire" (Acts 2.3) recall the creation, the Flood, and many manifestations of God, especially that to Moses at Sinai. Acts also recalls the baptism of Jesus (Luke 3.21–22): the flame of the Spirit rests on each of the apostles, as the dove of the Spirit did on Jesus.

Peter's first speech

The account of the coming of the Spirit is followed by a speech by Peter, explaining what it implied (Acts 2.14–40). Following Luke's general account for the spread of the Church, this sermon is addressed to Jews. It begins by claiming that God's promises to his people have been realized through the ministry, death, and resurrection of Jesus, and various biblical passages, in particular the prophet Joel, are quoted in support. The presence of the Holy Spirit, which the hearers have witnessed, is the sign of Jesus' exaltation and glory, and the apostles' message is authenticated because they are the witnesses of his resurrection and ascension. Through the rite of baptism, they are empowered to offer forgiveness of sins and the gift of the Holy Spirit to those who will take heed and repent. This is a promise not only for Jews but for any whom God may summon.

The Prophet Joel *(ca. 1510), by Michelangelo (1475–1564); in the Sistine Chapel, Rome. Peter's first speech includes an extensive quote from Joel (Acts 2.17–21, quoting Joel 2.28–32).*

Peter's first address sets the pattern for the general theology of the other speeches in Acts. It has often been claimed that these discourses represent the actual preaching of the first apostles. However, some specifically Lucan themes suggest that, in their present form, they are Luke's own compositions. For example, in this first sermon of Peter, proof of Jesus' divine mission is said to be provided by his miracles and signs (Acts 2.22). This is a regular theme of Luke's gospel, as is Peter's claim that everything that happened to Jesus was the result of God's "definite plan and foreknowledge" (Acts 2.23). But whatever their origin, the speeches in Acts represent important evidence for how the early Church understood the person and work of Jesus.

The result of the outpouring of the Spirit onto the apostles was that they were able to "speak in other languages" (Acts 2.4), a phenomenon witnessed by "devout Jews from every nation under heaven" who are living in Jerusalem (Acts 2.5). Luke lists the nations they represent (Acts 2.9–11): they are from both inside and outside the confines of the Roman empire and are depicted primarily as Jews from the widespread Dispersion of the late centuries BCE. Luke also mentions the presence of proselytes (Acts 2.10), Gentiles who had been converted to Judaism as the result of vigorous and successful Jewish propaganda. "Speaking in tongues," or "glossolalia" was a common phenomenon in the churches founded by Paul, well before the probable date of the composition of Acts. In these cases, however, it did not involve the ability to speak foreign languages, but the uttering of unintelligible, ecstatic speech which could even give the impression of madness. Luke seems to hint at this when he records that some of the onlookers thought that the apostles were drunk (Acts 2.13). Later references in Acts to speaking in tongues (Acts 10.46; 19.6) do not suggest that foreign languages were involved.

The apostles would not have needed to speak in the pilgrims' native tongues, since they would all have known a lingua franca, either Aramaic or Greek. Luke may have seen the events of Pentecost as a reversal of the Tower of Babel story (Gen. 11.1–9; see p.28). The story of the Tower of Babel tells how human presumption brought about the use of different languages which led to division in the world. The proclamation of the gospel, which all can understand, brings human beings together again, restoring their original harmony in a new community comprising, "everyone whom the Lord our God calls to him" (Acts 2.39).

PETER IN ACTS

GAMALIEL

Gamaliel the Elder, who appears in Acts 5, was a renowned rabbi of the first century CE. He was a member of the great Pharisee dynasty of Hillel and, according to tradition, served as president of the Sanhedrin. He represented the liberal interpretation of the Jewish Law that characterized the Hillel school, advocating more freedom of movement on the Sabbath and greater protection for women in divorce proceedings. According to Acts 22.3, the apostle Paul was his pupil.

Gamaliel's reputation for learning and tolerance is born out by his speech in Acts, in which he advises the Sanhedrin to leave Peter and the apostles alone, for "if this plan or this undertaking is of human origin, it will fail; but if it is of God, you will not be able to overthrow them" (Acts 5.38–39). It is entirely consistent with Luke's message that Gamaliel, a Pharisee, should show a not wholly unfavorable attitude toward the Christians. In spite of his frequent criticisms of the Jews, Luke was anxious to present Christianity as the legitimate successor of Judaism, especially as represented by the influential Pharisaic party. The Pharisees shared with the Christians a belief in the resurrection of the dead. Their opponents, the Sadducees, denied the possibility of resurrection, and twice hauled the apostles before the Sanhedrin (Acts 4 and 5). Paul later exploited the division between the two groups over the resurrection issue (Acts 23.6–10; see also pp.166–67).

In his discourse in Acts, Gamaliel refers to two messianic pretenders, Theudas and Judas, placing Theudas first. In fact, Theudas's revolt occurred long after that of Judas. This is probably a simple error by Luke and it does not affect the force of Gamaliel's argument.

The government of the early Church in Jerusalem was in the hands of the first twelve apostles, and it is Peter who appears as the undoubted leader and the spokesman of the Christian community in its confrontations with the religious authorities. He is depicted as a powerful wonder-worker: the mere falling of his shadow on the sick is said to be enough to heal them (Acts 5.15). Later in Acts, handkerchiefs and aprons which have been in contact with the apostle Paul are seen to possess similar curative properties (Acts 19.12). The first evidence of the apostles' ability to work "signs and wonders" comes immediately after the Pentecost story: this is the healing of a crippled beggar at the Beautiful Gate of the Temple, when Peter and John are attending one of the regular hours of prayer (Acts 3.1–10). The story follows the regular pattern of healing miracles in the gospels and elsewhere, mentioning the severity of the affliction, its cure, and the effect on the bystanders. The particular power inherent in Peter's person is brought out in the story: like Paul in Acts 14, he commands the cripple to stand up and walk, and his hands convey strength to the man's feet and ankles (Acts 3.6–8). It is sometimes suggested that this account betrays a knowledge of medicine, which supports the view that the author of Acts was the Luke that is referred to in Colossians 4.14 as "the beloved physician." However, the language is not really technical enough to warrant this conclusion.

The healing of the beggar is followed by Peter's second speech (Acts 3.12–26), which, like the first (see p.355), discusses the fulfillment of God's promise to send the Messiah, and the necessity to repent "so that your sins might be wiped out" (Acts 3.19). This speech stresses that the crucifixion of Jesus was the responsibility of the Jews, although Peter concedes that they acted in ignorance (Acts 3.17), as Jesus also acknowledged in Luke's gospel (Luke 23.34). As a result of this preaching, Peter and John are arrested by the Temple authorities (Acts 4.3). This marks the first of Peter's three imprisonments, which are narrated in increasingly dramatic terms. After a night in jail, the two apostles are brought before the council (Sanhedrin), where Peter makes a third speech (Acts 4.8–12). They are let off, on the condition that they are "not to speak or teach at all in the name of Jesus" (Acts 4.18). Peter and John refuse to obey this order, but they are released anyway "because of the people, for all of them praised God" for the miracle of the healed cripple.

The subsequent success of the Christian mission leads to the imprisonment of the whole apostolic college (Acts 5.18), which is then freed through the intervention of an angel (Acts 5.19). Luke's account here is modeled on a common framework for stories of prison escapes used by Classical authors such as Euripides and Ovid. Eventually the apostles appear again before the Sanhedrin, and the pattern is repeated: there is another speech from Peter (Acts 5.29–32) and, on the advice of the rabbinic teacher Gamaliel (see sidebar, left), the accused are released after an admonitory flogging and another order to stop preaching in the name of Jesus (Acts 5.40–41).

The account of Peter's third imprisonment in Acts 12 is a fine example of Luke's narrative powers. On this occasion, Peter alone is arrested, not by the Temple authorities, but as part of a persecution of leading Christians by Herod Agrippa I (ruled 37–44 CE), who, by winning the favor of the emperors Caligula and Claudius, had become client king of almost all the territory that was ruled by his grandfather Herod the Great (see map on p.137). Peter was probably detained in the Antonia fortress, the barracks next to the Temple. The vivid and detailed story of Peter's release by an angel (Acts 12.7–10) again follows the pattern of other prison escapes in both biblical and nonbiblical writings. The iron gate to the city opens "of its own accord" (Acts 12.10). There are similar occurrences in Greek literature from Homer onward, and the first-century Jewish historian Josephus recorded that during the great Jewish revolt of 66–73 CE, the great east gate of the Temple opened by itself.

Peter's happy escape by divine help is skillfully contrasted with the divine judgment visited on his persecutor. Because he "had not given glory to God," Herod is struck down and "eaten by worms" (Acts 12.23). Being eaten by worms is a form of death that is frequently mentioned by ancient writers. In particular, Luke may have had in mind the fate of the second-century BCE Hellenistic ruler Antiochus IV Epiphanes (2 Macc. 9.9; see pp.132–33). Herod, who was popular among Jews if not Christians, did in fact die suddenly, at Caesarea, in 44 CE. The circumstances of his death clearly made a great impression on his contemporaries: the account by Josephus agrees with that in Acts, both in general outline and in some details.

Herod Agrippa I (10 BCE–44 CE), a persecutor of the early Church, portrayed on one of his own coins.

St. Peter Healing with his Shadow *(Acts 5.15), a fresco by Tommaso Masaccio (1401–1428) in the Brancacci chapel of the church of Santa Maria del Carmine, Florence; ca. 1425.*

THE JERUSALEM CHURCH

The Death of Ananias, *from the Mortlake Tapestries, based on cartoons by Raphael (1483–1520) for tapestries in the Vatican. According to Acts, Ananias and his wife Sapphira sold a property and kept some of the proceeds that they had promised to donate to the Church. The tapestry depicts the moment after Peter has publicly condemned Ananias: "Now when Ananias heard these words, he fell down and died" (Acts 5.5). Sapphira later met the same fate.*

At intervals throughout Acts, Luke gives what may be described as "editorial summaries." They are particularly frequent in the early part of the book and give an idealized picture of the general life and development of the earliest Christian community in Jerusalem. Christians are shown as devout Jews, who attend the Temple every day at the regular hours of prayer (Acts 3.1). Luke says that they often share communal meals in their homes, when they break bread together (Acts 2.46). This ritual probably took place as part of an ordinary meal, but since in his gospel Luke says that Jesus broke bread at the Last Supper (Luke 22.19), it is likely to have included the practice that was later separated out as the Eucharist. The earliest Christian community, then, was a religious fellowship group of a kind common within Judaism, and it continued the fellowship that Jesus had established with his disciples.

Luke emphasizes the unity and joy of this Christian society. The whole company of believers is said to be "of one heart and soul" (Acts 4.32). Here, Luke seems to echo similar expressions found in Greek writers, who praise the ideal of universal friendship which, they claim, existed at the beginning of human history. In the same way, Luke describes the ideal state of harmony that characterized the Church in its earliest days.

It has sometimes been asserted that Acts shows the beginnings of later Church organization, with its emphasis on tradition and succession. But, in fact, the book provides little evidence of any clear or uniform ecclesiastical structures or procedures of worship. The leadership of the Jerusalem Church at first rested with the twelve apostles chosen by Jesus, with Peter at their head and Matthias in place of the traitor Judas Iscariot (Acts 1.26). But the followers of Jesus are represented as making collective decisions on important occasions. Later, in Acts 15, authority appears to be shared by apostles and, following Jewish tradition, "elders." This is probably because persecution (Acts 11.19; 12.1) had forced several of the apostles into exile: the exiles may even have included Peter himself (see Acts 12.17 and p.367). At the Apostolic Council (Acts 15.6–29; see p.367), the leader of the Church is clearly James, Jesus' brother. There is

The seven Hellenists

Acts records a rapid increase in the number of converts in Jerusalem: in a short period, Church membership is said to have grown from one hundred twenty (Acts 1.15) to over eight thousand (Acts 2.41, 4.4). This led to problems in coping with those who were in need, as many believers there were poor. Subsequently, other churches had to establish a charitable fund.

Sebaste, ancient Samaria, rebuilt in Greco-Roman style by Herod the Great. Philip, one of the seven Hellenists, may have preached here (Acts 8).

Matters came to a head with a dispute between the "Hebrews" and the "Hellenists." The "Hellenists" were Greek-speaking Jews (Gentiles had not been admitted to the Church at this time), as opposed to Aramaic-speaking "Hebrews." The Hellenists complained that their widows were losing out in the daily distribution of rations (Acts 6.1). The apostles decided that they themselves should be able to devote all their time to prayer, and called for "seven men of good standing" to be chosen to oversee food distribution (Acts 6.3–4). The community is then said to have elected seven men of the Hellenist party (Stephen, Philip, Prochorus, Nicanor, Timon, Parmenas, and Nicolaus), and the apostles solemnly commissioned them by the laying on of hands (Acts 6.6). The seven have been regarded as the first deacons, the clerical order which, in the early Church, was entrusted with the care of the poor and sick. But the laying on of hands conferred on the seven the authority of the apostles, and the Hellenists are not recorded as administrators but as preachers and missionaries. Two of them, Stephen and Philip, are said to have played a particularly active role (see pp.360–63), and Stephen, according to Acts, was the first Christian martyr.

evidence to suggest that, for a period of time, other members of Jesus' family exercised a kind of dynastic leadership in Jerusalem. Christian groups gathered for worship in each other's homes, and the "house church" became the typical meeting place of the early Christian communities. Worship was markedly spontaneous, and was driven by the impulse of the Holy Spirit: Acts records a prayer that was uttered in unison, when the participants were filled with the Spirit and "the place in which they were gathered together was shaken," as if by an earthquake (Acts 4.24–31).

According to Acts, one of the most striking features of the early Jerusalem Church was its common ownership of goods (Acts 2.32). This concept was a central element in the Utopian societies envisaged by many Greek thinkers, such as Plato, and it was practiced by some Jewish groups, for example the Essenes and the Qumran sect (see p.139 and p.169). However, it was not as universal in the Jerusalem Church as the author of Acts appears to suggest: the mother of John Mark, for example, had her own house, with at least one servant (Acts 12.12–13). Selling one's possessions and devoting the proceeds to a common fund administered by the apostles was a voluntary, though highly laudable, act. It was done at the prompting of the Spirit with the object of providing relief to those in need. Acts recounts two contrasting stories on this theme, about the virtuous Barnabas, who sold a field and gave all the proceeds to the Church (Acts 4.37), and the wicked Ananias and Sapphira (see picture on opposite page). At Qumran, those joining the community had to hand over all their possessions to the common pool, and anyone who concealed personal belongings was temporarily excommunicated. Behind this practice lies the old biblical concept of devoting something to God: anything so dedicated could never be taken back.

THE DEATH OF STEPHEN

Stephen, one of the seven who were appointed to oversee the distribution of food among the Hebrews and Hellenists (see p.359), was the first follower of Jesus to suffer death for the faith. The story of his martyrdom in Acts 6 and 7 falls into two parts: the account of his trial and death by stoning (Acts 6.8–15, 7.54–60), and his speech to the Sanhedrin, or council (Acts 7.1–53). The interpolated address is only loosely connected with the trial and stoning, and is probably an example of anti-Jewish polemic which Luke included in Acts as a speech of defense before the Jewish authorities. Such speeches occur regularly in Luke's work.

Stephen's death was occasioned by internal disputes among his fellow Greek-speaking Jews: whether his opponents had several synagogues or only one in Jerusalem is uncertain, but they clearly comprised Jews from North Africa and Asia Minor who had settled in the city. The narrative of the trial closely parallels that of the trial of Jesus in the gospels: the Hellenists suborn false witnesses, who accuse Stephen of blasphemy and of predicting that Jesus would destroy the Temple of Jerusalem (Acts 6.13–14). The charge against Jesus of seeking to destroy the Temple is not mentioned in Luke's gospel and Luke has probably transferred this accusation to the trial of Stephen. In the gospel, Jesus is condemned directly after his statement about the Son of Man seated at God's right hand (Luke 22.69). Similarly, the final fury of the crowd is aroused against Stephen when he has a vision of the Son of Man standing at the right hand of God (Acts 7.55). (The title "Son of Man" occurs only here in the New Testament outside the gospels.) Stephen's petition for the forgiveness of his killers, and his prayer that Jesus may receive his spirit (Acts 7.59–60), recall Jesus' words from the cross in Luke's gospel (Luke 23.34, 23.46).

How far the stoning of Stephen was legally authorized is unclear, because, under Roman rule, the Sanhedrin was probably no longer able to impose the death penalty. There is no mention of a formal sentence before the crowd rushed at Stephen and proceeded to stone him, so it may have been a simple case of lynching. But there is evidence that the Sanhedrin

Stephen Preaching *(left) and* Stephen Addressing the Council *(right), by Fra Angelico (ca. 1387–1455), in the chapel of Nicholas V in the Vatican, Rome.*

tried to revive its power to impose capital punishment whenever it had the opportunity to do so. The historian Josephus says that the execution of James, Jesus' brother, was prompted by members of the Sanhedrin, who took advantage of the interval in 62 CE between the death of one Roman procurator and the arrival of another (see p.388). Complaints were made, and the incoming procurator deposed the high priest. In the case of Stephen, the Jewish leaders may have felt that they could gamble on the Roman power turning a blind eye to his execution.

Stephen's address to the Sanhedrin (Acts 7) is the longest speech in Acts and marks an important stage in what Luke sees as the process of separating Christianity from Judaism. Most of Stephen's speech is related to the allegation that he had foretold the destruction of the Temple. He argues that Israel's history had been a record of continual disobedience to God. The people consistently opposed Moses and turned to other gods. Finally, they constructed the Temple, which was a mistake from the beginning, since "the Most High does not dwell in houses made with human hands" (Acts 7.48). There were Jewish groups, such as the community at Qumran (see p.139 and p.169), which were unfavorable toward the institution of the Temple, but Stephen seems to represent a radical strain within the Hellenist Christian community. He expresses a view that goes beyond Luke's own generally more favorable view of the Temple, and in the New Testament, Stephen's position is closest to that of the letter to the Hebrews (see pp.388–89). In his final words, Stephen turns directly on his hearers, accusing them of still resisting the Holy Spirit, just as their ancestors had done (Acts 7.51–53). Whatever the actual circumstances of Stephen's execution, for Luke it represents the rejection by the nation of the true Messiah, and therefore the nation's own rejection by God.

St. Stephen, *by Stefano Sassetta (ca. 1392–1450 or 1451). Medieval artists usually portrayed Stephen as a young man, often holding a book (the gospels, to symbolize his preaching).*

Persecution after Stephen's death

At the close of the story of Stephen's martyrdom, the author introduces "a young man named Saul," who looked after the coats of the stoning crowd (Acts 7.58) and approves of Stephen's execution (Acts 8.1). This is the first mention of the future apostle Paul (Saul was his Hebrew name). According to Acts, Stephen's death sparked off a severe persecution of the Jerusalem church, in which Paul took the lead (Acts 8.1).

This persecution was directed primarily against the particular group of Hellenists (Greek-speaking Jewish Christians) to which Stephen himself had belonged. They were forced to leave the capital, while "the apostles," presumably the twelve, were left undisturbed. Barnabas, a Greek-speaking Jew from the Diaspora, who made a large contribution to the Church (Acts 4.36–37), seems to have remained in Jerusalem, where he later introduced Paul to the apostles (Acts 9.27). Barnabas acted as a link between the Jerusalem Christians and the communities created in the Gentile world as a result of missionary expansion.

The persecution was at first confined to Jerusalem, because the refugees were apparently able to preach freely elsewhere (Acts 8.4–5). According to Acts 9.31, the Church was able to build up its strength in Judea, Galilee, and Samaria (see pp.362–63). The high priest authorized Paul/Saul to go to Damascus to arrest Christians – probably some of those who had fled Jerusalem – and bring them to Jerusalem for trial (Acts 9.1–2). Damascus was outside the jurisdiction of the Jewish authorities, but there is evidence in 1 Maccabees and in the historian Josephus that the high priest had the power to request the extradition of offenders against the Jewish Law.

PHILIP AND SIMON MAGUS

For Luke, the author of Acts, the death of Stephen and the persecution that followed it (see pp.360–61) had positive consequences: the spread of the gospel from Jerusalem to Judea and Samaria. According to Acts, the Samaritan mission was undertaken by Philip, one of the seven Hellenists ordained by the apostles (see p.359). Philip preached in "a city of Samaria" (Acts 8.5) which may have been Sebaste, built in Greco-Roman style by Herod the Great on the site of the ancient city of Samaria (some versions of Acts say that Philip went to "*the* city of Samaria"; see p.359). Another likely base for his mission would have been the Samaritan religious center of Neapolis, near the ancient city of Shechem (modern Nablus).

Acts says that Philip performed many acts of healing in Samaria (Acts 8.4–7). The inhabitants of this region were particularly receptive to such miracles, since for some time they had been captivated by a practitioner of magical arts, or *magus,* called Simon, known in biblical tradition as Simon Magus (Acts 8.9). Jesus' disciples often came into competition with apparently similar wonder-workers. The Samaritans recognized Simon as someone with divine powers, but Philip's cures are said to have been more numerous and striking, and won many converts. Simon, too, was impressed by Philip's deeds: he was converted and baptized, and proceeded to join Philip in his work (Acts 8.12–13).

The second part of this story brings out the special authority of the twelve apostles. In Acts, water baptism and the gift of the Holy Spirit are closely linked, but not identical: others could baptize, but only the apostles, represented by Peter and John, could confer the Holy Spirit, which they did by laying hands on the Samaritan converts (Acts 8.16–17). This may have had some physical result, such as speaking in tongues (see p.355), because Acts relates that when Simon "saw" that Peter and John had the power to pass on the Spirit, he tried to buy the same power for himself (Acts 8.18–19 – hence the word "simony" for the buying or selling of a spiritual office). Peter severely castigated Simon for his presumption (Acts 8.20–23), and although Acts describes Simon as repenting (Acts 8.24), it was Peter's harsh denunciation of him that was always remembered in Christian tradition. Beginning with the Christian writer Justin in the second century CE, Simon Magus was seen as the root of the Gnostic heresy and as an antichrist. He was said to have been accompanied by a woman called Helena, who was originally a prostitute from Tyre, but who, in the manner of Gnostic speculation, was considered by Simon Magus to be a divine emanation from his own mind. From the confrontation with Peter in Acts, there developed a whole string of legends of wonder-working duels between Simon and the apostle in various cities of the Roman empire, until, it was said, Simon finally met an ignominious end.

A second story about Philip, his meeting with the Ethiopian eunuch (Acts 8.26–40), occurs after his return from Samaria to Jerusalem with Peter and John. The narrative appears to have been influenced by the story of the prophet Elijah (see pp.90–2). Like him, Philip is summoned to undertake a journey by the angel of the Lord (Acts 8.26; compare 2 Kings 1.3) and is mysteriously snatched away after his mission is completed (Acts 8.39; compare 2 Kings 2.11). According to Acts, Philip meets a eunuch, a high official of Candace, queen of the Ethiopians, on the road from Jerusalem to Gaza. "Candace" is actually a title used by a number of queens of the kingdom of Meroe, in what is now Sudan. The eunuch "had come to Jerusalem to worship" and "was reading the prophet

Isaiah," (Acts 8.27–28), so he was presumably either a convert to Judaism or a person on the point of conversion. At the eunuch's request, Philip explains the scriptural passage he is reading, which is from Isaiah 53.7–8. Philip interprets it in Christian terms, and proclaims to the eunuch "the good news about Jesus" (Acts 8.35). This is the first time that the New Testament explicitly identifies Jesus with the figure of the suffering servant in Isaiah 53 (see p.106), and the chapter became a key text in early Christian preaching. The eunuch was then baptized (Acts 8.38). The story of his conversion appears to reflect the baptismal practice of the early Church. The candidate was instructed in the faith (Acts 8.35), then made a formal request to be baptized (Acts 8.36), followed by a confession of belief. Some versions of Acts include the confession: "I believe that Jesus Christ is the Son of God" (Acts 8.37).

The fact that the convert is both a eunuch and an Ethiopian may have symbolic significance. The Jewish Law technically excluded eunuchs from entering the Temple precincts and taking part in worship, but Isaiah 56.4–5 says that eunuchs who keep the covenant will find their place in the house of God. Acts possibly sees this condition as now being fulfilled. Several verses in the Psalms and prophets speak of people from Ethiopia turning to Yahweh and bringing offerings: it may be significant that the Ethiopian eunuch was in charge of the royal treasury.

After baptizing the eunuch, Philip is said to have been "snatched away" by "the spirit of the Lord" (Acts 8.39). According to Acts he then reappeared in the town of Azotus (ancient Ashdod), near the Mediterranean coast, from where he conducted an evangelistic mission as far as the Roman port of Caesarea (Acts 8.40). Philip appears to have taken up residence in Caesarea, because he is later said to be living there with four unmarried daughters who possessed the gift of prophecy (Acts 21.8–9). At about this time, Peter left Jerusalem and established himself in the predominantly Greek port of Joppa (Acts 9.43). These moves by Philip and Peter may reflect the Church's desire to preach in the less strongly Jewish coastal areas of Palestine. The gospel might receive a warmer welcome here than in what had become the hostile environment of Jerusalem.

The theater at Caesarea. The city was built in Greco-Roman style by King Herod the Great and named for the emperor Augustus Caesar. An important port, after Herod's death it became the seat of the Roman procurators of Judea (see also p.158).

Simon Magus Offering Money to St. Peter, *by Liberale da Verona (ca. 1445–ca. 1525).*

Royal tombs in the Nabatean capital city of Petra, south of the Dead Sea. A people of Arab origin, the Nabateans dominated southern Syria and northern Arabia from ca. 90 BCE. Their kingdom prospered as an ally of Rome until 106 CE, when it was absorbed into the Roman empire.

THE CALLING OF PAUL

There are three accounts in Acts of the "conversion" of the apostle Paul on the road to Damascus (see p.361). The fullest and most dramatic version occurs in Acts 9 during the story of the persecution of Christians following the martyrdom of Stephen. Paul, who is still referred to by his Hebrew name of Saul at this stage, was "breathing threats and murder against the disciples" (Acts 9.1). In his anti-Christian fervor he is said to have undertaken a mission to Damascus to bring "any who belonged to the Way" back to Jerusalem. Saul was nearing Damascus when "suddenly a light from heaven flashed around him" (Acts 9.3), causing him to fall to the ground. According to Acts, he heard a voice saying " 'Saul, Saul, why do you persecute me?' " (Acts 9.4) and, after asking who it was, received the reply: "I am Jesus, whom you are persecuting. But get up and enter the city, and you will be told what to do" (Acts 9.5). Saul is blinded by the vision and regains his sight only three days later, immediately prior to his baptism (9.17–18).

The other two accounts in Acts of the conversion are in speeches by Paul himself (Acts 22.6–11; 26.12–18). A few allusions in Paul's letters also appear to refer to this event: for example, in Galatians 1.15–16 he writes of his calling through God's grace and of seeing the risen Jesus, which set him on his mission to the Gentiles (and gave him the status of an apostle). Paul's words essentially agree with the story told by Luke in Acts, but the apostle gives no connected version of what happened.

All three accounts in Acts mention the supernatural light and the voice that cause Paul and his companions to fall to the ground. This is a common feature of accounts of visionary experiences in Jewish writings of the period. The *Testament of Job*, dating from around the beginning of the Common Era, provides a close parallel with Acts. Job says: "While I was asleep, there came to me a loud voice with a very great light, saying, 'Job, Job.' And I said, 'Here am I'; and he said, 'Get up, and I will show you who this is whom you wish to know' ... and when I heard, I fell down on my bed." Rabbinic writings frequently mention the *bath qol*, a mysterious voice by which God sometimes communicates with human beings.

Scholars have attempted to provide a psychological explanation for Paul's experience, suggesting that it may have been the resolution of an interior conflict between his strict Judaism (he was a Pharisee by training; see Acts 26.5) and the impression made on him by witnessing the persecution of Christians, especially the death of Stephen. This view can be no more than speculative, but it may have some support in Paul's quotation of a popular Greek proverb in the account of the conversion he gives to Herod Agrippa: "it hurts you to kick against the goads" (Acts 26.14). This suggests that even before his conversion his conscience had been pricking him over his role in persecuting Jesus' followers. Paul's letters reveal him as a person often torn by strong inner tensions. He appears to have been subject to ecstatic and visionary experiences: Acts also records other visions (Acts 22.17–21; 27.23–24).

There are discrepancies between Acts and Paul's letters in their accounts of the immediate aftermath of his experience on the Damascus road. In Acts, Paul is blinded by the heavenly light, but is cured three days later by the disciple Ananias and baptized a Christian (Acts 9.8–18; 22.11–16). In his letters, Paul writes that, after God's revelation to him, he went to Arabia without consulting a single person and subsequently returned to Damascus, only going to Jerusalem three years later to contact Peter and James, Jesus' brother (Gal. 1.16–17). This account differs from that in Acts, which records Paul as preaching in Damascus and then escaping to

PAUL'S BACKGROUND

In Acts, Paul is represented as saying that he was a native of Tarsus, a true-born Jew, a Pharisee, and a pupil of the famous rabbi Gamaliel (see p.356) in Jerusalem (Acts 22.3). In his letters, Paul states that he had been circumcised, belonged to the tribe of Benjamin, and had been trained as a Pharisee (Phil. 3.5). Paul's writings show considerable familiarity with the outlook and methods of first-century rabbinic Judaism.

Tarsus was rightly described by Paul as "no mean city." It was the capital of the Roman province of Cilicia and a prosperous town, known for the making of tents, which accounts for the fact that Paul earned his living as a tentmaker (Acts 18.3). Even more importantly, it was a center of intellectual life and produced many outstanding philosophers. This would account for the Hellenistic influences in Paul's writings and for his, at least superficial, acquaintance with the popular teaching of groups such as the Stoics and Cynics.

Thus, Paul was a Diaspora Jew and a native Greek-speaker, which may explain his involvement in the affair of Stephen, who came from a similar background. Paul also enjoyed the privilege of being born a Roman citizen and had a Latin name, Paul, as well as the Hebrew name Saul. It is not known how his family obtained this citizenship, but the picture in Acts of the status and privileges it conferred accords with Roman legal practice in the first century CE (see, for example, Acts 22.25–29).

Jerusalem, where he joined the other disciples and continued "speaking boldly in the name of the Lord" (Acts 9.19–28). It is possible that the author, Luke, has telescoped events, omitting Paul's time in Arabia, in which he had no particular interest.

In Acts, Paul escapes from Damascus by being lowered down the city wall in a basket, because the Jews wanted to kill him and were watching the city gates (Acts 9.24–25). This escape is also mentioned by Paul in his second letter to the Corinthians, where he attributes the danger he faced to the commissioner of King Aretas (2 Cor. 11.32–33). This was Aretas IV (ruled 9 BCE–40 CE), king of the powerful Nabatean state (see picture, opposite and map on p.369). At this time Aretas evidently controlled Damascus, which was intermittently a Nabatean possession. The Damascus Jews may have enlisted the royal commissioner's support in their pursuit of Paul, an action paralleled elsewhere in Acts. It is also possible, assuming that Luke has left out the Arabian visit, that Paul's escape took place on his second trip to Damascus (Gal. 1.17). His preaching in Arabia, much of which formed part of Aretas's kingdom, could have provoked the Nabatean authorities, who sought to arrest him when he next set foot in their territory.

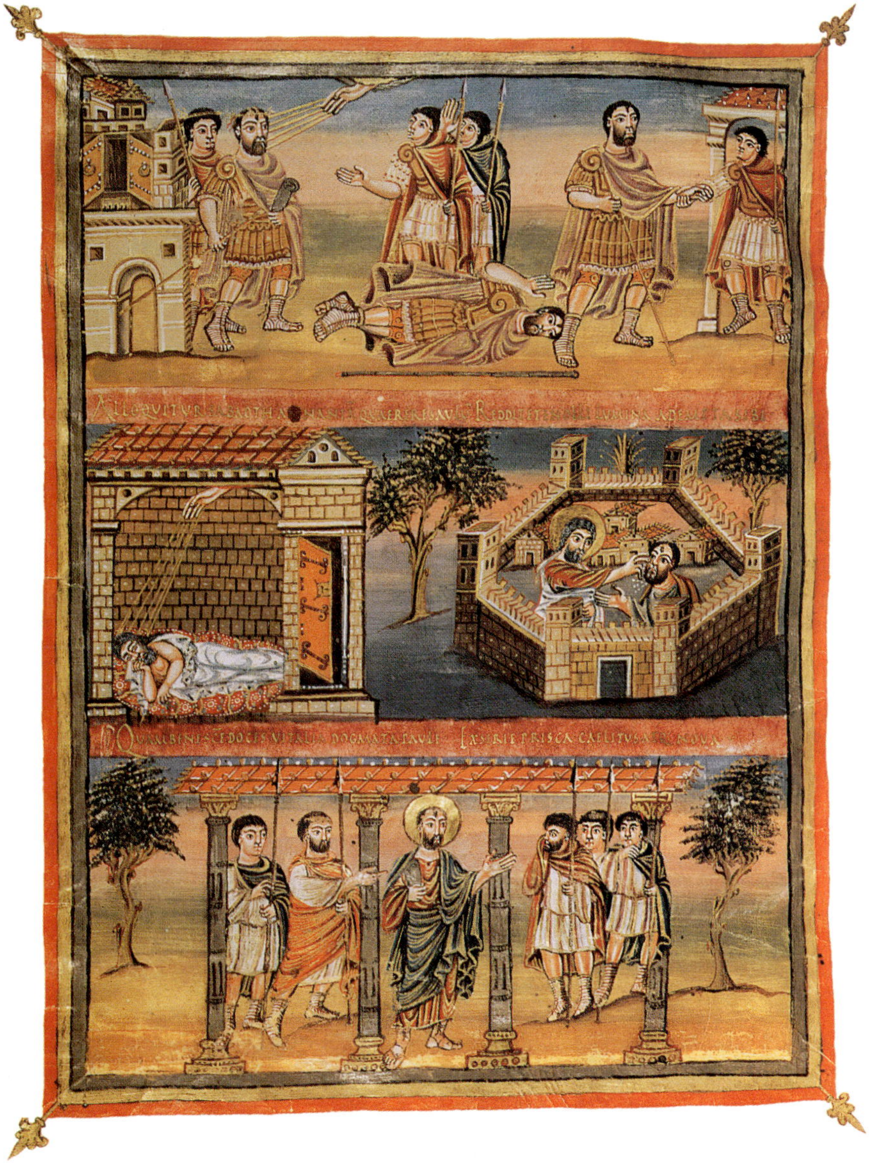

The Conversion of Paul *(top) and* Scenes of Paul Preaching, *from a bible made in 843–851* CE *for the French king, Charles the Bald. Paul is portrayed as a high official in Roman military dress.*

PETER AND CORNELIUS

Peter's conversion of a Roman centurion, Cornelius, at Caesarea is related in Acts 10. For the author of Acts, this was an important landmark in the spread of the Christian message: Luke's narrative credits Peter with the inauguration of the mission to the Gentiles, and shows that he was able to defend his action successfully against the objections of the Jewish Christians at Jerusalem.

Luke's narrative deals with two related issues that faced the Church in its early days. One was the question of whether, or on what terms, non-Jews could become members of the Church. For Jewish Christians, such as the earliest Jerusalem community, the only thing that distinguished Christians from other Jews was their recognition of Jesus as Messiah. They were still subject to the Jewish Law, and Gentiles who became believers had to accept all its provisions, in particular circumcision. This was always a great source of contention for non-Jews, and it was an issue with which Paul had to wrestle, particularly in his letter to the Galatians.

The other issue was the question of table fellowship. By this time, the regulations insisting on kosher meat and laying down which animals could be eaten were a central feature of Judaism, and Jews were forbidden

Roman officers of the imperial bodyguard (the Praetorian Guard); a marble relief of the 2nd century CE.

from eating with Gentiles who did not observe these rules. This created a problem when Jewish and Gentile Christians were together, especially in relation to the Eucharist or when sharing a meal.

Some members of the early Church felt that Jesus had established a new order of things which superseded the strict application of Jewish dietary laws. In Mark's gospel, Jesus says "whatever goes into a person from outside cannot defile" (Mark 7.18), which the evangelist interprets: "Thus he declared all foods clean" (Mark 7.19). Paul took the same position, although he respected the consciences of those who thought otherwise. Before his meeting with the Gentile Cornelius, Peter has a vision in which he sees a great sheet lowered from heaven. It contains "all kinds of four-footed creatures and reptiles and birds of the air" (Acts 10.11–12), in other words, the whole animal world. The divine voice proclaims that all these creatures have been made clean (Acts 10.15). For Acts, this nullification of the food laws means that there is now no distinction between Jew and Gentile. When Peter goes to see Cornelius, he tells him: "You yourself know that it is unlawful for a Jew to associate with or visit a Gentile; but God has shown me that I should not call anything profane or unclean" (Acts 10.28).

St. Peter Enthroned, *by Tommaso Masaccio (1401–1428); in the Brancacci chapel, Florence (see p.357).*

However, the real justification for the admission of Gentiles into the Church is the descent of Holy Spirit on them. Acts records that while Peter is still preaching to Cornelius and his friends and family, "the Holy Spirit fell upon all who heard the word" (Acts 10.44). The circumcised – that is, Jewish – believers with Peter are amazed to hear the audience "speaking in tongues and extolling God," a sign that "the gift of the Spirit had been poured out even on the Gentiles" (Acts 10.45–46; compare Acts 2.4). In Acts, the gift of the Spirit usually follows baptism, but on this exceptional occasion it precedes it.

For the author of Acts, the sequel to Peter's meeting with Cornelius serves to align Peter and Paul with respect to the mission to the Gentiles, and culminates in the meeting known as the Apostolic Council in Jerusalem in Acts 15. Before this, there is an account of how Gentiles were being evangelized in Antioch by refugees from persecution (Acts 11.20). Anxious, as always, to oversee all missionary operations, the Jerusalem Church sent Barnabas to Antioch as their emissary. He gave his approval to what was happening (Acts 11.22–23) and later brought Paul to Antioch to join him in preaching the gospel. Trouble arose, however, after Barnabas and Paul returned to Antioch at the end of their first missionary journey (Acts 14.26; see p.370). Some Jewish Christians came to Antioch and began teaching the necessity of circumcision, prompting Paul and Barnabas to go to Jerusalem to settle the question with the Church, then headed by the apostle James, Jesus' brother (Acts 15.1–2).

Peter reappears to address the Apostolic Council on the issue of circumcision. His appearance is rather abrupt and comes after he has been absent from the narrative since the dramatic story of his arrest and escape from prison, at the end of which it is said, a little mysteriously, that he "went to another place" (Acts 12.3–17). Before the apostles and elders of the Church, he refers to his own calling to preach to the Gentiles, arguing that God "testified to them by giving them the Holy Spirit, just as he did to us" (Acts 15.8), presumably a reference to his conversion of Cornelius. He questions the need to impose special requirements on non-Jews (Acts 15.9–12). Peter is followed by Barnabas and Paul, who also report on their mission to the Gentiles (Acts 15.12). In response, the council decrees that Gentile converts need not be circumcised, but it takes a stricter line in the matter of table fellowship. Gentile Christians must abstain from food that has first been offered to idols, and observe the key Jewish ban on eating meat that had not been drained of blood. The Council adds another demand: abstention from fornication, probably meaning sexual immorality in general (Acts 15.19–20).

THE APOSTOLIC COUNCIL IN PAUL'S LETTER TO THE GALATIANS

Paul paints a different picture of the Apostolic Council in what appears to be his account of the same events in Galatians 2.1–10, which is generally agreed to have been written earlier than Acts. According to Paul, Peter's mission had always been aimed at Jews and Paul's at the Gentiles. Paul claims that the Council, including Peter (here Paul uses Peter's Aramaic name, Cephas), had agreed that this situation should continue (Gal. 2.7–9). Paul relates that Peter had visited Antioch and had taken his meals with Gentiles, until some messengers from James caused him to desist. Paul strongly rebukes Peter for this "hypocrisy" (Gal 1.13–14). The versions of Acts and Galatians can be partly reconciled if the appearance of Peter in the Acts account is spurious and he was not in fact present at the Apostolic Council (see also pp.362–63).

THE MISSION OF PAUL

The story of the expansion of Christianity in the first century CE *is largely bound up with the career of Paul, the former persecutor of Christians who underwent a dramatic calling to the faith (see pp.364–65). Little is known of the work of the other apostles, or about how the new religion reached such areas as Egypt or the East beyond the Roman empire. However, Paul's tireless propagation of the faith is vividly recorded in Acts and in the letters which he wrote to new Christian communities (see pp.376–91). He traveled widely on his mission and may have ended his career, according to one strong tradition, in the imperial capital, Rome.*

A ministrant and the god Silenus, from a house at Pompeii, Italy, believed to have been used by a mystery cult.

THE ROMAN WORLD

Paul's journeys took him through the Roman provinces at a time when the empire had almost reached its greatest extent and the reigns of the emperors Augustus, Tiberius, and Claudius (see table on p.369) had created a stable and peaceful state. Compared with elsewhere in the ancient world, travel within the empire was easy and safe, as a result of a system of paved roads linking the provinces and the chief cities, as well as the extensive sea routes that were vital for the commercial life of the Mediterranean region. Paul and his companions traveled by road, apparently mainly on foot, and frequently by sea. According to Acts, Paul often came into contact with the well-established Roman system of provincial administration, which maintained law and order. A Roman citizen himself, he had dealings with the highest imperial officials, such as Gallio, the proconsul (governor) of Achaia and brother of the Roman statesman and philosopher Seneca (Acts 18; see also p.371), and Sergius Paulus, the proconsul of Cyprus (Acts 13). He also came into contact with the governors of less important provinces, such as the procurators of Judea, and with local administrators, such as the Asiarchs (officials of the province of Asia) at Ephesus, and the politarchs (city rulers) of Thessalonica.

Paul carried the gospel above all to the Greek-speaking cities of the eastern Mediterranean, and it was there that Christianity enjoyed its main success. These cities had a cosmopolitan population, and the composition of their churches reflected a wide range of social and ethnic backgrounds. It is sometimes thought that the early urban Christian communities consisted largely of the economically poor and socially deprived. However, recent studies have shown that most of the members of the early Church pursued gainful occupations and, in modern terms, they could fairly be described as "middle class."

One factor that assisted the success of the Christian mission was the wide variety of religious belief and practice in the Greco-Roman world. Official religion centered on the city temples, dedicated to the Olympian deities of the Greeks, or to the Roman deities with whom they were identified. In the provinces, the worship of the Roman emperor also grew up, as an expression of loyalty to Rome. Increasingly popular in the Roman empire in Paul's day were "mystery cults," often of Near Eastern origin, such as that of Artemis of Ephesus, which Paul encountered (see p.370). Like Christianity, they offered initiates the assurance of immortality and a more intense personal spiritual experience than the public rituals of the official religion. There were also a number of quasi-religious philosophical schools, such as the Pythagoreans and the Epicureans, whose adherents assembled in small groups in houses. Their doctrines were propagated by itinerant teachers, whom Christian preachers would have resembled in many ways. However, the new cult of Christianity enjoyed one advantage over the mystery religions and the philosophical schools: its organizational strength, which allowed each individual Christian group to see itself as part of a greater international society, the Church.

Jews in the Roman empire

Paul was born a Jew and a Roman citizen in the city of Tarsus in Asia Minor. Judaism was recognized by the Roman state as a *religio licita* ("permitted religion") and its members were allowed special privileges, such as exemption from military service and the right to observe the sabbath, although Rome disapproved of proselytism and sometimes took steps to check it. The Jews were based in the cities, where they often formed a large, wealthy, and influential segment of the population, in many cases of long standing. Generally they were strongly attached to their ancestral traditions and anxious to preserve them in a Gentile environment.

The first Christians, such as Paul, were Jews. As missionary activity spread from Palestine, Christian evangelists began to preach in the synagogues, as Paul is recorded as doing in Acts (though in his letters he states that his ministry was only to Gentiles). However, Acts claims that Diaspora Jews (those living outside their ancestral homeland of Palestine) were generally hostile to him and his followers. This is probably because Paul's overtures to the Gentiles and readiness to dispense with distinctive Jewish practices (especially circumcision) were seen as a threat to Jewish identity. But among those attending Diaspora synagogues were those described in the New Testament as "God-fearers," Gentiles attracted to Judaism by its monotheism and high ethical code, but not prepared to accept all the obligations of a full Jewish convert. Many of these converted to Christianity, which offered Jewish monotheism and morality, without what were seen as the disadvantages of circumcision and food taboos.

ROMAN EMPERORS IN NEW TESTAMENT TIMES

All dates are approximate and CE except where stated.

Augustus	27 BCE–14
Tiberius	14–37
Gaius (Caligula)	37–41
Claudius	41–54
Nero	54–68
Galba; Otho;	
Vitellius	68–69
Vespasian	69–79
Titus	79–81
Domitian	81–96

A statue of the fertility goddess Artemis of Ephesus (2nd century CE).

ARTEMIS OF EPHESUS

The account of Paul at Ephesus in Acts 19 paints a vivid picture of the popular Hellenistic cult of Artemis of Ephesus. She was originally a version of the widespread Near Eastern mother goddess, the patron of nature and fertility, and quite distinct from the Greek Artemis or the Roman Diana, with whom she came to be identified. Her original shrine was a primitive sanctuary at the mouth of the Cayster river, long predating the foundation of Ephesus on the river by Greek settlers. By New Testament times Artemis was worshiped in "all Asia," that is, Asia Minor (Acts 19.27). Ephesus was her "temple keeper" (Acts 19.35), in other words the site of her chief temple, a magnificent building that was reckoned among the Seven Wonders of the World. Ephesus was a great pilgrimage center, where, as at all such places in any age, there was a great trade in religious objects. The "silver shrines" made by Demetrius and other craftsmen (Acts 19.24) were either miniatures of the primitive sanctuary of the goddess, or of the classical temple, showing her cult image in a niche. The image, "the statue that fell from heaven" (Acts 19.35), was probably a meteorite; several other examples of meteorites becoming cult objects are known. However, Artemis was usually represented as a woman with many breasts, symbolizing her power as a fertility goddess (see picture).

PAUL'S JOURNEYS IN ACTS

Journeys undertaken by heroic figures appear frequently in the mythology of ancient Greece and other cultures. In the Bible, the heroic wayfarer is Paul, who undertakes at least four journeys on his mission to spread the gospel (see maps on p.369 and p.371). In common with other epic travelers, Paul faces many threats and dangers: Acts vividly relates how Paul is stoned and left for dead at Lystra on his first journey (Acts 14.19). Like the Greek heroes Odysseus and Jason, the apostle has to overcome supernatural evil forces, represented in the Bible by the sorcerer Bar-Jesus or Elymas (Acts 14.6–11). Paul also performs miracles which boost his authority: when he makes a cripple walk, he and his companion Barnabas (see p.367) are hailed as the Greek gods Hermes and Zeus, probably local deities that were identified with those of the official Greek pantheon (Acts 14.8–18). Paul was thought to be Hermes, the divine messenger, because he took the lead in speaking of Jesus, and Barnabas was Zeus, the head of the pantheon, probably because he was physically more imposing than Paul. In one of his letters, Paul speaks of a permanent bodily "weakness" (2 Cor. 12.7–8), and the mid-second-century Acts of Paul describes him as small, balding, and bow-legged.

According to Acts, Paul's itinerary was determined by the Holy Spirit. However, the fact that Barnabas was a Cypriot may be the reason why Cyprus was the first port of call on the first journey. The remainder of the mission, related in Acts 13–14, mainly involved cities in the southern part of the Roman province of Galatia, in what is now Turkey. One member of Paul's mission, John Mark, evidently refused to go with Paul beyond Pamphylia. This subsequently led to a break between Barnabas and Paul, who refused to take John Mark on his second mission (Acts 15.37–39).

In Acts, Paul's speeches are central to his mission and each is carefully crafted by Luke to fit the occasion. His first speech (Acts 13.16–41) is delivered in the local synagogue at Pisidian Antioch and is reported at length as a model of his synagogue addresses. It is distinctly Jewish in flavor: like the speeches of Peter in Acts 2 (see p.355) and Stephen in Acts 7 (see pp.360–61), it surveys Israel's history and quotes Scripture. In contrast, the speech at Lystra, Paul's first to a wholly Gentile audience (Acts 14.15–17), is brief and speaks of God in broad terms as the divine hand which "made the heaven and the earth and the sea and all that is in them" and sends "rains from heaven and fruitful seasons."

After the first journey, Paul and Barnabas travel from Antioch to attend the Apostolic Council in Jerusalem (see p.367). They return to Antioch with Judas Barsabbas and Silas, who are assigned by the council to take its decree (Acts 15.23–29) to the Gentile Christians in Syria and Cilicia, which were apparently evangelized by Paul shortly after his conversion (see Gal. 1.21). From Antioch, Paul sets out on his second missionary journey, recounted in Acts 15–18. It was considerably longer than the first and its primary object was to revisit the churches established during the first journey and assess their progress. One reason for the success of the Christian movement was the creation in this way of an international organizational structure which bound the various communities together under the supervision of an apostolic founder. After falling out with Barnabas, who left for Cyprus, Paul chose Silas as his companion, perhaps implying that the terms of the council decree were now to be extended to the new congregations of southern Galatia.

On the second journey, Paul continues to preach first to Jews, with some success: Jews are converted at Thessalonica (Acts 17.4) and at Beroea (Acts 17.11–12), and the president of the synagogue is converted, together with his entire household, at Corinth (Acts 18.8). Out of consideration for Jewish sensibilities, Paul has a half-Jew, Timothy, circumcised when he is recruited to his mission (Acts 16.3). However, Acts depicts the Diaspora Jews as generally hostile toward the gospel; the author often seeks to stress that the spread of the mission to the Gentiles was a consequence of its rejection by Jews (as for example at Acts 18.6).

Supernatural guidance of the missionaries is even more prominent on the second journey: the Holy Spirit prevents them from traveling to Asia and Bithynia and a vision directs Paul to preach in Macedonia (Acts 16.6–9). Heathen magic is again routed when the "spirit of divination" is expelled from a slave girl at Philippi (Acts 16.16–18). The author pinpoints certain historical events, such as the emperor Claudius's expulsion of the Jews from Rome, probably around 49 CE, and Gallio's proconsulship of Achaia (southern Greece), which he held probably in 52 CE (see also p.368). Typically for Acts, the narrative of this journey portrays the Roman authorities as favorably disposed toward the Christians: when Paul and Silas are jailed at Philippi, the magistrates act against them only from fear of mob violence, and detain them briefly. When they discover that Paul and his companions are Roman citizens, they realize that they have acted illegally in having them flogged, and apologize (Acts 16.20–39). Later, Paul's appearance before Gallio at Corinth confirms that Paul's mission was not a crime in Roman eyes (Acts 18.12–17).

A calmer and more elegiac note distinguishes the narrative of Paul's third journey, related in Acts 18–21. It begins with another visit to the churches of Galatia and Phrygia, where Paul's mission had begun, but its main focus is on his stay of over two years at Ephesus, the chief commercial city of Asia Minor. Paul's fellow tentmakers, Aquila and Priscilla, who had originally joined him at Corinth on his second journey (Acts 18.2–3), were already at Ephesus. They are joined by Apollos, an eloquent and learned man from Alexandria in Egypt and follower of John the Baptist, who, however, "taught accurately the things concerning Jesus." After Paul's arrival, a group of twelve disciples of the Baptist are also integrated into the Church (Acts 19.1–7).

Acts portrays Paul's Ephesus period as one of considerable success. When he meets the usual Jewish hostility in the synagogue, he simply hires a lecture hall, where his message reaches a large audience (Acts 19.9–10). Rival itinerant Jewish exorcists are vanquished (Acts 19.13–16), scrolls containing magical spells – a speciality of Ephesus – are burned (Acts 19.19), and the agitation of the silversmiths who make idols of the local goddess, Artemis (see sidebar on opposite page), comes to nothing after a warning from the town clerk (Acts 19.23–41). These last three episodes are told with a touch of humor. Later, at Troas, there is a picture of the Church's distinctive commemoration of the Resurrection on the first day of the week, with a sacred meal and preaching. On this occasion, appropriately, Paul restores to life a boy who had fallen to his death from a window sill when Paul's extended preaching sent him to sleep (Acts 20.7–12).

The narrative of Paul's third journey contains three passages where the author, Luke, uses the first person "we" instead of the third person "he" and "they" (Acts 20.5–7; 20.13–15; 21.1–18). These passages seem to show that Luke accompanied Paul on some of his travels. There are other theories, such as the possibility that Luke drew on a travel diary kept by one of Paul's companions. However, there is no significant difference in style between the "we" passages and the material that precedes and follows them. The use of "we" may simply be a stylistic device, lending the story directness and realism by portraying the narrator as a participant. All three passages – together with a fourth "we" section at Acts 27.1–28.16 – give accounts of sea voyages, which were a favorite theme of Hellenistic writers.

PAUL'S FIRST JOURNEY
(Acts 13.4–14.26)

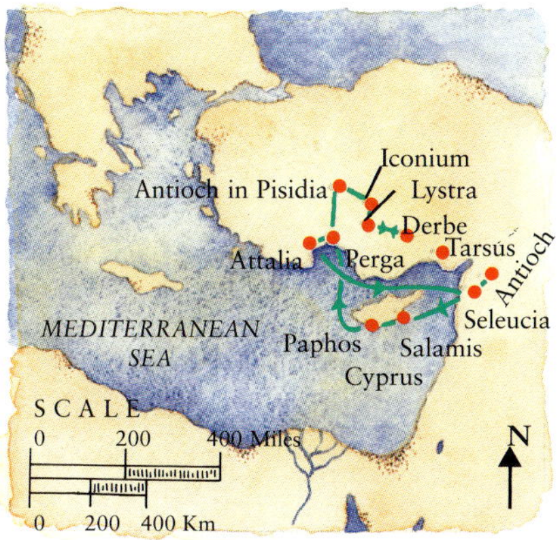

PAUL'S SECOND JOURNEY
(Acts 15.40–18.22)

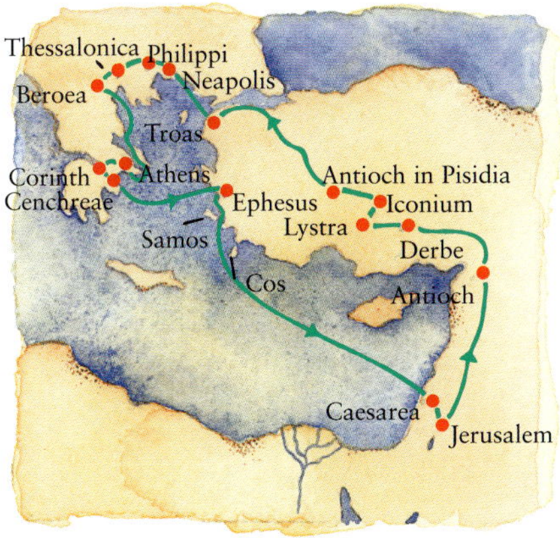

PAUL'S THIRD JOURNEY
(Acts 18.23–21.17)

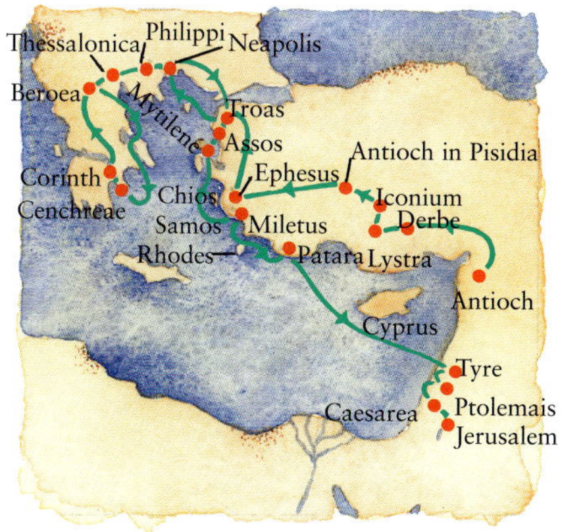

St. Paul, *by Martino de Bartolommeo (1369–1434). Paul is portrayed here holding a sword, symbolizing the tradition that he was beheaded at Rome under the emperor Nero (see also p.378 and pictures on pp.375 and 377).*

PAUL ON TRIAL

A dominant theme in the account of Paul's third journey (see p.371) is the apostle's determination to revisit Jerusalem, and then go to Rome (Acts 19.31). His motives are not explained, but the story is fraught with foreboding, especially when Paul takes his leave of the Ephesian church leaders at Miletus (Acts 20.18–35). His speech contains a farewell apologia for his missionary work, a prophecy that only imprisonment and hardship await him in the future, and the sad statement that the elders will never see him again. The ominous tone grows more urgent as Paul receives warnings from the Holy Spirit at Tyre (Acts 21.4), and Caesarea, where the prophet Agabus (see Acts 11.28) dramatically warns Paul that the Jerusalem Jews will deliver him to the Gentiles (Acts 21.11). But Paul remains determined to go to Jerusalem, and his companions finally have to accept that Paul's fate is in God's hands (Acts 21.14).

The account of Paul's arrival in Jerusalem parallels in some ways the earlier narrative of the Council of Jerusalem (see p.367). Like that account, but unlike Paul's own letters, it shows him as being on good terms with the leaders of the Jerusalem Church, who in turn welcome his work among the Gentiles (Acts 21.19–20a). It is apparently only now (Acts 21.25) that Paul learns of the terms of the council's letter to the Gentile Christians (see Acts 15.23–29). Paul is represented as a faithful Jew, although the Jerusalem leaders are aware that many doubt this (Acts 21.20b–21). To prove his loyalty to Judaism, Paul agrees to perform a special act of devotion (Acts 21.23–24). Acts records that Paul undertook this ritual at Cenchreae (Acts 18.18). In the Temple, Paul is spotted by some Jews from Asia, the scene of his third mission, who accuse him of the same crimes as those brought against Stephen (Acts 6.13). They also claim that Paul has taken Gentiles ("Greeks") into the inner court of the Temple, which non-Jews were forbidden to enter on pain of death (see picture, below). Like Stephen, Paul faces being stoned by an indignant mob, but he is rescued by Roman troops stationed in the Antonia fortress, immediately north of the Temple (Acts 21.31–35; see map on p.152).

Luke's repeated emphasis on how the Romans protected Paul against Jewish hostility (see p.371) appears again in the following narrative. Claudius Lysias, the Roman tribune (commandant) allows Paul to address

A Greek warning inscription from the Temple of Jerusalem, one of several fixed to the balustrade or low wall separating the Court of Gentiles from the most sacred areas of the Temple (see map on p.152). It reads: "Foreigners [Gentiles] are forbidden from entering through the balustrade into the enclosure around the sanctuary. Anyone found doing so will be to blame for the death that will follow."

the crowd. His speech goes well until he speaks of his mission to the Gentiles, which infuriates his hearers so much that Lysias has to bring him into the barracks "to be examined by flogging" (Acts 22.24). But because of Paul's Roman citizenship, the tribune releases him and orders a formal hearing before the Sanhedrin, the council of Jewish elders. Paul reduces this body to disorder by skillfully playing on the theological differences between its Sadducee and Pharisee members (see pp.166–67), and Lysias once more has to rescue the apostle (Acts 23.10). The tribune then learns of a plot to kill Paul and decides to transfer the matter to a higher authority, the Roman procurator (governor) at Caesarea.

Paul is sent to Marcus Antonius Felix, who held office from 52–60 CE (see table on p.138) and was married to a Jew, Drusilla, a daughter of King Herod Agrippa I. After five days, members of the Sanhedrin arrive to lay charges against Paul, and their lawyer, Tertullus, opens the prosecution case with a speech in the Hellenistic rhetorical style (Acts 24.1–8). Paul then gives his own account of events in the Temple, denying all the accusations and claiming that the real issue is the resurrection of the dead (Acts 24.20–21). Felix adjourns the case until he can hear testimony from Lysias, but no more is said of this move and it may only have been a pretext. A few days later, Felix and Drusilla interview Paul, but when Paul turns to questions of "justice, self-control, and the coming judgment," Felix is said to be "frightened" and ends the interview. He keeps Paul under open arrest for two years, hoping to extract a bribe from him (Acts 24.26). This behavior accords with the unfavorable portrayal of Felix's character by Roman historians.

Felix is succeeded as procurator (in 60 CE) by Porcius Festus, who reopens Paul's case. He asks Paul if he is willing to be tried in Jerusalem (Acts 25.9), and in response Paul exerts his right, as a Roman citizen, to be heard before the emperor himself (Nero). Festus accepts, and the process is set in train which will bring Paul to his ultimate goal: Rome (Acts 25.10–12).

Paul and Herod Agrippa II

Shortly after Paul's interview with Festus, Acts relates that the procurator receives a visit from Herod Agrippa II, the client king of territories to the north and east of Palestine, and his sister (and lover) Bernice (Acts 25.13). Agrippa asks to hear Paul, who begins his address with a rhetorical flourish, praising the king (Acts 26.2–3). Paul summarizes his own career as presented in Acts, ending with an affirmation of Jesus' death and resurrection, and the proclamation of the gospel to all humanity. Agrippa says that Paul almost persuades him to be a Christian, and asserts the apostle's innocence. In his view, Paul could have been freed if he had not appealed to Rome (Acts 26.32). But Paul's appeal to the emperor (see main text) commits him to being taken to Rome to be heard before the imperial tribunal.

A coin of Herod Agrippa II (ruled 50–ca. 100 CE), a great-grandson of Herod the Great and the last monarch of the Herodian dynasty.

PAUL'S JOURNEY TO ROME

The account in Acts 27–28 of Paul's voyage to Rome, especially his shipwreck off Malta (see sidebar, left), is one of the most dramatic pieces of writing in the New Testament. The narrative of the voyage, together with a few other sections of the book, is told in the first person plural, but this may simply be a stylistic device (see p.371). It reveals a good knowledge of Mediterranean geography and climate, and it has been described as one of the most informative documents for our knowledge of ancient seamanship. On the other hand, it stands in a long literary tradition, going back to Homer's *Odyssey*, in which accounts of a Mediterranean voyage almost invariably included the depiction of a storm and a shipwreck. In fact, much of the vocabulary of the *Odyssey* became part of the traditional way of recounting nautical stories, and traces of its style have been detected in Acts. The story has also been influenced by the Hellenistic genre known as the *periplus*, an account of a coasting voyage, of which a considerable number of examples remain. Luke's narrative can be compared with the work *The Ship* by the second-century CE author Lucian of Samosata, which covers some of the same geographical area (see map on p.369).

Paul and other prisoners sail for Italy, probably sometime between 60 and 62 CE (the period of office of the procurator Porcius Festus), in the custody of a military guard headed by a centurion. The ship calls first at Sidon, where Paul is allowed to visit friends, another manifestation of the friendly attitude of Roman officialdom toward him (Acts 27.3). Next, the party proceeds to Myra in Licia, where they transship into a vessel from Alexandria, which Acts 27.38 shows to have been a corn ship. It would have been sailing on a regular route from Egypt, Rome's chief source of grain, to the imperial capital. The ship reaches Fair Havens (modern Kaloí Liménes) in Crete at a time when further progress is dangerous: the narrator says that the "Fast" (Yom Kippur, the Jewish Day of Atonement in October) has passed (Acts 27.9) and, according to Roman writers, the dangerous season for navigation lasted from September 14 to November 11. The owner of the ship, the state contractor for the transport of corn, is determined to press on to a safe winter haven, but the ship is overtaken by a violent storm. At this point Paul receives a divine vision to reassure him that the ship's company will survive and that he himself will reach Rome (Acts 27.23–24). After a detailed and vivid description of the storm, the vessel is finally lost, but the ship's company escape and land safely on Malta (Acts 27.44). They winter on Malta for three months (see sidebar, left), since navigation in the Mediterranean was considered impossible from mid-November to the end of January.

The following spring, Paul is loaded with marks of respect by the local inhabitants and furnished with necessary supplies to continue his voyage. He embarks on another grain ship, with the figurehead of the "Twin Brothers," a reference to Castor and Pollux, the twin sons of the god Zeus (the Roman Jupiter), who were the patrons of navigation and commonly worshiped by sailors. After calling at Syracuse in Sicily and Rhegium in the extreme south of mainland Italy, the party finally disembarks at Puteoli (modern Pozzuoli) near Naples.

Paul's itinerary from Puteoli to Rome, via Appii Forum (Forum of Appius) and Three Taverns, is well-known from the Roman authors Cicero and Horace, as well as from a world map of the third or fourth century CE. The goal and the significance of the journey is summed up in the last words of Acts 28.14: "And so we came to Rome." The program of the author of Acts, laid out in Acts 1.8, is to chart the spread of

PAUL IN MALTA

After their escape from shipwreck, Paul and his companions are welcomed by the native inhabitants of Malta (Acts 28.2). Because of the bad weather, they light a bonfire, and as Paul puts sticks on it, a viper fastens onto his hand. The Maltese believe that this is divine punishment for a murderer and expect Paul to die, but when he shakes off the snake and is unharmed, they assume that he must be a god. Following this episode, Paul is received by Publius, the chief magistrate of the island, another example of the way in which Paul is represented throughout Acts as receiving sympathetic treatment from the Roman authorities. During a three-day stay in Publius's house, Paul lays hands on his father and eases his fever and dysentery. He also heals a number of other sick people.

Today there are no poisonous snakes in Malta, and perhaps there never were any. Paul's ability to resist snake poison and to cure illness may have been included to show him as typical missionary disciple, in accordance with Jesus' promise to the disciples at Mark 16.18: "if they handle snakes or drink any deadly poison, they will come to no harm; and the sick on whom they lay their hands will recover." The whole narrative is designed to honor Paul. Here, as elsewhere, he is recognized as a divine manifestation (Acts 14.11–12).

A clay imprint representing a Phoenician deity. In the story of Paul and the viper the local inhabitants expect "justice," in Greek diké, *to punish the apostle. The Maltese were of Phoenician origin, so* diké *probably refers to a Phoenician-Maltese deity who is given a Greek title by the author.* Diké *was the name of the Greek goddess of justice.*

Christianity from its original home in Palestine throughout the civilized world. This development reaches its climax when Paul is able to proclaim the gospel in Rome itself, the center of the empire.

The final chapter of Acts stresses two of the author's central themes. One is his positive attitude to the Roman power. Implicitly, Luke shows that the universal *Pax Romana*, the "Roman Peace," with the freedom and ease of travel that it ensured, facilitated the spread of the Christian faith and the consolidation of the Church. Explicitly, he shows repeatedly how the imperial representatives always treat Paul with impartial justice and protect him from his accusers, so that he is confident of a favorable hearing before the supreme tribunal of the empire. At Rome, Paul is not imprisoned but merely put under a mild form of house arrest, living for two years at his own expense and preaching the gospel "openly and without hindrance." Luke's second great theme is the rejection of the gospel by the Jews and its acceptance by the Gentiles. This is the subject of Paul's final interview with the Roman Jews (Acts 28.23–29).

Acts does not relate Paul's eventual fate, but there is a strong Christian tradition that he suffered martyrdom at Rome, perhaps during the persecution of Christians that took place under the emperor Nero in 64 CE. The author's silence about Paul's death may reflect his desire to bring his work to a rhetorical climax, with Paul's unfettered proclamation of the faith in the Imperial City.

Christians and Jews in Rome

Paul encountered one group of Christians at Puteoli (Acts 28.14) and another at Rome. He had previously written a letter to the Roman church (see p.383), which indicates that it was already of some strength. Its existence shows how Christianity must have expanded through the activities of other apostles, and by migration: those addressed by Paul in his letter have Greek, Roman, and Jewish names.

The Roman Christians formed a respectable segment of society. They probably included slaves and a few of the aristocracy, but basically they were what today might be described as middle-class. Paul's letter mentions the "household" of two men, and greets Prisca and Aquila, who had a house large enough for a Christian assembly to meet in. It was in the houses of members of the community that Christians gathered for worship. The famous Roman catacombs were not secret meeting places, as is often suggested, but simply burial sites, which would not have provided sufficient space for corporate worship. At least three "house churches" remain in Rome beneath the present churches of San Martino ai Monti, Santa Pudenziana (named traditionally after a certain Pudens who is said to have entertained St. Peter), and the saints Giovanni e Paolo.

St. Paul, *an enamel and gilt roundel from a 10th-century Venetian book cover. Paul has been portrayed since at least the 6th century as a balding, dark-haired man (see also pictures on pp.372 and 377).*

In Paul's day the Jews of Rome were more numerous, more influential, and longer established than the Christians. The development of the community really began with Pompey's capture of Jerusalem in 63 BCE, when he brought numerous slaves back to Rome. Many subsequently gained their freedom and established a colony in Trastevere, the area on the left bank of the Tiber, and later in other parts of the city. The Jews rapidly became an important element in Roman life: in the time of Augustus (27 BCE–14 CE) they numbered in the thousands. The historian Josephus relates that eight thousand Jews greeted a Jewish delegation from Palestine in 4 BCE. Their prominence is seen in the attacks on them by Roman writers, such as the satirist Juvenal, and along with members of other oriental cults they were now and again expelled from the city by imperial decree. But the community continued to flourish – for example, many Jews arrived after the fall of Jerusalem in 70 CE – until the last years of the empire.

LETTERS

Of the twenty-seven books of the New Testament, no less than twenty-one are called letters, or epistles (from the Latin epistola, *a letter). Most of them are attributed to early Church leaders; thirteen of them are ascribed to the apostle Paul alone. Letters were the means by which Church leaders were able to keep in touch with the scattered Christian congregations. The letters offered guidance on theology and pastoral care, advice on local difficulties, and warnings against certain practices and abuses. The last book of the New Testament, Revelation, is also a letter, although its extraordinary visionary character places it in the genre called apocalyptic (see pp.130–31).*

NEW TESTAMENT EPISTLES

The epistles (letters) that were sent out by the early Church to the far-flung Christian community may have been influenced by Jewish practice. The New Testament epistles recall missives that were despatched by the central Jewish authorities to communities in the Diaspora, discussing the proper observance of religious festivals and fasts. One letter from the Jerusalem Jews to their kinsfolk in Egypt, enjoining them to celebrate the new festival of Hanukkah (Dedication; see p.134), is preserved in 2 Maccabees 1–2; it is close in form and style to several of Paul's epistles.

Paul's correspondence would have been written on papyrus sheets, which were then rolled up and tied for transmission. The contents were dictated to a secretary, one of whom, Tertius, is mentioned by name in the letter to the Romans (Rom. 16.22). Paul sometimes added a postscript in his own hand, perhaps to make clear that the document really was from him. There was an efficient postal service in the Roman empire, but this was confined to official communications. Groups or individuals either had to employ their own couriers or entrust their letters to someone who happened to be traveling to the required destination. In ancient times, the bearer of a letter had an important role, often supplementing the written communication with further information or instructions from the sender. Paul often appointed delegates to carry his correspondence: he sent Timothy and Titus to the Corinthians (1 Cor. 4.17, 16.10–11; 2 Cor. 7.6–16, 8.16–18, 23–24). These same delegates would then bring a reply and other news back to the sender (2 Cor. 7.6–16).

The New Testament epistles make use of common Hellenistic and Jewish letter-writing forms, especially in their opening and closing greetings. They begin with the name of the sender, followed by the name of the recipient (for example, 1 Cor. 1.1–2; compare 2 Macc. 1.1). Greek letters usually employed the salutation "greetings," literally "rejoice," but Jews substituted or added the more typically Hebraic word "peace" (see, again, 2 Macc. 1.1). Paul does not use "greetings," but the distinctively Christian term "grace," which he couples with "peace" to form his most common salutation: "Grace to you and peace from God our Father and the Lord Jesus Christ" (Rom. 1.7 and so on). A prayer for the readers' health is often found, and an assurance of intercession for them in prayer (as in Rom. 1.9). There may be expressions of thanksgiving for past commendable conduct or for the faith of the communities the author is addressing (Rom. 1.8; 1 Cor. 1.4–7; Phil. 1.3–5; Col. 1.3–4; 1 Thess. 1.2–4; 2 Thess. 1.3). Significantly, Paul omits such praise in his letter to the Galatians, which is perhaps the most passionate and urgent of the epistles (see p.382). Stock polite formulas, such as "I appeal to you" and "You will do well to," introduce requests or injunctions. The letters conclude with often quite elaborate farewell greetings from the writer and his companions to those whom he is addressing. In all these respects, the New Testament writers reflect common Greco-Roman habits.

Although twenty-one of the writings in the New Testament are presented as literary epistles, they are not all of the same type and reflect the different kinds of letter that were common at the time. There was the purely personal letter, from one individual to another; Paul's letter to Philemon may belong to this category, although this is also addressed to "Apphia our sister, to Archippus our fellow soldier, and to the church meeting in your house" (see p.385). The third letter of John, from "the elder to the beloved Gaius" is another example of such personal correspondence.

There were also formal letters, intended for a wider audience, such as a particular church or community, which dealt with broader concerns and issued advice or directions to the readers. Paul's own letters combine the formal and more personal forms and were intended to be read during public worship. Some are of considerable length, and their quotations from Scripture, creeds, hymns, and other religious teachings, give them a distinctive character. At the same time, parts of them often reproduce conventional features of Hellenistic personal correspondence.

However, while Paul's letters are examples of real correspondence with individual communities, other writings that the New Testament labels "letters" are in reality more like general treatises. For example, the "letter" to the Ephesians (which may or may not be by Paul) is actually an encyclical, in other words a circular, intended for a number of churches in Asia Minor (see pp.386–87). The "letter" to the Hebrews is in fact a sermon, and contains no hint of conventional letter forms until its final verses. The "letter" of James is an example of *paranesis*, offering advice on living wisely and well (see pp.388–89). The Pastoral Letters (see pp.378–79) belong to a category of writings called "Church Order": they are largely concerned with handing down advice to particular churches on pastoral and practical matters, although they employ the literary form of a personal letter.

St. Paul, *Hungarian School, ca. 1500. The depiction of the apostle with a full head of hair and a long (rather than trimmed) beard reflects a different tradition from that represented in the image on p.375; that on p.372 appears to combine both traditions. Here, as on p.372, he carries a sword as a symbol of his supposed martyrdom (see p.378). In all three he holds the gospels, symbolizing his evangelical mission.*

Greco-Roman letters

All the letters in the Bible, and the majority of those from the Greco-Roman world, have survived only in literary contexts. But modern archaeological discoveries have produced a number of original letters, such as those from the cities of Mari, Tell El-Amarna, Lachish, Elephantine, and those dating from the first-century Jewish revolt of Simon Bar Kochba. Of particular interest for the New Testament are papyrus letters of the same period from Egypt and other arid regions, which have been preserved by the climate. They are private correspondence, often of quite ordinary individuals, and show that many of the formal elements that characterize the New Testament letters were in common use.

A more elaborate style of correspondence was produced by prominent public figures, such as the Roman statesmen Cicero and Seneca. Their letters, like those of Paul, were collected for publication. Such letters were often treatises intended for a wide circle of readers, dealing with philosophical, political, or moral issues. Letter-writing was viewed as a branch of the art of rhetoric, and handbooks have survived that provide appropriate letter forms for particular occasions. Fictitious letters could be produced for literary purposes or to sway those who might read them. Paul himself had to warn the Thessalonians not to be taken in by a missive purporting to be from him (2 Thess. 2.2). Historians felt free to make up letters and speeches that they considered to be appropriate to a particular character: examples of this kind of letter are found in the book of Revelation addressed to the seven churches of Asia (Rev. 1.4–3.22).

The Martyrdom of St. Paul, *from the workshop of Pacino di Buonaguida (active 1303–1309). According to tradition, Paul was beheaded with a sword. His head is said to have bounced three times, causing three fountains – the Tre Fontane in Rome – to spring from the earth.*

THE PASTORAL LETTERS

The New Testament does not relate the ultimate fate of either Peter or Paul. But according to a well-established tradition, especially early and strong in the case of Peter, both apostles were martyred at Rome during the emperor Nero's persecution of Christians in 64 CE. How Peter might have come to be in the city is unknown, but at the end of Acts, Paul is said to be in Rome, preaching the gospel "with all boldness and without hindrance" after his eventful journey from Palestine (see pp.374–75). He is said to have lived under a mild form of house arrest for two years (Acts 28.30–31), presumably waiting for his appeal to the emperor (see p.373) to be heard. But nothing further is said about the outcome of the appeal and Acts does not say that Paul was freed. According to one theory, at the end of the two years, he may have been freed, either because his accusers failed to press charges or through an act of imperial clemency. Another theory claims that the author may have omitted Paul's execution because he wished to end his work on a positive note. After all, the goal stated at the beginning of Acts has been achieved: the gospel is being preached in Rome.

One tradition, at least as early as the fourth-century CE Christian historian Eusebius, states that after the events recounted in the last chapter of Acts, Paul was released, resumed his missionary work, and finally returned to Rome, where he was martyred. Support for this tradition has often been found in three epistles, the first and second letters to Timothy and the letter to Titus (see box on opposite page). These are known as the "Pastoral Letters," because they offer guidance to the recipients on the pastoral care of their churches. The letters depict journeys by Paul in Asia Minor, Macedonia, Crete, and Greece. It is difficult to reconcile these travels with

The Martyrdom of St. Peter *(ca. 1550), by Michelangelo Buonarroti (1475–1564), a fresco in the Pauline chapel of the Vatican, Rome. In the traditional story, Peter is crucified under Nero in Rome. It is said that he considered himself unworthy to die in the same way as Jesus, and insisted on being crucified upside down. Like most artists from the 4th century onward, Michelangelo depicts the senior apostle as a tall, gray-haired man of great physical vigor.*

the career of Paul as related in Acts and his other letters. The journeys must therefore be ascribed to a later period of Paul's life: a passage in 2 Timothy may refer to his release from a first imprisonment in Rome (2 Tim. 4.16–17). However, this reconstruction presumes that the Pastoral Letters are in fact by Paul, a view that has been widely challenged. Most scholars now believe that they were written some considerable time after the apostle's death. The authors of the letters may have sought to reassert Pauline teaching in the face of problems in the churches that Paul had founded. Nevertheless, the Pastoral Letters may contain fragments from genuine, lost, Pauline letters, such as the names and deeds of particular individuals. There are also possibly genuine personal details, such as the reference to a cloak and notebooks left at Troas (2 Tim. 4.13). The authors may have included such details to give the letters a sense of authenticity.

The style and vocabulary of the Pastoral Letters differ considerably from those of Paul's undoubtedly genuine letters; they recall the works of Christian writers of the late first and early second centuries CE. The theological outlook of the Pastoral Letters also seems to be different in many ways from that of Paul. For example, "faith," used by the apostle in the sense of "an act of trust," becomes in the letters "*the* faith," the body of Christian doctrine. There is little mention of the work of the Spirit, which is central in the thought of the authentic Paul. Church organization appears to be considerably more developed than it does in Paul's other letters, with bishops, elders, and deacons. Again, this reflects the situation in the Church of around the end of the first century CE.

In defense of Pauline authorship, it has been said that if the Pastoral Letters date from late in Paul's life, then some of the developments in ecclesiastical structure that they indicate may already have begun. Also, the letters attack what seems to be the first real appearance of the Gnostic heresy, and Paul may have had to adapt his language and theological approach to meet this new threat to the Church.

Timothy and Titus

One argument against Paul's authorship of the Pastoral Letters is that they are addressed to individuals and not to Christian congregations, unlike all his other letters except Philemon. A later author might have employed the names of Timothy and Titus, both venerated figures in the early Church, to give authority to his own teaching.

Timothy, a native of Lystra who was chosen by Paul to accompany him on his missionary travels (Acts 16.3), appears frequently in Paul's letters (for example, Phil. 2.19–23). He was a close associate of Paul in his evangelistic work and also someone for whom the apostle felt a deep personal affection (see, for example, Phil. 2.22). Even if Paul did not write the warm words addressed to Timothy in 1 and 2 Timothy (such as 2 Tim. 1.3–4), they certainly reflect Paul's attitude. Paul employed Timothy as his personal emissary to the churches in Thessalonica and Corinth when he could not visit them himself (1 Thess. 3.2; 1 Cor. 4.17), and it is possible that Timothy could have assumed special charge of one or more of the Pauline congregations when Paul was confined in Rome. The author of the Pastoral Letters evidently knew the names of Timothy's mother and grandmother (2 Tim. 1.5).

Unlike Timothy, Titus is not mentioned in Acts, but he too was a "partner and co-worker" of Paul (2 Cor. 8.23). He accompanied Paul on an important visit to Jerusalem (Gal. 2.1), he too was an emissary of Paul's to Corinth (2 Cor. 7–8), and in particular he took the lead in the work of collecting contributions for the Jewish Christians at Jerusalem (2 Cor. 8). Whether the general picture of him in the letter to Titus can be regarded as coming from Paul is doubtful. However, the letter's reference to Titus's missionary work in Dalmatia and Crete, which is also mentioned in 2 Timothy, may represent an authentic tradition (2 Tim. 4.10; Titus 1.5). The author of the letter tells Titus that "Cretans are always liars, vicious brutes, lazy gluttons" (Titus 1.12). This is a quotation from a poem by the sixth-century BCE Cretan poet Epimenides. Paul is reported to have used the same poem in his speech at Athens (Acts 17.22–31).

LETTERS TO GREECE

A 4th-century monument on the ancient Via Egnatia (Egnatian Way), along which Paul would have traveled. It was the main road linking Thessalonica and other cities of northern Greece to the Adriatic (see map on p.369).

In the New Testament, Paul's letters are not arranged according to when they were written, but roughly in order of length. There is some dispute as to their exact chronological order, so it is difficult to use them to reconstruct Paul's life. It is also hard to see exactly how they fit into the picture of Paul that is presented in Acts.

However, it is generally accepted that the first Pauline letter is 1 Thessalonians, the first letter to the church at Thessalonica (modern Salonica) in northern Greece. It was probably written from Corinth in 50 CE by Paul and his fellow missionaries Silas (Silvanus) and Timothy. Paul visited the city during his second missionary journey, recorded in Acts 16–18. His teaching at the synagogue there attracted a good number of converts, but opposition from Jewish authorities forced him to leave (Acts 17.1–9). The letter to the Thessalonians, written subsequently, thus gives an interesting picture of a Christian community at an early stage. Addressed in the letter as a "church," the Thessalonian Christians had been suffering persecution. The letter begins with a thanksgiving, in characteristic epistolary style, in which Paul expresses his gratitude for the community's "work of faith and labor of love and steadfastness of hope in our Lord Jesus Christ" (1 Thess. 1.3), and exhorts them to persevere in the future.

In the letter, Paul offers guidance on three issues of concern to members of the Thessalonian church. He entreats them to avoid fornication, to control their bodies, and reject the sexual license of the Greco-Roman world, for "God did not call us to impurity but in holiness" (1 Thess. 4.3–7). He reminds them to be good citizens, to mind their own affairs and work to make a living, "so that you may behave properly toward outsiders and be dependent on no one" (1 Thess. 4.11–12). And he reassures them "by the word of the Lord" about the second coming of Jesus, which was seen as imminent, saying that those Christians who had already died would not be left behind but would, in fact, rise before the living, so that all would be "caught up in the clouds together ... to meet the Lord" (1 Thess. 4.13–18).

The second letter to the Thessalonians is the subject of much scholarly disagreement. Some argue that it was in fact written before 1 Thessalonians, while others hold that the differences between it and the first letter mean that it cannot have been written by Paul. Nevertheless, the second letter seems to take up two of the concerns of the first. The idea of the second coming of Christ was continuing to cause problems, but now some teachers were claiming that it had already occurred. This perhaps reflects the view, typical of later Gnosticism, that the Resurrection was a purely spiritual experience. In response, Paul reminds the Thessalonians of the apocalyptic concept of the "rebellion," which must precede the Messiah's advent (2 Thess. 2.3). The arrival of the Day of the Lord is being delayed by a "lawless one," who will enthrone himself in the Temple and claim to be God (2 Thess. 2.4). The imagery is much the same as in Mark 13, and reflects the depiction of the persecuting Hellenistic king Antiochus Epiphanes in the book of Daniel (see pp.130–33).

The concern with work also echoes 1 Thessalonians. Some Christians thought that because the coming of Jesus was very near or had in fact come, there was no point in their continuing to earn a living. Paul rejects such an attitude, pointing to himself as an example (2 Thess. 3.9). When he and his companions were among the Thessalonians, they worked for their daily bread, even though they might have expected others to support them. Paul condemns this attitude and tells his readers in no uncertain terms that "anyone unwilling to work should not eat" (2 Thess. 3.10). He exhorts them not to be "weary in doing what is right" (2 Thess. 3.13).

The letters to Corinth

More than any of Paul's writings, the two letters to the Corinthian church provide a vivid picture of an early Christian congregation. They were written from Ephesus, probably ca. 55 CE, to the church at Corinth which Paul had planted during his second missionary journey (Acts 16–18). The letters pose various literary problems, especially 2 Corinthians, which is probably made up of several different letters which were sent at various times. The precise course of events is thus not particularly easy to determine, but the issues and debates that faced a young church in a great cosmopolitan city are vividly depicted.

The Corinthian community was rent by divisions between followers of different evangelists, and at the beginning of the first letter, Paul appeals for unity, for adherence to no one teacher except Christ (1 Cor. 1.10–17). Next, Paul addresses the issue of sexual behavior. Essentially, he asserts the authority for Christians of the Jewish moral code. He orders the excommunication of a man who, contrary to the Jewish Law, had married his father's wife, and gives his views concerning marriage and divorce (1 Cor. 5–7). He then turns to another problem posed by the pagan environment: whether Christians could eat meat that had been offered to idols. Again, Paul's concern for unity is evident. In this matter, each should act according to his own conscience and not judge others (1 Cor. 8–9).

Questions of worship and belief occupy the remainder of Paul's letter. By this time, the eucharist had clearly become the central Christian celebration, but the communal meal in which it was set was in danger of exhibiting the excesses which often accompanied Greco-Roman festivities. "Speaking in tongues" was also leading to disorder in public worship and was becoming an occasion of self-indulgence. Paul does not forbid the practice, but stresses that other gifts are necessary, especially, in a famous passage, love (1 Cor. 13). What is required is a fully communal worship, which will bind the whole congregation together, and this demands that "all things should be done decently and in order" (1 Cor. 14.26–40). To this end, "women should be silent in the churches," in accordance with the Jewish Law (1 Cor. 14.33–36). Finally, some people in Corinth were denying the resurrection: presumably, like some of the congregation at Thessalonica, they denied the resurrection of the body, and understood the concept of resurrection in a purely spiritual sense. Once again, Paul adopts a mediating position: there will, at the final end, be a real resurrection, but of a new, transformed, and spiritual body, fitted for the new age (1 Cor. 15.1–58).

The second letter to the Corinthians does not add a great deal to the general picture of the community that was provided in the first letter, except to show the continuing seriousness of its divisions. Paul's first letter had apparently had little effect and, in the last three chapters of the second letter, he abandons the polite epistolary conventions to vent his anger and frustration. He threatens the Corinthians with the force of his displeasure on another visit.

The Bema, *the ancient public tribunal at Corinth, Greece. It was probably here that Paul faced Gallio, the Roman proconsul (see Acts 18.12–17).*

GALATIANS AND ROMANS

Abraham Prepares to Sacrifice Isaac, *a mosaic floor from the 6th-century* CE *synagogue of Beth-Alpha in northern Israel. In the letters to the Galatians (Gal. 3–4) and to the Romans (see especially Rom. 4), Paul draws extensively on the story of Abraham and his faith. He says that "the promise that he would inherit the world did not come to Abraham or to his descendants through the law but through the righteousness of faith" (Rom. 4.13). This was demonstrated through Abraham's readiness to sacrifice his son at God's behest (see p.37).*

Two of Paul's letters, Galatians and Romans, are often considered together. Both are concerned with the separation of Christianity from Judaism, which was one of the most significant results of Paul's ministry. The letter to the Galatians was probably among the earliest of Paul's epistles, written ca. 48 CE, although it has also been dated as late as 55 CE. The date of the letter to the Romans (see box on opposite page) is unknown, but it may be a later elaboration of ideas first addressed in Galatians.

The separation of the two religions seems to be found for the first time in the letter to the Galatians, in which Paul argues that faith alone can lead a person to salvation. Just who the "Galatians" were is much disputed. They were possibly the inhabitants of a broad region of north and central Turkey, called Galatia after the Celts who had settled in the area ca. 250 BCE. It is more likely, however, that they lived farther south, in the more narrowly defined region which since 25 BCE had been the Roman province of Galatia. There is no evidence that Paul ever visited the northerly region, but he traveled throughout the Roman province on his three missionary journeys, evangelizing the cities of Pisidian Antioch, Iconium, Lystra, and Derbe (Acts 13.14–14.23; see pp.370–71).

The strong tone of the Galatian letter may reflect the special attachment he felt to these cities, where his work had first borne fruit, and which he now felt were in danger of being led away from the gospel. Unlike his other letters, Galatians has no introductory thanksgivings, but the opening is followed abruptly by a forceful statement of his concern: "I am astonished that you are so quickly deserting the one who called you in the grace of Christ" (Gal. 1.6). It was in Galatia that Paul's mission to the Gentiles had begun, but now his Gentile converts were being won over by rival Jewish-Christian teachers, telling them that they could not be saved unless they accepted the Jewish Law and, in particular, its requirement of circumcision. These teachers seem to have combined the Law with an elaborate angelology and mystical speculation, similar to that found at the community of Qumran (see p.139 and p.169). Paul goes so far as to accuse the Galatians of reverting to their former belief in the "elemental spirits" that governed the universe (Gal. 4.9).

Paul's argument is that there is no reason that the Law should be imposed on Gentile converts, for "a person is justified not by the works of

The letter to the Romans

Many of the themes of the letter to the Galatians recur, though in a fuller and more carefully nuanced way, in the letter to the Romans, which was probably written shortly after. Essentially a treatise or essay, rather than a letter proper, it sums up Paul's theology and, as such, stands apart from his other undisputed writings.

Romans is also unique because it was not sent to a community that Paul himself had founded. He writes that it is his ambition to take the gospel to places where the name of Christ has not been heard, not wanting to "build on someone else's foundation" (Rom. 15.20). This raises the question of the exact occasion and purpose of his writing. In the first chapter, Paul appears to be assuming responsibility for evangelizing the whole Greco-Roman world, and writes that he has long planned to visit Rome and would now hope to do so (Rom. 1.11, 13). Paul may have felt that the Christians in Rome lacked a proper organizational structure: Paul does not use the word "church" outside the last chapter (the authenticity of which is disputed). It may be that the Roman community had been disrupted by the expulsion of the Jews from Rome that was ordered by the emperor Claudius in 41 or 49 CE. Those who were expelled could well have included Jewish Christians still linked with the synagogues there.

The letter may be seen as an attempt to lay a "foundation" for the Roman church and, not least, to avoid the tensions between Jewish and Gentile Christians which had arisen elsewhere. In it, Paul develops further the doctrine of justification by faith alone, one of the key themes of Galatians. His famous message that "a person is justified by faith apart from works prescribed by the law" (Rom. 3.28) is to be understood in the context of the relationship of Jew and Gentile in the church: the Jewish Law divided them, but a common faith in Jesus would unite them. Jewish Christians and Gentile Christians are sinners (Rom. 2.12–3.20), yet all can achieve salvation (Rom. 3.21–31). Toward the end of the letter is a discussion of Israel's future. Paul likens the Gentiles to wild olive shoots grafted onto an olive tree to replace branches that had broken off, that is, Jews who have rejected the gospel. In the end, however, "all Israel will be saved" (Rom. 11.17–26).

After setting out the theological basis for the Church, Paul turns to the attitudes of the Roman community in its everyday dealings: mutual harmony and tolerance among its own members; loyal obedience to the state; and the fulfillment of social obligations.

Top: *A 1st-century bust of the emperor Claudius (ruled 41–54 CE).*

Bottom: *It is possible that Paul wrote Romans from Corinth. This 1st-century inscription from the city bears the name of an official called Erastus, who may be the treasurer mentioned in Romans 16.23.*

the law but through faith in Jesus Christ" (Gal. 2.15). He does not disown his own Jewishness (Gal. 2.15), and he recognizes that the Law had its value "before faith came," in the sense that it served to convict human beings of their sinfulness (Gal. 3.19–24). On the other hand, he calls it a curse (Gal. 3.10–12), because, as he sees it, it is impossible to observe its commands fully. With the coming of Christ (Gal. 5.2–4), Paul writes, this curse has been lifted (Gal. 3.14), and the authority of the Law has come to an end (Gal. 3.25). Salvation is attained only through faith in Christ, a teaching developed more fully in Romans. In Galatians, Paul sets out a radical concept of Christian, and indeed human, freedom. The believer is delivered from old allegiances, whether Jewish or Gentile, because the gospel transcends all human differences: "there is no longer Jew or Greek, there is no longer slave or free, there is no longer male or female; for all of you are one in Christ Jesus" (Gal. 3.28).

THE CAPTIVITY LETTERS

A cell in the Roman-period prison of Philippi, believed to be on the same site as the cell in which Paul was detained, according to Acts 16.23–24.

Four of Paul's letters, Philippians, Philemon, Colossians, and Ephesians, are known as the "Captivity Letters," because in each case the author portrays himself as being imprisoned (Phil. 1.7, 12.14; Philem. vv. 1, 10; Col. 4.3; Eph. 3.1). The letters are related in other ways: Colossians and Ephesians, in particular, are connected both by their ideas and wording. They mention names that also occur in the letter to Philemon (see box on opposite page); these include Epaphras (Philem. v. 23; Col. 4.12), who may have founded the church at Colossae. The letter to Philippi lacks such close ties with the other three, except for the mention of Timothy in its opening greeting (compare Col. 1.1).

Much debate has centered on the place of composition, especially in the case of the letter to the Philippians. It is generally agreed that Paul was the author of the letter. He visited Philippi, a leading city of the Roman colony of Macedonia, on his second missionary journey (Acts 16), and the church he established there was his first foundation on the mainland of Europe. Some have suggested that the letter may have been sent from Rome or Caesarea, both places in which Paul was imprisoned. If the references in the letter to the "imperial guard," or Roman praetorium (Phil. 1.13), and to "those in the emperor's household" are taken to mean the imperial palace and Caesar's entourage, they would point to Rome as the point of origin. However, these references could equally apply to the official residence of a provincial governor and thus be applicable to Caesarea, the seat of the procurator of Judea.

Another school of thought claims that the letter was written from Ephesus, where Paul could have been imprisoned during his two-year stay (Acts 19.10). In the letter, Paul writes that he hopes to send his companion Timothy to the Philippians, "so that I may be cheered by news of you" (Phil. 2.19). Such a return journey by Timothy would have been difficult if he had had to travel from as far away as Rome or even Caesarea. If Paul were imprisoned at Ephesus, however, a return journey to Philippi would have been much more straightforward: Paul had traveled the same route himself on his third missionary journey (see p.371). Timothy was evidently closely associated with Ephesus, overseeing the Church's mission there according to 1 Timothy 1.3. Also, the Philippian church heard of Paul's imprisonment and felt that it was worthwhile to send one of its own members, Epaphroditus, as an aide to the apostle. Epaphroditus became ill and news of his illness reached Philippi, because Epaphroditus subsequently heard that his colleagues were worried for him (Phil. 2.25–26). The passage seems to imply that traffic between Philippi and the place of Paul's imprisonment was fairly regular and straightforward: there is no mention of the kind of travelers' perils faced by Paul in the account of his journey to Rome in Acts.

The warm and intimate tone of the letter to the Philippians contrasts with that of the correspondence to Galatia and Corinth (see pp.381–83). Paul speaks of his prayers for the Philippians (Phil. 1.3–11), and assures them that he will return to Philippi after his release from prison (Phil. 1.19–36). He thanks the Philippians for the financial support that they, alone, had given him in the early days of his ministry (Phil. 4.22), and expresses his appreciation of Epaphroditus (Phil. 2.25–30). Although he has to warn the church at Philippi against "evil workers" who insist on circumcision (Phil. 3.2–3), the general picture in the letter is of a harmonious and active community. Uniquely in Paul's indisputably genuine letters, "bishops" and "deacons" are addressed as the church leaders (Phil. 1.1), pointing to an already clearly organized ecclesiastical structure, at least in

Philemon and slavery

The letter to Philemon is addressed not only to Philemon but also to the church that meets in his house and to Apphia and Archippus. However, the entire content of the letter concerns Philemon and his slave, Onesimus.

Onesimus had run away from, and perhaps also robbed, his master. He had been put in prison, where he had met Paul and been converted to Christ. Paul had become deeply attached to him: he writes of how Onesimus had become "useful" (Philem. v. 11), playing on the slave's name, which means "useful" or "beneficial" in Greek. However, Paul believed strongly that all Christians should be good citizens and respect the legal and social order. This is probably why he decided to return Onesimus, bearing this letter to his master Philemon, who apparently lived at Colossae in Asia Minor: Paul sends greetings (v. 23) from five fellow prisoners who are also mentioned at the end of the letter to the Colossians.

Roman law prescribed the harshest penalties for runaway slaves, sometimes even death. But Paul does not simply ask for clemency or seek to tell Philemon his duty. Rather, he appeals to the common faith shared by both master and slave, and asks that Onesimus be received back as a brother "both in the flesh and in the Lord" (v. 16). Paul promises to repay Philemon for whatever Onesimus may have stolen, and seems to hint that Philemon might even consider returning the slave to him to continue to help him in prison (vv. 13–14).

Slavery was a widespread and accepted feature of the Roman world, but in the first century CE attitudes were changing. The emancipation of slaves, which gave them full civil rights and the possibility of Roman citizenship, occurred on a considerable scale, and the increasing egalitarianism preached by philosophers, such as the Stoics, affected the way in which the legal institution of slavery came to be regarded. As the letter to Philemon reflects, the early Church accepted the institution of slavery and taught that slaves should be obedient to their masters and perform their duties continuously (see also Eph. 6.5–6; Col. 3.22). But masters were to treat their slaves fairly and to give them their freedom if the opportunity arose (for example, Col. 4.1; 1 Tim. 6.1–2; Titus 2.9–10). Christian authors denounced the more brutal aspects of slavery, such as the slave trade (1 Tim. 1.10). Christianity also preached a much more radical doctrine which was to lead to the repudiation of slavery. For Paul, "in Christ" there was no distinction between slave and free (Gal. 3.28). Jesus had himself adopted the "form of a slave" (Phil. 2.7) and this was to be the pattern for Christians. Paul describes himself as a servant and prisoner of Christ (Rom. 1.1; Phil. 1.1) and proclaims that any slave who received his call to be a Christian would be free in the Lord, and, equally, a free person is a slave in the service of Christ.

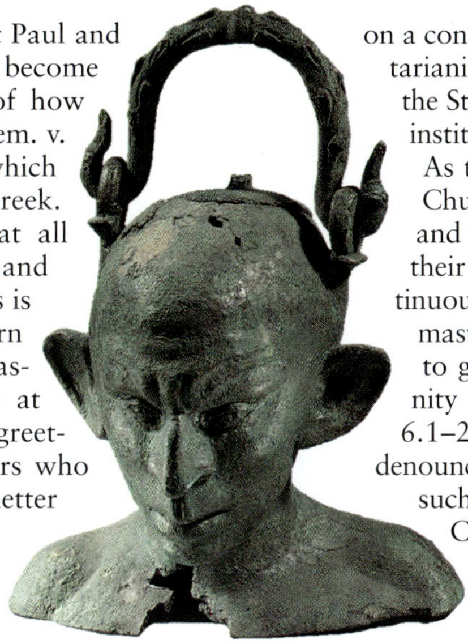

Top: *A 1st-century* CE *Greek inscription recording the foundation of a synagogue, possibly the one for freedmen (liberated slaves) mentioned in Acts 6.9.*

Bottom: *A 2nd-century Roman bronze and lead vase portraying a Syrian slave.*

Philippi. Philippians 2.6–11, which is the most famous passage in the letter, contains an early Christian hymn, which Paul adopts and modifies in order to demonstrate how the imitation of Christ is the model for the life of the believer. The hymn is important as showing how rapidly the doctrine of the person of Christ developed in the early church. Jesus is seen as preexistent, "in the form of God" (Phil. 2.6), but in spite of his divinity, he chose to take "the form of a slave" and to be born in human form (Phil. 2.7). The hymn appears to combine the Jewish concept of divine Wisdom (see pp.120–21) with the figure of the Suffering Servant in the book of Isaiah (see p.106), whom Christians understood as prefiguring the suffering Christ.

COLOSSIANS AND EPHESIANS

ETHICAL LISTS

In Martin Luther's German translation of the Bible, two sections have the heading *Haustafeln*, household tables or codes (Col. 3.18–4.1; Eph. 5.21–6.9). Very similar passages occur elsewhere in the New Testament, particularly in 1 Peter, and all seem to follow a broadly common pattern. Known as "ethical lists," they address believers in pairs according to their position in the household – wives and husbands, children and fathers, slaves and masters – and set out the mutual duties called for within each relationship. They are derived from catalogs of such duties in both Classical and Jewish sources, but the motivating clauses attached to them are distinctively Christian. In writings that may have been produced considerably later than Paul's lifetime, such as the Pastoral Letters, there are lists dealing specifically with positions in the Church, whether officers (bishops, elders, and deacons) or Church members (the old, the young, and widows).

Alongside the household and community catalogs, there are also lists of vices to be shunned and virtues to the embraced. These, too, reflect a widespread Greco-Roman ethical background, but again they are infused by the particular Christian concepts of love and faith, as in Colossians 3.14, which bids: "Above all, clothe yourself with love, which binds everything together in perfect harmony."

The letters to the churches of Colossae and Ephesus (see box, below) are closely related: the latter appears to incorporate about a quarter of the contents of the former, and both are perhaps the most disputed documents in the New Testament. Scholars differ sharply as to whether they were written by Paul or by a later author or authors who used and developed genuine Pauline concepts.

Colossians, at least, can claim strong grounds for Pauline authorship. The city of Colossae in Asia Minor had not been evangelized by the apostle himself but, according to the letter, by his fellow worker Epaphras (Col. 1.7–8). This probably occurred during the time of Paul's ministry in nearby Ephesus (Acts 19; see pp.370–71), probably ca. 52–55 CE. Several other individuals mentioned in Paul's letters are associated with the place, including Philemon (see p.385). Colossians has the regular form of one of Paul's indisputably genuine letters and contains authentic details such as a mention of the neighboring towns of Laodicea and Hierapolis.

The purpose of the letter was to alert the Colossians to the danger of false teachers, who sought to captivate them "through philosophy and empty deceit, according to human tradition, according to the elemental spirits of the universe, and not according to Christ" (Col. 2.8). This teaching was probably a kind of Jewish mysticism such as affected other Pauline churches. One verse appears to accuse the author's opponents of angel-worship (Col. 2.18), but this may mean that they claimed to have a visionary experience of angels in their worship. There is a precedent for this in the so-called "Angelic Liturgy" of the community at Qumran (see p.139). The earthly worshipers there viewed themselves as sharing in the worship conducted in heaven by the angels.

The letter to the Ephesians

The Pauline authorship of Ephesians is highly debatable. Regular epistolary features are lacking and the letter does not appear to address the problems in a particular congregation, in the way that Paul's other correspondence does. The words "in Ephesus" in the opening verse are not found in some of the most important early manuscripts of the New Testament, and this has led to the view that the document was really an encyclical, intended for circulation to a group of churches in Asia Minor, of which Ephesus was perhaps the center. It is the first of the seven churches of Asia Minor addressed in Revelation (see p.392). Also, the vocabulary is uncharacteristic: the letter contains some ninety words that are not found in Paul's other writings.

The 1st-century CE odeon *(small theater) at Ephesus in western Asia Minor (modern Efes, Turkey).*

In some respects, Ephesians seems to reflect a situation later than that of Paul's time. The conflict of Jew and Gentile, which so much exercised Paul, is long past: the very "secret" of the gospel is now the union of Jew and Gentile in the one body of the Church.

Ephesians carries even further the teaching found in Colossians 1 about the cosmic Jesus (Eph. 1.20–23; see main text on opposite page). The Ephesian letter contains reminiscences of almost every one of Paul's letters, but it seems to be looking back on them, and reads like a digest of the great themes of his preaching. Probably, then, the work should be viewed as a preservation and interpretation of Paul's ideas, created to meet the needs of the church when the living witness of the first apostles had passed away.

To counteract this teaching, and in order to reject the divinity of any figure but Jesus, the writer of the letter presents a picture of the cosmic Christ, especially in Colossians 1.15–20. These verses represent a hymn, originally in praise of Wisdom and probably Jewish, which is reinterpreted to refer to Jesus. Jesus is described as "the firstborn of all creation" (Col. 1.15) and depicted as the head of the universal Church (Col. 1.18). It has been argued that the language and theology of this passage differ significantly from that of Paul's authentic letters – for instance, elsewhere Paul only employs the term "church" to refer to a local congregation.

Another aspect of Colossians that has raised doubts about its Pauline authorship is its teaching about the end of the world and the universal resurrection of the dead. Elsewhere in Paul's writings, this final consummation of Jesus' victory is regarded as still to come, but Colossians appears to take the view that resurrection is already realized for the believer (Col. 3.1–4). It is possible that a later writer is attempting to cope with the problem of the delay in the second coming of Christ, whose imminent return had been expected in the Church's early days.

A host of angels (see main text on opposite page) hovers above the head of Christ in The Crucifixion *by Giotto (ca. 1266–1337), one of his frescoes for the Scrovegni chapel, Padua, ca. 1305.*

JEWISH CHRISTIANITY

The letter to the Hebrews and the letter of James are both, in different ways, closely linked to Jewish traditions. The distinctive characteristic of Hebrews is that it seeks throughout to show that Jesus is the true fulfillment of Judaism's history and faith. The title "to the Hebrews" was not part of the original work and the letter's author is not known; it does not claim to be by Paul. The writer was clearly very learned, trained in Hellenistic rhetorical methods and in using the Septuagint, the Greek translation of the Hebrew Scriptures.

The work is both a profound theological treatise and a genuine letter, addressed to a particular community and its problems. However, just what this community was and where it was situated remains the subject of much discussion. Because the letter sends greetings from "those from Italy" (Heb. 13.24), and because its earliest attestation is at Rome around 90 CE, it has often been suggested that it was sent to a Jewish Christian group in Rome. Attention has also been drawn to the similarities between Hebrews and the literature that came from the Greek-speaking Jewish community at Alexandria in Egypt, such as the Wisdom of Solomon and the work of the philosopher Philo (see p.126). More recently, a study of the texts from Qumran (see p.139) has led some experts to suggest that Hebrews is addressed to members of the Church in Palestine who had converted to Christianity from a strand of Judaism that stood outside the mainstream, such as the Qumran community and the Essenes (see p.139). If this theory is correct, these converts had probably not adequately understood the real nature of Christianity and were in danger of returning to their old beliefs.

Angels were central to the thinking of the Qumran community and it was widely believed that angels would usher in the end of the world (see, for example, Revelation). The recipients of Hebrews appear to have shared a similar belief. Hence, the author of Hebrews begins by demonstrating that Jesus is superior to all angels, and that God "did not subject the coming world" to them (Heb. 2.5). He then proceeds to argue that Jesus is also greater than Moses. Above all, Jesus transcends the whole

The Martyrdom of James, *by Lorenzo Monaco (ca. 1370–ca. 1422). According to the historian Josephus, the brother of Jesus was martyred in ca. 62* CE *on the initiative of the high priest Ananus, who took advantage of the gap between the death of one Roman procurator, Festus, and the arrival of another, Albinus. It is probable that otherwise only the Romans had the authority to impose capital punishment (see pp.246–47).*

Melchizedek

An important feature of the letter to the Hebrews is the role of Melchizedek, whose significance, says the author, is to be understood only by those well instructed in the faith. The story of Melchizedek, the priest king of Salem who blessed Abraham (Gen. 14.18–20; see p.33), is said to demonstrate the superiority of Melchizedek's office, because "it is beyond dispute that the inferior is blessed by the superior" (Heb. 7.7). The letter also claims that Jesus is "a priest forever, according to the order of Melchizedek" (Heb. 7.17, quoting Ps. 110). This means that Jesus is superior to Abraham and also to the Levitical priesthood, for "Levi himself was still in his ancestor's loins when Melchizedek met him" (Heb. 7.9–10).

The writer of Hebrews describes Melchizedek in terms that go well beyond Genesis: he has "neither beginning of days nor end of life, but resembling the son of God, he remains a priest forever" (Heb. 7.3). This language appears to reflect a strand of Jewish apocalyptic writing. For example, a fragmentary text discovered at Qumran portrays Melchizedek as a heavenly savior and an angelic being, immortal and nonhuman. He is referred to as *elohim*, the usual Hebrew word for "God," but here meaning one of the members of the divine heavenly assembly (see sidebar on p.21). In Hebrews, however, the word "resembling" shows that Melchizedek is similar to but not the equal of Jesus, whose superiority to all angels has been established earlier in the letter (see main text).

Abraham Presents Prisoners and Booty to Melchizedek *(Gen. 14.20), from the Psalter of St. Louis (French, ca. 1270).*

Jewish priestly and sacrificial system. He alone is the "great high priest" (Heb. 4.14), and only his sacrifice, not the sacrifices of Judaism, can truly make an atonement for human sins. Faith in Jesus and in his saving work is the way to salvation. The significance of the heroic figures of Israel is that they lived by faith, looking to the promises now fully realized in Christ. The letter's recipients are exhorted always to look to Jesus; this will both sustain them under persecution in this life and give them the perfect reward of their faith in the hereafter.

The letter of James is traditionally attributed to James, one of the brothers of Jesus, and the leader of the early Jewish Christian community in Jerusalem (Acts 15; see pp.358–59). It may date from around the early forties CE. The attribution is not impossible, but many scholars think that the work was written by someone else and dates from the end of the first century CE. It is addressed to "the twelve tribes," a reference to the traditional tribes making up the nation of Israel, and so, like Hebrews, it is probably directed at Jewish converts to Christianity. Although the style contains many characteristics reminiscent of the Hebrew or Aramaic languages, the letter is written in good Greek, and has many points of contact with literary and philosophical forms current in the Hellenistic world. For example, it contains what is called *paranesis*, exhortation of an ethical, practical nature, which was common in philosophical treatises and in Jewish writings of the Diaspora. The letter is also a diatribe, a short ethical treatise of the sort that was typical of the Cynic school of philosophers.

The author's prime concern is the unity and harmony of a community that is evidently under a degree of stress. The letter emphasizes the positive value of the testing of faith and endurance, and the danger to the wellbeing of the community that arises from gossip, backbiting, and envy. Rich people who seek to behave as if they were superior to their poorer fellows are roundly condemned.

FAITH AND WORKS

In James 2.14–26, the author apparently puts good works before faith, claiming: "faith by itself, if it has no works, is dead" (James 2.17). This passage, which led Martin Luther to tear the letter to James from every Bible he came across, has often been seen as a direct attack on Paul's central doctrine of "justification by faith," whereby people are saved by their faith, not by their deeds. But it is possible that the author of James was using the terms "works" and "faith" in a different way from Paul. In James, "works" could mean acts of charity, rather than Paul's sense of strict (but not necessarily sincere) adherence to the letter of the law. Similarly, "faith" in James may simply mean belief in the existence of God, rather than the total commitment to and trust in God that is Paul's understanding. Viewed in this light, the issue in James becomes less theological than practical: essentially, the author is discussing the merits of hospitality in a Christian, as at James 2.15–16.

St. Peter Baptizing New Converts, *a fresco of ca. 1427 by Tommaso Masaccio (1401–1428).*

PETER, JUDE, AND JOHN

The last five of the New Testament epistles are of uncertain authorship, but are attributed to well-known figures of the early Church: the apostle Peter; the apostle John, son of Zebedee (see box on opposite page); and Jude, the brother of Jesus. The first of the two letters of Peter is written to scattered communities over a wide area of Asia Minor. They are addressed as "the exiles of the Dispersion" (1 Pet. 1.1), which suggests that they were mainly Jewish Christians living outside Palestine. The letter is clearly an encyclical (a circular for wide distribution), written from the city of Rome, which goes by the name "Babylon," as in Revelation (see pp.392–94). If it really is by Peter, it provides evidence for his missionary activity, of which little is heard elsewhere in the New Testament (see pp.366–67). It would also lend support to the very early tradition that he was martyred during an otherwise unrecorded visit to Rome. However, some have objected that the literary Greek of the letter is too sophisticated for a man who had begun his career as a Galilean fisherman. But this fact does not necessarily disprove Peter's authorship, because his style could have been corrected by the scribe Silvanus, or Silas, who actually wrote the letter down (1 Pet. 5.12). Besides, Peter had long since left his first vocation behind by the time of the letter's composition.

The letter is written to encourage Christians who evidently feel isolated in a hostile environment, where they are "aliens and exiles" (1 Pet. 2.11). They have suffered persecution from their neighbors and the civic authorities, who "are surprised that you no longer join them in the same excesses of dissipation" (1 Pet. 4.4). The letter mentions "the fiery ordeal that is taking place among you" (1 Pet. 4.12), the choice of words perhaps indicating that the persecution was localized. However, if this refers to a more severe and general attack by the Roman state, the author could mean the persecution instigated by the emperor Nero in 64 CE, in which Peter himself is traditionally said to have died. It has also been suggested that the author lived much later than Peter at the time of the persecution of 112 CE in Asia Minor under the emperor Trajan (98–117 CE).

In view of their trials, Peter exhorts his readers to lead lives that give no cause for offense, to bind together and love one another, even in the face of further attacks (1 Pet. 2.11–12; 4.7–11). Their calling is to follow Jesus, who is presented as the figure of the Suffering Servant in the book of Isaiah (see p.106). Peter assures them that their afflictions will not endure for long, for Christ will soon return (1 Pet. 1.5–6; 4.7; 5.10).

It is widely accepted that 2 Peter is not by the apostle but is one of many writings produced within the early Church and deliberately attributed to one of its famous founders. It reflects a situation that existed only after Peter's death, when Christianity faced the problems of moving from a Jewish to a predominantly Gentile environment. There is no general consensus as to its date, although 2 Peter 3.4 says that the false teachers who deny Christ were first condemned "long ago": this implies that the letter was written after the first generation of Christians, ca. 80–90 CE or later. The reference to Paul's letters as "scriptures" (2 Pet. 3.16) also suggests that 2 Peter was written at least after Paul's death (which took place perhaps ca. 60–65 CE), and therefore probably after Peter's death as well.

The work opens with a standard form of address used in letters of the period (see p.376). It also takes the form of a farewell testament, a genre that was common in Jewish literature. Typically, these "testaments" claimed to be the final thoughts of biblical figures. In the style of such testaments, 2 Peter purports to have been written at a time when Peter saw his death as imminent (2 Pet. 1.14). It includes a summary of his teaching

(2 Pet. 1.3–11), as well as a final message, here bitterly denouncing the work of false teachers (2 Pet. 2.1–3.7). These teachers seem to have been people who wished to rid Christianity of certain features, particularly the apocalyptic hope of Jesus' return (2 Pet. 3.3–4). The author explains that the delay in the second coming appears lengthy only from a human perspective, whereas "with the Lord one day is like a thousand years, and a thousand years are like one day" (2 Pet. 3.8). God, he says, is providing time for sinners to repent (2 Pet. 3.9).

One reason for viewing 2 Peter as a comparatively late work is the use it makes of the letter of Jude (for example, compare 2 Pet. 2.1–18 and Jude vv. 4–13). The writer of Jude describes himself (v. 1) as the "brother of James," generally taken to mean James the brother of Jesus. Whether or not the author really was another of Jesus' brothers, Jude almost certainly has a Jewish Christian and Palestinian origin. It is not a real letter but a general tract, devoted entirely to combating the false teaching which it believes has infected the Christian community. This teaching is not very clearly described, but it involves licentious behavior (Jude vv. 4, 7) and disrespect toward angels (v. 8). The polemic against false teaching is based on the old Scriptures, and on the Hebrew rather than the Greek Septuagint. Jude sees biblical episodes in which God punished his opponents (vv. 5, 7, and 11) as prophesies of the fate awaiting the heretics of his own day. He is familiar with apocalyptic Jewish literature from Palestine, and quotes from one such work, the first book of Enoch (vv. 14–15). He also refers to a legend about the death of Moses that may once have formed the ending of a work known as *The Testament of Moses* (v. 9).

The letters of John

The three letters traditionally attributed to the author of the Fourth Gospel contain no real clues as to their authorship and background. Apart from its traditional title, 1 John is anonymous, and the writer of the other letters describes himself only as "the elder." All three have shared themes and vocabulary, and they have been credited to John because of their many resemblances to John's gospel. The opening of 1 John recalls the prologue to the gospel, and significant terms in the gospel, such as "life," "light," and "love," are prominent in the letters, especially 1 John. However, there are also important differences, and authorship should perhaps be ascribed to a "circle of John" rather than to a single author.

St. John the Evangelist, *by Pedro Berruguete (Spanish, ca. 1450–1504). The evangelist, to whom the letters of John are traditionally ascribed, is accompanied here by his traditional symbol, an eagle.*

The first letter of John is much longer than the other two and deals with those who deny that Jesus "has come in the flesh" (1 John 4.2). This appears to anticipate the second-century CE Docetic heresy, which held that Christ's body was only apparent, not real: 1 John strongly asserts Jesus' full and real humanity. It also pleads for the church to be a harmonious body, bound by mutual love. Both themes are also emphasized in 2 John, which is addressed to a church personified as "the elect lady." It is linked to 3 John by their common author, "the elder," although the third letter is written to an individual called Gaius. He is asked to provide the elder's envoys with hospitality, refused by Diotrephes, the leader of the congregation to which they had been sent.

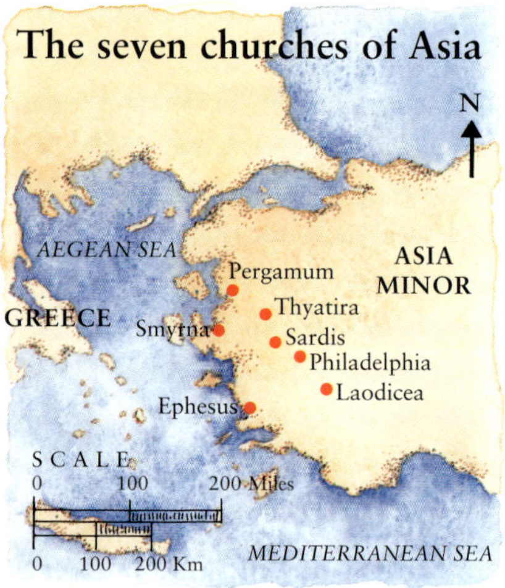

THE SEVEN CHURCHES

Revelation begins with individual letters to seven congregations in the Roman province of Asia, opposite the island of Patmos (see map, above). Apart from the great church of Ephesus, founded by Paul, only here in the New Testament are we given any details of Christian life in these centers. They were all important administrative centers and they are listed in a circle, from south to north and back again. However, the number seven is a symbol of perfection and completeness (see main text, right) that is meant to represent the entire Church and, although each congregation has its own letter, this is also intended for all "the churches."

The author shows a good knowledge of the setting and traditions of each particular city, and he has a specific message for every Christian congregation. Three of the churches are warned against false teachers, described as Nicolaitans. Little is said of their vices, but they are linked with Balaam and Jezebel (see p.61), and accused of advocating sexual license and eating food sacrificed to idols, problems which also faced Paul. The reference to Pergamum as "where Satan is enthroned" may be a warning against emperor worship: Pergamum was the first center of such worship in Asia Minor. But the general picture is of reasonably peaceful and well-established groups which are, however, in danger of complacency and succumbing to the temptations of their religious and social environment.

REVELATION

The Revelation to John, also called the book of Revelation and the Apocalypse, has always proved to be a difficult book to interpret, and it has been interpreted in many ways over the centuries. A modern reader may be puzzled by the apparently bizarre symbolism, and even repelled by the intense hatred and bloodthirstiness which it displays. Many people have seen the work as an authoritative prediction of the future, and have endeavored to deduce from it a date for the second coming of Christ and the end of the world, and have sought to identify the evil beings that it depicts with various historical figures, such as Napoleon or Hitler.

Biblical scholars now generally try to clarify Revelation with reference to the particular historical background against which it was written, and see it in the context of a long literary tradition. The book is, in fact, a letter, intended to be read in the churches to which it is addressed (see sidebar, left). It gives an account of what it claims is a revelation or vision of the imminent future, which God has given the author. In Greek, "revelation" is *apokalypsis* and the work is an example of the genre called "Apocalyptic," which was common in Judaism at around the beginning of the Common Era. It is found elsewhere in the Bible, for example in the book of Daniel (see pp.128–31). Revelation is, however, distinctively Christian, and the only instance of an entire apocalypse in the New Testament, although apocalyptic passages occur in several other writings there (see, for example, pp.334–35).

The author names himself as "John," and says that he received his revelation on the island of Patmos, where he claims to have been imprisoned "on account of the word of God and the testimony of Jesus." Patmos is known to have been used by the Romans as a penal colony. John (Hebrew *Y[eh]ohanan*, Greek *Iohannes*) was a common name, and the author of Revelation is possibly best thought of as an early Christian prophet. However, nearly every apocalypse claimed some great figure from the past as its author, and Revelation may deliberately want the reader or listener to think that it was the work of the apostle John, son of Zebedee. In fact, since at least the second century CE, the "John" of Revelation has traditionally been identified with the apostle, who is also supposed to have written the Fourth Gospel and the letters of John (see box on p.391). Quite apart from the problem of authorship in the case of the letters, it is difficult to see the same hand in all these works, although there are certain links between them.

The language of Revelation is unique. The author can write good Greek, but his style is often ungrammatical and includes many turns of phrase derived from Hebrew or Aramaic, probably with the object of aligning the style of his book with the older Scriptures. Revelation is carefully constructed and pervaded by a symbolic numerology, which was common both in Jewish writings and in the Greco-Roman world. The basic numbers are three, four, and seven, all of which signify completeness and perfection, as does twelve (three times four) which represents the twelve tribes of Israel and the twelve apostles of Jesus. In Revelation, groups of seven feature many times: seven letters to scholars (Rev. 1–3), seven seals (Rev. 5.1), seven visions, seven bowls of wrath (Rev. 16.1), as well as seven angels and seven trumpets (Rev. 8.2). Three disasters ("woes": Rev. 9–16) are followed by the final deliverance (Rev. 19–22) to make up the number four. There are four living creatures around God's throne (Rev. 4.6) and four destructive horsemen (Rev. 6.2–8), figures derived from the four winds. The "New Jerusalem,"the perfect messianic city, has twelve gates for the twelve tribes (Rev. 21.12) and twelve foundations for the twelve apostles (Rev. 12.14), and the number twelve is also the basis of its

Rome in the New Testament

The attitude of the book of Revelation to the Roman state contrasts in certain respects with that found elsewhere in the New Testament. In spite of the arguments of some scholars, Jesus does not seem to have aligned himself with groups such as the Zealots who advocated armed resistance to Rome: he advocated the paying of taxes to Caesar and the co-existence with the Empire of God's kingdom, because it was not of this world. The enigmatic instruction of Jesus in Luke to his followers to buy a sword may suggest that some Christians participated in the great Jewish revolt of 66–74 CE, but it is clear that most of them did not. Acts consistently brings out the comparatively friendly attitude of Roman officials toward Christians in the face of Jewish hostility. For Paul, the authorities are God's agents for the maintenance of justice and order, and the general teaching of the New Testament letters is that Christians should be loyal, law-abiding citizens, and pray for the welfare of their rulers.

At the same time, Christians believed that the second coming of Christ would mean the end of all earthly authority and this view finds extreme expression in Revelation. The author views Rome exclusively as the embodiment of emperor worship, to accept which is to deny the sovereignty of God: the "beast" which symbolized the empire is the agent of Satan. Christians owe no loyalty to Rome and soon only respond with endurance and suffering: they are not to fight against it, for God's action alone will soon excuse its fall. Here the author may also be expressing the outlook of marginalized groups and people in the empire for whom the Roman state appeared not as a civilizing authority but as an instrument of oppression.

A coin of the emperor Vespasian issued after the fall of Jerusalem to his son Titus in 70 CE*. It shows a female slave and bears the Latin words* IUDAEA CAPTA – *"Captive Judea."*

dimensions: twelve thousand furlongs and one hundred forty-four (twelve times twelve) cubits (Rev. 21.16–17). There are twenty-four elders (Rev. 1–3) and one hundred forty-four thousand of the elect, twelve thousand from each of the tribes of Israel (Rev. 4–8).

The famous "number of the beast," six hundred sixty-six (Rev. 13.18), is an example of Jewish numerology. Hebrew letters also function as numbers, and the number 666 is reached by adding up the Hebrew letters which transliterate *Kaisar Neron* – the Greek for "Emperor Nero" (see sidebar on p.394). The number six falls short of the perfect number, seven: the Roman emperor might claim divine status, but he is in fact no more than an imperfect human being (see also box, above).

The rich and all-pervading symbolism of Revelation is an amalgam of three sources: the Bible, Jewish apocalyptic literature, and the mythology of the ancient Near East. Particularly important is the author's use of Scripture. There are allusions to and reminiscences of almost every book of the Hebrew Scriptures on every page, but the imagery from Daniel (see pp.128–31) and Ezekiel is particularly powerful. For example, the description of Jesus in the opening vision (Rev. 1.7; 1.13–16) is a combination of features of Daniel's "Son of Man" and the divine figure in Ezekiel's first vision. The author reinterprets, for his own purposes, many great biblical themes, such as the Creation and the Exodus from Egypt, and he also draws on Isaiah's understanding of the return of the exiles from Babylon as a new Exodus and new Creation. Rome becomes Babylon (Rev. 14.8 and later), a symbol of evil political power in the Bible (see p.29), and it is predicted that, like Babylon, Rome will fall. In contrast, Jerusalem, the holy city, becomes a heavenly city and the center of the new age (Rev. 21.1–2).

Although all the symbols of Revelation are found in the old Scriptures, their presentation echoes the way in which they were elaborated in Jewish

THE DATE OF REVELATION

The early Church believed that Revelation was written during the reign of the Roman emperor Domitian (81–96 CE). Domitian certainly insisted on the divinity of the imperial line, and emperor worship, the supreme object of attack in Revelation, was universal throughout Asia Minor in his time. However, it is very doubtful if Domitian, as is often thought, persecuted Christians who refused to worship him, at least on any large scale. The attacks on believers mentioned in the letters to the Seven Churches (see sidebar on opposite page) are attributed to Jewish hostility, not the Romans (see, for example, 2.9).

The description of Nero, "the beast," reflects a widespread legend that he had not really died (in 68 CE), but was about to return with a great army from the East (see Rev. 13.3). Often the author seems to present future events in terms of the past: the depiction of the Gentile attack on Jerusalem seems to refer to the Jewish War of 66–74 CE. The list of seven kings, of whom five have fallen (Rev. 17.9–10), may refer to the chaotic conditions in the Roman empire directly after Nero's death (there were five emperors in the space of a year). Hence the reign of Domitian and conditions in Asia Minor in his time remain a likely background for Revelation.

A bronze bust of the emperor Nero, the "beast" of Revelation (see below).

literature around the beginning of the Common Era. The central role played by angels reflects the developed angelology of such texts and the author knows the myth of the fallen angels, which is prominent in the traditions of Enoch. His picture of worship in heaven (Rev. 8.3–5) recalls similar concepts found in the Dead Sea Scrolls from Qumran (see p.139). It is possible that some of the details are modeled on the Christian liturgy of his day, which he may have viewed as patterned on the angels' worship. Images such as the Lamb (Rev. 5.6), the beast from the sea (Rev. 13), and the dragon (Rev. 12) also derive from Jewish traditions. Behind them lie the even older traditions of ancient mythology. The dragon is the chaos monster of Mesopotamian myths (see p.16; pp.20–1), identified in Revelation with Satan (Rev. 12.9). The episode of the woman clothed with astral symbols whose child is threatened by the dragon (Rev. 17) is based on a myth about a mother goddess, and this concept may underlie the contrasting depictions of Babylon the harlot (Rev. 17), and Jerusalem the bride (Rev. 21). The author is also influenced by the Greco-Roman world, especially by its astrology and cosmogony. It has been suggested that the work is structured on the form of the Greek drama, which would have been performed in the theaters of the cities to which it was addressed.

THE NUMBER OF THE BEAST

In Revelation 13.18, the author says: "Let anyone with understanding calculate the number of the beast, for it is the number of a person. Its number is six hundred sixty-six." In Hebrew, letters are also used as numbers; the figure 666 is reached by adding up the numerical values of the Hebrew letters *Qsr Nrwn*, which transliterate the Greek *Kaisar Neron* ("Emperor Nero"):

Q	=	*100*
S	=	*60*
R	=	*200*
N	=	*50*
R	=	*200*
W	=	*6*
N	=	*50*
		666

The Apocalypse (Judgment Day), *a 15th-century Russian icon (Novgorod School).*

A BOOK-BY-BOOK SUMMARY OF THE BIBLE

THE HEBREW SCRIPTURES/ OLD TESTAMENT

The books of the Hebrew Scriptures are summarized below in the order generally followed in Christian Bibles.

Genesis

The title of the first book, Genesis, comes from Greek and means "origin," a good indication of its character: it describes the origins of the world and of the Israelite nation. God creates the universe in six days (see pp.20–1). In the Garden of Eden, the first humans commit the Original Sin, and are cast out into the world (see pp.20–1). Their firstborn son, Cain, murders his shepherd brother, Abel (see pp.24–5). Generations later, Noah and his family are deemed by God to be the only humans worthy of being spared in a universal deluge. Noah's family and the animals he has been instructed to save repopulate the earth.

After attempting to build the Tower of Babel, the people of the world are scattered (see pp.28–9), and Genesis moves on to the story of the ancestors of Israel (see pp.30–45). The first of them, Abraham, leaves Mesopotamia for Canaan. God promises Abraham and his descendants, the Israelites, the land of Canaan as a homeland in perpetuity (see p.31). Abraham's faith is tested in the so-called "Sacrifice of Isaac" (see p.37). Isaac marries Rebekah, and the family prospers in hard times. The younger of their two sons, Jacob, tricks his brother Esau out of his inheritance and flees to the land of his relatives (see pp.38–9). Jacob dreams of a ladder leading to heaven (see p.39). He first marries Leah and then Rachel, and, by them and their two female servants, fathers twelve sons, who become the founders of the twelve tribes of Israel (see p.41). Jacob himself is renamed "Israel" (see p.40).

Jacob-Israel's eleventh and favorite son, Joseph, is sold by his jealous brothers and ends up in Egypt, where he rises to prominence by interpreting Pharaoh's dreams (see pp.44–5). During a famine, Joseph's brothers arrive to buy grain and do not recognize Joseph at first. Eventually they are reconciled, and the brothers settle down to a prosperous new life in Egypt.

Moses at the Burning Bush (Exod. 3.2).

Exodus

The title is from the Greek *exodos*, meaning "departure," and the book relates the events surrounding the departure of the Israelites from Egypt and the years of wandering that followed, during which God handed down most of their laws.

Many years after the death of Joseph and his brothers, their descendants have become no better than slaves in Egypt. Pharaoh is alarmed at their numbers and orders the death of all newborn males. One Israelite couple has a son, Moses, who is abandoned on the Nile in a reed basket. However, Pharaoh's daughter rescues Moses and adopts him (see p.46).

Moses is forced to flee after killing an Egyptian, and following a dramatic encounter with God (Yahweh) at the Burning Bush (see pp.48–9), he becomes the leader of his people. God gives him and his brother, Aaron, miraculous powers with which to convince Pharaoh to let the Israelites leave Egypt for the Promised Land of Canaan. Pharaoh is obdurate in the face of nine plagues imposed on his land, and only releases the Israelites after the tenth plague, the death of the firstborn of each Egyptian family. (see pp.50–1). This last plague sees the institution of the Israelite festival of Passover (see also p.52).

The liberated Israelites head for the wilderness that lies between Egypt and the Promised Land, but they are pursued by Pharaoh's troops. The waters miraculously part, enabling them to cross the sea, but Pharaoh's pursuing troops are swept away (see pp.52–3).

In the wilderness, God gives the Israelites manna and quails to eat, and water springs from a rock for them to drink. Joshua becomes the Israelite military commander.

Moses goes up to meet God on Mount Sinai, where he receives the Ten Commandments or Decalogue (see p.54) and a series of other laws. He comes down to find the people feasting around an idol, the Golden Calf. Enraged, he breaks the tablets on which the divine Laws are inscribed. Some Israelite leaders are purged. Moses once more goes up Mount Sinai, and two more tablets of Law are divinely inscribed, renewing the Covenant. Subsequently, the construction, furnishings, and consecration of the Tabernacle – God's sanctuary – are described in detail, as are the vestments of its priests (see pp.54–9).

Leviticus
The book of Leviticus is primarily concerned with the laws given by God to Moses on a range of ritual and other religious matters (the title of the book means "of the Levites," the Israelite priestly tribe). These laws cover burnt offerings and sacrifices (see pp.116–17); the investiture and duties of priests; ritual cleanness; the commemoration of the Day of Atonement (Yom Kippur; see p.112); and the preservation of holiness in everyday life and in the feasts of the liturgical calendar.

Numbers
God orders a census of the twelve tribes of Israel in Sinai: the census is taken and the results are given at length (hence the name of this book). Further divine laws are promulgated.

The tribal leaders under Moses make ritual offerings, and the Levites are formally consecrated as a priestly clan. The decision is taken to leave Sinai and cross the desert wildernesses in the direction of the Promised Land (see pp.60–1). The Israelites set out, following the "Cloud of Yahweh." Soon, however, there are rumblings of discontent among the people, who are dissatisfied with their lot. Despite reports from scouts sent out by Moses that the land of Canaan is "flowing with milk and honey," there is outright rebellion against Moses and God. Yahweh is angered, and Moses only manages to appease him after God makes it clear that some of the senior Israelites, including Moses himself, will not reach the Promised Land.

A second serious rebellion among the Israelites is divinely punished by earthquake and plague, which kill thousands. Trouble occurs yet again when the Israelites stop for a time at Kadesh-barnea, where they have to withstand military attacks from the local Canaanites. Some of the Israelites begin to worship local idols, and God sends a plague that kills twenty-four thousand Israelites.

The military commander, Joshua, is appointed Moses' deputy. The Israelites invade the land of Midian (see p.47), and most of its inhabitants are slaughtered. More divine laws are promulgated.

Deuteronomy
Previous Israelite history and ritual observance is recapitulated and elaborated, hence the title of the book, which means "Second Law" (see p.101).

At the end of the book, Moses issues orders to the Israelites to prepare to enter the Promised Land, and makes a battle speech enjoining them to have faith in Yahweh. On Mount Nebo, Moses blesses the twelve Israelite tribes, and then dies, within sight of the Promised Land (see p.62).

Joshua
Following Moses' death, God confirms Joshua's command over his chosen people, and preparations are made to enter the Promised Land. Spies are sent into the city of Jericho, and although their presence is suspected, they are kept hidden at the house of Rahab the prostitute. After the spies have returned to Joshua, the Israelites cross the Jordan into Canaan (see pp.62–3). Jericho is the first city to fall to the Israelites, and all its inhabitants, apart from Rahab and her family, are put to the sword (see pp.64–5). Next to be taken is the city of Ai, followed by other cities and towns in Canaan. The whole territory is divided among the Israelite tribes, and the book concludes with Joshua leading the people in a reaffirmation at Shechem of the Covenant with God (see p.62). At the end of a long life, Joshua dies.

Judges
The opening chapters of Judges (see pp.66–7) present a picture of the early period of settlement in Canaan. Sometimes the Israelites fight and conquer the indigenous peoples, sometimes they live peacefully alongside them. Sometimes they abandon Yahweh and adopt the gods of their new neighbors, but each time this happens, God is angered and inflicts punishment on the Israelites.

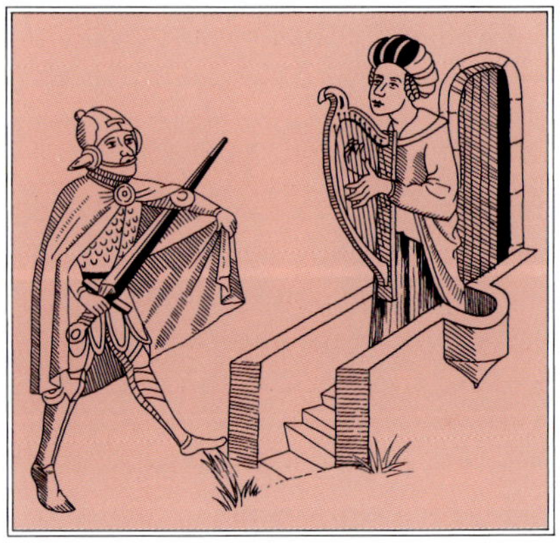

Jephthah and his daughter (Judg. 11.30–40).

Eventually, however, God hears his people's pleas and sends a heroic deliverer, or "judge," to reverse Israel's misfortunes. The first two judges, Othniel and Ehud, are dealt with briefly. The third judge, Deborah, and her military commander, Barak, rout the forces of their enemy Sisera, who is killed by Jael, the wife of Heber the Kenite. Sisera's death evokes the celebrated Song of Deborah and Barak (see p.68).

A generation later, the judge Gideon (see p.68) similarly routs the Midianites, but afterward Israel relapses into idolatry. Another crisis is ended through Gideon's successor, Jephthah, who defeats the Ammonites. However, in his triumph Jephthah vows to sacrifice the first creature that he sees on his return home: unhappily for him it is his daughter, his only child.

The judge Samson (see p.69), is a more solitary hero. He takes on the Philistines, although he also marries one, Delilah. She discloses the secret of Samson's great strength – his long hair – to her own people, who seize Samson and blind him. He gains his revenge in one last act of strength, which causes the Philistine temple to collapse, killing himself and all his enemies.

A time now comes when there is neither judge nor king, and the solidarity of the Israelites weakens. Following a mass rape at Gibeah by members of the tribe of Benjamin, the Benjaminites are almost wiped out by the other tribes.

Ruth

The folktale-like story of Ruth is placed among the historical books between Judges and 1 Samuel in Christian Bibles, because of its thematic links to both: it is set in the time of the judges and tells the story of a great-great grandmother of King David, who features prominently in Samuel. In Christian belief, she is therefore an ancestor of Jesus. Ruth is also a moral work and in the Jewish Bible it usually appears after Proverbs.

Ruth is the Moabite widow of an Israelite husband. She accompanies her mother-in-law, Naomi, back to Naomi's home town, Bethlehem in Judah. There, Ruth comes under the protection of their kinsman, Boaz, who, after addressing himself to the legal and social formalities involved, marries her. Their son, Obed, is King David's grandfather (see p.118).

1 Samuel

The history of the Israelites resumes with the birth of Samuel, the last and greatest of the judges, to the previously barren Hannah (see pp.70–1). At an early age, Samuel is placed with the priest Eli for religious training, and it is soon evident that he has been called to serve God.

David and Goliath (1 Sam. 17.49).

When Samuel reaches adulthood, the Israelites are defeated by their coastal neighbors, the Philistines (see p.71), who capture the ark of the Covenant, the dwelling place of God. They take the ark to the temple of their god, Dagon, in the city of Ashdod. But a mysterious plague of cancers immediately strikes the citizens, and the ark is hastily moved to another city. But the plague breaks out there too, and also in a third city. Finally the Philistines send the ark back to the Israelites, complete with gold offerings of appeasement.

It is another twenty years before Samuel becomes the judge or leader of Israel. Many years after that the people decide that they would prefer to be ruled by a king. God, through Samuel, warns them of the disadvantages of monarchy, but they are adamant. God reluctantly consents to their request, and sends Samuel to select Saul, of the tribe of Benjamin, to be the first king of the Israelites (see pp.72–3). Even before he is officially made king, Saul proves his worth by leading a successful attack on the Ammonites.

Saul triumphs over a great number of Israelite enemies, including the Philistines. Nevertheless, there is friction between Samuel and Saul, which ultimately leads to the latter's downfall (see pp.74–5). Saul is mentally tormented, and he employs the shepherd boy David, son of Jesse, to be both his armor bearer and the harpist that soothes him in times of stress. Unknown to him, God has already instructed Samuel to anoint David as Saul's successor.

The Philistine armies return, and their champion, the giant Goliath, challenges the Israelites. Armed only with a slingshot, David defeats the giant and kills him. David becomes so popular that Saul is both jealous and afraid of him. David inflicts further defeats on the Philistines, and his success enrages Saul even more. Finally, Saul tries to kill David, who flees the court with the assistance of his great friend Jonathan, Saul's son. About two years later, Saul and Jonathan are both in battle against the Philistines on Mount Gilboa. Jonathan is killed and Saul, badly wounded, kills himself.

2 Samuel

David laments the deaths of Saul and Jonathan. He is anointed king of the southern tribe of Judah. Seven years later, after a war between Judah and the followers of Saul's dynasty, David becomes king of the united Israelite nation. He captures Jerusalem from the Jebusites, makes the city his capital, and installs in it the ark of the Covenant (see pp.76–8).

Various military victories follow and David acquires a small empire (see p.77). He commits adultery with Bathsheba, the wife of Uriah, one of his officers, and ensures that Uriah is killed in battle. He incurs divine anger for this behavior, and God's displeasure is conveyed by the prophet Nathan. God's punishment is that David's first child by Bathsheba dies; but she bears another, Solomon.

David's last years are marked by court intrigue and rebellions fomented by his many offspring (see p.78). At one stage, his son Absalom is in virtual control of the kingdom, but he is killed by David's generals, despite David's continued love for him. There are also times of famine, and times when David addresses psalms of praise to God. The book ends with David, following divine command, erecting an altar on the threshing floor of Araunah the Jebusite – the site of the future Temple of Jerusalem.

1 Kings

Before his death, David appoints Solomon his successor. After a succession struggle (see p.79), Solomon is anointed king. He effects multiple political marriages, notably with the daughter of the pharaoh of Egypt, and permits foreign faiths to be practiced, even in Jerusalem. But he also builds a magnificent Temple to God in the city (see pp.84–5). Its construction takes thirteen years before it is finally dedicated.

Solomon's wealth and wisdom (see pp.80–1) become renowned, and the queen of the prosperous Arab state of Sheba comes to visit him (see p.81). But Solomon also institutes forced labor, and there are rumblings of popular discontent. A revolt under Jeroboam is quelled only with difficulty before Solomon dies (see pp.86–7).

After Solomon's death, political and religious factionalism divide the kingdom, with the northern tribes breaking away from the southern tribal areas of Judah and Benjamin, the heartlands of David and Solomon's dynasty. Two kingdoms are established: Judah in the south, and Israel in the north (see p.89). Compiled and edited primarily by people with connections to Judah and its capital, Jerusalem, the biblical history is generally more favorable toward the southern kingdom.

During the reign of King Ahab of Israel, the prophet Elijah becomes a prominent figure (see pp.90–1). He foretells a drought and relates it to the ungodliness of the king of Israel. Ahab is a fine warrior who is married to a Phoenician, Jezebel, a devout worshiper of the god Baal. Elijah performs miracles both to reinforce his authority and to confound the rival prophets of Baal.

Ahab displays great military prowess against Israel's enemies. But God is angered by his deceitful appropriation of a vineyard through the murder, at Jezebel's instigation, of its owner, Naboth. Elijah predicts terrible deaths for both king and queen, which come to pass as foretold. Jezebel outlives Ahab, but when her death comes it is particularly grisly (see p.91).

2 Kings

After a miraculous crossing of the Jordan, the prophet Elijah is taken up to heaven, and his mantle passes to his servant Elisha, who recrosses the Jordan and proceeds to perform further miracles. Elisha accurately forewarns the king of Israel against military raids by enemies. Elisha can do nothing, however, to avert the famine caused by the Aramean siege of the capital of Israel, Samaria.

Elisha then becomes resident prophet at the courts of a succession of kings. One is Jehu, who is responsible for the assassination of surviving members of Ahab's dynasty, including his son, Jehoram, and his widow, Jezebel, together with all the priests and prophets that serve Jezebel's god Baal. After Elisha dies, according to the Bible, there is no prophet in the land for another sixty years or so.

The kingdom of Israel falls to the Assyrian king, Shalmaneser. The residents of the capital, Samaria, are deported and the city is repopulated with eastern foreigners (see pp.94–5). The Bible relates that, about a decade later, King Hezekiah of Judah (see pp.98–9) is also attacked by the Assyrians. The prophet Isaiah, who is active during Hezekiah's reign (see p.99) reassures the king that, for a period at least, Judah is safe, but also warns that a time is coming when the residents of Judah will be carried off into exile in Babylon.

After Hezekiah, the lengthy reign of King Manasseh is dominated by the shadow of the Assyrians, and the Bible accuses Manasseh of idolatry (see p.100). His successor, King Josiah (see pp.100–02) undertakes a program of religious reform, during which the "book of the law of Moses," possibly the core of what is now the book of Deuteronomy, is said to be "rediscovered" in the Temple (see p.101).

Josiah falls in battle against the Egyptians, who set up a puppet regime, which is overthrown by the Babylonians (see p.102). The deportation of the citizens of Jerusalem and the confiscation of most of the city's treasures follow. Within eleven years, however, the remaining people of Judah rebel against Babylon. Jerusalem is at once besieged, captured, pillaged, and destroyed. This time, the Bible reports, all of its people are taken away into captivity in Babylon (see pp.106–07).

1 Chronicles

The first and second books of Chronicles are largely based on the earlier historical books, but they are considered of value because of the way in which they re-present and reinterpret the events of Israel's history in the light of the author's contemporary world (Judah under Persian rule after the return of the Babylonian exiles; see pp.108–11). The first third of 1 Chronicles gives genealogies from Adam to the time of the return from Exile. The remainder concentrates on the reign of David.

2 Chronicles

The last book in the Jewish Bible. The first nine chapters of 2 Chronicles recount the reign of Solomon. The remainder relates the history of the two kingdoms until the Exile and the beginning of the restoration of Judah under the Persian king Cyrus, who allows the exiles to return to rebuild the Temple (see pp.108–11).

Ezra

The books of Ezra and Nehemiah deal with the history of Judah after the return from Exile. They were considered as one book until around 300 CE, when they were divided as they are now. Both men were probably active in the reign of Artaxerxes I of Persia (465–425 BCE; see pp.110–11). Much of Ezra and all of Nehemiah are recounted in the first person.

Ezra opens with the decree of

Artaxerxes commissions Ezra (Ezra 7).

Cyrus, king of Persia, that those who wish to may leave Babylon and return to Jerusalem to rebuild the Temple. The returning exiles are listed.

Rebuilding work on the Temple begins. There is some opposition to the returned exiles, and work is halted temporarily. But, encouraged by the prophets Haggai and Zechariah, the Jewish authorities appeal to Cyrus's successor, Darius, whose archives confirm the original royal decree. The Temple is completed and rededicated.

Darius's successor, Artaxerxes, sends Ezra, a Jewish official of the Persian government, to Judah to ensure that the Jewish law is being strictly observed. Ezra finds that many of the formerly exiled families have been intermarrying with non-Jews, and puts a stop to the practice.

Nehemiah

Some eighty-five years after the return from Exile, Nehemiah, the Jewish cupbearer to the Persian king Artaxerxes, is moved to hear of the reputedly dilapidated state of Jerusalem. The king commissions him to go and supervise repairs. He surveys the damage and organizes those who are to be responsible for specific areas of work. However, Nehemiah encounters opposition from other Persian officials and there are delays in the rebuilding work in the city.

Other problems include social privations and various intrigues. But, finally, the city wall is once more in place, with gates, watchtowers, and a citadel.

Ezra is invited to rededicate the city by reading from the book of Moses. The occasion turns into a mass celebration of the Feast of Succoth (Tabernacles or Booths), followed, some days later, by a ceremony of atonement.

Nehemiah reports back to Artaxerxes. The next time Nehemiah returns to Jerusalem, he moves to counteract numerous irregularities in the operation and upkeep of the Temple.

Esther

Like Ezra and Nehemiah, the book of Esther is a story set in the time of the Persian empire (see pp.124–25). However, there is little to link it to authentic history apart from the name of the king in the story, "Ahasuerus," who could be any of several Persian rulers called Xerxes or Artaxerxes (see p.109).

Ahasuerus gives a grand banquet at his capital, Susa, but his queen, Vashti, refuses to attend. The king summarily puts her aside. The beautiful Esther, a young Jewish woman brought up by her uncle Mordecai, is chosen to replace her. But Mordecai makes an enemy of the king's chancellor, Haman, who determines to eliminate all Jews in the empire. He persuades the king to decree death to "a certain people" who keep their own laws.

Mordecai prompts Esther to go to the king and invite Ahasuerus and Haman to her own banquet. There, she reveals that she, the queen, is under threat of death from the king's own decree, and that it is Haman's doing. Horrified, the king rescinds his decree and orders Haman to be hanged on the very gallows he has set up for the Jews. Mordecai is promoted to chancellor, and the Jews are given license to take revenge on their enemies in the empire. In plotting to destroy the Jews, Haman had cast lots (*purim*); Esther's triumph is therefore celebrated in a new Jewish festival, called Purim.

Job

God allows Satan to test Job to see if he will remain unquestioningly faithful in the face of adversity. Job subsequently suffers various misfortunes, deprivations, and bereavements. Three of his friends arrive to offer sympathy, or at least intellectual discussion on the subject of divine justice. Job protests his innocence and rails against his fate. A fourth character, Elihu, appears, and attempts to vindicate his own view of

Job defends himself (Job 3–31).

God's mysterious ways. God himself intervenes to speak to Job. He tells him that for humans to discuss how God functions is presumptuous, since God is utterly beyond all mortal understanding. Job is humbled. God also reproaches the three friends and orders them to make a special sacrifice. Finally, God restores Job, bringing him even greater happiness and prosperity than he had enjoyed before (see pp.122–23).

Psalms

The Psalter or book of Psalms is a collection of varied types of liturgical works, such as hymns, supplications, praises, and songs of thanksgiving. They are addressed to God and expressed in poetic language, often of great majesty and beauty. Some are accompanied by instructions for musical accompaniment or indications as to their purpose. Many are attributed to King David (see p.115).

Proverbs

A collection of traditional sayings and popular maxims on such themes as correct behavior, godly thoughts, purity in mind and worship, the avoidance of sinners, and the quest for wisdom. This book includes a lengthy list of aphorisms attributed to King Solomon and his counsellors (see p.120).

Ecclesiastes

The author, who claims to be Solomon himself, discourses on the nature of existence in God's universe, and on eternal values. Everything about one's life on earth is "vanity and a chasing after wind." A world order exists, but we cannot know it; our only certainty is death. The conclusion to this searching, skeptical, and intensely personal work is that, while people can never know the secret of existence, human integrity makes our stay on earth tolerable. This allows us to enjoy to the full any benefits God may send.

King David singing Psalms (see the preambles to Pss. 3, 18, and others).

Song of Solomon

A poetic dialogue between a woman and her male lover – sometimes called the bride and the groom – expressed in heightened erotic language, and with interpolations by a chorus of "daughters of Jerusalem." It may or may not have been intended as a spiritual allegory (see p.125).

Isaiah

The book of Isaiah is in three distinct parts, although it purports to be the prophecies of one man, Isaiah, who was active in the reign of Hezekiah (see p.99, p.106, and p.111).
The first part probably represents the work of Isaiah himself. In it, he warns that Judah will inevitably suffer because of its religious inadequacy. Jerusalem, now a den of vice and idolatry, will be destroyed, but later renewed through the visitation of Yahweh. He foretells the coming of a savior, and describes the awesome power of God. Although

Judah is to be overwhelmed and its population deported, a remnant will in time return. In due course, Judah's enemies will suffer for their actions, as will the inhabitants of many of the regions around Judah, even as far away as Egypt.

The prophet attacks the wickedness of humanity and declares that the people of Zion will triumph. Salvation is in the hands of God.

The Assyrian king Sennacherib attacks Judah, but is driven off. King Hezekiah recovers from illness.

Isaiah 40–55 is a work of the Babylonian Exile, by an anonymous prophet who is referred to as "Second Isaiah." King Cyrus of Persia, he claims, will be God's instrument. There is a description of a figure called "the servant of the Lord" who, it is said, will rise up from insignificance among the people to bring justice to the nations. Israel will be freed, the land restored, and monotheism reinstituted: Yahweh will be God of all, judge of the world. There is to be a new covenant for a new Jerusalem, a new heaven and a new earth in which all worship Yahweh.

Chapters 56–66 are another distinct section, "Third Isaiah," dating in origin from the period just after the Exile. It depicts widespread religious and moral abuses, and promises divine retribution, so that the glory of God and his chosen people be shown in its true greatness.

Jeremiah

God calls Jeremiah, who lived in the period just before the Babylonian Exile (see p.103), to preach of the doom and destruction of Israel on account of the religious and moral impurity of its people. Even the priesthood is lax and corrupt. The Israelites are urged to repent and turn once more to God. Foreign invasion is regrettably inevitable: the Jews will suffer, their weak faith providing no security.

Jeremiah is threatened for his words but continues his diatribe. He lambasts the people and graphically depicts the horrors of war and deportation. Babylon is to be the instrument of Yahweh's wrath.

But all is not lost. There will come a "branch" of David – a member of the royal line of Judah – who will reign as true king. Israel and Judah will be restored and will once more worship God and revere their king. There will be a new covenant for a renewed Jerusalem, rebuilt in splendor.

Jeremiah is arrested for his outspoken views and is imprisoned until Jerusalem is besieged and falls to the Babylonians. Many of the city's inhabitants are deported, but Jeremiah is allowed to remain. However, following the assassination of the Babylonian governor of Judah, the prophet is taken off to Egypt by remnants of the former army of Judah "for his own protection." Jeremiah protests that all this means is that Egypt will in turn be invaded by Babylon. This, according to the Bible, is exactly what takes place.

Lamentations

Also called the Lamentations of Jeremiah, reflecting its traditional attribution to that prophet (see p.106). The author utters five carefully constructed dirges for those who have died in the fall of Jerusalem. The city mourns, the people wail in anguish, but there remains hope and trust in God.

Ezekiel

Before the fall of Jerusalem, Ezekiel (see p.106) is commissioned by God to speak out against the wickedness and idolatry of Israel. He lambasts false prophets and lists the sins committed by the nation throughout its history. Yahweh's sword is sharpened and polished, and the Babylonians will wield it. Many nations will suffer, even Egypt. Jerusalem falls, but in a vision Ezekiel sees the bones of Israel rise from the ground and acquire new flesh. The nation, he predicts, will be restored by Yahweh to its own land, and David's line will reign again. Ezekiel then relates his vision of the reconstructed Temple in Jerusalem. He describes rituals for festivals that are to be reinstituted, and appends some notions of the allocation of territory among the remnants of the twelve tribes of Israel.

Daniel

Daniel (see pp.128–31) is said to be one of four young Jewish boys taken in the sack of Jerusalem by King Nebuchadnezzar and brought up during the Exile at the royal court in

Daniel interprets Nebuchadnezzar's dream of the great statue (Dan. 2.31–45).

Babylon. Through prayer, Daniel is able to reveal to the king the meaning of a dream about a great statue. Daniel and his friends gain prestige in Babylon. The king has a golden idol made and demands that all should worship it. But three of Daniel's friends (Shadrach, Meshach, and Abednego) refuse, and are thrown into a blazing furnace. To the king's amazement, they survive unharmed through divine intervention.

Nebuchadnezzar has another dream. Daniel interprets it as a warning that the king will lose his reason until he recognizes God. This prediction soon comes to pass.

Some time later, during a feast given by King Belshazzar, fiery writing mysteriously appears on the wall of the banqueting hall. Daniel interprets it to mean that the king will die and his empire will fall to the Persians and Medes. That night, Belshazzar is assassinated.

Belshazzar's successor, the Persian king Darius, is inveigled by his courtiers into issuing a decree that all prayer should be addressed to him. When Daniel refuses to pray to him, he is thrown into a pit of lions – but emerges safely, preserved by God's angel. The penitent king throws the courtiers to the lions instead.

Then it is Daniel's turn to dream: he has apocalyptic visions, most of which are messianic in content (the "Son of Man" is a recurrent expression). The visions probably reflect the turbulent events in Judah under the Seleucid empire in the second century BCE, the time when the book of Daniel is thought to have been put together.

Hosea
The prophet Hosea (see p.97) was probably active ca.740–730 BCE. He is told by God to take a prostitute as a wife. He is then asked to love a woman as God loves Israel. Hosea's experience with his wife or wives (whether one or two women are involved is open to discussion) is a symbol of God's relationship with his people. God's bride, Israel, has become a faithless whore, corrupt, occasionally professing insincere repentance, though more usually ruled by sinful desires (especially true of her kings, nobles, and priests). But after a display of his anger and jealousy, God will yet restore the one nation he loves above all others.

Joel
According to the book of the prophet Joel, God promises to rid Judah of a plague of locusts, and to restore the prosperity of the devastated land. The plague is symbolic of God's even more devastating judgment of the world on the last day. However, for those who repent, this will herald a great outpouring of divine blessing (see also p.355).

Amos
Amos (see p.96) was active under Jeroboam II of Israel (786–784 BCE), a prosperous time. The prophet denounces the evil committed by the peoples on every side of Judah and Israel. But he is also aware of the corruption, ostentatious luxury, faithlessness, fornication, and obstinacy of his own people. There cannot be salvation without repentance. The "day of the Lord" is coming, and dire punishment is on its way: but the glory of the house of David will one day be restored.

Obadiah
The book of Obadiah is the shortest work in the Hebrew Scriptures/Old Testament. The prophet is scathing about the Edomites for invading Judah after the destruction of Jerusalem by the Babylonians in 587/6 BCE. But the coming "day of the Lord" will turn the tables on Edom, when Israel is restored to its full might and glory.

Jonah
God instructs Jonah (see p.118) to go to Nineveh in Assyria and warn the inhabitants that their wickedness will lead to their destruction. But Jonah is reluctant to obey his call, flees to Joppa, and takes a ship in the opposite direction. A storm blows up, for which Jonah accepts blame, and, at his own request, is thrown overboard. Swallowed by a giant fish, Jonah is vomited ashore, and heads for Nineveh. There he preaches the imminent destruction of the city. The citizens repent and renounce

Jonah emerges from the fish (Jon. 1.10).

their ways, and God does not destroy the city. Jonah indignantly demands to know of God what the point of all his efforts has been. Through a sign, Yahweh demonstrates that he is the God of all nations, who will show concern even for those who are not Israelites if they repent of their sins.

Micah
Micah (see p.97) prophesied in the last decades of the northern Israelite kingdom of Israel (ca. 735–725 BCE). The book of Micah, which includes

writing by, among others, an anonymous contemporary, forecasts destruction for both Israel and the southern kingdom, Judah. But afterward there will be liberation and restoration, led by a national savior who will be born, like King David, in Bethlehem in Judah. Present problems are the result of corruption and faithlessness, for which the people should seek God's forgiveness.

Nahum

The book of Nahum is the only prophetic writing that actually calls itself a book in the text; it may be a liturgy of the Jerusalem Temple (see p.95). Nahum is a brilliant poetic expression of joy at the prospect of the destruction of Nineveh, the capital of the hated Assyrian empire, which fell to the Babylonians and Medes in 612 BCE. Nineveh, a city steeped in blood and debauchery, will be utterly wiped out; Judah and Israel will be restored.

Habakkuk

Habakkuk complains to God for letting lawlessness go unpunished. He foresees invasion by the Babylonians (Chaldeans) as the instrument of divine retribution (he was probably active during the period of Babylonian expansion, ca. 610–600 BCE). In reply, God reassures the prophet of the coming judgment. The prophet then utters a public prayer expressing his trust and joy in God in the face of anguish.

Zephaniah

The Bible says that Zephaniah was a descendant of King Hezekiah of Judah who was active in the reign of King Josiah (640–609 BCE; see pp.100–02). The prophet foresees the approach of the "day of the Lord," on which Judah will be destroyed and Jerusalem sacked and pillaged. Even humble repentance for sin may not be enough to mitigate God's anger against every citizen. But in due course, Israel will be raised up again to triumph over her present enemies and oppressors. There will be shouts of joy and psalms of exultation in Zion. The exiles will return, and all those remaining alive on earth will be Yahweh's people. Zephaniah 1.14–15 inspired a famous medieval Latin poem called *Dies Irae*, which became part of the Latin Requiem Mass.

Haggai

Haggai and Zechariah prophesied in the period after the return from Exile in Babylon, in the early years of Darius (522–486 BCE). Haggai (see p.108) is appalled that people continue to live in fine houses while God's Temple still lies in ruins. Zerubbabel, the governor of the Persian province of Judah and a person of Judean royal descent, organizes a work party to start rebuilding. Haggai declares that God has chosen Zerubbabel for a position of greatness.

Zechariah

Zechariah (see p.108) receives several divine visions that together indicate God's intention to restore the Promised Land to his people, and to see the Temple rebuilt under the direction of Zerubbabel. Zion must rejoice in the renewed interest of God and listen to his words. Jerusalem will be great again, and God's people will be universally respected and admired. A savior-king is coming who will rule a kingdom of peace stretching to the ends of the earth.

Zechariah's final vision is apocalyptic, and features the final battle of Jerusalem. God is victorious: from that time, all nations worship him and do his will.

Malachi

Malachi, who was probably active ca. 475 BCE (after Haggai and Zechariah but before Ezra and Nehemiah), rages against the corrupt worldliness of the priesthood, whose teachings and customs are causing many to stumble from the path of righteousness. Moreover, idolatry and divorce are permitted. The "great and terrible day of the Lord" is coming when every sinner will be purified like molten gold and silver, or burned up like stubble. God declares that he will send a messenger before him to pave the way for his arrival: the great prophet Elijah will appear to turn people to God so that they may be saved. Christians have traditionally understood the book of Malachi as a work containing important prefigurations of the coming of Jesus. For this reason, the Old Testament places the prophetic books last, so that Malachi immediately precedes the New Testament.

THE APOCRYPHA/ DEUTEROCANONICAL BOOKS

Tobit

Tobit, a godly man, becomes blind. His son, Tobias, sets out for Media, to his kinsman Gabael's house, to collect some family savings. His guide and companion is the mysteriously omniscient Azariah. At the Tigris River, Azariah helps Tobias to catch a great fish, the innards of which, Azariah says, have powerful properties. Azariah reveals that they are to spend the first night of the journey at the house of another kinsman, Raguel, whose daughter Sarah is by right available for marriage to Tobias. But Tobias knows that Sarah is plagued by an evil spirit who has already killed seven suitors, and demurs. Azariah tells Tobias how to drive off the demon using the fish's heart and liver, and on arrival at Raguel's house, Tobias duly asks for Sarah's hand in marriage. He is accepted, and goes to spend the night with her. Meanwhile, Raguel digs a grave

Tobias and Azariah (the angel Raphael) catch the fish in the Tigris (Tob. 6.4).

outside for Tobias, whom he supposes must be the demon's next victim. The next morning, Azariah's charm has worked and the couple are formally betrothed. Azariah is sent on to collect the savings and to bring Gabael and his family back for the wedding. After a full fortnight of celebrations, Tobias, Sarah, and Azariah set out for Tobias's home.

Tobit and his wife Anna are overjoyed and relieved at their son's return. They are even happier when Tobias, on Azariah's instruction, uses the fish's gall to cure Tobit's blindness. At the ensuing feast, Tobit and Tobias wonder how they can possibly reward Azariah. But Azariah reveals that he is in fact the archangel Raphael, who has been both testing Tobit's faith and rewarding his virtue. He ascends to heaven as his hosts prostrate themselves in awe.

Tobit, Anna, Tobias, and Sarah live happily until the end of their days.

Judith

Probably composed during the oppressive rule of Antiochus Epiphanes (see pp.132–33), the book of Judith relates how King Nebuchadnezzar (here called the ruler of Assyria) defeats the Medes. He then sends his general, Holofernes, to punish the local Israelites for refusing to support him. Holofernes lays siege to the town of Bethulia. One of its citizens, the godly widow Judith, is determined not to give in. After fervent prayer she puts on her brightest clothes, leaves the town, and makes her way to Holofernes' camp. She offers to help him defeat her people, and proposes staying in the camp until this is achieved. Four nights later, alone in a tent with the drunken Holofernes, Judith decapitates him with his own sword. She runs back to Bethulia with his head and rouses the citizens, who attack and vanquish the Assyrians. All give thanks to God (see also p.125).

Additions to Esther

The Septuagint, the Greek version of the Jewish Bible, includes six passages in the book of Esther for which no Hebrew originals survive:

1. Mordecai dreams of coming events and warns the king of two treacherous eunuchs (inserted before Esther 1.1).

2. The text of the king's decree

Judith with Holofernes' head (Jud. 13.9).

eliminating the Jews in the empire is cited (inserted after 3.13).

3. Mordecai and Esther pray to God for deliverance (inserted after 4.17).

4. Esther approaches the king to seek his understanding (replaces 5.1–2).

5. The text of the king's edict annulling his former decree is cited (inserted after 8.12).

6. Mordecai realizes the meaning of his initial dream (inserted after 10.3).

Wisdom of Solomon

The author, who claims to be King Solomon, contemplates the nature of wisdom in relation to religious faith and to everyday life. He contrasts the earthly lives of the godless and the faithful, and their different destinies. The author understands God as the ultimate Wisdom, and reviews Israelite history in the light of that understanding (see p.120 and p.125).

Sirach (Ecclesiasticus)

A collection of sayings on a wide range of subjects. Wisdom, personified as a woman, is extolled. The author also expounds on the glory of God and ends with a hymn of thanksgiving (see p.121).

Baruch

Baruch, a follower of Jeremiah, is in Babylon with the exiles. He prays to God, acknowledging the faithlessness and corruption that he assumes to be the reason for the Jews' present sufferings, and in repentance entreats God's mercy. God has chastised Israel, but will surely also restore the nation and rebuild Jerusalem.

Letter of Jeremiah

This text is usually included as the last chapter of Baruch and purports to be from the prophet Jeremiah. The Babylonian Exile, Jeremiah says, will be long but not permanent. The exiles should not pick up bad habits, such as idolatry. Foreign idols cannot tell right from wrong; they cannot even be relied upon to sanctify a vow or curse. They are simply inanimate objects and should be shunned.

Additions to Daniel

1. The Prayer of Azariah and the Song of the Three Jews (or **Three Young Men**)
Shadrach, Meshach, and Abednego, Daniel's three friends, address a hymn of praise and repentance to God as they sit in the fierce heat of the furnace to which they have been condemned (inserted after Dan. 3.32 in the Septuagint).

2. Susanna and the Elders
Two lecherous elders, thwarted in their desire to have intercourse with the virtuous Susanna, have her brought to trial for her life on false charges of adultery. She is sentenced to die, but Daniel intervenes and demonstrates that the elders' evidence is false. The elders are put to death (Dan. 13 in the Septuagint).

3. Bel and the Dragon (or **Serpent**)
King Cyrus is aghast at Daniel's scorn for the statue Bel, to which great quantities of food and drink are offered daily. Daniel shows the king that it is not the idol that consumes the offerings but the priests and their families, who sneak into the sanctuary by night through a secret door. The angry king has the priests executed. Daniel destroys the idol. He later annihilates a dragon worshiped by the Babylonians, for which the king is forced by the mob to throw him into a den of lions. But the lions do not harm Daniel, and he is freed by Nebuchadnezzar, who throws Daniel's enemies to the lions instead. They are devoured at once. (Dan. 14 in the Septuagint).

1 Maccabees
An account of the history of the Jews under Alexander the Great and his successors, especially the Seleucid king Antiochus IV Epiphanes (reigned 175–164 BCE). The book recounts his persecutions and the rebellions led by the Maccabees (see pp.132–35). Antiochus defiles the Temple of Jerusalem and persecutes the Jews. Two years later he issues a decree abolishing most of Judaism's distinct features. The old priest Mattathias takes up arms to defend the faith. Following his death, his son Judas Maccabeus takes over command and wins a succession of victories, after which the Temple is purified and reconsecrated, a ceremony celebrated annually in the Jewish festival of Hanukkah. Judas is killed in battle, after having concluded a treaty with the Romans. His brother Jonathan succeeds him, and is appointed high priest, but the Seleucids retake Jerusalem and the Temple, and Jonathan is killed. His brother Simon succeeds, regains Jerusalem, and inaugurates a brief period of prosperity before being treacherously assassinated. The book ends with the accession of John (Hyrcanus) to the leadership of the Maccabee dynasty (see pp.134–35).

2 Maccabees
Several episodes recounted in 1 Maccabees are embellished for moral and religious effect. The book's central theme is the eternal sanctity of the Temple and of the true faith. Steadfastness in faith is exemplified by gruesome martyrdoms. A reference to the resurrection of the dead (2 Macc. 12.43–45) influenced Christian theology.

3 Maccabees
The events of 3 Maccabees precede those of 1 Maccabees by about half a century. Ptolemy IV Philopator, the Greek king of Egypt, defeats Antiochus III of Syria in battle and then tours the temples of his domains. By a miracle, he is prevented from entering the Temple of Jerusalem, and, enraged, he orders a persecution of the Jews in Egypt. In Alexandria, the Jews are rounded up and five hundred elephants are maddened with wine and let loose on them. But another miracle takes place and the elephants trample the Egyptians instead. Ptolemy finally repents of his persecution and frees the Jews in his kingdom.

4 Maccabees
A more philosophical tone pervades this work. Its author sets out to show not only how total obedience to the Jewish Law corresponds to the cardinal virtues, but also how such obedience may represent the triumph of spirit over bodily sensation. Martyrdoms recounted in 2 Maccabees are held up as examples of how unwavering faith leads to salvation.

1 Esdras
An alternative rendering of eleven chapters of 2 Chronicles, the whole of the book of Ezra, and a chapter or so of Nehemiah. It also contains some additional material, in particular an ancient Zoroastrian parable about "the strongest thing in the world," which, after lengthy discussion, turns out to be Truth.

2 Esdras
A partly Jewish, partly Christian book that properly belongs to the genre called apocalyptic (see pp.130–31). The work discusses the resurrection of the dead and the Messiah who will appear in glory

and reign for four hundred years, at the end of which he and all humanity will die. But within another seven days, the righteous dead of all times will be resurrected and welcomed into the new and glorious Jerusalem.

Prayer of Manasseh

A penitential psalm purporting to be a prayer addressed to God by King Manasseh of Judah (see p.100), in which he regrets his former apostasy and hopes for divine forgiveness.

Psalm 151

A psalm supposedly composed by David after his defeat of the giant, Goliath (see p.74). David extols himself as God's champion, the leader of a resurgent Israel.

THE NEW TESTAMENT

Matthew

The gospels of Matthew, Mark, and Luke are closely related and are referred to collectively as the Synoptic Gospels (see p.189). Each gospel recounts the life, works, teachings, death, and resurrection of Jesus. Matthew is the work of a Jewish Christian who sees in Jesus the Messiah. Jesus' coming, Matthew claims, has been foretold in the Scriptures. Jesus represents the fulfillment of God's promises, the inauguration of a new Covenant, and the coming of the kingdom of heaven. Matthew opens with a genealogy of Jesus. Unique to his gospel are the stories of the visit of the Magi after Jesus' birth, the Massacre of the Innocents, the Flight into Egypt (see pp.206–07), and the Sermon on the Mount (although Luke has a similar but much shorter passage; see p.279). The evangelist includes frequent quotations from the Hebrew Bible.

Jesus rises from the tomb (Matt. 28.6), as the guards (Matt. 27.66) sleep.

Mark

The shortest and possibly the earliest of the gospels. Its author restricts himself to the bald facts as much as possible. Nonetheless, Jesus' major burdens – hostility from the authorities and incomprehension on the part of his disciples – are well depicted. Mark's account begins with Jesus' baptism and ends abruptly after the appearance of Jesus to the two Marys at the tomb (16.8). From 16.8 the gospel has been completed by a different author.

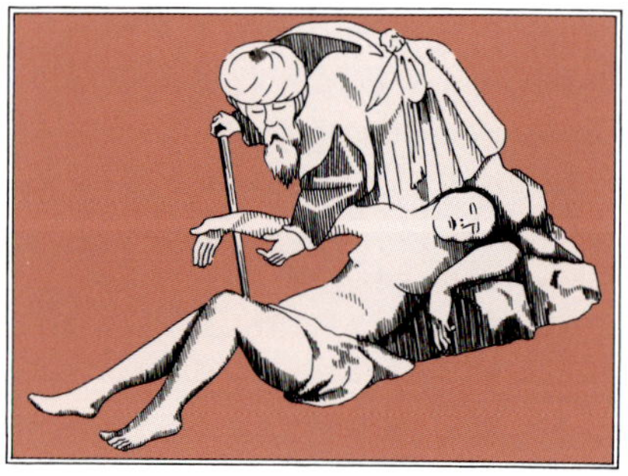

The Samaritan tends the injured man on the Jericho road (Luke 10.30–37).

Luke

Luke is a literary Hellenistic author, whose gospel is the first of two volumes, the second being Acts (see below). Together they recount the history of the faith from the birth of John the Baptist to the preaching of the apostle Paul in the capital of the Roman empire. Luke strives throughout to lend his account historical authenticity. His message is primarily addressed to Gentiles, and he therefore tones down the specifically Jewish aspects of Jesus' life and teachings. A major theme is the compassion and forgiveness of God through Jesus, by means of which salvation is open to all.

Numerous episodes are unique to Luke, such as the annunciation of the birth of the Baptist (see p.198); the presentation of Jesus in the Temple (see pp.208–09); the story of Jesus among the Temple teachers (see p.208); many of the best known parables, such as the stories of the Good Samaritan and the Prodigal Son (see pp.266–69).

John

The most mystical of the evangelists, John – traditionally identified as the apostle John, son of Zebedee – seems to have drawn on a different tradition of Jesus' life and teachings than the Synoptics (see pp.184–87). The first part of John's gospel (chs. 2–12) revolves largely around six extended discourses that explain six miracles. The rest of the gospel is notable for a further series of speeches by Jesus (see pp.284–85). Unlike the other gospels, John portrays Jesus as someone who regularly visited Jerusalem for the important Jewish festivals; in the Synoptics, Jesus makes only one main visit, at the end of his life.

Acts of the Apostles

Luke the evangelist (see above) continues his story in his second volume, Acts. He describes how the apostles receive the Holy Spirit at Pentecost and at once begin preaching to the nations (see pp.354–55). Several of the apostles (although not all of the twelve are mentioned in Acts) perform miracles (see pp.356–57), and soon the authorities are trying to stop them. The first follower of Jesus to be martyred is Stephen, a prominent activist, who is arrested, condemned, and stoned to death. The young Saul/Paul, a Pharisee from Tarsus in Asia Minor, is present at the stoning and approves of it (see pp.360–61).

Paul escapes from Damascus by being lowered down the city wall (Acts 11.25).

On his way to arrest Christians in Damascus, Saul/Paul experiences a vision that brings about a dramatic change of heart: he is baptized and begins preaching the gospel, becoming himself the target of persecution (see pp.364–65).

Congregations of followers of Jesus spring up outside Palestine, notably at Antioch in Syria, from where Paul and his colleague Barnabas embark on a missionary journey to Asia Minor. Paul makes further missionary journeys to Asia Minor and Greece (see pp.370–71). Before his second journey, he attends an important council of Church leaders at Jerusalem. The council agrees that Gentile converts to Christianity in Syria and Asia Minor need not comply with strict Jewish requirements such as circumcision and the food laws (see p.367).

After his third journey, Paul returns to Jerusalem, where he is persecuted by Jewish authorities. As a Roman citizen, Paul appeals to the Roman authorities and eventually wins the right to put his case to the emperor (see pp.372–73). He sails for Rome (see pp.374–75), and Acts ends with Paul under mild house arrest in the imperial capital, preaching the gospel. Luke says nothing further about his appeal or ultimate fate (see pp.378–79).

Romans

In his letter to the Roman church, Paul says that faith in God's truth and justice leads to the salvation of all Christians, whether their background be Jewish or Gentile. The new Israel is the successor to the old Israel, but is not by any means restricted to Israelites. Faith guarantees salvation – deliverance from sin and death. People must love one another, and love those who act against them. The secular law should be obeyed (see p.383).

1 Corinthians

Paul writes to the church at Corinth calling for unity in the face of factionalism. He addresses sexual morality, marriage, divorce, the Eucharist, and the importance of love (see p.381).

2 Corinthians

Probably a composite of several Pauline letters, 2 Corinthians expresses, among other things, Paul's frustration that his first letter has apparently had little effect (see p.381).

Galatians

Paul launches into this letter with an expression of astonishment that the Galatian church should be turning from the true gospel so soon. The Galatians should ignore those who say that Christians must follow the Jewish Law and be circumcised. Paul insists that Jewish traditions are not compulsory for Christians: faith in Jesus is more important than the works of the Law (see pp.382–83).

Ephesians

Paul is traditionally said to be the author of this letter, but this is doubtful. Its author states that believers are neither Jews nor Gentiles: all are Christians, part of God's household. The author calls for mutual respect between owners and slaves, employers and laborers.

Philippians

The letter to the Philippian church is generally agreed to be by Paul. It is personal and affectionate in tone. He thanks God for the work of the Philippians in spreading the gospel, and prays that their love for each other continues to increase so that, in unity and humility, they may all work together for salvation. But he also warns them against "evil workers" who are insisting on the necessity of circumcision (see pp.384–85).

Colossians
The letter to Colossae is probably, but not certainly, by Paul. If he is the author, it was possibly sent to Colossae at the same time as the letter to Philemon (see below). Colossians portrays Jesus as a cosmic figure, "the firstborn of all creation," the supreme head of the universal Church. The letter enjoins its recipients to hold fast to Jesus, because, it says, Jesus has redeemed all people and forgiven them their sins. Paul calls upon the members of the Colossian church to abandon the desires and temptations of the flesh, which represent a person's past existence (see p.386).

1 Thessalonians
The first letter to the church at Thessalonica is often believed to be the first of Paul's letters. He thanks God for the faith shown by those he addresses, who he says have been an example to everyone in the face of adversity. He also calls upon them to refrain from fornication and sexual license, and to be upright, law-abiding citizens who are prepared to work for a living. He gives reassurance about the imminence of Jesus' second coming (see p.380).

2 Thessalonians
The authorship of the second letter to the Thessalonians has aroused much debate, with many rejecting Paul as the author. However, it picks up on themes covered in 1 Thessalonians, such as the second coming of Jesus. The second coming is being delayed, the author claims, by a "lawless one," who will occupy the Temple and claim to be God (see p.380).

1 Timothy
The first of the "Pastoral Letters," which deal with the running of the Church and care of the Christian faithful (see p.378). The authorship of this and the following two letters is disputed, unlike most of Paul's undoubtedly genuine letters. The author tells Timothy that Jesus came into the world to save sinners, and if Jesus could show mercy to the greatest sinner (Paul, who began as a persecutor of the faith), then he can do so to anybody who has faith in him.

Congregational leaders must manage people and be able to teach by example and through mutual respect. The author gives instructions about widows, elders, and slaves. In fighting for their faith, the faithful will win eternal life (see p.379).

2 Timothy
The second of the Pastoral Letters. The author, who is possibly not Paul, calls upon his correspondent, whom he once more addresses in very warm terms, to use the strength that comes with the grace of Jesus to bear witness to the gospel. As a teacher of the gospel, he should be prepared to endure suffering, as the author does, for if the faithful hold firm they will reign with Jesus. The author entreats Timothy to avoid the sort of specious debates and discussions that lead people astray. He should abide by what he has been taught and knows to be true (see p.379).

Titus
The third and last of the Pastoral Letters. Again, Paul's authorship is open to question. The author tells his correspondent to appoint church elders in Crete as he had formerly instructed. The elders must teach sound doctrine in order to counter the teachers of Jewish myths. He goes on to give examples of such sound doctrine and the behavior that goes with it.

The author gives instructions to live a life of decency; lack of decorum, the author writes, scarcely befits those who are awaiting the second coming of Jesus. His correspondent should insist on respectful behavior (see p.379).

Philemon
Paul wrote the letter to Philemon from prison, where he had met and converted Onesimus ("Useful"), Philemon's runaway slave. Paul sent Onesimus back home with the letter, which asks Philemon, a leader of the church at Colossae, to take Onesimus back (the letter may have been sent to Colossae at the same time as the letter to the Colossians). He urges Philemon to treat Onesimus not as a slave but as a new brother in Jesus.

Paul offers restitution for anything

The apostle Peter, to whom the letters of Peter are attributed.

Onesimus may have stolen when he escaped, and perhaps hints that Philemon might free the slave to continue to work for the author in prison (see p.385).

Hebrews
The author of the letter to the Hebrews is unnamed. The letter shows how Jesus represents the fulfillment of God's promises to Israel. His sacrifice alone atones for the sins of humankind. Salvation comes through faith in him and his works (see pp.388–89).

James
This letter is traditionally said to be from James, the brother of Jesus. The author addresses a group of Jewish Christians, who are told to consider their trials as a privilege, and temptation as an opportunity to do right. They should assist the poor, especially if they themselves are comfortably off (see p.389).

1 Peter
The first of two letters traditionally attributed to the apostle Peter. The author offers encouragement to the faithful in the face of local hostility. They should love one another in total honesty and follow Jesus (see p.390).

2 Peter
This letter is generally accepted not to be by Peter. The author claims that he does not have long for this world. He denounces false teachers and says that the expectation of Jesus' second coming must never be abandoned.

The two-horned beast, and its worshipers on earth (Rev. 13.11–12).

1 John
The first of three letters traditionally attributed to the apostle John, son of Zebedee. The author denounces those who deny that Jesus appeared in the flesh, and calls upon those addressed to be bound together in mutual love (see p.391).

2 John
This brief letter is from an author calling himself "the elder." Believers must love one another and not be deceived by those who say that Jesus never came in the flesh (see p.391).

3 John
The author of 3 John also calls himself "the elder." It is addressed to "Gaius" and accuses the leader of Gaius's church of lack of hospitality and of spreading false accusations.

Jude
The author is said to be Jude, a brother of Jesus. He exhorts those addressed to keep the faith and beware of false teachers (see p.391).

Revelation (The Apocalypse)
Traditionally attributed to the apostle John, son of Zebedee, Revelation is in the form of a letter to seven churches in Asia Minor. The author sees an apocalyptic vision of a great sacrificial Lamb. The Lamb receives a scroll from God and breaks the seven seals on it one by one: the first four seals produce four apocalyptic horsemen, the next two raise the dead, and the last brings silence. Seven angels then blow their trumpets in sequence: the first six blasts cause destruction on earth; the seventh joins heaven together with what remains. A woman in childbirth appears: the child is taken to heaven. The angels under the archangel Michael defeat a seven-headed dragon. A terrible beast emerges. Its lesser companion (see picture, above) deceives the world into worshiping it.

The day of judgment breaks. Seven angels empty bowls of plague representing God's anger on to the world and over the beast. The cities of the world collapse and vanish. Babylon, the "Great Whore," burns and the world laments her passing. Songs of victory resound in heaven. The new age begins – after which Satan is released for a short time before his ultimate end. Then there is a new heaven and a new earth, and on the earth a new, messianic city of Jerusalem (see pp.392–94).

GLOSSARY

Apocrypha Writings that are not universally regarded as part of the canon of Scripture. These include Jewish Apocrypha, such as Judith, Tobit (see pp.124–25) and the books of the Maccabees (see p.135), which stand outside the Jewish canon and the canons of some Christian churches. In most cases they are works found in Greek in the Septuagint (see below) but for which no Hebrew original existed at the time of the formation of the canon, even if they were probably originally written in Hebrew, such as Sirach (or Ecclesiasticus; see p.121) and 1 Maccabees. In the Roman Catholic canon many of these writings are called Deuterocanonical, that is, they are acknowledged as distinct from the main body of Scripture but not as inferior in value. Christian Apocrypha include early Christian writings not incorporated into the New Testament, such as apocryphal gospels, acts and letters.

Apocryphal Of or pertaining to, or derived from, the Apocrypha.

Aramaic The Semitic language of Aram (Syria). It is closely related to Hebrew (see below), which it had largely displaced as the everyday language at least of northern Palestine (see below) by the first century CE. It was almost certainly the language spoken by Jesus and his disciples. Aramaic and its dialect, Syriac, are still spoken in some rural areas of Syria. Syriac is the language of the Syrian Christian church (see also p.92 and p.352).

Canaanites In the Bible, the term can mean any of the pre-Israelite inhabitants of Palestine. More specifically, it often refers to the Phoenicians, the seafaring people of the coastal area that is now part of Syria, Lebanon and Israel. Before the discovery of many Canaanite writings at the ancient site of Ugarit (modern Ras Shamra, Syria), the Bible was the chief source of knowledge about Canaanite beliefs and deities, such as Baal (see p.66).

Christ see **Messiah**

Christology Doctrine or teaching pertaining to the person of Christ, in particular the union of his human and divine natures.

Confession A profession of faith, such as that made by the apostle Peter to Jesus.

Davidic Of or pertaining to King David, ruler of Israel ca. 1000-ca. 965 BCE.

Deuterocanonical see **Apocrypha**

Deutero-Isaiah An alternative name for the biblical author known as Second Isaiah (Greek *deuteros*, "second"; see also p.106).

Diaspora, Dispersion The settlement of Jews outside their ancestral homeland of Palestine, a process that began with the Babylonian conquest of Jerusalem in the early sixth century BCE (see pp.104–07).

Eschatology A doctrine that looks for and anticipates the imminent end of the world. Adjective: eschatological.

Evangelist One who tells the "good news" (Greek *evangelion*) of the coming of Christ. The term is applied in particular to the authors of the four canonical gospels.

Fourth Gospel The gospel of John, in contradistinction to the three synoptic gospels (see below).

Hebrew The language of the Israelites. In the later centuries BCE, it was predominantly displaced as the vernacular language of northern and coastal Palestine (see below) by its Semitic relative, Aramaic (see above), and by Greek. However, as the original language of the Jewish Scriptures, it remained in liturgical, priestly and scholarly use. In the late nineteenth century, Hebrew was revived as a spoken language as part of the Zionist movement. Today, as the official language of the modern state of Israel, it serves to unify a Jewish population of many linguistic backgrounds.

Hebrew Bible, Hebrew Scriptures The Hebrew writings constituting the Jewish Bible. The Old Testament, the first part of the Christian Bible, consists of the Hebrew Scriptures (ordered differently from the Jewish Bible) with or without the Apocrypha (see above), depending on denomination.

Hellenism The widespread adoption of Greek language and culture in the Near East in the period following the conquests of Alexander the Great (356–323 BCE), when the region was largely ruled by the Greek dynasties that succeeded him. The so-called Hellenistic period was the era from ca. 300 BCE until the coming of the Roman empire (see pp.126–27; pp.132–33).

Josephus Flavius Josephus (37-ca. 100 CE), a Jewish historian and a key source for our knowledge of Judaism around the time of Jesus. His four extant works are *The Jewish War, The Antiquities of the Jews, Against Apion* (a riposte to an anti-Jewish tract), and the autobiographical *Life*.

Law In the present book, the term "law" almost always refers to the Jewish (Mosaic) law, or Torah.

Messiah Hebrew, "Anointed One." In Jewish and Christian theology, the Messiah is the savior figure who was sent by God to herald the end of the present world and the beginning of the divine kingdom. In Christian theology the Messiah is Jesus, who is therefore known as Christ, from *Christos* (or *Khristos*), a Greek title that translates the word Messiah. Adjective: messianic.

Mishnah A compilation of, and commentary on, those Jewish legal traditions not found in the Bible. Produced ca. 200 CE by the great rabbi Judah the Prince, the Mishnah in turn gave rise to a wealth of commentary and interpretation that was collected and codified in the Talmud (see below).

Mosaic Of or pertaining to Moses, used especially in reference to the Jewish law, or Torah (see below).

New Testament or **New Covenant** The second part of the Christian Bible. It consists of writings which, in Christian belief, bear witness to the covenant (testament) made between God and humanity in the person, ministry, death and resurrection of Jesus. The New Testament is said to represent God's final and supreme covenant with the world, supplementing and at the same time superseding the covenant of the Old Testament (see below). The books of the New Testament fall into three main categories: gospels; Acts of the Apostles (pp.352–75); and letters (the epistles and Revelation; pp.376–94).

Old Testament The first part of the Christian Bible, which, in Christian belief, bears witness to the covenant (testament) made between God and humanity before the coming of Jesus. The Old Testament consists of the books of the Jewish Bible, with or without the Apocrypha (see above), depending on tradition. There is some variation in the order of books between the Jewish Bible and the Old Testament (see also **New Testament**).

Palestine The region bounded roughly by the River Jordan to the west, the Negeb Desert to the south and the Golan Heights of Syria to the north. The name means "land of the Philistines" and was originally given by the Greeks to the coastal area occupied by the Philistines (see p.71). "Palestine" and "Palestinian" are used in this book as purely geographical terms without political connotations.

Passion The suffering (Latin *passio*), both mental and physical, of Jesus in the last twenty-four hours of his life, from the agony in Gethsemane to the Crucifixion.

Pauline Of or pertaining to the apostle Paul.

Pentateuch Greek *Pentateuchos*, "Five-Part Work." The first five books of the Hebrew Bible, Genesis, Exodus, Leviticus, Numbers, Deuteronomy. It is also known as: the Torah (see below); the book of Moses; the book of the Law; and the book of the Law of Moses.

Philo Philo of Alexandria (ca. 15 BCE–50 CE), a Jewish philosopher whose writings, in particular on the Logos concept (see pp.328–29), were very influential in the early Church.

Postexilic Of the period after the return to Judah, in the late sixth century BCE, of the Jewish exiles in Babylon.

Pseudepigrapha Religious writings outside the Jewish and Christian canons, Apocrypha, and the corpus of rabbinic works. They are often attributed to a biblical figure, such as Enoch.

Rabbinic, rabbinical Of or pertaining to the rabbis (Jewish teachers and interpreters of the Law) and their teachings.

Rabbinic age, rabbinic era The term given to an era (generally taken to be from the late first century CE to the early seventh century CE) in which the great rabbis (religious teachers) of Judaism, such as Yohanan ben Zakkai, Akiva, and Judah the Prince, were active. The rabbinic age saw the production of the Mishnah (see above) and the Talmud (see below).

Septuagint The Greek translation of the Hebrew Bible, so called because it was supposedly undertaken by seventy scholars (Latin *septuaginta*, "seventy") at Alexandria in Egypt (see p.126). The Septuagint, which contains writings regarded as non-canonical by Jews and as apocryphal or deuterocanonical by some Christian traditions, is the Old Testament of the Greek Orthodox church.

Synoptic Gospels (synoptics) The gospels of Matthew, Mark, and Luke. "Synoptic" (Greek *sunoptikos*) literally means "seen together": these three gospels share so many textual similarities that they may be set out in parallel and fruitfully compared.

Synoptists The authors of the synoptic gospels (see above).

Talmud The Mishnah plus the corpus of rabbinic commentary on it. There are two versions, one produced in Palestine ca. 400 CE (the "Jerusalem" Talmud) and one in Mespotamia ca. 500 CE (the "Babylonian" Talmud).

Temple The Temple of Jerusalem, the focus of Jewish religious life until 70 CE. The First Temple was built by King Solomon and destroyed by the Babylonians ca. 587 BCE; it was rebuilt following the exile in Babylon and lavishly refurbished by King Herod the Great. This Second Temple, the one Jesus knew, was destroyed by the Romans in 70 CE and never rebuilt.

Torah Hebrew, "instruction, direction." In a strict sense, the first five books of the Hebrew Bible, containing the 633 commandments (*mitzvot*) that form the basis of the Jewish law, transmitted by God to Israel through Moses. It is supplemented by the "oral Torah," various regulations not found in the Bible and codified in the Mishnah and Talmud.

Zion, Mount The hill of Jerusalem upon which stands the City of David and the Temple Mount. By extension, Zion can also mean Jerusalem.

FURTHER READING

THE BIBLE (GENERAL)

Introductions

Alter, Robert, and Frank Kermode. *The Literary Guide to the Bible*. London: Fontana, 1989.

Anderson, Bernard W. *The Living World of the Old Testament*. London: Longman, 1988.

Bartlett, John R. *The Bible: Faith and Evidence*. London: British Museum, 1994.

Childs, Brevard S. *Introduction to the Old Testament as Scripture*. London: SCM Press, 1983.

——. *The New Testament as Canon: An Introduction*. Philadelphia: Fortress, 1985.

Clements, R. E., ed. *The World of Ancient Israel*. Cambridge: Cambridge University Press, 1995.

Court, John M., and Kathleen M. Court. *The New Testament World*. Englewood Cliffs, New Jersey: Prentice-Hall, 1990.

Eissfeldt, Otto. *The Old Testament: An Introduction*. New York and Evanston: Harper and Row, 1965.

Koester, Helmut. *Introduction to the New Testament*. Philadelphia: Fortress, 1982.

Kümmel, Werner G. *Introduction to the New Testament*. London: SCM Press, 1977.

Metzger, Bruce M. *The New Testament: Its Background, Growth, and Content*. Nashville, Tenn.: Abingdon, 1983.

Rendtorff, Rolf. *The Old Testament: An Introduction*. London: SCM Press, 1985.

van der Woude, ed. *The World of the Old Testament*. Grand Rapids, Mich.: Eerdmans, 1989.

Biblical Interpretation, Textual Criticism, and Translation

Ackroyd, P. R., C. F. Evans, G. W. H. Lampe, and S. Greenslade. *The Cambridge History of the Bible*. 3 vols. Cambridge: Cambridge University Press, 1988.

Anderson, G. W., ed. *Tradition and Interpretation*. Oxford: Clarendon Press, 1979.

Coggins, R. J., and J. L. Houlden. *A Dictionary of Biblical Interpretation*. London: SCM Press, 1992.

Epp, Eldon Jay, and George W. MacHae, eds. *The New Testament and its Modern Interpreters*. Atlanta: Scholars, 1989.

Kenyon, Frederic. *Our Bible and the Ancient Manuscripts*. New York: Harper and Brothers, 1958.

Knight, Douglas A., and Gene M. Tucker, eds. *The Old Testament and its Modern Interpreters*. Philadelphia: Fortress, 1984.

Kraft, Robert A., and George W. E. Nickelsburg, eds. *Early Judaism and its Interpreters*. Philadelphia: Fortress, 1986.

Kugel, James, and Rowan A. Greer. *Early Biblical Interpretation*. Philadelphia: Westminster and John Knox, 1986.

Levenson, Jon D. *The Hebrew Bible, the Old Testament, and Historical Criticism*. Louisville, Ky.: Westminster and John Knox, 1993.

Metzger, Bruce M. *The Text of the New Testament: its Transmission, Corruption, and Restoration*. Oxford: Oxford University Press, 1995.

Morgan, Robert, and John Barton. *Biblical Interpretation*. Oxford: Oxford University Press, 1992.

Neill, Stephen, and N. T. Wright. *The Interpretation of the New Testament, 1861–1986*. New York: Oxford University Press, 1988.

Nida, E. A. *The Book of a Thousand Tongues*. Rev. ed. New York: American Bible Society, 1972.

Orlinsky, Harry M., and Robert G. Bratcher. *A History of Bible Translation and the North American Contribution*. Atlanta: Scholars, 1991.

Wurthwein, E. *The Text of the Old Testament*. London: SCM Press, 1980.

Literary Background

Ackroyd, P. R., A. R. C. Leaney, and J. W. Packer, gen. eds. *Cambridge Commentaries on Writings of the Jewish and Christian World 200BC to AD200*. Cambridge: Cambridge University Press, 1985–.

Barrett, C. K., ed. *The New Testament Background: Selected Documents*. London: SPCK, 1987.

Charlesworth, James H., ed. *The Old Testament Pseudepigrapha*. 2 vols. London: Longman & Todd, 1985.

Dalley, S. *Myths from Mesopotamia: Creation, the Flood, Gilgamesh and Others*. Oxford: Oxford University Press, 1991.

Gibson, J. C. L., ed. *Canaanite Myths and Legends*. Edinburgh: T. and T. Clark, 1978.

Gray, John. *Near Eastern Mythology*. London: Hamlyn, 1969.

Hennecke, E. *New Testament Apocrypha*. 2 vols. Nashville, Tenn.: Westminster and John Knox, 1991.

Leick, G. *A Dictionary of Ancient Near Eastern Mythology*. New York: Routledge, 1991.

Ogilvie, R. M. *The Romans and their Gods*. London: Hogarth, 1986.

Pritchard, James B., ed. *Ancient Near Eastern Texts Relating to the Old Testament; The Ancient Near East in Pictures Relating to the Old Testament*. Rev. ed. Princeton, NJ: Princeton University Press, 1970.

Ringgren, Helmer. *Religions of the Ancient Near East*. Philadelphia: Westminster, 1973.

Saggs, H. W. F. *The Greatness that was Babylon*. London: Sidgwick and Jackson, 1988.

Shafer, B., ed. *Religion in Ancient Egypt: Gods, Myths, and Personal Practice*. New York: Routledge, 1991.

Stone, Michael E., ed. *Jewish Writings of the Second Temple Period: Apocrypha, Pseudepigrapha, Qumran, Sectarian Writings, Philo, Josephus*. Philadelphia: Fortress, 1984.

Vermes, Geza. *The Dead Sea Scrolls in English*. Sheffield: JSOT, 1987.

Vernant, J. P. *Myth and Society in Ancient Greece*. New York: Zone Books, 1989.

Wiseman, D. J., ed. *Peoples of Old Testament Times*. Oxford: Clarendon Press, 1975.

History and Archaeology

Ben-Tor, Amnon, ed. *The Archaeology of Ancient Israel*. New Haven, Conn.: Yale University Press, 1991.

Garbini, Giovanni. *History and Ideology in Ancient Israel*. London: SCM Press, 1988.

Herrmann, Siegfried. *A History of Israel in Old Testament Times*. Philadelphia: Fortress, 1981.

Jagersma, Henk. *A History of Israel from Alexander the Great to Bar Kochba*. London: SCM Press, 1985.

Kenyon, Kathleen M. *The Bible and Recent Archaeology*. Rev. ed. London: British Museum, 1987.

Miller, J. Maxwell, and John H. Hayes. *A History of Ancient Israel and Judah*. London: SMC Press, 1986.

Soggin, J. Alberto. *An Introduction to the History of Israel and Judah*. London: SCM Press, 1993.

de Vaux, Roland. *The Early History of Israel*. London: Darton, Longman & Todd, 1978.

Wilkinson, John. *Jerusalem as Jesus Knew it: An Archaeological Guide to the Gospels*. London: Thames & Hudson, 1978.

Wright, G. Ernest. *Biblical Archaeology*. London: Gerald Duckworth & Co., 1962.

Anthropology, Sociology, and Folklore

Gaster, Theodor H. *Myth, Legend, and Custom in the Old Testament*. New York and Evanston: Harper and Row, 1969.

Gottwald, N. K. *The Tribes of Yahweh: A Sociology of the Religion of Liberated Israel, 1250–1000BC*. Maryknoll, New York: Orbis, 1979.

Lang, B., ed. *Anthropological Approaches to the Old Testament*. Philadelphia: Fortress, 1985.

Lemche, N. P. *Early Israel: Anthropological and Historical Studies on the Israelite Society before the Monarchy*. Leiden: Brill, 1985.

Meeks, W. A. *The First Urban Christians: The Social World of the Apostle Paul*. New Haven, Conn.: Yale University Press, 1994.

Niditch, Susan. *Folklore and the Hebrew Bible*. Minneapolis, Minn.: Fortress, 1993.

Rogerson, J. W. *Anthropology and the Old Testament*. Sheffield: Sheffield Academic Press, 1984.

Stambaugh, John E., and David L. Balch. *Social World of the First Christians*. Philadelphia: Westminster, 1986.

de Vaux, Roland. *Ancient Israel: Its Life and Institutions*. London: Darton, Longman & Todd, 1986.

Wilson, R. R. *Sociological Approaches to the Old Testament*. Philadelphia: Fortress, 1984.

Geography

Aharoni, Yohanan. *The Land of the Bible: A Historical Geography*. Rev. ed. Philadelphia: Westminster, 1980.

Bahat, Dan. *The Illustrated Atlas of Jerusalem*. London: Macmillan, 1990.

Baly, Denis. *The Geography of the Bible*. Rev. ed. Philadelphia: Fortress, 1987.

Brueggemann, W. *The Land: Place as Gift, Promise, and Challenge in Biblical Faith*. Philadelphia: Fortress, 1986.

May, Herbert G. *Oxford Bible Atlas*, 3rd ed., rev. by John Day. New York: Oxford University Press, 1984.

Religion, Theology, and Literature

Blenkinsopp, Joseph. *The Pentateuch: An Introduction to the First Five Books of the Bible*. London: SCM Press, 1992.

Coggins, R., A. Phillips, and M. Knibb. *Israel's Prophetic Tradition*. New York: Cambridge University Press, 1982.

Conzelmann, Hans. *An Outline of the Theology of the New Testament*. New York: Harper and Row, 1969.

Cross, Frank Moore. *Canaanite Myth and Hebrew Epic: Essays in the History of the Religion of Israel*. Cambridge, Mass.: Harvard University Press, 1973.

Dunn, J. G. D. *Unity and Diversity in the New Testament*. London: SCM Press, 1990.

Eichrodt, Walther. *Theology of the Old Testament*. 2 vols. London: SCM Press, 1978–9.

Engnell, Ivan. *Critical Essays on the Old Testament*. London: SCM Press, 1970.

Golka, Friedemann W. *The Leopard's Spots: Biblical and African Wisdom in Proverbs*. Edinburgh: T. and T. Clark, 1993.

Hanson, P. D., ed. *Visionaries and their Apocalypses*. Philadelphia: Fortress, 1983.

Hasel, G. F. *New Testament Theology: Basic Issues in the Current Debate*. Grand Rapids, Mich.: Eerdmans, 1978.

Hengel, Martin. *Judaism and Hellenism*. 2 vols. London: SCM Press, 1981.

Hooke, S. H., ed. *Myth, Ritual and Kingship*. Oxford: Clarendon Press, 1958.

Kraus, Hans-Joachim. *Worship in Israel: A Cultic History of the Old Testament*. Richmond, Va.: John Knox, 1966.

Mowinckel, S. *The Psalms in Israel's Worship*. 2 vols. Sheffield: Sheffield Academic Press, 1992.

Nickelsburg, George W. E. *Jewish Literature between the Bible and the Mishnah*. Philadelphia: Fortress, 1981.

Otzen, B., H. Gottlieb, and K. Jeppesen. *Myths in the Old Testament*. London: SCM Press, 1980.

Patrick, Dale. *Old Testament Law*. London: SCM Press, 1986.

von Rad, Gerhard. *Old Testament Theology*. 2 vols. London: SCM Press, 1975.

Smith, Mark S. *The Early History of God: Yahweh and the Other Deities in Ancient Israel*. San Francisco: Harper and Row, 1990.

de Vaux, Roland. *Studies in Old Testament Sacrifice*. Cardiff: University of Wales Press, 1964.

Whybray, R. N. *The Intellectual Tradition in the Old Testament*. Berlin and New York: de Gruyter, 1974.

Reference

Achtemeier, Paul J., ed. *Harper's Bible Dictionary*. San Francisco: Harper and Row, 1985.

Botterweck, G. Johannes, and Helmer Ringgren, eds. *Theological Dictionary of the Old Testament*. Grand Rapids, Mich.: Eerdmans, 1977.

Buttrick, George A., and K. Crim, eds. *The Interpreter's Dictionary of the Bible*. 5 vols. Nashville, Tenn.: Abingdon, 1976.

Freedman, David Noel, et al. *The Anchor Bible Dictionary*. 6 vols. New York: Doubleday, 1992.

Kittel, Gerhard, and Gerhard Friedrich, eds. *Theological Dictionary of the New Testament*. Grand Rapids, Mich.: Eerdmans, 1985.

Metzger, Bruce M., and Michael D. Coogan. *The Oxford Companion to the Bible*. Oxford: Oxford University Press, 1994.

Peake, A. S. *Commentary on the Bible*. Edinburgh: Thomas Nelson, 1962.

Roth, Cecil, ed. *Encyclopaedia Judaica*. New York: Macmillan, 1972.

JESUS CHRIST

General Studies

Bornkamm, G., *Jesus of Nazareth*. New York: Harper and Row; London: Hodder and Stoughton, 1960.

Bowden, John. *Jesus: the Unanswered Questions*. London: SCM Press, 1988.

Bultmann, R. *Jesus and the Word*. New York: Scribner; London: Collins, 1934, 1958.

Charlesworth, J.H. *Jesus within Judaism*. New York and London: Doubleday, 1988.

Conzelmann, H. *Jesus*. Philadelphia: Fortress Press, 1973.

Crossan, J. D. *The Historical Jesus: the Life of a Mediterranean Jewish Peasant*. San Francisco: Harper; Edinburgh: T. and T. Clark, 1991.

Harvey, A. E. *Jesus and the Constraints of History*. Philadelphia: Westminster; London: Duckworth, 1982.

Moule, C. F. D. *The Origin of Christology*. Cambridge: Cambridge University Press, 1977.

O'Collins, G. and D. Kendall. *Focus on Jesus*. Leominster, England: Gracewing (Fowler Wright Books), 1996.

Sanders, E. P. *The Historical Figure of Jesus*. London: Penguin, 1993.

Schillebeeckx, E. *Jesus: an Experiment in Christology*. New York and London: Collins, 1979.

Stanton, G. N. *The Gospels and Jesus*. Oxford: Oxford University Press, 1989.

Theissen, Gerd and Annette Merz. *The Historical Jesus: a Comprehensive Guide*. London: SCM Press, 1998.

Wright, N. T. *Jesus and the Victory of God*. Philadelphia: Fortress Press, 1996.

——. *The New Testament and the People of God*. Philadelphia: Fortress Press, 1992.

Vermes, Geza. *Jesus the Jew*, 2nd ed. London: SCM Press, 1983.

——. *Jesus and the World of Judaism*. London: SCM Press, 1983.

——. *The Religion of Jesus the Jew*. London: SCM Press, 1993.

The Setting

Bahat, D. *The Illustrated Atlas of Jerusalem*. New York: Simon and Schuster; London: Macmillan, 1990.

Downing, F. G. *The Christ and the Cynics*. London: SCM Press, 1988.

Hengel, Martin. *The "Hellenization" of Judaea in the First Century after Christ*. Philadelphia: Trinity Press International; London: SCM Press, 1989.

Jeremias, J. *Jerusalem in the Time of Jesus*. Philadelphia: Fortress Press; London: SCM Press, 1984.

Jones, A. H. M. *The Herods of Judaea*. Oxford: Clarendon Press, 1938.

Josephus, Flavius. *Works*. 10 vols., trans. and ed. by H. StJ. Thackeray, R. Marcus, and L. Feldman. London and Cambridge, Mass.: Loeb Classical Library, 1926–65.

Nickelsburg, George W. E. *Jewish Literature between the Bible and the Mishnah*. Philadelphia: Fortress Press; London: SCM Press, 1981.

Pfeiffer, R. H. *History of New Testament Times*. New York: Harper and Brothers, 1949.

Rousseau, John. J, and R. Arav. *Jesus and His World*. Philadelphia: Fortress Press; London: SCM Press, 1996.

Sanders, E. P. *Jesus and Judaism*. London: SCM Press, 1985.

Schürer, E., G. Vermes, F. Miller, and M. Black. *The History of the Jewish People in the Age of Jesus Christ*. 3 vols. Edinburgh: T. and T. Clark, 1973–87.

The Life

Borg, M.J. *Jesus: A New Vision*. San Francisco: Harper and Row, 1987.

Burridge, Richard A. *Four Gospels, One Jesus?* London: SPCK, 1994.

Catchpole, D. *The Trial of Jesus*. Leiden: Brill, 1971.

Craig, W. L. *The Son Rises: The Historical Evidence for the Resurrection of Jesus*. Chicago: Moody, 1981.

Finegan, J. *Handbook of Biblical Chronology*. Princeton, NJ: Princeton University Press, 1964.

Hengel, M. *Crucifixion in the Ancient World and the Folly of the Message of the Cross*. Philadelphia: Fortress Press; London: SCM Press, 1977.

——. *The Charismatic Leader and his Followers*. Edinburgh: T. and T. Clark, 1981.

Hoehner, H. W. *Chronological Aspects of the Life of Christ*. Grand Rapids, Mich.: Zondervan, 1977.

Jeremias, J. *The Eucharistic Words of Jesus*. New York and London: Scribner, 1966.

Kee, H. C. *Miracle in the Early Christian World*. New Haven, Conn.: Yale University Press, 1983.

Klasser, William. *Judas: Betrayer or Friend of Jesus?* London: SCM Press, 1997.

Légasse, Simon. *The Trial of Jesus*. London: SCM Press, 1997.

Ludemann, Gerd. *The Resurrection of Jesus*. London: SCM Press, 1996.

Lunny, W. J. *The Sociology of the Resurrection*. London: SCM Press, 1989.

Marxsen, W. *The Resurrection of Jesus of Nazareth*. Philadelphia: Fortress Press; London: SCM Press, 1970.

Metzger, B. M. *The Canon of the New Testament*. Oxford: Oxford University Press, 1987.

Millard, A. R. *Discoveries from the Times of Jesus*. Oxford: Lion, 1990.

Sanders, E. P., *Jesus and Judaism*. London: SCM Press, 1985.

Sanders, E. P., and Margaret Davies. *Studying the Synoptic Gospels*. Philadelphia: Trinity Press International, 1990.

Sherwin-White, A. N. *Roman Society and Roman Law in the New Testament*. Oxford, Clarendon Press, 1963.

Spong, J. S. *Born of a Woman*. San Francisco: HarperCollins, 1992.

Stanton, G. N. *Gospel Truth? Today's Quest for the Jesus of Nazareth*. San Francisco: HarperCollins, 1995; London: Fount, 1997.

Twelftree, G. H. *Jesus the Exorcist*. Tübingen: Coronet Books, 1993.

Van der Loos, H. *The Miracles of Jesus*. Leiden: Brill, 1965.

Vermes, G. *The Dead Sea Scrolls*. Sheffield: JSOT, 1987.

Webb, Robert. *John the Baptist in the Gospel Tradition*. Cambridge: Cambridge University Press, 1968.

Wenham, David, ed. *The Jesus Tradition outside the Gospels*. Sheffield: JSOT, 1984.

Wenham, D. and C. L. Blomberg, eds. *The Miracles of Jesus*. Sheffield, England: JSOT, 1986.

Wink, W. *John the Baptist in the Gospel Tradition*. Cambridge: Cambridge University Press, 1968.

Winter, P. *On the Trial of Jesus*. Berlin and New York: De Gruyter, 1974.

The Teachings

Banks, R. J. *Jesus and the Law in the Synoptic Tradition*. Cambridge: Cambridge University Press, 1975.

Beasley-Murray, G. R. *Jesus and the Kingdom of God*. Grand Rapids, Mich.: Eerdmans, 1986.

Davies, W. D. *The Setting of the Sermon on the Mount*. Cambridge: Cambridge University Press, 1964.

Dodd, C. H. *The Interpretation of the Fourth Gospel*. Cambridge: Cambridge University Press, 1953.

Evans, C. F. *The Lord's Prayer*. London: SCM Press, 1963.

France, R. T. *Jesus and the Old Testament*. London: Tyndale Press, 1971.

Jeremias, J. *Rediscovering the Parables*. London: SCM Press, 1966.

——. *The Prayers of Jesus*. Naperville, Ill.: Allenson; London: SCM Press, 1967.

McArthur, H. K. and R. M. Johnston. *They Also Taught in Parables: Rabbinic Parables from the First Centuries of the Christian Era*. Grand Rapids, Mich.: Zodervan, 1990.

Manson, T. W. *Jesus and the Non-Jews*. London: Athlone Press, 1955.

Perkins, P. *Jesus as Teacher*. New York and Cambridge: Cambridge University Press, 1990.

Perrin, N. *The Kingdom of God in the Teaching of Jesus*. Philadelphia: Westminster; London: SCM Press, 1963.

Strecker, G. *The Sermon on the Mount: on Exegetical Commentary*. Nashville, Tenn.: Abingdon; Edinburgh: T. and T. Clark, 1988.

Interpretations

Altizer, Thomas, J. J. *The Contemporary Jesus*. Albany, N.Y.: State University of New York Press, 1997.
Bammel, E. and C. F. D. Moule, eds. *Jesus and the Politics of His Day*. Cambridge: Cambridge University Press, 1984.
Barker, Margaret. *The Risen Lord: The Jesus of History as the Christ of Faith*. Edinburgh: T. and T. Clark, 1996.
Bonino, J. M. *Faces of Jesus: Latin American Theologies*. London: Orbis Books, 1984.
Borsch, F. H. *The Son of Man*. Grand Rapids, Mich.: Eerdmans; London: SPCK, 1983.
Brandon, S. G. F. *Jesus and the Zealots*. Manchester: Manchester University Press, 1967.
Buber, Martin. *Two Types of Faith: A Study of the Interpenetration of Judaism and Christianity*. New York: Harper Torchbooks, 1961.
Cullmann, O. *Jesus and the Revolutionaries*. New York: Harper and Row, 1970.
Daniélou, J. *A History of Early Christian Doctrine, vol. 1: The Theology of Jewish Christianity*. London: Burns and Oates, 1964.
Dodd, C. H. *The Founder of Christianity*. London: Collins, 1971.
Fiorenza, Elizabeth, S. *Jesus: Miriam's Child, Sophia's Prophet*. London: SCM Press, 1995.
Grillmeier, A. *Christ in Christian Tradition*. Nashville, Tenn.: Westminster John Knox Press, 1996.
Hagner, D. A. *The Jewish Reclamation of Jesus: an Analysis and Critique of Modern Jewish Study of Jesus*. Grand Rapids, Mich.: Zondervan, 1984.
Hahn, F. *The Titles of Jesus in Christology*. New York: World; London: Lutterworth Press, 1969.
Hamilton, William. *A Quest for the Post-Historical Jesus*. London: SCM Press, 1993.
Kramer, W. *Christ, Lord, Son of God*. London: SCM Press, 1966.
Leivestad, R. *Jesus in His Own Perspective*. Minneapolis: Augsburg Press, 1987.
Linders, B. *Jesus, Son of Man*. Grand Rapids, Mich.: Eerdmans; London: SPCK, 1983.
Meier, J. P. *A Marginal Jew: Rethinking the Historical Jesus*. 2 vols. New York and London: Doubleday, 1991, 1994.
Pagels, Elaine H. *The Gnostic Gospels*. London: Penguin Books, 1982.
Parrinder, G. *Jesus in the Qur'an*. London: Sheldon Press, 1976.
Reiser, M. *Jesus and Judgement*. Minneapolis: Augsburg Press, 1967.
Riches, J. K. *Jesus and the Transformation of Judaism*. London: Darton, Longman and Todd, 1980.
Rudolph, K. *Gnosis: the Nature and History of Gnosticism*. San Francisco: Harper and Row; Edinburgh: T. and T. Clark, 1983.
Stanton, G. N. *Jesus of Nazareth in New Testament Preaching*. Cambridge: Cambridge University Press, 1974.
Sweetman, J. W. *Islam and Christian Theology*. 4 vols. London: Lutterworth Press, 1945–1967.
Witvliet, Theo. *The Way of the Black Messiah*. London: SCM Press, 1987.

Jesus in Art

Baggley, J. *Doors of Perception: Icons and their Spiritual Significance*. London and Oxford: Mowbray, 1987.
Dionysius of Fourna. *The Painter's Manual*. Rev. ed., trans. by P. Hetherington (1974). Redondo Beach, Calif.: Oakwood Publications, 1989.
Every, G. *Christian Mythology*. Rev. ed. London: Hamlyn, 1987.
Kuryluk, E. *Veronica and her Cloth*. Cambridge, Mass., and Oxford: Basil Blackwell, 1991.
van der Meer, F., and C. Mohrann, *Atlas of the Early Christian World*. Trans. by M. F. Hedlund and H. H. Rowley. London: Nelson, 1966.
Ouspensky, L. and V. Lossky, *The Meaning of Icons*. Trans. by G. E. H. Palmer and E. Kadloubovsky. Crestwood, N.Y.: St Vladimir's Seminary Press, 1989.
Robinson, S. I. *Images of Byzantium: Learning about Icons*. London: Loizou Publications, 1996.
Schiller, G. *Iconography of Christian Art*. 2 vols., trans. by J. Seligman. London: Lund Humphries, 1971.
Speake, J. *The Dent Dictionary of Symbols in Christian Art*. London: J. M. Dent, 1994.
Tudor-Craig, P. "The Iconography of Corpus Christi", in S.E. Porter, M.A. Hayes and D. Tombs, eds., *Images of Christ: Ancient and Modern*. Roehampton Institute, London, Paper 2. Sheffield: Sheffield Academic Press, 1997.
Weitzmann, K. *The Icon: Holy Images, Sixth to Fourteenth Century*. London: Chatto and Windus, 1978.

Reference

Achtemeier, Paul J., ed. *Harper's Bible Dictionary*. San Francisco: Harper and Row, 1985.
Buttrick, George A., and K. Crim, eds. *The Interpreter's Dictionary of the Bible*. 5 vols. Nashville, Tenn.: Abingdon, 1976.
Coggins, R. J. and J. L. Houlden. *A Dictionary Interpretation*. Philadelphia: Trinity; London: SCM Press, 1990.
Freedman, David Noel, et al. *The Anchor Bible Dictionary*. 6 vols. New York: Doubleday, 1992.
Kittel, Gerhard, and Gerhard Friedrich, eds. *Theological Dictionary of the New Testament*. Grand Rapids, Mich.: Eerdmans, 1985.
Metzger, Bruce M. and Michael D. Coogan, eds. *The Oxford Companion to the Bible*. New York: Oxford University Press, 1993.
Peake, A. S. *Commentary on the Bible*. Edinburgh: Thomas Nelson, 1962.
Roth, Cecil, ed. *Encyclopaedia Judaica*. New York: Macmillan, 1972.

INDEX

Page references to main text, boxed text and margins are in roman, to captions in *italics*. References to the glossary (pp.410–11) have the suffix g. Where reference material occurs in text and captions on the same page, the text reference is given preference.

A

B

C

D

E

I

J

K

L

M

Q

R

S

T

U

V

W

X

Y

Z

PICTURE CREDITS

The publishers wish to thank the following for their kind permission to reproduce the illustrations in this book:

KEY:

b below; **c** center; **t** top; **l** left; **r** right

Axiom:	Axiom Photographic Agency, London
AA:	The Art Archive, London
BAL:	Bridgeman Art Library, London
BM:	British Museum, London
DBP:	Duncan Baird Publishers, London
ES:	Eitan Simanor, Jerusalem
RHPL:	Robert Harding Picture Library, London
HPL:	Hutchison Picture Library, London
PEF:	Palestine Exploration Fund, London
ZR:	Zev Radovan, Jerusalem

Page 1 AA/Sant' Apollinare in Classe, Ravenna
2 BAL/Pierpont Morgan Library, New York
3 BAL/Museo Basilica San Marco, Venice
8 ZR
10 BAL/British Library, Add 14761
11 BAL/British Library, London, Add 14761
14 BAL/Bible Society, London
17 BAL/Museo Basilica San Marco, Venice
18 BAL/British Library, London, Or 1404
20 BAL/British Library, London, Roy 19 D III f.3
21 BAL/British Library, London
23 BAL/Museo Diocesano de Solsona, Lerida
24 BM
25t DBP
25b BAL/Valley of the Nobles, Luxor (Thebes)
27t BAL/Victoria & Albert Museum, London
27b Staatliche Museen, Berlin
28 BAL/Private Collection
29 BM
31 RHPL
33t DBP
33b PEF
34t ZR
34b ZR
35 BAL/BM, Add 54180 f.136b
36 BAL/San Vitale, Ravenna
37 AA/Museum of Turkish & Islamic Arts, Istanbul
38t BAL/Österreichische Nationalbibliothek, Vienna
38b PEF
39 BAL/British Library, London
40 ZR
41 PEF
42 BAL/Fitzwilliam Museum, University of Cambridge
43 BAL/Fitzwilliam Museum, University of Cambridge
45 Sonia Halliday Photographs, Weston Turville
47l BAL/Valley of the Kings, Luxor (Thebes)
47r BAL/Musée du Louvre, Paris
49 BAL/Musée Condé, Chantilly, Ms 9/1695 f.12
51t BAL/Fitzwilliam Museum, University of Cambridge
51b BAL/Victoria & Albert Museum, London
52 BAL/Egyptian National Museum, Cairo
54 BAL/Dahlem Staatliche Gemäldegalerie, Berlin
55 Corbis, London
56 Sonia Halliday Photographs, Weston Turville
57t BAL/Monastery of St. Catherine, Mount Sinai
57b AA/Musée du Louvre, Paris
58t AA/Musée du Louvre, Paris
58b BAL/Private Collection
59 ZR
60 ZR
61t BAL/Musée de la Chartreuse, Douai
62 ZR
64t BAL/Bibliothèque Nationale, Paris
64b RHPL
65 ZR
66t BM
66b RHPL
67 ZR
68t AA/Archaeological Museum, Aleppo
68b PEF
69 BAL/British Library, London, Kings 5 f. 20r
70 ZR
71t ZR
71b BAL/Medinet Habu
73 BAL/Victoria & Albert Museum, London
74l BAL/British Library, London, Arundel 155 f.93
74r Francis/HPL
75 BAL/Kunsthistorisches Museum, Vienna
76t Corbis, London
76b ZR
78t ZR
78b BAL/Fitzwilliam Museum, University of Cambridge
79t BAL/Bibliothèque Nationale; Grec 139 f.136v
79b ZR
80 BAL/BM, Roy 15 D III f.285
81t BAL/Agnews & Sons, London
81b ZR
82t BAL/BM
82b ZR
83 Pignières/Sipa/Rex Features, London
84 BAL/British Library, London, Add 11639 f.522r
85t PEF
85b From an original drawing by Dr. Leen Ritmeyer
86 Regent/HPL
88 ZR
90 BAL/St. Peter's, Leuven
91t BM
91b BM
92 BAL/Museum of the History of Religion, St. Petersburg
93t BAL/Musée du Louvre, Paris
93b PEF
94t & b AA
95 AA/Musée du Louvre, Paris
96 BAL/Museo Catedralico, Cuenca
97l BAL/Bibliothèque Nationale, Paris, Fr 13091 f.29v
97r BAL/British Library, London, Harl 2803 f.264
98 PEF
99 Corbis, London
100 BAL/Victoria & Albert Museum, London
101 BM
102 Goebell/ZR
103 BAL/Musées Royaux des Beaux-Arts de Belgique
104 BAL/Museo Real Academia de Bellas Artes, Madrid
105 ZR
107t BAL/Lambeth Palace Library, London, Ms 3f. 258
107b BAL/Musée du Louvre, Paris
108 AA
109 Schörke/ZR
111t BAL/Biblioteca Medicea-Laurenziana, Florence
111b Jackson/RHPL
114t BAL/British Library, London, Ms 368.f.66
114b ZR
115 ZR
116 ZR
117t BAL/British Library, London, Add 27210 f.11
117b BAL/Chartres Cathedral
118t AA/Museum of Turkish & Islamic Arts, Istanbul
118b BAL/Musée du Louvre, Paris
119 ZR
120 BAL/Musée du Louvre, Paris
121 BAL/Musée du Louvre, Paris
122t BAL/Museo e Gallerie Nazionali di Capodimonte, Naples
122b BM
123 DBP
130 BAL/Victoria & Albert Museum, London
125 BAL/Musée Condé, Chantilly
127t Pate/HPL
127b Scala, Museo Nazionale, Naples
128 BAL/Kunsthistorisches Museum, Vienna
129 BAL/Christie's, London
130 BAL/British Library, London, Add 11695 f.240
131 BM
133t BAL/Private Collection
133b BAL/Bibliothèque Nationale, Paris
134t BAL/Musée des Beaux-Arts, Nantes
134b ZR
136 ZR
138l Corbis. London
138r ZR
139 Sonia Halliday Photographs, Weston Turville
140 BAL/Musée Condé, Chantilly
142 AF Kersting, London
143 ES/Axiom
144 ES/Axiom
146 ES/Axiom
147 ES/Axiom
148 ES/Axiom
149 Chris Bradley/Axiom
150 ZR
151 ES/Axiom
153 AF Kersting, London
154 AA/Museo Nazionale, Rome
155 ES/Axiom
156 ES/Axiom
158tl ES/Axiom
158bl Erich Lessing/AKG London
159 Michael Holford, London/Brobinskoy Collection
161 Superstock, London
163tr Erich Lessing/AKG London
163bl AA/Sant' Apollinare Nuovo, Ravenna
164 ES/Axiom
165 Superstock, London
166 AA/Basilica Sant' Angelo in Formis, Capua
167 ZR
168 BAL/Caylus Anticuario, Madrid
169 Sonia Halliday Photographs, Weston Turville
170 ZR
172 ZR
173 ES/Axiom
174tl ES/Axiom
174tr ES/Axiom
175 BAL/Musée d'Art et d'Histoire, Geneva
176 AA/Musée du Louvre, Paris
177 Erich Lessing/AKG London

178 Erich Lessing/AKG London
179 BAL/Musée du Louvre, Paris
180 AA/Kariye Camii, Istanbul
182 BAL/Bibliothèque Nationale, Paris
183 AA/Basilica Sant' Angelo in Formis, Capua
184 James Morris/Axiom
185 BAL/British Library, London
186 BAL/Lambeth Palace Library, London
187 Birch/Sonia Halliday Photographs, Weston Turville
188 ZR
189 BAL/Bibliothèque Nationale, Paris
190 BAL/Ashmolean Museum, Oxford
191 BAL/Museo de Santa Cruz, Toledo
193 BAL/Museo di San Marco dell'Angelico, Florence
194 BAL/Richardson & Kailas Icons, London
195 ES/Axiom
196 ES/Axiom
197 BAL/Museo Nacional del Prado, Madrid
198 ES/Axiom
199 AA/National Gallery, London
201 BAL/Noortman (London) Ltd
202 BAL/Victoria & Albert Museum, London
203 AA/Sant' Apollinare Nuovo, Ravenna
204 ES/Axiom
205 BAL/Museo di San Marco dell'Angelico, Florence
206 ES/Axiom
207 Chris Bradley/Axiom
208 Superstock, London/Scrovegni Chapel, Padua
209 BAL/Galleria Querini-Stampalia, Venice
210 ZR
211 ES/Axiom
212 BM
213 AA/Museo Nacional del Prado, Madrid
214 ES/Axiom
215 BAL/Musée du Louvre, Paris
216 Sonia Halliday Photographs, Weston Turville
217 AA/Baptistery of the Arians, Ravenna
218 ES/Axiom
219 BAL/Fitzwilliam Museum, University of Cambridge
220 BAL/Museo de Arte de Catalunya, Barcelona
221 ES/Axiom
222 BAL/Keble College, Oxford
223 ES/Axiom
224 BAL/Musée du Louvre, Paris
225 ES/Axiom
226 ES/Axiom
227 AA/Sant' Apollinare Nuovo, Ravenna
229 ES/Axiom
230 BAL/Roudnice Lobkowicz Collection, Nelahozeves Castle
231 ES/Axiom
232 BAL/Musée Condé, Chantilly
233 ES/Axiom
234 BAL/Museo Nacional del Prado, Madrid
235t ZR
235b BAL/Kunsthistorisches Museum, Vienna
236 ES/Axiom
237 ES/Axiom
238 ES/Axiom
239 BAL/Hermitage, St. Petersburg
240 AA/Scrovegni Chapel, Padua
241 ES/Axiom
243 BAL/Museo di San Marco dell' Angelico, Florence
244 BAL/Museo Nacional del Prado, Madrid
245 ES/Axiom
246 BAL/Duomo, Siena
247 ZR
248 BAL/Museum of Art, Novgorod
249 ES/Axiom
250 ZR
251 Scala, Florence/Galleria d'Arte Moderna, Florence
252 ES/Axiom
253 BAL/The Fine Art Society, London
254 ZR
255 BAL/Koninklijk Museum voor Schone Kunsten, Antwerp
256 AA/Cathedral Treasury, Turin
257 BAL/Hermitage, St. Petersburg
258 Michael Holford, London
259 BAL/Museo di San Marco dell' Angelico, Florence
260 BAL/Musée du Petit Palais, Avignon
261 ES/Axiom
262 ES/Axiom
263 BAL/Musée des Beaux-Arts, Lyons
264 BAL/Christie's Images, London
265 AA/Sant' Apollinare Nuovo, Ravenna
266 BAL/Christie's Images, London
267 AA/Santa Maria Capua Vetere
268 BAL/Christie's Images, London
269 BAL/Courtauld Institute Gallery, London
270 Sonia Halliday Photographs, Weston Turville
271 ES/Axiom
272 Chris Bradley/Axiom
273 AA/Musée des Beaux-Arts, Rouen
274 BAL/Musée des Beaux-Arts, Caen
275 ES/Axiom
276 BAL/Lambeth Palace Library, London
277 ES/Axiom
278 AA/Galleria degli Uffizi, Florence
279 ES/Axiom
280 Michael Holford, London
281 ES/RHPL
282 BAL/Johnny van Haeften Gallery, London
284 ES/Axiom
285 BAL/Hermitage, St Petersburg
286 ES/Axiom
287 AA/Santa Costanza, Rome
288 ES/Axiom
289 BAL/British Library, London
290 AA/National Gallery, London
292 Chris Bradley/Axiom
293 AA/Basilica Sant' Angelo in Formis, Capua
294 ES/Axiom
295 BAL/Musée National de la Renaissance, Ecouen
297 Superstock, London
298 ES/Axiom
299 AA/Cathedral, Anagni
300 BAL/Musée du Louvre, Paris
301 Held/Sonia Halliday Photographs, Weston Turville
302 BAL/Hermitage, St. Petersburg
303 BAL/Musée du Louvre, Paris
304 Michael Holford, London/Brobinskoy Collection
305 BAL/Castle Museum and Art Gallery, Nottingham
306 BAL/Abbey Church, Beaulieu-sur-Dordogne
307 BAL/St Martin, Colmar
308 BAL/Forbes Magazine Collection, New York
309 BAL/British Library, London
310 AA/Basilica Sant' Angelo in Formis, Capua
311 AA/Sant' Apollinare Nuovo, Ravenna
312 BAL/Richardson & Kailas Icons, London
313 BAL/Museo Nacional del Prado, Madrid
314 BAL/Scrovegni Chapel, Padua
315t BAL/Städelsches Kunstinstitut, Frankfurt-am-Main
315b BAL/Musée du Louvre, Paris
316 BAL/Richardson & Kailas Icons, London
317 BAL/Ca' d'Oro, Venice
318 BAL/St. Peter's, Vatican City
319 BAL/Musée du Louvre, Paris
320 AA/National Gallery, London
321 Sonia Halliday Photographs, Weston Turville
322 BAL/Cathedral, Cefalù
323 BAL/Vatican Museums and Galleries
324 Moroney/Axiom
325 BAL/Musée Condé, Chantilly
326 BAL/Hermitage, St. Petersburg
327 Gillham/RHPL
328 Sonia Halliday Photographs, Weston Turville
329 BAL/Musée du Louvre, Paris
330 AA/Santa Costanza, Rome
331 Sonia Halliday Photographs, Weston Turville
332 ES/Axiom
333 AA/Cenacolo Santa Apollonia, Florence
334 Michael Holford, London/Bardo Museum, Tunis
335 BAL/Pierpont Morgan Library, New York
336 AA/Sant' Apollinare Nuovo, Ravenna
337 Wolman/Tony Stone Images, London
338 ES/Axiom
339 AA/National Gallery, London
340 ES/Axiom
341 BAL/Musée d'Unterlinden, Colmar
342 BAL/Musée de l'Oeuvre de Notre Dame, Strasbourg
343 BAL/Richardson & Kailas Icons, London
344 BAL/Chester Beatty Library and Gallery of Oriental Art, Dublin
346 ES/Axiom
347 BAL/Musée Condé, Chantilly
348 BAL/Canterbury Cathedral
349 BALMusée du Louvre, Paris
350 BAL/Museo Correr, Venice
351 BAL/Cathedral of the Annunciation, Moscow
352 BAL/Bible Society, London
353 BAL/Museo d'Art de Catalunya, Barcelona
354 BAL/Scrovegni Chapel, Padua
355 BAL/Sistine Chapel, Vatican
357l BAL/Brancacci Chapel, Sta. Maria del Carmine, Florence
357r ZR
358 BAL/Belvoir Castle, Leicestershire
359 RHPL
360 BAL/ Nicholas V Chapel, Vatican
361 BAL/Pushkin Museum, Moscow
363t ZR
363b BAL/Fitzwilliam Museum, University of Cambridge, Ms 36-1950 f.49.v
364 Goebbell/ZR
365 BAL/Bibliothèque Nationale, Lat 1 f.386v, Paris
366 BAL/Louvre, Paris
367 BAL/Brancacci Chapel, Sta. Maria del Carmine, Florence
368 BAL/Villa dei Misteri, Pompeii
370 Sonia Halliday Photographs, Weston Turville
371 Sonia Halliday Photographs, Weston Turville
372t BAL/York City Art Gallery
372b PEF
373 ZR
374 ZR
375 BAL/Biblioteca Marciana, Venice
377 BAL/Magyar Nemzeti Galeria, Budapest
378t BAL/Fitzwilliam Museum, University of Cambridge
378b BAL/Pauline Chapel, Vatican
380 ZR
381 ZR
382 ZR
383t BAL/Louvre, Paris
383b ZR
384 ZR
385t DBP
385b BAL/Louvre, Paris
386 ZR
387 BAL/Scrovegni Chapel, Padua
388 BAL/Louvre, Paris
389 BAL/Bibliotheque Nationale, Paris
390 BAL/Brancacci Chapel, Sta. Maria del Carmine, Florence
391 BAL/Convent of S. Tomas, Avila
393 ZR
394t ZR
394b BAL/Tretyakov Gallery, Moscow.